THE LITERATURE
of
THE LEWIS AND CLARK EXPEDITION

THE LITERATURE
of
THE LEWIS AND CLARK EXPEDITION
A BIBLIOGRAPHY AND ESSAYS

ESSAYS BY

STEPHEN DOW BECKHAM

BIBLIOGRAPHY BY

DOUG ERICKSON

JEREMY SKINNER

PAUL MERCHANT

LEWIS & CLARK COLLEGE

Portland, Oregon

Published by Lewis & Clark College
0615 S.W. Palatine Hill Road, Portland, Oregon 97219
www.lclark.edu
© 2003 by Lewis & Clark College

ISBN: 0-9630866-1-8
Library of Congress Control Number: 2002116566

Copyeditor Teri Cettina
Designers Robert Reynolds and Letha Gibbs Wulf,
   Reynolds Wulf Inc.
Photographers Jeff Krausse and Robert Reynolds

This book was typeset in Adobe Garamond Expert
and Berthold Garamond by Letha Gibbs Wulf.
It was printed by Dynagraphics and bound
by Lincoln and Allen.

Printed in the United States of America.

The contents of this book were developed under a grant
from the U.S. Department of Education. However, these contents
do not necessarily represent the policy of the Department of
Education, and readers should not assume endorsement
by the federal government.

Contents

Plates and Photographs 6

Foreword 7

Acknowledgments 9

Usage Notes 12

Introduction 15

Chapter One
The Expedition's Traveling Library 23

Chapter Two
Early Expedition-Related Publications 65

Chapter Three
Patrick Gass, First in Print 87

Chapter Four
Taking Literary License: Surreptitious and Apocryphal Narratives 119

Color Plates 144

Chapter Five
Editing the Expedition Journals 145

Chapter Six
General Histories, Centennial Publications,
and Children's Literature, 1803–1905 205

Chapter Seven
A Twentieth-Century Publications Checklist 229

Sources Cited 286

Index 301

Plates and Photographs

Color plates, following page 144:

Plate I *Sagittaria sagittifolia*, Benjamin Smith Barton, *Elements of Botany* (Philadelphia 1803)

Plate II Title page, *Dictionary of Arts and Sciences* (London 1754–55)

Plate III Plate, John Miller, *An Illustration of the Sexual System* (London 1779)

Plate IV Aaron Arrowsmith, "A Map Exhibiting all the New Discoveries" (London 1802)

Plate V George Vancouver, "A Chart shewing part of the Coast of N.W. America" (London 1798)

Plate VI Thomas Jefferson, *Message from the President* (Washington, D. C. 1806)

Plate VII Broadside, Jefferson's Message, *National Intelligencer* (Washington, D. C. 1806)

Plate VIII Paper wraps, Patrick Gass, *Voyage des Capitaines Lewis et Clarke* (Paris 1810)

Plate IX Title page, Patrick Gass, *A Journal of the Voyages and Travels* (Philadelphia 1810 2nd state)

Plate X Plates, Patrick Gass, *A Journal of the Voyages and Travels* (Philadelphia 1810 2nd state)

Plate XI Digest, Patrick Gass, *A Journal*, in *Neue historische und geographische Gemählde* (Vienna 1811)

Plate XII Map, Patrick Gass, *A Journal of the Voyages and Travels* (Philadelphia 1812)

Plate XIII Frontispiece and title page, *The Travels of Capts. Lewis & Clarke* (Philadelphia 1809)

Plate XIV Map, *The Travels of Capts. Lewis & Clarke* (London 1809)

Plate XV Plate, "Sioux Krieger," *Die Reisen der Capitaine Lewis und Clarke* (Libanon [Lebanon], Pa. 1811)

Plate XVI Plates, "Captains Lewis and Clark, Returned," *An Interesting Account of the Voyages* (Baltimore 1812)

Plate XVII Original boards, vol. 2, *History of the Expedition* (Philadelphia 1814)

Plate XVIII Map, *Reize naar de Bronnen* (Dordrecht 1816–18)

Plate XIX Swords, bludgeon, canoe paddle, January 1, 1806, Codex J, Coues-Anderson Manuscript Transcript

Plate XX Plate, "Pehriska-Ruhpa," *Original Journals*, vol. 5 (New York 1904–05)

Plate XXI Plate, "Scalp Dance of the Minatarres," *Original Journals*, vol. 1 (New York 1904–05)

Plate XXII Plates, *Scenes in America* (London 1821)

Plate XXIII *Clarkia pulchella*, Frederick Pursh, *Flora Americae Septentrionalis* (London 1814)

All illustrations in this volume are from items in or on loan to the Lewis & Clark College Collection.

Contemporary photographs taken along the expedition route:

Page 2 Upper Lochsa River, Idaho

Page 9 Wapato *(Sagittaria latifolia)*, the root of which was a diet staple for Native Americans

Page 19 Missouri Breaks, Montana

Page 24 Gates of the Rocky Mountains, Missouri River, Montana

Page 66 Madison River, Montana, two miles before it joins the Jefferson and Gallatin Rivers to form the Missouri River

Page 88 Bitterroot Range looking east from Bald Peak, Idaho

Page 120 Petroglyphs near Buffalo Eddy, Snake River, Idaho

Page 146 Mount Hood, Oregon

Page 206 Columbia River near Skamokawa, Washington

Page 230 Haystack Rock, Cannon Beach, Oregon

Page 286 Basalt flow along Yakus Creek, on the Lolo Trail, Idaho

Page 302 Bitterroot *(Lewisia rediviva)*, first collected by Meriwether Lewis on July 1, 1806

Foreword

As much as any one person could, Thomas Jefferson embodied the American Enlightenment. He lived and promoted its core claims: the triumph of reason, the rightness of nature, and the improvement of society through knowledge. Informed by these ideals, Jefferson wrote his instructions to Meriwether Lewis, directing him to find a navigable waterway from St. Louis to the Pacific Ocean, to make contact with the Indians he encountered, and to document all that he observed en route.

Each of Jefferson's orders revealed his true hope that the mission would go beyond discovering whether the "Northwest Passage" was fact or fantasy. He wanted to learn about the people, plants, animals, geology, and climate of the West. He wanted to put to rest the myths about the western region, so truth could reign and the improvement of the United States could follow. Like his hero Francis Bacon, Jefferson believed that wisdom begins with the patient gathering of facts, the careful sorting of those facts into rational categories, and a determination not to impose preconceptions on nature, but instead to let nature teach us how to live. Like John Locke, Jefferson believed that studying people living in a natural state, or nearly so, would teach something about the fundamentals of civilization and permit the reformation of society in the name of nature and simplicity. Like Isaac Newton, Jefferson also believed that the universe was balanced and orderly, and that man's chief duty was to discern the natural laws that underlie all surface appearances. His orders for the expedition reflected these values.

Jefferson could not make the westward journey himself, but he sent a trusted associate to do the work on his behalf. Meriwether Lewis took his role quite seriously. He was an amateur with a gift for careful observation. His sense of mission governed his every action and at times appeared to overwhelm him. Had he lived to publish his narrative, he would today be seen as a scientist and exemplar of the Enlightenment, rather than an adventurer.

Under Jefferson's guidance, Lewis had been schooled by the leading American scholars of the period. Lewis's co-captain, William Clark, was a frontiersman of great resourcefulness, a master of boatcraft, and a talented surveyor and cartographer. As a team, Lewis and Clark have been called the "writingest" explorers of all time because of their extensive journals, field notes, annotated maps, and letters. It is clear they were also among the "readingest" of all explorers. They carried with them a small reference library carefully preserved against the exigencies of a transcontinental river voyage. They packed books that would help them classify plant and animal species, determine the names and composition of minerals, and ascertain the latitude and longitude of key features of the western landscape. They even carried a four-volume general encyclopedia. The journals attest to the use of the traveling library in helping them make their scientific observations and determinations. With these books, Lewis, Clark, and their Corps of Discovery embarked on a journey of questioning, examining, and reasoning. They engaged in ambitious, descriptive scientific inquiry.

Lewis and Clark's journey revealed fascinating information about the West. Clark mapped a critical portion of it—the Missouri watershed and the lower reaches of the Clearwater, Snake, and Columbia Rivers. His map, published in 1814, was a major contribution to the emerging cartography of western North America. Lewis's labors included linguistics, ethnography, botany, and zoology. He described tribal cultures, collected word lists, ascertained commercial potentials, and opened diplomatic relations with more than fifty tribes and bands. Lewis documented hundreds of plants and animals. In many instances his observations and collections of specimens were the first made of dozens of species. Lewis's herbarium of dried plants is today housed at the Academy of Natural Sciences in Philadelphia.

Over several decades, Lewis & Clark College has assembled a remarkable collection of expedition-related books, maps, manuscripts, illustrations, and ephemera. We are proud of this collection, both for the evidence it offers about the American embrace of the Enlightenment as the foundation for Lewis and Clark's expedition and for the library's potential to serve students and the scholarly community in the decades ahead.

This book represents years of research and teaching by the College's librarians and historians into the expedition and the texts written about this inaugural exploration by land across the American West. The annotated bibliography, filled out with interpretive essays on the historical setting and context of publication, is our gift to scholarship and to the bicentennial observances of the Lewis and Clark Expedition.

Michael Mooney
President
Lewis & Clark College

Acknowledgments

Much of the research for the historical essays in this volume occurred in the Aubrey R. Watzek Library and Paul L. Boley Law Library of Lewis & Clark College. The support of the staff at these research centers is much appreciated.

Securing other information for the essays entailed work at several institutions. The opportunity to consult books, maps, manuscripts, biographical directories, census records, and databases helped drive this venture. Appreciation is therefore extended to the Pennsylvania Historical Society, Free Library, Library Company, and the American Philosophical Society of Philadelphia; the Library of Congress, especially the divisions of Rare Books, Family History and Genealogy, and Government Documents; Beinecke Library, Yale University; and the Huntington Library and Art Gallery in San Marino, California.

At several points, the essays in this book required work in French, German, and Dutch. Professors Dinah Dodds and Klaus Engelhardt of Lewis & Clark College assisted in the German and French translations, respectively. Leonoor Swets Ingraham, director of the Clark College Library and a bibliographer of Lewis and Clark Expedition publications, translated Dutch publications about the expedition into modern English with verve and enthusiasm.

The staff of the Office of Bicentennial Planning and Events extended special service to this project through moral support, critiques of drafts, and determination to keep ventures on schedule. Thanks are thus extended to Holly Bard, Michael Ford, Sherry Manning, and Rachael Vorberg-Rugh. Invisible but essential to these undertakings are staff members in the Division of College Relations who have helped secure the funding for bicentennial planning and projects. To those who worked on grant proposals and underwriting of these ventures—thank you. My daughter, Ann-Marie C. Beckham, and my father, Dow Beckham, read and critiqued the full typescript. For their good eyes and insights, I am most grateful.

Special appreciation is extended to Clay Jenkinson, humanities scholar in residence at Lewis & Clark College and actor/scholar presenting Thomas Jefferson and Meriwether Lewis. Jenkinson's insight, critiques, and pressing of the agenda helped make this book happen. Most significantly, the support of Michael Mooney, Lewis & Clark College president, and Scott Staff, vice president for college relations, for these ventures turned a proposal into a book.

Stephen Dow Beckham

First acknowledgments must go to Roger Wendlick. When I met Roger many years ago in the upstairs room of Great Northwest Books in downtown Portland, I had no idea how he would change my life. My friendship with him over the last few years is filled with admiration for one of the leading authorities on the printed history of Lewis and Clark. Roger is my mentor, and still the person to whom I look for answers about the Corps of Discovery. His hard work and perseverance led to the most remarkable collection of Lewis and Clark–related materials ever assembled by one individual, a great story in and of itself. Special thanks to Phil Wikelund and John Henley of Great Northwest Books for introducing me to Roger.

Jim Kopp, library director at Lewis & Clark College's Aubrey R. Watzek Library, has been a great supporter, friend, confidante, and boss. This project could not have been accomplished without his leadership and goodwill.

Many others have helped along the way. In the world of book dealers, Charles Seluzicki, Roger and Elsa Roberts of Hawthorne Boulevard Books, Mark Wessel of Wessel and Lieberman Books, Vic Zojack of Tavistock Books, Curt Bench of Benchmark Books, Michael Ginsberg of Ginsberg Books, Bob Clark of Arthur H. Clark Co., Clarence Wolf of George S. MacManus Company, Ludd Trozpek, Eugene L. Vigil of Antiquariat Botanicum, Sue West and Michael Powell of Powell's Books, among many others, have provided invaluable service. William Reese of William Reese Company has been patient and forthcoming in sharing his vast knowledge of the American West. Brian Booth and James Kidd, M.D., deserve special thanks for their generosity and friendship to the Special Collections team.

Irving Anderson, George Tweney, and Eldon Chuinard, M.D., are all owed a great debt of gratitude for assembling and compiling their fine libraries. Collectively with Roger Wendlick, they have produced one of the finest collections of Lewis and Clark materials in existence. I am honored to have known all these gentlemen, and to have considered all of them my friends. I must also mention that my earliest introduction to Lewis and Clark scholarship was through historian Fred Gowans, my first mentor in the subject and my continuing source of information and encouragement. When it comes to this project itself, working with colleagues Jeremy Skinner and Paul Merchant has been an undiluted pleasure.

Finally, I wish to thank my wife, Stacy Johnson Erickson, and my three boys—Nicholas, Colton, and Joseph—for putting up with all of my time away from them, and for giving me the love and support throughout this project that only a good family can provide.

Doug Erickson

The Lewis & Clark College Special Collections staff wishes to acknowledge the following libraries and their staffs for assistance with items described in the volume, and for providing prompt and helpful answers to our questions: At the Library Company of Philadelphia, Cornelia S. King and John VanHorn; at Portland's Multnomah County Library, Jim Carmin, special collections librarian; at the University of British Columbia, A.A. Dell Rosario, archives librarian; at the American Philosophical Society, Robert Cox, librarian; at the Academy of Natural Sciences, Rick McCourt; at the Houghton Library, Harvard University, Jennie Rathbun; at the Beinecke Library, Yale University, George Miles; at the University of Washington, Carla Rickerson, Sandra Kroupa, and Karyl Winn; at the California Academy of Sciences, Laura Burkhart, reference librarian.

We also received valuable assistance from library and special collections staff at the University of California at Berkeley, Stanford University, University of California at Davis, University of California at San Francisco, Reed College, University of Portland, Lewis and Clark Trail Heritage Foundation, and the New York Public Library.

Stephen Allie, director of the Fort Leavenworth Colonial Army Museum, and Billy Maxwell, interpreter at the Lewis and Clark Interpretive Center in Great Falls, Montana, both provided valuable insights on military-related texts carried by Lewis and Clark. Clay Jenkinson, humanities scholar in residence at Lewis & Clark College, generously shared his wide range of knowledge and his perspective on the Corps of Discovery. John Logan Allen offered valuable insights on maps carried by Lewis and Clark. Stephen Tufte, assistant professor of physics at Lewis & Clark College, gave timely assistance in understanding questions of astronomical observation. Gary Moulton, editor of the Lewis and Clark Journals in the thirteen-volume standard edition, has provided wise and patient help on Lewis and Clark Expedition questions for many years.

Deborah Bosket and Clara Stemwedel of Lewis & Clark College's Watzek Library interlibrary loan staff helped us immeasurably with their efficient process-ing of our numerous requests. Laura Ayling, Mark Dahl, Elaine Gass, Joanna Haney, Elaine Heras, Daniel Kelley, and Betty Ann Smith of the Watzek Library's reference staff helped locate numerous reference works. Sandra Beehler, Nancy Black, and Linda Dunne, acquisitions and collection development librarian and staff, were of great assistance. Our hard-working student assistants—Adam Seluzicki, Katie Chrislip, Emilia Carley-Roe, and Elizabeth Palmer—have helped us with many tasks along the way. We also acknowledge the friendly assistance of the College's Information Technology staff, in particular Mike McNamara, Zachary Spiller, and Christopher Stevens.

The following people have provided steady support throughout this project: the Bicentennial Committee at Lewis & Clark College: Stephen Beckham, Holly Bard, Michael Ford, Rachael Vorberg-Rugh, Evan Williams, Kim Stafford, Linda Tesner, Ron Lansing, and Daniel Rohlf. The Lewis & Clark College administration, President Michael Mooney, Provost Jane Atkinson, and Vice President for Finance Mervyn Brockett deserve warm thanks for their vision and support for both the special collections department and this project.

The visual elegance of this book is thanks to the unerring eyes and hands of Robert M. Reynolds, designer and photographer of the large scenic photographs, and his design associate Letha Wulf. Jeff Krausse produced excellent photographs of objects in Lewis & Clark College's collection of expedition materials. Judy McNally, associate vice president for public affairs and communications, coordi-nated the publication process for the College. We are especially grateful for the keen editorial eye of Teri Cettina and the keyboard skills of Wendy Leith.

Our greatest debt, however, is to the pioneering scholars of the printed material related to the Lewis and Clark Expedition: Elliott Coues, Paul Cutright, Donald Jackson, Victor Paltsits, Carl Wheat, and the bibliographic team of Henry Wagner, Charles Camp, and Robert Becker.

Doug Erickson
Jeremy Skinner
Paul Merchant

Usage Notes

Bibliographic Entries

In the first five chapters of this book, each bibliographic item described has its own number and descriptive title, followed when necessary by a short, general comment. Each full title-page transcription, which is set off in colored type, reproduces the exact capitalization, italics, punctuation, and spelling of the original publication, with line breaks indicated by vertical strokes. The "Collation" sections provide the format and dimensions (height only, in centimeters) of each item and a listing of the contents, by inclusive page numbers, followed by subjects.

Measurements of maps, many of which fold out from the original volumes, are given in centimeters in this bibliography, width before height. The "Plate" descriptions reproduce the original spellings and, when revealing, punctuation of any listed captions.

In some cases, the "References" section of the bibliography includes abbreviated citations. The most frequent references can be located in their entirety in "Sources Cited" as follows: Coues: the bibliography presented as the introduction to volume 1 of his four-volume *History of the Expedition*; Graff: the Graff Collection catalog, edited by Colton Storm; Jackson: references to his edition of *Letters of the Lewis and Clark Expedition*, or to his article on the traveling library, as indicated; Paltsits: introductory bibliography for the Thwaites eight-volume edition of *Original Journals of the Lewis and Clark Expedition*; Thwaites: his eight-volume edition of *Original Journals*, with volume number indicated; and Wagner-Camp-Becker: the 1982 fourth edition of *The Plains & the Rockies*.

Items in chapters 6 and 7, which are catalogs of later nineteenth-century and twentieth-century Lewis and Clark materials, are presented slightly differently. Each entry includes information about the author, title, place of publication, and date, followed by a brief description (when helpful), and references to further editions.

Historical Spellings

Unusual, dated, and incorrect spellings appear occasionally in this volume, particularly within quotations in the historical essays and within titles in the annotated bibliography. For instance, William Clark's name is sometimes spelled "Clarke." Geographical names were often misspelled; there are multiple versions of "Louisiana" on maps and in publications. Variable spellings were quite common prior to the publication of Noah Webster's dictionary in 1828.

Because the original spellings provide historical context and help differentiate between similar items in the bibliography, they have been maintained. Language within quotes is punctuated as originally printed.

Lewis and Clark Journal Quotations

All quotations from Lewis and Clark's original journals are drawn from Gary E. Moulton's *The Journals of the Lewis and Clark Expedition* (1983–2001). Capital letters have sometimes been added to these quotes at the beginning of sentences. All other material from the explorers' journals is quoted as spelled and punctuated in the Moulton edition.

Introduction

Through careful planning, Lewis & Clark College has assembled one of the finest print collections in the world relating to the Lewis and Clark Expedition. This undertaking affirms the institution's name and motto—*explorare, discere, sociare* (to explore, to learn, to work together). The College emphasizes the importance of the life of the mind, critical exploration of ideas and information, qualities of leadership and character, and the embracing of adventure. The library acquisitions regarding the expedition have been the product of both fortune and friendship. It was the College's good fortune to have an administration and Board of Trustees willing to invest in materials that meshed appropriately with the institution's name and mission of teaching the liberal arts and sciences. In addition, the friendship of a number of scholars and collectors of rare books helped drive the acquisition of the collections now housed in the Heritage Room of the Aubrey R. Watzek Library.

"Books are also magnets, with the power to attract people," wrote Lawrence Clark Powell, longtime librarian of the University of California at Los Angeles (UCLA). "A single book may have this magnetic force, and when hundreds and thousands of books are brought together in bookshops and libraries, their power is increased, so that such a place of bookish concentration possesses an irresistible attraction for readers and collectors." This magnetic force has helped shape Lewis & Clark College's collections on the American West. The holdings include materials on exploration, fur trade, missions, settlement, Spanish borderlands, development of towns and cities, the environment, conservation, and literature.

Early Acquisitions

In 1920, Caroline Gray Kamm, the widow of a steamboat magnate, gave twelve thousand dollars to the College, partly to facilitate library development. In 1928, three years before her death at age ninety-one, she gave her family library to the College. Her bequest included William H. Gray's *A History of Oregon*, a book written by her father; six volumes of Hubert Howe Bancroft's *Chronicles of the Builders of the Commonwealth* (1891–92), a series of biographies of wealthy business leaders of the Pacific Slope; and other works especially related to American settlement of the Oregon Country. Kamm's parents were among the earliest Euro-American missionaries and settlers to live in the area.

In time, the College acquired George Catlin's *North American Indians* in two volumes (Edinburgh, 1926), Henry Rowe Schoolcraft's *Information Respecting the History Condition and Prospects of the Indian Tribes of the United States* in five volumes (Philadelphia, 1853–56), and Charles Wilkes's *Narrative of the United States Exploring Expedition During the Years 1838, 1839, 1840, 1841, 1842* in five volumes plus atlas (Philadelphia, 1845). The Wilkes set came from the library of Peter Gerard Stuyvesant, while the Schoolcraft set was a discard from the Boston Public Library, valued on May 1, 1928, at fifteen dollars.

Western History Materials

With the hiring in 1950 of Professor Arthur Throckmorton to teach courses on American West and Pacific Northwest history, the Lewis & Clark College faculty gained a colleague who annually expended part of his book budget on materials to support his courses. Throckmorton's death at a young age in 1962 interrupted this acquisition program. It renewed, however, in 1977 with the hiring of Professor Stephen Dow Beckham and the development of a regular complement of survey courses, seminars, and field-based programs concerned with the history of the American West and Native Americans.

In 1978, Edmund and Anna Hayes of Portland gave twenty-one thousand dollars to triple-match a grant of seven thousand dollars from the National Endowment for the Humanities. These funds were to help Beckham develop a collection to support his curriculum. As a result, the Watzek Library began to acquire books, periodicals, microfiche, and microfilms at a steady pace. These included federal census schedules (1850–1920) for the Pacific Northwest, the Smithsonian Institution's microfilm edition of the papers of John Peabody Harrington regarding his fieldwork with Pacific Northwest tribes, and the large microform publication of *The Plains and the Rockies*, a collection founded on the Wagner-Camp bibliography of the same title. Other acquisitions included field correspondence of the Bureau of Indian Affairs for California, Oregon, Washington, and Idaho (1848–1874), runs of important regional newspapers, the Oregon Territorial Papers, and reprints of out-of-print county and regional histories from University Microfilms. Purchases facilitated by the Hayes gift still carry a special bookplate with the library's logo owl, illustrated in the Northwest Coast style by Chief Lelooska.

Acquisitions in the Watzek Library were developed along with a parallel program in the College's Paul L. Boley Law Library. The law purchases included on microfiche the entire Congressional Serial Set, expert witness testimony in 280 cases adjudicated by the Indian Claims Commission, the Congressional Information Service Index in ninety volumes, Charles J. Kappler's *Indian Laws and Treaties*, and other materials to support the College's environmental law and Indian law programs.

Frederick William Beinecke of New York City initiated the College's Lewis and Clark Expedition collection with a boxed copy of *The Field Notes of Captain William Clark 1803–1805* (1964), edited by Ernest Staples Osgood. On June 12, 1966, Beinecke presented the volume to the College elegantly encased in a green leather clamshell box with gold tooling that identified the volume, author, donor, and date. Beinecke, founder of the S & H Green Stamp Stores, was also an avid collector of Western Americana and a primary force behind creation of the Beinecke Library at Yale University. Beinecke was a Yale graduate who developed a passionate interest in Western history. He spent millions of dollars purchasing books, maps, photographs, and manuscripts for the library bearing his name on the New Haven campus.

Laurence L. Shaw, a lumber executive born in 1908 in Mill City, Oregon, and a graduate of Stanford University, served as a trustee of Lewis & Clark College. In 1973, Shaw and his wife, Dorothy, gave the *History of the Expedition Under the Command of Captains Lewis and Clark* (Philadelphia, 1814), appraised at six thousand dollars, to Lewis & Clark College's Watzek Library. This remarkable two-volume set, bound in original boards, had previously been owned by Frederick Beinecke but was deaccessioned from the Yale collection. This gift became a powerful fulcrum for further Lewis and Clark acquisitions.

The Shaws were collectors of Western Americana for more than forty years. In 1983, they donated their books and endowment funds to establish the Shaw Historical Library at the Oregon Institute of Technology in Klamath Falls. Their collection focused on logging, sawmilling, railroads, exploration, and Native Americans.

Annually since 1986, the *Journal of the Shaw Library* has published documents and new historical research about the Klamath Basin area.

In 1981, Eldon G. "Frenchy" Chuinard, M.D. (1904–1993), an orthopedic surgeon in Portland, proposed putting his research collection about the Lewis and Clark Expedition on loan to Lewis & Clark College. Chuinard, a 1925 graduate of the University of Puget Sound and a 1934 graduate of the University of Oregon Medical School, had maintained a decades-long fascination with the Corps of Discovery. He translated that interest into years of service to the Lewis and Clark Trail Heritage Foundation. He penned articles and wrote *Only One Man Died: The Medical Aspects of the Lewis and Clark Expedition* (1979). In addition to maintaining his orthopedic practice, Chuinard taught as a clinical professor at the University of Oregon medical school in Portland, published twenty-two scientific papers, and lectured widely to audiences at medical schools around the world.

The Chuinard collection was a library shared by Chuinard's entire family: his wife, his daughter, and his son, Robert Chuinard, M.D. In 1981, the family agreed that the time was right for the books to be placed at the College, where they might be used by students and other researchers interested in the expedition. Chuinard's passion for the Lewis and Clark Expedition created a ritual: he often began his day by reading a selection from the expedition journals of that same date. In a letter on October 19, 1981, Chuinard pressed Leonoor Ingraham, then director of the Watzek Library: "I would like you to consider, too, in future plans and developments, the creation of a Lewis and Clark Corner in your library, with copies of Lewis and Clark paintings, maps, bronzes, copies of the portraits of Jefferson, Lewis and Clark—all for the purpose of visually enhancing the aura for the visiting scholars and our own students."

On December 17, 1981, Chuinard and his son, Robert, transferred 161 books and 208 journals, pamphlets, and reprints about the Lewis and Clark Expedition to the College. The Chuinards also gave one thousand dollars toward cataloging the materials. Each piece of the Chuinard collection carries a special bookplate: a copy of Lewis's drawing of *Berberis aquifolium* (Oregon grape) found on February 12, 1806, at Fort Clatsop. The books' move to the campus did nothing to slow Chuinard's passion for the subject or his book collecting. In 1982, he paid Warren R. Howell of John Howell Books, San Francisco, six thousand dollars for the "edition de luxe" of Thwaites's *Original Journals of the Lewis and Clark Expedition 1804–1806* with hand-tinted plates, a printing of fifty copies. The books were added within days to the holdings at the College.

Each year, Chuinard added more titles to the collection, as well as maps, framed portraits of Lewis and Clark, and other items. On December 29, 1986, Robert Chuinard executed a deed of gift of the entire library to the College. "We spent many happy hours together in bookstores from Charlottesville, Virginia to San Francisco, California in search of many of these priceless volumes," he wrote. The younger Chuinard continued: "We have shared our thoughts and opinions of the Expedition in countless discussions based on our reading of this material." The elder Chuinard's purchases and gifts continued for many years. He visited his donated collection at the Watzek Library a last time in January 1992, when he was eighty-seven.

In 1983, the College secured another highly significant addition to its resources on the American West. John Walton Caughey (1902–1997) and his wife, LaRee Caughey (1902–1996), of Los Angeles gave thirty-two hundred volumes to the

Watzek Library. The books were part of their research and reading library, which John Caughey used to write and edit thirty books, seven of them with LaRee. A 1923 graduate of the University of Texas, Caughey briefly taught high school before entering the University of California at Berkeley, where he earned his master's and doctoral degrees under the mentoring of Herbert Eugene Bolton. In 1930, Caughey joined the faculty of the Department of History at the University of California at Los Angeles (UCLA), where he taught for forty years. His courses were in American history, especially that of California, the American West, and the American Indian.

Caughey's initial research focused on the Spanish borderlands from Florida to California. He wrote extensively on the Gold Rush, overland emigration, Native Americans, civil rights, and civil liberties. The latter subject emerged as a twenty-year commitment, when he was fired by the regents of the University of California for refusing to take their loyalty oath during the McCarthy Era. Although removed from his post at UCLA, Caughey continued to teach graduate students in seminars in his home. He also retained his role as the state's expert witness in the tidelands oil litigation in federal court, and persisted as editor of the *Pacific Historical Review*. While at the helm of this journal for twenty-seven years, he monitored the new histories of the western United States and built a remarkable library of works of current scholarship, as well as classics on exploration and travel. In 1954, Caughey was restored to his professorship at UCLA and awarded full salary plus interest for the years of his suspension. His essay, "A University in Jeopardy," in *Harper's Magazine* (1950) and his eloquent treatise, "A Plea to the Regents of the University of California," were landmarks in the loyalty-oath controversy.

Caughey taught American history to millions of Americans. For more than sixty years his book, *California: The History of a Remarkable State*, was the premier college textbook on the subject. He also wrote elementary and college history texts. His biggest success in textbook writing came when he coauthored *Land of the Free*, an American history text for eighth graders, with John Hope Franklin of the University of Chicago and Ernest May of Harvard University. The book gained initial statewide adoption in New York, Texas, and California, and was used in many other states following its publication in 1965. The work was both acclaimed and criticized because it integrated poor and minority populations into the history of the United States in text and illustrations. Caughey also mentored dozens of master's and doctoral students, wrote hundreds of book reviews, and authored more than seventy articles for scholarly journals. One of his former students, Stephen Dow Beckham, suggested to the Caugheys that their library would remarkably strengthen the Western history holdings at Lewis & Clark College. They agreed.

Special works in the Caugheys' library included the Quivera Society publications, narratives of Spanish exploration edited by Herbert Eugene Bolton, Henry Raup Wagner's works on cartography and the maritime voyages along the West Coast of North America, and numerous works of fiction and poetry by Western authors. The Caugheys' great love of literature was confirmed in their coedited literary anthology, *California Heritage*. Caughey was also biographer of Hubert Howe Bancroft, founder of the Bancroft Library at the University of California at Berkeley, and "author" of the *History of the Pacific States*. The Caughey collection included the thirty-nine volumes of "Bancroft's Works," each with Caughey's title-page notations about contributions from Bancroft's research staff. The

Caugheys' library included fine-press and limited editions published by the Grabhorn Press, Ward Ritchie Press, and Grant Dahlstrom. The Caughey library significantly broadened and deepened the Western history holdings of the Watzek Library. The John and LaRee Caughey Foundation has, in recent years, also made endowment gifts to Lewis & Clark College for library acquisitions.

In 1988, the heirs of Francis D. Haines Sr. gave to the College his library of 297 books about the Columbia Plateau—the sprawling interior of the Pacific Northwest. Haines was born in 1899 in Buchanan, West Virginia, but grew up on his parents' homestead near Clancy, Montana. After service in World War I, where he was wounded at Verdun, he earned a bachelor's degree in engineering from Montana State College and later a master's degree from the University of Montana. Haines's commitment to history developed while he worked as a school principal and superintendent. During the summer of 1935, Haines met Walter Prescott Webb while enrolled in a summer course at Harvard University. Webb advised him to seek admission to the University of California at Berkeley to study with Herbert Eugene Bolton. Haines went on to earn his Ph.D. in 1938 with Bolton, then taught until his retirement in 1966. Haines's last fifteen years of teaching were at Oregon College of Education, now Western Oregon State University in Monmouth, Oregon.

Haines's dissertation on the Nez Perce tribe was published as *Red Eagles of the Northwest* (1939). Significantly revised, the book reappeared as *The Nez Percés: Tribesmen of the Columbia Plateau* (1955). Haines also wrote *The Story of Idaho* (1942), *The Appaloosa Horse* (1950), and *Oregon in the U.S.A.* (1955). Because of these interests, the Haines collection included the multi-volume Pacific Railroad Surveys with handsome, colored plates and maps printed prior to the Civil War, as well as numerous books about Columbia Plateau tribes. Haines's love of horses was confirmed both in his book on the Appaloosa and the long run of the periodical *Western Horseman*, which was added to the College's holdings. Keith Woodard, a Haines grandson and alumnus of Lewis & Clark College, helped facilitate this gift.

In the 1990s, the forces for development of the Watzek Library grew dramatically through the College presidency of Michael Mooney. A historian and scholar of the Renaissance, Mooney realized that the Watzek Library needed significant new shelf space, study rooms, and upgraded electronic access. In 1992, Dr. Robert B. Pamplin Jr., chair of the Board of Trustees, made a one-million-dollar pledge to kick off the library expansion project. The "Chairman's Challenge" brought students, faculty, and staff into an intense day of athletic competition and community-building. The success of this fund-raising initiative led in 1995 to the doubling in size of the Watzek Library, the construction of a new Heritage Room to house Special Collections, and the Ronna and Eric Hoffman Gallery of Contemporary Art on a lower level of the new building.

With the facilities in place, President Mooney then posed the question: could Lewis & Clark College become the world's primary center for research on the Lewis and Clark Expedition? Could it augment its existing collections and garner first-rank status on this subject? Douglas Erickson, head of the College's Special Collections and an active member of the Lewis and Clark Trail Heritage Foundation, believed that the deed could be done. Using his connections with rare-book dealers, Erickson soon met Roger Wendlick, a Portland book collector. Friendship between the two led to the College's good fortune when, in 1998, by purchase and gift, the Wendlick library of Lewis and Clark materials came to the Watzek Library.

A construction worker by trade, Wendlick became committed to building a Lewis and Clark Expedition collection in 1984. He had previously assembled memorabilia—plates, pitchers, mugs, cigar boxes, post cards, and miscellany—associated with the Lewis and Clark Centennial Exposition of 1905. When he lost interest in the eleven hundred items he had acquired, Wendlick sold them and began buying books. For the next fourteen years, he pursued the agenda with single-minded purpose. His ambitious goal was to acquire every edition of each printed item by or about the expedition. His coverage ranged from primary to secondary works, biographies of expedition members, accounts of those who helped prepare Lewis for the field, studies of the tribes encountered, books and maps in the expedition's traveling library, and government documents mentioning or reporting on the expedition. He also collected magazine accounts and reviews of books published about the Corps of Discovery printed between 1803 and 1817. The Wendlick holdings also included numerous pamphlets, articles, and juvenile literature about the expedition printed in the twentieth century.

Wendlick was not a formal scholar. He secured one year of college at Portland State University. In addition, his steady work of six days a week in the construction business left him little time to read and enjoy the books that filled both his shelves and a hulking Mosler safe with double fireproof doors. However, his determination to acquire the finest library on the expedition was relentless. Several times, in fact, he mortgaged his home to finance book purchases. He rationed out his paychecks over many months to pay William Reese for a premier 1814 Biddle-Allen edition of the journals he found in 1992 at the dealer's counter at the Los Angeles Antiquarian Book Fair. He traveled, searched, shopped, and closed deals. He worked his way through the editions of the Patrick Gass journal, obtained the rare Dutch edition of the Biddle-Allen narrative, and, whenever possible, upgraded his collection to printings in fine condition or possessing special associational value. He also obtained fascinating contemporary newspaper notices about the departure and return of the expedition, confirming strong public interest in the venture.

Then, as he phrased, "it was time for these children—my books—to come to college." Lewis & Clark College's Watzek Library became their new home, and Wendlick came with them, serving as a volunteer collection curator in the Heritage Room. In a marvelous moment of serendipity, Wendlick's passionate labors to build a magnificent private library focused on a single theme coincided precisely with the College's mission to catapult its holdings on the expedition to the first rank.

In 1999, Brian and Gwyneth Booth gave to the College the only reported copy of a broadside, *National Intelligencer Extraordinary*, printed in Washington, D.C., on December 2, 1806. The publication announced the success of the Lewis and Clark Expedition to the residents of the nation's capital. Brian Booth, a Portland attorney, patron of the arts, and founder of Literary Arts, felt that this special ephemeral publication would have a good home in Lewis & Clark's Heritage Room. A publication in three columns, the broadside presented the report of President Jefferson to Congress on the latest intelligence of the Western exploring expeditions.

For nearly thirty years, the Lewis and Clark Trail Heritage Foundation kept a mailbox at the campus post office. Every week, Chuinard, Robert Lange (long-time editor of *We Proceeded On*, the foundation's journal), and Irving Anderson gathered for a cup of coffee, to open the mail, discuss their research, and plan

Oregon chapter activities. Anderson (1920–1999), a career employee with the Bureau of Land Management, lived directly across the street from the campus. His passion was to research the poorly documented history of Sacagawea, her husband, and son. In time, Anderson's essays appeared in *American West, South Dakota History, Oregon Historical Quarterly*, and *We Proceeded On*. These shorter pieces led to an important work, *A Charbonneau Family Portrait: Biographical Sketches of Sacagawea, Jean Baptiste, and Toussaint Charbonneau* (1988, revised 1992). Anderson also worked as consultant to the Department of the Treasury, United States Mint, researching the image of Sacagawea for the gold one-dollar coin that was issued in 2000.

After his death in 2000, the family of Irving Anderson donated to the College his research library: 130 books and twenty-five cubic feet of archival material on the expedition. The volumes reflect Anderson's years of reading and notetaking. Many publications are filled with 3" x 5" file cards with notes, marking passages or subjects he wanted to consult further. The Anderson collection also included periodical articles published in the twentieth century and helped fill out more of the College's holdings of these more ephemeral materials.

Also in 2000, George H. Tweney (1916–2000), an author, aeronautical engineer, pilot, and longtime Seattle dealer in rare books, received confirmation from his doctor that he had only a few months to live. As a result, Tweney made a number of decisions about the disposition of his books. His library included a fine Jack London collection. Tweney and Hensley C. Woodbridge had compiled and written *Jack London: A Bibliography* (554 pages, 1966, revised 1973). These materials went to his alma mater, Michigan State University. His magnificent collection of printed materials related to Samuel Johnson and James Boswell was to remain with his family. As author of the bibliography *The Washington 89*, Tweney had previously identified from his collection what he considered the most important eighty-nine books published about the state or by residents of the state. This list and his essays became a guide for a number of regional book collectors.

Another part of Tweney's library was a Lewis and Clark Expedition collection. In it was a one-of-a-kind work: the Coues-Anderson manuscript facsimile of the original Lewis and Clark journals from the American Philosophical Society in Philadelphia. In 1892, Elliott Coues had commissioned Mary B. Anderson to copy the thousands of pages of the journals (For further detail, see chapter 5). Unlike the originals, the only marks on the Coues-Anderson manuscript are those of Coues. He worked with the portion of the journey up the Missouri River in 1804, in anticipation of editing the manuscripts he had discovered well-preserved but forgotten in Philadelphia. Coues, however, became diverted by other projects and died before he could complete the project. Tweney found Coues's materials in 1970 in a New York bookstore back room. Tweney paid one hundred dollars for the box, brought it to Seattle, and promptly had the facsimile placed in sixteen custom-made boxes.

Interestingly, Tweney had helped mentor Wendlick during his collecting years. Now their friendship and Tweney's waning health persuaded him to consider selling his collection to join the Wendlick collection at the College. This important acquisition was made in spring 2000. It deepened again the already-diverse holdings in the Heritage Room and added the unique Coues-Anderson manuscript to the College's expedition materials.

In 2001, James Kidd, M.D., retired pathologist from the Children's Hospital of Chicago and collector of Western Americana, made a highly important gift to the College of multiple volumes by French explorer Duflot de Mofras. A diplomat, historian, and scholar, de Mofras traveled for the French government in 1840 to examine conditions on the West Coast of North America from Mexico to Alaska. His two years of explorations entailed examination of harbors, terrain, and settlements. He wrote a general descriptive work that filled in the details of Euro-American activities in the Pacific Northwest subsequent to the Lewis and Clark Expedition. Kidd's gift to Lewis & Clark College included the French edition in original boards, *Exploration du Territoire de l'Orégon, des Californies et de la Mer Vermeille* . . . , printed by Arthus Bertrand (Paris, 1844), and its accompanying atlas with twenty-six engraved maps. "Carte Du Rio Colombia" identified Indian villages and settlements from "Cap San Roque ou Désappointement" to Fort Vancouver. In addition, Kidd's gift included translator Marguerite Eyer Wilbur's personal copies of the two-volume English-language edition printed on white Chippendale text paper in an edition of four hundred copies. The translated edition, *Duflot de Mofras' Travels on the Pacific Coast,* was printed in 1937 by Fine Arts Press (Santa Ana, California).

Books are part of the glue that helps hold together civilization. Unlike oral tradition, books can communicate through a skip of generations. For instance, interest in the Lewis and Clark Expedition was intense in the United States and Western Europe between 1803 and 1817, then it waned and was barely sustained by the occasional reprinting of Archibald M'Vickar's 1842 abridgement of the Biddle-Allen edition in the Harper Family Library. The expedition's centennial increased interest in the event, and a flood of new publications marked the years 1893 to 1905. The pace then slackened, but renewed with the sesquicentennial in 1953–56, and again waned. Now, with the advent of the expedition's bicentennial, the flood of materials surges again.

The Lewis & Clark College Collection documents part of the larger fabric of the human experience in western North America. The materials were assembled with the understanding that Jefferson's vision for the expedition was couched in the eighteenth-century Enlightenment, and that he approached the exploration of the West with practical, commercial, diplomatic, and scientific objectives. His remarkable letter of instruction, penned on June 20, 1803, to Meriwether Lewis confirmed the breadth of his vision and designs for the young nation he had helped create. The holdings at Lewis & Clark College document two hundred years of coming to terms with a remarkable event: an overland expedition that helped craft a continental nation. These volumes speak to ordinary people carrying out a mission with extraordinary consequences. They also document the soundness of a clear mission, quality leadership, attention to detail, and perseverance in the face of immense adversity.

Chapter One
The Expedition's Traveling Library

Essay 25
Bibliography 43

1a Books Consulted in Advance or Carried on the Expedition
1a.1 *Dictionary of Arts and Sciences* 1754-55
1a.2 Antoine-Simon Le Page du Pratz, *History of Louisiana* [1763], 1774
1a.3 Benjamin Rush, *Directions for Preserving the Health of Soldiers* 1778
1a.4 John Miller's *Linnæus* 1779, 1789
1a.5 *The Articles of War*, Issued Annually
1a.6 Richard Kirwan, *Elements of Mineralogy* [1784], 1794, [1810]
1a.7 Patrick Kelly, *Introduction to Spherics and Nautical Astronomy* 1796, 1801
1a.8-9 Nevil Maskelyne, *Tables Requisite* 1766-1802; *Nautical Ephemeris* 1804-6
1a.10 Benjamin Smith Barton, *Elements of Botany* 1803
1a.11 Alexander Mackenzie, *Voyages* 1802
1a.12 Andrew Ellicott, *Journal* 1803

1b Maps Carried on the Expedition
1b.1 Antoine-Simon Le Page du Pratz, "Louisiana" [1763], 1774
1b.2 Aaron Arrowsmith, "New Discoveries" 1802
1b.3 Nicholas King, Manuscript Map of Western North America 1803
    1b.3(i) Guillaume de l'Isle, "Carte de la Louisiane" [1718]
    1b.3(ii) James Cook, "Chart of the Northwest Coast of America" 1784
    1b.3(iii) George Vancouver, "Part of the Coast of N.W. America" 1798
    1b.3(iv) Alexander Mackenzie, "America Between Latitudes 40 and 70 North" 1801
    1b.3(v) Andrew Ellicott, Maps of the Mississippi River 1803

1c Other Manuscript Maps Carried on the Expedition
1c.1 James Mackay, Map of the Missouri River from St. Charles to the Mandan Villages 1797
1c.2 John Evans, Map of the Missouri 1797
1c.3 Antoine Soulard, Map of the Missouri to the Osage 1803
1c.4 [Antoine Soulard], Map of Upper Louisiana, Copied from a Spanish Original ca. 1794–1803

1d Examples of Other Manuscript Materials in the Traveling Library
1d.1 Jean Baptiste Truteau, *Journal Extracts* Translated by Jefferson 1803
1d.2 Robert Patterson/Meriwether Lewis, *Astronomy Notebook* 1803, 1805, 1806
1d.3 John Evans and James Mackay, *Journal Extracts* Translated by John Hay 1804

The Expedition's Traveling Library

A diverse collection of maps, books, and manuscripts accompanied
the expedition on its westward journey. The library included important
resources related to geography, navigation, taxonomy, medicine, military
procedures, and native populations.

While many of the labors and adventures of the Lewis and Clark Expedition are
well known, the party's role in carrying the first library across North America in
1804–6 has remained obscure and incompletely documented.[1] The books and
maps in their kit confirmed both the intellectual purposes of their labors and
also the captains' commitment to mount their observations and descriptions with
as much accuracy and detail as they could muster. This traveling library was a
modest portent of the development of great research libraries that, in subsequent
decades, shaped the life of the mind in the United States. In a substantial way,
the library's weight was physical as well as intellectual. The books were sufficient
to fill a full saddlebag for a horse and were part of the dead weight in the keel-
boat's hold so laboriously moved up the Missouri and in the pirogues taken to
that stream's headwaters. Books were also essential baggage taking up space in
the dugouts during the explorers' travels to the great Columbia River west of
the mountains. Lewis and Clark gave hearty meaning to the term "travelers
who put books in their baggage."

As secretary and confidante of President Thomas Jefferson, Lewis had ample
opportunity—fortunately—to become familiar with Jefferson's research into the
care and storage of paper documents. On January 16, 1796, Jefferson wrote to
George Wythe (ca. 1726–1806), a mentor, jurist, and lifelong friend, and described
his ambitious project to collect the printed laws of Virginia. Some of the documents were in such fragile condition that they were disintegrating into powder.
"These I preserve," wrote Jefferson, "by wrapping & sewing them up in oiled
cloth, so that neither air nor moisture can have access to them." Jefferson referred
to these documents as "precious monuments of our property, and our history."[2]
Because of his concern for preserving longitude and latitude data recorded during
the expedition, Jefferson admonished Lewis to keep two documentary copies. He
added: "A further guard would be that one of these copies be on the paper of the
birch, as less liable to injury from damp than common paper."[3] Jefferson's own
work on document preservation, his remarkably tender care for the books in his
library, and his worries about the susceptibility of the written record to the ravages
of moisture and time encouraged Lewis and Clark to take special precautions
with their traveling library of maps, books, journals, and field notes.

Lewis's shopping lists contain a few clues that suggest how the books and
maps were handled. Presumably, the maps were cut, mounted on linen for preservation and ease of handling in the field, and folded—perhaps for carrying in a
leather case. Possibly as a barrier to moisture, the books were wrapped and placed
in a wood box. Lewis purchased in Philadelphia "20 yds. Oil Linnen for wrapping
& securing Articles" and thirty "Oil Cloth bags well painted."[4] Upon the expedition's return to St. Louis, Clark forwarded a set of books—the expedition's four-
volume dictionary—along with two Indian wallets and natural history specimens
in "a Hat Box."[5] This container may have made the entire journey and, for a time,

1 The initial identification
and discussion of the
materials consulted and
taken on the expedition
appears in Jackson, "Some
Books Carried" (1959) and
*Thomas Jefferson & the Stony
Mountains* (1981:132–134).

2 Peterson, *Thomas Jefferson*,
1031–1032.

3 Jackson, *Letters*, 1:62–63.

4 Ibid., 1:71, 74

5 Thwaites, *Original Journals*,
6:280.

> "The object of your
> mission is to explore
> the Missouri River
> and such principal
> stream of it, as by its
> source and commu-
> nication with the
> waters of the Pacific
> Ocean . . . may offer
> the most direct and
> practicable water
> communication
> across this continent
> for the purpose of
> commerce."
>
> Thomas Jefferson
> to Meriwether Lewis,
> June 20, 1803

held the captain's handsome uniform hat with feathered decoration. Subsequently, the hat box served as a secure container for books.

The contents of the traveling library were influenced by the individuals who trained Meriwether Lewis in his duties for the expedition. Thomas Jefferson was the central figure in this enterprise. An ardent bibliophile, Jefferson assembled three libraries during his lifetime: the first was destroyed in a fire; the second was sold to Congress in 1815 to replace its library destroyed by the British Army during the War of 1812–14; and the third was the collection from his retirement years at Monticello. It is not surprising that a number of books and maps consulted or carried by Lewis and Clark were in Jefferson's second library.[6] Other experts instructed Lewis, advised on materials, and lent him books. These counselors included Albert Gallatin, Henry Dearborn, Andrew Ellicott, Benjamin Smith Barton, M.D., Caspar Wistar, M.D., Benjamin Rush, M.D., and Robert Patterson. Jefferson's notice to those assisting Lewis was articulated in his letter to Benjamin Rush on February 28, 1803: "Capt. Lewis is brave, prudent, habituated to the woods, & familiar with Indian manners & character. He is not regularly educated, but he possesses a great mass of accurate observation on all the subjects of nature which present themselves here . . . . For this purpose I ask the favor of you to pre-pare some notes of such particulars as may occur in his journey & which you think should draw his attention & enquiry."[7]

Books

The *Dictionary of Arts and Sciences*, a four-volume work first printed in 1754–55 and sometimes referred to as *Owen's Dictionary*, was a core part of the traveling library. Thomas Jefferson had a copy of *A New and Complete Dictionary of Arts and Sciences* . . . published in 1763–64 by William Owen at Homer's Head in Fleet Street, London. Jefferson probably purchased the four volumes while living in Paris. He referred to the set in a 1785 letter to a teacher at William & Mary College. Jefferson greatly valued *Owen's Dictionary* and on October 4, 1809, wrote to Samuel R. Demaree: "I am not acquainted with Rees's Encyclopedia; but I suppose it inferior to the British published by Dobson. but Owen's is a very good supplement to any collection of particular treatises, & costs in England but 8. Dollars . . . ."[8]

Ephraim Chambers (ca. 1680–1740) compiled and published in 1728 in two folio volumes the *Cyclopaedia, or an Universal Dictionary of Arts and Sciences*. The son of a farmer, Chambers had settled in London as a young man and was apprenticed to John Senex, a maker of maps and globes who encouraged Chambers's interest in general knowledge. Chambers's work gained considerable attention and secured his election to the Royal Society in 1729. His *Cyclopaedia* went through a number of revisions and editions, a French translation becoming the foundation for Diderot's and D'Alembert's great *Encyclopaedia*.[9] In 1778, Abraham Rees (1743–1825) took over revisions of the Chambers work. He added extensive new material and, from 1781 to 1786, published it in four volumes. Rees gained memberships in the Royal Society, Linnean Society, and American Philosophical Society as a consequence of his work. In 1802, Robert Carr printed the first American edition of *The New Cyclopaedia; or, Universal Dictionary of Arts and Sciences* for John Conrad in Philadelphia. In 1798, Thomas Dobson of Philadelphia published yet another work—*Encyclopaedia; or, A Dictionary of Arts, Science, and Miscellaneous Literature*—a volume dismissed by

6 Sowerby, *Catalogue*, ix–xiii.

7 Jackson, *Letters*, 1:18–19.

8 Sowerby, *Catalogue*, 5:153.

9 Espinasse, "Ephraim Chambers," *Dictionary of National Biography*, 4:16–17.

Jefferson, who considered it inferior. Thus, though there were several multi-volume encyclopedias or dictionaries in print by 1803, it remains likely that Lewis and Clark packed the four-volume *Owen's Dictionary* in their traveling kit.

William Owen (d. 1793) first came to public notice in 1748 with publication of a pamphlet, *The Remembrances*, by George Cadwallader. In 1749, "W. Owen, bookseller," was in business on St. James Street, but his enduring address was at "Homer's Head," Fleet Street, where he ran a bookshop for more than forty years. On July 6, 1752, Owen was tried but acquitted for selling a pamphlet setting forth the sufferings of Alexander Murray, who had interfered in a parliamentary election. Owen probably considered himself fortunate when the House of Commons voted *The Case of Alexander Murray, Esq.*, and found that he did not publish the pamphlet it deemed "an impudent, malicious, scandalous and seditious libel." For many years, Owen published with W. Goadby *An Account of the Fairs Held in England and Wales* and also the *Book of Roads*. These volumes went through numerous editions. In 1781, Owen was named a Master of the Stationers' Company.[10]

On March 13, 1806, Lewis wrote a description at Fort Clatsop about the "common Salmon and red Charr." His language was precise: "the eye is large and the iris of a silvery colour the pupil black. the rustrum or nose extends beyond the under jaw and both the upper and lower jaws are armed with a single series of long teeth which are subulate and infleted near the extremities of the jaws . . . ."[11] An entry in *Owen's Dictionary* contains nearly parallel wording: "The common salmo, or salmon, with the rostrum extending beyond the lower jaw, is an inhabitant of both the sea and rivers. . . the eyes are round, and their iris of a silvery colour, with a faint admixture of green; the pupil is black."[12] Although the match is not exact, this passage suggests Lewis used *Owen's Dictionary* while on the shores of the Pacific.[13]

The most definitive evidence of *Owen's Dictionary* being included in the traveling library appeared in William Clark's journal on January 21, 1804. Clark "Defined the word Sense:"

> It is a faculty of the Soul, whereby it perceived external Objects, by means of the impressions they make on certain organs of the body. These organs are Commonly reconed 5, Viz: the Eyes, whereby we See objects; the ear, which enables us to hear sounds; the nose, by which we receive the Ideas of different smells; the Palate, by which we judge of tastes; and the Skin, which enables us to feel—the different forms, hardness, or Softness of bodies.[14]

Clark's definition is identical to that for "SENSE" in *Owen's Dictionary*, with one change in verb tense, omission of "the cutis, or" (the reference to skin), spelling of "reckoned," and use of the number 5 rather than the word "five."[15]

Antoine-Simon Le Page du Pratz (ca. 1695–1775) resided in Louisiana from 1718 to 1734. His book about his North American experiences was in Thomas Jefferson's library and in the traveling collection of the Corps of Discovery.[16] Trained in engineering, architecture, and astronomy, du Pratz secured land near Natchez, Mississippi, as part of a colonization venture organized by John Law and the Company of the West. He resided among the Indians and may have fathered children by native women. In 1728, he moved to New Orleans to manage a plantation. He lived there during and after an Indian revolt—the Natchez Massacre of 1729—and later returned to France. In a dozen installments between September 1751 and February 1753, he published his "Memoire sur la Louisiane," a prelude

"You will therefore endeavor to make yourself acquainted, as far as a diligent pursuit of your journey shall admit, with the names of the nations and their numbers; the extent and limits of their possessions; their relations with other tribes or nations; their language, traditions, monuments."

Thomas Jefferson to Meriwether Lewis, June 20, 1803

10 Plomer and Bushnell, *A Dictionary*, 187–188.

11 Moulton, *The Journals*, 6:410.

12 Society of Gentlemen, *A New and Complete Dictionary*, 4:2792.

13 Jackson, "Some Books Carried," 12.

14 Moulton, *The Journals*, 2:161.

15 Society of Gentlemen, *A New and Complete Dictionary*, 4:2866–2867.

16 Sowerby, *Catalogue*, 4:237.

to the expanded narrative in three octavo volumes *Histoire de la Louisiane* (1758). Du Pratz described conditions in Louisiana and his exploration to the Great Plains. He became best known, however, for his ethnographic sketch of the Natchez tribe, an account included in John R. Swanton's *Indian Tribes of the Lower Mississippi Valley* (1911) and used extensively in courses on North American ethnography. The work, "severely abridged and rearranged," was translated and published in two volumes in London as *The History of Louisiana, or of the Western Parts of Virginia and Carolina . . .* (1763).[17] The four parts of this work included the French in Louisiana, the country and its products, the natural history of Louisiana, and the natives of Louisiana.[18]

Meriwether Lewis borrowed a copy of the second English edition of 1774 in one volume from Benjamin Smith Barton. The copy is in the Library Company of Philadelphia and bears the inscription:

> Dr. Benjamin Smith Barton was so obliging as to lend me this copy of Monsr. Du Pratz's history of Louisiana in June 1803. It has been since conveyed by me to the Pacific Ocean through the interior of Continent of North America on my late tour thither and is now returned to it's proprietor by his Friend and Obt. Servt. Philadelphia, May 9th, 1807 Meriwether Lewis.[19]

The captains also needed a manual of medical instruction for treating ailments and accidents in the field. Benjamin Rush, M.D., (1746–1813) of Philadelphia provided basic information to Lewis in the spring of 1803. Educated at the College of New Jersey (later Princeton), Rush returned to Philadelphia in 1761 and began a medical apprenticeship with John Redman and attended lectures at the University of Pennsylvania. In 1766, Rush traveled to Scotland and enrolled in the renowned medical school at the University of Edinburgh where, in 1768, he received his degree. Rush then spent a residency at St. Thomas's Hospital, London, and visited France. In 1769, he entered medical practice in Philadelphia and in 1771 gained appointment to the first professorship in chemistry at the College of Philadelphia. During the Revolutionary War, Rush served in the Second Continental Congress, signed the Declaration of Independence, and was commissioned as surgeon general of the Middle Department of the continental army. His criticism of disorganization and corruption in army hospitals led to tensions and his resignation. For the remainder of his life, Rush was a leading physician, author, and teacher at the University of the State of Pennsylvania.[20]

During his tenure with the army, Rush wrote an eight-page pamphlet, *Directions for Preserving the Health of Soldiers* (1778). Used during the war, the Rush guide (originally published in a periodical in 1777) went through numerous printings and was re-issued in 1865 "for the Union Army, waging the Second War of Independence."[21] Rush was a learned man who wrote on many topics: extraction of maple sugar, medical practices of American Indians, women's education, temperance, capital punishment, inoculation for smallpox, and mental illness. A collection of his essays, *Medical Inquiries and Observations*, was published in four volumes in 1804 in Philadelphia. It is likely that, as a military unit, the Corps of Discovery carried Rush's *Directions*. On June 11, 1803, Rush wrote out for Lewis a set of eleven "Rules of Health." Copies survive in the Jefferson papers, Library of Congress, and in Rush's "commonplace book" at the American Philosophical Society.[22] Well documented in the expedition's supplies were "Dr. Rush's Bilious Pills," the "thunderbolts" that purged the intestines of all contents and which the good doctor

17 Sayre, "Antoine-Simon Le Page du Pratz."

18 Sowerby, *Catalogue*, 4:237.

19 Jackson, *Letters*, 2:695.

20 Sullivan, "Benjamin Rush," *American National Biography*, 19:72–75.

21 Sabin, *A Dictionary of Books*, 130.

22 Jackson, *Letters*, 1:54–55.

prescribed as a curative for a variety of ailments.[23]

In outfitting the expedition in Philadelphia, Lewis recorded in June 1803 his purchase of crayons, sealing wax, books, maps, charts, blank vocabularies (for recording Indian words), a variety of scientific instruments, and "Miller's edition of Lineus in 2 vol."[24] Lewis had obtained the works of Karl von Linné, the Swedish botanist and taxonomist, translated from Latin to English by John Miller and published in London. The first volume, *An Illustration of the Sexual System, of Linnæus* (1779), was "Sold at the Authors House in Dorset-Corner near Parliament Street and at the Principal Booksellers." The octavo edition of 1779, purchased by Lewis, had a handsome frontispiece with a Latin quotation from Genesis 1:12 and a cameo portrait of von Linné.[25]

Born Johann Sebastian Müller (ca. 1715–1790) in Nuremeberg, Miller (his anglicized name) immigrated to England in 1744 with his brother Tobias, an architectural engraver. He settled in London and worked for the remainder of his life as an engraver, especially of botanical subjects. In 1759, Miller published a prospectus for one hundred prints, a "curious Collection of Plants and Insects," the plants to be classified by Philip Miller of the Chelsea Garden and the insects by the system of Dr. Linnæus. The 1779 octavo edition, *An Illustration of the Sexual System, of Linnæus*, carried by the Corps of Discovery, contained 106 colored plates and a quotation from Linnæus promising a second volume. That edition, *An Illustration of the Termini Botanici, of Linnæus*, was published in London in 1789. These two works, translated from Latin into English and supported with dozens of hand-tinted, engraved plates, were a labor of love for John Miller. They were also valuable guides for Lewis as he wrote descriptions of plants he viewed and collected during the expedition. Miller later produced hundreds of additional botanical plates, as well as illustrations for Milton's *Paradise Lost* and Gray's *Poems*.[26]

Because of its organization as a military expedition, it is also highly likely that the Corps of Discovery carried the *Regulations for the Order and Discipline of the Troops . . . the Articles of War* (1794).[27] The British first published rules of conduct for naval military personnel in the 1650s, amended them in 1749, and revised them again in 1757. In 1778, Parliament adopted "Rules and Articles for the better Government of Our Horse and Foot Guards, and all other Our Forces, in Our Kingdoms of Great Britain and Ireland, Dominions beyond the Sea, and Foreign Parts." The "Articles" contained twenty sections of rules on a range of topics such as mutiny, quarters, disposition of the effects of deceased personnel, and administration of justice.[28]

The American military manual was the creation of German-born Frederich W. A. von Steuben (1730–1794). Trained under the harsh discipline of Frederick the Great, Steuben served as a staff officer during the Seven Years War, rising to captain and holding a post in the Prussian general headquarters. Rumors about his sexual orientation, a matter not clearly sustained, drove Steuben from Austria in 1776 and to the United States in 1777. Armed with letters of introduction from Benjamin Franklin and Silas Deane, he joined the American forces under George Washington at Valley Forge. In short order, this officer—who initially knew no English—transformed the farmers and shopkeepers facing British regulars and mercenaries into the continental army. He addressed almost every aspect of soldier life: sanitation, drill, food preparation, and conduct. Washington named Steuben

23 Chuinard, *Only One Man Died*, 133, 155–156.

24 Jackson, *Letters*, 1:70.

25 O'Donoghue and Boulger, "John Miller," *Dictionary of National Biography*, 13:414.

26 Ibid., 13:413–414.

27 Jackson, *Stony Mountains*, 134.

28 "Royal Navy Articles of War–1757," www.hmsrichmond.org/rnarticles; "Articles of War–1778," www.cvco.org/sigs/reg64/articles.

in 1778 the Inspector General of the army, a position he ably held for the duration of the war. During the winter of 1778–79 Steuben wrote the army's *Blue Book*, also known as the *Regulations for the Order and Discipline of the Troops of the United States.* Philander D. Chase, Steuben's biographer, has noted: "The manual became an indispensable guide for the Continental army and remained in active use by U.S. soldiers until the War of 1812, going through more than seventy editions."[29] Steuben's volume was approved by Congress in March 1779 and printed for issue to the army.[30]

The precise edition of the *Articles of War* in the traveling library is not known. However, matters of military discipline probably compelled the captains to consult this work. On March 30, 1804, while at Camp Dubois on Wood River, Clark instituted a court martial of a man for stealing expedition supplies. He wrote: "I red the orders on Parade this evening."[31] Whether or not he referred to Steuben's manual is not clear. On May 17, 1804, however, John Ordway recorded the proceedings of the court martial of John Collins. He wrote: "The Court are of oppinion that the Prisnair is Guilty of all charges alledged against him it being a breach of the rules & articles of War and do Sentence him to receive fifty lashes on his naked back."[32]

Richard Kirwan (1733–1812) was another author represented in the expedition's traveling library. Jefferson owned works by Kirwan, including *An Estimate of the Temperature of different Latitudes* (1787), *The Manures most advantageously applicable to the various Sorts of Soils . . .* (1796), and "Observations on Coal-Mines" in *The Transactions of the Royal Irish Academy* (1789). Lewis purchased Kirwan's *Elements of Mineralogy.* The first edition was printed in London in 1784. It was expanded in a second edition of two volumes in 1794, likely the edition carried by the Corps of Discovery. A chemist and natural philosopher, Kirwan was born in Galway, Ireland. An eager Latin student, Kirwan entered a Jesuit novitiate in 1754 in St. Omer but returned to Ireland in 1755 when his elder brother died in a duel. From 1777 to 1787, Kirwan resided in London and moved in the society of intellectuals. He was elected in 1780 to the Royal Society and in 1782 was awarded the Copley Medal for his papers on chemical affinity.[33]

The utility of Kirwan's *Elements of Mineralogy* was in its descriptions of minerals and some of their uses. Kirwan, like von Linné, presented a classification system to readers: "Minerals in their strictest signification denote only such substances as are found in mines, such as Metals, Semi-metals, Sulphur and Salts; but in a more extensive sense, they denote all fossils that do not belong either to the vegetable or animal kingdoms, and consequently Stones and Earths, all of which are comprehended under the Denomination of the *Mineral kingdom*." Kirwan divided the kingdom into four parts: Earths and Stones, Salts, Inflammable Substances, and Metallic Substances. Of special interest for novices in the field, he included an appendix of "Geological Observations" wherein he defined mountains, theorized about the antiquity and origin of mountains, provided a formula for determining their height (a calculation based on temperature and barometric readings), and discussed petrifications (fossils) and volcanoes. He also laid down observations on the structure of mountains: entire, stratified, homogenous, heterogeneous, and confused. His book was an excellent source for those attempting to come to terms with what they found in nature.[34]

An example of Kirwan's use in the expedition journals appeared on January 7, 1806, in Clark's discussion of climbing Tillamook Head in coastal Oregon. He wrote: ". . . there is a Strater of white earth (which my guide informed me) the

29 Chase, "Friedrich Wilhelm von Steuben," *American National Biography*, 20:689–691.

30 Palmer, *Washington, Lincoln, Wilson*, 52.

31 Moulton, *The Journals*, 2:183.

32 Ibid., 236.

33 Clerke, "Richard Kirwan," *Dictionary of National Biography*, 11:228–230.

34 Kirwan, *Elements of Mineralogy*.

neighboring indians use to paint themselves, and which appears to me to resemble the earth of which French Porcelain is made; I am confident that this earth Contains argill, but whether it Contains Silex or magnesia, or either of those earths in a proper perpotion I am unable to deturmine."[35] Kirwan, writing on "Arenaceous Quartz or Sand," noted: "It is of various colours and incapable of forming a mass or hardening with water, the purest is white, the minute particles of which, when inspected through a lens are transparent. It is seldom perfectly pure; Mr. *Achard* says that the fine white sand of *Freyenwald*, which is used in porcelain manufactories contains 1/3 of its weight of argill and calcareous Earth . . . ."[36] The parallels between these narratives strongly suggest that Clark's journal entry was shaped by reading Kirwan during his weeks at Fort Clatsop.

Another scientific work in the traveling library was *A Practical Introduction to Spherics and Nautical Astronomy* (1796) by Patrick Kelly (1756–1842), published in a second edition in 1801, also in London. Kelly's primary objective was to provide lunar distances to facilitate the determination of longitude at sea. With it, he engaged in an expansive discussion of this "new method of calculating this important problem." Long-time master of the "Mercantile School" in London, Kelly wrote persuasively in the "Preface" of the *Practical Introduction*:

> Astronomy is allowed to be the most useful as well as the most sublime science that ever engaged the human attention, and the proper foundation of this study is Spherics; for all the heavenly bodies are spherical, or nearly so, and the concave expanse which invests our globe, and in which those bodies appear at equal distances from the eye, is represented by a sphere, upon which circles are drawn, and arcs and angles measured with perfect mathematical precision. Thus the most important problems, both of Astronomy and Navigation, are performed; such as finding the time of the rising, setting, &c. of the heavenly bodies, finding the variation of the compass by azimuths and amplitudes, the latitudes by altitudes, and the longitude by the lunar observations.[37]

The tenth essay in Kelly's volume, "Upon Longitude.–General Remarks upon the Longitude, with a comparative View of the various Methods of determining this important Question," was his *tour de force*. "The great object of Nautical Astronomy," wrote Kelly, "is to tell at all times *the place where the ship is*; in other words, to find the latitude and longitude." Viewing heavenly bodies at sea, he argued, provided the only visible means of such determinations and "the surest means, even at land." The easy solution to this critical determination was an accurate timepiece, yet, in spite of advances such as the chronometers crafted by John Harrison, Kelly said "they cannot be supposed such infallible guides to the longitude as the heavenly bodies."[38]

Although a variety of means existed to determine longitude in 1796, all depended on time based on the standard at Greenwich Observatory. Nevil Maskelyne's *Nautical Almanac*, calculated for the Greenwich meridian, facilitated fixing longitude. "Here the time is shewn when various celestial appearances take place under the above meridian," wrote Kelly, "and as those appearances are seen nearly at the same moment of absolute time in every part of the world where they are visible, *the difference between the observed time of any phenomenon and the computed time in the almanacs will give the longitude*."[39] Kelly acknowledged that observations of the eclipses of the moons of Jupiter and of solar eclipses, by the sun's declination, by the moon's culminating, and by the "occulation of a fixed star" also

"Beginning at the mouth of the Missouri, you will take observations of latitude and longitude at all remarkable points on the river, and especially at the mouths of rivers, at rapids, at islands, and other places and objects."

Thomas Jefferson to Meriwether Lewis, June 20, 1803

35 Moulton, *The Journals*, 6:178.

36 Kirwan, *Elements of Mineralogy*, 106; Wendlick, "In Search."

37 Kelly, *A Practical Introduction*, iii.

38 Ibid., iii., 184–210.

39 Ibid., iii., 186.

created opportunities for fixing longitude. His preferred method–that which was the primary purpose of his book–was the lunar mode. Kelly laid out his approach in nine carefully crafted pages. "The most practical method that has been yet adopted for determining the problem," he wrote, "is by the lunar observation . . . ."[40] Kelly's volume provided two examples of how "To project a Lunar Observation Stereographically, and thence to estimate the true Distance," four examples of how to "Form the Line of Correction and the Moon's horizontal Parallax, to find the Second or parallactic Correction," six rules "For working the Lunar Observations," a rule "From the True Lunar Distance and the Time to find the Longitude" (using the *Nautical Almanac*), a fold-out page with a formula for "A New Method of working the Lunar Observations," and a blank with all the critical data identified for "A Formula for working the Lunar Observations."

Robert Patterson (1743–1824), one of Lewis's instructors in navigational observations, had provided him with an astronomical notebook for lunar calculations. His intended method was what may be termed "Patterson's Problem 4th," a system for calculating the altitude of a body, estimated longitude, and time.[41] The method had three ingredients: the watch time of a lunar-distance measurement; the watch time of noon established by equal-altitude measurements; and previous knowledge of latitude (determined by a noon-altitude measurement). Kelly's manual on lunar-distance measurements, Maskelyne's *Nautical Almanac* (developed for the year), *Tables Requisite*, and possibly the *Journal of Andrew Ellicott* (1803), which demonstrated his use of the "Patterson's Problem 4th" method, all supported Lewis and Clark's efforts to record latitude and longitude.[42]

Jefferson laid down explicit expectations for the captains to secure accurate readings keyed to primary geographical features: "Beginning at the mouth of the Missouri, you will take ~~careful~~ [strikeout as in original document] observations of latitude and longitude, at all remarkeable points on the river, & especially at the mouths of rivers, at rapids, at islands, & other places & objects distinguished by such natural marks & characters of a durable kind, as that they may with certainty be recognized hereafter." Jefferson then re-emphasized the point: "Your observations are to be taken with great pains & accuracy, to be entered distinctly & intelligibly for others as well as yourself, to comprehend all the elements necessary, with the aid of the usual tables, to fix the latitude and longitude of the places which they were taken . . . ."[43]

Nevil Maskelyne (1732–1811), Britain's Astronomer Royal, compiled the astronomical tables in the traveling library. A graduate of Trinity College, Cambridge, Maskelyne secured several degrees, was elected to his college in 1757, and became a member of the Royal Society in 1758. A stipend for serving as rector of the parish of North Runcton in Norfolk allowed Maskelyne to devote his energies to astronomical observations and tabulations. In 1761, the Royal Society sponsored his trip to St. Helena to observe the transit of Venus. Although the planet was obscured by clouds, Maskelyne remained on the island for ten months recording the tides. In 1763, based on experiments in determining longitude by lunar distances, he published *The British Mariner's Guide*. In 1763, Maskelyne sailed to Barbados to test the accuracy of John Harrison's fourth chronometer, an assignment for the Board of Longitude. Harrison was a dogged inventor and master clockmaker. He found approval of his chronometers a frustrating and expensive process. After being appointed Astronomer Royal in 1765, Maskelyne founded the *Nautical*

40 Kelly, *A Practical Introduction*, iii., 187–188.

41 Preston, "The Accuracy," 177.

42 For another discussion of Lewis and Clark's efforts to determine key geographical positions, see Starr, "Celestial Navigation Basics," and Bergantino, "Revisiting Fort Mandan's Longitude."

43 Jackson, *Letters*, 1:62.

Almanac and Astronomical Ephemeris (1767) and supervised its publication for the next forty-five years. In 1766, he issued the *Tables Requisite to Be Used with the Astronomical and Nautical Ephemeris.* The demand was so great that ten thousand copies sold immediately. Maskelyne brought out new editions in 1781 and 1802.[44]

Derek Howse, Maskelyne's biographer, observed: "And it is largely because of the worldwide success of that publication [the *Nautical Alamanac* and the *Tables Requisite*] in the eighteenth and nineteenth centuries that the world's system of longitude and time reckoning should today be based on the Greenwich meridian." Maskelyne's devoted labors in making the calculations and seeing them published lasted beyond his death, for the annual compilations of 1811 to 1815 were also Maskelyne's work. Through his residency at Greenwich from 1765 to 1811 and his use of the Greenwich meridian as the base for his publications, he brought all positional reckoning to his doorstep. At times, however, the towering stature of the Astronomer Royal appeared imperious and capricious, especially in his dogged resistance to Harrison's inventive chronometers and his decades-long effort to win the prize announced in the Longitude Act of 1714 for a "Practicable and Useful" means of determining longitude.[45]

Another of Lewis's pre-expedition mentors in Pennsylvania was the ambitious, overworked, often ill, and brilliant Benjamin Smith Barton (1766–1815). A physician and botanist, Barton was a member of a survey team engaged in 1785 to define the western boundary of the state. That adventure instilled in him a lifelong fascination with history and American Indian languages and led to Barton's *New Views of the Origin of the Tribes and Nations of America* (1797). In this volume, Barton reviewed the origin theories of Native Americans and concluded: "Future researches will doubtless discover it in the vast countries (unknown to philosophers; traversed but by traders and by Jesuits) which are comprehended between the Mississippi and the Pacific-Ocean." Barton felt that comparative linguistic studies might shed light on the antecedents of the tribes of the Western Hemisphere.[46]

Barton studied medicine at the University of Edinburgh from 1786 to 1788 and won a prize for his assessment of the medicinal affects of black henbane, but did not take a degree. In 1789, he began his work in Philadelphia and secured a professorship at the College of Philadelphia (subsequently the University of Pennsylvania), where he taught botany, natural history, and materia medica. Jefferson sent Lewis to study with Barton in 1803 and Lewis subsequently carried Barton's teaching text with him to the Pacific. Barton dedicated his *Elements of Botany: or, Outlines of the Natural History of Vegetables* (1803) "To the Students of Medicine, in the University of Pennsylvania, and to the Lovers and Cultivators of Natural History, in Every Part of the United States."[47]

Barton's major botanical work opened with a poetic stanza from "The Pleasures of Imagination:"

But not alike to every mortal eye
Is this great scene unveil'd, For since the claims
Of social life, to different labours urge
The active powers of man; with wise intent
The hand of NATURE on peculiar minds
Imprints a different bias, and to each
Decrees its province in the common toil.

"Other objects worthy of notice will be the soil and face of the country, its growth and vegetable productions, especially those not of the United States."

Thomas Jefferson to Meriwether Lewis, June 20, 1803

44 Clerke, "Nevil Maskelyne," *Dictionary of National Biography*, 12:1299–1301.

45 Sobel, *Longitude*, 8, 166–167.

46 Barton, *New Views of the Origin*, lvii.

47 Thomas, "Benjamin Smith Barton," *American National Biography*, 2:287–288.

To some she taught the fabric of the sphere,
The changeful moon, the circuit of the stars,
The golden zones of heaven: to some she gave
To weigh the moment of eternal things,
Of time, and space, and fate's unbroken chain,
And will's quick impulse: OTHERS BY THE HAND
SHE LED O'ER VALES AND MOUNTAINS, TO EXPLORE
WHAT HEALING VIRTUE SWELLS THE TENDER VEINS
OF HERBS AND FLOWERS; OR WHAT THE BEAMS OF MORN
DRAW FORTH, DISTILLING FROM THE CLIFTED RIND
IN BALMY TEARS. But some to higher hopes
Were destin'd.[48]

Barton organized his volume for easy reference by students and researchers in the field. The first section examined the parts of a plant: roots and bulbs, trunks, leaves, and the fulcra (flowering parts). He based his analysis on the sexual system of von Linné but also invoked Erasmus Darwin's *Zoonomia*, writers of classical antiquity, and observations of a few modern travelers. The third part of Barton's work was a discussion of the Linnæan sexual system, identifying twenty-four classes of plants and their features. The appendix contained seventeen classificatory systems (rudimentary botanical keys) and thirty plates. The work was filled with descriptive terms and means to permit a would-be botanist to carry out plant identifications in the field.[49]

The use of Barton's work on the expedition was confirmed by Clark's November 4, 1805, entry on the estuary of the Columbia River: "This root they call *Wap-pa-to* which the *Bulb* of the *Chinese* cultivate in great quantities called *Sa-git ti folia* or common arrow head–. it has an agreeable taste and answers verry well in place of bread."[50] Barton wrote: "SAGITTARIA sagittifolia, or Common Arrow-head . . . . This bulb, when boiled or roasted, is agreeable food, and the plant is cultivated by the Chinese."[51] On January 10, 1805, Clark again wrote: "They bring *Wap-pa-to* root (which is Sagittifolia or the Common *arrow head* which is Cultivated by the Chinees) to Sell."[52] On April 8, 1806, near the head of the Columbia estuary, Lewis encountered the salmonberry, *Rubus spectabilis*. He wrote: "this bryer is of the class Polyandria and order Polygynia."[53] Barton discussed "Class XIII. Polyandria. Many Males," a grouping of plants that contained many stamens and divided into seven orders, including "Polygynia."[54] Again, it appears that the captains were using Barton's book in crafting their observations.

Barton was a good choice to mentor Lewis. His fascination with North America resounded in his writings. In an 1812 reprint of his "New Views of the Origin of the Tribes and Nations of America," an essay in Bradford & Inskeep's *The Port Folio*, Barton wrote:

To the naturalist, in particular, the new world presented a prospect that was peculiarly inviting. It opened to him a field of research unparalleled in extent, and rich in every thing he had been accustomed to value. Its spacious plains and lofty mountains, formed and ornamented in the munificence of nature, had been hitherto trodden only by the foot of the savage; its animal, vegetable, and mineral productions had attracted none but the savage eye.
To sources like these he was eager for access, conscious that they would abundantly remunerate his toils.[55]

Andrew Ellicott (1754–1820) served as another of Lewis's teachers. A surveyor,

48 Barton, *Elements of Botany*, 2.

49 Ibid.

50 Moulton, *The Journals*, 6:17.

51 Barton, *Elements of Botany*, Appendix, 35.

52 Moulton, *The Journals*, 6:195.

53 Ibid., 7:94.

54 Barton, *Elements of Botany*, 60–65.

55 Barton, "New Views," *The Port Folio* 7, no. 6: 508–9.

mathematician, and astronomer, Ellicott was reared in a Quaker family. He joined his father and uncles in clockmaking, milling, and making mathematical instruments. In 1780, he calculated and published the ephemerides for *The United States Almanack* and in that decade participated in a number of important boundary surveys, a labor that increasingly occupied his time. In 1796, President Washington hired Ellicott to survey the boundary between the United States and Florida.[56] His field notes documented his labors as a surveyor, traveler, observer, and an American figure confronting strong Spanish opposition. *The Journal of Andrew Ellicott . . .* was published with six maps in 1803 by Thomas Dobson and printed by Budd & Bartram in Philadelphia. The appendix to Ellicott's volume contained dozens of observations of weather, temperature, sunrise, sunset, and astronomical data (altitudes of the sun, emersions and immersions of the satellites of Jupiter, zenith distances of stars, lunar observations, and determinations of latitude and longitude). Ellicott confirmed his powers of observation, navigation, and genius in his stunning *Journal.*[57]

On March 6, 1803, Ellicott wrote to President Jefferson: "Your agreeable favour of the 26th Ult. has been duly received, and the contents noted. I shall be very happy to see Captn. Lewis, and will with pleasure give him all the information, and instruction, in my power. The necessary apparatus for his intended, and very interesting expedition, you will find mentioned in the last paragraph of the 42d page of my printed observations made in our southern country [the Florida boundary region], a copy of which I left with you." Ellicott's counsel was that Lewis should "acquire a facility, and dexterity in making the observations; which can only be attained by practice; in this he shall have all the assistance I can give him with the aid of my apparatus."[58]

Although not enumerated among the books purchased in Philadelphia, it is likely that Lewis and Clark carried the recently published account of a journey across North America—Alexander Mackenzie's *Voyages from Montreal,* first published in 1801. Jefferson learned of this publication in January 1802 from Caspar Wistar.[59] On January 27, 1806, while at Fort Clatsop, Lewis described the venereal disease that afflicted Silas Goodrich. His statement was virtually a paraphrase of Mackenzie's account. In "Some Account of the Chepewyan Indians," Mackenzie wrote:

> The venereal complaint is very common; but though its progress is slow, it gradually undermines the constitution, and brings on premature decay. They have recourse to superstition for their cure, and charms are their only remedies, except the bark of the willow, which being burned and reduced to powder, is strewed upon green wounds and ulcers, and places contrived for promoting perspiration. Of the use of simples and plants they have no knowledge; nor can it be expected, as their country does not produce them.[60]

In writing about Goodrich, Lewis, who referenced the Chippewa with whom he had had no contact, wrote:

> I cannot learn that the Indians have any simples which are sovereign specifics in the cure of this disease; and indeed I doubt very much wheter any of them have any means of effecting a perfect cure. when once this disorder is contracted by them it continues with them during life; but always ends in decipitude, death or premature old age; tho' from the uce of certain simples together with their diet, they support this disorder with but little inconvenience for many years, and even enjoy a tolerable health; particularly so among the

56 Bedini, "Andrew Ellicott," *American National Biography,* 7:415–416.

57 Ellicott, *Journal of Andrew Ellicott . . . .*

58 Jackson, *Letters,* 1:23.

59 Jackson, *Thomas Jefferson,* 95.

60 Mackenzie, *Voyages,* 1:152–153.

Chippeways who I believe are better skilled in the uce of those simples than any nation of Savages in North America.[61]

Jefferson's library contained the two-volume edition of Mackenzie's *Voyages from Montreal* (1802 edition).[62] The work included vocabularies of Indian languages in both volumes and, in some ways, was a precursor for Lewis's construction of "A List of the Names of the different Nations & Tribes of Indians Inhabiting the Countrey on the Missourie and its Waters . . . ," a section of his "Fort Mandan Miscellany" forwarded to Jefferson in the spring of 1805. Mackenzie, for example, identified the yield of pelts and skins by type and discussed their sales, particularly to China.[63] Lewis included data on monetary values of furs, types of pelts, and locations where a trade might best be prosecuted—a faint echo of Mackenzie's information.[64] The *Gazette* in New Orleans on July 17, 1805, carried information brought down the Missouri from Fort Mandan. In the discussion of the expedition's advance upstream in quest of the Great Falls, the account noted: "The descriptions given by McKenzie of the headwaters of this river are true." This offhand comment suggests that Mackenzie's travel account was probably in the traveling library at Fort Mandan during the winter of 1804–05 and was read in anticipation of the adventures ahead.[65]

Additional evidence that Lewis and Clark carried Mackenzie's *Voyages from Montreal* appeared in Lewis and Clark's "A Statistical View of the Indian Nations inhabiting the Territory of Louisiana and the Countries Adjacent to its northern and Western boundries." The data was appended as a table in Jefferson's *Message from the President* (1806). Lewis and Clark assessed the Assiniboin, Kinistanoes, Crees, Chipaways and other peoples not encountered during the expedition's ascent of the Missouri. They provided information on the furs they harvested, dollar values of pelts, their residency, and other data. While it is probable they obtained some of this information from Indians, voyageurs, and fur trappers at the Mandan villages, Mackenzie's book is another logical source. Their use of such terms as "Lake Winipicque" and "Lake Manitauber" were remarkably similar to Mackenzie's "Lake Winnipic" and "Lake Manitaubos," though, in light of their spelling, this evidence cannot be weighed too heavily.[66]

In addition to books, the expedition's traveling library also contained numerous manuscripts. These included extracts from the journal of Jean Baptiste Truteau, who in 1794–95 had ascended the Missouri to explore, barter for furs, and visit the Mandan villages. His narrative provided valuable information on tribal distribution, character, travel conditions, and trade opportunities. Jefferson forwarded a translation he made of Truteau's account to Lewis on November 16, 1803.[67] Patterson prepared an astronomy notebook of thirty pages for Lewis. The manuscript is now in the Breckenridge Collection, Missouri Historical Society.[68] The traveling library also contained extracts from the journals of John Evans and James Mackay, explorers of the Missouri River in the late 1790s, as translated for Lewis by John Hay, who appended information from his own travels.[69]

Maps

Considerable interest has arisen about the maps consulted and carried by the Corps of Discovery. Useful essays on this subject include Carl Wheat's "Geographic Pig-in-a Poke," "First Cartographic Fruits of the Lewis and Clark Expedition," and "Lewis and Clark Maps" in *Mapping the Transmississippi West*, vol. 2 (1958); John Logan Allen's "Preparing the Attempt on the Passage" in *Passage*

61 Moulton, *The Journals*, 6:239–240.

62 Sowerby, *Catalogue*, 4:249.

63 Mackenzie, *Voyages*, 1:31.

64 Moulton, *The Journals*, 6:388–389.

65 Nasatir, *Before Lewis and Clark*, 2:761–763.

66 Thwaites, *Original Journals*, 6:80–113.

67 Nasatir, *Before Lewis and Clark*, 257–311; Jackson, *Letters*, 1:136.

68 Moulton, *The Journals*, 1:16; 2:564–565.

69 Jackson, *Letters*, 1:155–157.

Through the Garden (1975), Gary E. Moulton's "Introduction," *Atlas of the Lewis & Clark Expedition, The Journals of the Lewis and Clark Expedition*, vol. 1 (1983), and Guy Meriwether Benson's *Exploring the West from Monticello: A Perspective in Maps from Columbus to Lewis and Clark* (1995). Collectively, these essayists have identified a basic set of maps that made up the expedition's traveling library and also suggested the maps the team consulted. The maps carried by the Corps of Discovery included the following:

Antoine-Simon Le Page du Pratz, "A Map of Louisiana, with the course of The Mississippi," 1763.

This map was in the English translation of du Pratz's book, *The History of Louisiana, or of The Western Parts of Virginia and Carolina . . .* (1763), first published in Paris in 1758. A French military engineer, du Pratz (ca. 1695-1755) lived in Louisiana from 1718 to 1734 and, during the period, made a five-month exploration of the territory. With reasonable accuracy, his map showed the lower Missouri and Mississippi Rivers. In chapters 16–19, vol. 1, du Pratz described an exploration that took him to the Great Plains.[70] Lewis carried Benjamin Smith Barton's copy of this book and map in the expedition library.[71]

James Mackay, [Untitled map of the Missouri River], 1797.

A Scottish explorer and surveyor, Mackay (ca. 1759–1822) was well-educated, fluent in French and Spanish, a violinist, and, after 1776, an employee of the North West Company in Canada. He first visited the Mandan villages on the upper Missouri River in 1787 and mapped part of the region west to the Rockies. Mackay settled in St. Louis in the mid-1790s, where he became a Spanish subject and worked for the Missouri Company. He was ordered by Baron de Carondelet to drive the British from the Mandan villages, establish forts, and explore to the Pacific Ocean. Accompanied by John Evans, a young Welshman, Mackay set out with thirty-three men in four pirogues in 1795 to ascend the Missouri. He built Fort Charles in Nebraska and sent Evans to forge relations with the tribes and seek the ocean. The two-year exploration of Mackay and Evans, while it did not pass the Rockies, produced valuable journals and maps about the Missouri watershed and the tribes living in the region.[72]

When the United States acquired Louisiana Territory in 1803, Mackay remained in Missouri. He later served as a judge and member of the territorial legislature. On January 10, 1804, he visited William Clark at Camp Dubois to share what he knew about the geography, tribes, and diplomatic challenges facing the Corps of Discovery in its ascent of the Missouri River. Mackay's advance intelligence proved extremely useful to the captains in orienting themselves during their journey and anticipating challenges in Indian relations.[73]

The Mackay map carried by Lewis and Clark has been a subject of intense discussion. Its identity as the map found in the early 1900s in the Office of Indian Affairs is ably assessed by John Logan Allen in *Passage Through the Garden*.[74] This map came to William Clark at Camp Dubois from William Henry Harrison. It showed the Missouri River upstream to the Mandan villages. Allen concluded "it was almost certainly a copy of a map drawn by James Mackay during his travels on the Missouri in the summer of 1797, or drawn from data that resulted from those travels and supplemented with information from John Evans."[75]

"Capt. Lewis is brave, prudent, habituated to the woods, & familiar with Indian manners & character. He is not regularly educated, but he possesses a great mass of accurate observation on all subjects of nature."

Thomas Jefferson to Benjamin Rush, February 28, 1803

70 Sayre, "Antoine-Simon Le Page du Pratz."

71 Benson, *Exploring the West*, map 22.

72 Perry, "James Mackay," *American National Biography* (1999), 14:245.

73 Ibid., 245–246; Moulton, *The Journals*, 1:6; 2:154; Jackson, *Letters*, 1:135.

74 Allen, *Passage Through the Garden*, 141–142.

75 Ibid., 141–142.

John Evans, [Set of seven maps showing the Mackay-Evans explorations between the mouth of the Missouri and the Mandan villages], 1797.

Evans (1770–1799) was a wandering Welsh explorer who came to North America in 1792 to seek "Welsh Indians" allegedly residing deep in the interior of the continent. These "white Indians" were reported to be the descendants of Madog, the son of Welsh King Owain of Gwynedd, and his followers. Madog purportedly sailed to North America in 1170, first entering via Mobile Bay and living variously in the Southeast and the Ohio Valley before leading his followers up the Missouri.[76] In the spring of 1793, Evans walked from Baltimore to St. Louis, where he was imprisoned by the Spanish. He was eventually released and obtained employment with the Missouri Company. With James Mackay, Evans made a two-year exploration (1796–97) of the Missouri watershed, mapping it for nearly 1,400 miles to the Mandan villages of North Dakota.[77]

On January 13, 1804, Jefferson wrote to Lewis that he enclosed "a map of the Missouri as far as the Mandans 12 or 1500. miles I presume above it's mouth. . . . It is said to be very accurate, having been done by a Mr. Evans by order of the Spanish Government. But whether he corrected by astronomical observations or not we are not informed." Jefferson mentioned this map nine days later in a second letter to Lewis. It is fair to assume that the Evans map was in Lewis's travel kit.[78] Lewis wrote on December 28, 1803, to Jefferson from Cahokia, Illinois, that he had "obtained three maps." He continued: "I have also obtained Ivins's and Mac Kay's journal up the Missouri, it is in French & is at present in the hands of Mr. Hay, who has promised to translate it for me. . . ."[79] Lewis was thus also seeking textual information from the Mackay-Evans explorations to supplement the cartographic data.

Antoine Soulard, "a general Map of Uper Louisiana" or "A Topogra[phical] Sketch of the Missouri and Upper Missisippi; Exhibiting the various Nations and Tribes of Indians who inhabit the Country: Copied from the Original Spanish MS. Map," 1795; and an unidentified map "of the interior of the country lying between the Missouri and New Mexico" copied for Lewis from Soulard's collection.

Soulard was born in 1766 in France and served for a time in the French navy. In 1794, he settled in St. Louis and, until the American takeover in 1804, was a captain of the militia, adjutant to the lieutenant-governor of Upper Louisiana, and surveyor-general for St. Louis and Ste. Genevieve.[80] In December 1803, Meriwether Lewis called on Soulard and found him an amiable, willing informant. However, Soulard was fearful of retribution from the French government if he permitted Lewis to copy the Spanish census data of 1800. Soulard had a map collection and from it Lewis may have obtained two copies. The first, described by Lewis as "a General Map of Uper Louisiana," was reproduced in the Thwaites atlas (1908, map 2) and in the Moulton atlas (1983, map 4). The map bears the caption, "A Topogra[phical] Sketch of the Missouri and Upper Missisippi; Exhibiting the various Nations and Tribes of Indians who inhabit the Country: Copied from the Original Spanish MS. Map." The map provides information about several forks of the Missouri, tribal distribution, and data on the country running west from Lake Superior to Lake-of-the-Woods, Lake Winnipeg, and the Rocky Mountains. Symbols denote "Wandering Nations" and "Fixed or Permanent"

76 Williams, *Madog.*

77 Nasatir, *Before Lewis and Clark*, 1:98–107.

78 Wheat, *Mapping the Transmississippi West* (1957), 1:161–162.

79 Jackson, *Letters*, 1:155; Quaife, "Extracts," 185–210.

80 Nasatir, *Before Lewis and Clark*, 1:370.

tribes and a note claims that at the Great Bend of the Missouri the country between "is only 20 miles across." Moulton has referred to this work as "Soulard's Map of 1795." The English copy with annotations in Clark's handwriting is in the William Robertson Coe Collection, Yale University.[81]

The second map, the details about which are not exactly known, was referred to by Lewis in a letter to Jefferson written on December 28, 1803: "When I extended my inquiries to the geography of the country and asked for such information as he felt himself at liberty to give me on that subject, particularly of the interior of the country lying between the Missouri and New Mexico," wrote Lewis, "he shewed me a manuscript map, imbracing a portion of the Mississippi, the Missouri from it's junction with this river to the mouth of the Osages, and the last named river in it's whole extent. . . ." Lewis prevailed on Soulard to have the map copied. Soulard agreed, provided that the merchant who owned the map granted permission. This "Osage River map" has not been found but may have been carried by the captains.[82]

Aaron Arrowsmith, "A Map Exhibiting All the New Discoveries in the Interior Parts of North America," 1795, updated in 1802.

Aaron Arrowsmith (1750–1823) was a well-known engraver of maps that showed the road systems of England and Wales. A stickler for accuracy, Arrowsmith drew on the best information he could secure. His first map of North America, engraved in 1795, was founded on the extensive collection of manuscript maps and journals of the Hudson's Bay Company, Great Trinity Lane, London. The explorations of Peter Fidler in 1792, Samuel Hearne in 1770–72 west of Hudson's Bay, Alexander Mackenzie's journey to the Arctic Ocean in 1789, and Vancouver's charting in 1792 of the North Pacific Coast were all important sources of information. The primary element of myth in Arrowsmith's map was his identification of the "Stony Mountains" as a single chain of peaks running like a backbone through the western third of the continent. This presentation persisted in the 1802 update, but that map—carried by the explorers—had new and useful information gleaned from Mackenzie's *Voyages* (1801). That volume covered his several explorations into the Northern Rockies as well as to the Pacific Ocean in July 1793.[83]

Arrowsmith became the leading publisher of maps in Great Britain by the end of the eighteenth century. His skills were in rendering large-scale accuracy to maps founded on primary sources. His maps ranged from the Arctic to the Galapagos and were often updated following the receipt of new information. He also executed and published the much-used *Atlas of Southern India* (1822). His sons and nephew John Arrowsmith, a founder of the Royal Geographical Society, continued his business for most of the nineteenth century.[84]

Nicholas King, Map of the Western Part of North America, 1803.

Commissioned in March 1803 by Secretary of the Treasury Albert Gallatin to execute a map based on established authorities and recent explorations, Nicholas King consulted several maps to create a highly useful cartographic representation of known features. Gallatin wrote: "I have requested Mr. King to project a blank map to extend from 88° to 135° West longitude from Greenwich & from 30° to 55° north latitude; which will give us the whole course of the Mississippi and the whole coast of the Pacific ocean within the same latitudes together with a sufficient

"The observations on which Arrowsmith has constructed his map of the northern part of this country, were all calculated in England."

Andrew Ellicott
to Thomas Jefferson,
March 6, 1803

81 Moulton, *The Journals*, 1:5, map 4.

82 Jackson, *Letters*, 1:150, 155n; Allen, *Passage Through the Garden*, 148.

83 Benson, *Exploring the West*, maps 30 and 31.

84 Coote, "Aaron Arrowsmith," 1:595–596.

"The white perogue
of the captains
hoisted Sail as the
wind blew fair. . . .
She filled ful of
water. . . . Some
of the paper and
nearly all the books
got wet, but not
altogether Spoiled."

Joseph Whitehouse,
Missouri River in Montana,
May 14, 1805

space to the North to include all the head waters of the Port Nelson River." [85]

Into this outline, Gallatin instructed King to insert data drawn from several sources. These included Guillaume de l'Isle's "Carte de la Louisiane et du Cours du Mississipi" (1718), John Mitchell's "A Map of the British and French Dominions in North America . . ." (1755), James Cook's "Chart of the NW Coast of America and NE Coast of Asia explored in the years 1778 & 1779" (1784), George Vancouver's "A Chart shewing part of the Coast of N.W. America" (1798), David Thompson's "A map showing the Great Bend of the Missouri" (1798), Alexander Mackenzie's "A Map of America between Latitudes 40 and 70 North, and Longitudes 45 and 180 West, Exhibiting Mackenzie's Track" (1801), Aaron Arrowsmith's "A Map Exhibiting all the New Discoveries in the Interior Parts of North America" (1802), and Andrew Ellicott's "Map of the Mississippi River" (1803). King also consulted maps by Jean Baptiste Bourguignon d'Anville (1697–1782), a French cartographer who used reports of French traders, missionaries, and explorers to craft several maps of North America. The maps by d'Anville included "Carte de la Louisiane" (1732) and "Amerique Septentrionale" (1746). In 1787, Thomas Jefferson purchased seven of d'Anville's maps and in correspondence with Gallatin discussed the usefulness of d'Anville's work for showing the lower Mississippi. [86]

Lewis knew the importance of these base maps and, in spite of King's use of them in creating the synthetic map for his use, he tried to purchase a number of them prior to the expedition. Lewis reported to Jefferson on May 29, 1803, from Philadelphia that he had been unable to purchase a map by d'Anville and added: "The maps attached to Vancouver's voyage cannot be procured seperately from that work, which is both too costly, and too weighty, for me either to purchase or carry." [87]

King (1771–1812) emigrated in 1794 to the United States from England. He worked as a surveyor in Philadelphia and Washington, D.C. His synthetic map showed a number of features of the Missouri River, made no speculation about the Rocky Mountains except to show a few isolated peaks, and provided excellent detail on the configuration of the Northwest Coast from Cape Blanco to central British Columbia. King's map, which made the journey to and from the Pacific Ocean with the Corps of Discovery, is in the Geography and Map Division of the Library of Congress. [88]

Lewis's Tracings from Vancouver's Charts

In 1803, Lewis reported to Jefferson the obstacles in purchasing and carrying Vancouver's charts in the expedition's traveling library. He prefaced his observations, however, by writing: "You will receive herewith inclosed some sketches taken from Vancouver's survey in a haisty manner, but I believe they will be found sufficiently accurate to be of service in composing the map, which Mr. Gallatin was so good as to promise he would have projected and compleated for me." [89]

Gary Moulton, editor of *The Journals of the Lewis & Clark Expedition* (1983–2001), wrote: "Lewis had with him on the expedition copies of Vancouver's maps." [90] It is perhaps more accurate to suggest that Lewis likely carried with him *sketches* of Vancouver's charts. The Nicholas King map, based on Vancouver, Cook, and other sources, provided no detailed information about the Columbia estuary. If Lewis and Clark had carried Vancouver's charts, they would probably have noted such a feature as Vancouver Point, a place denominated by William Broughton during his reconnaissance of the estuary nearly 110 miles upstream from the Pacific.

85 Allen, *Passage*, 74; Jackson, *The Letters*, 1:28.

86 Jackson, *Letters*, 1:28; Benson, *Exploring the West*, maps 14A and 14B.

87 Jackson, *Letters*, 1:53.

88 The King map is reproduced in Moulton, *The Journals*, 1: map 2.

89 Jackson, *Letters*, 1:53.

90 Moulton, *The Journals*, 1:16 n., 6:47 n.

Clark's journal, however, confirms that the Corps of Discovery had some specific cartographic data based on Vancouver's accounts. On November 15, 1806, he wrote: ". . . in full view of the *Ocian* from *Point Adams* to Cape Disapointment, I could not See any Island in the mouth of the river as laid down by Vancouver. The Bay which he laies down in the mouth is imediately below me." Clark also wrote the previous day: "The Canoe returned at dusk half full of water, from the waves which dashed over in passing the point Capt Lewis is object is also to find a Small Bay as laid down by Vancouver just out of the mouth of the Columbia River."[91] Since Lewis had made sketches from Vancouver's charts, it is probable he included copies in the traveling library, because Nicholas King's map of 1803 provided no details of the mouth of the Columbia River. King's map identified only Mt. Rainier, Mt. St. Helens, and Mt. Hood; the "River Oregan" (the Columbia estuary); and notable capes along the shoreline of Oregon and Washington.[92] Arrowsmith's map, however, clearly showed the small bay inside (east of) Cape Disappointment and faintly indicated a large sandbar near the mouth of the river.[93] Vancouver's detailed chart, "Entrance of Columbia River," showed no island, but his overview "A Chart shewing part of the Coast of N.W. America" showed a large island lying in the estuary immediately east of the harbor entrance. The sandbars of the tidal estuary were perhaps misread as an island by Lewis when he executed his "haisty sketches."[94]

The feat of carrying books, manuscripts, and maps across the continent for scientific purposes affirmed the commitment of the Lewis and Clark Expedition to the goals of the Enlightenment. The captains sought, as fully as possible, to identify, classify, and collect the phenomena of the natural world. In addition, the books in their baggage also became the first lending library in the American West. The evidence is slim but conclusive. On February 18, 1805, Francois-Antoine Larocque, a French-Canadian fur trader in the employ of the North West Company, wrote in his journal: "Went down to Fort Mandan, in the morning, to Return a Book I had borrow'd, & to see if there was any particular news. Arrived there at 3 P.M. & Remain'd the whole day."[95] Larocque, on a second trip from River Fort de la Bosse on the Assiniboine River during the summer of 1805, explored the Yellowstone River and wrote the first detailed account of the Crow Indians. Fluent in both French and English, but preferring to write in French, Larocque had found something of interest in the books at Fort Mandan. Which book Larocque borrowed is not known, but his journal confirms that there was a library worth considering on the plains of North Dakota during the winter of 1804–05.[96]

The journals written at Fort Clatsop suggest that the books by Kirwan, Barton, and Mackenzie, Miller's volumes of *Linnæus*, and *Owen's Dictionary* made the full trip. Lewis's note in Barton's copy of du Pratz's *History of Louisiana* confirms that he took the book to the West Coast and returned it to Philadelphia. Not all the books in the traveling library, however, made the journey to the shores of the Pacific Ocean.

On June 26, 1805, at the portage around the Great Falls of the Missouri, Lewis wrote: "Capt. C. also scelected the articles to be deposited in the cash consisting of my desk which I had left for that purpose and in which I had left some books, my specimens of plants minerals &c. collected from fort Mandan to that place." Clark noted similarly: ". . . a few Small lumbersom articles Capt Lewiss Desk and Some books & Small articles in it."[97] On July 13 of the following year, Lewis returned to this site, opened the cache, and wrote: "found my bearskins

91 Moulton, *The Journals*, 6:46, 50.

92 Moulton, *The Journals*, 1:map 2.

93 Arrowsmith, "A Map Exhibiting All the New Discoveries. . . ."

94 Vancouver, "A Chart shewing part of the Coast of N.W. America. . . ."

95 Wood and Thiessen, *Early Fur Trade*, 149.

96 Hazlitt, "The Journal," 3-26.

97 Moulton, *The Journals*, 4:334-335.

"Capt. C. also scelected the articles to be deposited in the cash consisting of my desk which I had left for that purpose and in which I had left some books, my specimens of plants minerals &c. collected from fort Mandan to that place."

Meriwether Lewis,
Great Falls, June 26, 1805

entirely destroyed by the water, the river having risen so high that the water had penitrated. all my specimens of plants also lost. the Chart of the Missouri fortunately escaped. opened my trunks and boxes and exposed the articles to dry. found my papers damp and several articles damp." [98] Lewis did not account for the fate of the stored books.

The traveling library of the Corps of Discovery facilitated the observations of tribes, geography, flora, fauna, and minerals of the American West. The eyes of the party were open to possibilities. Their minds were quick to discern what was new, different, and unusual. The Enlightenment and its principles of order and classification resounded in the works they carried. Their adventures were founded on a quest for knowledge, and they took with them some of the best tools of their day to achieve those objectives.

98 Moulton, *The Journals*, 8:107.

The Expedition's Traveling Library: Bibliography

Lewis and Clark's traveling library was the first of its kind. Assembled to assist the captains in their travels, it comprised the latest English-language research at the time on botany, geology, medicine, and astronomy. The texts included plates, maps, tables, and scientific catalogs. This library influenced and shaped the way Lewis and Clark described their expedition.

We know the current location of only one of these books: the French explorer du Pratz's *History of Louisiana*, loaned to Lewis in 1803 by Benjamin Barton and returned in 1807 with a friendly inscription by Lewis to Barton. This copy resides at the Library Company in Philadelphia. None of the other books actually carried on the expedition are known to have survived.

We do, however, know the titles of a handful of books requisitioned by Lewis (Jackson, *Letters*, items 53 and 57). These volumes, more fully discussed in an earlier article by Jackson ("Some Books Carried"), can be considered the core items of the traveling library. They are listed below, along with other books and maps that were carried, or are likely to have been consulted. As part of the preparation for the expedition, Jefferson instructed Lewis to consult with five Philadelphia scholars, all leaders in their fields: botanist Benjamin Smith Barton, astronomer Andrew Ellicott, mathematician Robert Patterson, physician Benjamin Rush, and anatomist Caspar Wistar. Their recommendations undoubtedly contributed to Lewis's choices of materials to carry.

Each identification of a text or map connected to the expedition is accompanied by one or more items, under the heading "Document(s)," identifying a direct association with the Corps of Discovery. The height of each book is given in centimeters. In map measurements, width precedes height.

1a Books Consulted in Advance or Carried on the Expedition
1a.1 *Dictionary of Arts and Sciences* 1754–55 [Color plate II]
A NEW AND COMPLETE | DICTIONARY | OF | ARTS and SCIENCES; | COMPREHENDING ALL | The Branches of Useful Knowledge, | WITH | ACCURATE DESCRIPTIONS as well of the | various MACHINES, INSTRUMENTS, TOOLS, FIGURES, | and SCHEMES necessary for illustrating them, | AS OF | The Classes, Kinds, Preparations, and Uses of NATURAL | PRODUCTIONS, whether ANIMALS, VEGETABLES, | MINERALS, FOSSILS, OR FLUIDS; | Together with | The KINGDOMS, PROVINCES, CITIES, TOWNS, and | other Remarkable Places throughout the WORLD.| Illustrated with above Three Hundred COPPER-PLATES, | curiously engraved by Mr. JEFFERYS, Geographer and Engraver to | his Royal Highness the Prince of WALES. | The Whole extracted from the Best AUTHORS in all Languages. | By a SOCIETY of GENTLEMEN. | *Huc undique Gaza* | *Congeritur* VIRG. | [rule] | VOL. I. [II.] [III.] [IV.] | [double rule] | LONDON: | Printed for W. OWEN, at Homer's Head, in Fleet-street. | MDCCLIV. [MDCCLV.]

Collation: Four volumes, 8vo., 22 cm. xvi, 3538 pages, 302 leaves of plates. Vols. 1–3 appeared in 1754, vol. 4 in 1755.

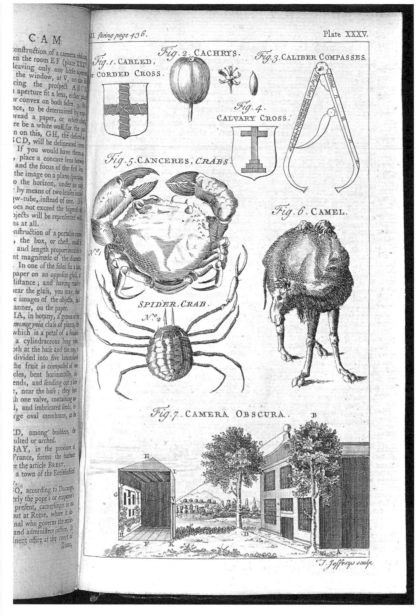

Document: "a Hat Box containing the 4 vols. of the Deckinsery of arts an ciences" from "Memorandum of articles forwarded to Louisville by Capt. Clark in care of Mr. Wolpards," St. Louis, 1806 (Moulton, Jackson).

References: William Clark, *Journals*, Codex N, 1–2 [the word in Clark and Anderson may read "Deckensery"]; Jackson, "Some Books," 11–12; Moulton, 8:419, 419 n.

Description: The dictionary returned to Louisville by Clark after the expedition's return is very likely to have been the four-volume dictionary listed here, with the plural "Sciences" in its title. Jackson notes verbal parallels between entries in the journals and definitions in this publication, particularly in the descriptions of the salmon and the ibex. The definition of the word "sense" was copied nearly verbatim from this dictionary. Owen issued a second edition in four volumes in 1763-64. The only other four-volume English dictionary "of arts and sciences" that might have been carried is the very large (44 cm. tall) folio of Chambers, published by Abraham Rees, London, 1786. Apart from its unwieldy size, there seems to be no direct correspondence between the journals and this set, entitled *Cyclopædia: or Universal Dictionary of Arts and Sciences.*

Lewis & Clark College Collection: Eight parts in four volumes, incomplete. The following parts are present: 1(1); 2(1, 2); 3(2); 4(2). Bookplate of 1768, name erased. Wendlick: Eight parts in four volumes, complete (on loan to the collection). Early binding, with raised bands; L. Hogdson bookplate.

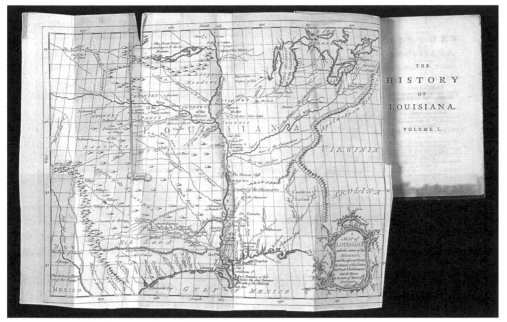

1a.2 Antoine-Simon Le Page du Pratz, *History of Louisiana* [1763], 1774

[First Edition] THE | HISTORY | OF | LOUISIANA, | OR OF | THE WESTERN PARTS | OF | VIRGINIA and CAROLINA: | CONTAINING | A Description of the Countries that lye | on both Sides of the River *Missisipi:* | WITH | An Account of the Settlements, Inhabitants, | Soil, Climate, and Products. | [rule] | Translated from the FRENCH, | (lately published,) | By M. LE PAGE DU PRATZ; | WITH | Some NOTES and OBSERVATIONS | relating to our COLONIES. | [rule] | In TWO VOLUMES. | [rule] | VOL. I [II] | [double rule] | LONDON, | Printed for T. BECKET and P. A. DE HONDT | in the Strand. MDCCLXIII.

Collation: Two volumes, 8vo., 16.5 cm. Vol. 1: Unpaginated half title and title leaves; [i]–xlii preface, followed by eight pages of description of Harbour of Pensacola; i–vii contents and one page of advertisements; 1–368 text. Pagination: 1–197, Book 1; 199–368, Book 2; Two folding maps in vol. 1: "A Map of Louisiana with the course of the Missisipi. . . 1757" (33.5 cm. x 25.5 cm.) facing the half title; "Louisiana" (17.5 cm. x 14.5 cm.) facing p. 1. The engraver of the first map is given as Palmer. This map is discussed at 1b.1. Vol. 2: Unpaginated half title and title leaves, and contents; 1–108, Book 3; 109–272, Book 4.

[Second Edition] THE | HISTORY | OF | LOUISIANA, | OR OF | THE WESTERN PARTS | OF VIRGINIA AND CAROLINA: | Containing a DESCRIPTION of the | Countries that lie on both Sides of the River MISSISIPPI: | With an ACCOUNT of the | SETTLEMENTS, INHABITANTS, SOIL, | CLIMATE, AND PRODUCTS. | [rule] | Translated from the FRENCH | of M. LE PAGE DU PRATZ; | With some

Collation: One volume, 8vo., 21 cm. Map bound before title: 33.5 cm. x 25.5 cm. Four unnumbered leaves containing title page; blank; three leaves of contents; [i]–xxxvi preface; map: 17.5 cm. x 14.5 cm. Text pagination: [1]–117, Book 1; 119–223, Book 2; 225–290, Book 3; 291–387, Book 4.

Documents: "Dr. Benjamin Smith Barton was so obliging as to lend me this copy of Monsr. Du Pratz's history of Louisiana in June 1803. It has been since conveyed by me to the Pacific Ocean through the interior of Continent of North America on my late tour thither and is now returned to it's proprietor by his Friend and Obt. Servt." Meriwether Lewis, Philadelphia, May 9, 1807. (Jackson, *Letters*). "This once powerful nation [Paducas] has, apparently, entirely disappeared; every inquiry I have made after them has proved ineffectual. In the year 1724, they resided in several villages on the heads of the Kansas river, and could, at that time, bring upwards of two thousand men into the field (see Monsr. Dupratz history of Louisiana, page 71, and the map attached to that work)." (Lewis, in "A Statistical View," from Jefferson's Message of 1806, A. & G. Way edition), p. 64. "DuPratz must have been badly informed as to the Cane opposed this place" (Clark, journal entry of July 5, 1804: Moulton, 2:351 and n. 5 explaining Clark's misunderstanding).

References: Benson et al., item 22; Cutright, "Du Pratz," 31–35; Jackson, "Some Books," 9–10, and *Letters*, item 441.

Description: "Thomas Jefferson owned this [1763] edition of Le Page du Pratz's work and used it as a reference source as he prepared his treatise on Louisiana. Meriwether Lewis borrowed an English edition of this work from Benjamin Smith Barton, his botany tutor in Philadelphia, and took it on the expedition to the Pacific. Several references to Le Page du Pratz's work appear in the journals of the expedition" (Benson, et al.). Barton's copy was the 1774 second London edition, in one volume. The folding maps are the same in the first two editions.

Lewis & Clark College Collection: Wendlick: First edition 1763. Two volumes, half leather with marbled boards, raised bands, gold stamping and tooling, all edges marbled. Bookplates of Paul E. Bechet.

1a.3 Benjamin Rush, *Directions for Preserving the Health of Soldiers* 1778
Rush, Benjamin. *Directions for Preserving the Health of Soldiers Recommended to the Consideration of the Officers of the Army of the United States.* Lancaster [Pennsylvania]: John Dunlap, 1778.

Collation: Eight-page pamphlet, 18 cm.

Document: "I am thankful to you for your attention to Capt. Lewis while at Philadelphia and the useful counsels he received from you." Jefferson to Rush, June 24, 1803 (Jackson, *Letters*).

References: Jackson, *Letters*, item 50, and *Stony Mountains*, 134.

Description: The treatise was "first published in the *Pennsylvania Packet*, no. 284 (1777). Rush was ordered by the Board of War to republish this work in a small pamphlet, with such additions and alterations as he thought proper. (Cf. 'Extract from the minutes' of the Board of War, Sept. 5, 1777, on p. [2]). This [Dunlap, 1778] is apparently the first separate edition" (information from Online Computer Library Center database). "No doubt the expedition also carried at least one medical treatise and the current edition of the rules and articles of war." (Jackson, *Stony Mountains*). As part of his training with Rush, Lewis probably used one or both of the early editions of Rush's *Medical Inquiries and Observations*, the two-volume first edition (1789, 1793) or the five-volume expanded edition (1794–98).

Lewis & Clark College Collection: A facsimile of the 1778 pamphlet, and the first edition of Rush's *Medical Inquiries and Observations*, described above.

1a.4 John Miller's *Linnæus* 1779, 1789 [Color plate III]

Vol. 1: [Engraved title page] [ornament] AN [ornament] | ILLUSTRATION | of the | SEXUAL SYSTEM, | of | *LINNÆUS,* | by | IOHN MILLER. | [engraving] | LONDON. | Vol. I. | *Published as the Act directs,* | *& Sold at the Authors House in Dorset-Court near Parliament-* | *Street and at the Principal Booksellers.* | MDCCLXXIX. [ornament]

Vol. 2: [Engraved title page] [ornament] AN [N reversed] [ornament] | ILLUSTRATION | of the | TERMINI *BOTANICI,* | OF | *LINNÆUS,* | by | IOHN MILLER. | Vol: II. | [engraved flourish] | Published as the Act directs. | *& Sold at the Authors House, N°. 20, Vauxhall Walk, Lambeth.* | MDCCLXXXIX. | *NB. Where also may be had the first Vol. of the above & the Folio* | *Edition of the Illustration of the Sexual System.*

Collation: Vol. 1: One volume, 8vo., 23 cm. Frontispiece, designed and engraved by John Miller; 1–8 preface; 1–[107] text, with facing plates. Vol. 2: One volume, 8vo., 23cm. Three leaves: title page and verso, two pages of preface; [blank]; Plate 1; 1–86 [i.e. 104] text, with 85 plates; [blank]; errata page.

Document: "1 Miller's edition of Lineus in 2 Vol:" Lewis's List of Requirements, June 30, 1803 (Jackson).

Reference: Jackson, *Letters*, item 53 and n. 3.

Description: A two-volume translation of works by Linnæus, illustrating his methods of classification. The engraved frontispiece in the first volume is by John Miller, who translated the text. The engraved title pages and plates are probably also by Miller (born Johann Sebastian Müller), whose preface (p. 3) describes the plates and text as being closely linked. Barton may well have steered Lewis toward these volumes; he acknowledges borrowing material from Miller on page x of his *Elements of Botany*.

Among the small number of other Linnæan texts in English available to the expedition, one in particular should be mentioned: the two-volume *Elements of Natural History; Being An Introduction to the* Systema Naturae *of Linnæus*, published in 1801–1802 by Cadell and Davies in London and William Creech in Edinburgh. (The same publishers were also responsible for the two-volume Mackenzie *Voyages* of the same year, almost certainly carried on the expedition.) This text contains the only known source for Lewis's first full description on May 27, 1806, of the

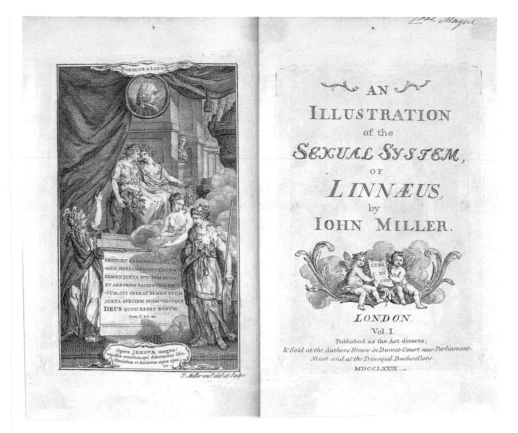

woodpecker named after him, (Moulton, 7:293): "the tongue is barbed, pointed, and of an elastic cartilaginous substance." Compare *Elements* 1, 173: "By means of these elastic cartilages the birds of this genus thrust out their filiform tongue to catch insects. . . . their sharp pointed and barbed tongue enables them to extract insects from their lurking places in trees."

This connection is more suggestive than absolutely conclusive, and further research is needed on the Linnæan texts consulted by Lewis. There were two other English versions of the *Systema Naturae* in print by 1802, both of them translations from the German version by Johann Gmelin: those of Robert Kerr (1792) and William Turton (four volumes in 1802, three further volumes in 1806). Other relevant Linnæan texts may await discovery.

Lewis & Clark College Collection: Miller, vol. 1: Early half-leather edition with marbled boards, rebacked with leather spine. *Elements of Natural History*, 1801–1802, both volumes, original boards.

1a.5 *The Articles of War,* Issued Annually

REGULATIONS | FOR THE | ORDER AND DISCIPLINE | OF THE | TROOPS
OF THE UNITED STATES. | TO WHICH IS PREFIXED, | THE ARTICLES OF
WAR, | THE | MILITIA LAW OF THE UNITED STATES, | AND THE | MILITIA
LAW OF SOUTH-CAROLINA. | [rule] | ALSO, IS ADDED, | THE MANUAL
EXERCISE, AND EVOLUTIONS | OF THE | CAVALRY: | AS | PRACTISED IN
THE LATE AMERICAN ARMY. | [rule] | The Plates corrected by an Officer in the
late American Army, | at present in this State. | [rule] | *CHARLESTON*: | Printed
and Sold by *W. P. YOUNG*, FRANKLIN'S-HEAD, | No. 43, BROAD-STREET,
| −1794.−

Document: "A violiation or Disobediance shall be Subject to Such punishment as derected by the articles of War. . . . This Court will act agreeable to the rules and regulations of the Articles of War and Such others as may be established by the Said Cpt L. & C. from time to time" (William Clark; full text in Moulton). "No doubt the expedition also carried at least one medical treatise and the current edition of the rules and articles of war" (Jackson).

References: Jackson, *Stony Mountains,* 134; Moulton, 2:163.

Description: The *Articles of War* were reprinted in many editions, probably annually, up to the time of Lewis and Clark's departure. The Lewis & Clark College Collection possesses a copy of the text, printed with *Regulations for the Order and Discipline of the Troops. . . .* (Charleston: W. P. Young, 1794). This text contains regulations for a court martial, of the kind followed by Clark in his notes excerpted above. Later editions modify and expand these regulations.

Lewis & Clark College Collection: Microfiche, Boley Law Library; photocopy in Special Collections.

1a.6 Richard Kirwan, *Elements of Mineralogy* [1784], 1794, [1810]

[First Edition] ELEMENTS | OF | MINERALOGY. | BY | RICHARD KIRWAN, Esq; F.R.S. | [device] | LONDON: | Printed for P. ELMSLY, in the *Strand.* | M.DCC.LXXXIV.

Collation: One volume, 8vo., 22 cm. title; [1]–xviii preface and contents; [1]–412 text. Three tables, 398–412.

[Second Edition] ELEMENTS | OF | MINERALOGY. | [rule] | BY | RICHARD KIRWAN, Esq. F.R.S. & M.R.I.A. | OF THE ACADEMIES OF STOCKHOLM, UPSAL, | BERLIN, MANCHESTER, PHILADELPHIA, &c. | [rule] | SECOND EDITION, | WITH CONSIDERABLE IMPROVEMENTS AND | ADDITIONS. | [rule] | VOL. I. | EARTHS AND STONES. | [rule] | LONDON: | PRINTED BY J. NICHOLS, | FOR P. ELMSLY, IN THE STRAND. | [rule] | M DCC XCIV. | Vol. II. | SALTS, INFLAMMABLES, AND METALLIC | SUBSTANCES. | rule] | LONDON: | PRINTED FOR P. ELMSLY, IN | THE STRAND. | [rule] | M, DCC, XCVI.

Collation: Two volumes, 8vo., 22 cm. Vol. 1: [i] half title with blank verso; [iii] title page with blank verso; v–xvi preface; xvii–xxvii contents; [blank]; xxix–xxxi two errata leaves [1]–510 text. Vol. 2: [i] half title with blank verso; [iii] title page with blank verso; v–xvi contents; [xvii] errata leaf with blank verso; [1]–529 text. Table 1 (four foldouts), 2, and 3 (single foldouts) bound following 485.

[Third Edition] ELEMENTS | OF | MINERALOGY. | [rule] | BY | RICHARD KIRWAN, ESQ. | P.R.I.A.F.R.S.L. & E. | OF THE ACADEMIES OF STOCKHOLM, UPSAL, BERLIN, MANCHESTER, | PHILADELPHIA, &c. | [rule] | THE THIRD EDITION.| [rule] | IN TWO VOLUMES. | VOL. I. | *EARTHS AND STONES.* | [rule] | *LONDON:* | PRINTED FOR J. MACKINLAY, 87, STRAND. | [rule] | 1810. | Vol. II. | *SALTS, INFLAMMABLES, AND METALLIC* | *SUBSTANCES.* | rule] | *LONDON:* | PRINTED FOR J. MACKINLAY, 87, STRAND. | [rule] | 1810. |

Collation: Two volumes, 8vo., 22 cm. Vol. 1: title with printer's notice on verso ("London: Printed by B. M'Millan, Bow Street, Covent Garden"); [v]–xxiv preface of second edition and contents; [1]–452 text. Vol. 2: title with blank verso; [v]–xiv contents; [1]–459 text. Table 1 (two foldouts) and 2 (one foldout), 421–6.

Document: "Kirwan's Mineralogy," Summary of Purchases, Journal of the Military Storekeeper at Philadelphia, Journal C, June 6, 1803 (Jackson).

References: Jackson, *Letters*, item 57 and n. 3: Wendlick, "In Search of the White Earth," Portland: Oregon Chapter of the Lewis and Clark Trail Heritage Foundation, 2002.

Description: Published in three early editions: the first in one volume (1784); a second in two volumes (1794); containing additional material; and the third, a close reprint of 1794, and carrying that edition's preface, in 1810. Roger Wendlick has established a strong likelihood that Lewis and Clark carried the enlarged second edition of 1794.

Lewis & Clark College Collection: Wendlick 1: First edition, modern half leather, marbled boards, raised bands and tooling; ownership inscription of J. J. Simpson on title page. Wendlick 2: Third edition, early half leather, marbled boards, gold stamping; ownership stamps of Devon and Exeter Institution.

1a.7 Patrick Kelly, *Introduction to Spherics and Nautical Astronomy* 1796, 1801

[First Edition] A | PRACTICAL INTRODUCTION | TO | *SPHERICS* | AND | *NAUTICAL ASTRONOMY.* | BEING | AN ATTEMPT TO SIMPLIFY THOSE USE- FUL | SCIENCES. | CONTAINING, | AMONG OTHER ORIGINAL MATTER, THE DISCOVERY OF A | PROJECTION FOR CLEARING THE LUNAR DISTANCES, | IN ORDER TO FIND THE | *LONGITUDE AT SEA*; | WITH | A NEW METHOD OF CALCULATING THIS IMPORTANT | PROBLEM. | [rule] | BY P. KELLY, | MASTER OF FINSBURY SQUARE ACADEMY, LONDON. | [rule] | *La Trigonométrie Spherique est la véritable Science de l'Astronome.* | M. DE LA LANDE, TOM 3, p. 540. | [rule] | *LONDON:* | Printed for J. JOHNSON, St. Paul's Church-Yard, and G. G. and J. | ROBINSON, Pater-noster-Row. | [rule] | MDCCXCVI.

Collation: One volume, 8vo. 23.5 cm. [i]–xiv title, preface, contents; xv errata with blank verso; [1]–210 text. Contains fifty-two engraved figures.

[Second Edition] A | PRACTICAL INTRODUCTION | TO | *SPHERICS* | AND | NAUTICAL ASTRONOMY. | BEING | AN ATTEMPT TO SIMPLIFY THOSE USEFUL | SCIENCES. | [rule] | THE SECOND EDITION, | AUGMENTED AND IMPROVED. | [rule] | By P. KELLY, | MASTER OF FINSBURY-SQUARE ACADE- MY, LONDON. | [decorative rule] | *La Trigonométrie Spherique est la véritable Science de l'Astronome.* | M. DE LA LANDE, TOM. 3, p. 540. | [rule] | London: | *Printed by J. Crowder, Warwick-square;* | FOR J. JOHNSON, AND F. AND C. RIVINGTON, IN ST. PAUL'S | CHURCH-YARD, AND G. G. AND J. ROBINSON, PATER-NOSTER- | ROW. | [rule] | 1801.

Collation: One volume, 8vo., 25 cm. [i]–xvi title, dedication, preface, contents; [1]–201 text; [201]–215 appendix on time-keepers; [216] advertisement. Contains fifty-four engraved figures.

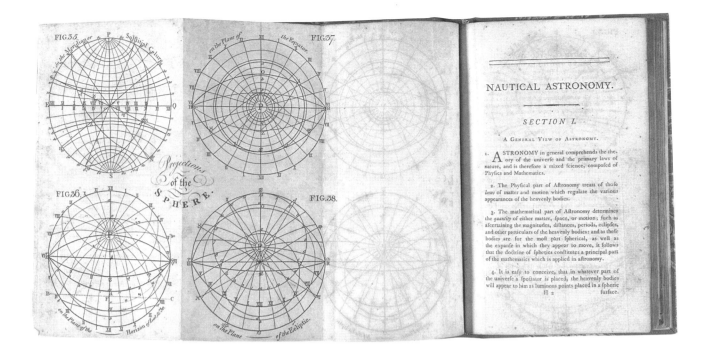

Document: "Kelleys Spherics" Summary of Purchases, Journal of the Military Storekeeper at Philadelphia, Journal C, June 6, 1803 (Jackson, item 57). Either Ellicott or Patterson probably suggested to Lewis the purchase of Patrick Kelly's *Nautical Spherics*. Patterson's letter to Jefferson (Jackson, item 22) describes calculations very similar to those in Kelley, pp. 188 ff.

References: Jackson, *Letters*, items 19, 22, and 57 (with n. 5).

Description: The second London printing, for J. Johnson 1801, was "augmented and improved," and could have been carried by Lewis and Clark. It includes a new appendix on time-keepers. Further editions of *Spherics* were issued after the start of the expedition, in 1805, 1813, and 1822. Lewis was trained by Ellicott (Jackson, item 19) in the techniques of setting an artificial horizon for celestial measurements, establishing a mean meridian by observations before and after noon, calculating latitudes, and recording data for later determination of longitudes.

Lewis & Clark College Collection: Wendlick: 1796 Edition: Half leather with marbled boards, raised bands, gold stamping on spine. Ownership inscription of John Levering, August 2, 1810. 1801 Edition: Half calf, damaged marbled paper, bumped spine. Ownership inscription of John Grave on title page.

1a.8–9 Nevil Maskelyne, *Tables Requisite* 1766–1802; *Nautical Ephemeris* 1804–6
1a.8 Maskelyne's *Tables*
Tables Requisite to Be Used with the Astronomical and Nautical Ephemeris. Published by Order of the Commissioners of Longitude. London. Printed by W. Richardson and S. Clark, 1766. [Author: Nevil Maskelyne.]

Document: "1 Requisite Tables," Summary of Purchases, Journal of the Military Storekeeper at Philadelphia, Journal C, June 6, 1803 (Jackson, item 57).

1a.7 Patrick Kelly,
Introduction to Spherics and Nautical Astronomy
1796

Description: Maskelyne's compilation of *Tables Requisite* first appeared in 1766, and was reprinted in 1781, 1799, and 1802. All three reprints claimed to have been corrected and improved; the 1802 reprint by T. Bensley may have been carried on the expedition.

Lewis & Clark College Collection: Print from microform of Maskelyne's Tables, as included in John Garnett, *Tables Requisite to Be Used with the Nautical Ephemeris, for Finding the Latitude & Longitude at Sea.* New Brunswick, N. J., 1806. Also: William Croswell, *Tables, for Readily Computing the Longitude.* Boston: I. Thomas and E.T. Andrews, 1791. Boley Law Library microfiche.

1a.9 *Nautical Ephemeris* 1804–6
The Nautical Almanac and Astronomical Ephemeris for the Year 1804.
London: Second edition, Commissioners of Longitude, 1803.

Document: "1 Nautical Ephemeris," Summary of Purchases, Journal of the Military Storekeeper at Philadelphia, Journal C, June 6, 1803 (Jackson, item 57).

References: Benson et al., 72–73; Jackson, *Letters,* items 32, 37, and 57 with nn. 1 and 2; "Books Carried," 5; Preston, *passim.*

Description: The *Tables Requisite* and *Nautical Ephemeris* were designed to be used together; Maskelyne's *Tables* provided the tabulations necessary for determining latitude and longitude. The annual volumes of the *Nautical Ephemeris* indicated the sun's changing location in the heavens for each day of the year. Lewis may have attempted to purchase all available *Tables* for the years of the expedition. The British *Nautical Almanac* was published between 1781 and 1804; Garnett began his reprints of the *Almanac* in 1803 (Jackson, "Books Carried"). Jefferson recommended that Lewis contact Garnett on April 30, 1803, and May 16, 1803 (Jackson, *Letters,* items 32 and 37).

Lewis & Clark College Collection: Print from microform of 1804, 1805, and 1806 almanacs, published by John Garnett in each preceding year.

1a.10 Benjamin Smith Barton, *Elements of Botany* 1803 [Color plate I]
ELEMENTS OF BOTANY: | OR | OUTLINES OF THE NATURAL HISTORY | OF | VEGETABLES. | ILLUSTRATED BY THIRTY PLATES. | [rule] | BY BEN-JAMIN SMITH BARTON, M. D. | PROFESSOR OF MATERIA MEDICA, NATURAL HISTORY, AND BOTANY, | IN THE UNIVERSITY OF PENNSYLVANIA. | [rule] | PHILADELPHIA: | PRINTED FOR THE AUTHOR. | [rule] | 1803.

Collation: One volume, 8vo., 22.5 cm. Folding frontisplate; title page, with university lecture advertisement on verso; dedication, dated February 28, 1803, backed with additional lecture advertisements; [v]–xiv preface and errata page; half title backed with poem extract; [1]–302 text, part 1; [blank]; [1]–32 text, part 2; [1]–168 text, part 3; [1]–58 separately paginated appendix and explanation of plates; thirty pages of plates, some folding.

Document: "1 Copy Bartons Bottony (pd. by C.L.)," Summary of Purchases, Journal of the Military Storekeeper at Philadelphia, Journal C, June 6, 1803 (Jackson).

References: Jackson, *Letters,* item 11 and item 57, n. 4.

Description: Lewis studied under Barton at Philadelphia (Jackson), and carried Barton's copy of du Pratz on the journey. Barton presumably recommended to Lewis his recent work, *Elements of Botany,* and taught Lewis how to press, dry, and preserve the plants discovered along the trail. The Academy of Natural Sciences in Philadelphia possesses the volume used to instruct Lewis, a field book composed by Barton from plant samples, each described in appropriate Linnæan terminology.

Lewis & Clark College Collection: Wendlick: Half leather with marbled boards, raised bands, gold stamping to red spine label; 1934 bookplate of Horticultural Society of New York.

1a.11 Alexander Mackenzie, *Voyages* 1802

VOYAGES | FROM | MONTREAL, | ON THE RIVER ST. LAURENCE, | THROUGH THE | CONTINENT OF NORTH AMERICA, | TO THE | FROZEN AND PACIFIC OCEANS; | *In the Years* 1789 *and* 1793; | WITH A PRELIMINARY ACCOUNT | OF THE RISE, PROGRESS, AND PRESENT STATE OF | THE FUR TRADE | OF THAT COUNTRY; | WITH ORIGINAL NOTES AND AN APPENDIX BY BOUGAINVILLE, | MEMBER OF THE FRENCH SENATE; | ILLUSTRATED WITH MAPS; | BY ALEXANDER MACKENZIE, ESQ. | VOL. I. [II.] | [rule] | *LONDON:* | PRINTED FOR T. CADELL, JUN. AND W. DAVIES, STRAND; | COBBETT AND MORGAN, PALL-MALL; AND W. CREECH, | AT EDINBURGH; | BY R. NOBLE, OLD-BAILEY. | [rule] | M.DCCC.II.

Collation: Two volumes, 8vo., 20 cm. Vol. 1: [i]–xiv frontispiece, title, dedication, preface; facing [1] folding map "America"; [1]–162 "General History of the Fur Trade"; map; [163]–284 "Journal of a Voyage"; [285]–290 contents. Vol. 2: half title with blank verso; title with blank verso; map; [5]–210 [for 310] text; [311]–332 notes, appendix, contents.

Documents: In a letter of June 17, 1803, to New York book dealer James Cheetham, Jefferson requested a copy of Mackenzie's journals published in London in 1802: "I have understood there is to be had in New York an 8vo Edition of McKenzie's travels with the same maps which are in the 4to edition: I will thank you to procure it for me. The American 8vo edition is defective in it's maps, and the English 4to edition is too large & cumbersome" (Jackson, item 44). A July 17, 1805, report in the Louisiana *Gazette* (sent from Lexington, Kentucky) confirms the use of Mackenzie by Lewis and Clark: "The descriptions given by Mackenzie of the headwaters of this river are true" (Nasatir). A Spanish commentator confirms the association: "They have to pass toward the source six nations of Indians among which last is that called Serpent which they mistrust; they believe they will make the second winter quarters on the Pacific Ocean; they have sent various curiosities of plants, birds, etc. and among them some deposits of minerals; the diary and map of it they have given and they have for corroboration the description given by McKenzie, which seems to be that of the deceased Loisel sent to you in letter number 47 of September 30, 1804" (Marqués of Casa-Calvo, July 19, 1805, in Nasatir). Mackenzie's Knisteneaux, Algonquin, and Chipeweyan vocabularies are a possible model for Jefferson's blank vocabularies, filled out by Lewis and sent to Jefferson from St. Louis (Jackson, 142, 207; Thwaites). Barton's *New Views of the Origin of the Tribes and Nations of America* (1797) contained a comparative list of fifty-four words. Also, Lewis and Clark's compilation "A Statistical View," composed at Fort Mandan in the winter of 1804–05, contains information on tribes farther to the north, not seen on the expedition. This information could only have come from other traders, or from the one published account, which was Mackenzie's. The folding map facing [1] in vol. 1 was a contributor to King's manuscript map.

References: Jackson, *Letters*, items 44, 142, 207 (p. 323); Nasatir, 1:760–64; Thwaites, 7:408–10.

Description: This is the two-volume 1802 London octavo second edition, described in Jefferson's letter, above. The one-volume London quarto of the previous year was judged too bulky to be taken on the expedition.

Lewis & Clark College Collection: Wendlick: Two volumes, half leather with gold stamping and tool work on spine.

1a.12 Andrew Ellicott, *Journal* 1803

THE | JOURNAL | OF | ANDREW ELLICOTT, | LATE COMMISSIONER ON BEHALF OF THE UNITED STATES | DURING PART OF THE YEAR 1796, THE YEARS 1797, | 1798, 1799, AND PART OF THE YEAR 1800: | FOR | DETERMIN-ING THE BOUNDARY | BETWEEN THE | UNITED STATES | AND THE | POS-SESSIONS OF HIS CATHOLIC MAJESTY | IN AMERICA, | CONTAINING | *OCCASIONAL REMARKS* | ON THE | SITUATION, SOIL, RIVERS, NATURAL PRODUCTIONS, | AND DISEASES OF THE DIFFERENT COUNTRIES | ON THE | OHIO, MISSISSIPPI, AND GULF OF MEXICO, | WITH | SIX MAPS | Comprehending the Ohio, the Mississippi from the mouth of the Ohio to the Gulf of | Mexico, the whole of West Florida, and part of East Florida. | TO WHICH IS ADDED | AN APPENDIX, | Containing all the Astronomical Observations made use of for determining the boundary, | with many others, made in different parts of the country for settling the geogra- | phical positions of some important points, with maps of the boundary | on a large scale; likewise a great number of Thermometrical | Observations made at different times, and places. | [rule] | Philadelphia: PRINTED BY BUDD & BARTRAM, | FOR THOMAS DOBSON, AT THE STONE HOUSE, | NO. 41, SOUTH SECOND STREET. | [rule] | 1803.

Collation: One volume, 4to., 26 cm. [i]–viii title page, copyright, preface ([iii]–vii); [viii blank]; [1]–299 journal; [1]–151 separately paginated appendix, "Astronomical and Thermometrical Observations;" [blank]; errata page. Plates: six foldout charts in text; eight foldout plates in appendix. Text: Plate A: Ohio River; B: Ohio River; C: Mississippi River; D: Mississippi River; E: Southern Boundary of the United States; F: Southern Boundary of the United States. Appendix: eight untitled illus-trations of surveying methods.

Documents: "Mr. Lewis's first object must be, to acquire a facility, and dexterity, in making the observations; which can only be attained by practice; in this he shall have all the assistance I can give him with the aid of my apparatus." Ellicott to Jefferson, March 6, 1803 (Jackson). "Altitude of the [Sun]'s Center at time of Obsert. by Mr. Elicot's formula–" Lewis, journal entry for February 23, 1805, at Fort Mandan (Moulton).

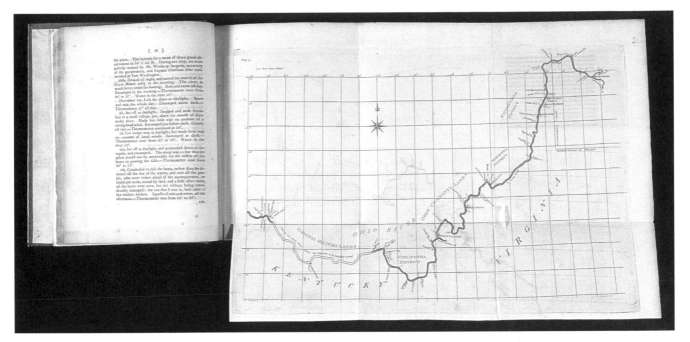

1a.12 Andrew Ellicott,
Journal 1803

References: Jackson, *Letters,* item 19; Moulton, 3:301.

Description: Lewis studied under Ellicott, whose charts of the Mississippi were used by Nicholas King in his map for Lewis and Clark. See below, 1b.3(v). The astronomical and thermometrical measurements taken along the journey clearly follow Ellicott's instructions, and are modeled on those in the appendix to Ellicott's *Journal.*

Lewis & Clark College Collection: Full leather, raised bands with original red leather label pasted to spine. Appendix signature "f" misbound before signature "d."

1b Maps Carried on the Expedition

The Corps of Discovery also carried and consulted maps along the route. Important scholarship has been published on this subject, most notably the work of John Logan Allen and Carl Wheat. An excellent survey, with reproductions of many of the maps, is also available in Benson, Irwin, and Moore's *Exploring the West from Monticello: A Perspective in Maps from Columbus to Lewis and Clark.* Many of the manuscript maps listed below are reproduced and discussed in vol. 1 of Moulton's edition of the Lewis and Clark journals.

1b.1 Antoine-Simon Le Page du Pratz, "Louisiana" [1763], 1774

Du Pratz, Le Page. "A Map of Louisiana, with the course of The Missisipi." In *The History of Louisiana, or of the Western Parts of Virginia and Carolina.* London: 1763. 33.5 x 25.5 cm [Illustrated on p. 45.]

Document: "see Monsr. Dupratz history of Louisiana, page 71, and the map attached to that work," Lewis and Clark, "A Statistical View," from Jefferson's Message of 1806 (A. & G. Way edition), p. 64.

References: Allen, plate 16; Benson et al., item 22; Wheat, 1:73, 215.

Description: This volume is described in 1a.2. The map presents good information on the courses of the Mississippi and lower Missouri Rivers. However, it shows an upper Missouri flowing through prairies north of the Rocky Mountains, which no doubt encouraged Jefferson (who owned this edition of Le Page du Pratz) and Meriwether Lewis in their belief in a navigable river system to the West Coast. This belief was supported by Vancouver's chart, 1b.3(iii).

Lewis & Clark College Collection: Wendlick: Described in 1a.2. Barton's copy was the second London edition (1774) in one volume. The Wendlick copy is the two-volume first edition of 1763. The maps are the same in both editions.

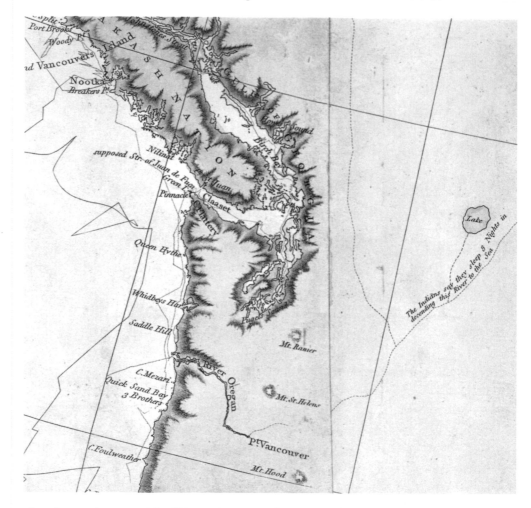

1b.2 Aaron Arrowsmith, detail from "New Discoveries" 1802

1b.2 Aaron Arrowsmith, "New Discoveries" 1802 [Color plate IV]
Arrowsmith, Aaron. "A Map Exhibiting all the New Discoveries in the Interior Parts of North America," London, 1795, "with Additions to 1802." 145 x 123 cm.

Document: "I now began more than ever to suspect the varacity of Mr. Fidler or the correctness of his instruments. for I see that Arrasmith in his late map of N. America has laid down a remarkable mountain in the chain of the Rocky Mountains called the tooth nearly as far South as Latitude 45°, and this is said to be from the discoveries of Mr. Fidler". Lewis, journal entry of June 8, 1805 (Moulton, 4:266–267).

References: Allen, plate 16 and pp. 74–80, 98–105; Benson et al., item 30; Heckrotte, pp. 16–20; Wheat, 1:178, 249.

Description: This five-foot-wide chart is the largest and most influential map carried on the expedition. The second edition, with "Additions to 1802," containing new information given to Arrowsmith by Peter Fidler, a Hudson's Bay Company employee, about the great bend of the Missouri and its headwaters, was the first to incorporate the topography of Mackenzie, Vancouver, and Cook from their published travels and voyages.

Aaron Arrowsmith was the premier cartographer of his time. The new additions to 1802 included information from Fidler, Cook, Vancouver, and Mackenzie. In addition to being carried on the journey, Arrowsmith's map was essentially the basis for Nicholas King's manuscript chart (see following item). "Arrowsmith's 1802 map of North America was the most comprehensive map of the West available to Jefferson and Lewis and it was probably the most important map used in the planning of the expedition." (Benson, et al.). The map exists in two states, described by Heckrotte. The difference between the two states is most easily seen in the wide loop of the Red Deer River reaching east to longitude 110°W, just above the 50th parallel. In the first state, this part of the river runs almost north-south. Another point of difference can be seen due east of the Juan de Fuca Strait, above the legend noting that the Indians sleep eight nights in descending the river from the mountains to the sea. Here, a lake is present in the second state, but not the first.

Lewis & Clark College Collection: Original map, 1802 edition (second state), framed and displayed in the Heritage Room, Lewis & Clark College Special Collections. On loan from Roger Wendlick. The collection also contains (from Wendlick) three of the four maps from Arrowsmith's 1804 *A New and Elegant General Atlas* described in Wheat, 2:4–11 (missing the "Spanish Dominions"). This atlas almost certainly appeared too late to be carried on the expedition.

1b.3 Nicholas King, Manuscript Map of Western North America 1803
King, Nicholas. Map of the western part of North America, 1803. In the collection of the Geography and Map Division of the Library of Congress.

Document: "I have requested Mr. King to project a blank map to extend from 88 to 126° West longitude from Greenwich and from 30° to 55° north latitude." Albert Gallatin to Jefferson, March 14 1803 (Jackson).

References: Allen, plate 21, and pp. 97–103; Benson et al., item 31; Jackson, *Letters*, item 21; Moulton, 1:map 2 and p. 5.

Description: Nicholas King was commissioned by Albert Gallatin to compose a new map for the Lewis and Clark Expedition. He was instructed to use information from the works of Ellicott, Cook, Vancouver, Arrowsmith, Mackenzie, Thompson, Mitchell, d'Anville, and de l'Isle in compiling his map (Benson et al.). King prepared maps for other travelers, including one from the survey of William Dunbar found in some copies of Jefferson's 1806 Report to Congress (2b.1).

The Lewis & Clark College Collection contains original copies of the following contributors to King:

1b.3(i) John Senex
version of de l'Isle
"Carte de la Louisiane"
[1718]

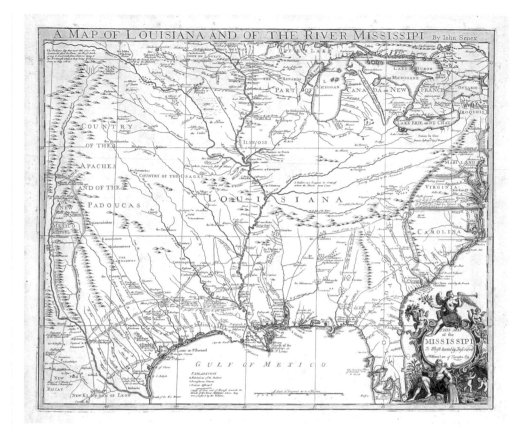

1b.3(i) Guillaume de l'Isle, "Carte de la Louisiane" [1718]

De l'Isle, Guillaume. "Carte de la Louisiane et du Cours du Mississipi," 1718.

Lewis & Clark College Collection: Senex, John. "A Map of Louisiana and of the River Mississipi. This Map of the Mississipi is most humbly inscribed to William Law of Lawreston Esq." 1719. Reprinted in *A New General Atlas: Containing a Geographical and Historical Account of All the Empires, Kingdoms, and Other Dominions of the World: with the Natural History and Trade of Each Country. Taken from the Best Authors, Particularly Cluverius and Others. The Maps Are All Engraven or Revised by Mr. Senex.* London: D. Browne, 1721. 58 x 48.5 cm. This map is an anglicized version of de l'Isle. Original map, framed and displayed in the Heritage Room, Lewis and Clark Special Collections. On loan from Roger Wendlick.

Reference: Wheat, 1:66, 205.

1b.3(ii) James Cook, "Chart of the NW Coast of America" 1784

Cook, James. "Chart of the NW Coast of America and NE Coast of Asia explored in the Years 1778 & 1779." In *A Voyage to the Pacific Ocean.* London: 1784. 67 x 39.5 cm.

Reference: Benson et al., item 25

Description: "Cook's chart of the Pacific coast served as a chief reference source for Nicholas King" (Benson et al.) even though its usefulness was limited by the omission of the mouth of the Columbia. Cook also drew Vancouver Island as part of the coastline. The Asian coasts are drawn from a Russian chart.

Lewis & Clark College Collection: Original chart, framed and displayed in the Heritage Room, Lewis & Clark College Special Collections. Wendlick copy.

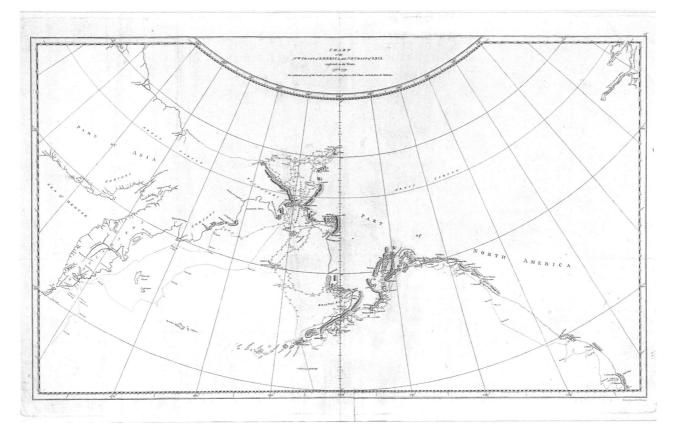

**1b.3(iii) George Vancouver, "Part of the Coast of N.W. America" 1798
[Color plate VI]**
Vancouver, George. "A Chart shewing part of the Coast of N.W. America." In
A Voyage of discovery to the North Pacific ocean, and Round the World. London: 1798.
57.5 x 75.5 cm.

Document: "examine if a Bay is Situated near the mouth of this river as laid
down by Vancouver," Clark, journal entry of November 14, 1805 (Moulton, 6:47).

Reference: Benson et al., item 26; Jackson, *Letters,* item 40.

Description: British commander George Vancouver explored and mapped the
Northwest Coast as captain of the *Discovery.* However, the major river of the
West was first entered by American Robert Gray, captain of the *Columbia,* in 1792.
After seeing Gray's chart, Vancouver returned to the Columbia in the same year,
and his lieutenant, Broughton, navigated his ship *Chatham* to Point Vancouver. In
preparing for his expedition, Lewis traced Vancouver's chart (Jackson), which was
also used by Nicholas King in compiling his manuscript map. Lewis's tracing(s)
may well have been carried on the expedition (see introductory essay). Broughton's
sighting of the Cascade mountain chain encouraged him to place the Continental
Divide too far to the west, an error repeated by Mackenzie (see following item),
deceiving Jefferson and Lewis in their assumptions about a river route to the coast.

Lewis & Clark College Collection: Original chart from Wendlick, framed and
displayed in the Heritage Room, Lewis & Clark College Special Collections.

**1b.3(ii) James Cook,
"Chart of the NW Coast
of America" 1784**

1b.3(iv) Alexander Mackenzie, "America Between Latitudes 40 and 70 North" 1801
Mackenzie, Alexander. "A Map of America between Latitudes 40 and 70 North, and Longitudes 45 and 180 West, Exhibiting Mackenzie's Track From Montreal to Fort Chipewyan & from thence to the North Sea in 1789. & to the West Pacific Ocean in 1793." In *Voyages from Montreal, on the River St. Laurence, through the Continent of North America to the Frozen and Pacific Oceans; In the Years 1789 and 1793.* London: 1801. 78 x 44 cm.

Reference: Allen, 119ff.; Benson et al., item 27; Wheat, 1:174, 248.

Description: Sir Alexander Mackenzie was the first European explorer to reach the Northwest Coast by an overland route. His description of the Continental Divide as no higher than three thousand feet encouraged Jefferson's belief in an easy crossing. "Moreover, Mackenzie's urgent recommendations that the British government secure control of the Pacific Northwest probably also hastened President Jefferson's authorization of an expedition to the Northwest" (Benson et al.). Mackenzie's mapping of the upper course of a river (the Fraser) that he believed to be the Columbia (named by him the "Tacoutche Tesse or Columbia") was followed by Arrowsmith (1b.2) in his 1802 Additions.

Lewis & Clark College Collection: Wendlick copy, original map, framed and displayed in the Heritage Room, Lewis & Clark College Special Collections. This map is also found in vol. 1 of the two-volume set described at 1a.11.

1b.3(v) Andrew Ellicott, Maps of the Mississippi River 1803
Ellicott, Andrew. Maps published in *The Journal of Andrew Ellicott*. Philadelphia: 1803. King would have made use of the two charts (C and D) of the Mississippi.

Document: "In this [King's map] I intend to insert the course of the Mississipi as high up as the Ohio from Ellicot's [chart]." Gallatin to Jefferson, March 14, 1803 (Jackson).

References: Benson et al., item 28; Jackson, *Letters*, item 21.

Description: The printed journal of Lewis's astronomy and surveying tutor, Andrew Ellicott, probably carried on the expedition (see above, 1a.12), contained accurate maps of the Mississippi as far north as the Great Lakes, identifying its confluences with the Ohio and the Missouri.

Lewis & Clark College Collection: Contained in the volume described at 1a.12.

1c Other Manuscript Maps Carried on the Expedition
1c.1 James Mackay, Map of the Missouri River from St. Charles to the Mandan Villages 1797
References: Allen, 140; Jackson, *Letters*, item 93; Moulton, 1:6; Wheat, 1:161, 246.

Description: There has been considerable discussion by scholars regarding the source of this map, which was found in William Clark's papers in the Office of Indian Affairs, Washington, D.C., in 1916. The map shows Mackay's route on the Missouri River in 1797. It appears to have been sent to Clark by William Henry Harrison on November 13, 1803, and carried on the expedition. The map is reproduced in the Moulton *Atlas,* map 5.

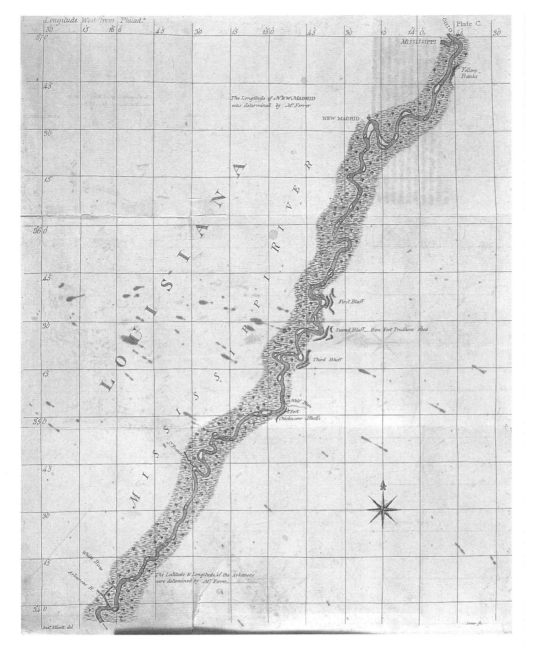

1b.3(v) Andrew Ellicott,
Mississippi River 1803

1c.2 John Evans, Map of the Missouri 1797

Document: "I now inclose you a map of the Missouri as far as the Mandans, 12.
or 1500. miles I presume above it's mouth. It is said to be very accurate, having
been done by a Mr. Evans by order of the Spanish government." Jefferson to
Lewis, January 13, 1804 (Jackson, item 103).

References: Allen 137; Jackson, *Letters*, items 93 n. 3, and item 103; Moulton,
1:6; Wheat, 1:161, 245. The map is first reproduced in Annie Heloise Abel, "A
New Lewis and Clark Map," *The Geographical Review* 1, 5 (1916): 329–45 (offprint
at Lewis & Clark College).

Description: Lewis and Clark carried a set of seven maps showing the Mackay-
Evans explorations from the mouth of the Missouri to the Mandan villages. There
has been much speculation about the procurement of these maps, with the fullest
coverage in Allen and Moulton. The maps are reproduced in the Moulton *Atlas*.

1c.3 Antoine Soulard, Map of the Missouri to the Osage 1803

Map of the mouth of the Missouri to the mouth of the Osage, by Antoine Soulard (Manuscript copy by Lewis, 1803).

Document: A map "imbracing a portion of the Mississippi, the Missouri from it's junction with this river to the mouth of the Osages, and the last named river in it's whole extent" Lewis to Jefferson, December 28, 1803 (Jackson).

References: Allen 148; Jackson, *Letters*, item 100; Moulton, 1:5.

Description: Allen, Jackson, and Moulton provide evidence that Soulard gave Lewis permission to copy this map. No map of this description now exists.

1c.4 [Antoine Soulard,] Map of Upper Louisiana, Copied from a Spanish Original ca. 1794–1803

"A General Map of Uper Louisiana," from a lost Spanish original of 1794.

References: Allen, 148; Aubrey Diller, "A New Map of the Missouri River Drawn in 1795." *Imago Mundi*, 12 (1955): 175–80; Jackson, *Letters*, item 100 and n. 6; Moulton, 1:5; Wheat, 1:157–8.

Description: Lewis acquired this map in St. Louis before the departure of the expedition up the Missouri. According to John Logan Allen, "This map has not been identified beyond all doubt but it is probably a copy of a map drawn by Antoine Soulard." (Allen, 148) The copy, titled "A Topogra[phical] Sketch of the Missouri and Upper Missisippi; Exhibiting the various Nations and Tribes of Indians who inhabit the Country: Copied from the Original Spanish MS. Map," was found in William Clark's papers, and now resides in the Coe Collection at Yale. Reproductions of the map can be found in Thwaites (8, plate 2), Moulton (1, plate 4), and Allen (plate 25).

1d Examples of Other Manuscript Materials in the Traveling Library

Lewis and Clark carried a number of manuscript materials as a part of their traveling library. The following items were used by the explorers in their journals or published reports.

1d.1 Jean Baptiste Truteau, *Journal Extracts* Translated by Jefferson 1803

Document: "I inclose you also copies of the treaties for Louisiana, the act for taking possession, a letter from Dr. Wistar, & some information collected by myself from Truteau's journal in MS. all of which may be useful to you." Jefferson to Lewis, November 16, 1803 (Jackson).

References: Jackson, *Letters*, item 94 and n. 3; Sowerby, 4:340. A different text of Truteau's description of the Upper Missouri is reprinted in full in Nasatir, 2:376ff.

Description: Jefferson's translation from Jean Baptiste Truteau, Indian agent for the Illinois trading company, among the Ricaras on the Missouri, is transcribed in full in Jackson. Truteau's notes on individual tribes are a clear source for Lewis and Clark's "A Statistical View," first published in Jefferson's *Message* of 1806 (2b.1). Truteau's organization of materials is a model for Lewis's greatly expanded and updated reports, and in at least one case—the Grand Osages—Lewis quotes Truteau's numbers and language directly: "The Grand Osages. . . . They furnish 20.000 skins of the small deer" (Truteau), "Grand Osâge. . . . [The species of peltries, furs and other articles which they annually supply or furnish] 20.000. . . Principally skins of the small deer, black bear, some beaver, and a few otters and rackoons" (Lewis).

1d.2 Robert Patterson/Meriwether Lewis, *Astronomy Notebook* 1803, 1805, 1806
Document: "By Mr. Patterson's Altd. [Sun]'s Center at time of observation—" Lewis, journal entry of February 23, 1805, at Fort Mandan (Moulton, 3:301).

References: Moulton, 2:564f.; Preston, 176f. and n. 16.

Description: Robert Patterson's Astronomy Notebook of thirty pages, containing instructions for measuring lunar distances, with additional notations by Lewis, was carried on the expedition (Preston). This notebook is now housed as the Meriwether Lewis Astronomy Notebook in the Breckenridge Collection, Missouri Historical Society, item C1074 (description in Moulton).

1d.3 John Evans and James Mackay, *Journal Extracts* Translated by John Hay 1804
Document: "I have also obtained Ivins's and Mac Kay's journal up the Missouri, it is in French & is at present in the hands of Mr. Hay, who has promised to translate it for me" Lewis to Jefferson, December 28, 1803 (Jackson).

References: Jackson, *Letters,* item 100; Moulton, 1:5; Thwaites, 1:4. A translation of Mackay's Spanish journal is reprinted in Nasatir, 1:354–365. See the discussion also in Allen, 43–44. Frederick J. Teggart surveys the relationship of Truteau, Evans, and Mackay (all three employees of the Spanish Company of Explorers of the Missouri) with the leaders of the expedition ("Notes Supplementary to Any Edition of Lewis and Clark," Reprinted from the *Annual Report of the American Historical Association for 1908,* Vol. 1: 183–195).

Description: John Hay provided Lewis with information of his own on the Red and Assiniboine Rivers, and translated journal entries by Evans and Mackay describing the upper Missouri (Moulton, Thwaites).

Chapter Two
Early Expedition-Related Publications

Essay 67
Bibliography 75

2a Initial Funding of the Expedition

2a.1 Jefferson's Confidential Request for Funds, January 18, 1803

2a.2 Act for Extending the External Commerce of the United States,
February 28, 1803

2a.3 Act Authorizing Jefferson to Take Possession of the Louisiana Territory,
October 22, 1803

2a.4 Report of the Committee of Commerce, March 8, 1804

2b Jefferson's Report to Congress, February 19, 1806

2b.1 A. & G. Way, Washington 1806

2b.2 Duane, Washington 1806

2b.3 Gales and Seaton, Washington 1832 (reprint of 2b.1)

2b.4 Hopkins and Seymour, New York 1806

2b.5 Marschalk, Natchez 1806

2b.6 Phillips, London 1807

2b.7 Journal and Newspaper Publications Relating to Jefferson's February Report

2c Documents Relating to the Return of the Expedition

2c.1 Clark's Letter to His Brother, September 23, 1806

2c.2 Jefferson's Message to Congress, December 2, 1806

2c.3 Newspaper Editions of Jefferson's December 2, 1806, Message

2c.4 A Bill Making Compensation to Lewis and Clark, January 23, 1807

Early Expedition-Related Publications

Initial U.S. government documents about the Lewis and Clark Expedition
provided the first glimpses of the project's goals and progress.

As a government-financed, military reconnaissance, the Lewis and Clark Expedition
gained notice in several official United States publications. Intense public interest
in the adventures of the Corps of Discovery also inspired several publishers to
reprint reports of the explorations for general consumption by eager readers. These
early publications confirmed American and European curiosity about the interior
of North America—a great *terra incognita* two hundred years ago.

The expedition was one of many important explorations at that time. The travels to the Arctic and Antarctic to determine whether or not the earth was hollow
with openings at its poles, the quest to find the headwaters of the great Missouri
and Mississippi Rivers, the treks through deserts and jungles to ascertain the sources of
the Nile and Congo, and the descent through the Grand Canyon of the Colorado—
all of these journeys were nineteenth-century ventures that drew public and private
funds. The secrets of distant lands beckoned to the adventuresome and to armchair
travelers alike. Readers in the United States and abroad devoured the accounts of
those who dared to go where few had gone before.

The first printed information about the expedition came in 1803, when Samuel
Harrison Smith (1772–1845) published a notice of President Jefferson's letter to
Congress. The letter forwarded the report from the Secretary of War about establishing trading houses among Indian tribes, obtaining land cessions, and marking
tribal boundaries. The *Journal of the House of Representatives* merely observed that on
January 18: "A message in writing, was received from the President of the United
States, by Mr. Lewis, his secretary . . . ." The letter vaguely hinted that "further
progress in marking boundaries and in new extinguishments of title" would require
"some appropriations of money."[1] The *Journal of the Senate, 1801–1809*, printed by
A. and G. Way, Washington, D.C., contained the same cryptic passage.[2] The text
of Jefferson's letter remained "in confidence" until published in 1828 by Duff
Green in the *Journal of the Executive Proceedings of the Senate . . . .*[3] By that date, tensions with Spain and Britain had cooled and Spain was no longer a contender for
any lands in the American West.

The confidential message of January 18, 1803, contained Jefferson's design for
the expedition. "The river Missouri, and the Indians inhabiting it," he wrote, "are
not as well known as is rendered desirable by their connexion with the Mississippi,
and consequently with us." Jefferson continued:

> An intelligent officer, with ten or twelve chosen men, fit for the enterprize and
> willing to undertake it, taken from our posts, where they may be spared without
> inconvenience, might explore the whole line, even to the Western Ocean,
> have conferences with the natives on the subject of commercial intercourse,
> get admission among them for our traders, as others are admitted, and return
> with the information acquired, in the course of two summers.

Jefferson argued: "The interests of commerce place the principal object within
the constitutional powers and care of Congress, and that it should incidentally
advance the geographical knowledge of our continent, cannot but be an additional
gratification."[4]

> "I wish to mention
> to you in confidence
> that I have obtained
> authority from
> Congress to under-
> take the long desired
> object of exploring
> the Missouri &
> whatever river,
> heading with that,
> leads into the
> Western ocean."
>
> Thomas Jefferson
> to Benjamin Rush,
> February 28, 1803

1 *The Journal of the House
of Representatives*,
2:124–125.

2 *The Journal of the Senate*,
2:44–45.

3 *The Journal of the Executive
Proceedings*, 1:437–439.

4 Ibid. This publication contained the text of Jefferson's
letter of January 18. It was
published by Duff Green, a
member of President Jackson's
"kitchen cabinet." The letter
next appeared in *American
State Papers, Class II, Indian
Affairs* (1832).

Smith first earned Jefferson's attention while serving as secretary of the American Philosophical Society in Philadelphia. Smith's essay on education, presented to the Society, caught Jefferson's eye. In 1800, the president-elect encouraged Smith to relocate to the new capital. Smith agreed and set up his printing shop and residence on New Jersey Avenue between D and E streets, Southeast. On August 27, 1800, he began printing the Georgetown *Centinel of Liberty*, and on October 31, 1800, the triweekly *National Intelligencer and Washington Advertiser*. Smith edited the latter newspaper until 1810, sold his interests in 1813, and spent his remaining years in banking.[5] The extensive correspondence of the Smith family, and the diaries and commonplace books of his wife, Margaret Bayard Smith, document the social, cultural, and political life of Washington, D.C., in the first third of the nineteenth century.[6]

Andrew and George Way, printers of the *Journal of the Senate*, were also from Philadelphia. In 1799, the firm of Way and Groff printed Benjamin Smith Barton's *Fragments on the Natural History of Pennsylvania* and in 1800, Barton's *A Memoir Concerning the Disease of Goitre*. The promise of government printing contracts drew Way and Groff to Washington, D.C. In August 1802, Joseph Groff left the firm. Andrew Way Jr. and George Way remained as principals. However, George Way, who died in 1819, spent more of his energy in the manufacturing of glass. Following his brother's death, Andrew Way continued running both companies, taking in Jacob Gideon as a printing partner in 1822. The firm continued as Way and Gideon until 1834, when Way followed his brother in devoting his remaining years to glass manufacturing.[7]

Duff Green (1791–1875), publisher in 1828 of Jefferson's confidential message to Congress requesting funds for the expedition, was a veteran of the War of 1812, a merchant, land speculator, lawyer, and Missouri politician. In 1823 he purchased the *St. Louis Enquirer* and in 1824 bought the *United States Telegraph* in Washington, D.C. Green attacked President John Quincy Adams and campaigned ruthlessly for Andrew Jackson. In 1829 he became an official publisher for Congress and a personal adviser to President Jackson. In 1830 Green established the *Washington Globe*. Although he broke with Jackson and lost his congressional patronage as printer in 1832, Green remained involved in national affairs for many years. The *Journal of the Executive Proceedings of the Senate*, printed by Green in 1828, included documents from the first to the nineteenth Congress.[8]

On February 28, 1803, within four weeks of receipt of Jefferson's "confidential message," Congress appropriated funds to underwrite the expedition:

An ACT for extending the external commerce of the United States. BE it enacted by the Senate and House of Representatives of the United States of America, in Congress assembled, That the sum of two thousand five hundred dollars be, and the same is hereby appropriated for the purpose of extending the external commerce of the United States, to be paid out of any money in the treasury not otherwise appropriated.

The statute carried the signatures of Nathaniel Macon, Speaker of the House; Aaron Burr, vice president and president of the Senate; and Thomas Jefferson.[9]

On October 22, 1803, President Jefferson sought consent from Congress to implement the terms of the agreement with France to purchase Louisiana Territory. At issue were claim payments of American citizens against France, and the appropriation of $11.25 million to pay the French Republic. The measure passed,

5 The *Journal of the House of Representatives*, 2:v–vi; McMurtrie, *A History of Printing*, 2:267–268.

6 Smith, "The Papers."

7 McMurtrie, *A History of Printing*, 2:268–269; Ancestry.com [George Way], viewed August 17, 2001; *The Journal of the Senate*, 2:iv.

8 Silbey, "Duff Green," *American National Biography*, 9:484–485.

9 *The Laws of the United States of America*, 6:215.

thus authorizing one of the greatest real estate deals in modern history. The proceedings regarding this authorization appeared in the *Journal of the House of Representatives* (Eighth Congress, First Session), printed in 1803 by Samuel Harrison Smith, and the *Journal of the Senate* (Eighth Congress, First Session) printed in 1803 by William Duane & Son of Washington, D.C.[10]

On March 8, 1804, the House Committee of Commerce and Manufactures reported on its enquiry into the "Expediency Authorising the President of the United States, to Employ Persons to Explore Such Parts of the Province of Louisiana, as He May Deem Proper." The Committee wrote:

> It is highly desirable that this extensive region should be visited, in some parts at least, by intelligent men. Important additions might thereby be made to the science of geography. Various materials might thence be derived to augment our knowledge of natural history. The government would thence acquire correct information of the situation, extent and worth of its own dominions, and individuals of research and curiosity would receive ample gratification as to the works of art and productions of nature which exist in those boundless tracts.

The report concluded: "The two enterprising conductors of this adventure, captains Lewis and Clark, have been directed to attempt a passage to the western shore of the South Sea; from them on their return in 1805, a narrative full of instruction may be expected." The report was included in the House documents of the Eighth Congress, First Session.[11]

Jefferson had to stretch his political philosophy to justify the purchase of Louisiana. The Constitution was mute on increasing the size of the United States. As a devoted advocate of agrarian democracy, however, Jefferson perceived the acquisition of the sprawling heartland as buttress to the future of the nation. The purchase of Louisiana resolved the critical matter of U.S. control over New Orleans and also insured the free and ready passage of commerce from the great valleys of the Ohio, Tennessee, and Mississippi Rivers to a world market. To ascertain the prospects of these newly acquired lands, Jefferson dispatched three expeditions in 1803–4. The Lewis and Clark party was to explore the Missouri to its headwaters and beyond and became the best-known exploring team. Less dramatic in their missions and accomplishments, but nevertheless important, were the explorations of William Dunbar and George Hunter in 1804 on the Red, Black, and Washita Rivers. Thomas Freeman, a civil engineer and astronomer, and Peter Custis, a botanist, also explored nearly six hundred miles of the Red River before being turned back by the Spanish.[12]

On February 19, 1806, Jefferson shared the results of these labors, and notes on the Indians of the southern part of Louisiana collected by John Sibley of Natchitoches, in his *Message from the President of the United States, Communicating Discoveries Made in Exploring the Missouri, Red River and Washita . . . .* In 1806 Andrew and George Way of Washington, D.C., first printed the document.[13]

The *Message from the President* contained much interesting information: a letter authored by Meriwether Lewis at Fort Mandan on April 17, 1805; Lewis and Clark's "Statistical View" and "Historical Sketches," including documentary material about the tribes and the party's ascent of the Missouri River to North Dakota; Sibley's letter of April 10, 1805, to General Henry Dearborn; and "Distances up Red River," "Observations," and "Meteorological Observations" related to the

10 *The Journal of the House of Representatives*, 3:31–61; *Journal of the Senate*, 3:10–29.

11 *Report of the Committee of Commerce and Manufactures*, 3–4.

12 Rowland, *Life, Letters and Papers of William Dunbar*, 137–141, 187–192.

13 *Message from the President* (Washington, D.C., 1806); Allen, *Passage Through the Garden*, 371n. Jefferson's letter of February 19, 1806, also appeared in *The Journal of the Senate*, 5:144–147, printed by William Duane and Son, Washington, D.C., 1805 [printed in 1806].

explorations of the southern part of Louisiana Territory. Some copies, printed for the use of the Senate, included Nicholas King's "Map of the Washita River in Louisiana from the Hot Springs to the Confluence of the Red River." King based his map on the surveys of William Dunbar.[14]

Jefferson's *Message from the President* attracted considerable attention. In addition to the Way edition, the document was printed in 1806 by George F. Hopkins and Seymour (first name unknown) of New York, Andrew Marschalk of Natchez, and Richard Phillips of London.[15] Hopkins had begun his career as a newspaper publisher. In 1792, he entered a short-lived partnership with Matthias Day & Company to print the *New-Jersey State Gazette*. In 1795, Hopkins took over *Arnett's New-Jersey Federalist*, renamed it the *New-Jersey Federalist*, and later renamed it again as the *Genius of Liberty*. Hopkins ceased publication of his newspaper early in 1796 and relocated to New York City, where he began publishing the *Minerva*. In 1802, Hopkins, who operated a bookstore at Washington's Head, 118 Pearl Street, published the first American edition of Alexander Mackenzie's *Voyages from Montreal*, an octavo edition of 296 pages.[16] Hopkins and Seymour reprinted the *Message from the President* with some abridgement, cutting Lewis and Clark's "Historical Sketches" from the Washington, D.C., edition and reducing Lewis's letter from Fort Mandan to "an extract." [17]

Andrew Marschalk changed the title of Jefferson's report to *Discoveries Made in Exploring the Missouri, Red River and Washita . . . .*[18] Unlike the Washington, D.C., and New York editions, this version included "Extracts from the Appendix to Mr. Dunbar's Journal." The publication, probably issued in a limited press run, has become the rarest of all printed items addressing the Lewis and Clark Expedition.[19] Marschalk may have printed this work at the behest of William Dunbar, a resident of Natchez, Mississippi. He may have also sensed a market for selling the report of explorations along the southern boundary of Louisiana Territory.

Born in New York to Dutch parents, Marschalk (1767–1838) traveled to England as a young man and learned the art of printing. When he returned in 1790, he imported a press and settled in Philadelphia. The following year, he sold his press and enlisted in the army to fight in the Ohio Valley Indian wars. He later served in artillery and engineer operations. In 1797, he was with the forces who descended the Mississippi to take possession of former Spanish outposts. While still in the military, Marschalk repurchased his press and shipped it, and a great deal of type, to Walnut Hills, Mississippi. In 1797–98, he printed "The Galley Slave," a broadside ballad. This small item was one of the first printed works issued in the lower Mississippi region. The following year, he published *Paine Detected, or the Unreasonableness of Paine's Age of Reason*, a volume deemed Mississippi's first book. Also in 1799, Marschalk published the *Territorial Laws of Mississippi*.[20]

Marschalk left the army in 1802 and settled in Natchez, where he founded the *Mississippi Herald and Natchez Gazette*, the fourth newspaper in the territory. During his labors as a newspaper publisher and printer, Marschalk reprinted Jefferson's message. For the next thirty years, Marschalk worked in the trade and as a writer, renaming and merging his newspaper repeatedly, while nurturing a volatile public persona. Never a man to duck a controversy, Marschalk was involved in several libel suits. However, the power of the press proved costly for Marschalk. Beset by financial problems, he solicited $3,500 in 1832 from Nicholas Biddle of

14 *Documents Relating to the Purchase*, 2.

15 *Message from the President* (New York, 1806); *Discoveries Made in Exploring*; *Travels in the Interior Parts*.

16 McMurtrie, *A History of Printing*, 2:235, 239; Mackenzie, *Voyages from Montreal*.

17 *Message from the President* (New York, 1806).

18 *Discoveries Made in Exploring the Missouri . . . .*

19 Seven copies of Marschalk's pamphlet are currently known: three at Yale University and single copies at the New York Public Library, Newberry Library, Case Western Reserve Library, and the British Museum Library.

20 Welsh, "Andrew Marschalk," 1–8, 18, 20.

Philadelphia. Biddle had served as writer of the 1814 narrative about Lewis and Clark's explorations. In return for a loan, Marschalk was willing to pledge his full support for the Bank of the United States, of which Biddle was president, then under assault by the Andrew Jackson administration. Biddle needed friends but not risky loans, so he refused Marschalk's plea. Without Biddle's financial assistance, Marschalk was forced to sell his publishing operations in 1833. He died five years later at Washington, a village near Natchez.[21]

The text of the *Message from the President* was also published in London as a single work and in the fifth volume of a travel set. J. G. Barnard, a bookseller located at 57 Skinner Street, Snow Hill, London, printed *Travels in the Interior Parts of America* for Richard Phillips (1767–1840) of 6 Bridge Street, Blackfrairs, London.[22] This was the first European publication containing any substantive information about the Lewis and Clark Expedition and the Red River country. The small volume proclaimed: "never before published in Great Britain."

Phillips had a strong interest in tales of exploration in distant lands. In 1805, he launched *A Collection of Modern and Contemporary Voyages and Travels*. Phillips included the accounts of the explorations of Louisiana Territory from the *Message from the President* in this multi-volume 1807 set. The adventures of Lewis and Clark, Dunbar, and Hunter thus joined Francois Marie Perrin du Lac's *Travels Through the Two Louisianas*, Gavriil Sarytschew's *Account of a Voyage of Discovery to the North-East of Siberia*, Georg Reinbeck's *Travels from St. Petersburgh*, Francis B. Spilsbury's *Account of a Voyage to the Western Coast of Africa*, and Edward S. Waring's *Tour to Sheeraz*.[23] Perrin du Lac (1766–1824) had preceded Lewis and Clark in 1802 when he ascended the Missouri to its confluence with the White River. His narrative sought to persuade the French that riches awaited those who ousted the British from the fur trade with tribes on the upper Missouri and Mississippi Rivers.[24]

Further indication of widespread interest in the expedition was obvious in *Message from the President* extracts printed in journals and newspapers. The journals quoting this information included the *Evening Fire-Side; or, Literary Miscellany* (Philadelphia, 1805–06), *Medical Repository* (New York, 1805–06), *The Repertory* (Boston, 1806), *The Monthly Anthology, And Boston Review* (Boston, 1806), and the *1809– 1810 Omnium Gatherum, A Monthly Magazine* (Boston).[25]

The Corps of Discovery returned to St. Louis a year before the eventual Phillips publication of Jefferson's *Message*. On September 23, 1806, Lewis wrote proudly to President Jefferson: "In obedience to your orders we have penetrated the Continent of North America to the Pacific Ocean, and sufficiently explored the interior of the country to affirm with confidence that we have discovered the most practicable rout which dose exist across the continent by means of the navigable branches of the Missouri and the Columbia Rivers."[26] Lewis also drafted a letter that William Clark dispatched to one of his brothers. However, the document was clearly intended for the press. The letter discussed the route traversed, considerations of travel by water, and the economic potentials. "I consider this tract across the continant of emence advantage to the fur trade," wrote Clark, "as all the furs collected in 9/10ths of the most valuable furr country in America may be conveyed to the mouth of the Columbia and shiped from thence to East indias by the 1st of August in each year." This letter spread the news of the success of the expedition and its primary findings. Between October 9 and November 3, it was published in the *Palladium* and the *Western World* (Frankfort), the *Pittsburgh Gazette*

"By the return of a party which we send from this place with dispatches, I do myself the pleasure of giving you a summary view of the Missouri, &c."

William Clark, Fort Mandan, to William Henry Harrison, April 2, 1805

21 Welsh, "Andrew Marschalk," 62–63.

22 Todd, *A Directory of Printers*, 10.

23 *A Collection of Modern and Contemporary Voyages and Travels*, 5; Issitt, "Introducing Sir Richard Phillips."

24 Nasatir, *Before Lewis and Clark*, 1:111.

25 The bibliographic collation that follows enumerates a fuller listing of journal and newspaper notices of the expedition.

26 Jackson, *Letters*, 1:320.

and the *National Intelligencer* (Washington, D.C.).[27] The letter was also included in 1806 in *The Monthly Anthology, And Boston Review*, a periodical of philosophy, religion, history, arts, and manners published by Munroe & Francis in Boston.[28]

The return of the expedition prompted President Jefferson to report again to Congress, this time on December 2, 1806. "The expedition of Messrs. Lewis and Clarke, for exploring the river Missouri, and the best communication from that to the Pacific ocean, has had all the success which could have been expected," he wrote. "They have traced the Missouri nearly to its source, descended the Columbia to the Pacific ocean, ascertained with accuracy the geography of that interesting communication across our continent, learned the character of the country, of its commerce and inhabitants; and it is but justice to say, that Messrs. Lewis and Clarke, and their brave companions, have, by this arduous service, deserved well of their country." Jefferson took considerable pride in the accomplishments of the Corps of Discovery. The president's message was printed in 1806 by A. & G. Way and by Duane & Son of Washington, D.C.[29] It also appeared in a periodical, *The Weekly Inspector* (New York), on December 6, 1806.[30]

A number of American newspapers carried notice of Jefferson's December 2 confirmation of the Corps of Discovery's success. First to publish the notice was Samuel Harrison Smith's *National Intelligencer* on December 2. Under the headline "National Intelligencer Extraordinary," Smith issued the full text of the president's message to Congress as a broadside in three columns. The copy at Lewis & Clark College is the only one known to exist.[31]

Lewis arrived in Washington, D.C., in the last week of December 1806. Samuel Harrison Smith's *National Intelligencer* heralded his return: "Few expeditions have been conducted with more patience, perseverance, or success; and we have no doubt but that the curiosity of the reader will be fully satisfied by the statements, which we understand, it is the purpose of captain Lewis to lay before the public at as early a day as is compatible with the necessary arrangements for a work of such importance." Residents of the city rallied to host a public dinner to honor Lewis "evincive of the high sense and affectionate esteem they entertain for him." Lewis's entourage included a tribal delegation from the upper Missouri River. On January 1, 1807, Lewis and his new friends attended the theater, where they observed a series of performances: dancing; Mr. Manfredi performing the "Drunken Dragoon" on a tightrope; clowns; tumbling children; the "Egyptian Pyramid"; and a finale—"GRAND INDIAN DANCE IN CHARACTER." According to the advertisement for the evening's events: "The Chief of the Mandans, and Osage INDIANS will dance several dances of character and the great Culumes Dance, which has never been performed before." Presumably, the performance had never occurred before in the nation's capital.[32]

On January 23, 1807, Congress considered payment for services rendered by the Corps of Discovery. A. & G. Way published *Documents Accompanying a Bill Making Compensation to Messieurs Lewis and Clarke and Their Companions, Presented the 23d January, 1807*. The slender document contained a letter from Willis Alston Jr. to Secretary of War Henry Dearborn requesting guidance to Congress on compensation. Dearborn's letter of January 14 recommended land grants of 320 acres to all privates and non-commissioned personnel, one thousand acres to Clark, and fifteen hundred acres to Lewis. However, the letter noted that Lewis wished no distinction in the amount of land, even though Clark had held the rank of

27 Jackson, *Letters*, 1:326–330.

28 *The Monthly Anthology, And Boston Review*, "Political Cabinet," 6–8.

29 *The Journal of the House of Representatives*, 6:9–17; *The Journal of the Senate*, 6:8–21.

30 *The New York Weekly Inspector* 1, no. 15: 121, 132–136.

31 *National Intelligencer and Washington Advertiser*, December 2, 1806.

32 Ibid., December 31, 1806.

lieutenant. Lewis's letter of January 15 forwarded a roll of those who had traveled to the Pacific. He also singled out for consideration Richard Warfington and John Newman, who had served in the ascent of the Missouri. An oversize, folding table presented "A Roll Of the men who accompanied captains Lewis and Clarke on their late tour to the Pacific ocean, through the interior of the continent of North America, shewing their rank, with some remarks on their respective merits and services." [33] The letters of Alston, Dearborn, and Lewis, but not his "roll," were also printed on the front page of the *National Intelligencer* on February 2, 1807. [34]

Lewis enumerated twenty-nine men for consideration for compensation by Congress. Interestingly, he listed the deceased Charles Floyd but omitted the manservant York and Sacagawea, the Shoshone interpreter. Lewis crafted "remarks" on eight. Of Touisant Charbono, as Lewis spelled his name, he wrote: "A man of no peculiar merit; was useful as an interpreter only, in which capacity he discharged his duties with good faith from the moment of our departure from the Mandans, on the 7th of April, 1805, until our return to that place in August last, and received as a compensation 25 dollars per month, while in service." He concluded with a general affirmation:

> With respect to all those persons whose names are entered on this roll, I feel a peculiar pleasure in declaring, that the ample support which they gave me under every difficulty; the manly firmness which they evinced on every necessary occasion, and the patience and fortitude with which they submitted to and bore the fatigues and painful sufferings incident to my late tour to the Pacific ocean, intitles them to my warmest approbation and thanks; nor will I suppress the expression of a hope, that the recollection of services thus faithfully performed, will meet a just reward, in an ample remuneration on the part of our government. [35]

The full text of *Documents Accompanying a Bill* (1807) was reprinted in *American State Papers* (1832). [36]

On January 23, 1807, the House of Representatives heard the first reading of the compensation bill. [37] The Senate next considered the matter and concurred with the House on a "do pass" recommendation. [38] The act approving land warrants to those listed on Captain Lewis's roll, as well as to Richard Warfington and John Newman of the Missouri River leg of the expedition, passed Congress and gained Jefferson's signature on March 3. The law provided that the lands selected, including sixteen hundred acres each to Lewis and Clark, be located in the public domain west of the Mississippi River. [39] Congress further authorized double pay for all of the roster personnel during the expedition. The act was included in *The Laws of the United States of America*, vol. 8, published in Washington, D.C., in 1807 with no printer listed. [40] The act providing land warrants and listing the names of the Corps of Discovery was also reported in the *National Intelligencer* on March 11. [41]

The earliest publications on the Lewis and Clark Expedition clearly documented the deliberate but cautious manner in which Thomas Jefferson at last achieved his long-frustrated plans to explore the North American interior. Under the guise of the "Commerce Clause" for finding a water route to the Pacific and quelling discontent among the Indian tribes, Jefferson laid plans for a remarkable expedition with multiple objectives. The initial publications flowing from the presses of Samuel Harrison Smith, Andrew and George Way, and William Duane and Son in Washington, D.C., did not disclose Jefferson's detailed instructions to Captain

"We have not lost a man sence we left the Mandans a circumstance which I assure you is a pleasing consideration to me."

William Clark to [George Rogers Clark?], September 23, 1806

33 *Documents Accompanying a Bill.*

34 *National Intelligencer and Washington Advertiser,* February 2, 1807.

35 *Documents Accompanying a Bill.*

36 *American State Papers,* 12:207–209.

37 *The Journal of the House of Representatives,* 6:191.

38 *The Journal of the Senate,* 6:245–247.

39 Lewis & Clark College holds a file documenting Patrick Gass's repeated efforts over the next sixty years to obtain additional public domain lands.

40 *The Laws of the United States of America,* 8:294–295.

41 *National Intelligencer and Washington Advertiser,* March 11, 1807.

42 Jefferson's remarkable letter of instructions to Lewis is in the Jefferson Papers, Library of Congress. The letter is reproduced in Jackson, *Letters*, 1:61–66.

Lewis. However, it later became clear that far more than commerce and Indian relations were on Jefferson's mind on June 20, 1803. On that day he articulated his grand vision—an expedition to document geography, mineralogy, botany, zoology, Indian cultures and languages, and trade opportunities. The president's personal letter to Lewis (later revealed in his "Life of Captain Lewis" for the 1814 Biddle-Allen narrative) confirmed his true intentions and his hunger for information about things not yet known to a wider world.[42]

The Corps of Discovery's journey to the Mandan villages on the plains of North Dakota, as well as the reports of Dunbar, Hunter, and Sibley about southern Louisiana Territory, spawned a second round of publications in 1806–07. Most of this material was also embedded in the *Message from the President*, the report to Congress on the progress of explorations. Lewis's letter from Fort Mandan, the "Statistical View" on the Indian tribes, and other materials were printed in Washington, D.C., New York, Natchez, and London. Eager publishers tapped this data to meet public interest. The *Message from the President* also provided grist for the creation of several surreptitious and apocryphal accounts about the expedition in later years. Likewise, newspaper and periodical editors printed extracts of these accounts.

Upon the return of the expedition, the letter of William Clark, drafted for him by Lewis on September 23, 1806, in St. Louis, provided confirmation of the success of the venture. Jefferson's message to Congress of December 2, 1806, however, gave official notice of the Corps of Discovery's remarkable transit across the continent. Shortly thereafter, an appreciative Congress moved deliberately to identify and compensate those who had engaged in such singular service to their nation. That an African-American, York, had made the trip and participated in all of the hardships and duties drew no notice, nor did the role of the female interpreter, Sacagawea. Both were below the horizon of recognition in the first decade of the nineteenth century. Their "discovery" was left to later generations who looked at the expedition through different eyes and perspectives.

Early Expedition-Related Publications: Bibliography

The following catalog attempts to list all known U.S. House of Representatives and Senate publications that summarize congressional activity on the expedition's initial funding, Jefferson's 1806 progress report, and reports of the Corps of Discovery's safe return. This listing also includes related contemporary publications held at Lewis & Clark College in the Boley Law Library or in the Watzek Library's Special Collections. In addition to the printed texts listed below, some congressional materials can be researched at the Library of Congress Web site (www.loc.gov).

2a Initial Funding of the Expedition
2a.1 Jefferson's Confidential Request for Funds, January 18, 1803

On January 18, 1803, President Jefferson sent a confidential message to both houses of Congress requesting funds for an expedition that would help promote commerce with Indian tribes along the Missouri River. This message was recorded in confidence for the members of Congress, and the printed proceedings of the House and Senate note the delivery of the message. It was not made available to the public in printed form until 1828.

JOURNAL | OF THE | HOUSE OF REPRESENTATIVES | OF THE | *UNITED STATES,* | AT THE | SECOND SESSION | OF THE | SEVENTH CONGRESS. | IN THE | TWENTY-SEVENTH YEAR | OF THE | INDEPENDENCE OF THE UNITED STATES. | [rule] | CITY OF WASHINGTON: | PRINTED BY SAMUEL HARRISON SMITH [no date].

Description: On January 18, 1803, "A message, in writing, was received from the President of the United States, by Mr. Lewis, his secretary. . . ."

Lewis & Clark College Collection: Glazier reprint, *Journal of the House of Representatives, 1801–1809,* 2:124f.

JOURNAL | OF THE | SENATE | OF THE | United States of America: | BEING THE | SECOND SESSION | OF THE | SEVENTH CONGRESS, | *BEGUN AND HELD AT THE CITY OF WASHINGTON,* | *DECEMBER* 6, 1802, | AND IN THE TWENTY-SEVENTH YEAR OF THE SOVE- | REIGNTY OF THE SAID UNITED STATES. | [rule] | Washington: | PRINTED BY A. AND G. WAY. | [rule] | 1802.

Description: On January 18, 1803, "Two written messages were received from the President of the United States, by Mr. Lewis, his secretary; the first a confidential message, which was read, as is stated on the executive record. *Ordered,* that it lie for consideration. On motion, that it be printed for the use of the Senate."

Lewis & Clark College Collection: Glazier reprint, *Journal of the Senate, 1801–1809,* 2:44f.

JOURNAL | OF | THE EXECUTIVE PROCEEDINGS | OF | THE SENATE | OF | THE UNITED STATES OF AMERICA: | From the commencement of the First, to the termination of the Nineteenth Congress. | VOLUME I. | [rule] | PRINTED BY ORDER OF THE SENATE OF THE UNITED STATES. | [rule] | WASHINGTON: | PRINTED BY DUFF GREEN. | 1828.

Description: On January 18, 1803, a report of a confidential message was delivered from President Jefferson to the "Gentlemen of the Senate, and of the House of Representatives." "The message was read. *Ordered,* That it lie for consideration" (437–439). On February 14, 1803, the same confidential message was "brought from the House of Representatives, by Mr. Nicholson and Mr. Bayard, a committee of that House," and read to the Senate. Additional consideration of this item appears on pp. 444f., the bill passing on February 22, 1803. It was signed into law by the president on February 28.

Lewis & Clark College Collection: Wendlick: The edition is limited (title page verso) to seven hundred copies. The confidential message is also reproduced in facsimile in the appendix of the Glazier reprint, *Journal of the Senate, 1801–1809,* 2:437–9, 443ff., and was reprinted in 1832 in *American State Papers, Class 2, Indian Affairs,* item 102, pp. 684–685 (microfilm and printout). The final disposition of the bill is recorded in the Glazier reprint, *Journal of the House of Representatives,* 2:331f.

2a.2 Act for Extending the External Commerce of the United States, February 28, 1803

[Volume title:] THE | LAWS | OF THE | UNITED STATES | OF | AMERICA. | [double rule] | VOL. VI. | [rule] | *PUBLISHED BY AUTHORITY.* | [rule] | WASHINGTON CITY. | [rule] | 1803. [Bound at end of volume following index, i–xxvi.]

[Half title:] [rule] | ACTS | PASSED AT THE | SECOND SESSION | OF THE | SEVENTH CONGRESS | OF THE | *UNITED STATES.* | [rule]

Description: Chapter 65, pp. 215ff. contains the text of the act: *"An ACT for extending the external commerce of the United States."*

Notices: *Columbian Centinel & Massachusetts Federalist* (Boston), April 2, 1803. Page 1, col. 2, "Miscellany of the Times" contains speculation on Congress's reasons for allocating twenty-five hundred dollars to Jefferson. Page 2, col. 3, a single paragraph notes that Lewis and Clark will soon be departing on political business to the Mississippi country.

Columbian Centinel & Massachusetts Federalist (Boston), September 24, 1803. Page 2, col. 1 article notes that Lewis and Clark will soon be departing from Louisville, Kentucky, to penetrate the Louisiana Territory and to ". . . ascertain the feasibility of making establishment on the sea."

Lewis & Clark College Collection: (*The Laws*) Wendlick: Original wraps, untrimmed.

2a.3 Act Authorizing Jefferson to Take Possession of the Louisiana Territory, October 22, 1803

JOURNAL | OF THE | HOUSE OF REPRESENTATIVES | OF THE | *UNITED STATES,* | AT THE | FIRST SESSION | OF THE | EIGHTH CONGRESS, | IN THE | TWENTY-EIGHTH YEAR | OF THE | INDEPENDENCE OF THE UNITED STATES. | [rule] | CITY OF WASHINGTON: | PRINTED BY SAMUEL HARRISON SMITH [no date].

Notice: *The Connecticut Courant* (Hartford), November 23, 1803. Page 2, col. 2 article notes that Congress had authorized President Jefferson to take possession of the Louisiana Territory.

Lewis & Clark College Collection: Glazier reprint, *Journal of the House of Representatives, 1801–1809*, 3:20ff.

JOURNAL | OF THE | SENATE | OF THE | *UNITED STATES OF AMERICA;* | BEING | The First Session | OF THE | EIGHTH CONGRESS, | *BEGUN AND HELD AT THE CITY OF WASHINGTON,* | *OCTOBER* 17, 1803. | AND | IN THE TWENTY-EIGHTH YEAR OF THE SOVEREIGNTY | OF THE SAID UNITED STATES. | [rule] | WASHINGTON CITY: | PRINTED BY WILLIAM DUANE & SON. | [dotted rule] | 1803.

Lewis & Clark College Collection: Glazier reprint, *Journal of the Senate, 1801–1809*, 3:8ff.

2a.4 Report of the Committee of Commerce, March 8, 1804

REPORT | OF | *THE COMMITTEE* | OF | COMMERCE AND MANUFACTURES, | WHO WERE INSTRUCTED, | *BY A RESOLUTION OF THIS HOUSE,* | OF THE | 18th ULT. | "TO ENQUIRE | INTO THE | *EXPEDIENCY OF AUTHORISING* | THE | PRESIDENT OF THE UNITED STATES, | *TO EMPLOY PERSONS* | TO EXPLORE SUCH PARTS OF THE PROVINCE | OF | *LOUISIANA,* | AS HE MAY DEEM PROPER." | [rule] | 8th MARCH, 1804. | *Read, and ordered to be committed to a committee of the | whole House, on Wednesday next.* | [rule]

Reference: Paltsits, lxxxiv.

Description: Text on 3–7: "merely has an allusion to Lewis and Clark on p. 4, who are there designated as 'two enterprising conductors,' etc." (Paltsits).

Lewis & Clark College Collection: Tweney: Disbound section of report containing the commerce and manufactures component. Wendlick: Disbound copy of same report.

2b Jefferson's Report to Congress, February 19, 1806

This report was printed for Congress (2b.1 and 2b.2, reprinted 1832, 2b.3), and was printed for the public in 1806 and 1807 (2b.4–2b.6).

2b.1 A. & G. Way, Washington 1806 [Color plate VI]

MESSAGE | FROM THE | PRESIDENT OF THE UNITED STATES, | COMMUNICATING | *DISCOVERIES* | MADE IN EXPLORING | THE MISSOURI, RED RIVER AND WASHITA, | BY | *CAPTAINS LEWIS AND CLARK, DOCTOR SIBLEY,* | AND | MR. DUNBAR; | WITH | A STATISTICAL ACCOUNT | OF THE | COUNTRIES ADJACENT. | [rule] | FEBRUARY 19, 1806. | Read, and ordered to lie on the table. | [rule] | CITY OF WASHINGTON: | A. & G. WAY, PRINTERS | [dotted rule] | 1806.

Collation: One volume, 8vo., 22.5 cm. Title page [1]; [blank]; [3]–4 "Jefferson's Message"; [5]–8 Lewis's Fort Mandan letter, April 17, 1805; [9]–65 "A Statistical View"; [66]–86 "Historical Sketches"; 87–112 "Sibley's Letter to General Henry Dearborn, April 10, 1805"; 113–115 "Distances up Red River"; 116–171 "Observations"; [172]–[178] "Meteorological Observations." Folding chart, facing 30 "A. Siouxs Proper."

References: Coues, cvii–cvix; Graff, 4406; Paltsits, lxiii; Wagner-Camp-Becker, 5:1, 5:2.

Description: First printed in an edition of one thousand copies in Washington in 1806, this was Jefferson's Message to Congress. The report conveyed information sent back to Jefferson by the Corps of Discovery from the Mandan winter encampment of 1804–05. The information included data and specimens collected from the lower reaches of the Missouri, along with ethnographic descriptions of the Indians. The text appears in two states. One is designated "Read, and ordered to lie on the table." (Wagner-Camp-Becker, 5:1), and the other "Printed by order of the Senate." (Wagner-Camp-Becker, 5:2). It was standard procedure for presidential communications to be laid on the Speaker's table for promulgation by the Speaker. These documents were also printed by the Senate for its own use. Some of the Senate copies were issued with a map entitled "Map of the Washita River in Louisiana from the Hot Springs to the Confluence of the Red River" by Nicholas King, taken from the survey of William Dunbar. This map was reprinted in *Documents Relating to the Purchase and Exploration of Louisiana* (1904), a volume also held at Lewis & Clark College. The map and the title page textual variation are the only differences between the two government publications of 1806.

Notices: *Evening Fire-Side; or, Literary Miscellany* (Philadelphia) 2 (1805–1806): 28. The publication included extracts from President Jefferson's message to Congress. Not at Lewis and Clark College.

Medical Repository (New York), November/December 1805 and January 1806: 315–318. A proposal for "Lewis's Map of the Parts of North-America which lie between the 35th and 51st Degrees of North Latitude, from the Mississippi and the upper Lakes to the North Pacific Ocean."

The Repertory (Boston), March 7, 1806. Under the heading "National Legislator": report that on February 19, 1806, Congress ordered that "one thousand copies of the message, together with the accompanying communication, be printed for the use of the members."

Lewis & Clark College Collection: All first printing, designated "Read, and ordered to lie on the table." Tweney: Original boards untrimmed. Lacks the final table 23. Wendlick 1: Uncut and untrimmed, in a clamshell box. Wendlick 2: Facsimile map by Nicholas King (Dunbar survey of Washita River) laid in. Early binding with multiple blank leaves at end, and with spine titling: "1 | Lewis and Clark Discoveries | 1806 | Senate Library". Roger Wendlick was informed by George Tweney, previous owner of this item, that he had seen a similar copy with legislators' comments in the blank pages.

2b.2 Duane, Washington 1806 (dated 1805)

JOURNAL | OF | THE SENATE | OF THE | UNITED STATES OF AMERICA, | BEING THE | First Session | OF THE | NINTH CONGRESS, | BEGUN AND HELD AT THE CITY OF WASHINGTON, | DECEMBER 2, 1805, | AND | IN THE THIRTIETH YEAR OF THE SOVEREIGNTY OF THE | SAID UNITED STATES. | [double rule] | WASHINGTON CITY: | PRINTED BY WILLIAM DUANE AND SON. | [double dotted rule] | 1805.

Reference: Jackson, *Letters*, item 193.

Description: A letter from Thomas Jefferson to Congress dated February 19, 1806 (pp. 144–147), discussing Lewis and Clark's travels up the Missouri to Fort Mandan. This letter is included as the introduction to the full report to Congress printed by A. & G. Way in Washington in 1806 (2b.1).

Lewis & Clark College Collection: Disbound original, lacking title page, and Glazier reprint, *Journal of the Senate, 1801–1809,* 5:144–147.

2b.3 Gales and Seaton, Washington 1832 (reprint of 2b.1)

AMERICAN STATE PAPERS. | [rule] | DOCUMENTS, | LEGISLATIVE AND EXECUTIVE, | OF THE | CONGRESS OF THE UNITED STATES, | FROM THE FIRST SESSION OF THE FIRST TO THE SECOND SESSION OF THE | FIFTEENTH CONGRESS, INCLUSIVE: | COMMENCING MARCH 3, 1789, AND ENDING MARCH 3, 1819. | [rule] | SELECTED AND EDITED, UNDER THE AUTHORITY OF CONGRESS, | BY WALTER LOWRIE, Secretary of the Senate, AND | MATTHEW ST. CLAIR CLARKE, Clerk of the House of Representatives. | [rule] | VOLUME XII | [rule] WASHINGTON: | PUBLISHED BY GALES AND SEATON. | [rule] | 1832.

Reference: Wagner-Camp-Becker, 5:7.

Description: "Lewis and Clarke's Expedition. Communicated to Congress, February 19, 1806." Class 2, Indian Affairs, No. 113. Ninth Congress, First Session. pp. 705–743. This is a reprint of Jefferson's Report to Congress, A. & G. Way 1806 (2b.1).

Lewis & Clark College Collection: Microfilm and printout.

2b.4 Hopkins and Seymour, New York 1806

MESSAGE | FROM THE | PRESIDENT OF THE UNITED STATES, | COMMUNICATING | DISCOVERIES | MADE IN EXPLORING THE | *MISSOURI, RED RIVER, AND WASHITA,* | BY | CAPTAINS LEWIS AND CLARK, DOCTOR SIBLEY, | AND MR. DUNBAR; | WITH | A STATISTICAL ACCOUNT | OF THE | COUNTRIES ADJACENT. | [rule] | *READ IN CONGRESS, FEBRUARY* 19, 1806. | [rule] | *NEW-YORK:* | PRINTED BY HOPKINS AND SEYMOUR, | AND SOLD BY G. F. HOPKINS, NO. 118, PEARL-STREET. | [rule] | 1806.

Collation: One volume, 8vo., 21.5 cm. [1] title page; [blank]; [3]–4 "Message to the Senate and House by Jefferson, February 19, 1806"; [5]–8 extract of a letter from Lewis to Jefferson from Fort Mandan, April 17, 1805; [9]–47 "A Statistical View of the Indian Nations"; [48]–62 "Historical Sketches by Sibley"; 63–81 "Letter to Dearborn"; [82]–83 "Distances up Red River"; 84–125 "Observations"; 125–128 "Meteorological Observations". Folding chart facing 24: "A. Siouxs Proper."

References: Coues, cix; Graff, 4407; Paltsits, lxiii; Wagner-Camp-Becker, 5:3.

Lewis & Clark College Collection: Tweney: As issued, unbound, untrimmed, in half-leather clamshell box with raised bands and gold stamping on spine. Wendlick: Rebound in half leather with marbled boards and raised bands with gold stamping. New end papers front and rear. Inscription on title page: "New York Historical Society from Peter Burtswing."

New York Historical Society
4 from
Peter Buetts 1889

MESSAGE

FROM THE

PRESIDENT OF THE UNITED STATES,

COMMUNICATING

DISCOVERIES

MADE IN EXPLORING THE

MISSOURI, RED RIVER, AND WASHITA,

BY

CAPTAINS LEWIS AND CLARK, DOCTOR SIBLEY,

AND MR. DUNBAR;

WITH

A STATISTICAL ACCOUNT

OF THE

COUNTRIES ADJACENT.

READ IN CONGRESS, FEBRUARY 19, 1806.

NEW-YORK:

PRINTED BY HOPKINS AND SEYMOUR,

AND SOLD BY G. F. HOPKINS, NO. 118, PEARL-STREET.

1806.

2b.5 Marschalk, Natchez 1806

DISCOVERIES | MADE IN EXPLORING | THE MISSOURI, RED RIVER | AND WASHITA, | BY | *CAPTAINS LEWIS AND CLARK, DOCTOR SIBLEY,* | AND | WILLIAM DUNBAR, Esq. | WITH | A STATISTICAL ACCOUNT | OF THE | COUNTRIES ADJACENT. | [wavy rule] | WITH AN APPENDIX BY MR. DUNBAR | [wavy rule] | NATCHEZ: | PRINTED BY ANDREW MARSCHALK. | [dotted rule] | 1806.

Collation: One volume, 8vo., 20 cm. [1] title page with blank verso; [3]–4 "Message to the Senate and House from Jefferson, February 19, 1806"; [5]–8 Extract of Lewis's letter to Jefferson from Fort Mandan, April 17, 1805; [9]–64 "A Statistical View"; [one unnumbered page]; 65–83 "Historical Sketches" by Sibley; 84–109 Sibley Letter "To General Henry Dearborn," April 10, 1805; 110–12 "Distances up Red river"; 113–64 "Observations"; [165]–166, 159–169 [with repeated pagination] "Extracts from the Appendix to Mr. Dunbar's Journal"; 170–77 "Meteorological observations."

References: Coues, cx; Paltsits, lxiv; Wagner-Camp-Becker, 5:4.

Description: Presumably printed for William Dunbar in Natchez, Mississippi, in 1806, this edition includes for the first time "Extracts from the Appendix to Mr. Dunbar's Journal," but lacks the folding table "A. Siouxs Proper" of earlier editions. A very rare item.

Notice: *The Repertory* (Boston), October 3, 1806. Page 2, col. 3 report announces that a publication from Natchez on the new western territory by Lewis, Clark, Sibley, and Dunbar has appeared: "Our New Western country! Yes Mr. Smith, We have the map, and the Spaniards and Indians have ninety-nine hundredths of the soil."

Lewis & Clark College Collection: Microfiche, and bound facsimile from microfilm.

2b.6 Phillips, London 1807

TRAVELS | IN THE | INTERIOR PARTS OF AMERICA; | COMMUNICATING | *DISCOVERIES* | MADE IN EXPLORING | THE MISSOURI, RED RIVER AND WASHITA, | BY | *CAPTAINS LEWIS AND CLARK, DOCTOR SIBLEY,* | AND | MR. DUNBAR; | WITH | A STATISTICAL ACCOUNT | OF THE | COUNTRIES ADJACENT. | [rule] | *AS LAID BEFORE THE SENATE,* | BY THE | PRESIDENT OF THE UNITED STATES. | IN FEBRUARY, 1806, | AND NEVER BEFORE PUBLISHED IN GREAT BRITAIN. | [rule] | *LONDON:* | PRINTED FOR RICHARD PHILLIPS, 6, BRIDGE STREET, | BLACKFRIARS, | *By J. G. Barnard*, 57, *Snow-hill.* | [rule] | 1807.

Collation: One volume, 8vo., 21.5 cm. [1] title page; [blank]; [3]–4 Jefferson's Message to Congress, February 19, 1806; 4–7 Lewis's letter to Jefferson from Fort Mandan, April 17, 1805; 7–24, 17–39 [signature C repeated] "A Statistical View"; [40]–72 "Sibley's Historical Sketches, April 10, 1805"; 72–74 "Distances up Red River"; 74–113 "Observations"; 114–16 "Meteorological Observations." The folding table "A. Siouxs Proper" is bound between the two C signatures, facing p. 24 of first signature C, and followed by p. 17 of the second signature C.

References: Coues, cx; Paltsits, lxiv; Wagner-Camp-Becker, 5:6.

Description: The first overseas publication on Lewis and Clark, reprinted from the 1806 Washington edition by A. & G. Way (2b.1), and issued in vol. 5 of an eleven-volume subscription series compiled by Sir Richard Phillips (see transcript, below, of the fifth volume title page). The series was printed in eleven unbound volumes from 1804 to 1810, each volume issued with its own binding instructions. Most copies of this item are bound separately.

A | COLLECTION | OF | *MODERN AND CONTEMPORARY* | VOYAGES | AND | TRAVELS: | CONTAINING, | I. | TRANSLATIONS FROM FOREIGN LANGUAGES, OF VOYAGES | AND TRAVELS NEVER BEFORE TRANSLATED. | II. | ORIGINAL VOYAGES AND TRAVELS NEVER BEFORE PUBLISHED. | III. | ANALYSES OF NEW VOYAGES AND TRAVELS | PUBLISHED IN ENGLAND. | [rule] | VOL. V. | [rule] | *LONDON:* | PRINTED FOR RICHARD PHILLIPS, 6, NEW BRIDGE STREET, | BLACKFRIARS, | *By J. G. Barnard, 57, Snow Hill.* | [rule] | 1807. | [PRICE FIFTEEN SHILLINGS IN BOARDS.]

Lewis & Clark College Collection: Chuinard: Full leather with gilt spine and raised bands. Tweney 1: Half leather with spine label and plain covers. Bound by C. A. Carpenter Jr. of Shrewsbury, Massachusetts. Tweney 2: Half leather with marbled boards and gilt labeling on brown leather spine. New end papers. Wendlick: Half leather with marbled boards and gilt labeling on blue leather spine. New end papers.

2b.7 Journal and Newspaper Publications Relating to Jefferson's February Report
Columbian Centinel & Massachusetts Federalist (Boston), March 5, 1806. Page 1, col. 5, para. 5, "Ninth Congress: First Session—Captain Lewis" describes some details of the expedition, including when it began. It also notes that a letter and some maps had been sent to President Jefferson from the Mandan villages on April 7, 1805, and that the contents of this letter were being presented to both houses of Congress.

The Repertory, Boston, March 7, 1806. Page 1, col. 4, "National Legislature." The article is the same as that in the March 5, 1806, *Columbian Centinel & Massachusetts Federalist.*

New Hampshire Sentinel, March 15, 1806. Page 1, col. 3 article carries the same text as in the March 5, 1806, *Columbian Centinel & Massachusetts Federalist.*

"Literary, Philosophical and Geographical Intelligence." *The Panoplist; or the Christian's Armory* 1, 2 (April 1806): 514–517. Article includes copies of Jefferson's Letter to Congress, February 19, 1806, and Lewis's Mandan letter to Jefferson.

The Monthly Anthology, And Boston Review, Containing Sketches and Reports of Philosophy, Religion, History, Arts And Manners, 3 (1806): 39–92. The "Political Cabinet," printed as an appendix to *The Monthly Anthology,* contains the text of Jefferson's Report to Congress. This is described by Wagner-Camp-Becker in 5:5 and 5b as being a "full copy" of Marschalk's Natchez 1806 printing. The *Monthly Anthology* version, however, lacks Lewis and Clark's "A Statistical View of the Indian Nations." Also, Natchez is the only printing of the report to include the "Extracts from the Appendix to Mr. Dunbar's Journal." These are not reprinted in *The Monthly*

Anthology. A comparison of spellings indicates that this publication follows the text of the Washington 1806 edition of A. & G. Way (2b.1). The Lewis & Clark College Collection's Tweney copy is a bound compilation of *The Monthly Anthology* for 1806 and 1807, including the appendix of American State Papers designated "Political Cabinet." The Wendlick copy, disbound from the periodical, contains only the American State Papers portions, the "Political Cabinet."

Omnium Gatherum, A Monthly Magazine, Recording Authentick Accounts of the Most Remarkable Productions, Events, and Occurrences, in Providence, Nature, and Art (Boston) 1, no. 1 (1809–10). Lewis's letter to Jefferson from Fort Mandan, April 17, 1805, appears on pp. 10–11. The sections from Jefferson's report to Congress dealing with William Dunbar and John Sibley's explorations are printed in later sections of the *Omnium Gatherum* in the same year. See Wagner-Camp-Becker, 5:7, n. 5. The Lewis & Clark College Collection copy is an early binding, in a single volume for 1809–10, the complete run of issues.

2c Documents Relating to the Return of the Expedition
2c.1 Clark's Letter to His Brother, September 23, 1806
The Monthly Anthology, And Boston Review, Containing Sketches and Reports of Philosophy, Religion, History, Arts And Manners, 4 (1807): 6–8. "Political Cabinet," appendix to *The Monthly Anthology*.

Description: Contains the letter from Captain Clark in St. Louis to his brother, September 23, 1806, describing the expedition.

Lewis & Clark College Collection: See 2b.7 *The Monthly Anthology*.

2c.2 Jefferson's Message to Congress, December 2, 1806
JOURNAL | OF THE | HOUSE OF REPRESENTATIVES | OF THE | United States, | AT THE | SECOND SESSION | OF | *THE NINTH CONGRESS,* | IN THE | THIRTY FIRST YEAR | OF THE | *INDEPENDENCE OF THE UNITED STATES.* | [rule] | CITY OF WASHINGTON: | A. & G. WAY, PRINTERS. | [dotted rule] | 1806.

Description: Jefferson's Message to Congress of December 2, 1806, regarding the completion of the expedition and its success, appears on pp. 9–17.

Lewis & Clark College Collection: Glazier reprint, *Journal of the House of Representatives, 1801–1809*, 6:9–17.

JOURNAL | OF | THE SENATE | OF THE | UNITED STATES OF AMERICA; | BEING THE | Second Session | OF | THE NINTH CONGRESS, | BEGUN AND HELD IN THE CITY OF WASHINGTON, | DECEMBER 1, 1806, | AND | IN THE THIRTY FIRST YEAR OF THE SOVEREIGNTY OF | THE SAID UNITED STATES | [rule] | *WASHINGTON CITY:* | PRINTED BY DUANE & SON. | [rule] | 1806.

Description: Jefferson's Message to Congress of December 2, 1806, regarding the completion of the expedition and its success, appears on pp. 8–21.

Lewis & Clark College Collection: Glazier reprint, *Journal of the Senate, 1801–1809*, 6:8–21.

2c.3 Newspaper Editions of Jefferson's December 2, 1806, Message

National Intelligencer and Washington Advertiser, December 2, 1806. [Color plate VII] An "extraordinary" broadside printing of Jefferson's Message to Congress, December 2, 1806 (Wagner-Camp-Becker 5a). Some reprints of this text are listed below.

Lewis & Clark College Collection: Gift of Brian and Gwyneth Booth.

Baltimore American–Extra, December 3, 1806. A reprint of the previous item. Not at Lewis and Clark College.

The Weekly Inspector, New York, December 6, 1806. Another reprint (pp. 121, 132–6) of Jefferson's Message.

Lewis & Clark College Collection: Original newspaper.

Providence Gazette, Rhode Island, December 9, 1806. Another reprint. Not at Lewis and Clark College.

The Witness, Litchfield (Connecticut), December 10, 1806. Another reprint (p. 3) of Jefferson's Message.

Lewis & Clark College Collection: Original newspaper.

The Repertory, Boston, December 12, 1806. Another reprint (pp. 1, 2) of Jefferson's Message.

Lewis & Clark College Collection: Original newspaper.

Freeman's Friend, Saco (Maine), December 13, 1806. Another reprint (pp. 2, 3) of Jefferson's Message.

Lewis & Clark College Collection: Original newspaper.

2c.4 A Bill Making Compensation to Lewis and Clark, January 23, 1807

DOCUMENTS | ACCOMPANYING | *A BILL MAKING COMPENSATION* | TO | MESSIEURS LEWIS AND CLARKE, | AND | THEIR COMPANIONS, | PRESENTED | THE 23d JANUARY, 1807. | [rule] | WASHINGTON CITY: | A. & G. WAY, PRINTERS. | [dotted rule] | 1807.

Collation: [1] title page; [blank]; [4]–5 letter from Willis Alston, January 12, 1807; letter from H. Dearborn, January 14, 1807; [6]–8 letter from Meriwether Lewis, January 15, 1807. A foldout chart faces p. 8, titled "A Roll Of the men who accompanied captains Lewis and Clarke on their late tour to the Pacific ocean, through the interior of the continent of North America, shewing their rank, with some remarks on their respective merits and services."

Description: This is the first printed version of the bill that made compensation to Lewis and Clark. It is also the first printing of the expedition roster.

Notice: *New Hampshire Sentinel,* February 7, 1807. Page 2, col. 2, "House of Representatives" contains a one-sentence note that federal legislation would compensate Lewis and Clark for exploring the interior of Louisiana.

A Roll

Of the men who accompanied captains Lewis and Clarke on their late tour to the Pacific ocean, through the interior of the continent of North America, shewing their rank, with some remarks on their respective merits and services.

No.	NAMES.	RANK.	REMARKS.
1	John Ordnay,	Serjeant.	
2	Nathaniel Pryor,	ditto.	
3	Charles Floyd,	ditto.	Deceased the 20th of August, 1804; a young man of much merit. His father, who now resides in Kentucky, is a man much respected, though possessed of but moderate wealth. As the son has lost his life whilst on this service, I consider his father intitled to some gratuity, in consideration of his loss; and also, that the deceased being noticed in this way, will be a tribute but justly due to his merit.
4	Patrick Gass,	ditto.	Promoted to serjeant 20th of August, 1804, in the place of Charles Floyd, deceased; in which capacity he continued until discharged at St. Louis, November 10, 1806.
5	William Bratton,	Private.	
6	John Collins,	ditto.	
7	John Colter,	ditto.	
8	Pier Cruzatte,	ditto.	
9	Joseph Field,	ditto.	Two of the most active and enterprizing young men who accompanied us. It was their peculiar fate to have been engaged in all the most dangerous and difficult scenes of the voyage, in which they
10	Reuben Field,	ditto.	uniformly acquitted themselves with much honor.
11	Robert Frazier,	ditto.	
12	Silas Goodrich,	ditto.	
13	George Gibson,	ditto.	
14	Thomas P. Howard,	ditto.	
15	Hugh Hall,	ditto.	
16	Francis Labuicke,	ditto.	He has received the pay only of a private, though besides the duties performed as such, he has rendered me very essential services as a French and English interpreter, and sometimes also as an Indian interpreter; therefore, I should think it only just that some small addition to his pay, as a private, should be added, though no such addition has at any time been promised by me.
17	Hugh M'Neal,	ditto.	
18	John Sheilds,	ditto.	Has received the pay only of a private. Nothing was more peculiarly useful to us in various situations, than the skill and ingenuity of this man as an artist, in repairing our guns, accoutrements, &c. And should it be thought proper to allow him something as an artificer, he has well deserved it.
19	George Shannon,	ditto.	
20	John Potts,	ditto.	
21	John Bapteist La Page,	ditto.	Entitled to no peculiar merit; was inlisted at Fort Mandan, on the 2d of November, 1804, in order to supply the deficiency in my permanent party, occasioned by the discharge of John Newman. He performed the tour to the Pacific ocean, and returned to St. Louis, where he was discharged, in common with others, on the 10th of November last. As he did not perform the labours incident to the summer of 1804, it would be proper to give him the gratuity only of two thirds as much as is given to others of his rank.
22	John B. Thompson,	ditto.	
23	William Werner,	ditto.	
24	Richard Windsor,	ditto.	
25	Peter Wiser,	ditto.	
26	Alexander Willard,	ditto.	
27	Joseph Whitehouse,	ditto.	
28	George Drulyard,	Interpreter,	A man of much merit; he has been peculiarly useful from his knowledge of the common language of gesticulation, and his uncommon skill as a hunter and woodsman; those several duties he performed in good faith, and with an ardor which deserves the highest commendation. It was his fate also to have encountered, on various occasions, with either captain Clarke or myself, all the most dangerous and trying scenes of the voyage, in which he uniformly acquitted himself with honor. He has served the complete term of the whole tour, and received only 25 dollars per month, and one ration per day, while I am informed that it is not unusual for individuals, in similar employments, to receive 30 dollars per month.
29	Touisant Charbono,	ditto.	A man of no peculiar merit; was useful as an interpreter only, in which capacity he discharged his duties with good faith from the moment of our departure from the Mandans, on the 7th of April, 1805, until our return to that place in August last, and received as a compensation 25 dollars per month, while in service.

GENERAL REMARK.

With respect to all those persons whose names are entered on this roll, I feel a peculiar pleasure in declaring, that the ample support which they gave me under every difficulty; the manly firmness which they evinced on every necessary occasion, and the patience and fortitude with which they submitted to and bore the fatigues and painful sufferings incident to my late tour to the Pacific ocean, intitles them to my warmest approbation and thanks; nor will I suppress the expression of a hope, that the recollection of services thus faithfully performed, will meet a just reward, in an ample remuneration on the part of our government.

MERIWETHER LEWIS, *Capt.*
1st U. S. regt. Infantry.

CITY OF WASHINGTON, *January 15, 1807.*

Lewis & Clark College Collection: Wendlick: Half leather, marbled boards with gilt labeling on spine; new end papers. Text reprinted in *National Intelligencer and Washington Advertiser* for March 2, 1807 (microfilm).

AMERICAN STATE PAPERS. | [rule] | DOCUMENTS, | LEGISLATIVE AND EXECUTIVE, | OF THE | CONGRESS OF THE UNITED STATES, | FROM THE FIRST SESSION OF THE FIRST TO THE SECOND SESSION OF THE | FIFTEENTH CONGRESS, INCLUSIVE: | COMMENCING MARCH 3, 1789, AND ENDING MARCH 3, 1819. | [rule] | SELECTED AND EDITED, UNDER THE AUTHORITY OF CONGRESS, | BY WALTER LOWRIE, Secretary of the Senate, AND | MATTHEW ST. CLAIR CLARKE, Clerk of the House of Representatives. | [rule] | VOLUME XII | [rule] WASHINGTON: | PUBLISHED BY GALES AND SEATON. | [rule] | 1832.

Description: A reprint of Washington 1807 text (previous item), subtitled "Military Affairs", vol. 1, pp. 207–9, Ninth Congress, Second Session, No. 68: "Gratuities to the Officers and Men in the Expedition to the Pacific Ocean, Under Lewis and Clarke. Communicated to the House of Representatives, January 23, 1807."

Lewis & Clark College Collection: Wendlick: Original, detached from omnibus volume. Also on microfilm and printout.

JOURNAL | OF THE | HOUSE OF REPRESENTATIVES | OF THE | United States, | AT THE | SECOND SESSION | OF | *THE NINTH CONGRESS,* | IN THE | THIRTY FIRST YEAR | OF THE | *INDEPENDENCE OF THE UNITED STATES.* | [rule] | CITY OF WASHINGTON: | A. & G. WAY, PRINTERS. | [dotted rule] | 1806.

Description: "Mr. Alston, from the committee appointed on the second instant, presented, according to order, a bill making compensation to Messieurs Lewis and Clark, and their companions, which was received, and read the first time." January 23, 1807.

Lewis & Clark College Collection: Glazier reprint, *Journal of the House of Representatives, 1801–1809,* 6:191.

JOURNAL | OF | THE SENATE | OF THE | UNITED STATES OF AMERICA; | BEING THE | Second Session | OF | THE NINTH CONGRESS, | BEGUN AND HELD IN THE CITY OF WASHINGTON, | DECEMBER 1, 1806, | AND | IN THE THIRTY FIRST YEAR OF THE SOVEREIGNTY OF | THE SAID UNITED STATES | [rule] | *WASHINGTON CITY:* | PRINTED BY DUANE & SON. | [rule] | 1806.

Description: Pages 220ff. contain the discussion of *A Bill Making Compensation,* which passed the Senate on March 3, 1807.

Lewis & Clark College Collection: Glazier reprint, *Journal of the Senate, 1801–1809,* 6:220, 225f., 231, 234, 245.

[General title] THE | LAWS | OF THE | *UNITED STATES* | OF | AMERICA. | [rule] | VOL. VIII. | [rule] | [rule] | PUBLISHED BY AUTHORITY. | [rule] | WASHINGTON CITY: | [rule] | 1807. [Bound at end of volume.]

[half title] [rule] | ACTS | PASSED AT THE | SECOND SESSION | OF THE | NINTH CONGRESS | OF THE | UNITED STATES. | [rule]

Reference: Paltsits, lxxxvi.

Description: Chapter 77 is titled "AN ACT making compensation to Messrs. Lewis and Clarke, and their companions" (294–295). This is the final text of the act approved by both Houses of Congress and the President of the United States, March 3, 1807.

Lewis & Clark College Collection: Wendlick: Uncut, blue paper wraps; volume begins at unnumbered [219] and continues to 352. Text reprinted in *National Intelligencer and Washington Advertiser* for March 11, 1807 (microfilm), and in Jackson, *Letters,* item 244.

Chapter Three
Patrick Gass, First in Print

Essay 89
Bibliography 104

3.1 Cramer, Pittsburgh 1807
3.2 Budd, London 1808
3.3 Arthus-Bertrand, Paris 1810
3.4(a) Carey, Philadelphia 1810 (first state)
3.4(b) Carey, Philadelphia 1810 (second state)
3.5 Doll, Vienna 1811
3.6 Carey, Philadelphia 1811
3.7 Carey, Philadelphia 1812
3.8 Landes-Industrie-Comptoirs, Weimar 1814, 1815
3.9 Ells, Claflin, & Co., Dayton 1847
3.10 Request for Compensation
3.11 *The Life and Times of Patrick Gass*, 1859
3.12 Hosmer, Chicago 1904

Patrick Gass, First in Print

When details of the Lewis and Clark Expedition were slow
to appear in print, the journal of a sergeant on the journey
catapulted into notice.

Patrick Gass wrote the first book-length, published report of the explorations of
Lewis and Clark. On March 24, 1807, the *Pittsburgh Gazette* announced by prospectus
the availability of subscriptions for copies of *A Journal of the Voyages & Travels of
a Corps of Discovery* by Patrick Gass, "one of the persons employed in the expedition." The publisher, David M'Keehan (or McKeehan), operated a book and stationery store near the courthouse in Pittsburgh. The printer, Zadok Cramer, was a
thrifty bookseller and printer of the same city.[1] The prospectus announced a book
of approximately three hundred pages, bound in boards and priced at one dollar.[2]

The Gass *Journal* was on the market for seven years before the appearance
in 1814 of the narrative based on the journals of Meriwether Lewis and William
Clark. Meriwether Lewis did not write a word of his projected narrative. As printing, binding, and sales of the Gass volume moved forward between April and July
of 1807, Lewis went through the motions of preparing his and Clark's journals
for publication. He consulted scientific specialists, hired an illustrator—Frederick
Pursh, a German-born botanist—to make drawings of specimens, and laid substantial plans, but they were chimerical. He suffered one of the nation's most notable
cases of writer's block.[3] Thus, in the absence of Lewis's projected first-volume
narrative, the Gass *Journal* took off on a remarkable course of publication history.
Although it lacked the insight, reflection, and depth of geographic, ethnographic,
diplomatic, and scientific observations penned by Lewis and Clark, it and
Jefferson's brief *Message from the President* were the only accounts available for
seven years to describe the expedition's adventures. M'Keehan's rush to publication and spirited defense of his right to bring out the Gass *Journal* paid off, but
probably brought little benefit for Gass. The dutiful diarist received an initial payment for his journal and one hundred copies of the Pittsburgh printing. Although
he claimed he held the copyright, the registration in Pennsylvania was for David
M'Keehan.[4] Subsequent publishers likely ignored the copyright and printed with
impunity.

Patrick Gass was born July 12, 1771, at Falls Springs, Pennsylvania. Gass served
in the 1790s as a volunteer soldier and, in 1799, enlisted in the Army. When the
captains began recruiting personnel for the expedition, he was a member of the
First Infantry stationed at Fort Kaskaskia, Illinois. A carpenter, Gass performed
many useful labors during the expedition. When Sergeant Charles Floyd died
during the ascent of the Missouri River, the captains on August 26, 1804, named
Gass a sergeant in *"the corps of volunteers for North Western Discovery"*—a position
he held to the completion of the expedition.[5]

Gass was not the only journal writer among the enlisted men. Floyd kept a
diary until his illness and death. Robert Frazer, John Ordway, Joseph Whitehouse,
and possibly Nathaniel Hale Pryor also recorded their observations and experiences. A prospectus issued in October 1806, announced the forthcoming publication of Frazer's journal as a book of about four hundred pages, octavo, to sell at

1 In the Rare Book Division
   of the Free Library of
   Philadelphia is a volume,
   *The Hive: Or a Collection of
   Thoughts on Civil, Moral,
   Sentimental & Religious Subjects*
   (1804). The book bears a label
   reading "Sold at M'Keehan's
   Book and Stationary Store,
   Pittsburgh."

2 Jackson, "The Race to Publish
   Lewis and Clark," in Ronda,
   Voyages of Discovery, 210.

3 Jackson, *Letters*, 2:398–399,
   643.

4 MacGregor, *The Journals*, 18.

5 Moulton, *The Journals*,
   2:513; 3:14.

three dollars. The journal was never published nor are its whereabouts known. The surviving artifact is a manuscript at the Library of Congress, "A Map of the discoveries of Capt. Lewis & Clark from the Rockey mountain and the River Lewis to the Cap of Disappointment Or the Columbia River At the North Pacific Ocean By observation of Robert Frazer."[6] Pryor's journal, if written, has never appeared. Lewis and Clark paid three hundred dollars for Ordway's diary, precluding its publication and probably intending to tap it for further information to buttress their own accounts. Ordway wrote on 863 days, the most faithful of all expedition diarists. His account was not published until 1916 when edited by Milo M. Quaife.[7] The Whitehouse journal remained in manuscript until edited and published in 1905 by Reuben Gold Thwaites.[8]

There is no evidence that Gass had previously engaged in writing. His journal, like those of his compatriots, was the product of the urging of the two captains. Lewis wrote to Jefferson on April 7, 1805, from Fort Mandan: "We have encouraged our men to keep journals, and seven of them do so, to whom in this respect we give every assistance in our power."[9] In his prospectus for Gass's *Journal*, David M'Keehan identified the field collaboration that, in his opinion, gave credibility to Gass's writings:

> To recommend the correctness of this work, the publisher begs leave to state, that at the different resting places during the expedition, the several journals were brought together, compared, corrected, and the blanks, which had been unavoidably left, filled up; and that, since he became the proprietor, in order to render it more useful and acceptable, he has undertaken and completed the laborious task of arranging and transcribing the whole of it.

M'Keehan further included in the prospectus a passage from a letter written by Meriwether Lewis at St. Louis on October 10, 1806, wherein Lewis spoke to the merits, "manly firmness," and fortitude which Gass exhibited during "that long voyage."[10]

M'Keehan carefully laid out in the Gass prospectus the "Conditions" he wanted subscribers to consider:

I. This work will be published in one volume duodecimo; and is expected to contain near 300 pages.

II. The price to subscribers will be one dollar, handsomely bound in boards. As the expence, however, of publishing an edition sufficiently large to meet the demands for this work, including the original purchase money, will be very considerable; those who pay in advance, will be intitled to a discount of 12 1/2 per cent.

III. Those who obtain ten subscribers and become responsible for the payment of the subscription money shall receive one copy gratis. The work will be ready for delivery in two months from this date. Subscriptions will be received at the Store of the publisher, and at the Office of the Pittsburgh Gazette.[11]

M'Keehan's publication of the Gass *Journal* in 1807 was the preemptive strike of an opportunist who sensed an eager public ready to read about the adventures of the Corps of Discovery. The Gass *Journal* was in production in the printing shop of Zadok Cramer when M'Keehan learned of Lewis's announcement of his own three-volume work. On March 18, 1807, Lewis wrote in the *National Intelligencer* (Washington, D.C.) that "there were several unauthorized and probably

6 Jackson, *Letters*, 1:345–346.

7 Quaife, *The Journals*; Moulton, *The Journals*, 9:xvi–xvii.

8 Thwaites, *Original Journals*, 7.

9 Jackson, *Letters*, 1:232.

10 Ibid., 2:390–391.

11 Ibid., 2:391.

some spurious publications now preparing for the press, on the subject of my late tour to the Pacific Ocean by individuals entirely unknown to me." Lewis warned readers that these "impositions" might "depreciate the worth of the work which I am myself preparing for publication." He mentioned the imminent completion of a map of the route. Lewis's prospectus appeared on about April 1, 1807, from the press of John Conrad of Philadelphia. It announced a work of two parts in three volumes, each of four hundred to five hundred pages, and a third to embrace the scientific observations with a compendium of twenty-three Indian vocabularies. Lewis's prospectus also appeared in the *National Intelligencer* of March 23, 25, 27, 30 and April 1, and in the *Aurora* of March 23.[12] Smith and Maxwell of Philadelphia also published it on July 18, 25, and August 1, apparently as advertising supplements to *The Port Folio*.[13]

When M'Keehan read of Lewis's subscription list for the three volumes, he published a counterblast. M'Keehan wrote on April 7 to Lewis a defense of his "character and rights" and published his rejoinder on April 14 in the *Pittsburgh Gazette*. He took the offensive about the unauthorized Gass *Journal*. "Your rapid advancement to power and wealth," he charged of Lewis, "seems to have changed the polite, humble and respectful language of a *Sir Clement* into that of him who commands and dispenses favours; even your subscription lists, when you offer your learned works for publication must be 'promulgated.'[14]

M'Keehan then sharpened his spirited defense, alleging that Lewis had taken double federal compensation both as a member of the expedition and as secretary to Jefferson. And to make things hurt, M'Keehan alluded to some of Lewis's misfortunes during the expedition: the altercation with the Blackfeet on the Marias River and the prospect that Pierre Cruzatte's shot, which perforated Lewis's buttocks, might not have been accidental. M'Keehan went even further, asking: "Where was your journal during the session of Congress? Snug, eh! No notice is given in the government paper of an intention to publish it; - No warnings against impositions; - only a few proposals circulated among booksellers at a distance!" M'Keehan implied that Lewis had withheld his journal and the Clark map of the American West to make a fortune by their publication. In full fury, M'Keehan wrote mockingly in first person, as if Lewis were responding:

> I'll squeeze the nation first, and then raise a heavy contribution on the citizens individually: I'll cry down these one-volume journals, and frighten the publishers; and no man, woman, or child shall read a word about *my* tour, let me enquire by what high grant or privilege you claim the right of authorizing, licensing or suppressing journals or other publications concerning it?[15]

In April 1807, Cramer issued for M'Keehan *A Journal of the Voyages and Travels of a Corps of Discovery Under the Command of Capt. Lewis and Capt. Clarke of the Army of the United States*.[16] M'Keehan had probably rewritten and polished portions of the journal, but the absence of the original manuscript renders assessment of his editorial work impossible. M'Keehan added thirty explanatory notes; they are clearly in a different style than the journal. Some information provided clarification. Other data M'Keehan gleaned from Alexander Mackenzie's *Voyages from Montreal* (1801), a work he cited by the title of the volume's first part, *A General History of the Fur Trade from Canada to the North-west*.[17]

The publication of his diary catapulted the obscure Gass to national and international attention. The M'Keehan narrative, probably quite unlike the

12 Jackson, *Letters*, 2:385–386, 394–397.

13 Copies of the Smith and Maxwell prospectus of July 18 and 25 are held at Yale University; the August 1 prospectus is at the University of Pennsylvania.

14 Jackson, *Letters*, 2:395–408.

15 Ibid., 2:406–407.

16 M'Keehan's preface was dated March 26 and the copyright notice was April 11.

17 Mackenzie, *Voyages*, 1–162.

ordinary entries penned by Gass, gave a fairly detailed discussion of the route and adventures of the explorers in crossing North America. It is commonly assumed that the original Gass journal vanished, perhaps discarded by M'Keehan or disposed of when set in type at Cramer's printing shop.[18] On July 7, 1810, however, Nicholas Biddle wrote to William Clark: "I find that Gass's journal in the original manuscript is also deposited in our library, & at my service. Ordway's which is much better than Gass's is really very useful. . . ." [19]

The question arises as to what Biddle meant by "our library." Two conclusions are possible. Biddle may have referred to the collections of the Library Company of Philadelphia, the city's oldest library founded in 1732 by Benjamin Franklin, or to the collections of the American Philosophical Society where, eventually, the Biddle family deposited a number of the manuscripts relating to the expedition.[20]

David M'Keehan remains an obscure figure. Most who have written about the Gass *Journal* have provided only a few "possible" elements of biographical information on its publisher. New information, in part, remedies this situation.[21] M'Keehan was the fourth of five sons of Samuel McKeehan (1728–1800) of Cumberland County, Pennsylvania. The family was of Scotch-Irish descent and probably emigrated with the Presbyterian community from Newcastle, Delaware, into Pennsylvania in the early eighteenth century. David M'Keehan is likely the young man of that name who graduated from Dickinson College in 1787 and, according to family history, was admitted in December 1789 to the Bar of Mifflin County, Pennsylvania.[22] He perhaps first gained public notice when, on February 22, 1800, he delivered a George Washington birthday oration. His speech was subsequently published as a pamphlet at Washington, Pennsylvania, and, on March 8, 1800, by the *Pittsburgh Gazette*.[23]

By 1800, M'Keehan had settled in Pittsburgh and, for a time, operated a book and stationery business. Subsequent to publishing the Gass *Journal*, he located in New Orleans where, in June 1814, he edited and published the *Louisiana Gazette and New-Orleans Commercial Advertiser*. His printing house, located at No. 51 Chartres Street, brought out the newspaper three times a week. He advertised "Printing Every Description Executed at this Office." New Orleans was a place of excitement, tension, and conflict at the time of M'Keehan's residency. He was at the helm of the newspaper in October 1814, but by February 1815 the business had passed to Gordon G. Cotten. Whether M'Keehan sold out on the eve of the Battle of New Orleans in January 1815 or died is unknown. There are no extant issues of the newspaper to document the transition in ownership or M'Keehan's fate.[24]

Zadok Cramer, the printer, played a part in driving the publication of the Gass *Journal*. Born in 1773 in New Jersey, Cramer grew up in Washington, Pennsylvania. A fallen Quaker, he was a bookseller by trade and a drab Quaker by dress. In the spring of 1800, he announced in the *Pittsburgh Gazette* his plans to open a bookbindery. The death of John C. Gilkison in March changed Cramer's plans, for it presented him with the opportunity to purchase Gilkison's small bookstore, a venture financed by Hugh Henry Brackenridge. Coauthor with Philip Freneau of "The Rising Glory of America" (1771), a poem celebrating "that day when Britain's sons shall spread Dominion to the north and south and west from th' Atlantic to Pacific shores," Brackenridge was settling Gilkison's affairs. Cramer bought the business and announced to the residents of the "Western Country" that he would bind blank books and sell volumes of general interest.[25]

18 In 1997, for example, Carol Lynn MacGregor, editor and annotator of the Gass *Journal* and the Gass account book, wrote that the journal was lost. "The few clues on record about the Gass manuscript," she wrote, "have led nowhere." MacGregor, *The Journals*, 17–18.

19 Jackson, *Letters*, 2:551.

20 Neither of these libraries has current information confirming the holding of the Gass manuscript. Donald Jackson, whose research into these matters is legendary, dismissed this clue, noting of Biddle's report: "A curious statement, for the manuscript journal kept by Gass has not been found." The possibility that Gass's original journal will be discovered in Philadelphia or elsewhere cannot be ruled out.

21 Tombstone inscriptions, wills, and probate records link M'Keehan to relations in Cumberland County, Pennsylvania. The *Louisiana Gazette* confirms his residency in New Orleans.

22 Jackson, *Letters*, 2:391; Douglas, *The Families*, 277–298.

23 M'Keehan, *An Address*.

24 *Louisiana Gazette and New-Orleans Advertiser*, June 9, 1814; February 21, 1815.

25 Dahlinger, *Pittsburgh*, 161–183.

An ambitious proprietor, Cramer identified himself by the summer of 1800 as "Bookbinder and Publisher." Publishing came early; that fall, Cramer announced the first of a series of almanacs to be sold at "Philadelphia prices." As the Burr-Jefferson contest for the presidency gripped the nation and moved toward resolution in the House of Representatives, Cramer also announced plans to publish a history of the political struggle. In 1801, he began promoting the "Pittsburgh Circulating Library," a collection available from the shelves of his store for a fee. In time, Cramer's library became the Pittsburgh Library Company and grew to two thousand volumes.[26] Although his store served as the city's primary bookshop, Cramer also sold wallpaper, stationery, writing paper, Italian letter paper, quills, camel-hair pencils, inkstands, sealing wax, red and black ink powders, playing cards, and patent medicines.[27]

Cramer developed a compelling interest in the geography of the American West and in providing useful information for customers and readers. He moved naturally from *Cramer's Almanac* to creating *The Navigator*. Published in an era when the Ohio, Tennessee, and Mississippi Rivers were primary arteries of commerce, this work provided valuable river data and statistical information to shippers and travelers. The first volume appeared in 1801; Cramer updated and expanded it steadily. Because he initially had no press, Cramer's first *Almanacs* were printed in the nearby shop of John Israel, and *The Navigators* were printed by John Scull. In August 1805, Cramer purchased his own press and type and announced that henceforth he would print "literary and ecclesiastical works as may be most in demand."[28] The fifth edition of *The Navigator*, a volume of ninety-four pages with illustrations and maps, came out in 1806 and included "an account of Louisiana." The sixth edition of 1808 grew to 156 pages, to which he added "An Appendix Containing an Account of Louisiana, and of the Missouri and Columbia Rivers" with illustrations and maps. Cramer tapped the Gass *Journal* for specific information on the western watersheds. The eighth "improved and enlarged" edition of 1814, published by Cramer, Spear, & Eichbaum, grew to 360 pages and twenty-eight maps. It included an "Abridgement of Lewis and Clark's Expedition," based on the Gass *Journal* and including the recently published Biddle-Allen edition of the two captains' narratives.[29]

As business expanded, Cramer took on partners. The first, John Spear, assumed partial ownership in 1808. The retail store continued under Zadok Cramer's name and was also advertised as Zadok Cramer's Classical, Literary and Law Bookstore. William Eichbaum became a partner in 1810, having served for seven years as an apprentice in bookbinding.[30] Cramer, Spear, and Eichbaum published volumes of travel subsequent to the Gass *Journal*. In 1810, they issued in 504 pages Fortescue Cuming's *Sketches of a Tour of the Western Country Through the States of Ohio and Kentucky*. In 1814, the firm printed and published Henry Marie Brackenridge's *Views of Louisiana Together With a Journal of a Voyage Up the Missouri River in 1811*. Henry M. Brackenridge, the precocious son of Hugh Henry Brackenridge, had followed in the footsteps of Lewis and Clark and recorded these adventures.

Cramer preserved a record of his intellectual interests when, in 1810, he published in the *Pittsburgh Magazine Almanack* a catalog of the volumes in his bookshop. The inventory included numerous religious works (Bibles, testaments, and hymnals), works of poetry, law, and politics, and volumes of exploration and travel. Among the more exotic titles were James Bruce's *Travels to Discover the Source*

"The publisher hopes that the curiosity of the reader will be in some degree gratified; that the information furnished will not be uninteresting and that some aid will be furnished those who wish to acquire a Geographical knowledge of their country."

David M'Keehan, "Preface," *A Journal of the Voyages and Travels of a Corps of Discovery* (1807)

26 Dahlinger, *Pittsburgh*, 161–183.

27 Ibid., 185–186.

28 Ibid., 187.

29 Cramer, *The Navigator* (1814), 343–349.

30 Dahlinger, *Pittsburgh*, 188–189.

of the Nile (1790), John C. Ogden's *A Tour Through Upper and Lower Canada* (1799), Alexander Mackenzie's *Voyages from Montreal* (1801), George Anson's *A Voyage Round the World* (1749), and Patrick Gass's *A Journal of the Voyages and Travels of a Corps of Discovery* (1807). Cramer also stocked *A Geological Account of the United States* (1807) by James Mease.[31]

Zadok Cramer died in 1813. Both *Cramer's Almanack* and *The Navigator* survived him. William Eichbaum (1787–1866) helped Cramer's widow sustain the business. Born at Monte Cenis in Burgundy, Eichbaum had immigrated to the United States with his parents in 1793 and, in 1797, to Pittsburgh. His father, William Peter Eichbaum, was a skilled glassmaker. The younger Eichbaum served seven years with Cramer's firm and, at age twenty-three, was taken in as a partner to form the company of Cramer, Spear & Eichbaum. With Cramer's death, Eichbaum negotiated dissolution of the partnership and, in 1817, left the firm. For a number of years the publishing house of Eichbaum and Johnston printed almanacs, school books, religious tracts, and German-language calendars. Eventually Eichbaum left publishing and invested in a foundry, a bakery, and a commission business. Although devastated financially by the Pittsburgh fire of April 10, 1845, Eichbaum slowly recouped his investments until his death in 1866.[32]

Subsequent to Cramer's death, Cramer, Spear & Eichbaum also published *The Western Gleaner, or Repository for Arts, Sciences and Literature.* The journal attempted "to contribute towards promoting cheerfulness and improving the taste of our fellow citizens in the arts of imagination." The first issue in December 1813 made an interesting claim to the intellectual position of the firm, which had published the Gass *Journal* six years earlier.

> Our western countries are as yet but little exposed in a scientific respect. Thousands of discoveries will yet be made in the respective departments of zoology, botany, and mineralogy, and the economical, medical, and chemical uses of many of our productions remain yet to be investigated. Facts and observations relative to these various objects, will be carefully recorded by the *Gleaner*. The editor is fully sensible, how little either his personal circumstances or his abilities will admit of giving a considerable extent to his individual researches in so extensive a field; but he confidently relies on the liberal cooperation of every friend of science, and measures have already been taken to secure a permanent correspondence with some of the most distinguished characters.[33]

True to its promise, *The Western Gleaner* published in-depth reviews of scientific, literary, and geographical works of interest. These included in its first volumes a review of fifteen pages of H. M. Brackenridge's *Views of Louisiana*, published by Cramer, Spear & Eichbaum in three hundred pages; Thomas Jefferson's "Life of Captain Lewis" in vol. 1, no. 5 (April 1814); and a twenty-five-page review of the *History of the Expedition Under the Command of Captains Lewis and Clarke* (Philadelphia 1814) in vol. 1, no. 6 (May 1814). The publishing company founded by Zadok Cramer thus established good credentials as a firm promoting the understanding of the American West. By printing the Gass *Journal* for David M'Keehan, its *Almanack* and *Navigator* volumes, and its broad coverage in *The Western Gleaner*, the company brought to public notice major works about the previously unknown western lands.

31 *Cramer's Pittsburgh Magazine & Almanack* (1810).

32 Luckhardt, "Notable Printers," 22–27.

33 *The Western Gleaner*, 3–4.

M'Keehan's publication also sparked international interest in the Gass *Journal*. John Budd, a London bookseller, published the Gass volume in 1808 under the same title as the Pittsburgh edition. He proclaimed that he was "Bookseller to His Royal Highness the Prince of Wales," who, in 1811, was named regent when the insanity of his father, George III, appeared irreversible. Budd's shop was at 100 Pall Mall from 1805 to 1820. The successor firm, Budd & Calkin, moved to 118 Pall Mall and remained in business into the 1850s. Pall Mall became a highly fashionable London street in the seventeenth century, known for its grand houses and expensive shops. Fifty-two Pall Mall was the bookstore of Robert Dodsley, who suggested to Samuel Johnson the idea of compiling the English dictionary. Mrs. Fitzherbert, wife of George IV (the aforementioned Prince of Wales) lived from 1789 to 1796 at 105 Pall Mall. At the time of Budd's operations, the street featured fine coffee houses, clubs, private mansions, and quality shops selling clocks, books, and other items.[34]

Budd was a well-known publisher of legal books, public documents, and travel narratives. His specialties included letters on Catholicism, maritime rights, proceedings of court martials, currency and bullion issues, and pending treaties. In 1804, he published John Quincy Adams's *Letters on Silesia, Written During a Tour Through that Country in the Years 1800 and 1801*. More central to his fare were the volumes of *Cobbett's Parliamentary Register* and *Cobbett's Parliamentary Debates*. By 1808, Budd had published three of sixteen projected volumes of *Cobbett's Parliamentary History of England*.[35]

Budd contracted with the firm of Brettell & Company to print and bind the M'Keehan edition of the Gass *Journal*. John Brettell was a master printer who, from 1804 to 1812, had a shop at 4 Marshall Street, Golden Square, London. The printing shop subsequently moved to the Haymarket and, as Thomas Brettell & Company, continued into the 1870s.[36] Budd wrote an illuminating introduction, the "Advertisement by the English Publisher," to the first European edition of the Gass diary. Recognizing Gass's inferior status in the Corps of Discovery, he attempted to suggest that a sergeant's perspective might be more honest than one crafted by an officer.

> The following journal, though dry in style, cannot fail to prove interesting in the extreme to all those persons, who have either seen or read much of America, and who must naturally be desirous of knowing what is to be seen in those immense countries, which lie between the Mississippi and the Pacific Ocean, and through the whole extent of which the language of England will, in all human probability, be one day spoken and written, in spite of all the prejudices that can be brought to operate against it. The journalist appears to have been of inferior rank in the Expedition; but, with those who wish to know the *unadorned* truth, that circumstance is not likely to be lamented. From facts such as he records, the reader will be able to form a much more correct idea of the real estate of the country, than he would from a narrative, written under the influence of a desire to establish or confirm certain pre-conceived positions; not to mention another influence, too generally prevalent in America, namely, that of self-interest, for which there may be such ample scope of indulgence, in giving an account of countries, immediately adjoining that of a nation of land-jobbers.[37]

The Quarterly Review (London) carried notice in May 1809 of Budd's publication of the Gass *Journal*. The reviewer, confronted with the humble writing of Gass as

34 Brown, *London Publishers and Printers*, 27, 32; Weinreb and Hibbert, *The London Encyclopedia*, 578–579.

35 Budd's list of recent publications appeared in the final two pages of the edition of the Gass *Journal* (1810).

36 Brown, *London Publishers and Printers*, 24; Todd, *A Directory of Printers*, 24.

37 Gass, *A Journal of the Voyages* (London, 1808), iii–iv.

possibly polished by M'Keehan, lamented what he found:

> So few parts of the globe remain unexplored, especially in the temperate
> latitudes from 38° to 48°, that we looked forward to the discoveries of this
> corps with considerable expectation. Our hopes were somewhat checked in
> the outset when instead of sitting down to a magnificent quarto, with maps,
> plates, and 'all appliances and means to boot', as we had a right to expect
> from a plan executed under such auspices, we took up a shabby octavo, the
> production of a mere underling, and without one chart to guide the eye, or
> assist the memory. Led on, however, by the subject, we began the perusal
> of this journal, and, what we believe few can say who have seen the book,
> actually *finished* it.[38]

The English reviewer's assessment of the prosaic Gass *Journal* went for the
jugular. "It is curious to observe how ingeniously Mr. Gass has avoided whatever
could interest or amuse," he wrote. "All he says, we have no doubt, is strictly
true: at least, if intolerable dulness be a symptom of truth in narration, he has
amply vindicated his veracity." The reviewer captured the absurdity of what Gass
wrote in the following comment: "The appearance of a volcano a thousand miles
from the sea, and the death of a grey horse are recorded in the same breath, and
with equal faithfulness, brevity and indifference." The "sickening minutiae" made
it difficult for readers to wade through the Gass narrative. And, in light of this
volume, the reviewer found scientific observations even more wanting: "The longitude is not once determined–no means, or at least no attempt to observe with
this view the moon or the satellites of Jupiter is on record–no thermometrical or
barometrical information–no symptom of a single philosophical instrument being
on board, except the common sextant for ascertaining the latitude."[39] Gass, a man
with little education, had not described the laborious effort of the captains to
try to fix both longitude and latitude nor their recording of the temperatures of
springs until their last thermometer broke. The reviewer rightly found the volume
wanting in scientific information.

In 1810, the publisher Arthus-Bertrand, a bookshop at Rue Hautefeuille
No. 23, Paris, issued the Gass *Journal* in French. Bound in robin's-egg blue paper
wrappers mottled with light, black specks, the volume in its original condition
had a delicate spine label reading *Voyage des Capitaines Lewis et Clarke*. Antoine
Jean Noel Lallemant translated the text. Lallemant in 1798 had translated the
African explorations of Mungo Park and Daniel Houghton and, in 1804, translated
the African explorations of John Ledyard and Simon Lucas. Ledyard, an American
from Connecticut, had sailed to the Northwest Coast of North America with
James Cook from 1776 to 1779. In Paris in 1785, he met Jefferson, Franklin, and
John Paul Jones. In 1787, in part inspired by Jefferson's dreams of exploring the interior of North America, he set out from St. Petersburg for Siberia on a wild scheme
to gain passage to Alaska and then walk alone down the coast to a point where
he would then cross the continent to the Mississippi Valley. The Russians turned
Ledyard back on the shores of the North Pacific; he later disappeared in Africa.[40]

At the conclusion of his translation of the Gass *Journal*, Lallemant included
a copy of William Clark's letter of April 2, 1805, written at Fort Mandan to
Governor Harrison, and another penned on September 23, 1806, at St. Louis.
Mᵉ Vᵉ Jeunehomme of No. 20 Rue Hautefeuille printed the book. J. B. Tardieu
engraved the "Carte Pour Servir au Voyage des Cap.ᵉˢ Lewis et Clarke, à l'Océan

38 Review of *A Journal of the
Voyages and Travels, The
Quarterly Review* 1 (London,
1809): 294–295.

39 Ibid., 296.

40 Jackson, *Thomas Jefferson*,
45–52.

Pacifique." The map included the Gallatin, Madison, and Jefferson Rivers at Three Forks and the location of Fort Clatsop.[41]

Arthus-Bertrand included in the back of the Gass volume a catalog of libraries, purchased from estates, that featured works on science, travel, and exploration. In the decade prior to publishing Gass's diary, the store's book list included: Andre-Pierre Le Dru's *Travels to the Islands of Teneriffe, Trinity, Saint Thomas, Saint Croix and Puerto Rico* (1810); C. S. Sonnini's *Travels in Upper and Lower Egypt* and his *Travels in Greece and Turkey*; Chevalier Saint-Gervais's *Travels to Spain*; de Lantier's *Travels in Greece and Asia*; and M. F. Person's *Travels of Discovery in Australia*. Most of these titles were issued in two or three volumes, octavo. In works of science, Arthus-Bertrand had published Karl von Linné's *Système Sexuel des Végétaux* (1803) and a major work on plants by the taxonomist Antoine Laurent de Jussieu, *La Botaniste Cultivateur* (1803). Subsequent to the Gass volume, Arthus-Bertrand continued publishing works in the same specialty subjects. These included Prince Maximilian von Wied-Neuwied's *Travels to Brazil in the Years 1815, 1816 and 1817* (1821). In 1833–34, Maximilian and his Swiss artist friend, Karl Bodmer, ascended the Missouri on a remarkable hunting trip that yielded stunning portraits of Native Americans. These illustrations were subsequently reproduced in fine editions of the Lewis and Clark journals in 1904–05. Maximilian and Bodmer met Toussaint Charbonneau, then in his seventies, at Fort Clark where, he noted, the man was still chasing Indian women.[42]

In 1810, Mathew Carey of Philadelphia published the Gass volume. He reissued it a second time in 1810 and again in 1811 and 1812, confirming steady sales and sizable American interest in the expedition.[43] The Carey editions included six illustrations, an engraver's fanciful rendering of scenes and events mentioned in the journal. Although the plates had no authenticity, they gained frequent republication in the twentieth century, in part because of their pleasing, naive simplicity. Bibliographer Victor Hugo Paltsits was troubled by the plates and remarked: "the bear in the plate at page 239 of the 1810 edition looks like a Newfoundland dog; in the other editions he looks either like a pig or anything other than a bear."[44] Carey's reprints used new composition of type, introduced slight changes in the plates, and, in 1812, included a small, folded map, "Louisiana."

Born in Dublin in 1760, Mathew Carey secured an apprenticeship to the book trade at age fifteen. An omnivorous reader, he grew in intellectual power and published his first essay, a denunciation of dueling, in 1777 in the *Hiberian Journal*. Carey's views on the anti-Catholic penal code led to his flight to Paris. Fortuitously, there he met Marquis de Lafayette and Benjamin Franklin. For a time, Carey worked at Franklin's hobby press at Passy, France. A pioneer in printing and publishing during decades of residence in Philadelphia, Franklin, in his old age, could not resist the lure of type, ink, and enterprise of a press. After returning to Ireland, Carey was imprisoned for sedition. He was released in 1784, at which time he quietly and hastily immigrated to Pennsylvania. Carey borrowed four hundred dollars from Lafayette, who was then visiting the United States, to establish the *Pennsylvania Evening Herald* and enter the job press business.[45]

Carey's interest in geography and exploration ran deep and helped shape both his own writing as well as the titles he published. Significant in Carey's connection to the Lewis and Clark Expedition was his publication of Thomas

41 Gass, *Voyage des Capitaines* (Paris, 1810).

42 Maximilian's narrative was published in Thwaites, *Early Western Travels*, vols. 22–24 (1906). A more recent edition is Thomas and Ronnefeldt, eds., *People of the First Man* (1976), 8, 174.

43 Carey employed the identical title to the Pittsburgh edition of 1807, *A Journal of Voyages and Travels of a Corps of Discovery, Under the Command of Capt. Lewis and Capt. Clarke of the Army of the United States* . . . . Clarkin, *Mathew Carey*, 108–109.

44 Paltsits, "Bibliographical Data," in Thwaites, 1:lxi–xciii.

45 Green, "Mathew Carey," 381–383; Bradsher, *Mathew Carey*, 4–9.

"A comparison with other journals of the Lewis and Clark expedition shows that on many occasions exact wording was copied by two or more journals."

Carol Lynn MacGregor, *The Journals of Patrick Gass* (1997)

Jefferson's *Notes on the State of Virginia* (1794). This volume of 336 pages, containing a "Map of Virginia" by Samuel Lewis and engraved by James Smither, was Jefferson's only book and a notable contribution to learning. Jefferson recounted Virginia's history, assessed the state's natural resources, accounted for its native peoples, and described the first, scientific, archaeological investigations in America. In 1794–95, Carey published in two volumes William Guthrie's *A New System of Modern Geography*. This work contained significant, new information on North America, the probable contribution of Jedidiah Morse. Carey also published his own works. These included *Carey's American Atlas: Containing Twenty Maps and One Chart* (1795), *Carey's American Pocket Atlas* (1796), *Carey's Minor American Atlas* (1802), and *General Atlas* (enlarged in several editions between 1796 and 1818 to include fifty-eight maps).[46]

Carey became America's first commercial publisher. At the time he printed the Gass diary, he had his printing shop and bookstore at Nos. 118–122 Market Street. In 1814, he moved to No. 121 Chestnut Street.[47] Carey's business plan emerged in the 1790s when, in order to meet market demand, he commissioned other printers to set type, print pages, and bind his books. He also hired Samuel Lewis, a skilled cartographer who later redrew William Clark's map of the American West, to assist in proofreading. Through calculated allocation of resources and energies, Carey dramatically reduced the time required to produce a book. In 1801, he began promoting book fairs in Philadelphia and New York modeled on those in Frankfurt and Leipzig. In 1802, he drafted the constitution for the American Company of Booksellers, an organization to facilitate the distribution and sale of books in the United States.[48]

Carey's impact on American intellectual life was substantial. Between 1785 and 1824, his company published 1,527 volumes. They ranged from the diary of Patrick Gass to Jonathan Swift's satirical *Travels Into Several Remote Nations of the World* (by Lemuel Gulliver) and Daniel Defoe's *The Life and Most Surprising Adventures of Robinson Crusoe* (1809). His presses issued "A Map of the Discoveries Made by Capts. Cook & Clarke in the Years 1778 & 1779 Between the Eastern Coast of Asia and the Western Coast of North America" (1809), Amos Stoddard's *Sketches, Historical and Descriptive of Louisiana* (1812), and George Heriot's *Travels Through the Canadas* (1813).[49]

The Gass volume was a minor event in the notable history of Mathew Carey's long career as a publisher and essayist. Appointed to the board of the Bank of the United States in 1811, a financial institution headed for many years by Nicholas Biddle (subsequently the primary author of the Lewis and Clark Expedition narrative published in 1814), Carey increasingly tried to influence national economic policy. In the 1820s, he authored pamphlets on tariffs and sought to shape public opinion in Pennsylvania on internal improvements. Carey's greatest legacies, however, are the volumes issued under his firm's name and the publishing company that succeeded him at death in 1838. His son, son-in-law, and other partners formed Lea & Blanchard at the time of Carey's demise. The firm continued publishing under various names into the twentieth century.[50]

Interest in the explorations of Lewis and Clark was intense, both in the United States and in western Europe. Anton Doll, a publisher and bookseller in Vienna, published the Gass volume in 1811 in J. B. Schütz's *Neue historische und geographische Gemählde, oder Charakteristiken merkwürdiger Personen . . .* , [*New*

46 Carey, *Catalogue of Books* (1810).

47 *Biographies of Successful Philadelphia Merchants*, 147–148.

48 Shuffleton, "M. Carey and Company," *American Literary Publishing Houses*, 72–75.

49 Clarkin, *Mathew Carey*, 96–127.

50 Shuffleton, "M. Carey and Company," *American Literary Publishing Houses*, 72; Green, "Mathew Carey," 382–383.

Historical and Geographical Paintings or Characters of Noteworthy Persons . . .],
Part 6, "Bericht Über die Erforschungsreise des Lauses der Flüsse Missuri und
Columbia" [Report of the Explorations of the Rivers Missouri and Columbia].
A series of twelve volumes bound in six, the work included an interesting
summary of travel narratives, with several in the Western Hemisphere:
Krusenstern's voyages of 1803–06, Alexander Von Humboldt's and Felix d'Uzara's
travels in South America, Ledru's trip to the West Indies, and the Gass diary.[51]

J. B. Schütz crafted an "Introduction" to the Gass *Journal* and broke the
narrative into three parts. He opened with the observation:

> The closer acquaintance we made by this report of a large part of the enor-
> mous distances of North America has an even more enjoyable importance
> because these are areas rather fortunately already inhabited by half-civilized
> people. The discovery of the connection of the innermost area with the
> Pacific Ocean will in the future have consequently important results for the
> fur trade, and, which should be taken into consideration even more, for the
> uplifting of the natives. The crowded, though complete excerpt which we
> have made of this report, is therefore worthy of consideration.

Schütz then summarized the journey, converting distances from English to
German miles, thrilling over the abundance of wildlife, identifying the savagery
of the Indians, and commenting on the scenic wonders. Items selected for discussion included geography, ethnography, and travel conditions. Describing the
encounter with the Shoshone on August 17, 1805, for example, Schütz wrote:

> Their information brought about the location of the source of the Columbia,
> which was at a distance of a quarter mile from the Jefferson. This is also the
> strange place where two rivers have their source, one of which emptied into
> the Pacific and the other into the Gulf of Mexico. The natives of this area
> were very poor but courageous. Fish and berries were their nourishment and
> their huts were bad. These people were willing guides.[52]

Schütz gleaned from the Gass diary essential geographical information,
which he offered to readers:

> The great result of the journey in short: The Missouri is 3,096 English (844
> German) miles long and navigable; then the Jefferson begins, navigable for
> 744 miles (187 German). Then for 340 English (92 German) miles overland
> of which 140 (38 German) miles is over terrible, partly covered with eternal
> snow, mountains. The Columbia is easily navigable and, from its mouth,
> China is reached earlier than going from Canada to England, which is very
> important for fur traders. Nearly the whole traveled area is rich in valuable
> products of the animal and plant kingdoms, and the rather numerous, peace-
> ful natives approach civilization. The government of the United States can
> count this area, according to its length and width of 150 and 900 German
> miles, clandestinely their own and is at least authorized to protest against
> any other civilized nation's claims. They want to have this area known to be
> a part of Louisiana and had the expedition started from there, but before it
> really claims this area as its own, one cannot duly call it New Louisiana.[53]

The firm of Anton Doll both printed and sold books. Its owners were the
brothers Alois Doll (1767–1826) and Anton Doll (1772–1812). In the 1790s, the
company published scientific literature. Among its works was the multi-authored
Methode der Chemischen Nomenklatur für das Antiphlogistische System [*System of*

51 Schütz, *Neue historische und
geographische Gemählde . . .* ;
Mayer, *Wiens Buckdrucker-
geschichte, 1482–1882*, 299;
Frank, "Anton Doll," *Lexikon
des Gesamten Buchwesens*,
2:336.

52 Schütz, *Neue historische und
geographische Gemählde . . .* ,
116.

53 Ibid., 120.

Chemical Nomenclature for the Antiphlogisten System] (1799). In 1807, the firm published Francois Marie Perrin du Lac's *Reise in die Beyden Louisianen Unter die Wilden Völkerschaften am Missouri, Durch die Vereingten Staaten und die Provinzen am Ohio, in den Jahren 1801, 1802, und 1803 . . .* [*Travels in the Two Louisianas Among the Savage Peoples of the Missouri, Through the United States and the State of Ohio in the Years 1801, 1802 and 1803 . . .*].[54] Du Lac's travels described his ascent of the Missouri in 1802 from St. Louis to the White River, a narrative that drew heavily from the writings of Jean Baptiste Truteau and Pierre Antoine Tabeau.[55]

In 1814, Philip Christoph Weyland (1765–1843) crafted a version of the Gass *Journal* in German. Weyland had translated the travels of Giuseppe Acerbi in Finland and Sweden (1803), Francois R. J. de Pons' travels in South America (1808), and Zebulon M. Pike's travels in the Louisiana Territory and New Spain (1813). In the case of Gass's account, Weyland presented a summary rather than a translation. Landes-Industrie-Comptoirs in Weimar, Germany, published the account as *Tagebuch einer Entdeckungs-Reise durch Nord-America, von der Mündung des Missuri an bis zum Einfluss der Columbia in den Stillen Ocean, Gemacht in den Jahren 1804, 1805 und 1806. . . .* [*Diary of an Exploring Trip Through North America, from the Mouth of the Missouri to the Outlet of the Columbia to the Pacific Ocean, Made in the Years 1804, 1805 and 1806 . . .*]. The Gass narrative was most likely published as a separate volume in 1814 and reissued the following year in *Neue Bibliothek der wichtigsten Reisebeschreibungen zur Erweiterung der Erd- und Völkerkunde in Verbingdung mit Einigen Anderen Gelehrten Gesammelt . . .* [*New Library of the Most Important Travel Descriptions for the Enlargement of Geography and Anthropology in Connection with Some Other Scholars . . .*]. The works were collected and edited by Friedrich Justin Bertuch of Weimar. In 1815, the Gass narrative, in most instances, was bound with Jacob Morier's *Reise Durch Persien, Armenian und Klein-Asien Nach Constantinopel, in den Jahren 1808 und 1809* [*Travels Through Persia, Armenia, and Asia Minor to Constantinople in the Years 1808 and 1809*].[56]

Weyland retained Thomas Jefferson's message as a preface to the book, asserting that it set the stage for the Gass narrative of the expedition. He wrote:

> This endeavor is here so much more important and interesting since it is directed towards the as yet undiscovered and with deep darkness-covered regions in the interior of America. The present journal is therefore of undisputable value and deserves, beside the nearly simultaneous travels through the western regions of North-America of Pike, whereof last year also a translation at this publishers appeared, the first place among the explorations of those unknown regions. The extensive description of this travel itself, which will comprise three volumes and an atlas [per the Lewis prospectus of 1807], has either not appeared or at least have not come to the continent of Europe. So far only the present journal is available, which a participant of the trip, Sir Patrick Gass, has issued in the English language.[57]

Weyland's elevation of Sergeant Patrick Gass to "Sir Patrick Gass" might have pleased David M'Keehan as much as it might have driven Meriwether Lewis to fits of raving! The remainder of Weyland's brief introduction was a rough paraphrase of M'Keehan's explanation that the journal had emerged from sessions of comparison and correction in the field. "All information contained herewithin deserves the more acceptance," he concluded, "as the author had the full trust of both supreme leaders of the expedition."[58]

54 Frank, "Anton Doll," *Lexikon des Gesamten Buchwesens*, 2:336.

55 Nasatir, *Before Lewis and Clark*, 2:706–712.

56 William Reese, dealer in Western Americana, noted in a catalog: "This German edition of the Patrick Gass narrative of the Lewis and Clark expedition is perhaps the rarest contemporary edition of any of the accounts of the journey, with the possible exception of the Natchez edition of Jefferson's 1806 message." Reese offered a copy in 2001 for $6,500. Reese, *206 New Acquisitions*, Item 77. Volumes translated by Weyland are listed in *World Catalog* and the *National Union Catalog*.

57 Gass, *Tagebuch einer Entdeckungs-Reise*, vi–vii.

58 Ibid.

Landes-Industrie-Comptoirs was the "Publishing House of State" and in steady production of literary, travel, and scientific works since 1791. Volumes describing exploration of exotic lands dominated its new book list. In the decade prior to printing the Gass volume, the press brought out works on travels in Senegal, Morocco, French Guiana, Surinam, New South Wales, Europe's North Cape, Sweden, Seeland, Turkey, Persia, and Egypt. The publishing house also issued atlases and single maps. The daily observations of "Sir Patrick Gass" were in good company when printed in Weimar.[59]

Friedrich Justin Bertuch (1747–1822), the volume editor, had studied theology at the University of Jena, then turned to law, natural history, and literature. His patron, Baron Ludwig Heinrich of Weimar, encouraged his work in literature and translation, notably the first German edition of Cervantes' *Don Quixote* (1775–77). Bertuch's labors as secretary and steward of the finances of the Duke Karl August of Weimar consumed much of his time. In 1776, he founded a school in Weimar's "Red Castle," administered after 1788 by Johann W. von Goethe. In 1778, he transformed an old sharpening mill into a paper and coloring plant, laying the foundation for Landes-Industrie Comptoirs, a state-operated publishing house founded in 1791 to employ cartographers, artists, and printers. For these contributions, Bertuch was awarded "princely privilege." In spite of the interruptions of war in 1806, Landes-Industrie Comptoirs published numerous works for several decades.[60]

The publication of the Gass diary in Weimar was its last printing for thirty-three years. Then, on the fortieth anniversary of its publication in Pittsburgh (1847), the firm of Ells, Claflin & Company of Dayton, Ohio, reprinted the book. The volume had a new title, claiming more than the original had intended: *Lewis and Clarke's Journal to the Rocky Mountains In the Years 1804, -5, -6; As Related by Patrick Gass, One of the Officers in the Expedition.* The contents were not the journals of Lewis and Clark, but merely a reprinting of the Gass narrative. The publisher celebrated a "New Edition with Numerous Engravings," thirteen in total, including fanciful events such as "Lion and Buffalo Fight," and generic settings such as "Moon Light on the Western Waters." The work made no reference to David M'Keehan and his role in publishing the first edition nor to the fact that Gass was yet living in Wellsburg, West Virginia.[61]

Publishing the Gass diary was Benjamin Franklin Ells's second attempt to address the Lewis and Clark Expedition. In 1840, he issued *The Journal of Lewis and Clarke, to the Mouth of the Columbia River . . .* , an illustrated version of the surreptitious history allegedly written by William Fisher and published by James Sharan in 1812 in Philadelphia. Benjamin Franklin Ells (1805/6–1874) was the son of Benjamin and Clarissa (Wyles) Eells of Hartford, Connecticut.[62] In the 1830s, he established himself as an author, publisher, and bookstore operator in Dayton, Ohio. His books included *The Dialogue Grammar* (1834) [printed at Hanover College Press in Indiana], *The Dialogue Arithmetic* (1836), *A History of the Romish Inquisition* (1835), *The Bible Prayer Book* (1835), *The Pleasing Speller and Definer* (1842), and other works.[63]

B. F. Ells's interest in the American West led to his firm's publication in 1848–49 of *The Western Miscellany*. "Our object in getting up this periodical," he wrote, "is to furnish a course of cheap and useful reading, of a healthful literary and moral character, and of such variety as to be adapted to the capacities of reading

59 *World Catalog's* listings by publisher provides an extensive run of works published by Landes-Industrie Comptoirs in Weimar.

60 Heinemann, *Ein Kaufmann*; Kaiser, "Friedrich Justin Bertuch als Verleger," www.weimar-klassik.de/projekte/eli_240d.html; "Friedrich Justin Bertuch," Geschichte Mitteldeutschlands, DREFA-Projektgruppe, www.mdr.de/geschichte/archiv/personen/bertuch

61 Gass, *Lewis and Clarke's Journal.*

62 The family surname changed from Eells to Ells in the migration to Dayton, Ohio.

63 Erastus Ells, possibly a son of B. F. Ells, married Sarah Mercy Claflin in 1850 in Dayton. This marriage suggests that kinship as well as business were probably involved in the firm of Ells, Claflin & Company. Wright, *Genealogy*; Ancestry WorldTree, "Benjamin Franklin Ells," viewed August 17, 2001.

members of all families." The first volume of *The Western Miscellany* included recipes, advice on grammar, historical vignettes, biographical sketches of notable figures, and tales of exploration and travel. Among the articles was the "History of Oregon" which drew from the travels of Jonathan Carver, David Douglas, and William Slacum; the histories of Washington Irving; and, by reference, the adventures of Lewis and Clark.[64] Ells, Claflin & Company published eccentrically. The firm's new book list in 1847 included *Collyer's Manual on Phrenology*, *A Guide to Cabinet Makers*, John A. McClung's *Sketches of Western Adventure*, *The World to Come*, and the Gass *Journal*.

The entrepreneurial ambitions of David M'Keehan established Gass as one of the prominent voices about the Lewis and Clark Expedition. The humble sergeant and carpenter was published between 1807 and 1847 in Pittsburgh, Philadelphia, Vienna, London, Paris, Weimar, and Dayton. Gass took pride in his accomplishments. In 1829, he wrote to John Eaton, Secretary of War, seeking continuation of his pension for the loss of an eye while serving in the War of 1812. He noted parenthetically: "And permit me to add here that in the years 1804, 5 & 6 I accompanied Captains Lewis and Clarke to the Pacific Ocean, and on our return had, published my dailey Journal, which book I am informed is honored with a place in the Library of Congress."[65]

By dint of longevity, Gass became a figure of public interest. He married in 1831 at age sixty, fathered seven children, and in his ninth decade, became the subject of a biography, *The Life and Times of Patrick Gass* (1859).[66] The biographer, John Gabriel Jacob (1826–1903), was editor and publisher with J. A. Smith of *The Wellsburg Herald* and *The Panhandle Farmer*.[67] A copy of the biography in the Library Company of Philadelphia includes an inscription, "March 28th, 1859, Respectfully yours Patr. Gass." Jacob and Smith, who forwarded the signed biography to the library, reported:

> According to request, we transmit your autograph of Patrick Gass, the sole survivor of the age of 88, of the Lewis & Clark Exploring Expedition in 1804-5-6. The penmanship is not of the best, nor the arrangement in the most approved style, neither is the spelling to be highly commended, but the autograph is probably more of a curiosity as it is, than if more systematically written and arranged."[68]

Gass died in 1870 at the age of 99. He was the last of the Corps of Discovery. Years before his death, public interest in the expedition had dimmed. Not until the quickening of interest at the time of the expedition's centennial did the Gass volume come back into print. James Kendall Hosmer, author of *The Story of the Louisiana Purchase*, crafted a new introduction and prepared an index. A. C. McClurg & Company, a Chicago publisher featuring history, historical fiction, and western writers, brought out *Gass's Journal of the Lewis and Clark Expedition* (1904).[69] The sergeant's narrative found a new audience and would continue to be reprinted several times over the next century.

The question arises: was the Gass diary deserving of so many printings and translations into French and German? The simple answer is no. The critical matter, however, is that Lewis's failure to write his narrative and Clark's inability to craft a book created a situation wherein the Gass *Journal*, revised and published by M'Keehan, captured a market. When nothing else appeared in print and a public clamored for information, publishers producing works on exploration and

64 *The Western Miscellany* (Dayton, Ohio), 1 (July 1848).

65 Jackson, *Letters*, 2:646–647.

66 Moulton, *The Journals*, 2:513.

67 Norona and Shelter, *West Virginia Imprints*, 252–253.

68 Jacob, *The Life and Times of Patrick Gass*.

69 Gass, *Gass's Journal*.

travel turned to what was available. In spite of its humdrum recitation of trivial events, the Gass narrative laid out the bare bones of a singularly significant transit across North America. Thus, as prosaic and tedious as it was, the work met a need and earned a niche in world travel literature. Had the Gass volume remained the only primary account in print on the expedition in the nineteenth century, its importance would be certain. However, even when it was eclipsed by the appearance in 1814 of the Biddle-Allen narrative based on the journals of Lewis and Clark, the Gass *Journal* remained a volume of interest and useful information.

Patrick Gass, First in Print: Bibliography

The following publications all derive from the *Journal* of Patrick Gass, member of the Corps of Discovery, as edited by David M'Keehan. The location of the original journal is not known, but it may still exist, possibly in Philadelphia. The most recent editor of Gass's *Journal*, Carol Lynn MacGregor, comments (p. 18) that searches since 1904 for the original manuscript have been unsuccessful.

M'Keehan, Gass's choice as editor, undoubtedly transcribed and possibly polished the journal of the relatively uneducated Gass for publication, and M'Keehan added discursive notes of his own, in a quite different style from the plain narrative of the text. M'Keehan's long letter to Lewis, published in the *Pittsburgh Gazette*, defending his publication of the journal, will be of interest to any student of nineteenth-century invective. It is reprinted in full by Jackson (*Letters*, item 264), and reveals a writer of considerable wit and energy, quite unlike the narrator of the Gass text. Moreover, since Gass's surviving account books show him to have been literate, financially competent, and careful, there is little reason to suppose that M'Keehan significantly altered Gass's basic narrative.

J. G. Jacob's 1859 *Life and Times of Patrick Gass* summarizes the editorial process as follows (p. 141): "McKeehan presented his materials in the raw state, almost, and undigested, just as they were noted down by the author,–frankly stating in his preface, that 'neither he or Mr. Gass had attempted to give adequate representations of the scenes portrayed.' Mr. Gass received the copy-right of the work, and one hundred copies of the first edition, while McKeehan received as his compensation, the balance of the edition, which he disposed of, to some profit." The number printed in the first edition is not on record. The copyright, however, never belonged to Gass, whatever he may have believed. It was recorded to M'Keehan, and remained his through all the Mathew Carey reprints. The arrangement was presumably made with that publisher, who acknowledged M'Keehan's title to copyright as late as 1812.

The Gass *Journal* was reprinted several times in the twentieth century. Some of these publications included new prefaces and introductions, like James Hosmer's 1904 edition (3.12), and that of Earle R. Forrest (Ross and Haines 1959), who also wrote a pamphlet entitled *Patrick Gass: Lewis and Clark's Last Man* (publisher Mrs. A.M. Painter, Independence, Pennsylvania, 1950). Carol MacGregor has reprinted the journal, along with Gass's account books from 1826 to 1837 and 1847 to 1848 (Missoula: Mountain Press, 1997). Gary Moulton included Gass as vol. 10 of his thirteen-volume *Journals of the Lewis and Clark Expedition*. Hosmer's 1904 edition was reprinted by Lone Wolf Press in 2000.

3.1 Cramer, Pittsburgh 1807

A JOURNAL | OF THE | VOYAGES AND TRAVELS | *OF A CORPS OF DISCOVERY*, | UNDER THE COMMAND OF CAPT. LEWIS AND CAPT. | CLARKE OF THE ARMY OF THE UNITED STATES, | FROM | *THE MOUTH OF THE RIVER MISSOURI THROUGH THE | INTERIOR PARTS OF NORTH AMERICA | TO THE PACIFIC OCEAN*, | DURING THE YEARS 1804, 1805 & 1806. | CONTAINING | An authentic relation of the most interesting transactions | during the expedition,–A description of the country,– | And an account of its inhabitants, soil, climate, curiosities |

and vegetable and animal productions. | [rule] | *BY PATRICK GASS*, | ONE OF THE PERSONS EMPLOYED IN THE EXPEDITION. | [rule] | WITH | GEOGRAPHICAL AND EXPLANATORY NOTES | BY THE PUBLISHER. | [rule] | [COPY-RIGHT SECURED ACCORDING TO LAW.] | *PITTSBURGH*, | PRINTED BY ZADOK CRAMER, | FOR DAVID M'KEEHAN, PUBLISHER AND | PROPRIETOR .... 1807.

Collation: One volume, 18mo., 17 cm. [i]–ix title page, Pennsylvania copyright to David M'Keehan, April 11, 1807; half title; publisher's preface dated March 26, 1807; [11]–262 text.

References: Coues, cxvii–cxix; Graff, 1516; Paltsits, lxxi; Wagner-Camp-Becker, 6:1.

Description: The first printing of a journal by a member of the Lewis and Clark Expedition, its title page naming the exploration team as the "Corps of Discovery" for the first time in print.

Notices: *The Monthly Anthology, And Boston Review* 4 (December 1807): 682, "Catalogue of New Publications for December," first item: "A Journal of the Voyages and Travels of a Corps of Discovery, under the command of Captains Lewis and Clarke, of the Army of the United States, from the Mouth of the Missouri through the Interiour parts of North-America, to the Pacifick Ocean, during the years 1804, 1805, and 1806. By Patrick Gass, one of the persons employed in the expedition. With Geographical and Explanatory Notes by the publisher. Price one dollar."

The Navigator; Containing Directions for Navigating the Monongahela, Allegheny, Ohio and Mississippi Rivers . . . . To Which Is Added an Appendix, Containing an Account of Louisiana, and of the Missouri and Columbia Rivers, as discovered by the Voyage under Capts. Lewis and Clark. Eighth Edition–Improved and Enlarged. Pittsburgh, Published and Sold by Cramer, Spear and Eichbaum . . . 1814. This compilation by Zadok Cramer, printer of the 1807 first edition of the *Journal*, began in 1801 as a small pamphlet on the navigation of the Ohio (Paltsits, lxxxvi), and first included in its 1808 sixth edition a digest of Gass's *Journal*. Paltsits (lxxxvii) summarizes its subsequent reprints. In the eighth edition (1814, as described above from the Lewis & Clark College Collection copy) and in subsequent editions, an expanded text appears on pp. 343–9, headed "Abridgement of Lewis and Clark's Expedition." The eighth edition is also available at Lewis & Clark College in a Readex Microprint volume.

Lewis & Clark College Collection: Chuinard: Rebound by Lloyd Wallis & Lloyd in full leather, with raised bands and gilt edges. Half title bound before title. Tweney 1: Original state in excellent condition. Tweney 2: Rebound in blue and gold marbled boards with handwritten paper label on spine. Wendlick 1: David M'Keehan's family copy, with signatures of Benjamin M'Keehan (front endpaper) and John Alexander M'Keehan (rear endpaper), and detailed letter of provenance from knowledgeable Ohio book dealer Ernest Wesson laid in. Original state; half leather, with marbled boards and gilt titling on spine. Wendlick 2: William Dunbar family copy with signatures: "W Dunbar | 1829 Forest | Willy Dunbar from his | affectionate Mother | M. F D. | Forrest April– | 1831." (William Dunbar Sr., whose southern travels form part of Jefferson's Report, died at his plantation, The Forest, south of Natchez, in October 1810.) Original state; signature C missing, supplied from another copy.

3.1 Cramer, Pittsburgh 1807. M'Keehan family copy.

3.2 Budd, London 1808

A | JOURNAL | OF THE | VOYAGES AND TRAVELS | OF | *A CORPS OF DISCOVERY,* | UNDER THE COMMAND OF CAPTAIN LEWIS AND | CAPTAIN CLARKE, OF THE ARMY OF | THE UNITED STATES; | FROM THE MOUTH OF THE | RIVER MISSOURI, | THROUGH THE | *Interior Parts of North America,* | TO THE PACIFIC OCEAN; | DURING THE YEARS 1804, 1805, & 1806. | CONTAINING | An Authentic Relation of the most interesting Transactions during | the Expedition: A Description of the Country: And an | Account of its Inhabitants, Soil, Climate, Curiosities, | and Vegetable and Animal Productions. | [rule] | By PATRICK GASS, | One of the Persons employed in the Expedition. | [rule] | PITTSBURGH: PRINTED FOR DAVID M'KEEHAN. | LONDON: RE-PRINTED FOR J. BUDD, BOOKSELLER TO | HIS ROYAL HIGHNESS THE PRINCE OF | WALES, PALL-MALL. | 1808.

Collation: One volume, 8vo., 22 cm. [i]–iv title page, backed by imprint of Brettell & Co. Printers; [iii]–iv advertisement by the English publisher, dated April 18, 1808; [1]–9 preface by the American publisher, dated March 26, 1807; [blank]; [11] half title; 13–381 text; [383]–[384] advertisements leaf (Tweney).

References: Coues, cxix; Graff, 1517; Paltsits, lxxi; Wagner-Camp-Becker, 6:2.

Description: A London printing directly based on Philadelphia 1807.

Notice: *The Quarterly Review* 1 (February and May 1809): 293–304: "A Journal of the Voyages and Travels of a Corps of Discovery, under the Command of Captains Lewis and Clarke, from the Mouth of the River Missouri, through the interior Parts of North America, to the Pacific Ocean. By Patrick Gass, one of the Persons employed on the Expedition. pp. 381. 8vo. Pittsburgh, printed. London, re-printed. Budd. 1808." The Lewis & Clark College Collection copy (Wendlick) is the sixth edition reprint, John Murray, 1827.

Lewis & Clark College Collection: Chuinard: Rebound in half calf with marbled boards. Tweney: Original leather, re-backed. Contains advertisement leaf. Bookplate of Mrs. Hamilton Nisbet. Wendlick: Untrimmed full calf, a fine copy. Unrelated map (North America, engraved by B. Baker, Islington) laid in. Bookplate of Rev. Nathaniel S. Thomas.

3.3 Arthus-Bertrand, Paris 1810 [Color plate VIII]

VOYAGE | DES CAPITAINES | LEWIS ET CLARKE, | *DEPUIS l'embouchure du* | *MISSOURI, jusqu'à l'entrée* | *de la COLOMBIA dans L'OCÉAN PACIFIQUE;* | FAIT DANS LES ANNÉES 1804, 1805 et 1806, | PAR ORDRE DU GOUVERNEMENT DES ÉTATS-UNIS: | CONTENANT | Le Journal authentique des Événements les plus remar- | quables du Voyage, ainsi que la Description des | Habitants, du Sol, du Climat, et des Productions | animales et végétales des pays situés à l'ouest de | l'Amérique Septentrionale. | *Rédigé en Anglais par PATRICE GASS, Employé dans* | *l'Expédition;* | Et traduit en Francais par A. J. N. LALLEMANT, | l'un des Secrétaires de la Marine. | AVEC DES NOTES, DEUX LETTRES DU CAPITAINE CLARKE, | ET UNE CARTE GRAVÉE PAR J. B. TARDIEU. | [wavy rule] | A PARIS, | CHEZ ARTHUS-BERTRAND, Libraire, rue Hautefeuille, n° 23. | [rule] | 1810.

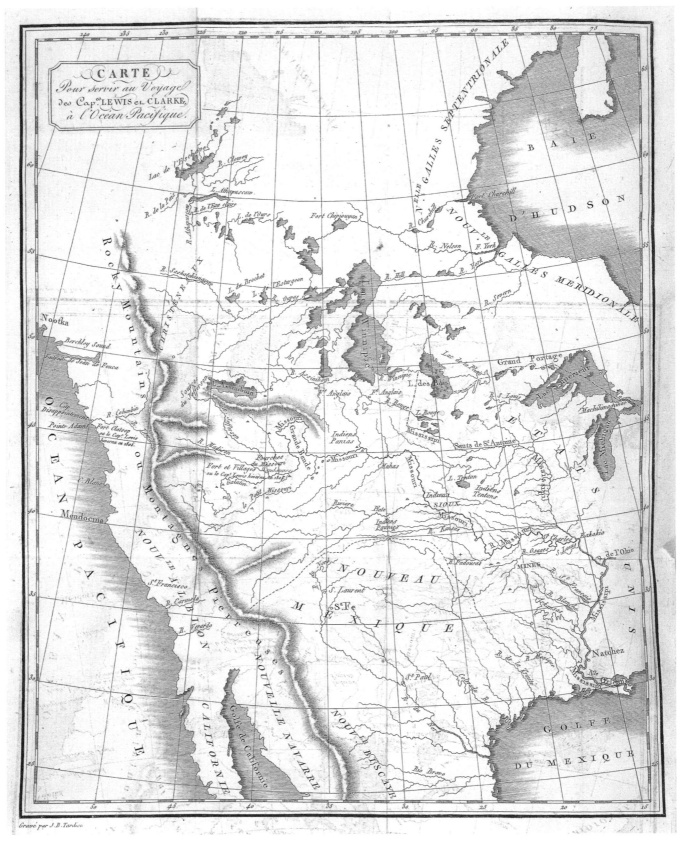

3.3 Map from Arthus-Bertrand, Paris 1810

Collation: One volume, 8vo., 21 cm. [i]–xvii: half title "VOYAGE DES CAPITAINES LEWIS ET CLARKE"; publisher's advertisement "Voyages qui se trouvent chez le même Libraire"; full title page; [blank]; "Message du Président des États-Unis, Aux Deux Chambres du Congrès"; [blank]; "Préface de l'Éditeur Américain. [1]–415 text "Journal d'un Voyage de Découvertes à Travers L'Amérique Septentrionale"; 416–22 "Lettre du capitaine Clarke à s. E. le Gouverneur Harrison"; 423–32 "Lettre du capitaine Clarke à son frère le general Clarke"; 433–43 "Table des Chapitres" [Contents]; map, originally placed following 443. In the Chuinard copy in original wraps are found two separately paginated advertisement supplements: [1]–20 "Extrait du Catalogue du Fonds de Librairie"; [1]–8 "Ouvrages Nouveaux qui se Trouvent à Paris."

Plates: Map, engraved by J. B. Tardieu ("Carte pour servir"), reproducing closely the Neele map in the London 1809 surreptitious account (4a.2). Bound at the end of the text in copies in original wraps and Chuinard 2. Bound before the first page of text in Wendlick. Missing in Tweney 2.

References: Coues, cxx; Graff, 1519; Paltsits, lxxii; Wagner-Camp-Becker, 6.3.

Description: A translation by A. J. N. Lallemant, following London, 1808, with the addition of the message from the President, Clark's two letters, a map, and some minor editorial notes.

Lewis & Clark College Collection: Chuinard 1: Streeter copy (3124), in original wraps. Contains map and twenty-eight pages of advertisements, from which selections appear in the advertisement page on [i]. Original ownership label of M[adam]e Porchon de Bonval; later owner Edward Eberstadt & Sons, 1938. Chuinard 2: Rebound in yellow boards, worn leather spine. Chuinard bookplate. Contains map. Tweney 1: Original wraps. Tweney bookplate laid in. Contains map. Tweney 2: Period full leather, with blue marbled endpapers, front board detached. Pencil inscription of George W. Cable library, November 7, 1925. Lacks map. Wendlick: Rebound in green marbled boards. Half leather. Contains map. Houecourt bookplate.

3.4(a) Carey, Philadelphia 1810 (first state)

A | JOURNAL | OF THE | VOYAGES AND TRAVELS | *OF A CORPS OF DISCOVERY,* | UNDER THE COMMAND OF CAPT. LEWIS AND CAPT. | CLARKE OF THE ARMY OF THE UNITED STATES, | FROM | *THE MOUTH OF THE RIVER MISSOURI THROUGH THE* | *INTERIOR PARTS OF NORTH AMERICA* | *TO THE PACIFIC OCEAN,* | During the Years 1804, 1805, and 1806. | CONTAINING | An authentic relation of the most interesting transac- | tions during the expedition,–A description of | the country,–And an account of its inhabi- | tants, soil, climate, curiosities and ve- | getable and animal productions. | [rule] | *BY PATRICK GASS,* | ONE OF THE PERSONS EMPLOYED IN THE EXPEDITION. | [rule] | WITH GEOGRAPHICAL AND EXPLANATORY NOTES. | [rule] | [*Copy-Right secured according to Law.*] | [rule] | *PHILADELPHIA:* | PRINTED FOR MATHEW CAREY, | NO. 122, MARKET-STREET. | [rule] | 1810.

Page.60.

Captain Clark & his men building a line of Huts.

Page.95.

Captain Clark and his men shooting Bears.

Collation: One volume, 12mo., 17.5 cm. Frontispiece of "A Canoe Striking on a Tree." [i]–viii title page, with blank verso; [iii]–viii "Preface by the Publisher of the First Edition"; 9 half title page "Journal of the Voyages and Travels of a Corps of Discovery"; [blank]; 11–262 text.

Plates: Frontispiece "A Canoe Striking on a Tree" (originally intended to face 220, as noted in upper right corner of engraving); facing 26 "Captains Lewis & Clark holding a Council with the Indians"; facing 60 "Captain Clark & his men building a line of Huts"; facing 95 "Captain Clark and his men shooting Bears"; facing 239 "An American having struck a Bear but not killed him, escapes into a Tree"; facing 245 "Captain Lewis shooting an Indian."

The illustrator, not an engraver of distinction, has remained anonymous. Clarkin (item 583) compares his work to the plates in Carey's 1809 *Cabinet of Momus*: "The drawings are indeed crude. If one were to judge by their execution, one would say that this 'artist' and that of the Gass volume on the Lewis and Clark Expedition were one and the same." The same engraver was very likely used for Carey's 1809 *Life of George Washington* by M. L. Weems. This volume is in the Lewis & Clark College Collection. The engraving style is similar, and both series show in their captions a distinctive lengthened serif on lower-case ascenders.

References: Coues, cxxi; Graff, 1518; Wagner-Camp-Becker, 6:4.

Description: A reprint by Philadelphia publisher Mathew Carey of M'Keehan's edition. This is the first printed account of the expedition to include plates. Its text is a page-by-page reprint of Cramer 1807, almost a facsimile of that edition. Minor corrections (for example that of "has" to "have" in the preface, directly above the signature A2) and occasional modernizations of spelling ("cheerfulness" for "chearfulness" in the same location of the following unsigned page) appear throughout.

The title page and its verso exist in two states. In the first state, Carey's title page states no edition and makes no mention of the six engravings, the edition's main claim to originality. The reprint of Cramer's 1807 preface, following the title's blank verso, does acknowledge him as the "Publisher of the First Edition." The second state of the title page claims this as the second edition (ignoring London 1808 and Paris 1810, if the latter was already in print), draws attention to the engravings, and reprints for the first time on its verso the M'Keehan copyright notice of 1807. Both states are listed by Howes, G77; Sabin, 26741; Shaw-Shoemaker, 20185; and Streeter, 6123.

3.4(b) Carey, Philadelphia 1810 (second state) [Color plates IX and X]

A | JOURNAL | OF THE | VOYAGES AND TRAVELS | *OF A CORPS OF DISCOVERY*, | UNDER THE COMMAND OF CAPT. LEWIS AND CAPT. | CLARKE OF THE ARMY OF THE UNITED STATES, | FROM | *THE MOUTH OF THE RIVER MISSOURI THROUGH THE* | *INTERIOR PARTS OF NORTH AMERICA* | *TO THE PACIFIC OCEAN*, | During the Years 1804, 1805, and 1806. | CONTAINING | An authentic relation of the most interesting transac- | tions during the expedition,—A description of | the country,—And an account of its inhabi- | tants, soil, climate, curiosities and ve- | getable and animal productions. | [rule] | *BY PATRICK GASS*, | ONE OF THE PERSONS EMPLOYED IN THE EXPEDITION. | [rule] | WITH GEOGRAPHICAL AND EXPLANATORY NOTES. | [rule] | *SECOND EDITION*–WITH SIX ENGRAVINGS. | [rule] | [*Copy-Right secured according to Law.*] | [rule] | *PHILADELPHIA:* | PRINTED FOR MATHEW CAREY, | NO. 122, MARKET-STREET. | [rule] | 1810.

Collation: One volume, 12mo., 17.5 cm. Frontispiece of "A Canoe Striking on a Tree." [i]–viii title page, backed by Pennsylvania copyright to David M'Keehan, April 31, 1807; [iii]–viii "Preface by the Publisher of the First Edition"; 9 half title page: "Journal of the Voyages and Travels of a Corps of Discovery"; [blank]; 11–262 text.

References: Coues, cxxi; Graff, 1518; Paltsits, lxxii; Wagner-Camp-Becker, 6:5.

Plates: As in 3.4(a).

Lewis & Clark College Collection (both in second state): Wendlick: Original leather. Map laid in, not belonging to this title. Contains a thirty-six page catalogue of books by Mathew Carey at end of volume. Ownership inscriptions of Lewis Baily, Reuben Baily, and (erased) Ellis Coates. Chuinard: Rebound. Contains Chuinard bookplate.

3.5 Doll, Vienna 1811 [Color plate XI]

Neue | historische und geographische | Gemählde, | oder | Charakteristiken merk-würdiger Personen | und Darstellungen wichtiger Begebenheiten | unserer Zeit; | nebst | Schilderungen | der durch neuesten Schicksale ausgezeichne- | ten, neu entdeckten oder näher untersuchten | Länder und Völker. | [rule] | Bearbeitet | von | J. B. Schütz. | [rule] | Viertes Bändchen. | [rule] | Wien, [1811.] | Im Verlage bey Anton Doll.

Description: Twelve volumes bound as six, 12mo., 18 cm. First four volumes undated; vols. 5 to 12 dated 1811. The fourth volume contains (pp. 108–121) a digest in German of Patrick Gass's *Journal*. The spellings "St. Jean" of May 25, 1804 (English text "St. John's"), "Tenton" of September 24, 1804 (English "Tinton"), and "Mandanne" of November 30, 1804 (English "Mandan") are clear indications that the digest derives from the French edition of 1810. The compiler Schütz also collaborated with the same publisher, Anton Doll of Vienna, in a twelve-volume geographical collection of 1808, under the general title *Allgemeine Erdkunde für denkende und gebildete Leser*.

Lewis & Clark College Collection: Acquired in 2000.

3.6 Carey, Philadelphia 1811

JOURNAL | OF THE | VOYAGES AND TRAVELS | OF | A CORPS OF DISCOVERY, | *Under the command of Capt. Lewis and Capt. Clarke* | *of the army of the United States*, | FROM THE MOUTH OF THE RIVER MISSOURI THROUGH | THE INTERIOR PARTS OF NORTH AMERICA | TO THE PACIFIC OCEAN, | During the Years 1804, 1805, and 1806. | CONTAINING | An authentic relation of the most interesting transactions | during the expedition; a description of the country; | and an account of its inhabitants, soil, cli- | mate, curiosities, and vegetable | and animal productions. | [rule] | BY PATRICK GASS, | *One of the persons employed in the expedition.* | [rule] | WITH GEOGRAPHICAL AND EXPLANATORY NOTES. | [rule] | THIRD EDITION– WITH SIX ENGRAVINGS. | [rule] | [Copy-right secured according to Law.] | [rule] | PRINTED FOR MATHEW CAREY, | NO. 122 MARKET STREET, | PHILADELPHIA. | [rule] | 1811.

Collation: Same as 1810, apart from changes of edition and date on title page.

Plates: Identical in number, titles, and placing to 1810 edition.

References: Coues, cxxi–cxxii; Graff, 1520; Paltsits, lxxiii–iv; Wagner-Camp-Becker, 6:6.

Description: A close copy of 1810, apparently reset throughout, but with possible use of standing type in some later pages.

Lewis & Clark College Collection: Wendlick: Original leather. Ownership inscription of Joseph Pinney.

3.7 Carey, Philadelphia 1812 [Color plate XII]

JOURNAL | OF THE | VOYAGES AND TRAVELS | OF | A CORPS OF DISCOVERY, | *Under the command of Capt. Lewis and Capt. Clarke* | *of the army of the United States,* | FROM THE MOUTH OF THE RIVER MISSOURI THROUGH THE | INTERIOR PARTS OF NORTH AMERICA TO | THE PACIFIC OCEAN, | During the Years 1804, 1805, and 1806. | CONTAINING | An authentic relation of the most interesting transactions during the expedi- | tion; a description of the country; and an account of its inhabitants, | soil, climate, curiosities, and vegetable and animal productions. | [rule] | *BY PATRICK GASS,* | One of the persons employed in the expedition. | [rule] | WITH GEOGRAPHICAL AND EXPLANATORY NOTES. | [rule] | FOURTH EDITION–WITH SIX ENGRAVINGS. | [rule] | [Copy-right secured according to Law.] | [rule] | PRINTED FOR MATHEW CAREY, | NO. 122, MARKET-STREET, | PHILADELPHIA. | [dotted rule] | 1812.

Collation: Same as 1810 and 1811, apart from changes of edition and date on title page, a folding map (in some copies) facing the title page, and a double-sided leaf of reviews, signed A, substituting for the original half title.

Plates: As in 1810 and 1811. The unsigned map, titled "Louisiana," is apparently a remainder sheet from the 1805 *Carey's American Pocket Atlas* (Wheat, 2:13f.).

References: Graff, 1521; Paltsits, lxxiv; Wagner-Camp-Becker, 6:7.

Description: As with 1811, a close reprint of 1810, but showing evidence of further resetting in the early pages but apparent use of standing type (from 1811) in later signatures.

Notices: The two-sided leaf of reviews collects extensive quotations from the *Eclectic Review,* the *Record of Literature, The Monthly Anthology, And Boston Review* for June 1809, the New York *Medical Repository,* Aiken's *Annual Review,* vol. 7, and *The Quarterly Review* for May 1809. The full text of the *Quarterly Review* notice is available in the original at the Lewis & Clark College Collection (see 3.2).

Lewis & Clark College Collection: Chuinard 1: Three-quarter leather rebind, with review leaf bound in at the end. Lacks map. Ownership inscription of J[o]hn Peale Atkinson. Chuinard 2: Full original leather, re-backed. Contains map. Review leaf bound into front. Inscription: "Eunis and." Wendlick: Full leather rebound by Brentano Bros. Contains map. Two sets of preliminaries (sig. A) bound in, the second set correct (with review leaf substituted for half title) and the first set in some disorder. The frontispiece has been transferred to 220, following the incorrect instructions on the plate.

3.8 Landes-Industrie-Comptoirs, Weimar 1814, 1815

Tagebuch | einer | Entdeckungs-Reise | durch | Nord-America, | von | der Mündung des Missuri an bis zum Einfluss der | Columbia in den stillen Ocean, | gemacht | in den Jahren 1804, 1805 und 1806, | auf | Befehl der Regierung der Vereinigten Staaten, | von | den beiden Capitäns Lewis und Clarke. | [rule] | Uebersetzt | von | Ph. Ch. Weyland. | [rule] | Mit einer Charte. | [rule] | Weimar, | im Verlage des H. S. privil. Landes-Industrie-Comptoirs. | 1814.

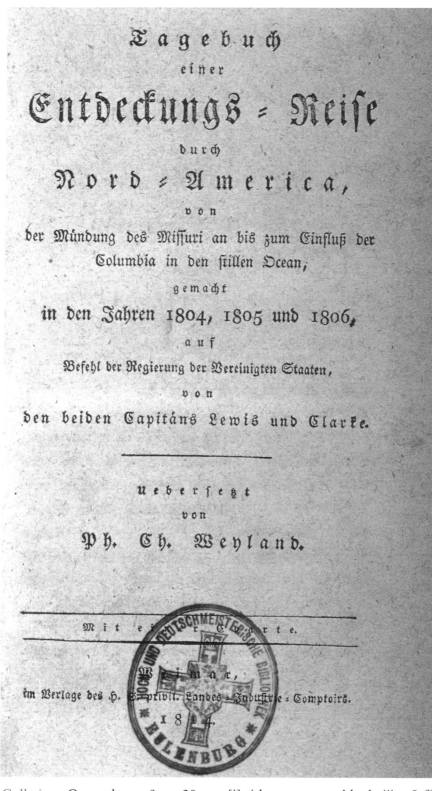

Collation: One volume, 8vo., 20 cm. [i] title page, verso blank; iii–v Jefferson's
January 18, 1803, Message to Congress; vi–viii German translator's introduction,
identifying the narrator as "Sir Patrick Gass"; ix–x contents; [1]–345 half title;
[blank]; Gass's Journal; [346]–352 Clark's letter to Harrison from Fort Mandan;
[353]–362 Clark's letter to his brother from St. Louis; folding map.

References: Coues, cxxvii; Paltsits, lxxiv–lxxv; Wagner-Camp-Becker, 6:8.

Description: A full translation of the Paris edition of 1810, by Philipp Christoph Weyland. The (unsigned) map is re-engraved from the J. B. Tardieu map in the 1810 Paris edition, following it closely, retaining its French captions and identical title in cartouche: "Carte Pour Servir au Voyage des Cap.es Lewis et Clarke, à l'Océan Pacifique."

This 1814 text is reprinted in 1815, apparently from the same type, as the first part of a volume entitled *Neue Bibliothek der wichtigsten Reisebeschreibungen zur Erweiterung der Erd- und Völkerkunde*, a new library of geographical and anthropological studies, edited by Dr. F. J. Bertuch, and published by the same Weimar publishing house, this volume being the second in the series. The other item in the volume prints Jacob Morier's 1808–1809 travels in Persia and Asia Minor, paginated [i]–vi, [1]–210, followed by a map of Asia Minor. Collation of the *Tagebuch* text as above, except that a series title page replaces that of 1814, with a summary of the volume contents on verso. The 1814 title page is bound in opposite that of 1815.

A further omnibus volume in the special collections at the University of Washington, Seattle, contains both of the above items, followed by Morier's second travels in Persia, 1810–1816, appearing in 1820 (again as vol. 2 of Bertuch's *Neue Bibliothek*) from the same publishing house. This collates (with separate pagination) as [i]–x, [1]–454. It seems likely that the Lewis and Clark translation was first issued separately in 1814, then in gradually enlarged omnibus editions in 1815 and 1820. The translator, Philipp Christoph Weyland (1765–1843) of Weimar, translated a number of volumes for the same Weimar publishing house. The compiler, Friedrich Justin Bertuch (1747–1822), was also of Weimar.

Lewis & Clark College Collection: Wendlick 1814: Half leather, with gilt on spine, marbled boards; Eulenberg bookplate. Wendlick 1815: Second edition, published with Jacob Morier's travels. Green half leather with marbled boards and series label on spine. Marbled endpapers. Ownership label of Johann Baptist Zitz of Mainz, died 1829. English translations of 1815 title page and German translator's preface laid in.

3.9 Ells, Claflin, & Co., Dayton 1847

LEWIS AND CLARKE'S | JOURNAL | TO THE | ROCKY MOUNTAINS | In the years 1804,-5,-6; | AS RELATED BY | PATRICK GASS, | ONE OF THE OFFICERS IN THE EXPEDITION. | [rule] | New Edition with Numerous Engravings. | [rule] | DAYTON, | PUBLISHED BY ELLS, CLAFLIN, & CO. | 1847. [rule]

Collation: One volume, 12mo., 19 cm. Frontispiece on verso of [i]; [blank]; [iii] title page, backed with copyright notice and start of preface; v–viii remainder of preface; [blank]; portraits of Lewis and Clark (x and xi); [blank]; [13]–238 text; one leaf of advertisements.

Plates: Frontispiece "The Beaver Dam" [1840: "A Beaver Dam"] signed "Grosvenor"; [10] "Captain Lewis"; [11] "Captain Clarke"; [23] "Water-which-cries or the weeping stream"; [27] untitled plate of apparent koala bear; 40 untitled plate of waterfall [1840, "Falls"]; [47] untitled plate of an Indian [1840, "Indian Hunter"]; [51] untitled Indian dwellings and canoe [1840, "Indian Canoe and Fishing Lodge"]; [62] untitled plate of Indians hunting buffalo [1840, "Indian Amusements"]; [79] untitled plate of river rapids [1840, "Rappids"]; [91] untitled plate of man chased by bear [1840, "Escape from a Bear"]; [98] "Lion and Buffalo Fight"; [117] untitled plate, the White Cliffs of the Missouri [1840, "White Cliffs"]; [131] untitled plate, two dogs, three horses, and six people [1840, "Prairie on Fire"]; [151] "Moon Light on the Western Waters" [1840, same title]; 173 untitled plate, fashioning a canoe, signed "Grosvenor" [1840, "A Kinstenaux Indian"]; [196] "Burning a Prisoner–See Note" [1840, "Burning a Prisoner"].

References: Graff, 1522; Paltsits, lxxv; Wagner-Camp-Becker, 6:9.

Description: New edition with numerous engravings. In many cases, these are recycled out of the 1840 surreptitious item from the same publishers. (See 4c.4.) The engraver, Grosvenor, has not been securely identified, but the memoirs of stone engraver Watson Stewart describe a young Troy, Ohio, stone-dresser in 1847, C. H. Grosvenor, who might conceivably have been an apprentice wood engraver in nearby Dayton six years earlier. This C. H. Grosvenor went on to a command in the Ohio militia in the Civil War.

Lewis & Clark College Collection: Wendlick: Original cloth. Inscription of Joseph Kinney Hudson, Ohio, 1868. Tweney 1: Early leather, re-backed. Inscription of J. C. W. Seymour. Tweney 2: Early leather, re-backed. Inscribed sheet laid in, dated 1850. Chuinard: Rebound in canvas with leather spine title. Inscription of W. F. Burrell.

3.10 Request for Compensation
3.10(a) 32nd Congress, 1st Session. House Report No. 56. Patrick Gass.
To accompany H.R. No. 152. January 29, 1852.
Document: "The Committee on Private Land Claims, to whom was referred the petition of Patrick Gass, report: That the petitioner asks an appropriation of three hundred and twenty acres of land, to be located by him anywhere on the public domain of the United States, where the same could be located by anyone entitled to bounty land."

Description: The petition briefly summarizes Gass's career, with a comment on his journal: "He was appointed sergeant by Lewis and Clark, and kept a daily journal of the transactions of the corps of exploration, and a full and homely, yet graphic description of the country through which they passed. This journal spoke with its native and forcible simplicity to the people of the west, long before the voluminous and expensive work of Lewis and Clark was published, and it con-tributed much to the feeling and the fact that made Oregon a part of the country." Gass received 320 acres in 1807 with the other expedition members, 160 acres for services in the War of 1812, and an additional 320 acres as result of this further petition in 1854 (Jackson, *Letters*, item 411; Moulton, 10:xviii). Earle R. Forrest suggests, in his memoir of 1850, that at least part of the land was lost through non-payment of taxes.

Lewis & Clark College Collection: Photocopy of House document, among the Chuinard papers.

**3.10(b) 33rd Congress, 1st Session. House Report No. 215. Patrick Gass.
To accompany H.R. No. 419. June 23, 1854.**

Document: "That the petitioner asks an appropriation of 320 acres of land. . . .
This is the amount of land granted by government to the actual settlers in
Oregon, and the petitioner predicates the equity of his claim to this bounty on
the just and reasonable ground that he was one of the original explorators of
that distant country; that his bravery, zeal and devotion aided materially in the
discovery of the Oregon river and its principal tributaries, under Lewis and Clark."

Description: The congressional decision granting Patrick Gass's claim for
compensation.

Lewis & Clark College Collection: Photocopies of House documents, with record
of the bill's Senate and House enactment on August 4, 1854. Also available in
the Lewis & Clark College Collection are copies of minutes of debates relating to
this bill, as reported in the *Congressional Globe* for 1854, vol. 28, parts 2 (p. 1495)
and 3 (pp. 1867–8, 1888, 1912, 1928, 1984, 2135, 2205–6, 2208).

3.11 *The Life and Times of Patrick Gass*, 1859
THE | LIFE AND TIMES | OF | PATRICK GASS, | NOW SOLE SURVIVOR | OF
THE OVERLAND EXPEDITION TO THE PACIFIC, | UNDER LEWIS AND CLARK,
IN 1804-5-6; | ALSO, | A SOLDIER IN THE WAR WITH GREAT BRITAIN, FROM |
1812 TO 1815, AND A PARTICIPANT IN THE | BATTLE OF LUNDY'S LANE. |
TOGETHER WITH | GASS' JOURNAL OF THE EXPEDITION CONDENSED;
| –AND– | SKETCHES OF SOME EVENTS OCCURRING DURING THE | LAST
CENTURY IN THE UPPER OHIO COUNTRY, | BIOGRAPHIES, REMINISCENCES,
ETC. | [rule] | BY J. G. JACOB. | [rule] | JACOB & SMITH, | PUBLISHERS AND
PRINTERS, WELLSBURG, VA. | 1859.

Collation: One volume, 12mo., 18.5 cm. Frontispiece: portrait engraving of
Patrick Gass; title page, backed by copyright page; [iii]–v preface; [vi]–vii, table
of contents; [9]–280 text.

Plates: Frontispiece, portrait wood engraving of Patrick Gass, "From an
Ambrotype by E. F. Moore, Wellsburg [W. Virginia]"; facing 59 "Mandan
Indians"; facing 108 "Big White-Ball Costume"; facing 248 "Going to Church in
Old Times".

References: Coues, cxxiii; Graff, 2183; Paltsits, lxxvi; Wagner-Camp-Becker, 6:10.

Description: Preface dated January 1859. The text covers the life of Patrick Gass,
by 1859 the last surviving member of the Corps of Discovery, as told to J. G.
Jacob. The edition was reprinted in 2000 by Lone Wolf Press.

Lewis & Clark College Collection: Chuinard: Original (rust) binding, loose front
hinge, ex-library. Tweney 1: Original (green) binding. Owner's inscription of
R. M. Haney. Tweney 2: Original (rust) binding. Two inscriptions of Joseph E. Glass
of Wellsburg, West Virginia, December 20, 1874, on back end papers. Wendlick:
Original (dark brown) binding, inscribed by publisher to John R. Doneher,
April 21, 1859.

It appears from the copies in the Lewis & Clark College Collection that *The Life and Times of Patrick Gass* was bound in various cloth bindings at the time of publication. All three colors (brown, rust, and green) of cloth used have the identical blind stamping to the covers. The publisher's presentation copy was dark brown with gilt titling.

3.12 Hosmer, Chicago 1904

GASS'S JOURNAL | OF THE | LEWIS AND CLARK EXPEDITION | By Sergeant Patrick Gass | ONE OF THE PERSONS EMPLOYED IN THE EXPEDITION | Reprinted from the edition of 1811, with facsimiles of the original | title-page and the five original illustrations, a repro- | duction of a rare portrait of Gass, and | a map of the Lewis and | Clark route. | With an analytical Index, and an Introduction | By James Kendall Hosmer, LL.D., | Author of "The Story of the Louisiana Purchase," etc. | [rule] | CHICAGO | A. C. McCLURG & CO. | 1904

Collation: One volume, 4to., 25 cm. (large paper), 21.5 cm. (trade). [i] half title, with limitation page verso (large paper) and advertisement verso (trade); unnumbered portrait frontispiece, facing title [iii], with copyright page verso; [v] facsimile of 1811 Carey title page, with M'Keehan 1807 copyright verso; [vii]–viii publisher's note; [ix] contents; [blank]; [xi] list of illustrations; [blank]; [xiii]–xvi introduction; [xlvii]–liii preface to first edition; [1]–288 text; [289]–298 index, followed by four pages of advertisements.

Plates: Frontispiece, portrait of Patrick Gass from the 1859 *Life and Times of Patrick Gass* (3.11). The six illustrations (following) derive from one of the Carey editions of 1810–1812; facing 30 "Captains Lewis & Clark holding a Council with the Indians"; facing 76 "Captain Clark & his men building a line of Huts"; facing 120 "Captain Clark and his men shooting Bears"; facing 164 "A Canoe Striking on a Tree"; facing 208 "An American having struck a Bear but not killed him, escapes into a Tree"; facing 250 "Captain Lewis shooting an Indian."

References: Paltsits, lxxvi; Wagner-Camp-Becker, 6:10, note.

Description: An edition closely following the M'Keehan text of 1807, in its Carey reprint with illustrations, and reproducing the title and copyright pages of the 1811 Carey. The edition was issued in two states, copyrighted September 15, 1904: an unlimited trade edition, top edge gilt, and in large paper, limited to seventy-five copies.

Lewis & Clark College Collection: Trade Edition: Chuinard: Original condition, with Chuinard bookplate. Bought from Wright Howes, January 1959. Tweney: Original condition, rubbed boards. Wendlick: Original condition; Paul Steinbrecher bookplate.

Large-Paper Edition: Chuinard: Rebound in green buckram, all edges gilt; no. 13 of 75. Tweney: Original condition, untrimmed; no. 16 of 75. Wendlick: Original condition, untrimmed; Bartlett bookplate; no. 43 of 75.

Chapter Four
Taking Literary License: Surreptitious and Apocryphal Publications

Essay 121
Bibliography 133

4a Hubbard Lester
4a.1 Lester, Philadelphia 1809
4a.2 Longman, London 1809
4a.3 Reclam, Leipzig 1811

4b German-American Digest Versions
4b.1 Stöver, Libanon [Lebanon], Pennsylvania 1811
4b.2 Bärtgis, Friedrichstadt [Frederick], Maryland 1812

4c William Fisher
4c.1 Sharan, Philadelphia 1812
4c.2 Miltenberger, Baltimore 1812
4c.3 Mauro, Baltimore 1813
4c.4 Ells, Dayton 1840

4d George Phillips, *Travels in North America*
4d.1 Bentham, Dublin 1822
4d.2 Smith, Dublin 1824
4d.3 Rivington, London 1831
4d.4 SPCK, London 1846

Taking Literary License: Surreptitious and Apocryphal Narratives

Intense public interest inspired publication of a unique genre of alleged accounts of the Lewis and Clark Expedition.

The dearth of information on the adventures of the Corps of Discovery spawned a remarkable literature: the creation of seemingly authentic, but not quite honest, accounts of the travels of Lewis and Clark. These works–which began to appear in 1809–all contained elements of accuracy, but their compilers pillaged and pasted. They seldom gave credit to their sources of information and they presented data about Indian tribes and experiences totally unrelated to the adventures of the Corps of Discovery. All of these works were founded on truthful accounts, except the apocryphal narrative of George Phillips. Phillips's *Travels in North America* (1822) was in a class of its own for the license it took in fabricating a travel tale around a core of factual data.

The motives of the surreptitious and apocryphal account writers were surely pecuniary. The consequences for the reading public were interesting reading but also confusion and misinformation. Scholars and book collectors have reacted to these narratives with both outrage and fascination. In *A History of the Lewis and Clark Journals*, Paul Cutright denounced these works: "each a dark and uncomely smudge on the well-favored countenance of the fourth estate."[1] Elliott Coues, editor of the Biddle-Allen edition of the journals, was more vehement. He condemned each of them as a "notable literary forgery." Referring to the plagiarism of Jonathan Carver's *Travels* to construct the fictitious accounts, he concluded: "This miserable trick, by which Carver was robbed and ethnology travestied, has misled every bibliographer."[2]

The primary sources used to create these narratives are easily identifiable. First was the *Message from the President*, used to impart governmental endorsement and authenticity. Dated February 19, 1806, Thomas Jefferson's report informed Congress of the first leg of the expedition. It included information about the travels from Camp Dubois on Wood River to Fort Mandan, the winter passed on the plains of North Dakota, and the tribes living along the Missouri River. Jefferson included Meriwether Lewis's letter of April 7, 1805, from Fort Mandan, and Lewis and Clark's "A Statistical View," a table providing several categories of data on the tribes of the Missouri watershed. Another part of Jefferson's communication to Congress was data on the tribes of Louisiana south of the Arkansas River, and conditions and distances covered along the Red River by John Sibley. Jefferson also included observations by William C. Dunbar and George Hunter during their explorations of the Red and Washita Rivers.[3] The president had also dispatched Sibley, Dunbar, and Hunter to gain information on the Louisiana Purchase.

A second source was a letter penned by William Clark at St. Louis on September 23, 1806, reporting his return from the Pacific coast. The letter was copied in contemporary newspapers.[4] Jonathan Carver's *Travels Through the Interior Parts of North America in the Years 1766, 1767, and 1768* (1778) was a third source. Carver (1710–1780) had explored the upper Mississippi watershed and Lake

"And then came the counterfeit editions, or Apocrypha, at least eight or nine of them. One by one, over a period covering almost half a century, they appeared."

Paul Cutright, *A History of the Lewis and Clark Journals* (1976)

1   Cutright, *A History*, 33.

2   Coues, *History*, 1:cxii.

3   The various documents forwarded to Congress in February 1806 were published as *Message from the President of the United States Communicating Discoveries Made in Exploring the Missouri, Red River and Washita* . . . and were printed in Washington, D.C.; Natchez, New York; and London (1806–07). A potential pillager of specific information about portions of Louisiana Territory thus had useful information at hand by the spring of 1806.

4   Jackson, *Letters*, 1:325–330.

Superior. Thwarted in his efforts to find the "Western Ocean" by hostilities between the Sioux and Chippewa tribes, he went to London to write his book and seek compensation for his labors. His narrative described nearly five thousand miles of travels and numerous tribes; it provided useful but irrelevant information about the route followed by Lewis and Clark. The fourth source, also an authentic narrative, even if far to the north of Lewis and Clark's journey, was Alexander Mackenzie's *Voyages From Montreal* (1801). A fifth source, available by July 1807 was the journal of Patrick Gass. Even though this account provided detailed information of explorations west from Fort Mandan, very little from Gass appeared in the surreptitious narratives published between 1809 and 1813.

In 1809, Hubbard Lester of Philadelphia published *The Travels of Capts. Lewis & Clarke, by Order of the Government of the United States, Performed in the Years 1804, 1805 & 1806 . . .* , a work of nearly three hundred pages selling at $1.62 1/2. The full, rambling title claimed that the work contained accounts of the Indian tribes "who inhabit the Western part of the Continent"; Lewis and Clark's "A Statistical View"; a "Map of the Country inhabited by the Western tribes of Indians"; and five engraved portraits of tribal chiefs. The volume's introduction invoked the explorations of Captain James Cook and Alexander Mackenzie but was filled with verbosity sufficient to turn away most discerning readers. "It cannot fail of giving pleasure to the Philanthropic mind," wrote the essayist:

> to behold implements of agriculture put in the hands of the uncivilized Barbarian, to provide and protect him from the precarious reliance on the chase for a scanty sustenance. The time is not far distant, in all moral probability, when the uncultivated wildes of the interior part of the Continent, which is now only inhabited by the tawney sons of the Forest, and the howling beasts of prey, will be exchanged for the hard votaries of agriculture, who will turn those steril[e] wildernesses into rich cultivated and verdant fields.[5]

To try to give this account utility, the compiler included a "Statement of the Commerce of the Missouri"; a brief roster of fur-bearing animals by numbers of skins and values; and "An Estimate of the Produce of the Several Mines," implying that fabulous mineral wealth was abundant, even though the statistics documented only the production of lead. The eight-page vocabulary of the Knisteneaux, or Cree, was simply appropriated from Mackenzie. The greatest incongruities of the volume were the irrelevant inclusions of William Buchan's "History of Master Edward," and "Anecdotes," a brief passage about George Washington. These last pages were simply filler and had nothing to do with the expedition. The five plates were wholly fanciful and absurd, but the map showed at least some use of the Gass *Journal*, for it named the Jefferson, Madison, and Gallatin Rivers and gave an approximate location for the "Snake Indians."[6]

Who was Hubbard Lester? There was an American by this name, the son of Elihu and Nancy Lester, born October 5, 1790, at Alford, Massachusetts.[7] Nothing beyond name connects a nineteen-year-old from Massachusetts with *The Travels of Capts. Lewis & Clarke*. City directories and 1800 and 1810 decennial census schedules for Philadelphia list no one named Hubbard Lester. It is probable that "Hubbard Lester" was a pseudonym. Whoever this publisher was, he was clever. The "Recommendation of the President" in this volume appeared to be Thomas Jefferson's endorsement, though it was nothing of the kind. It was merely a subterfuge to entice purchasers. Biologist and historian Paul Cutright, who found

5 Lester, *The Travels*, vii.

6 Ibid.

7 The genealogical trace of Hubbard Lester is found at www.familysearch.org. Viewed August 1, 2001.

nothing redeeming in this work, saved his greatest spleen, however, for "Travels to the Pacifick Ocean," that part of the book whereof he wrote "we find the false heart, lungs, and other visceral parts of this shoddy composite. It constitutes 140 of the total of 300 pages, and is the portion which the compiler leans on most heavily to justify his title . . . ." [8]

The hunger for information on the expedition sometimes superseded editorial judgment. In 1809, the venerable publisher Longman, Hurst, Rees, and Orme printed a British edition of *The Travels of Capts. Lewis & Clarke*. The volume had no plates or irrelevant "Anecdotes," but included the "Map of the Country Inhabited by the Western Tribes of Indians." The edition showed a nodding acquaintance with the Gass *Journal*, for it explained that the expedition's horses were left with the Indians during the descent of the Columbia and, when the cache near Canoe Camp on the Clearwater River was disinterred by floodwaters, the Nez Perce had saved its contents and turned them over on the return of the explorers. A note on p. 63 referenced another source, William Hubbard's *A Narrative of the Indian Wars in New-England . . .* (1775). The London edition, printed by C. Stower of Paternoster Row, London, was, for the most part, a reprint of Lester's volume. It included a section on the Knisteneaux (Cree) language taken from Mackenzie but dropped the Algonquin word list from that table. [9]

Interest in Louisiana Territory and the Lewis and Clark Expedition was not confined to speakers and readers of English in the United States. During the eighteenth century, German-speaking Protestants had poured into Pennsylvania, Maryland, Delaware, and Virginia. Many had fled the sectarian conflicts between Lutherans and Catholics in the Rhineland. Others were driven by an eagerness to obtain affordable and sizable tracts of land for themselves and their children. Some were members of German sects and established Amish, Schwenkfelder, Mennonite, Moravian, Dunker, and other pietist communities. An active German-language press developed in the wake of this immigration. Publishers issued newspapers, hymnals, religious tracts, testaments, schoolbooks, and works of history and travel for German readers in the United States. [10]

Lebanon, Pennsylvania, emerged as an important community for German publications. [11] In 1799, Jacob Schnee began publishing in the village by issuing a small volume on fruit culture. In 1809, Schnee published a biography of Georges de Benneville, a French champion of the Reformation who had settled in Berks County in 1745. In 1807, Schnee founded the *Freimuthige Libanoner* [*Candid Libanoner*], a newspaper purchased in 1809 by Jacob Stöver and renamed *Der Libanoner-Morgenstern* [*Lebanon Morning Star*]. The grandson of Rev. John Casper Stöver, a Lutheran clergyman, Stöver in 1811 printed and sold a German version, *Die Reisen der Capitaine Lewis und Clarke; unternommen auf Befehl der Regierung der Vereinigten Staaten in den Jahren 1804, 1805 und 1806 . . . [The Travels of Captains Lewis and Clarke; Undertaken by the Order of the Government of the United States in the Years 1804, 1805 and 1806]*. [12] Stöver (1787–1862) was a prominent citizen of the Lebanon Valley. He published the newspaper from 1809 to 1837, served from 1830 to 1834 in the Pennsylvania legislature, and at the time of publishing *Die Reisen* was actively engaged in producing job press books and pamphlets. [13]

A stitched pamphlet of sixty pages, Stöver's volume contained four fanciful portraits of Indians, each image reversed from those in Hubbard Lester's pamphlet. Stöver reduced Jefferson's letter to Congress to a single paragraph but

8   Cutright, *A History*, 34–35.

9   *The Travels of Capts. Lewis & Clarke* (London: 1809).

10 Cazden, *A Social History*, 8.

11 This community was known as Steitze and as Libanon in the eighteenth and early nineteenth centuries. Martin Luther had used the term Libanon in his German Bible (Miller, "The German Newspapers," 1910:137).

12 Croll, "Lebanon County Imprints," 4, 6, 8, 25; Shenk, *A History*, 1:68; Miller, "The German Newspapers," 137, 147.

13 Bierman, "Lebanon County," 366; Croll, "Lebanon County Imprints," 4, 6.

reproduced the full "Recommendation." The "Statistical View" was heavily abridged, abbreviating some entries and dropping others. The essay, "Ueber den Ursprung der Indianer"[Origin of the Population of the Indians] was, as in the case of Hubbard Lester's volume, lifted from Jonathan Carver's *Travels* (1778). Even though the edition was shorter than Lester's original, it included the incongruous appendix "Anecdote" about George Washington.[14]

In 1811, Carl Heinrich Reclam, a publisher in Leipzig, included an abridgement of the surreptitious narrative as part six, *Resultate der Reise der Capitäne Lewis und Clarke ben Missouri Entlang bis zur Sud-See [Outcome of the Travel of Captain Lewis and Clark to the Missouri Along to the South Sea]*, pp. 169–230, in *Allgemeines historisches Archiv [General Historical Archive]*. The volumes were edited by Hans Karl Dippold and Friedrich August Koethe. Professor Johann Severin Vater (1771–1826) of Konigsberg (Kaliningrad, Russia), made the cuts and provided brief annotations. Vater was co-editor with Friedrich Justin Bertuch (1747–1822) of the *Allgemeines Archiv für Ethnographie und Linguistik [General Archive for Ethnography and Linguistics]* (1808), author of several works of religious history, and author of *Untersuchugnen Über Americka's Bevölkerung aus dem Alten Kontinente dem Herrn Kammerherrn Alexander von Humboldt [Investigations Concerning America's Inhabitants from the Old Continent by the Gentleman Alexander von Humboldt]* (1810).[15]

This surreptitious work omitted the letter of President Jefferson, Lewis's letter from Fort Mandan, and considerable other information. The volume copied portions of Jefferson's *Message from the President* as printed in Philadelphia (1809) and London (1809). Confirmation of the use of the 1809 editions appears in citing "Rakansas River" rather than "Arkansa River," as in the *Message from the President* printed in Washington, D.C. (1806), Natchez (1806), New York (1806), and London (1807). Unlike the surreptitious works printed in Philadelphia, London, and Lebanon, the Leipzig narrative included annotations from Antoine Le Page du Pratz's *Histoire de la Louisiane* (1758) and the *Bibliotheque Americaine* (1807).[16]

The name Reclam has remained familiar for two centuries in European book publishing. Karl Heinrich Reclam, not to be confused with the nineteenth-century physician and author of the same name, was a book dealer and publisher in Leipzig. Starting in about 1800, he published numerous medical and natural history volumes. His son, Anton Philipp Reclam, born in 1807, became a publishing magnate in the 1840s. Reclam's "Universal Library" made available the works of great thinkers at modest prices. With that success, he expanded his publishing into popular literature and established a firm that printed low-priced books through the twentieth century.[17]

The *Allgemeines historisches Archiv* was edited by Hans Karl Dippold (d. 1811), professor of history at the University of Danzig, and Friedrich August Koethe, professor of philosophy at the University of Jena. A theologian, Koethe (1781–1850) had studied in Leipzig, took his advanced degree in Jena, taught until 1819, and then held church positions and worked as a writer of theology and educational materials. Dippold was the author of *Skizzen der Allgemeinen Geschichte [Sketches of General History]* (1811) and the translator of William Coxe's *History of the House of Austria* (1810).[18] The inclusion of the surreptitious narrative about the Lewis and Clark Expedition was presumably done by accident, not solely to make money. Other selections in the *Allgemeines historisches Archiv* included reputable histories of such subjects as the Roman occupation of the Rhine and the history of King Karl V with the Protestants.

14 *Die Reisen der Capitaine Lewis und Clarke.*

15 World Catalog lists Vater's extensive publications. His volume, *Untersuchungen Über Americka's Bevölkerung . . .* was in the library of Thomas Jefferson; a surviving copy bears Jefferson's initials. Bertuch included selections from the Gass *Journal* in *Neue Bibliothek der der Wichtigtsten* (Weimar 1815).

16 *Resultate der Reise.*

17 *Allgemeine Deutsche Biographie*, 53:246; Fischer, "Philipp Reclam, Jun.," *Lexikon*, 6:203–204.

18 Wesseling, "Friedrich August Koethe," *Biographisch-Bibliographisches Kirchenlexikon*, 4:298–299; "Hans Karl Dippold," World Catalog.

In 1812, the surreptitious account appeared again in German, published by Matthias Bärtgis of Friedrichstadt (Fredericktown), Maryland. The title, *Die Reisen der Capitaine Lewis und Clarke; unternommen auf Befehl der Regierung der Vereinigten Staaten in den Jahren 1804, 1805 und 1806 . . .* [*The Travels of Captains Lewis and Clarke; undertaken by the Order of the Government of the United States in the Years 1804, 1805 und 1806 . . .*] was identical to the pamphlet published by Jacob Stöver, and further confirmed a strong interest in the exploration of the western portions of North America among German-speaking Americans. Like Stöver, Bärtgis was a printer, newspaper publisher, and an active figure in the German-American community. He was born in 1750, the son of Michael and Catherine (Echterenach) Bärtgis of Lancaster, Pennsylvania. As a young man, Bärtgis wanted to learn the printing craft. He secured an apprenticeship with William Bradford, the well-known Philadelphia printer and father of Samuel Fisher Bradford, who published the Biddle-Allen edition of the journals in 1814. According to family tradition, Bärtgis served in the early phases of the Revolutionary War as a soldier in the battle at Germantown.[19]

Bärtgis began his trade in Lancaster, where he resided from 1776 to 1781. In approximately 1779, he established a press in Fredericktown where, in 1784, he published a popular handbook of family veterinary medicine, *Der Erfahrene americanische Haus-und-Stall Arzt* [*The Experienced American House and Stable Doctor*]. He also initiated that year a new line of almanacs, *Der Verbesserte Hoch-Deutche Americanische Land und Staats Calendar für 1785* [*The Improved High German American Nation and States Calendar for 1785*]. The following year, 1786, Bärtgis founded two newspapers—the *Maryland Chronicle* and *Bärtgis's Marylandiche Zeitung*. Although his newspapers had broken runs and changes in name, Bärtgis remained an active publisher, alone and with partners, until 1820. His longest-running newspaper was *Bärtgis's Republican Gazette*, 1800–24, a publication continued for a time by his son, Mathias E. Bärtgis.[20] Described as a good printer but "not a brilliant writer," Bärtgis knew German, English, French, and Latin. He owned and operated a paper mill on the Tuscarora River, where he resided at his death in 1825. Bärtgis also ran an active job press and published more than two dozen volumes during his career, including several almanacs, a "pocket companion" of legal advice, schoolbooks, *The History of the American Revolution in Scripture Style* (1823) by Richard Snowden, and the solitary pamphlet on Lewis and Clark's travels.[21]

Another surreptitious account, allegedly written by William Fisher, Esquire, was published by James Sharan and printed in Philadelphia by James Maxwell in 1812. It sold for $1.25. The title, *New Travels Among the Indians of North America; Being a Compilation, Taken Partly from the Communications Already Published, of Captains Lewis and Clark . . .* , admitted that the book was a compilation and was "taken partly from other authors." The contents included the one paragraph "Recommendation" of Thomas Jefferson and an "Introduction" that was a paraphrase of that in the surreptitious volumes published in 1809 in Philadelphia and London. Fisher wrote with the same gratuitous but hollow language of Hubbard Lester: "The advantages, that arise from the discoveries of unknown regions, are too numerous to be mentioned," he noted. "They arise one after another in continual succession. Geography, Civilization, Humanity, and the Arts and Sciences, received aid from them."[22] The *New Travels* included Clark's letter from Fort Mandan of April 2, 1805; Clark's letter

19 Wheeler, *The Maryland Press*, 57–59.

20 Brigham, *History and Bibliography*, 258–260; McMurtrie, *A History of Printing*, 2:129–130.

21 Scharf, *History of Western Maryland*, 1:528.

22 Fisher, *New Travels*, ii–xi.

"The first press or printing-office brought to Frederick County was introduced by Matthias Bartgis, of Philadelphia, and opened by him in North Market Street, Frederick Town."

J. Thomas Scharf, *History of Western Maryland* (1882)

"Whereas the compiler, editor, thief or whatever he may have been, of the London and Philadelphia editions of 1809, retired behind an anonym, William Fisher not only stole his productions bodily . . . but also formally announced himself as the author of the same."

Elliott Coues, *History of the Expedition* (1893)

from St. Louis of September 23, 1806; data on the tribes that was identified as taken from the pen of Alexander Mackenzie; the "Statistical View"; and the irrelevant fillers about Master Neddy and George Washington. The volume was little more than a reprint of the book of Hubbard Lester with a new author and a more honest title.[23]

Who was William Fisher? Pennsylvania records raise several prospects: William Fisher (1773–1847) of Heidelberg Township, Berks County; William Fisher (b. 1782) of Allegheny; William Fisher (b. 1776) of Rehrersburg, Berks County; William Fisher (b. 1760) of Chester; William W. Fisher, a merchant residing in 1807 at No. 33 Arch Street, Philadelphia; William Logan Fisher (1781–1862), a prominent Quaker and woolens manufacturer of Germantown; and William S. Fisher (1777–1814), a Methodist minister of Germantown.[24] Although the name is right and the dates suggest that such a man could have compiled this account, there is no reason to make a case for any of these figures. In fact, William Fisher and Hubbard Lester were probably the convenient pseudonyms of a wily publisher.

The publisher of William Fisher's volume was James Sharan. In light of Sharan's fabulous autobiography, alleged travels, and other publishing ventures, he emerges as a prospect to be William Fisher and possibly also Hubbard Lester. Sharan was born in 1762 to John Sharan, a carpenter who resided near Liverpool. Sharan claimed that as a youth of ten years old he was impressed into service as a cabin boy: "Thus was I stolen from my parents when a lad; I lost all the kindness of my friends, all the satisfactions of a settled life, left my family inconsolable agonies, and became a rambler of the world."[25]

Sharan wrote that from 1772 to 1777, he sailed frequently to North America and from Halifax to the West Indies. During a sea battle in the Revolutionary War he was hit by a falling yard and, left an invalid, was put ashore in New York City in August 1778. The following year, Sharan, age seventeen, became an apprentice wheelwright in Shippenberg, Pennsylvania. When his master died, he moved to Charleston, South Carolina, and in 1784, to Philadelphia. With no explanation about his source of capital, Sharan claimed that he began purchasing furs, which he shipped to Edinburgh and Dublin. He peddled the furs in exchange for linens he imported to the United States. Although this was a plausible enterprise, this story was buttressed more with filler than fact. Sharan wove a number of essays into his autobiography, including "England," "History of the Revolutionary War," and "Scotland." His ready appropriation of general information is quite reminiscent of the Hubbard and Fisher narratives.[26]

Sharan wrote that he made an epic western journey in 1787, exploring East Florida, visiting New Orleans, and sojourning for some time with the Choctaws. Then came an interesting admission:

> I continued my route up the Mississippi, until I arrived at the junction of the Missouri and that river–first it was my intention to have proceeded eastward, but by some unaccountable mistake, I took the wrong course and continued in it until I met with a party of hunters, who informed me of my mistake, and advised me to return home. They told me that if I persisted I should be found by the Osage Indians, from whom I should never escape. Judging it prudent to adopt their advice, I turned my face towards the United States.[27]

Having seen the lower Missouri country, Sharan told of his travels among the Indians of the Great Lakes. He inserted a chapter, "Falls of Niagara." He then

23 Fisher, *New Travels*, ii–xi.

24 *Poulson's American Daily Advertiser*, Sept. 6, 1814; *The True American Commercial Advertiser*, April 30, 1807; "William Fisher," http://www.familysearch.org. Viewed August 13, 2001.

25 Sharan, *The Adventures*, 12.

26 Ibid., 39–97.

27 Ibid., 99.

described his passage through upstate New York and New England, his travels from New York City to Pittsburgh, a sailing trip down the Ohio, and his overland journey to view the "Natural Bridge," a section in which he freely appropriated passages from Jefferson's *Notes on the State of Virginia*. Nineteen days later he was in Charleston, concluding his epic narrative with the boast that he had covered ten thousand miles "principally on foot, and alone" in twenty-two months.[28]

Had Sharan terminated his adventures at this point, they might have seemed credible. However, he was an inveterate spinner of tales and had more to tell. Sharan reported that in 1789 he headed to Guinea in West Africa with a cargo of clothing, trinkets, tobacco, and candy. He claimed he was kidnapped in North Africa by the Moors, had numerous misadventures, escaped, and in 1791 returned to New York. He used his African misfortunes to insert several pages about the lifestyle of the Moors who had imprisoned him. On another voyage, during the summer of 1791, Sharan told of his explorations of Egypt. "Only one of these two pyramids is open for inspection," he noted, "that which stands most to the northward. You enter into this building on the north-side–after which you clamber up unto a large kind of vault where there is a tomb."[29]

With no explanation about his business affairs or financing, Sharan then claimed to have sailed in 1792 to the Cape of Good Hope and on to Macao and Canton. Determined to penetrate China to view the "forbidden city" in Peking, he wrote: "I must be dressed in the Chinese fashion, my face coloured to deceive the officers, and above all that I should never speak to any person, but always appear to be dumb." After a variety of adventures in China, Sharan said he then visited St. Helena and Copenhagen, where he sold coffee and made $2,500. He visited Rome, Leghorn, and Gibraltar, returning to the United States. Sharan concluded his fantastic autobiography with the observation:

> From that period [1792] unto the present time [1808], I have been unsettled, sometimes in one part of the United States, and at another time in the opposite extremity. I have visited every part of the Union. I have watched the settlements of uncultivated wilds. I have seen the lands tenanted by the Indians transferred into the hands of American citizens–I have seen plenty and human society succeed desolation and the haunts of the wild beasts, and can now rejoice that amid so many dangers and difficulties through which I have passed, I am still blessed with seeing liberty, and prosperity reign throughout our beloved country.[30]

Sharan offered his book through subscription. He provided a long list of purchasers–including Mathias Bärtgis of Fredericktown. Sharan's autobiography is full of borrowed passages, including "The Rock Bridge," "Cape of Good Hope," "Nangan," "Great Wall of China," "St. Helena," and "Copenhagen," among others.[31] His gratuitous appropriation of information without citation and spinning of fantastic adventures appeared entirely in line with the craftsmanship of Lester and Fisher, the pseudonymous "compilers" of the surreptitious accounts.

Could James Sharan have compiled and published Hubbard Lester's *The Travels of Capts. Lewis & Clarke* (1809)? Most certainly. He lived, at least for a time, in the Philadelphia area. He published *The Adventures of James Sharan* (1808) in Baltimore. He soon published several more titles in Philadelphia: William Smyth's *The New American Clerk's Instructor* (1810); *New Travels Among the Indians of North America* (1810); John Howard's *The Family Instructor* (1813); and *John*

28 Sharan, *The Adventures*, 107–119.

29 Ibid., 121–163.

30 Ibid., 225.

31 Ibid., 118–119, 165–167, 178–185, 191–192, 203–205, 207–208.

Howard, Philanthropist (1815). He also had dealings with printers producing German-language editions. In 1810, for example, he contracted with Ambrose Henkel of New Market, Virginia, to print in English *A New and Most Elegant Oration for the Fourth of July, Not Yet Delivered*—possibly another of his essays penned under the pseudonym Pilolutheros. By dint of his entrepreneurial activities, penchant for fabricated adventures, appropriation of information, location, and connections with the German printers Bärtgis and Henkel, Sharan emerges as a top candidate to have crafted the surreptitious expedition accounts published between 1809 and 1813. As to his later life, nothing is known. Following publication of *The Polar Star, and Centre of Comfort* (1816) in New York, Sharan vanished.

Surreptitious accounts about Lewis and Clark were extremely popular in 1812. In addition to the publications in Fredericktown and Philadelphia, a third edition came from the press of Anthony Miltenberger in Baltimore, Maryland. The volume by William Fisher had obtained a new title, *An Interesting Account of the Voyages and Travels of Captains Lewis and Clark, in the Years 1804, 1805 and 1806.* Its lengthy subtitle claimed that it contained "very entertaining anecdotes, and a variety of other useful and pleasing information." Unlike publishers of other surreptitious accounts, Miltenberger provided a frontispiece and two full-page portraits: "Captains Lewis and Clark, Returned." Imagined works of an engraver, the images nevertheless appeared to give a stamp of approval to the volume.[32]

Anthony Miltenberger was a printer and stationer at 10 North Howard Street in Baltimore. The neighborhood was commercial and, to a degree, literary. In 1810, the Baltimore Circulating Library was located at 69 North Howard and from 1814 to 1816, at 63 North Howard.[33] Miltenberger had a somewhat attenuated career as a printer and publisher. His presses produced *The Little Merchants* (1811), a work of juvenile fiction; *The Holy War, Made by King Shaddai Upon Diabolus* (1812), a book of 310 pages by John Bunyan; Emanuel Swedenborg's *A Treatise Concerning Heaven and Hell* (1812); *An Interesting Account of the Voyages and Travels of Captains Lewis and Clarke* (1812); and a short-lived periodical—*The Halcyon Luminary and Theological Repository*—which appeared from January 1812 to December 1813.[34]

Yet another American surreptitious edition about the Lewis and Clark Expedition appeared in 1813. Philip Mauro reprinted a volume nearly identical to that of Anthony Miltenberger. It bore the same title: *An Interesting Account of the Voyages and Travels of Captains Lewis and Clarke . . . .* Again, it was the work of the pseudonymous William Fisher. In this publication, the plates differed from earlier printings. The frontispiece had portraits, "Captain Clark" and "Captain Lewis," identical to those in Miltenberger's edition. New illustrations included: "The Bear Pursueing His Assailant," "An Indian Destined to Death" [a scene of a man being burned alive], "St Dennie Attacking the Natchez Indians," and "A View on the Washita." As in previous editions, several pages about George Washington, the Sioux Indians, and the lamentable "Master Edward" concluded the volume.[35]

Philip Mauro dealt in real estate, groceries, and miscellany. In 1804, he worked as a music and language teacher, offering instruction in pianoforte and flute at Semme's Tavern in Georgetown. At the time of Captain Lewis's return to Washington, D.C., in December 1806, Mauro ran a grocery store selling oranges, lemons, limes, apples, candies, and candles. In 1811, he put up for sale all his household effects, his pianoforte, and eight lots on Pennsylvania Avenue within

32 Avid readers might discover, as in other printings, that "Master Edward," confined to the filler at the end of the book, "died without a groan," the victim of "improper food, tight or expensive clothing, and want of fresh air and exercise," if these things mattered in the history of western exploration. Fisher, *An Interesting Account* (Baltimore, 1812), frontispiece, 319–325.

33 Silver, *The Baltimore Book Trade*, 14, 42.

34 Miltenberger was probably the son of George Miltenberger, "gentleman," residing on Pratt Street in 1810, and of Catherine Miltenberger, a widow of the same address in 1812. *Baltimore Directory for the Year 1812 . . .*, 53; *Baltimore Directory and Register for 1814–15 . . .*, 132.

35 Fisher, *An Interesting Account*, (Baltimore, 1813).

five blocks of the "President's Mansion" to settle on North Eutaw Street in Baltimore. Two years later he was residing at 10 North Howard, the same address as that of the printing office of Anthony Miltenberger.[36]

In 1813, Mauro posted an advertisement announcing the sale of the Franklin Printing Office, Book and Stationery Store at 10 North Howard Street and the auctioning of the print shop and all books and stationery on hand. The following year, Mauro dissolved his partnership with Oliver H. Neilson & Company in Baltimore to return to Washington, D.C., where he opened an auction house. Mauro found his calling in the nation's capital, where he peddled real estate and hosted periodic auctions of furniture and other real property. In June 1829, he was elected to the Common Council of Washington, D.C., and a few months later, he and his son moved their auction rooms to new quarters. There is no trace of Mauro publishing any book other than the surreptitious volume in Baltimore in 1813.[37]

The eight surreptitious volumes published between 1809 and 1813 had in common a great deal of shared content, even when their titles differed. An entirely new and quite wonderful fabricated account of the Lewis and Clark Expedition surfaced in 1822 in Dublin. George Phillips's *Travels in North America* was in a class by itself and it secured a long shelf life and interesting reputation. Christopher Bentham, Eustace Street, Dublin, printed this work. The 1822 edition featured a woodcut of a turtle on the title page, a frontispiece of three men in a mine, and plates of no relevance whatsoever to the travels of Lewis and Clark. They included: "Inside of Hut," "Falls of Niagra," "View of Icebergs," and "Meeting of English and Esquimaux"![38] The work next appeared in Dublin in 1824, printed by Brett Smith, who had a shop on Mary Street. The volume of 180 pages retained all four plates of the 1822 edition and featured a woodcut of a walrus on the title page.[39]

This book was presented as the biography of George Phillips, a world traveler who had sojourned for a number of years in South America. During his travels, Phillips allegedly visited the fabled silver mines of Potosi, the rivers Amazon, Orinoco, and La Plata, and the "famed mountains of Cotopaxi and Chimborazo." Readers then learned that Phillips returned to Cork, Ireland, and that:

> Phillips was a religious man; his parents had imbued him with a fondness for devotion, and though some ungodly persons might be found to make light of it, the reader will not think the worse of him, and to pass a part of his time at least, in the *remote* and *imperfectly* explored parts of North America, he reflected with pain that he was voluntarily withdrawing himself from those places where Christians can offer up in a house of worship their united prayers. He resolved, however, to do all that he could to supply his loss; he brought with him a small portable copy of the Holy Scriptures, in order that he might read therein, and be warned from it of his duty, both to Him whose revealed will it contained, and to his fellow creatures, whom it commanded him to love as himself.[40]

This information was the heart and soul of the publication success of the Phillips apocrypha; it was allegedly the narrative of an evangelical Christian who had borne witness to the savages of the American West.

According to his narrative, Phillips made a second trip to the Western Hemisphere, visiting several islands in the West Indies, Veracruz, Mexico City, and New Orleans, where he reported that exports in 1817 totaled some £4 million sterling—an interesting date in light of his subsequent adventures. With a friend, Phillips

36 *National Intelligencer*, October 4, 1804; January 7, 1807; August 20, 1811.

37 Silver, *The Baltimore Book Trade*, 40, 44; *National Intelligencer*, August 13, 1812; June 3, 1829; October 9, 1829.

38 Phillips, *Travels* (Dublin, 1822).

39 Phillips, *Travels* (Dublin, 1824).

40 Ibid., 11.

then took passage on a steamboat to ascend the Mississippi, passing prosperous sugar-cane plantations and the town of Natchez, arriving fifteen days later at St. Louis. Here began his greatest adventure:

> As the expedition which Phillips had now joined, was one from which much interesting information was expected concerning the interior of the American Continent, as well as much future advantage to the inhabitants of the United States, by establishing a commerce with the native Indians for their furs, every thing was provided, as we have mentioned, which could contribute to its success; besides the leaders of the party, Captain Lewis, and Captain Clarke the other Commander, Phillips on his arrival at St. Louis, found twenty-three robust active young men, who had volunteered to accompany them, two French watermen, an Interpreter and his wife, to enable them to hold communication with the Indian tribes they might meet with in their course, a hunter, and a black servant, belonging to Captain Clarke. From these, three were appointed serjeants, and in addition, six soldiers and nine watermen, were to accompany them in order to assist in carrying the stores, and in repelling the attack of any hostile tribes of Indians.

The adventures of Phillips, as recounted in 1822 and 1824, clearly added "new" misinformation about the Lewis and Clark Expedition: a heretofore unidentified Irishman, George Phillips, had accompanied the party; and, Charbonneau and Sacagawea had joined the expedition at St. Louis, not at Fort Mandan in 1805.[41]

In his account, Phillips played an integral part in the Corps of Discovery. He found a nest of rattlers, observed black swans, saw the Northern Lights, and was in Lewis's advance patrol, which encountered the Shoshone near the Continental Divide. Unreported in any other account, he was integral to finding the site of Fort Clatsop: ". . . Phillips, by direction of the commanders, set out with five men, and after a fatiguing course at last pitched upon an eligible spot, about 200 yards from the water's edge, and 30 feet above the high tides . . . ." The chronology of these events was even more astonishing. The Lewis and Clark Expedition "arrived [at the mouth of the Columbia] on the 14th of November, 1815, and departed on the 23d of March, 1816, on their return, by the same route by which they had come out."[42] This was intriguing intelligence, for, according to the Phillips biography, the expedition had required more than a decade to cross the continent and was in the field some six years after Lewis's death on the Natchez Trace!

Also unreported in other histories of the expedition was the supposed decision by Phillips, during the return journey, to separate at Fort Mandan from the Corps of Discovery and, with a fur trader, to track easterly six hundred miles to Lake Superior. On his now solitary travels, Phillips explored the Atlantic seaboard, visiting cities from Boston to St. Augustine, before sailing to Europe and reuniting with his friends in Cork. His biographer included a bit of counsel for those considering this book:

> Let us hope that the reader does not part from Mr. Philips without regret. If he has followed him in his wanderings he must have learned at least one lesson from the perusal–We have all our allotted duties in life, and if they call into foreign lands we should not hesitate to obey, but whether we travel into Africa or America, through the burning deserts of the one or along the mighty rivers of the other, we travel but to little purpose unless we return with increased relish for home and its gratifications, and increased thankfulness to

41 Phillips, *Travels* (Dublin, 1824), 52–53.

42 Ibid., 92–94.

Providence for having placed us in a country where it must be our own fault if we do not enjoy every blessing which a mild climate, a fertile soil, and wise laws can bestow.[43]

This wonderful, irrelevant advice was founded on a fantasy linking an Irishman to the Corps of Discovery.

In spite of its egregious errors, the Phillips biography had a life of its own. It was next printed in 1831 in London by the venerable firm of C. J. G. & F. Rivington, "Booksellers to the Society for Promoting Christian Knowledge." With a "Moose Deer" on its title page, this edition preserved the original text but included a frontispiece, "Mexican Soldier," and two new plates: "Mexican Woman of Rank" and "Falls of Niagara."[44] In 1831, the publishing house of Rivington was run by Charles, John, George, and Francis Rivington, heirs to an eighteenth-century enterprise that had thrived for decades by concentrating on evangelical publishing. The firm had shops at 62 St. Paul's Churchyard and 3 Waterloo Place, Pall Mall, London. In the nineteenth century, the publishing house became notable for its acquisition and use of oriental typefaces, and for its ability to print books in 276 different languages.[45] Publication of the apocryphal Phillips biography was, presumably, solely a function of the firm's lucrative contract to print literature for the Society for Promoting Christian Knowledge. The group's publishing committee had erroneously perceived the Phillips biography as the authentic life and labors of an evangelical Christian.

A fourth printing of Phillips's *Travels in North America* was published by Richard Clay in 1846 in London. This edition excised Phillips's adventures in South America, dismissing them with the comment: "It is not necessary to mention the circumstances which induced Mr. Phillips, whose travels in South America have been already related, to undertake a voyage to North America, two years after his return home." The volume opened with Phillips's arrival in Barbados and proceeded as in the previous editions. Clay began printing in London in 1820 and, at the time of this publication, was located at 7 and 8 Bread Hill Street. His firm endured as R. Clay Son & Taylor, then R. Clay & Sons, Ltd., and was still in business in 1900, surviving Clay's 1877 death. At the time he printed *Travels in North America*, Clay employed twenty-six men and fourteen boys.[46]

Like the proverbial "bad penny," the surreptitious accounts perpetrated in Philadelphia between 1809 and 1812 came back in August 1840. Benjamin Franklin Ells, working with printer John Wilson in Dayton, Ohio, reissued the work under the title *The Journal of Lewis and Clarke, to the Mouth of the Columbia River Beyond the Rocky Mountains. In the Years 1804–5, & 6*. Ells posted an "ADVERTISEMENT" on the reverse of the title page justifying the reprint:

> The great demand for the Journal of Lewis & Clarke, has induced the re-publication of the work, with the additions of extensive and interesting notes, and numerous illustrations on wood. We have divided the work into Chapters, with appropriate citations; corrected much that was erroneous, in the Topography, and especially the Nomenclature and Orthography of the Proper Names, and the Philological errors, (of which there were many,) have been corrected, where it could be done, without too materially infringing the text.[47]

The changes to the volume, beyond editing, included the addition of several new plates. The portraits of "Captain Lewis" and "Captain Clarke," based on those in William Fisher's 1813 printing, were less detailed and reversed. Interspersed

"The apocryphal editions are today collectors' items only and, even though they bring fancy prices at auctions, are of no value whatever to historians."

Paul Russell Cutright, *A History of the Lewis and Clark Journals* (1976)

43 Phillips, *Travels* (Dublin, 1824), 180.

44 Phillips, *Travels* (London, 1831).

45 Brown, *London Publishers*, 162; Plomer, *A Short History*, 295–297; Rivington, *The Publishing Family*, xxi, 79–30, 112–113.

46 Phillips, *Travels* (London, 1846); Brown, *London Publishers*, 39; Howe, *The London Compositor*, 301; Todd, *A Directory of Printers*, 40.

47 *The Journal of Lewis and Clarke* (Dayton, 1840).

through the twenty-one chapters were fourteen plates, some of them familiar from earlier editions, others new, and none pertinent. The volume's "Appendix" raised irrelevance to a new height, providing the anecdote on George Washington; a selection from Rev. J. Hubbard's "Compilation of Indian History"; a brief essay, "The Indian Nurse"; and—quite beyond belief–the selection, "Great African Serpent, Killed by Regulus the Roman General." In spite of the claim of Ells to have "corrected much that was erroneous," the volume created new errors in the "Dictionaty [Dictionary] of Indian Words and Phrases," giving scant hope that this dictionary was accurate! Ells purged from the text the list of trees, shrubs, and plants growing along the Washita River that appeared in several of the earlier editions.[48]

48 *The Journal of Lewis and Clarke* (Dayton, 1840).

The surreptitious and apocryphal accounts of the Lewis and Clark Expedition thus appeared in thirteen printings between 1809 and 1846. They included three in German, two of which were published in the United States. Nine volumes were primarily founded on the *Message from the President*, Carver's *Travels*, and Mackenzie's *Voyages*, supplemented by selected letters penned by Lewis and Clark, with absurd concluding anecdotes. Four volumes were the fictional adventures of George Phillips, the intrepid Irish evangelical. Phillips's anonymous biographer was possibly a writer in Dublin, where *Travels in North America* first appeared. Although there is no confirming evidence about the identity of the pseudonymous Hubbard Lester and William Fisher of Philadelphia, James Sharan is a candidate for having crafted the primary text that was printed and reprinted with minor variations over three decades.

The surreptitious and apocryphal editions definitely found some readers. If they had not, there would have been little incentive for publishers to put these works on the market. The flurry of printings between 1809 and 1813–when eight of the thirteen editions appeared–confirms a pent-up interest in the adventures of the Corps of Discovery unmet by the Gass *Journal* and the limited notices issued by the federal government. In spite of frustrations they caused for bibliographers, these works are interesting additions to the literature of the expedition.

Taking Literary License: Surreptitious and Apocryphal Narratives Bibliography

The delay in publishing an official account of the expedition from the Lewis and Clark journals left a reporting vacuum, filled in 1809 by a pair of almost identical volumes published anonymously in Philadelphia and London. These compilations were made up of materials from various printed sources: the opening of Jefferson's 1806 Report to Congress (2b.1); Clark's St. Louis letter of September 1806 (2c.1), and accounts by Patrick Gass (1807), Jonathan Carver (1778), Alexander Mackenzie (1802), Lewis and Clark ("A Statistical View" from Jefferson's 1806 Report), and Doctor Sibley and William Dunbar (1806). These volumes played fast and loose with copyrights, and did not provide an adequate account of the promised "Travels of Capts. Lewis and Clarke." However, they did fulfill the other promise of their title pages: to provide accounts, borrowed from various published sources, of native American tribes in Canada and the northern and southern United States. This was the first attempt to assemble in one volume a range of authentic ethnographic material covering the continent. The accompanying map in these volumes is the first to include locations described by Lewis and Clark: Fort Mandan, the three forks of the Missouri River, and Fort Clatsop. The crude illustrations, on the other hand, are of no ethnographic value.

Cutright (*History*, 33:n. 1) assumes the priority of the Philadelphia publication over the London volume. This seems correct. The Philadelphia copyright date of April 17 well precedes the date of September 12 on Neele's map accompanying the London edition. (The advertisements dated December 1, 1808, in one of the Lewis & Clark College Collection London copies, Chuinard 1, are presumably offering somewhat older stock.)

The market for subsequent versions of this compilation continued to 1840, significantly beyond the time when actual editions of the Lewis and Clark journals had become available. No author is given for any of the publications in the compilation series, and the names of many of the printers or publishers seem to be pseudonyms.

4a Hubbard Lester

4a.1 Lester, Philadelphia 1809 [Color plate XIII]

THE | TRAVELS | OF | *Capts. Lewis & Clarke,* | BY ORDER OF THE | GOVERNMENT OF THE UNITED STATES, | PERFORMED IN THE YEARS 1804, 1805, & 1806, | BEING UPWARDS OF THREE THOUSAND MILES, FROM | ST. LOUIS, BY WAY OF THE MISSOURI, AND | COLUMBIA RIVERS, TO THE | PACIFICK OCEAN: | Containing An Account of the Indian Tribes, who inhabit | the Western part of the Continent unexplored, | and unknown before. | WITH COPIOUS DELINEATIONS OF THE MANNERS, CUS- | TOMS, RELIGION, &c. OF THE INDIANS. | COMPILED | *From various authentic sources, and Documents.* | TO WHICH IS SUBJOINED, | A Summary of the Statistical view of the Indian | Nations, from the Official Communication of | [rule] | MERIWETHER LEWIS. | [rule] | Embellished with a Map of the Country inhabited by | the Western tribes of Indians, and five Engravings | of Indian Chiefs. | [rule] | PHILADELPHIA: | PUBLISHED BY HUBBARD LESTER. | [dotted rule] | 1809. | Price—1 *dollar* 62 ½ *cts*

Collation: One volume, 12mo., 19.5 cm. Map; unpaginated frontispiece; [i]–xii title page; Pennsylvania copyright to Hubbard Lester of April 17, 1809; "Recommendation of the Expedition" by Jefferson; [blank]; Jefferson's Message (lacking the final three paragraphs relating to Sibley and Dunbar); [blank]; introduction; [1]–153 "New Travels Among the Indians"; 154–78 "A Statistical View"; 179–204 "Historical Sketches"; 204–28 "Their Origin"; 229–92 Dunbar and Hunter's "Observations"; 293–300 unrelated "Anecdotes."

Plates: Anonymous map, "Map of the Country Inhabited by the Western Tribes of Indians," preceding the frontispiece (Wendlick); frontispiece "Sioux Queen"; facing 48 "Mahas Queen"; facing 96 "Sioux Warrior"; facing 156 "Ottoes Chief"; facing 204 "Serpentine Chief." (Two plates found in facsimile at the University of California at Berkeley's Bancroft Library have erroneous captions: "Mahas King," and "Ottoes Queen," suggesting proof correction, leading to two states of the illustrations. This same Bancroft copy also contains the London 1809 map in facsimile.) No engraver is named for the rather crude plates. The map is also unsigned, though it is clearly based closely on that of Louisiana in the 1804 Arrowsmith and Lewis *Atlas* (Wheat, vol. 1, map facing p. 2, commentary on 5ff. and 13ff.), with added information on the Missouri and in the West (notably the naming of the Columbia River, and of Fort Clatsop) derived from the journal narratives, "the earliest published cartographic reflections of Lewis and Clark's great effort" (Wheat, 1:14). This map's title cartouche is an octagon.

References: Coues, cxi–cxii, cxiv; Paltsits, lxvi; Wagner-Camp-Becker, 8:1.

Description: This is the first in a long and mostly related series of unauthorized published accounts of the expedition. The copyright page and misleading "Recommendation" ([ii], [iii]) and the final anecdotes are not present in the London edition. Within the section "New Travels Among the Indians," pp. 1–23 are a synopsis based on Gass and others; pp. 24–35 contain Clark's letter to Governor Harrison, from Fort Mandan, April 2, 1805, and to his brother from St. Louis, September 23, 1806; pp. 35–119 gather miscellaneous materials; and pp. 119–153 are derived from Mackenzie, whose authorship is acknowledged.

Notices: Clark's letter to Governor Harrison first appeared in the *Telegraphe and Daily Advertiser*, Baltimore, for July 25, 1805 (Jackson, *Letters*, item 146). Clark's letter to his brother first appeared in the *Palladium*, Frankfort (Kentucky), for October 9, 1806 (Jackson, *Letters*, item 208). See also 2c.1 (*The Monthly Anthology*).

Lewis & Clark College Collection: Anderson: Damaged copy, lacking map, containing all plates. Chuinard: Rebound leather, with map, lacking all plates. Wendlick: Rebound three-quarter leather with marbled boards. Contains map and all plates. Streeter copy (Streeter, 3122). Early owner: T. W. Coit, New Rochelle.

4a.2 Longman, London 1809 [Color plate XIV]

THE | TRAVELS | OF | CAPTS. LEWIS & CLARKE, | FROM | *ST. LOUIS, BY WAY OF THE MISSOURI AND COLUMBIA RIVERS*, | TO THE | PACIFIC OCEAN; | PERFORMED IN THE YEARS 1804, 1805, & 1806, | BY ORDER OF THE | *GOVERNMENT OF THE UNITED STATES.* | CONTAINING | DELINEATIONS OF

THE MANNERS, CUSTOMS, | RELIGION, &c. | Of the Indians, | COMPILED FROM | *Various Authentic Sources, and Original Documents,* | AND | A SUMMARY OF THE STATISTICAL VIEW OF | THE INDIAN NATIONS, | FROM THE OFFICIAL COMMUNICATION OF | [rule] | MERIWETHER LEWIS. | [rule] | *Illustrated with a Map of the Country, inhabited by the* | *Western Tribes of Indians.* | [rule] LONDON: | PRINTED FOR LONGMAN, HURST, REES, AND ORME, | PATERNOSTER ROW. | 1809.

Collation: One volume, 8vo., 22.5 cm. Map; [i]–ix title page, Jefferson's Message (lacking the final three paragraphs relating to Sibley and Dunbar), introduction; [blank]; [1]–309 text: [1]–156 "New Travels Among the Indians"; 157–83 "A Statistical View"; 184–210 "Historical Sketches"; 210–37 "Origin"; 238–309 Dunbar and Hunter's "Observations." Chuinard 1 ends with sixteen pages of advertisements, dated "Dec. 1, 1808."

The map in this edition is engraved by Samuel John Neele, engraver of the map (based on that of Samuel Lewis) in the 1814 one-volume London quarto of the Biddle-Allen *Travels* (5a.2). It carries the imprint "Published Sep.^{tr} 12.th 1809, by Longman & Co. Paternoster Row. Neele sc. Strand." It is a close copy of the anonymous Philadelphia 1809 map, itself partly based on Samuel Lewis's "Louisiana" in the Arrowsmith and Lewis *Atlas* of 1804. It is to Samuel Lewis's credit that he was the engraver of the two earliest maps of the expedition. The London edition's map has a rectangular title cartouche with incurved corners, and omits the French and English names of the Rocky Mountains.

References: Coues, cxii–cxiv; Graff, 2479; Paltsits, lxvi–lxvii; Wagner-Camp-Becker, 8:2.

Description: A close reprint of the Philadelphia edition, with the omission of Jefferson's Recommendation (a deliberately misleading element in the earlier edition), with changes to the publisher's introduction, particularly in the early paragraphs, and with the omission of the plates and final anecdotes. This light editing showed some judicious cuts in extraneous material.

Notices: *The Edinburgh Review* 29 (October 1809): 244; *The Quarterly Review* 2, no. 4 (December 30, 1809): 468. Both notices give the price of the volume as 9 s[hillings].

Lewis & Clark College Collection: Chuinard 1: Original boards, untrimmed. Contains map. Ownership inscription of James Grant 1810. Chuinard 2: Full leather, untrimmed, repairs to title page. Inscription from Chuinard's son to his father. Contains map. Tweney: Original boards untrimmed. Contains map. Wendlick: Rebound in full leather. Contains map.

4a.3 Reclam, Leipzig 1811

Allgemeines | historisches Archiv | herausgegeben | von | Hans Karl Dippold, | Professor der Geschichte zu Danzig, | und | Friedrich August Koethe, | Dr. und Prof. der Philosophie zu Jena. | [rule] | Ersten Bandes Zweites Heft. | [rule] | Leipzig, | bei Carl Heinrich Reclam 1811. |

Description: This item is the separately bound, second part of the first volume in a series (this part only in the Lewis & Clark College Collection), pp. [165]–348. The format is octavo, 22 cm. Part 6, the first of nine items in this second part, occupies pp. 167–230, a narrative subtitled "6. Resultate der Reise der Capitäne Lewis und Clarke den Missuri entlang bis zur Süd-See." The compiler was Johann Severin Vater (1771–1826), a professor at Königsberg (Kaliningrad). His 1810 volume, derived from Humboldt, was in Jefferson's library. The selection and translation is confined to two perfectly authentic portions of the surreptitious editions: Lewis and Clark's "A Statistical View of the Indian Nations," and Sibley's "Historical Sketches of the Several Indian Tribes in Louisiana," first published in Jefferson's 1806 Report to Congress. In this case, the volume derived almost certainly from the London 1809 surreptitious volume (4a.2). Vater provides light annotation and a two-page general introduction to his translations.

Lewis & Clark College Collection: Chuinard, with his bookplate and an autograph note laid in.

4b German-American Digest Versions
4b.1 Stöver, Libanon [Lebanon], Pennsylvania 1811 [Color plate XV]

Die | Reisen | der Capitaine | Lewis und Clarke; | unternommen | auf Befehl der | Regierung der Vereinigten Staaten | in den Jahren 1804, 1805 und 1806, | über | eine Länderstrecke von mehr als 3000 Meilen, | von St. Louis, auf dem Missouri und | Columbia, nach dem stillen Meer. | Enthaltend: | Eine Beschreibung der Indianischen Völkerstämme, | welche den westlichen Theil von Nord-America, | der uns bisher unbekannt und unentdeckt | war, bewohnen. | Samt | einer statistischen Uebersicht der Indianer Nationen, | aus dem Official Bericht von | [rule] | Meriwether Lewis. | [rule] | [Mit vier Abbildungen Indianscher Könige.] | [rule] | Libanon, (P.) | Gedruckt bey Jacob Stöver.– 1811.

Collation: One volume, 18mo., 16.5cm. Title page; blank; [5]–11 "Empfehlung"; "Vorbericht"; "Reise nach dem stillen Meer"; 11–14 "Bericht des Capitains Clarke, in einem Briefe an den Gouvernör Harrison. Fort Madan, den 2. April, 1806"; 15–20 "Brief des Capitains Clarke an seinen Bruder. St. Louis, den 22. Sept. 1806"; 20–23 surreptitious account; 23–33 "Statistische Uebersicht"; 34–47 "Beobachtungen"; 47–51 "Louisiana"; 52–9 "Ueber den Ursprung der Indianer"; 59–60 "Anekdote"; 60 publisher's subscription call (for volume on Revolutionary War of 1778).

Plates: Facing 10 "Serpentine Chief"; facing 13 "Sioux Königin"; facing 21 "Sioux Krieger"; facing 25 "Mahas Königin."

References: Paltsits, lxvii; Wagner-Camp-Becker, 8:3.

Description: Issued in decorative marbled wraps. The first of two German-American imprints clearly derived from the 1809 Hubbard Lester surreptitious account in a digest form. (The borrowing is unambiguous in "Ueber den Ursprung der Indianer" from Lester's "Their Origin.") This edition includes plates, crude renderings imitated from four of the five in the Lester 1809 edition, but all reversed from their originals.

Lewis & Clark College Collection: Acquired by William Reese for the College at the Siebert Sale at Sotheby's October 28, 1999, item number 685. "Bottom of final 14 leaves of *Reisen* chewed. Marbled paper wrappers" [Siebert, 2:114]. Boxed.

4b.2 Bärtgis, Friedrichstadt [Fredericktown/Frederick], Maryland 1812

Die | Reisen | der Capitaine | Lewis und Clarke; | unternommen | auf Befehl der | Regierung der Vereinigten Staaten | in den Jahren 1804, 1805 und 1806, | über | eine Länderstrecke von mehr als 3000 Meilen, | von St. Louis, auf dem Missouri und | Columbia, nach dem stillen Meer. | Enthaltend: | Eine Beschreibung der Indianischen Völkerstämme, | welche den westlichen Theil von Nord-America, | der uns bisher unbekannt und unentdeckt | war, bewohnen. | Samt | einer statistischen Uebersicht der Indianer Nationen, | aus dem Official Bericht von | Meriwether Lewis. | [double rule] | [Mit Abbildungen Indianscher Könige. | [heavy rule] | Friedrichstadt: | Gedruckt bey M. Bärtgis,– 1812. |

Collation: One volume, 12mo., 17 cm. Title page; [blank]; [5]–11 "Empfehlung"; "Vorbericht"; "Reise nach dem stillen Meer"; 12–21 "Bericht des Capitains Clarke, in einem Briefe an den Gouvernör Harrison. Fort Madan, den 2ten April, 1806" and "Brief des Capt. Clarke an seinen Bruder. St. Louis, den 22ten Sept. 1806"; 21–4 surreptitious account; 24–36 "Statistische Uebersicht"; 36–51 "Beobach-tungen"; 51–56 "Louisiana"; 56–64 "Ueber den Ursprung der Indianer."

References: Paltsits, lxviii; Wagner-Camp-Becker, 8:4.

Description: Closely follows Stöver 1811 (4b.1), but without plates. However, plates are announced on the title page, in imitation of Stöver.

Lewis & Clark College Collection: Facsimile from microfiche.

4c William Fisher

The apocryphal work compiled by the presumably pseudonymous William Fisher is close in content to its 1809 Hubbard Lester progenitor, to the point of including both the misleading "Recommendation" from Jefferson and the irrelevant final anecdotes.

The Fisher compilation appears in two 1812 publications, in Philadelphia and in Baltimore, with no certain indication of precedence between the two. The Philadelphia edition contains in some of its copies two title pages, of very different style and tone. The second title page, with the spelling "Clarke," cruder in manner and tipped in as a separate leaf on heavier stock, announces a price, but gives no publisher or date, and has no copyright notice on its verso. The first title page, more sophisticated in its appearance and appeal to the "curious reader," gives publisher and date, and is backed by a copyright notice. "Clark" is correctly spelled. The "Dictionary of the Indian Tongue" claimed on this title page is taken verbatim from Mackenzie's *Voyages,* omitting the column of Algonquin vocabulary. The printing of the edition is relatively handsome, on a wide measure.

The Baltimore edition, acknowledging Fisher as author, but employing a different printer, uses the same blocks as Philadelphia for the portrait woodcuts (though with titles added), adapts the language of the second, less appealing, title page, following it even in an odd pattern of indentation, and lacks a copyright notice. The title also upgrades Fisher's claim to read "A Complete Dictionary of the Indian Tongue." The preliminaries are paginated in order, taking their guide from the irregularly paginated preliminaries of the Philadelphia edition. Baltimore is more crudely printed, on cheaper paper, to a narrower measure. These differences suggest the priority of Philadelphia, but with close contact between the two print shops, at least in the transfer of woodblocks from one to the other.

4c.1 Sharan, Philadelphia 1812

First title: NEW TRAVELS | AMONG THE | INDIANS OF NORTH AMERICA; | BEING | A COMPILATION, TAKEN PARTLY FROM THE COMMUNICATIONS ALREADY | PUBLISHED, OF | CAPTAINS LEWIS AND CLARK, | TO THE | PRESIDENT OF THE UNITED STATES; | AND | PARTLY FROM OTHER AUTHORS WHO TRAVELLED AMONG | THE VARIOUS TRIBES OF INDIANS. | CONTAINING | A VARIETY OF VERY PLEASANT ANECDOTES, REMARKABLY CALCULATED | TO AMUSE AND INFORM THE MIND OF EVERY CURIOUS READER; | WITH | A DICTIONARY OF THE INDIAN TONGUE. | COMPILED | BY WILLIAM FISHER, ESQR. | PHILADELPHIA: | PUBLISHED BY JAMES SHARAN. | J. Maxwell, printer. | 1812. |

Second title: THE | VOYAGES AND TRAVELS | OF | CAPTAINS LEWIS AND CLARKE, | IN THE YEARS 1804, 1805, AND 1806. | CONTAINING | AN ACCURATE ACCOUNT OF THEIR ADVENTURES, DU- | RING THREE YEARS AND FOUR MONTHS.– WHICH | WERE CHIEFLY CONFINED TO THE RIVER MISSOURI.– | THEN DESCENDED THE COLUMBIA TO THE PACIFIC | OCEAN.–ASCERTAINED WITH ACCURACY THE GEOGRA- | PHY OF THAT INTERESTING COMMUNICATION ACROSS | THE CONTINENT.–LEARNED THE CHARACTER OF THE | COUNTRY, ITS COMMERCE, SOIL, CLIMATE, ANIMAL AND | VEGETABLE PRODUCTIONS.– ALSO, THE MANNERS AND | CUSTOMS OF THE DIFFERENT TRIBES OF INDIANS | THROUGH WHICH THEY PASSED. | COMPILED BY WILLIAM FISHER, ESQ. | PRICE ONE HUNDRED AND TWENTY-FIVE CENTS. |

Collation: One volume, 12mo., 17.5 cm. Untitled portrait frontispieces on inner of unpaginated folded leaf; [i] first title page "NEW TRAVELS"; copyright on verso; separate leaf, with second title "THE VOYAGES AND TRAVELS"; verso blank; [iii] "Recommendation"; [iv]–[v] "Message"; [vi] blank; [vii]–xi introduction; xii "Estimate"; [13]–23 text; 23–27 Clark Mandan letter to Harrison; 28–35 Clark letter to his brother; 35–153 "Travels to the Pacific Ocean"; [154]–178 "A Statistical View"; [179]–204 "Historical Sketches"; 204–28 "Origin"; [229]–292 "Observations"; [293]–300 "Anecdotes".

References: Coues, cxv; Howes, F153a, aa; Paltsits, lxix; Wagner-Camp-Becker, 8:6.

Description: Paltsits notes "pagination of 155 is inverted in some copies. In most copies the second title page is lacking." In the Wendlick copy, both title pages are present. This is the only copy seen in this state.

Lewis & Clark College Collection: Chuinard: Rebound in a red vinyl-like binding with gold stamping on spine and new end papers. Description from book dealer catalog bound in after copyright page. Wendlick: Rebound in half leather with marbled boards and new end papers. Signature of Henry Stoddard on first title page.

4c.2 Miltenberger, Baltimore 1812 [Color plate XVI]

AN | INTERESTING ACCOUNT | OF THE | VOYAGES AND TRAVELS | OF | *CAPTAINS LEWIS AND CLARK*, | IN THE YEARS 1804, 1805, AND 1806. | GIVING A FAITHFUL DE SCRIPTION OF THE RIVER MISSOURI AND | ITS SOURCE–OF THE VARIOUS TRIBES OF INDIANS THROUGH | WHICH THEY PASSED–MANNERS AND CUSTOMS–SOIL–CLIMATE | –COMMERCE– GOLD AND SILVER MINES–ANIMAL AND VEGE- | TABLE PRODUCTIONS INTER- SPERSED WITH VERY ENTER- | TAINING ANECDOTES, AND A VARIETY OF OTHER USEFUL AND | PLEASING INFORMATION REMARKABLY CALCULAT- ED TO DE- | LIGHT AND INSTRUCT THE READERS–TO WHICH IS ADDED A | COMPLETE DICTIONARY OF THE INDIAN TONGUE. | BY WILLIAM FISHER, ESQ. | [rule] | *BALTIMORE.* | PRINTED BY ANTHONY MILTENBERGER, | *For the Purchasers.* | 1812.

Collation: One volume, 12mo., 17 cm. [i] blank; [ii]–[iii] portrait frontispieces titled CAPTAINS LEWIS AND | CLARK, RETURNED; [iv] blank; [v] title page with blank verso; [vii] "Recommendation from the President of the United States"; [viii]–[ix] "Message from the President"; [x]–xiv introduction; xv "Estimate"; [16]–27 text; 27–32 Clark Mandan letter to Harrison; 32–40 Clark letter to his brother; 40–168 "Travels to the Pacific Ocean"; 168–93 "A Statistical View"; [194]–220 "Historical Sketches"; 220–46 "Their Origin"; 246–318 "Observations"; [319]–326 "Anecdotes".

References: Coues, cxv; Howes, F153a; Paltsits, lxviii–lxix; Wagner-Camp-Becker, 8:5.

Description: A close reprint of Philadelphia 1812 (4c.1), from a different printer, but using the same woodblocks for the portrait frontispieces.

Lewis & Clark College Collection: Wendlick: Rebound in full leather. Inscriptions on title page of Nath. Potter and Augˢ J. Alberts.

4c.3 Mauro, Baltimore 1813

AN | INTERESTING ACCOUNT | OF THE | VOYAGES AND TRAVELS | OF | CAPTAINS LEWIS AND CLARKE, | IN THE YEARS 1804–5, & 6. | GIVING A FAITHFUL DESCRIPTION OF THE RIVER MISSOURI AND | ITS SOURCE– OF THE VARIOUS TRIBES OF INDIANS THROUGH | WHICH THEY PASSED– MANNERS AND CUSTOMS–SOIL | –CLIMATE–COMMERCE–GOLD AND SILVER | MINES–ANIMAL AND VEGETABLE | PRODUCTIONS. | Interspersed | *With very entertaining anecdotes, and a variety of | other useful and pleasing information, re- | markably calculated to delight and | instruct the readers.* | To which is added | *A complete Dictionary of the Indian Tongue* | [rule] | *BY WILLIAM FISHER, Esq.* | [rule] | *BALTIMORE:* | PRINTED AND PUBLISHED BY P. MAURO, | *Nᵒ. 10, North Howard St.* | 1813. |

Collation: One volume, 12mo., 17.5 cm. [Tipped to endpaper] "Captain Clark."; [i] "Captain Lewis."; verso blank; [iii] title page; verso blank; [v] "Recommendation"; [vi]–vii "Message"; [viii]–xi "Introduction"; [xii] "Estimate"; [13]–21 "Travels to the Pacific Ocean"; 22–25 Clark Mandan letter to Harrison; 26–32 Clark letter to his brother; 32–115 "Among the Indians"; [116]–124 "Examples of their Language"; [125]–137 "Some Account of the Chepewyan Indians"; [138]–161 "A Statistical View"; verso blank; [163]–184 "Historical Sketches"; [185]–204 "Origin"; [205]–259 "Observations"; 259–60 "Common Names"; [261]–266 "Anecdotes".

Plates: Frontispieces "CAPTAIN CLARK", "CAPTAIN LEWIS"; facing 35 "THE BEAR PURSUEING HIS ASSAILANT"; facing 79 "AN INDIAN DESTINED TO DEATH"; facing 176 "ST DENNIE ATTACKING the NATCHEZ INDI-ANS"; facing 215 "A VIEW ON THE WASHITA."

References: Coues, cxvi; Graff, 1331; Paltsits, lxix; Wagner-Camp-Becker, 8:7.

Description: A close reprint, from yet another printer, of the 1809–1812 lineage. The portrait vignettes of the two explorers are re-engraved in this volume by a more competent engraver. The edition includes plates not previously found in any other editions. Paltsits comments: "There are no pp. 125, 126, 149, 150, 179, 180, 209, 210; and pp. 173, 174 are repeated." Wagner-Camp-Becker does not list a plate opposite 176. This plate is present in both the Wendlick and Tweney copies; it is lacking in the Chuinard copy. Coues is not correct in his observation that the "Master Neddy" anecdote was dropped in this publication.

Lewis & Clark College Collection: Chuinard: Full leather tree calf with Chuinard bookplate. Foxing throughout. Tweney: Rebound in contemporary leather with new endpapers. Inscription reads "Presented to the Diagnothian society by C. S. Orth." Wendlick: Rebound in full leather with raised bands and gold stamping on spine. Stamp of Frank C. Deering inside front cover.

4c.4 Ells, Dayton 1840

THE | JOURNAL | OF | LEWIS AND CLARKE, | TO THE MOUTH OF THE COLUMBIA RIVER | BEYOND THE ROCKY MOUNTAINS. | IN THE YEARS 1804-5, & 6. | GIVING A FAITHFUL DESCRIPTION OF THE RIVER MISSOURI | AND ITS SOURCE-OF THE VARIOUS TRIBES OF INDIANS | THROUGH WHICH THEY PASSED-MANNERS AND CUS- | TOMS-SOIL-CLIMATE-COMMERCE-GOLD AND | SILVER MINES-ANIMAL AND VEGETABLE | PRODUCTIONS, &c. | NEW EDITION, WITH NOTES. | REVISED, CORRECTED, AND ILLUSTRATED WITH NUMEROUS | WOOD CUTS. | TO WHICH IS ADDED | A COMPLETE DICTIONARY OF THE INDIAN TONGUE. | [rule] | DAYTON, O. | PUBLISHED AND SOLD BY B. F. ELLS. | JOHN WILSON, PRINTER. | [dotted rule] | 1840.

Collation: One volume, 16mo., 17.5 cm. [i] blank; [ii] Portrait of Captain Lewis; [iii] Portrait of Captain Clarke; [iv] blank; [v] title page; [vi] copyright with advertisement; [vii] Jefferson's Message; [vii]–[viii] Additional Message; [ix]–xii preface; [15]–224 "Lewis and Clarke's Journal"; [225]–234 "Dictionaty [Dictionary] of Indian Words and Phrases"; 234–237 "Appendix"; [238]–240 contents.

Plates: [ii] "Captain Lewis"; [iii] "Captain Clarke"; [xxiv] "Moon-Light on the Western Waters"; [18] "Prairie on Fire"; [39] "Escape from a Bear"; [44] "Indian Hunter"; [68] "A Beaver Dam" signed by Grosvenor; [82] "Burning a Village"; [84] "Burning a Prisoner"; [98] "Falls"; [105] "A Kinstenaux Indian" signed by Grosvenor; [111] "Indian Canoe and Fishing Lodge"; [126] "Rappids."; [138] "Indian Amusements."; [176] "White Cliffs."; [222] "View on the Upper Mississippi."

References: Coues, cxvi–cxvii; Paltsits, lxx; Wagner-Camp-Becker, 8:8.

Description: Many of these plates appear again in the Ells, Claflin & Co. publication of Patrick Gass's *Journal* in 1847. The engraver signs as "Grosvenor" in two of the plates in this edition and the 1847 Gass volume. See 3.9 for plate comparison.

Lewis & Clark College Collection: Tweney: Rebound in full leather with blind stamping on covers, raised bands with gold stamping on spine, and with original spine label pasted on. Text is brittle. Wendlick: Original leather. Bright copy.

4d George Phillips, *Travels in North America*

The four printings between 1822 and 1848 of George Phillips's *Travels in North America* (two in Dublin followed by two in London) represent the one early example of a totally spurious account of the Lewis and Clark Expedition. The fifty or so pages devoted to the connection with Lewis and Clark are a fabrication, and can be regarded as entirely apocryphal.

4d.1 Bentham, Dublin 1822

TRAVELS | IN | NORTH AMERICA. | [rule] | [vignette (turtle)] | [rule] | Dublin: | Printed by Christopher Bentham, Eustace-street. | [rule] | 1822.

Collation: One volume, 12mo., 14.5cm. Leaf with frontispiece on verso (scene in a mine); Title page, verso blank; [9]–184 text.

Plates: [97] "INSIDE OF A HUT"; [130] "FALLS OF NIAGARA"; [144] "VIEW OF ICEBERGS"; [149] "MEETING OF ENGLISH AND ESQUIMAUX."

Reference: Wagner-Camp-Becker, 21c:1.

Description: Fictional account by George Phillips of his travels in North America, including a journey with Lewis and Clark from St. Louis to the Pacific and on the return as far as Fort Mandan. The Lewis and Clark portion of the books comprises pp. 48–104.

Lewis & Clark College Collection: Rebound in full leather with gold stamping on spine. Frontispiece pasted to leaf preceding title page. Acquired at auction of the Eric W. Wolf Collection in Bethesda, Maryland, September 16, 1999.

4d.2 Smith, Dublin 1824

TRAVELS | IN | NORTH AMERICA. | [vignette (walrus)] | DUBLIN: | PRINTED BY BRETT SMITH, MARY-STREET. | [rule] | 1824.

Collation: One volume, 12mo., 14.5cm. Frontispiece (scene in a mine) facing [3] title page; [blank]; [5]–180 text.

Plates: [93] "INSIDE OF A HUT"; [123] "FALLS OF NIAGARA"; [140] "VIEW OF ICEBERGS"; [145] "MEETING OF ENGLISH AND ESQUIMAUX."

Reference: Wagner-Camp-Becker, 21c:2.

Description: Completely reset text, following 1822, with minor alterations. The narrative dealing with Lewis and Clark occupies pp. 44–100. The woodcut frontispiece is from the same block as the 1822 edition, now badly worn. The plates are also from the same blocks as the 1822 volume.

Lewis & Clark College Collection: Wendlick: Full leather, tree calf, with gold stamp on spine.

4d.3 Rivington, London 1831

TRAVELS | IN | NORTH AMERICA. | [vignette ("Moose Deer")] | [rule] | LONDON: | PRINTED FOR C. J. G. & F. RIVINGTON, | *Booksellers to the Society for Promoting Christian Knowledge;* | ST. PAUL'S CHURCH-YARD, AND WATERLOO-PLACE. | [rule] | 1831.

Collation: One volume, 12mo., 14.5cm. Frontispiece, "Mexican Soldier," facing title page; [blank]; advertisement; [blank]; [1]–168 text.

Plates: Facing 38 "Mexican Woman of Rank"; facing 115 "Falls of Niagara."

Reference: Wagner-Camp-Becker, 21c:3.

Description: The narrative dealing with Lewis and Clark occupies pp. 39–92. The frontispiece and text woodcuts are new. The text follows the 1822 or 1824 editions, again with minor variants.

Lewis & Clark College Collection: Tweney 1: Original cloth binding, with blind stamping on covers. Inscription of John. Ed. Sheppard, Dec.er 1844. Tweney 2: Rebound in half leather with green marbled boards, gold stamp on spine. Inscription to Benjamin Smith, November 12, 1852. Stamp of Camp & Curtis, Mar. 1836 (or 1856) on inside cover. Wendlick: Rebound in half leather with red marbled boards, gold stamp on spine. A very similar binding to Tweney 2. Stamp of Smith & Son, Binders, 15, Albion buildings, Bartholomew Close. March, 1834 on inside cover.

4d.4 SPCK, London 1846

TRAVELS IN NORTH AMERICA. | [rule] | PUBLISHED UNDER THE DIRECTION OF | THE COMMITTEE OF GENERAL LITERATURE AND EDUCATION, | APPOINTED BY THE SOCIETY FOR PROMOTING | CHRISTIAN KNOWLEDGE. | [rule] | LONDON: | PRINTED FOR THE | SOCIETY FOR PROMOTING CHRISTIAN KNOWLEDGE; | SOLD AT THE DEPOSITORY, | GREAT QUEEN STREET, LINCOLN'S INN FIELDS, | AND 4, ROYAL EXCHANGE, AND | BY ALL BOOKSELLERS. | 1846.

Collation: One volume, 12mo., 14.5 cm. Frontispiece of various scenes, facing title page; printer's imprint (R. Clay); [1]–151 text.

Plates: [23] "WORKING IN A SILVER MINE"; [27] "CITY OF MEXICO"; [89] "CANADIAN BOATMEN"; 96 vignette of Niagara Falls; 102 vignette of Quebec; 104 vignette of horse and sleigh; 114 vignette of shipwreck on ice, engraver signature "Whimper"; 118 vignette of walrus; 135 vignette, "NEW YORK."

Description: The text dealing with Lewis and Clark occupies pp. 26–75. The first nine or so pages of the original narrative are abbreviated into two short paragraphs in this text, though some parts of the original text are followed closely. This edition is not described in any standard bibliography.

Lewis & Clark College Collection: Wendlick: Original cloth binding with blind stamping to covers.

Note: There is a reference in Wagner-Camp-Becker (p. 84 n.) to Sabin and Howes's citations of undated Dublin printings by John Jones and P. D. Hardy, the latter also noted in the *National Union Catalog.*

Plate II 1a.1. Title page, *Dictionary of Arts and Sciences* (London 1754–55)
Plate III 1a.4. Plate, John Miller, *An Illustration of the Sexual System* (London 1779)
Plate IV 1b.2. Aaron Arrowsmith, "A Map Exhibiting all the New Discoveries" (London

A NEW AND COMPLETE

DICTIONARY

OF

ARTS and SCIENCES;

COMPREHENDING ALL

The Branches of Uſeful Knowledge,

WITH

ACCURATE DESCRIPTIONS as well of the various MACHINES, INSTRUMENTS, TOOLS, FIGURES, and SCHEMES neceſſary for illuſtrating them,

AS OF

The Claſſes, Kinds, Preparations, and Uſes of NATURAL PRODUCTIONS, whether ANIMALS, VEGETABLES, MINERALS, FOSSILS, or FLUIDS;

Together with

The KINGDOMS, PROVINCES, CITIES, TOWNS, and other Remarkable Places throughout the WORLD.

Illuſtrated with above Three Hundred COPPER-PLATES, curiouſly engraved by Mr. JEFFERYS, Geographer and Engraver to his Royal Highneſs the Prince of WALES.

The Whole extracted from the Beſt AUTHORS in all Languages.

By a SOCIETY of GENTLEMEN.

——————— *Huc undique Gaza*
Congeritur——————— VIRG.

VOL. I.

LONDON:
Printed for W. OWEN, at Homer's Head, in Fleet-ſtreet.
MDCC LIV.

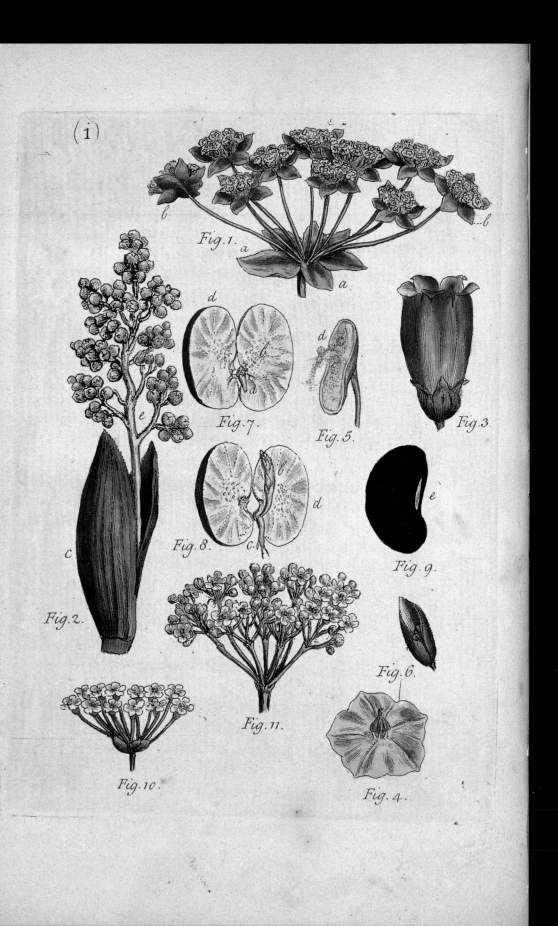

(1)

Fig.1. *a* *b* *a* *b*

Fig.7. *d* *b* *a*

Fig.5. *d*

Fig.3.

Fig.8. *b* *d* *c*

Fig.9. *e*

Fig.2. *c* *e*

Fig.6.

Fig.11.

Fig.10.

Fig.4.

Left: Plate V 1b.3 (iii). George Vancouver, "A Chart shewing part of the Coast of N.W. America" (London 1798)

low: Plate VI 2b.1. Thomas Jefferson, *Message from the President* (Washington, D. C. 1806)

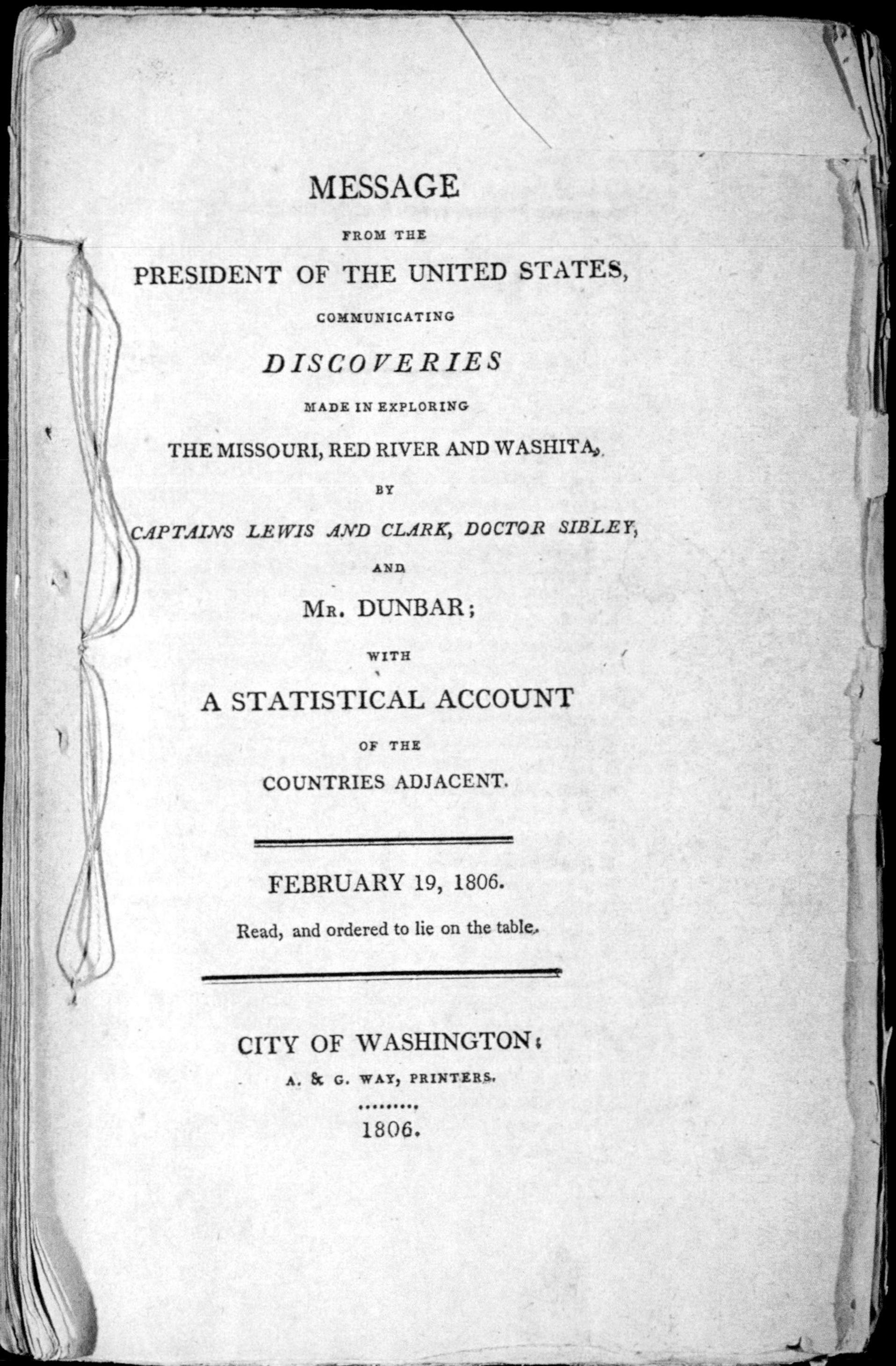

MESSAGE

FROM THE

PRESIDENT OF THE UNITED STATES,

COMMUNICATING

DISCOVERIES

MADE IN EXPLORING

THE MISSOURI, RED RIVER AND WASHITA,

BY

CAPTAINS LEWIS AND CLARK, DOCTOR SIBLEY,

AND

MR. DUNBAR;

WITH

A STATISTICAL ACCOUNT

OF THE

COUNTRIES ADJACENT.

FEBRUARY 19, 1806.

Read, and ordered to lie on the table.

CITY OF WASHINGTON:

A. & G. WAY, PRINTERS.

....

1806.

NATIONAL INTELLIGENCER EXTRAORDINARY, December 2, 1806.

THIS DAY, at 12 o'Clock, the PRESIDENT *of the United States communicated, by* Mr. Coles, *his Secretary, the following* MESSAGE *to both Houses of Congress.*

To the Senate and House of Representatives of the United States of America in Congress assembled.

IT would have given me, fellow Citizens, great satisfaction to announce, in the moment of your meeting, that the difficulties in our foreign relations, existing at the time of your last separation, had been amicably and justly terminated. I lost no time in taking those measures which were most likely to bring them to such a termination, by special missions, charged with such powers and instructions as, in the event of failure, could leave no imputation on either our moderation or forbearance. The delays, which have since taken place in our negociations with the British Government, appear to have proceeded from causes which do not forbid the expectation that, during the course of the session, I may be enabled to lay before you their final issue. What will be that of the negociations for settling our differences with Spain, nothing which had taken place, at the date of the last dispatches, enables us to pronounce. On the western side of the Mississippi she advanced in considerable force, and took post at the settlement of Bayou Pierre, on the Red river. This village was originally settled by France, was held by her as long as she held Louisiana, and was delivered to Spain only as a part of Louisiana. Being small, insulated, and distant, it was not observed at the moment of re-delivery to France and the United States, that she continued a guard of half a dozen men, which had been stationed there. A proposition however having been lately made by our commander in chief, to assume the Sabine river as a temporary line of separation between the troops of the two nations, until the issue of our negociations shall be known, this has been referred by the Spanish commandant to his superior, and in the mean time he has withdrawn his force to the western side of the Sabine river. The correspondence on this subject, now communicated, will exhibit more particularly the present state of things in that quarter.

The nature of that country requires indispensably that an unusual proportion of the force employed there should be cavalry, or mounted infantry. In order therefore that the commanding officer might be enabled to act with effect, I had authorised him to call on the Governors of Orleans and Mississippi, for a corps of five hundred volunteer cavalry. The temporary arrangement he has proposed may perhaps render this unnecessary. But I inform you with great pleasure, of the promptitude with which the inhabitants of those territories have tendered their services in defence of their country. It has done honour to themselves, entitled them to the confidence of their fellow citizens in every part of the Union, and must strengthen the general determination to protect them efficaciously under all circumstances which may occur.

Having received information that in another part of the United States a great number of private individuals were combining together, arming and organising themselves, contrary to law, to carry on a military expedition against the territories of Spain, I thought it necessary, by proclamation, as well as by special orders, to take measures for preventing and suppressing this enterprize, for seizing the vessels, arms, and other means provided for it, and for arresting and bringing to justice its authors and abettors. It was due to that good faith which ought ever to be the rule of action in public, as well as in private transactions; it was due to good order, and regular government, that, while the public force was acting strictly on the defensive, and merely to protect our citizens from aggression, the criminal attempts of private individuals to decide, for their country, the question of peace or war, by commencing active, and unauthorized hostilities, should be promptly and efficaciously suppressed.

Whether it will be necessary to enlarge our regular force, will depend on the result of our negociations with Spain. But as it is uncertain when that result will be known, the provisional measures requisite for that, and to meet any pressure intervening in that quarter, will be a subject for your early consideration.

The possession of both banks of the Mississippi reducing to a single point the defence of that river, its waters, and the country adjacent, it becomes highly necessary to provide, for that point, a more adequate security. Some position above its mouth, commanding the passage of the river, should be rendered sufficiently strong to cover the armed vessels which may be stationed there for defence; and, in conjunction with them, to present an insuperable obstacle to any force, attempting to pass. The approaches to the city of New Orleans, from the eastern quarter also, will require to be examined, and more effectually guarded. For the internal support of the country, the encouragement of a strong settlement on the western side of the Mississippi, within reach of New Orleans, will be worthy the consideration of the Legislature.

The gun boats, authorised by an act of the last session, are so advanced, that they will be ready for service in the ensuing spring. Circumstances permitted us to allow the time necessary for their more solid construction. As a much larger number will still be wanting to place our sea-port towns and waters in that state of defence to which we are competent, and they entitled, a similar appropriation for a further provision of them is recommended for the ensuing year.

A further appropriation will also be necessary for repairing fortifications already established, and the erection of such other works as may have real effect in obstructing the approach of an enemy to our sea-port towns, or their remaining before them.

In a country whose constitution is derived from the will of the people, directly expressed by their free suffrages, where the principal executive functionaries, and those of the legislature, are renewed by them at short periods, where, under the character of jurors, they exercise in person the greatest portion of the judiciary powers, where the laws are consequently so formed and administered as to bear with equal weight and favor on all, restraining no man in the pursuits of honest industry, and securing to every one the property which that acquires, it would not be supposed that any safeguards could be needed against insurrection, or enterprize, on the public peace or authority. The laws, however, aware that these should not be trusted to moral restraints only, have wisely provided punishment for these crimes when committed. But would it not be salutary to give also the means of preventing their commission? Where an enterprize is meditated by private individuals, against a foreign nation, in amity with the United States, powers of prevention, to a certain extent, are given by the laws. Would they not be as reasonable, and useful, where the enterprize preparing is against the United States?—While adverting to this branch of law, it is proper to observe that in enterprizes meditated against foreign nations, the ordinary process of binding to the observance of the peace and good behaviour, could it be extended to acts to be done out of the jurisdiction of the United States, would be effectual in some cases where the offender is able to keep out of sight every indication of his purpose which could draw on him the exercise of the powers now given by law.

The states on the coast of Barbary seem generally disposed at present to respect our peace and friendship. With Tunis alone, some uncertainty remains. Persuaded that it is our interest to maintain our peace with them on equal terms, or not at all, I propose to send, in due time, a reinforcement into the Mediterranean; unless previous information shall shew it to be unnecessary.

We continue to receive proofs of the growing attachment of our Indian neighbors, and of their disposition to place all their interests under the patronage of the United States. These dispositions are inspired by their confidence in our justice, and in the sincere concern we feel for their welfare. And as long as we discharge these high and honorable functions with the integrity and good faith which alone can entitle us to their continuance, we may expect to reap the just reward in their peace and friendship.

The expedition of Messrs. Lewis and Clarke, for exploring the river Missouri, and the best communication from that to the Pacific Ocean, has had all the success which could have been expected. They have traced the Missouri nearly to its source, descended the Columbia to the Pacific Ocean, ascertained with accuracy the geography of that interesting communication across our continent, learnt the character of the country, of its commerce, and inhabitants, and it is but justice to say that Messrs. Lewis and Clarke, and their brave companions, have, by this arduous service, deserved well of their country.

The attempt to explore the Red River, under the direction of Mr. Freeman, though conducted with a zeal and prudence meriting entire approbation, has not been equally successful. After proceeding up it about six hundred miles, nearly as far as the French settlements had extended, while the country was in their possession, our geographers were obliged to return without compleating their work.

Very useful additions have also been made to our knowledge of the Mississippi, by Lieutenant Pike, who has ascended it to its source, and whose journal and map, giving the details of his journey, will shortly be ready for communication to both Houses of Congress. Those of Messrs. Lewis, Clark and Freeman, will require further time to be digested and prepared. These important surveys, in addition to those before possessed, furnish materials for commencing an accurate map of the Mississippi and its western waters. Some principal rivers however remain still to be explored, towards which the authorisation of Congress, by moderate appropriations, will be requisite.

I congratulate you, fellow-citizens, on the approach of the period at which you may interpose your authority constitutionally, to withdraw the citizens of the United States from all further participation in those violations of human rights, which have been so long continued on the unoffending inhabitants of Africa, and which the morality, the reputation, and the best interests of our country, have long been eager to proscribe. Although no law you may pass can take prohibitory effect till the first day of the year one thousand eight hundred and eight, yet the intervening period is not too long to prevent, by timely notice, expeditions which cannot be compleated before that day.

The receipts at the Treasury, during the year ending on the 30th day of September last, have amounted to near fifteen millions of dollars; which have enabled us, after meeting the current demands, to pay two millions seven hundred thousand dollars of the American claims, in part of the price of Louisiana; to pay, of the funded debt, upwards of three millions of principal, and nearly four of interest, and, in addition, to reimburse, in the course of the present month, near two millions of five and an half per cent. stock. These payments and reimbursements of the funded debt, with those which had been made in the four years and an half preceding, will, at the close of the present year, have extinguished upwards of twenty-three millions of principal.

The duties composing the Mediterranean fund will cease, by law, at the end of the present session. Considering, however, that they are levied chiefly on luxuries, and that we have an impost on salt, a necessary of life, the free use of which otherwise is so important, I recommend to your consideration the suppression of the duties on salt, and the continuation of the Mediterranean fund, instead thereof, for a short time, after which that also will become unnecessary for any purpose now within contemplation.

When both of these branches of revenue shall, in this way, be relinquished there will still, ere long, be an accumulation of monies in the treasury beyond the instalments of public debt which we are permitted by contract to pay. They cannot then, without a modification, assented to by the public creditors, be applied to the extinguishment of this debt and the compleat liberation of our revenues, the most desirable of all objects. Nor, if our peace continues, will they be wanting for any other existing purpose. The question, therefore, now comes forward, to what other objects shall these surplusses be appropriated, and the whole surplus of impost after the entire discharge of the public debt, and during those intervals when the purposes of war shall not call for them? Shall we suppress the impost, and give that advantage to foreign over domestic manufactures? On a few articles of more general and necessary use, the suppression, in due season, will doubtless be right; but the great mass of the articles on which impost is paid, are foreign luxuries purchased by those only who are rich enough to afford themselves the use of them. Their patriotism would certainly prefer its continuance, and application to the great purposes of the public education, roads, rivers, canals, and such other objects of public improvement, as it may be thought proper to add to the constitutional enumeration of federal powers. By these operations, new channels of communication will be opened between the states; the lines of separation will disappear, their interests will be identified, and their union cemented by new and indissoluble ties. Education is here placed among the articles of public care, not that it would be proposed to take its ordinary branches out of the hands of private enterprise, which manages so much better all the concerns to which it is equal: but a public institution can alone supply those sciences, which though rarely called for, are yet necessary to compleat the circle, all the parts of which contribute to the improvement of the country, and some of them to its preservation. The subject is now proposed for the consideration of Congress, because, if approved, by the time the state Legislatures shall have deliberated on this extension of the federal trusts, and the laws shall be passed, and other arrangements made for their execution, the necessary funds will be on hand, and without employment. I suppose an amendment of the constitution, by consent of the states, necessary; because the objects now recommended are not among those enumerated in the constitution, and to which it permits the public monies to be applied.

The present consideration of a national establishment for education particularly, is rendered proper by this circumstance also, that, if Congress, approving the proposition, shall yet think it more eligible to found it on a donation of lands, they have it now in their power to endow it with those which will be among the earliest to produce the necessary income. This foundation would have the advantage of being independent on war, which may suspend other improvements by requiring for its own purposes the resources destined for them.

This, fellow-citizens, is the state of the public interests, at the present moment, and according to the information now possessed. But such is the situation of the nations of Europe, and such too the predicament in which we stand with some of them, that we cannot rely with certainty on the present aspect of our affairs, that may change from moment to moment, during the course of your session, or after you shall have separated. Our duty is therefore to act upon the things as they are, and to make a reasonable provision for whatever they may be. Were armies to be raised whenever a speck of war is visible in our horizon, we never should have been without them. Our resources would have been exhausted on dangers which have never happened, instead of being reserved for what is really to take place. A steady, perhaps a quickened pace, in preparations for the defence of our sea-port towns and waters, an early settlement of the most exposed and vulnerable parts of our country, a militia so organised that its effective portions can be called to any point in the union, or volunteers instead of them, to serve a sufficient time, are means which may always be ready, yet never preying on our resources until actually called into use. They will maintain the public interests, while a more permanent force shall be in a course of preparation. But much will depend on the promptitude with which these means can be brought into activity. If war be forced upon us, in spite of our long and vain appeals to the justice of nations, rapid and vigorous movements, in its outset, will go far towards securing us in its course and issue, and towards throwing its burthens on those who render necessary the resort from reason to force.

The result of our negociations, or such incidents in their course as may enable us to infer their probable issue; such further movements also, on our western frontier as may shew whether war is to be pressed there, while negociation is protracted elsewhere, shall be communicated to you from time to time, as they become known to me; with whatever other information I possess or may receive, which may aid your deliberations on the great national interests committed to your charge.

TH: JEFFERSON,

December 2, 1805.

à Me PORCHON DE BONVAL

Below: Plate IX 3.4 (b). Title page, Patrick Gass, *A Journal of the Voyages and Travels* (Philadelphia 1810 2nd state)

Right: Plate X 3.4 (b). Plates, Patrick Gass, *A Journal of the Voyages and Travels* (Philadelphia 1810 2nd state)

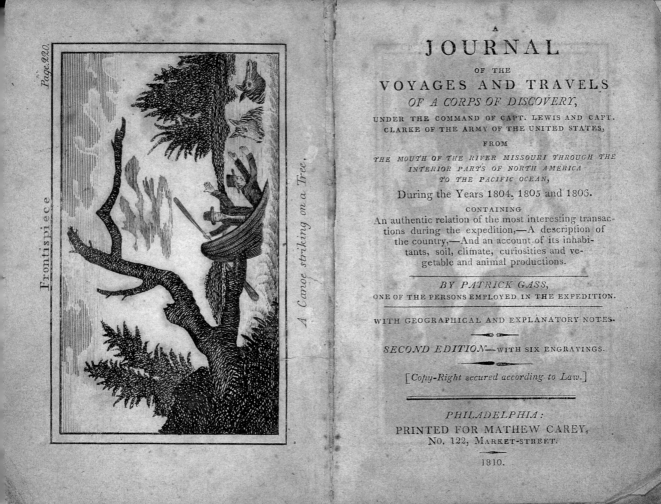

Page. 220.

Frontispiece

A Canoe striking on a Tree.

A

JOURNAL

OF THE

VOYAGES AND TRAVELS

OF A CORPS OF DISCOVERY,

UNDER THE COMMAND OF CAPT. LEWIS AND CAPT.
CLARKE OF THE ARMY OF THE UNITED STATES,

FROM

*THE MOUTH OF THE RIVER MISSOURI THROUGH THE
INTERIOR PARTS OF NORTH AMERICA
TO THE PACIFIC OCEAN,*

During the Years 1804, 1805 and 1806.

CONTAINING

An authentic relation of the most interesting transactions during the expedition,—A description of
the country,—And an account of its inhabitants, soil, climate, curiosities and vegetable and animal productions.

BY PATRICK GASS,

ONE OF THE PERSONS EMPLOYED IN THE EXPEDITION.

WITH GEOGRAPHICAL AND EXPLANATORY NOTES.

SECOND EDITION—WITH SIX ENGRAVINGS.

[*Copy-Right secured according to Law.*]

PHILADELPHIA:
PRINTED FOR MATHEW CAREY,
No. 122, MARKET-STREET.

1810.

An American having struck a Bear but not killed him, escapes into a Tree.

Captains Lewis & Clark holding a Council with the Indians

VI.

Bericht über die Erforschungsreise
des Laufes der Flüsse Missuri und Columbia.

Von Patrik Gaß.

(Die nähere Bekanntschaft, in welche uns dieser Reisebericht über einen beträchtlichen Theil der ungeheuren Strecken von Nordamerika setzt, hat eine um so erfreulichere Wichtigkeit, da es ziemlich beglückte, und schon von halbcultivirten Menschen bewohnte Gegenden sind, welche er umfaßt. Die Entdeckung der Verbindung des innersten Landes mit dem stillen Meere wird überdieß in der Folge mehrfache, für den Handel, und worauf man doch mehr Rücksicht nehmen sollte, für die Veredelung der Eingebornen bedeutende Resultate herbeyführen. Der gedrängte, jedoch vollständige Auszug, welchen wir von diesem Berichte gemacht haben, wird daher einer besonderen Erwägung würdig seyn.)

Erste Abtheilung.

Zweck der Reise. — Nordamerikanische Alterthümer. — Das neue Fort Mandanne. — Der Marienfluß. — Quellen des Missuri. —

Seit die nordamerikanischen Freystaaten durch Abtretung der Luisiana von Seite des französischen Reiches einen sehr beträchtlichen Zuwachs an Gebiet erlangt hatten, mußte ihnen daran liegen, das ganz Land vom 52 Breitengrade bis an die Grenze des Spanischen America kennen zu lernen, welches bis dahin noch von keinem Europäer durchwandert war.

Daher beschloß der republikanische Congreß den Capitän Meriwether Lewis vom 1. Infanterieregimente, und mit diesem den Lieutenant Clarke als zweyten Commandanten, in Gesellschaft eines gewissen Patrik Gaß, begleitet von einer gewissen Anzahl Leute, zur Untersuchung dieser Gegenden abzusenden. Die Aufgabe war, den Lauf des Missuri von seiner Ergiessung in den Mississippi bis zu seiner Quelle zu verfolgen, und, nachdem die Berge auf dem kürzesten Weg überschritten würden, den geradesten und leichtesten Wasserweg von diesen Bergen an bis in das stille Meer aufzufinden. Beyde Officiere sollten übrigens mit den Volksstämmen, die sie treffen würden, Handelsverbindungen vorbereiten.

Below: Plate XIII 4a.1. Frontispiece and title page, *The Travels of Capts. Lewis & Clarke* (Philadelphia 1809)

Right: Plate XIV 4a.2. Map, *The Travels of Capts. Lewis & Clarke* (London 1809)

SIOUX QUEEN.

W.R.Jones fc.

THE
TRAVELS
OF
Capts. Lewis & Clarke,

BY ORDER OF THE
GOVERNMENT OF THE UNITED STATES,
PERFORMED IN THE YEARS 1804, 1805, & 1806,

BEING UPWARDS OF THREE THOUSAND MILES, FROM
ST. LOUIS, BY WAY OF THE MISSOURI, AND
COLUMBIA RIVERS, TO THE
PACIFICK OCEAN:

Containing an Account of the Indian Tribes, who inhabit
the Western part of the Continent unexplored,
and unknown before.

WITH COPIOUS DELINEATIONS OF THE MANNERS, CUS-
TOMS, RELIGION, &c. OF THE INDIANS.

COMPILED

From various authentic sources, and Documents.

TO WHICH IS SUBJOINED,

A Summary of the Statistical view of the Indian
Nations, from the Official Communication of

MERIWETHER LEWIS.

Embellished with a Map of the Country inhabited by
the Western tribes of Indians, and five Engravings
of Indian Chiefs.

PHILADELPHIA:
PUBLISHED BY HUBBARD LESTER.
....
1809.
Price—1 dollar 62½ cts

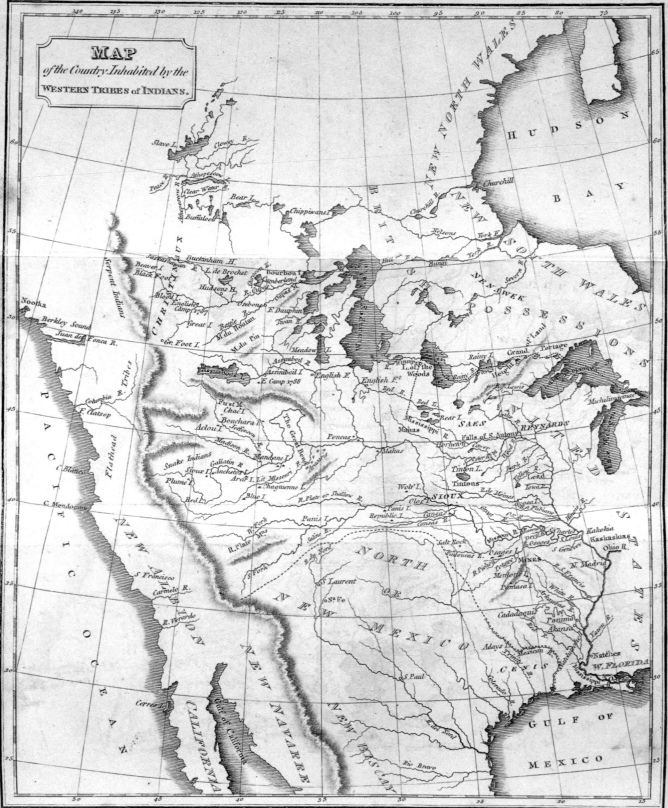

MAP
of the Country Inhabited by the
WESTERN TRIBES of INDIANS.

Published Sep.r 12th 1809. by Longman & Co Pater-noster Row.

Neele sc Strand.

Sioux Krieger.

CAPTAINS LEWIS AND   CLARK, RETURNED.

Plate XVII 5a.1. Original boards, vol. 2, *History of the Expedition* (Philadelphia 1814)

Plate XVIII 5a.4. Map, *Reize naar de Bronnen* (Dordrecht 1816–18)

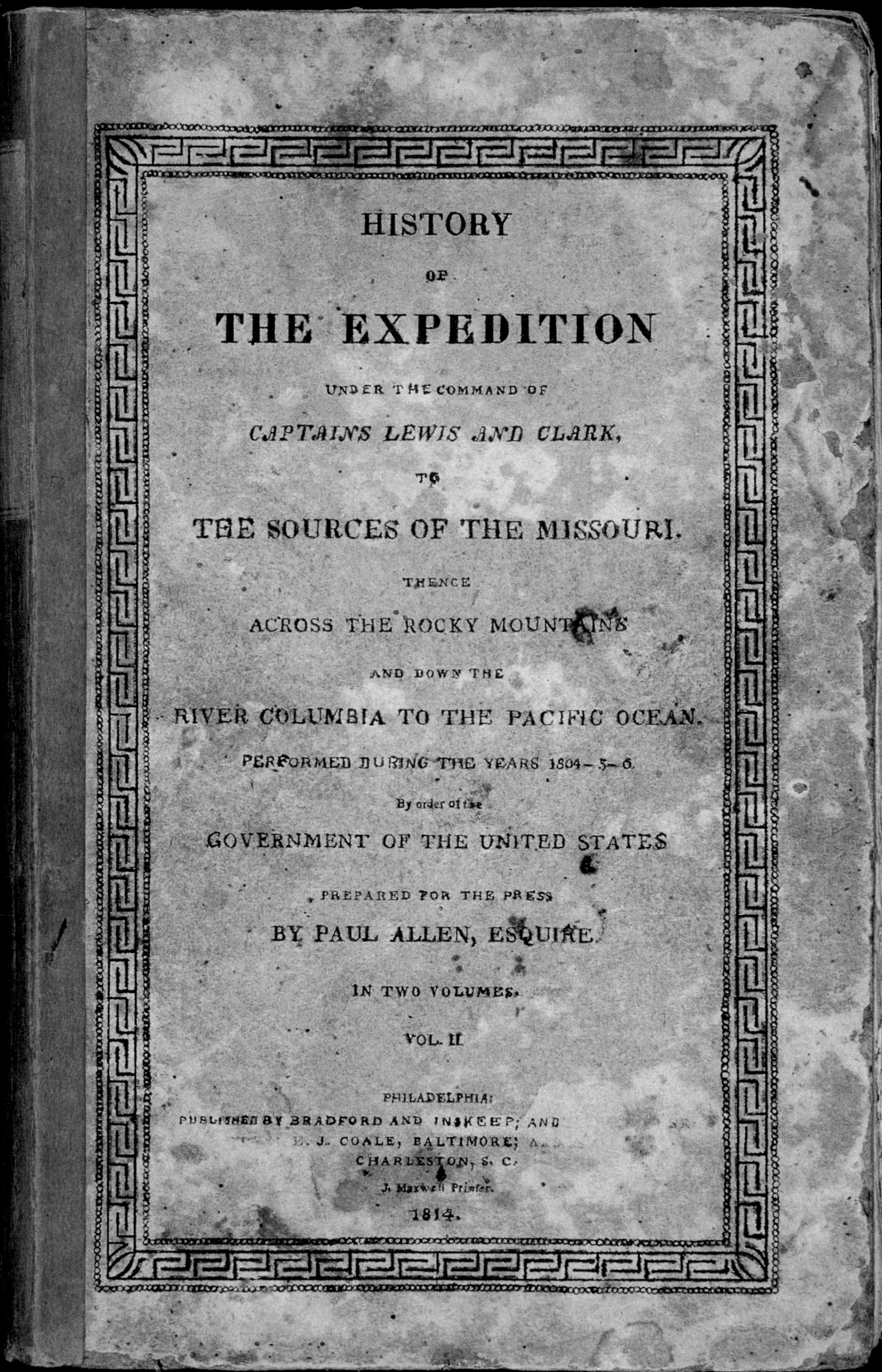
HISTORY
OF
THE EXPEDITION
UNDER THE COMMAND OF
CAPTAINS LEWIS AND CLARK,
TO
THE SOURCES OF THE MISSOURI.
THENCE
ACROSS THE ROCKY MOUNTAINS
AND DOWN THE
RIVER COLUMBIA TO THE PACIFIC OCEAN.
PERFORMED DURING THE YEARS 1804–5–6.
By order of the
GOVERNMENT OF THE UNITED STATES
PREPARED FOR THE PRESS
BY PAUL ALLEN, ESQUIRE.
IN TWO VOLUMES.
VOL. II.
PHILADELPHIA:
PUBLISHED BY BRADFORD AND INSKEEP; AND
J. COALE, BALTIMORE;
CHARLESTON, S. C.
J. Maxwell Printer.
1814.

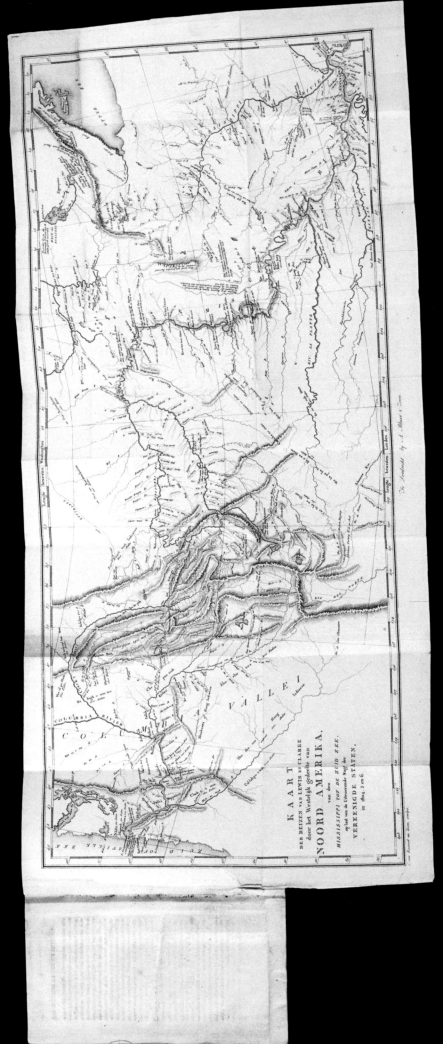

KAART
DER REIZEN VAN LEWIS EN CLARKE
door het Westelijk gedeelte van
NOORD AMERIKA.
van den
MISSISSIPPI TOT DE ZUID ZEE,
op lat van de Uitvoerende Magt der
VEREENIGDE STATEN,
in 1804, 5 en 6.

1

Codex J

[Wednesday] Fort Clatsop.
Tuesday January 1st 1806

Clatsop Paddle 5 feet long
4 In. greatest wiath of blade.

Quath-lah-poh the Swoard
3 feet in length. some of
them are near 4 feet in length
and 4½ inches in width at the
widest part. —

form of the wooden
bludgeon used by the
same people.

PEHRISKA-RUHPA

Moennitarri Warrior in the costume of the dog dance

43

46

44

47

45

48

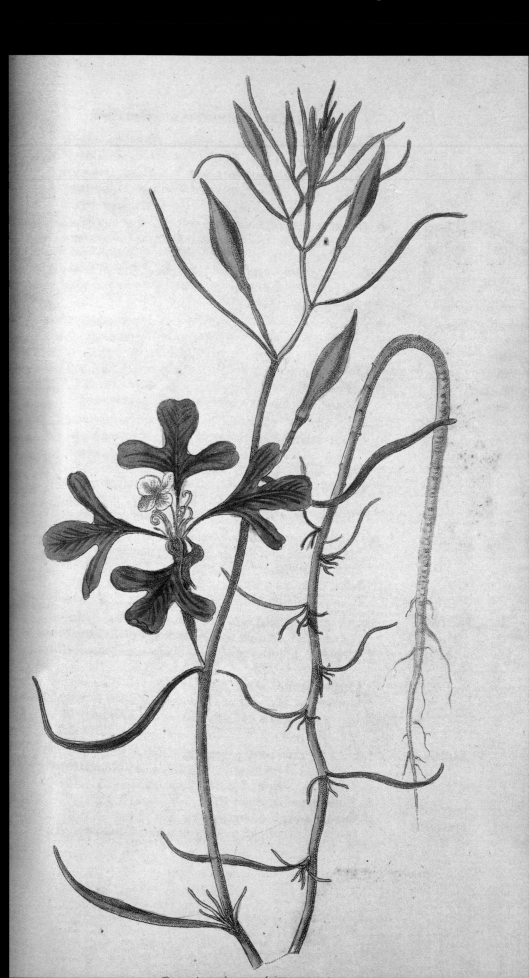

Chapter Five
Editing the Expedition Journals

Essay 147
Bibliography 171

5a The Biddle-Allen *History of the Expedition*
5a.1 Bradford and Inskeep, Philadelphia 1814
5a.2 Longman, London 1814
5a.3 Longman, London 1815
5a.4 Blussé, Dordrecht 1816-18
5a.5 Longman, London 1817
5a.6 Christie, Dublin 1817
5a.7 Mausberger, Vienna 1826
5a.8 Harper/M'Vickar, New York [Akron] 1842-1917
5a.9 McClurg/Hosmer, Chicago 1902-05, 1917, 1924
5a.10 New Amsterdam Book Company, New York 1902
5a.11 Barnes, New York 1903
5a.12 Barnes/McMaster, New York 1904
5a.13 Nutt, London 1905
5a.14 Allerton, New York 1922

5b Elliott Coues
5b.1 The Coues-Anderson Manuscript Transcript of the Journals
5b.2 Harper/Coues, New York 1893
5b.3 Other Publications by Coues on Lewis and Clark

5c James Davie Butler
5c.1 Butler, *The Journal of Charles Floyd* 1894
5c.2 Other Publications by Butler on Lewis and Clark

5d Reuben Gold Thwaites
5d.1 Thwaites, *Original Journals* 1904-5
5d.2 Other Publications by Thwaites on Lewis and Clark

5e Milo M. Quaife, *Journals of Lewis and Ordway* **1916**

5f Donald Jackson
5f.1 Jackson, *Letters of the Lewis and Clark Expedition* 1962, 1978
5f.2 Other Publications by Jackson on Lewis and Clark

5g Ernest Staples Osgood
5g.1 Osgood, *The Field Notes of Captain William Clark* 1964
5g.2 Other Publications by Osgood on Lewis and Clark

5h Gary E. Moulton
5h.1 Moulton, *The Journals of the Lewis and Clark Expedition* 1983-2001
5h.2 Other Publications by Moulton on Lewis and Clark

Editing the Expedition Journals

Several writers and editors crafted useful and commercially important narratives from Lewis and Clark's lengthy journals.

The untimely death of Meriwether Lewis on the Natchez Trace in October 1809 shattered the hopes of those anticipating a definitive narrative of the Lewis and Clark Expedition and an assessment of its scientific findings. However, other problems also arose. The Gass *Journal*, the work of a man with no literary aspirations or scientific interests, found a brisk market with editions in Pittsburgh (1807), London (1808), Philadelphia (1810, 1811, 1812), Paris (1810), and Weimar (1814). Surreptitious and apocryphal accounts about the expedition appeared in Philadelphia (1809) and London (1809) and several other locations thereafter. Benjamin Smith Barton, charged with assessing the flora and fauna collected and observed by the Corps of Discovery, was ill and plodding as he tried to craft the third volume announced in Lewis's prospectus of 1807. Frederick Pursh, engaged by Lewis to assist with the botanical studies, became discouraged with Barton's desultory efforts, moved to New York in 1809, and soon left the United States. Pursh took with him a significant collection of Lewis's specimens. In addition, John Conrad, the erstwhile publisher, had encountered financial reverses that drove him toward bankruptcy.[1]

As a result of all of these factors, Thomas Jefferson and William Clark experienced mounting anxiety about the necessity of publishing expedition reports. In 1810, Clark considered employing a man residing in Richmond, Virginia, to write the book. However, upon meeting Nicholas Biddle of Philadelphia, Clark wrote:

> I have calculated on your writing for me, and if you will undertake this work, Cant you Come to this place where I have my Books & memorandoms and stay with me a week or two; read over & make yourself thirily acquainted with every thing which may not be explained in the Journals? If you will come it may enable me to give you a more full view of those parts which may not be thirily explained and enable you to proceed without dificuelty.[2]

On receipt of Clark's letter, Biddle responded initially: "My occupations necessarily confine me to Phila., and I have neither health nor leisure to do sufficient justice to the fruits of your enterprize and ingenuity." Two weeks later, Biddle reversed his decision, finding better health, more time, and hearty encouragement from both Barton, who was to write the scientific assessment, and John Conrad, the publisher. "I will therefore very readily agree to do all that is in my power for the advancement of the work," he wrote, "and I think I can promise with some confidence that it shall be ready as soon as the publisher is prepared to print it."[3] The plan thus proceeded: Biddle was to work with the journals and field notes to craft a narrative of exploration and travel, while Barton was to take the scientific data and specimens and write a natural history.

The success of the project lay primarily with Nicholas Biddle, one of the brightest minds in America. Born in Philadelphia in 1786, Biddle entered the University of Pennsylvania at age ten and graduated at thirteen. He then studied at the College of New Jersey in Princeton, where he graduated in 1801 as valedictorian of his class. From 1804 to 1806, Biddle served as secretary to the American

1 For a general history of the crafting of the Biddle-Allen edition, published in 1814, see Cutright, "Nicholas Biddle," *A History*, 53–72; Jackson, *Letters*, 2:566, 577–578, 607–608.

2 Jackson, *Letters*, 2:494.

3 Ibid., 2:496.

4 Shade, "Nicholas Biddle," *American National Biography* (1999), 2:734–736.

5 Jackson, *Letters*, 2:497–545, 546.

6 Ibid., 2:547–548.

7 Ibid., 2:548–549.

8 Ibid., 2:562.

minister in Paris, traveled extensively, moved to London to serve as temporary secretary to American ambassador James Monroe, and in 1807 returned to Philadelphia. Biddle gained admittance to the Pennsylvania Bar Association in 1809 and was elected to the state legislature in 1810. He also became a regular contributor to the journal *Port Folio* and turned increasingly to a life of letters. This was the busy man who agreed in 1810 to William Clark's request that he transform raw notes into a book about the Corps of Discovery.[4]

To expedite his assignment, Biddle traveled in April 1810 to Fincastle, Virginia—the estate of Clark's father-in-law—to review with Clark the general plan of the work, borrow materials, and learn more about subjects that interested him or were incompletely documented. The sessions were immensely productive. Biddle recorded extensive notes based on his interviews with Clark. In all, Biddle spent nearly three weeks with Clark, an important collaboration that prepared Biddle quite well for crafting a narrative.[5]

Biddle retained the firm of C. and A. Conrad of Philadelphia to print a new prospectus for the publication—probably in May 1810. The prospectus announced subscriptions for *The History of the Expedition of Captains Lewis and Clarke, Through the Continent of North America, Performed During the Years 1804, 1805 and 1806, by order of the Government of the United States.* The announcement expressed regret at the delay incurred by the "melancholy fate of Captain Lewis" and dismissed the "several imperfect accounts of the journey" that had appeared in print. Biddle promoted a work in two parts: a narrative of the journey and an assessment of the scientific discoveries—the latter in the hands of Barton. Purchasers could secure either or both parts, paying ten dollars for the two volumes, octavo, of the first part (which included a map) and eleven dollars for the second part, sending their money to the Conrad firm at No. 30 Chestnut Street, Philadelphia.[6]

Biddle worked steadily from May 1810 to July 1811 to write a flowing narrative. He continued to correspond with Clark to secure additional information and, for a time, worked side by side with George Shannon, a veteran of the Corps of Discovery. Shannon, who had studied at the University of Lexington upon his return from the American West, traveled to Philadelphia in May 1810 to assist both Biddle and Barton.[7] Plans to salvage the aborted Lewis volumes for a natural history narrative, however, did not succeed. Barton's declining health and age precluded completing his assignment. Jefferson, long a friend, correspondent, and associate, tried to coax Barton to continue. He reminded Barton in September 1811 that John Bradbury's account of his western explorations had been printed and would soon be picked up in Europe, thus gaining public notice for first discoveries. "With respect therefore to your work, as well as Govr. Lewis's," he wrote, "I am anxious that whatever you do, should be done quickly." Again in April 1813, Jefferson wrote: "When shall we have your book on American botany, and when the 1st volume of Lewis & Clark's travels? Both of these works are of general expectation, and great interest, and to no one of more than to myself."[8]

Another calamity was the accelerating financial problems of the publisher. "That the firm of C. and A. Conrad and Co. for a long time previous to its failure, was in a state of extreme difficulty and embarrassment, was a matter of notoriety to every person acquainted with the parties," recalled Mathew Carey, the 1810–12 publisher of the Gass *Journal*. In October 1811, the press of creditors accelerated. Carey, who had loaned thirteen thousand dollars to Conrad, saw the problems as fatal and wrote: "John Conrad, early in November, informed me that he had executed securities in favour of Gray and Taylor, and Bradford and Inskeep, and myself, who were his principal creditors." The company collapsed in 1812.[9]

The bankruptcy of the Conrad firm involved an interesting nexus of publishers and printers of Lewis and Clark materials. Carey published the Gass *Journal* in 1810, 1811, and 1812. Conrad issued the prospectus in 1807 for the Lewis volumes and in 1810 for the Biddle and Barton volumes. Bradford and Inskeep ultimately published the Biddle-Allen edition in 1814. Tensions were high, especially when they involved money and the mercurial Mathew Carey. In the court proceedings against Edward Gray, Samuel F. Bradford (a principal in the firm of Bradford and Inskeep), and Robert Taylor in the bankruptcy of C. and A. Conrad and Co., Carey railed against other creditors. Writing of Edward Gray, Carey said:

> And further, never, were he to live an hundred years, can he wash himself clear of the damning fact, that on Tuesday the 26th of May, he *insidiously and fraudulently* strove to extort money from me to support C. and A. Conrad and Co. (after having before extorted money for the same purpose,) whose whole property he, and Robert Taylor, and Samuel F. Bradford, rapaciously seized three days afterwards.[10]

The bankruptcy of C. and A. Conrad and Co. became yet another impediment to publishing the primary documentation of the Corps of Discovery. On July 4, 1812, Biddle wrote to Clark: "I have been constantly endeavoring to commence the publication not only from a regard to the interests of both of us, but because while this work remained on my hands it interfered very much with all my other occupations, besides that the work would lose some of its interest by so much delay." Conrad's collapse compelled him to terminate business and abandon the project. "This misfortune," observed Biddle:

> is very much to be regretted on his account, & I am sorry that we did not know sooner that he would not be able to publish. But since things have taken this turn, it is perhaps better that the printing was not begun than that we should be entangled with his assignees, since now we can place it in other hands. I have already spoken to Mr. Bradford one of the best booksellers here & if we come to an arrangement we can soon print the work. I am in hopes that he will take it on the same terms as Mr. Conrad did . . . .[11]

In the fall of 1812, John Conrad tried to sell the manuscript, or at least find a publishing house willing to take what Biddle had crafted. In November, he wrote to Biddle that the firm of Johnson and Warner, stationers and booksellers at 147 Market Street, had "positively declined making any sort of offer for Genl. Clarkes book." He also reported that Thomas Dobson & Son, booksellers at 41 South Second Street, "appears to have little inclination to embark in the work and declines making any proposals for it." Conrad counseled Biddle to accept the offer of Bradford & Inskeep. "It is," he wrote, "I am confident the best bargain you can make for Genl. Clarke. The copyright I presume will be in him (Genl. C.) & I suppose he will derive the entire benefit of the sale of the M.S. in England."[12]

In March 1813, William Clark, then residing in Missouri Territory, assigned power of attorney to Nicholas Biddle to represent him in transactions with the publishers Bradford & Inskeep.[13] At this point, however, Biddle began to retreat from further work on the expedition history. He was eager to get on with his own

"You should know that the original 'Lewis & Clarke' was very badly edited from the rough field-notes of the explorers."

Elliott Coues to Francis Harper, July 17, 1892

9 Carey, *Narrative of the Proceedings*, 3, 11.

10 Ibid., p. 7.

11 Jackson, *Letters*, 2:577.

12 Ibid., 2:581.

13 Ibid., 2:583.

business affairs, politics, and other writing. Also, he had married in 1811 and, in 1812, assumed duties as editor of *The Port Folio*.[14] Biddle hired Paul Allen for five hundred dollars to complete the work of preparing the travel narrative for press. "This sum," concluded Donald Jackson, "indicates that Biddle left a considerable amount of work to be done."[15]

The role of Paul Allen in the final preparation of the expedition history became a controversial subject in 1893. At that time, Elliot Coues, who was preparing a reprint of the edition, assigned all work credit to Biddle and denigrated Allen. Coues wrote:

> I presume Mr. Paul Allen is mainly responsible for the shocking punctuation and other errors of the published pages. He had absolutely no joint authorship with Mr. Biddle; he had not the shadow of a claim that I can discover, to be even mentioned in connection with the work, much less to have his name on the title-page; he was a mere hack, who received $500 for some alleged or perhaps imaginary services, not discernible in the light of history.[16]

Allen deserved better treatment. Born in 1775 in Providence, Rhode Island, he came from a family prominent in politics. He graduated in 1793 from Brown University, where he earned a reputation as an orator. Allen's literary aspirations were in poetry; he published a collection, *Original Poems, Serious and Entertaining* (1801). He eventually settled in Philadelphia and became a writer for and editor of the *United States Gazette* and *The Port Folio*. In 1811, Allen began writing a biography of Charles Brockden Brown, an American novelist. He partially completed this assignment and saw into print one volume, a collection of most of Brown's unpublished manuscripts.[17]

The respective roles of Biddle and Allen were cogently examined in Lester J. Cappon's "Who is the Author of *History of the Expedition under the Command of Captains Lewis and Clark* (1814)?" In a review of the 1961 J. B. Lippincott reprint of this work, Cappon explored the textual complications of the 1814 volumes. He laid out authorship as clearly as anyone has ever stated it:

> The *History*, then, is not 'Governor Lewis's journal' (to quote Jefferson); nor is it a 'narrative of the journey' (to quote Allen) in the sense that its title implies to the modern reader. As day-by-day primary accounts of the expedition, the journals delineate its 'history' in the free use of that word, in their generation of our own, by persons who do not distinguish clearly between documentary history and the historian's history derived from the sources by a process of research, distillation, and interpretation. Biddle's 'succinct and circumstantial narrative,' as he called it, was the product of skillful, well-knit piecework rather than patchwork, of interpolation of his 'oral history' notes recorded from Clark and Shannon, and of his own sound sense of selection and continuity. With his feeling for the polite style young Biddle, an established literary editor and brilliant scholar, found sufficient reason, in accord with the standards of his time, to improve upon the vocabulary and phraseology of the explorers, to make the rough passages smooth. Some printed accounts of the expedition, both genuine and spurious, had already met with a favorable public response. One can well imagine that Biddle, immersed in the original records, found his task challenging as a literary and historical pursuit.[18]

Allen's role in preparing the manuscript was substantial. Feeling that the work needed more of a human-interest element, he solicited from Thomas Jefferson a

14 Shade, "Nicholas Biddle," *American National Biography* (1999), 2:734–736.

15 Jackson, *Letters*, 2:585.

16 Coues, *History of the Expedition*, 1:xvn; Coues, "Description of the Original Manuscript Journals," 33.

17 Kagle, "Paul Allen," *American National Biography* (1999), 1:337–338.

18 Cappon, "Who Is the Author," *William and Mary Quarterly* 19: 261.

biographical sketch of Meriwether Lewis. When Jefferson confirmed he would write it, Allen held up publication. Allen explained to Jefferson: "I am not apprehensive that the fulness of Your Biography will be an obstacle to its publication now that I have prevailed upon the Booksellers to procrastinate the volume. I wish very much to enliven the dullness of the Narrative by something more popular splendid & attractive."[19] Jefferson promptly wrote the sketch and forwarded it to Biddle, asking him to review the submission before passing it to Allen.

By September 1813, the long-deferred work was in the hands of typesetters. Biddle informed Jefferson: "about one half of the second & last volume of the narrative is printed & that the whole will appear shortly. The introductory notice of Govr. Lewis is very interesting & the account of the previous projects for exploring the country west of the Mississippi contains new & curious information."[20]

However, the project was not yet complete. Work slowed, then stopped. Bradford and Inskeep became involved in other printing. In December 1813, Paul Allen wrote to Jefferson that all was done but the weather diary in the appendix. He expressed appreciation for the Lewis biography and mentioned that, though he had seriously considered it, he had withheld inclusion of Alexander Wilson's moving account of Lewis's death to avoid wounding "the sensibility of surviving relatives & friends."[21]

On March 23, 1814, Biddle wrote to William Clark a fulsome report about the history of the expedition:

> I have at last the pleasure of informing you that the Travels are published—that they have sold very well I understand, and have been well thought of by the readers. Henceforward you may sleep upon your fame which must last as long as books can endure. Mr. Bradford has I presume sent you a copy of the work. The gentleman who revised & prepared it for the press, Mr. Allen is a very capable person, & as I did not put the finishing hand to the volumes I did not think it right to take from him the credit of his own exertions & care by announcing personally the part which I had in the compilation. I am content that my trouble in the business should be recompensed only by the pleasure which attended it, and also by the satisfaction of making your acquaintance which I shall always value.[22]

The years of waiting for details of the expedition were mostly worthwhile. Biddle and Allen—the latter of whose name, alone, appeared on the title page— had crafted a highly readable travel narrative. While they lacked significant scientific data, the two volumes provided extensive new information about the geography, native peoples, and economic prospects of the western two-thirds of North America. The crowning glory of the publication was William Clark's map, redrawn by Samuel Lewis—cartographer for Jefferson's *Notes on the State of Virginia*—and engraved by Samuel Harrison (1789–1818). This splendid work filled in the blank spaces and removed much of the mythology from western cartography. Gone was Aaron Arrowsmith's hypothetical single line of mountains, a western mirror image of the Appalachians. In their place were the convoluted ranges that tested the mettle and survival skills of the Corps of Discovery in their crossings from east to west and back again. The volume also included Jefferson's biography of Lewis and the appendix with Lewis's "Observations and reflections on the present and future state of upper Louisiana, in relation to the government of the Indian nations . . . A summary statement of the rivers, creeks and most remarkable places, their distances

"The printer, Inskeep, probably did the best he could with the copy furnished him, but it is wretchedly set up, the pointing in particular being terrific, the spelling often very funny, and the 'parts of speech' dislocated in a thousand places."

Elliott Coues to Francis Harper, July 17, 1892

19 Jackson, *Letters*, 2:584–586.

20 Ibid., 2:594–595.

21 Ibid., 2:597. Wilson, an ornithologist, visited the site of Lewis's death and grave and published a poignant narrative and poem about the experience. Slatkin, "Alexander Wilson," *American National Biography* (1999), 23:554–556.

22 Jackson, *Letters*, 2:598.

from each other, &c., . . . Estimate of the western Indians . . . Thermometrical observations, showing the rise and fall of the Mississippi (Missouri). . . Remarks and reflections [January 1, 1804, to August 22, 1806]." [23]

The volume's publisher, Bradford & Inskeep, maintained distinguished connections and was part of Philadelphia's thriving publishing industry. [24] Samuel Fisher Bradford (1776–1837) was the great-great-grandson of William Bradford, a printer who immigrated to America in 1682 and established a shop in 1683 in Philadelphia. William Bradford later moved to New York, gained appointment as Royal Printer, and in 1725 founded a newspaper. Successive generations entered the trade. Thomas Bradford, father of Samuel Fisher Bradford, returned to Philadelphia, founded the newspaper *True American and Commercial Advertiser*, and expanded the family's role in publishing. Samuel Fisher Bradford married Abigail Inskeep and became an important publisher of books in the first decade of the nineteenth century. [25]

Samuel Bradford was committed to publishing works of travel and exploration. One of his most ambitious moves was to begin production in 1802 of William Fordyce Mavor's *An Historical Account of the Most Celebrated Voyages, Travels, and Discoveries, from the Time of Columbus to the Present Period*. This series first appeared in London. Twenty volumes were published in 1796–97 and four more volumes appeared in 1801. The pace of production was inexorable. Between March 1802 and early 1804, Bradford brought out a new volume almost every fourth week, for a total of twenty-four volumes. Most of them were bound in blue boards and printed by Robert Carr. [26] The first volume contained selections from the writings of Columbus, Vespucci, Cortes, Pizarro, da Gama, Cabral, and Magellan. Volumes 6 and 7 were accounts of the three voyages of Captain James Cook. Bruce's search for the source of the Nile, Hearne's quest for the Northwest Passage in 1769 and 1772, Brissot de Warville's travels in the United States in 1788, the adventures of Mungo Park and John Ledyard in Africa, and many others made up this series. Each volume contained 260 to 300 pages. Mavor (1758–1837) wrote several of the titles in the series, including histories of the Arabs, and of India, Hindustan, Korea, and Japan. Select purchasers gained remarkable accounts of world exploration. [27]

Works of general interest and utility were also part of Samuel Fisher Bradford's inventory. These included *Dr. Rees' New Cyclopaedia* (1806), *The Ladies and Gentleman's Pocket Almanac* (1807), "A Map of the Territory of Orleans, Comprising West Florida, and a Part of the Mississippi Territory" (1807), and Vol. 3, *Atlas*, of the *American Artillerist's Companion* (1813). [28] As a writer, Bradford also translated from French to English the "Funeral Oration on Brother George Washington" (1800) and penned a spirited pamphlet, *The Imposter Detected, Or, a Review of Some of the Writings of 'Peter Porcupine'*" (1796). Mathew Carey was engaged in the same satirical debate with his works, *A Plumb Pudding for . . . Peter Porcupine* and *The Porcupiniad* (1799). [29]

Bradford's marriage to Abigail Inskeep brought him into several dealings with his father-in-law, John Inskeep (1757–1834), and with his wife's uncle, Abraham Inskeep (1752–1820), a New York publisher and bookdealer. A veteran of the Revolutionary War, John Inskeep was successively a Philadelphia tavern owner, china and glassware merchant, Philadelphia mayor (1800, 1805), judge, and longtime chief officer of insurance companies. In 1812, he purchased a partnership for his son, John Inskeep Jr., with Samuel Fisher Bradford, to create the firm of Bradford &

23 Biddle and Allen, *History of the Expedition*.

24 William McCulloch reported that in 1803 he found forty-five printing houses with eighty presses operating in the city. Of the printers, fifteen were also engaged in the retail book trade. McCulloch, "William McCulloch's Additions," *American Antiquarian Society Proceedings*, 93.

25 Purple, *Bradford Family*, 1–8.

26 Carr printed perhaps eighteen volumes. Tesseon & Lee and H. Maxwell printed some of the remaining six titles. Bradford, "Bradford Family Papers."

27 Bradford preserved records of his printing costs of this series. The first ten volumes ranged in payments to Robert Carr from $143.91 to $168.65, with the number of copies not known. Bradford, "Bradford Family Papers."

28 *The True American Commercial Advertiser* (Philadelphia), January 1, 1807.

29 Green, "Mathew Carey," *American National Biography* (1999), 4:381–383.

Inskeep on the west side of Third Street, below Market, in Philadelphia. Inskeep's interests lay, however, not in printing, publishing, and book selling, but in theology. He remained in the firm only four years, then departed for New Orleans to work as a minister. The younger Inskeep died there of the "malignant fever" in 1820.[30]

Pre-publication and review notices of the *History of the Expedition* appeared in *The Stranger* (Albany), March 12 and April 9, 1814, and in more lengthy accounts in *The Western Gleaner* (Pittsburgh), April and May, 1814, a journal published by the firm of Cramer, Spear & Eichbaum, publishers in 1807 of the Gass *Journal*. The editor of *The Western Gleaner* first printed in full Jefferson's "Life of Captain Lewis," presumably buying a bit of time to read the two volumes of the Biddle-Allen narrative. Then, in the May issue, he presented an ambitious and perceptive review of the work. The writer summarized the expedition and laid out its contributions: geographical information; prospects of the land, new animals, plants, and minerals; and insight into the nature of the Indian tribes. Expressing a bit of dismay about the richness of information, the reviewer then reminded himself that the book was "the *official* report of public men to their employers" and that "this minuteness of detail" gave "to the performance a stamp of candor and veracity, which, in the eyes of the philosopher, are the very requisites of similar compositions."[31]

The reviewer for *The Stranger* criticized many things. He lamented the absence of information on natural history and the Indian vocabularies: "These are to travels what episodes are to Poetry, and should be skillfully arranged by an author so as to revive the drooping attention. Notices of the Musquetoe, are, however, frequently made, and there seems to have been no opportunity missed, in which the incursions of these interesting little animals, are not introduced." He found the biography of Lewis "pompously displayed." And he tore into the editor:

> Mr. Allen, the editor, had no part in the expedition, and we look upon him, rather as an interloper, who wishes to share in the merits of the enterprize, without participating at all, in the difficulties of attending it. He has been known to the publick as a writer of verses, and some prose pieces; and it would appear that his merit has been acknowledged by the present *national work* being trust to his care. It has been whispered, that the government have taken no part in this publication. If this is the fact, there can be no excuse for it.[32]

For later generations interested in the labors of the Corps of Discovery, the reviewer's comments in *The Western Gleaner* about the failure to produce the third volume of scientific information are particularly relevant. In particular, the reviewer found fault with the "learned Professor," Barton. He wrote: "The works promised at various times by Barton would almost fill by themselves the shelves of a library. To quiet our anxiety, however, concerning this deluge of publications, the celebrated Professor tells us somewhere with great naivety, (we believe at the end of his fragments on the natural history of Pennsylvania) that the promises of authors are not to be taken any more literally, than the oaths of lovers." The reviewer quoted at length from the Biddle-Allen edition about grizzly bears, buffaloes, antelopes; the account of strange noises near the falls of the Missouri; Osage and Ricara tribe myths; and the ethnographic overview of the tribes at the mouth of the Columbia. The reviewer found the two-volume work worthwhile and concluded: "It will have been perceived, that the style is clear, simple and

30 Wallace, "Sketch of John Inskeep," 7; Crane and Dine, *The Diary*, 3:2169; *Poulson's American Daily Advertiser* (Philadelphia), September 27, 1820.

31 Jefferson, "Life of Captain Lewis," *The Western Gleaner* 1: 293–301; Review of *History of the Expedition* in *The Western Gleaner* 1: 350–354.

32 Review of *History of the Expedition* in *The Stranger* 1: 321–328.

unaffected. Digressions foreign to the subject are carefully discarded; nor is the work in any way tainted with the animosities of party-spirit."[33]

The Biddle-Allen edition was also reviewed in *The Analectic Magazine* (Philadelphia, 1815). The lengthy review provided an overview of the expedition and contained praise for the detailed journals kept by Lewis and Clark "judiciously" used by the editor to craft the narrative. What troubled this reviewer, however, was "disgust at the manner which certain typographical gentlemen in Philadelphia, and elsewhere" adopted in ramming together adjectives and nouns. "Their practice is to connect the two words as to make them appear as one word of two syllables," he wrote. To buttress his argument, he cited: Whitebrant creek, Whiteearth river, Yellowstone river, Goodhope island, Muscleshell river, Grapevines, and Chokecherries. He concluded his review by observing:

> This tasteless and niggardly innovation, offends, at the same moment, the sight, the sound, and the sense. It tends to obliterate the clearest vestiges of etymology, disfigures the features of the letter press, gives a vulgar and insignificant cast to the most dignified proper names, and has a continual proneness to mar the sound by its range and unnatural mixture of distinct words that were never made to be melted down into petty syllables, for the mere convenience of a work shop.[34]

The publishing house of Longman, Hurst, Rees, Orme, and Brown was next to print the Biddle-Allen narrative. With a new introduction by Thomas Rees and a new title—*Travels to the Source of the Missouri River and Across the American Continent to the Pacific Ocean*—the work began its transit through European publishing houses and bookstores. Momentum was quick, for within weeks of issue in Philadelphia and New York, Rees had crafted his comments, dated April 30, 1814. He wrote: "The present edition is printed nearly verbatim from the original; the sheets of which were forwarded to this country by the American Proprietors: the only liberty that has been taken with the language, has been merely the correction of a few inadvertent grammatical or typographical errors." Considering that portion of the appendix containing Lewis's "State of the Indian Nations" of "little interest for the British reader," Rees cut it. He also dropped Jefferson's "Life of Lewis" and Paul Allen's preface. Rees took the opportunity in his "Introduction" to mention the travel account of Zebulon Montgomery Pike, a work printed by Longman and listed in the firm's advertisement of recent titles. This London edition, in quarto, was offered at £2 12s 6d.[35]

The London edition, printed by John George Barnard, included Clark's large, fold-out map and plates after those of the American edition but re-engraved with some variations by Samuel John Neele (1758–1824).[36] Barnard was located at 27 Skinner Road in the Snow Hill District of London from 1807 to 1821. His printing establishment had been destroyed by fire in 1811, but he renewed work and executed the handsome London edition of the Biddle-Allen text.[37] Thomas Rees (1777–1864), who cut portions of the text and crafted the London preface, was the son of Josiah Rees, a younger brother of the publisher Owen Rees. Thomas Rees entered the book trade but withdrew in 1799 to study for the ministry. Between 1807 and 1832 he held a variety of religious appointments in London, but ultimately resigned and died in obscurity in Brighton. Rees was an expert in sixteenth-century antitrinitarian opinion, a collector of religious tracts, and author of several volumes of religious history as well as *The Beauties of South Wales, &c.* (1815).[38]

33 Review of *History of the Expedition* in *The Western Gleaner* 1: 355–375.

34 Review of *History of the Expedition* in *The Analectic Magazine* 5: 127, 233–234.

35 *Travels to the Source* (London, 1814); "New Publications for 1814," *The Edinburgh Annual Register* (1814), xxvi–xxvii.

36 *Travels to the Source* (London, 1814).

37 Todd, *A Directory of Printers*, 10.

38 Lee, "Thomas Rees," *Dictionary of National Biography*, 47:401–402.

The publishing house of Longman had its origins in London in 1724 with the labors and vision of Thomas Longman. Longman was an orphan from Bristol who apprenticed in the London book trade. Known as Longman, Hurst, Rees, and Orme (1804–1811), it published Hubbard Lester's surreptitious *Travels of Capts. Lewis and Clarke . . .* (1809). As Longman, Hurst, Rees, Orme, and Brown (1811–1823), it published the Biddle-Allen edition, *Travels to the Source of the Missouri River . . .* (1814). Longman, along with Rivingtons (publisher of the George Phillips apocrypha, *Travels in North America,* 1831), enjoyed two of the longest and most notable book publishing histories in England over the last three centuries. A crucial element of Longman's success was its decision to publish Ephraim Chambers' *Cyclopedia* in 1728. Longman gained control of this valuable work by buying out the other interests. The volume was in its fifth edition by 1746 and was revised and reissued by Abraham Rees between 1778 and 1786.[39]

Owen Rees, a brother of Thomas Rees, became a Longman partner in 1794 or 1797. In 1802, Longman Rees (as the firm was commonly known in that era) began publication of the *Annual Review* and also was a partial owner of *The Edinburgh Review.* Through these ventures, the company built an important list of authors, including William Wordsworth, Robert Southey, Samuel Taylor Coleridge, and Sir Walter Scott. Thomas Hurst and Cosmo Orme joined the publishing company as partners in 1804. Hurst turned out to be a scoundrel, got the firm into financial difficulties, was expelled from the partnership, and died in 1850 in a poor house. Generally, however, the company succeeded and was a major force for more than 250 years in the publishing and book trade of London's Paternoster Row.[40]

Longman Rees's 1814 edition of the Biddle-Allen narrative was the subject of an ambitious essay in *The Edinburgh Review* (1815). The reviewer found much in the work to be "minute, circumstantial, and unadorned," and, while accurate, "often heavy and uninteresting" but filled with "curious and valuable information concerning a tract of the earth that possesses many singularities." Several subjects caught the reader's attention. One was the Plains Indian "Buffalo Dance," a subject so fraught with lurid sexual content that Biddle rendered the passage in Latin, assuming that only scholarly eyes should consider the event. The reviewer found the dance "the most vile and indecorous amusement which we have any where seen described." As with other accounts, this reviewer, too, lamented the absence of more scientific data:

> The manner in which the scientific part was conducted, appears to merit commendation; though the want of a Barometer is an oversight hardly to be forgiven. We wish, too, that the astronomical apparatus had been more particularly described, and that the manner of finding the longitude had been more circumstantially detailed. Chronometers were used, and rectified, we presume, by lunar observation: But of this we should have been precisely informed; and the observations should have been given just as they were made, without reduction or correction of any kind.[41]

The Quarterly Review (London, October 1814–January 1815) also reviewed the first London edition of the Biddle-Allen narrative. The commentator wrote scornfully about the lack of scientific information, lamenting the absence of draftsmen and naturalists on the expedition and theorizing that such was "probably imputable to the spirit of an illiberal and parsimonious government." The reviewer reserved his greatest scorn, however, for the choices of place names inflicted by Lewis and

39 Briggs, "T. Longman," *The British Literary Book Trade,* 176–183.

40 Curwen, *A History,* 89–94; Feather, *A History,* 120; Rees, *Reminiscences,* 45–59.

41 Review of *Travels to the Source, The Edinburgh Review* 24: 412–438.

Clark on the landscape of the American West:

> Of all people who ever imposed names upon a newly discovered country the
> Americans have certainly been the most unlucky in their choice; witness
> Bigmuddy River, and Littlemuddy River, Littleshallow River, Good Woman
> River, Little Good Woman Creek, Grindstone Creek, Cupboard Creek,
> Biscuit Creek, Blowing Fly Creek, *cum multis aliis* in the same delightful taste.
> When this country shall have its civilized inhabitants, its cities, its scholars,
> and its poets, how sweetly will such names sound in American verse!

And, to provide a sample of future poetic prospects, the reviewer (whom Elliot
Coues later identified as Robert Southey) wrote:

> Ye plains where sweet Big-muddy rolls along,
> And Tea-Pot, one day to be famed in song,
> Where swans on Biscuit and on Grindstone glide,
> And willows wave upon Good Woman's side!
> How shall your happy streams in after time
> Tune the soft lay and fill the sonorous rhyme!
> Blest bards, who in your amorous verse will call
> On murmuring Pork and gentle Cannon-Ball;
> Split-Rock, and Stick-Lodge, and Two-Thousand-Mile,
> White-lime, and Cupboard, and Bad-humour'd Isle!
> Flow, Little-Shallow, flow! and be thy stream.
> Their great example, as it will their theme!
> Isis with Rum and Onion must not vie,
> Cam shall resign the palm to Blowing-Fly,
> And Thames and Tagus yield to great Big-Little-Dry.[42]

Regardless, Longman Rees found a good market for the Biddle-Allen narrative.
The book sold out in 1814, was reprinted in 1815 and 1817, all under the London
title, *Travels to the Source of the Missouri River*. In 1817 J. Christie of 170 James's
Street, Dublin, printed the *History of the Expedition Under the Command of Captains
Lewis and Clarke*. This work, in two volumes, derived directly, with some changes
in punctuation, from the Philadelphia edition and may have been underwritten
by Bradford and Inskeep. It retained the notice of the Pennsylvania copyright,
Jefferson's "Life of Lewis," and published for the first time the plate, "Principal
Cascade of the Missouri," which was drawn by Irish-born John James Barralet
(ca. 1747–1815). Meriwether Lewis had commissioned Barralet in 1807 to execute
drawings of the falls of the Missouri and Columbia.[43]

J. Christie of Dublin was a highly productive printer during a time when the
book trade of Ireland was collapsing. Ireland's clergy, land owners, and lawyers
were eager buyers of books. Works of history, biography, lexicography, and general essays found a strong market, especially when reprinted and sold at prices significantly less than in London. The factors that undermined the publishing enterprise were the brisk rise of reprints in the United States and England, an increase
in duty on paper imported into Ireland, and—catastrophically—the extension of
British copyright law in 1801 with the Act of Union. These events drove dozens
of printers and publishers out of business or to immigrate to other countries.[44]

J. Christie survived the bad times and was a regular publisher of works, many
of them reprints, in history, religion, and travels. In 1809, he published *The General
History of Ireland* by Geoffrey Keating and Dermod O'Connor; in 1810 Dennis

42 Review of *Travels to the Source*
in *The Quarterly Review*
12: 318, 335–336.

43 Lewis paid Barralet forty
dollars to execute two drawings of waterfalls. The originals have disappeared. In this
case, however, a Dublin plate
was used to engrave this
image, the first visual documentation of the falls of the
Missouri. Jackson, *Letters*,
2:462–463.

44 Cole, *Irish Booksellers*, 28–31,
148, 156.

Taffe's *An Impartial History of Ireland*; and in 1813 in eight volumes, *A History of the Earth and Animated Nature* by Oliver Goldsmith. Christie's most ambitious publishing project, however, was *The World Displayed; Or, A Curious Collection of Voyages and Travels, Selected from Writers of All Nations* (1814–1815), the reprinting of a work in ten volumes with plates and introductions by Christopher Smart, Oliver Goldsmith, and Samuel Johnson. The accounts included several voyages to the East Indies, narratives of explorations in quest of the Northwest Passage, Pocock's travels in Egypt, Moore's travels to Senegal and the interior of West Africa, and travel accounts in many countries in Europe. Following publication of the *History of the Expedition Under the Command of Captains Lewis and Clarke* (1817), Christie remained an active publisher, especially of volumes of religious history.[45]

The Dutch also had a thriving book trade and a public interested in exploration and travel. Popular fare included works on Dutch explorations in the East and West Indies, North America, Africa, and India. Dordrecht, Netherlands, was an important center of publishing and, since the 1720s, the site of a steady flow of works from the press of Abraham Blussé. The firm published the Biddle-Allen narrative as *Reize Naar de Bronnen van den Missouri en Door Het Vaste Land van America Naar de Zuidzee* [*Journey to the Sources of the Missouri and Across the Continent of America to the South Sea*]. The volumes in 1816 and 1817 bore the imprint of A. Blussé en Zoon (A. Blussé and Son), while the third, released in 1818, was published by Blussé en van Braam.[46]

Abraham Blussé (1726–1808) founded a printing dynasty that endured for four generations. For many years he was joined in the business by his son, Pieter Blussé Sr. (1748–1823), creating the firm of A. Blussé en Zoon. In the third generation, Pieter Blussé Jr. (1786–1869) married Clara Maria van Braam, the daughter and sole surviving child of Pieter van Braam (1740–1817), a publisher and poet who also resided in Dordrecht. The fourth generation of this publishing family was headed by Pieter van Braam Blussé (1809–1888). Between 1745 and 1823, the firm printed more than fourteen hundred titles.[47]

The firm of A. Blussé printed new books, reprinted other works, published dictionaries and grammars of modern languages, held the monopoly of printing lucrative lottery tickets, and produced a newspaper, edited after 1795 by Abraham Blussé Jr. (b. 1772), another son of Pieter Blussé Sr. Abraham Blussé had named his printing shop "Laurens Coster" in honor of the Dutchman many contended was the true inventor of moveable type. The largest single project undertaken by the firm was the publication in French of Count Georges L. Buffon's *Histoire Naturelle: Générale et Particulière* in nine volumes.[48] Buffon's contention that creatures in the Western Hemisphere were degenerate, both in vitality and size, had produced a lively exchange when Thomas Jefferson resided in France in the 1780s. In fact, part of Jefferson's determination to have Lewis and Clark collect natural history specimens was to set to rest, once and for all, Buffon's errors. At considerable trouble and expense, Jefferson obtained the skin, antlers, and skeleton of a moose. He presented the specimens to Buffon.[49]

Nicholas Godfried van Kampen (1776–1839) was responsible for translating the Biddle-Allen narrative into Dutch and writing an enthusiastic introduction to the work. Born near Haarlem, van Kampen endured the loss of his parents at a young age. While his father's nursery business was in the hands of guardians, he was well educated at Crefeld and Muhlheim. In 1795, following the sale of his

45 *World Catalog* enumerates more than thirty titles which bear the imprint of "J. Christie," Dublin.

46 *Reize naar de Bronnen van den Missouri.*

47 Baggerman, *Een Lot Uit de Loterij;* Van der Aa, "Abraham Blussé," *Biographisch Woordenboek,* 2:666–671; "Pieter van Braam," *Biographisch Woordenboek,* 3:1139–1141.

48 Van der Aa, "Abraham Blussé," *Biographisch Woordenboek,* 2:666–667.

49 Jackson, *Letters,* 1:47; 2:737.

father's business, he settled in Leiden to master the book trade and modern languages. Van Kampen wrote intermittently for newspapers in Leiden and Alphen. While in his early thirties, he was named librarian of the Bibliotheca Thysiana, a good position but one that provided little compensation. In 1815, he was named lecturer in High German languages at the University of Leiden and joined the Institute of P. de Raadst te Noortheij bij Leiden, where he helped teach Dutch history and literature to some of the finest pupils. Van Kampen next settled in Amsterdam in 1829 to teach literature and language at the "famous school," presumably the old university. He was, at the time of translating the Biddle-Allen narrative, a teacher, writer, and polymath, competent in multiple modern and ancient languages. At his death in 1839, van Kampen had written or translated seventy-six works about history, literature, and world travel.[50]

In the "Voorberight van den Vertaler" ["Preface of the Translator"], van Kampen reviewed major discoveries, addressing the continents and the explorers who made known distant and exotic lands. He then wrote:

> The fifth gap in our knowledge of the earth is the interior of North America. From the west bank of the River Mississippi to the South Sea, based on almost the entire length of this river, the knowledge of this land was based on uncertain rumors of fables such as by the famous Lahouton. But one could more readily expect the supplementing of this lacking piece because, not here like in Asia or in Africa with its deserts and suspicious tribes or like New Holland with its mountain ranges or finally such as South America with the slowness of an antiquated, almost died out government, nothing hindered it.[51]

Van Kampen described the United States as "a youthful republic sprouted out of European blood," which had opened commerce in all oceans and lands. As a consequence, he argued that the country could not remain indifferent about its unknown western frontier and that Jefferson, "no matter what you think of his political life," was a scholar and lover of knowledge who designed the expedition "to make an indispensable contribution."[52]

Van Kampen looked for comparable settings to describe to the reader, and found the great prairies of the interior of North America similar to the plains of southern Russia. He suggested that "both may be suitable places for European colonization," but argued that the primary mission of the United States was to find a land route to the Pacific Ocean to foster the fur trade with China. The expedition, he wrote, was mounted "under unspeakable difficulty and incomparable leadership" and represented one of the most significant renewals of explorations from previous times. The Dutch translator immersed readers in his enthusiasm: "Entire new discoveries were made by this journey. Never by Europeans, maybe by no human beings had these lands been explored. Imagine the fertile steppes of southern Russia for the first part of the journey. The prairie along the Missouri is a fertile desert crying for inhabitants other than the tribes which hunt and trap there." Van Kampen, who completely ignored the presence of Indian tribes, envisioned the rise of cities along the Missouri—"true European cities" he said, unlike those along the Dneiper.[53]

Not all of the Dutch preface was filled with praise for the Biddle-Allen narrative. "The account of this journey is most important and the communications are pleasurable for our countrymen who have any appreciation of the knowledge of

50 Van der Aa, "Nicholas Godfried van Kampen," *Biographisch Woordenboek*, K:15–25.

51 *Reize naar de Bronnen van den Missouri*, 1:vi–vii.

52 Ibid., 1:vii–viii.

53 Ibid., 1:ix–x.

the earth and the inhabitants," wrote van Kampen. "Although the writers were pre-eminently up to their task, it appears not much in the art of assembling succinct and lively discourse of their remarks. The diary lapses frequently to repetition and becomes expansive about unremarkable geographical features." To remedy these problems, van Kampen explained: "The translator has made it his obligation not to bother his readers by this [extraneous geographical information], and he fears still to have used the pruning knife too little, which one must only attribute to his scrupulous care to leave out nothing of importance, especially as pertains to the natural sciences."[54]

Van Kampen's approach to the volume was ambitious. He discussed reviews of the work in *The Quarterly Review* and *The Edinburgh Review* and tapped some of that information for his annotations. He reproduced the preface of the English publisher—the short essay by Thomas Rees—and retained the appendix as abridged in London. The map of the London edition crafted by Samuel John Neele was finely re-engraved by C. Baarsel en Zoon for this edition, translating a number of the place names for Dutch readers.[55]

A. Blussé en Zoon and Blussé en van Braam published numerous books of travel and exploration. Van Kampen's translation of the Biddle-Allen narrative joined James Wathen's *Reis naar Madras en China* (1816), Vasilii M. Golovin's *Mijne Lotgevallen in Mijne Gevangenschap Bij de Jappaners* (1817), Hinrich Lichtenstein's *Reizen in Het Zuidelijk Gedeelte Van Afrika* (1818), James Riley's *Verhaal van Het Verongelukken der Amesrikaansche Brik De Koophandel* (1818), and John Oxley's *Reizen in de Beinnenlanden van Australie* (1821), among several such works.[56]

A selection of the Biddle-Allen narrative concerned with the Shoshone, Flathead, and other tribes appeared in 1821 in Paris. Translated from either the 1815 or 1817 London editions (or possibly from the Dutch edition of 1816–1818), this account was *Indiens du Fleuve Colombia, Extrait du Voyage de Lewis et Clarke* [*Indians of the Columbia River, an Extract from the Travels of Lewis and Clark*] and was included in the long-running monthly periodical, *Nouvelles Annales des Voyages de la Géographie et l'Histoire, ou Recueil des Relations Originales Inédites* [*New Annals of Voyages, Geography, and History, or Compilation of Original Unedited Accounts*]. Published by Gide Fils, the *Annales*, from 1819 to 1870, provided narratives of worldwide explorations.[57] The bookstore of Gide Fils had an active publication program. It produced histories, natural histories, dictionaries, mysteries, and an extensive collection of exotic travel tales. Morier's explorations of Persia, Armenia, and Asia Minor, Golovin's voyage to Japan, and Parry's quest for the Northwest Passage were among the bookstore's separate volumes from 1818 to 1822. The selection from Lewis and Clark's travels thus fit comfortably into the firm's inventory.

The next version of the Biddle-Allen narrative was a heavily abridged selection in *Die wichtigsten neuern Land-und Seereisen* [*Significant New Land and Sea Travels*], selected by Wilhelm Harnisch (1787–1864) and published in Leipzig by Gerhard Fleischer (1820–29) as vol. 3 (1821) in a multi-volume set. It was next included as vol. 3 (1826) in a five-volume set of *Interessante Zimmerreise zu Wasser und zu Lande für wissbegierige Leser gebildeter Stände* (1826) [*Interesting Travels (at Home) to Water and Land for the Educated Reader of Cultured Position*], a series printed from 1826 to 1829 in Vienna. A second title page of vol. 3 of the Vienna edition more explicitly reads *Hearne's, Mackenzie's, Lewis und Pike's*

54 *Reize naar de Bronnen van den Missouri*, 1:xiii.

55 *Reize naar de Bronnen van der Missouri* (1816, 1817, 1818).

56 For a full listing of works of travel and exploration published by this firm, see *World Catalog*.

57 "Indians du Fleuve," *Nouvelles Annales* (1821), 8:119–165.

Entdeckungreisen im Innern Nord-Amerika's. Nebst einer Beschreibung der Nordwestküste und Neu-Spaniens [Hearne's, Mackenzie's, Lewis and Pike's Explorations in the Interior of North America and Also a Description of the Northwest Coast and New Spain]. Published by Anton Mausberger in Vienna, the volume included travel accounts about North America by Samuel Hearne, Alexander Mackenzie, Meriwether Lewis and William Clark, and Zebulon Montgomery Pike. A folding map, "Nord-Amerika mit Bezeichnung der Entdeckungsreisen . . ." identified numerous Indian tribes and locations, including "Mandanenburg" and "Clat-sop-burg."[58]

The Vienna edition of Lewis and Clark's travels filled seventy-seven pages and opened with an overview of the expedition. The four parts following were "Von St. Louis to den Mandenen" ["From St. Louis to the Mandans"], "Von den Mandenen bis zur Mundung der Columbia" ["From the Mandans to the Mouth of the Columbia"], "Von der Mundung der Columbia bis nach St. Louis" ["From the Mouth of the Columbia to St. Louis"], and "Bescreibung der Nordwestkuste America's" ["Description of the Northwest Coast of America"]. The frontispiece, a folding plate, illustrated an Indian dance at Mission San Jose in California, an image relevant only for the discussion of Alta California, a province of New Spain.[59]

Harnisch, the volume's editor, was a teacher and educational writer born in Wilsnack, Prussia, and educated in Halle and Frankfort-on-the-Oder. He became a devotee of the philosophy of Johann H. Pestalozzi, a Swiss educational theorist who stressed the importance of modern languages and outdoor learning. Harnisch earned a doctorate and taught in the methods of Pestalozzi in Berlin and Breslau, and, from 1822 to 1842, in Saxony. In 1842, Harnisch moved to Wolmirstedt Elbeu and continued as a teacher until his retirement in 1861. He wrote numerous educational books stressing the technique of Pestalozzi and the role of the "volksschule" ["folk school"] in Germany. In addition to the volume of North American travels, Harnisch also edited *Die wichtigsten neuern Land-und Seereisen für die Jungend* (1821–32) [*The Significant New Country-and-Ocean Travels for the Young*], a work issued in sixteen parts.[60]

The publisher of *Interessante Zimmerreise*, Anton Mausberger (1800–1844), was born in Vienna and was the son of Ludwig (1783–1823) and Theresia Mausberger. His father was a printer of books, calendars, and religious volumes. When Ludwig died, his widow took over the firm and ran it with her son, Anton. In 1828, Anton assumed complete ownership. The company primarily published German classics. In 1844, Mausberger disappeared from his home; his body was found on the banks of the Donau, perhaps the victim of suicide or murder. His widow, Francisca, then age twenty-three, took over the company and continued its operation.[61]

The publishing history of the Biddle-Allen edition suggests that there were more readers interested in the Lewis and Clark Expedition in Europe than in the United States. Between 1814 and 1826, the solitary printing by Bradford & Inskeep of Philadelphia stood in contrast to seven printings in Europe—five of them nearly complete reprints of the initial American edition. Perhaps, to some degree, four American editions of the Gass *Journal* had filled the market, but it was clear that Europeans had a strong interest in the lands, resources, and native peoples of the American West. Not until 1842 was the Biddle-Allen narrative reprinted in the United States and, in that instance, the work was an abridgement created by Archibald M'Vickar and published by Harper and Brothers of New York as *History of the Expedition Under the Command of Captains Lewis and Clarke* . . . .[62]

58 Harnish, *Interessante Zimmerreise.*

59 Ibid.

60 Bautz, "Wilhelm Harnisch," *Biographisch-Bibliographiches Kirchenlexikon* (1990), 2:570; "Wilhelm H. Harnisch," *Allgemeine Deutsche Biographie* (1907), 10:614–617.

61 Mayer, *Wiens Buckdruckergeschichte,* 203, 208–209.

62 *History of the Expedition Under the Command of Captains Lewis and Clarke, to the Sources of the Missouri* . . . (New York, 1842).

M'Vickar's goal was to produce a readable, short, two-volume version of the Biddle-Allen narrative for inclusion in the *Harper's Family Library*. This remarkable series grew to 187 titles in fifteen years, offering cheap copies (forty-five cents each) of popular works. The series ranged from Richard Henry Dana's *Two Years Before the Mast*, a classic sea voyage around Cape Horn to California in the years 1834 to 1836, to the writings of Herman Melville. *Harper's Family Library* was strong in history, biography, and travels, including sea voyages of Drake, Cavendish, and Dampier; South American explorations of Alexander von Humboldt; Russell's accounts of the Barbary States, Persia, Nubia, and Abyssinia; and other subjects.[63] Lewis and Clarke's *Travels. . .* became vols. 154 and 155 in the rapidly growing list. M'Vickar's role was to write a summary of the expedition, lift lengthy passages from the Biddle-Allen narrative (apparently as printed in Dublin, 1817), and to insert asterisks to denote omissions. The results were undistinguished, but for the next fifty years were the only text in print that drew directly from the writings of Lewis and Clark.[64]

Archibald M'Vickar (1785–1849) was one of seven sons born to John and Ann (Moore) McVickar of New York City. An Irish immigrant, John McVickar became a prosperous importer, bank director, and director of insurance companies. Archibald M'Vickar (formerly McVickar) graduated in 1802 from Columbia University and earned a second degree at Peterhouse, Cambridge University. He married Catherine A. Livingston, daughter of Henry B. Livingston, a lawyer and member of the U.S. Supreme Court. Nothing is known as to how M'Vickar gained the role of abridger of the Biddle-Allen narrative. He wrote no books, unlike his much better-known younger brother, Reverend John M'Vickar, professor of moral philosophy, rhetoric, and belles lettres at Columbia University.[65]

Between 1842 and 1917, Harper and Brothers printed as many as twenty editions of M'Vickar's version of the Biddle-Allen narrative, most in runs of about 250 copies. These filled a steady but rather insubstantial reading interest in the United States. Harper and Brothers, founded in 1817 by James and John Harper in New York City, was the largest printer of books in the United States by 1830. Another estimate ranked it in 1850 as one the three largest publishers in the world, producing books, pamphlets, and Harper's *New Monthly Magazine*. The firm's success stemmed from good marketing and adaptation of new technologies. Harper and Brothers were first (in 1833) to use steam-powered presses. Harper also printed and sold what the public wanted and grew prosperous through its popular reprints.[66]

In 1893, Elliott Coues edited and Francis Harper published the Biddle-Allen edition in four handsome volumes. An intense man of immense talent, Coues was three times married, twice divorced, the father of five children and, for a decade, a career officer in the United States Army. Born in 1842 in Portsmouth, New Hampshire, he was the son of Samuel Elliott Coues, a peace advocate and, after 1854, holder of a post in the U. S. Patent Office. Coues grew up in Washington, D.C. His friendship with Spencer Fullerton Baird, the distinguished assistant secretary of the Smithsonian Institution, helped him become accomplished in natural history. He began publishing articles in ornithology even as a teenager. In 1860, he participated in an expedition to Labrador. Coues earned a bachelor's degree at Washington Seminary in 1861, an M.D. from the National Medical College in 1863, and a Ph.D. from Columbia College (now George Washington University) in 1869. During his military service, Coues was on duty in the Southwest

"Some years ago I made a special study of the L. & C. literature, and I could therefore undertake the desired work with much confidence."

Elliott Coues to Francis Harper, June 23, 1891

63 Exman, *The Brothers Harper*, 20–21.

64 Ibid., 381–383.

65 McVickar and Breed, *Memoranda*; "Columbia College," *Cyclopedia of American Literature*.

66 Horsford, "Harper and Brothers," *Dictionary of Literary Biography*, 49:192–196.

and, from 1873 to 1876, served as naturalist and ornithologist on the Northern Boundary Commission in Dakota and Montana Territories. Coues wrote major monographs on birds and mammals during his service with Ferdinand V. Hayden of the U.S. Geological Survey of the Territories in the 1870s.[67]

In 1880, Coues became irritated by an Army posting for routine medical duty in Arizona. He angrily resigned his commission and became a professor of anatomy at the National Medical College, where he taught from 1881 to 1887. An ambitious researcher and writer, Coues also served as natural history editor of the *Century Dictionary* and author for the American supplement of the *Encyclopedia Britannica*. His contributions to these two references consisted of more than eight hundred articles. Coues also was an editor of several accounts of western explorations and travels. These included the ambitiously annotated journals of Alexander Henry, Zebulon Montgomery Pike, Charles Larpenteur, and Francisco Garcés. Coues traveled widely in Europe and the American West. In 1899, the year of his death, he participated with his third wife in the Smithsonian's photo- documentary expedition to the Rio Grande pueblos. He undertook this rigorous camping trip with Frederick Webb Hodge, George Parker Winship, and photographer Adam Clark Vroman.[68]

In 1891, Francis P. Harper solicited Coues's involvement in preparing a reprint of the Biddle-Allen narrative. Harper probably turned to Coues because of his bibliographical essay, "An Account of the Various Publications Relating to the Travels of Lewis and Clarke, with a Commentary on the Zoological Results of Their Expedition" (1876).[69] Coues felt his previous examination of Lewis and Clark literature had prepared him well for the assignment. "I could therefore undertake the desired worked with confidence. It would also be congenial work," he wrote to Harper. Shortly thereafter, however, Coues departed to the West to recover his health. He was greatly worn down from years of rigorous research and writing for *The Century Dictionary*. More than a year passed before Coues actually signed a contract with Harper and holed up in his secluded summer home in Cranberry, North Carolina, to craft his introduction, editorial notes, and new information.

Because he lacked a research library, Coues fired off a barrage of requests to Harper for books on travel and exploration and—at last—for a copy of the 1814 Biddle-Allen narrative. Coues found many deficiencies in the work as published in Philadelphia, and he laid them out for Harper:

> The printer, Inskeep, probably did the best he could with the copy furnished him, but it is wretchedly set up, the pointing in particular being terrific, the spelling often very funny, and the 'parts of speech' dislocated in a thousand places. Who, for example, would know that the word printed 'louservia' was meant for loup cervier (Canada lynx)? I think you will agree with me that it would *not* be desirable, even if it were possible, to 'recast' or 'rewrite' the book—for you must be able to assure your public that you are giving them the original genuine 'Lewis and Clarke,' without abridgment or alteration—yet I can in going over the book put in the necessary touches, to make 'the nouns and verbs agree,' etc., and thus insure some degree of literary excellence, without presuming to so much as recast a single sentence.[70]

Coues summoned all his energy to drive the project to early completion. Referring to working at "'lightning express' speed," he told Harper he had sifted and digested 3,056 pages of manuscripts from the American Philosophical Society

67 Brodhead, "Elliott Coues," *American National Biography*, 5:577–578.

68 Ibid.; Hodge, "Diary."

69 Coues, "An Account."

70 Cutright and Brodhead, *Elliott Coues*, 340–341.

and held "in mind every one of the thousands of minutiae requisite for my commentary." From this and other sources, Coues crafted voluminous notes—a mounting nightmare for Harper, who watched the Coues material grow and almost surpass the Biddle-Allen narrative in length. Coues also added three large folding maps, retained the original five charts, and pressed unsuccessfully for new illustrations of Indians, plants, animals, Sergeant Patrick Gass, and others. The work, while it retained much of the Biddle-Allen narrative, was heavily altered by Coues. He changed words and inserted punctuation. However, he also made several helpful contributions: an index, a valuable bibliographical introduction essay, a biological chapter drawn from Lewis's diary at Fort Clatsop, biographical memoirs of Clark and Gass, and a genealogical table of Clark's descendants.[71]

During his work on the Biddle-Allen narrative, Coues tracked down the original journals of Lewis and Clark. He found them in the library of the American Philosophical Society in Philadelphia, where they had been stored and forgotten since deposited there in 1818 by Nicholas Biddle. The lack of interest in these materials confirmed that the Lewis and Clark Expedition had slipped from public awareness. With the emergence in the 1880s of the graduate seminars of Herbert Baxter Adams at Johns Hopkins University and the development of history as a field of instruction in American colleges and universities, Coues's discovery became fortuitous. A new generation was poised to "re-discover" the adventures of the Corps of Discovery. To assist him in his editorial work, Coues persuaded the American Philosophical Society and its tenacious librarian, Henry Phillips Jr., to loan him manuscripts. Coues took these documents to Washington, D.C., in 1892 to study and organize them. The minutes of the American Philosophical Society of December 16, 1892, contain a sentence reading: "Dr. Elliott Coues presented a request for the loan of the Lewis & Clark Mss. which was granted." Shortly thereafter, Coues wrote to Harper: "I go home tomorrow with all those Manuscripts of L. & C., voted to be loaned to me by the Philosophical Society. If your prospectus is not out say in it that I have possession of all the original field note books of L. & C., with which to check the History as published in 1814, and that much new matter of the utmost importance will be incorporated in my notes, as the Biddle narrative is very little like the originals."[72]

On February 9, 1893, Coues wrote to Phillips at the American Philosophical Society: "The new edition is going on splendidly–great comfort in working on returns back of which *nobody* can go!" On July 30, Coues reported further to Phillips: "You may not be surprised to learn that from them, and other sources of new information, I have added as much more new matter to the Biddle edition as there was in the original."[73] In the course of his work, Coues embarked on what could have become an even more substantial project—the reproduction of the original journals of Lewis and Clark. Jefferson Kearny Clark, a descendant of William Clark, endorsed Coues's project. Coues hovered over the original notes and journals, "the mine opened in Phila.," as he referred to it in a letter to Harper. He continued:

> There are 18 bound note books, and 12 small parcels of other Mss., making in all 30 codices, and I think something like 2,000 written pages. Of course we shall not be idiotic enough to ever let the Mss. go out of our hands without keeping a copy. I have an expert copyist already at work, making an exact copy, word for word, letter for letter, and point for point. I do not know how the expense will come out; if you will authorize the expenditure of $150,

"You will rejoice to hear that I have found out all about the original manuscripts, through Judge Craig Biddle (son of Nicholas Biddle). Also lots of letters of Clark, etc."

Elliott Coues to Francis Harper, September 19, 1892

71 For a full discussion of Coues's labors while editing the Biddle-Allen narrative, see Cutright and Brodhead, Chapter 22, "Coues and Lewis and Clark," *Elliott Coues*, 339–363.

72 Ibid., 345.

73 Coues to Phillips, February 9 and July 30, 1893.

I will make up the balance, whatever it will be, and the copy thus become[s] our joint property. I think most probably, *after* our present edition, if that turns out as well as you have every reason to expect, you will want to bring out another volume reproducing the orig. Mss *verbatim*. It would be such a curiosity as the world has never yet seen and make a great sensation.[74]

Indeed! Coues could hardly contain his enthusiasm for the facsimile. "You know the discovery and utilization of the Mss. put a new complexion on the whole enterprise," he wrote to Harper. "I regard it now as one of the greatest and most novel things in literature, sure to make a great sensation, and be the corner stone of a grand reputation for you as a publisher."[75]

Coues was right, but he had not fully assessed what he had discovered. The Lewis and Clark writings, 1804-06, were one of the largest collections of manuscript material by American authors on a single subject written to that time. The journals, field notes, and correspondence exceeded the sermons of Puritan pastors, the diary of William Byrd of Westover, and histories of many other events. While the correspondence of Benjamin Franklin, Thomas Jefferson, and others ran to more pages and covered a far broader sweep of time, the Lewis and Clark manuscripts were in a class by themselves. Coues sensed this. At the same time, he treated the originals badly. He peeled off the brass clasps on the notebooks, declaring them "a nuisance," and gave some of them away as Christmas presents to friends.[76] He wrote freely on the original manuscripts and wrestled them into what he termed "perfect order," a series of thirty "Codices," each duly paginated. He reported on these labors—an egregious handling of original materials—in "Description of the Original Manuscript Journals and Field Notebooks of Lewis and Clark, on Which Was Based Biddle's History of the Expedition of 1804-06, and Which Are Now in the Possession of the American Philosophical Society in Philadelphia" (1893).[77]

Coues also initiated the copying process by employing his secretary, Mary B. Anderson, as scribe. He wrote to Francis Harper: "Meanwhile, however, let us simply possess ourselves of the copy, and we can talk about printing it later . . . . Better keep very dark about this." Cutright and Brodhead, in their biography of Coues, expressed discomfort with his "motives for covertly transcribing the manuscripts or the seemliness of his action," since the originals were the property of the American Philosophical Society and remarked "he had no license to copy them." "From his advice to Harper advocating secrecy about his action," they concluded, "it is quite evident he himself doubted its propriety."[78] In the letters exchanged between Coues and Harper on the matter of copying, Coues did not conceal this activity. On July 30, 1893, he laid out to American Philosophical Society librarian Henry Phillips Jr. exactly how he was handling the materials in his care:

Lest you have any anxiety about the L. and C. MSS., already longer in my hands than perhaps either of us expected they would be, I can assure you of their entire safety. On leaving home a month ago, they were placed in the fireproof vaults of the Safe Deposit Company of Washington, where only besides myself my private secretary has access to them; and only one vol. at a time can be taken out, for the purpose of copying. The new edition will be out next month; I will then bring the MSS. back to Philada. In person, upon my return from Chicago and a further West tour I shall make. They will be found in perfect order. You may not be surprised to learn that from them,

74 Coues to Phillips, February 9 and July 30, 1893.

75 Cutright and Brodhead, *Elliott Coues*, 345–346.

76 Coues to Phillips, December 20, 1892.

77 Coues, "Description of the Original Manuscript Journals."

78 Cutright and Brodhead, *Elliott Coues*, 346–347.

and other sources of new information, I have added as much more new matter to the Biddle edition as there was in the original. In making my formal acknowledgments to the A.P.S., I had also the pleasure of mentioning your name personally in the Preface. The work promises to be a great success; nearly the whole edition has been taken up by subscription before publication, showing a very widespread interest in our immortal explorers.[79]

Coues continued to take great interest in the facsimile crafted by Mary B. Anderson. In mid-December 1893, he wrote to Harper: "The copying of the L. & C. Mss. has been completed, and now we own the only cops. in existence after the original, made with great care & skill, and practically perfect. It is a very valuable piece of property!"[80] Coues did not return the Lewis and Clark manuscripts to Philadelphia until early in 1894. "If you will kindly advise me when the next two meetings will be held," he wrote to Phillips in December 1893, "I will present myself at one of them–probably the first. Meanwhile the papers are safe and intact in the vaults of the Safe Deposit Co. of this city."[81]

Coues anticipated editing the original journals into a major publication on the Lewis and Clark Expedition. However, Harper did not embrace the project. Instead, he persuaded Coues to edit the journals of Zebulon Montgomery Pike as his next project. Sometime, however, between 1894 and his death in 1899, Coues expended considerable effort toward studying and annotating the facsimile edition. Of particular utility was the *Map of the Missouri River From its mouth to Three Forks, Montana,* a work in eighty-four sheets printed by the Missouri River Commission, 1893–94.[82] In neat handwriting, Coues entered hundreds of notations from this river atlas on the facsimile. He recorded modern place names, distances in miles, inserted missing words, provided first names of some fur traders, and initiated the process of documentary editing. In some instances, he noted spellings that varied from those in the Biddle-Allen edition of 1814. Working with a fragment of Lewis's journal for September 16–17, 1804, for example, Coues wrote on the cover sheet of Codex Ba: "Copied page for page, line for line, word for word, letter for letter and point for point by M. B. Anderson Dec. 1892. Examined and compared with orig. ms. by me, E. Coues."

Francis Harper retrieved the facsimile after Coues's death in 1899 and took it to New York. There, the project–filed in sixteen folio boxes and wrapped in sheets identified in Coues's handwriting–lay forgotten for seventy years, perhaps because no one except Harper realized it existed. On a book-buying trip to New York City in 1970, George Tweney, a Seattle rare-book dealer, called on the firm of Lathrop Harper, Inc., in Manhattan. After visiting with Douglas Parsonage, who had worked for years for the firm, Tweney gained permission to browse. Tweney's tale continued:

'Come out into the workroom," [said Parsonage], 'I may have something of interest out there.' This was the room where incoming books were unpacked, and outgoing orders were prepared for shipment. Under the long work bench in a corner of the room, Parsonage pointed out a cardboard carton to me that seemed to be full of a jumble of loose papers, and scrawled on the side of the carton were the words 'Lewis and Clark.' He said, 'I don't know exactly what is in that box, but you are welcome to take a look.'

Upon returning home, I began to go through the papers page by page. Even then I did not really recognize their significance, but it wasn't hard for

---

"I go home tomorrow, with all those manuscripts of L. & C., voted to be loaned to me by the Philosophical Society."

Elliott Coues to Francis Harper, December 1892

79 Coues to Phillips, July 30, 1893.

80 Cutright and Brodhead, *Elliott Coues*, 352.

81 Coues to Phillips, December 13, 1893.

82 Missouri River Commission, *Map of the Missouri River.*

me to put all the pages in their proper order, and to discover that they were sequentially bundles of codices. Of course, I recognized their similarity to the Lewis and Clark manuscripts in the American Philosophical Society in Philadelphia, because I had seen those papers on several previous occasions. My 'find' easily sorted into all the codices, as I later discovered, and as they had been named by Elliott Coues. The pages are all uniformly 9" x 5 3/4" in size, and I later had them all enclosed in folding cases for safekeeping. There are a total of sixteen cases, some codices being short enough to include several or more in one case.[83]

The remarkable manuscript facsimile arrived at Lewis & Clark College in 2000 with the purchase of George Tweney's collection of materials relating to the Lewis and Clark Expedition.

Another special discovery in the 1890s was the unknown diary of Charles Floyd, the young lieutenant whose brief illness and death during the ascent of the Missouri River in 1805 had left indelible memories on the Corps of Discovery. The publication of this journal of May 14–August 18, 1804, was the editorial labor of Professor James Davie Butler (1815–1905), a teacher of Greek and Italian at the University of Wisconsin, Madison. Born in Rutland, Vermont, Butler earned degrees at Middlebury College in 1836 and Andover College in 1840. He did graduate study in Germany, taught for several years at Middlebury and Wabash College, and in 1858 joined the faculty of the University of Wisconsin. He became a good friend of his student, John Muir, the well-known American preservationist, whom he visited in California in 1869 on one of the first railroad trips across the United States. Butler was a regular contributor to historical journals, especially the *Transactions of the Wisconsin Academy of Sciences, Arts, and Letters* and the *Wisconsin Historical Collections*. He authored more than two hundred articles about his travels for a variety of magazines.[84]

Butler first peripherally addressed the Corps of Discovery when, in 1884, he wrote a brief sketch of John Colter for the *Magazine of American History*.[85] In his "golden years," Butler worked closely with Lyman Draper and Reuben Gold Thwaites, dynamic scholars associated with The State Historical Society of Wisconsin. In 1895, a decade before centennial enthusiasm about the Lewis and Clark Expedition began, Butler introduced and presented "The New Found Journal of Charles Floyd, a Sergeant Under Captains Lewis and Clark." The journal had been saved by the captains and sent to Floyd's family in Kentucky when the party returned from Fort Mandan in 1805. Thwaites found it in the Draper papers in 1893; how Draper had acquired the journal is unknown. Floyd's account covered the ascent of the Missouri River until his death in mid-August 1804, and was an important, new document to supplement the Biddle-Allen narrative. It was published in the *Proceedings of the American Antiquarian Society* and as a separate offprint, a rare pamphlet.[86]

As the centennial of the Lewis and Clark Expedition neared, interest in the labors of the Corps of Discovery mounted. Citizens planned parades and pageants, raised funds for statues, traveled by the tens of thousands to the Lewis and Clark Centennial Exposition in Portland, Oregon, and purchased books and pamphlets. In 1902, the New Amsterdam Book Company of New York reprinted the Biddle-Allen narrative in three volumes. The edition included Allen's preface, Jefferson's biographical sketch of Lewis, five plates, and the Samuel Lewis folding map as engraved in 1814 by Samuel Harrison. Additions to the work were portraits:

83 Tweney, "Elliott Coues on Lewis and Clark," 12–13.

84 "James Davie Butler," *The National Cyclopedia,* 9:190–191.

85 Butler, "John Colter."

86 Butler, "The New Found Journal," 225–252; Moulton, *The Journals,* 9:xvii.

Lewis as a frontispiece in vol. 1 and Clark as a frontispiece in vol. 2. The New Amsterdam Book Company printed the work three times in 1902.[87]

James Kendall Hosmer (1834–1927) prepared another reprint of the Biddle-Allen narrative, *History of the Expedition of Captains Lewis and Clark 1804-5-6 Reprinted from the Edition of 1814*. A. C. McClurg & Company of Chicago, a firm specializing in western history and fiction (including ten Tarzan books by Edgar Rice Burroughs), issued the work in two volumes in 1902, 1903, 1904, 1905, 1917, and 1924.[88] An 1855 Harvard graduate, Hosmer studied theology and was ordained a Unitarian minister. Following service in the Union Army, he left the ministry and became a professor of English, rhetoric, and German literature, teaching at Antioch College, the University of Missouri, and Washington University. From 1892 to 1904, he was librarian of the Minneapolis Public Library. During that period, he wrote or edited items related to the expedition or its historical context. These included a pamphlet, *Sacajawea Statue Association* (1900), *History of the Louisiana Purchase* (1902), the reprint of the Biddle-Allen narrative (1902), and *Gass's Journal of the Lewis and Clark Expedition* (1904). Hosmer also wrote biographies of New England colonial leaders, accounts of the Civil War, two novels, and numerous articles.[89]

Hosmer's work on the 1814 edition was minimal. While acknowledging the ambitious annotations in the Coues edition of 1893 as "a noble reprint," he reproduced none of them and contributed only an introduction of eighteen pages and an index. Hosmer used his introduction to the volume to make the case for the importance of Sacagawea, but without assessing the nature or variety of her contributions. "Her figure in the story of Lewis and Clark is very pathetic and engaging," he wrote. In laying out a new direction for the persona of this otherwise obscure figure, Hosmer added: "It is doubtful if the expedition could have pushed its way through without her." Others followed his cue in this brief essay, published in 1902. The process of building a public persona for the obscure, young Indian woman who accompanied the Corps of Discovery was now unleashed. Hosmer saw the expedition as helping fulfill America's destiny as a nation and setting the stage for Long, Frémont, Hayden, and other explorers.[90]

In 1903 and 1904, A. S. Barnes and Company of New York also reprinted the Biddle-Allen narrative as *History of the Expedition Under the Command of Captains Lewis & Clark to the Sources of the Missouri, Across the Rocky Mountains, Down the Columbia River to the Pacific in 1804-6 . . . .* The work, in three volumes, was in the company's Classics in American History series in 1903 and, in 1904, in its Trailmakers series. To give more credence, if not market appeal, the 1904 edition included a history of the Louisiana Purchase by John Bach McMaster, author of a multi-volume history of the United States, and volume introductions by Ripley Hitchcock.[91] A. S. Barnes and Company, founded in 1838 by Alfred Smith Barnes in Hartford, Connecticut, moved to Philadelphia in 1840 and to New York in 1845, and became a leader in publishing textbooks. In the early twentieth century, Ripley Hitchcock (1857–1918) served briefly as the firm's literary adviser, a position he also held with D. Appleton & Company (1890-1902), and after 1906, with Harper & Brothers. Hitchcock wrote *The Louisiana Purchase and the Exploration, Early History and Building of the West* (1903) and *The Lewis and Clark Expedition* (1905). Beginning in 1906, A. S. Barnes and Company renewed its textbook publishing business, which it had largely abandoned in 1890 following the death of A. S. Barnes.[92]

87 *History of the Expedition* (New Amsterdam Book Company, 1902).

88 *History of the Expedition* (McClurg,1902); Davis, "A. C. McClurg and Company," *Dictionary of Literary Biography*, 49(1):297-298.

89 Buck, "James Kendall Hosmer," *Dictionary of American Biography*, 9:244-245.

90 *History of the Expedition* (Chicago, 1904), 1:xxxiv-xxxv.

91 *History of the Expedition* (New York, 1903).

92 Wilkinson, "A. S. Barnes and Company," *Dictionary of Literary Biography*, 49(1):40-42; Harlow, "James Ripley Wellman Hitchcock," *Dictionary of American Biography*, 9:76-77.

93 *History of the Expedition* (London, 1905).

94 Armbrust, "David Nutt," *Dictionary of Literary Biography*, 106:228–229; Brown, *London Publishers*, 140.

95 *History of the Expedition* (New York, 1922).

96 Thwaites, *Original Journals*, 1.

97 Gale, "Reuben Gold Thwaites," *American National Biography*, 21:637–638.

98 These earlier bibliographies included: Coues, "An Account," and a revised version in *History*, 1:xvii–cxxxii; Sabin, *Dictionary of Books Relating to America*, 6:443, 7:181, and 10:31–313; Field, *Essay Towards an Indian Bibliography* (1873); Bancroft, *History of the Northwest Coast*, 2:7, 8, 31; Winsor, *Narrative and Critical History of America*, 7:556–558; and Miner, *The Literary Collector* (1902), 3:204–209.

In 1905, the firm of David Nutt, London, reprinted the edition prepared by A. S. Barnes and Company with the inclusion of McMaster's history of the Louisiana Purchase.[93] Nutt (1810–1863) founded a publishing house and bookstore in 1833 at 90 Bartholomew Close. By 1850, the firm was at 270–271 Strand. Nutt and his son, Alfred T. Nutt (1856–1910), became well-known for publishing religious and educational books. The firm particularly specialized in folklore and antiquities, especially volumes for the Folklore Society, the English Goethe Society, and the Irish Texts Society.[94] The Barnes edition was reprinted again by the Allerton Book Company, New York, 1922, in its American Explorers Series.[95]

The centennial of the expedition was a propitious time to release a major, new edition of the documents generated by the Corps of Discovery. Reuben Gold Thwaites (1853–1913) seized the project of editing the original manuscripts, which had been found in the American Philosophical Society library in Philadelphia in 1892 by Elliott Coues. Thwaites drove the enterprise forward with verve and talent to produce the *Original Journals of the Lewis and Clark Expedition 1804–1806 Printed from the Original Manuscripts*. One thousand copies first appeared in 1904–05 in three editions by Dodd, Mead & Company.[96]

Born in Dorchester, Massachusetts, to a farming family, Thwaites moved in 1866 with his English parents to Oshkosh, Wisconsin. He taught school, farmed, and worked as a newspaper writer before enrolling in 1874–75 as a "special" student at Yale University. He then returned to Oshkosh and worked for a decade as a newspaperman. He mastered writing, printing, and proofreading and also served as an assistant to Lyman C. Draper, secretary of The State Historical Society of Wisconsin. In 1887, he succeeded Draper and began a dramatic period of building the society's collections of manuscripts, books, and maps and welding the research library to the nearby educational programs of the University of Wisconsin. Thwaites inaugurated an ambitious publications program, traveled in the footsteps by foot and canoe of figures about whom he wrote, and mounted interviews with knowledgeable persons. His editing projects were monumental and included seventy-three volumes of *The Jesuit Relations and Allied Documents* (1896–1901), twenty-five volumes of *Proceedings of the State Historical Society of Wisconsin* (1888–1912), two volumes of Louis Hennepin's *New Discovery of a Vast Country* (1903), and thirty-two volumes of *Early Western Travels, 1748–1846* (1904–07). These projects were underway simultaneously with Thwaites's masterful reading of the handwritten narratives of Lewis, Clark, Whitehouse, and Floyd. He turned them, along with special reports and letters, into the *Original Journals of the Lewis and Clark Expedition*, comprising seven volumes and an atlas (1904–05).[97]

Thwaites wrote a lengthy introduction to the Lewis and Clark volumes. He placed the expedition in historical context and discussed the various journals, field notes, and correspondence he had assembled. He also included the bibliography of works by and about the expedition crafted by Victor Hugo Paltsits of the New York Public Library. The Paltsits enumeration of published works was a highly useful update from the Coues compilation of 1876, Coues's 1893 revision of the Biddle-Allen narrative, and other bibliographical treatments of the expedition by Sabin, Field, Bancroft, Winsor, and Miner.[98]

Thwaites presented information never before known about the labors of the Corps of Discovery. Because he was impeccable in his reading of the original handwriting of the manuscript journals and letters, he enabled readers to see the wide range of scientific and cartographic labors mounted by the captains. Although he was generous in his "Acknowledgments," Thwaites did not tell the whole story of the remarkable new materials he edited. Among his additions were "several important note-books by William Clark, together with an Orderly Book, a Field Book, the maps in the Atlas, and a number of letters, memoranda, etc." described as "the property of Mrs. Julia Clark Voorhis and Miss Eleanor Glasgow Voorhis" of New York. It was true that these Clark descendants permitted Thwaites to borrow and copy this information. Thwaites did not say how he found the documents.[99]

The discoverer of the additional materials was Eva Emery Dye, an indefatigable researcher from Oregon City, Oregon. Between 1899 and 1901, Dye was engaged in writing the historical novel, *The Conquest: The True Story of Lewis and Clark* (1902). At her own expense, Dye crisscrossed the United States to track down descendants of William Clark and collateral members of the family of Meriwether Lewis. Her quest was for documents and images. Ultimately, she found John O'Fallon Clark of St. Louis, who insisted he had shipped important materials to his aunt, Mrs. Jefferson K. Clark. "I sent them myself," he said. "They had lain for years in my grandfather's old secretary. I cleared them out and shipped the whole to the Jefferson K. Clarks in New York City. I doubt whether they ever looked into those boxes." Dye turned east, found the family, and looked into the boxes. She was elated with her "finds" and hurried west, stopping in Madison to tell Thwaites of her discoveries. Some months later, as he embarked on preparation of the *Original Journals,* Thwaites visited the Clark descendants in New York City and borrowed the critical documents found by Dye. Unfortunately he never reported how he found this trove of information. Years later, Dye ruefully remarked, "I, at one time, had the credit of discovering those documents."[100]

The Thwaites volumes—seven narratives and an atlas—became the standard text for the labors of the Corps of Discovery for the next eighty years. Thwaites attempted to print all the information he could find, laying in the daily "Course, Distance & refferences" logged by the captains, providing explanatory notes and cross-referencing information to the Gass *Journal,* tapping geographical information researched by Coues, and filling a volume with "Scientific Data." These reports on geography, ethnology, zoology, mineralogy, meteorology, and astronomy included notes by scholar collaborators. Thwaites also appended the "Miscellaneous Memoranda," several pages of notes and and financial information, including lists of "Sundries for Indian Presents" in the hand of William Clark.[101] The volumes were ambitious, scholarly, and immensely useful.

Dodd, Mead & Company invested considerable care in publishing the *Original Journals* in 1904–05. These included two hundred sets in fourteen parts with an atlas on Van Gelder handmade paper and Karl Bodmer's prints of the Indians; fifty sets in fourteen parts, with an atlas on Imperial Japan paper and Bodmer's prints hand-tinted in color; and 750 copies in the trade edition. Dodd, Mead & Company dated to 1839, when Moses W. Dodd left the ministry to enter book publishing. In 1870, Frank H. Dodd, a son of the founder, and Edward S. Mead, his cousin, took over the firm which, in 1876, became Dodd, Mead & Company. The firm continued its shift from publishing religious books to more and more general volumes, especially juvenile titles and American history. After Mead's death in 1894, Dodd increased the list of modern British writers. These included H. G. Wells, Joseph Conrad, and Agatha Christie. Between 1902 and

99 Thwaites, *Original Journals* (1904),1:ix, lix.

100 Bartlett-Browne, "Eva Emery Dye," (Ph.D. dissertation, University of Minnesota, St. Paul, Minnesota, 2002); "Celebrated Historian," *The Portland Oregonian*, November 11, 1923.

101 Thwaites, *Original Journals*, 7.

1904, the company published in seventeen volumes the *New International Encyclopedia* and sold more than fifty thousand sets of the work. The *Original Journals* were a noteworthy scholarly contribution for a publishing house better known for its fiction.[102]

The Biddle-Allen narrative of the explorations of Lewis and Clark rose in 1814 like the phoenix out of the ashes of Lewis's literary failings and the collapse of the firm of C. and A. Conrad and Co. The account was the prose of Nicholas Biddle as subjected to the editing of Paul Allen and the typographical inconsistencies of printer James Maxwell for the publishers—Bradford & Inskeep, Philadelphia, and Abraham Inskeep, New York. In spite of its deficiencies, the work held together; it told a remarkable story. Editors and translators pruned and corrected it and, on occasion, tapped it for summary abridgements. These gave the narrative a long shelf life that finally dimmed following the Civil War. Elliott Coues then renewed the narrative with his ambitious editing and Francis Harper's investment in the four-volume edition of 1893.

The new lease on life for the Corps of Discovery came with the centennial of the expedition. Between the Coues edition of the Biddle-Allen narrative in 1893 and 1922, there were ten printings of the account plus continued reprints by Harper through 1917 of the M'Vickar abridgement of 1842. Coues's discovery of the original manuscripts in Philadelphia and Dye's success in tracking down additional important documents held by the Clark descendants enabled Reuben Gold Thwaites, a diligent and talented editor, to launch the expedition for a second century of readers in the *Original Journals*. Thwaites's work was not eclipsed until the discovery of additional documents—William Clark's field notes found in 1953 in an old desk in an attic in St. Paul, Minnesota, and edited by Ernest Staples Osgood, and an expansive set of contextual letters researched and compiled in the 1960s by Donald Jackson.[103] This corpus of Lewis and Clark manuscripts ultimately became the primary text and source of notes for the new documentary edition, *The Journals of the Lewis and Clark Expedition*, edited by Gary B. Moulton (13 volumes, 1983–2001).

102 Ames, "Dodd, Mead and Company," 49(1):126–130.

103 For history about the discovery and editing of additional documents relating to the expedition, see Cutright, *A History*, 145–201.

Editing the Expedition Journals: Bibliography

5a The Biddle-Allen *History of the Expedition*

All nineteenth-century editions of the *History of the Expedition* have their origin in the text prepared directly from the Lewis and Clark journals by Nicholas Biddle and his successor Paul Allen. The Biddle-Allen text was published in Philadelphia in 1814 in two octavo volumes. The one-volume London quarto of the same year follows Philadelphia closely, as does the two-volume Dublin octavo of 1817. London 1815 (three octavo volumes) follows London 1814, as does the Dutch three-volume octavo issued in consecutive years from 1816 to 1818. Another London three-volume octavo edition in 1817 is closely based on its 1815 predecessor.

A quarter of a century later, in 1842, Harper and Brothers published a two-volume selection, based probably on the text of Dublin 1817; this selection was reprinted in at least twenty editions during the remainder of the century. The approach of the first centenary of the expedition gave rise to two reprints of Philadelphia 1814: the two-volume Hosmer in 1902, the first to contain an index, and a series of three-volume pocket editions, initiated by the New Amsterdam Book Company in 1902. The latter is notable for containing in a portable text the original plates and map, and two documents often omitted: Jefferson's "Life of Lewis" and the lengthy appendices of the first edition.

5a.1 Bradford and Inskeep, Philadelphia 1814 [Color plate XVII]

HISTORY | OF | THE EXPEDITION | UNDER THE COMMAND OF | *CAPTAINS LEWIS AND CLARK,* | TO | THE SOURCES OF THE MISSOURI, | THENCE | ACROSS THE ROCKY MOUNTAINS | AND DOWN THE | RIVER COLUMBIA TO THE PACIFIC OCEAN. | PERFORMED DURING THE YEARS 1804-5-6. | By order of the | GOVERNMENT OF THE UNITED STATES. | PREPARED FOR THE PRESS | BY PAUL ALLEN, ESQUIRE. | IN TWO VOLUMES. | VOL. I [II]. | *PHILADELPHIA:* | PUBLISHED BY BRADFORD AND INSKEEP; AND | ABM. H. INSKEEP, NEWYORK. | J. Maxwell, Printer. | 1814.

Collation: Two volumes, 8vo., 22 cm. Vol. 1: [i] title page, backed by copyright notice; [iii]–v Paul Allen's preface; [vi blank]; [vii]–xxiii Jefferson's "Life of Lewis"; [blank]; xxv–xxviii contents pages; [1]–470 text. Large folded map tipped in, usually opposite title page of vol. 1: "A Map of Lewis and Clark's Track, Across the Western Portion of North America From the Mississippi to the Pacific Ocean." Vol. 2: [i] title page, backed by copyright notice; [iii]–ix contents pages; [x blank]; [1]–522 text. Allen's preface is followed (vii–xxiii) by President Jefferson's "Life of Captain Lewis." The appendix (435–522) contains Lewis's "Observations and reflections on the present and future state of upper Louisiana, in relation to the government of the Indian nations . . . . A summary statement of the rivers, creeks and most remarkable places, their distances from each other, &c . . . . Estimate of the western Indians . . . . Thermometrical observations, showing also the rise and fall of the Mississippi (Missouri); . . . Remarks and reflections [January 1, 1804, to August 22, 1806]."

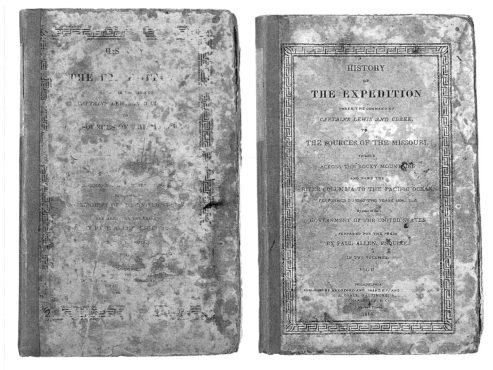

Plates: Vol. 1: Facing 63 "Fortification"; facing 261 "The Falls and Portage." Vol. 2: Facing 31 "Great Falls of Columbia River"; facing 52 "The Great Shoot or Rapid"; facing 70 "Mouth of Columbia River." The map was drawn by Samuel Lewis from Clark's original, and engraved by Samuel Harrison (1789–1818), who may also be the engraver of the plates.

References: Coues, cxxiii; Graff, 2477; Paltsits, lxxvii; Wagner-Camp-Becker, 13:1.

Description: The Philadelphia 1814 first edition of the journals had its origins in February 1810, when Clark sought the help of Nicholas Biddle of Philadelphia in editing the records of the Corps of Discovery (Wagner-Camp-Becker). Biddle's work, taken through the press by Paul Allen, was issued on February 20, 1814, in a sale of 1,417 perfect copies (of the original printing of two thousand) at six dollars for the two-volume set (Coues, xci–xcii). The covers of both volumes in original boards list two publishers in addition to Bradford and Inskeep: E. J. Coale of Baltimore and J. Hoff of Charleston (Siebert, item 802). In 1970, a census by Cappon and Berol of the extant copies in original boards was published by the Columbia University Libraries. Since that census, some of these copies have changed hands. Most recently, the Frank Siebert copy sold at Sotheby's in New York in October 1999. In 1973, a copy in original boards was donated to the Lewis & Clark College Collection by the Laurence L. Shaw Family of Klamath Falls, Oregon. Wendlick, Chuinard, and Tweney each had complete rebound copies of this important work in their collections. An early owner of the Wendlick copy was Isaac Chauncey, an admiral in the war of 1812. The front boards of the Chuinard copy bear the stamp of James Foshay, probably James A. Foshay, superintendent of the public schools of Los Angeles between 1895 and 1906.

Notices: "Proposals By C. & A. Conrad for Publishing the History of the Expedition of Captains Lewis and Clarke." Four pages, circa May 1810. Unique item, described and printed only in Jackson, *Letters*, item 327a, with a facsimile facing p. 132.

The Stranger (Albany) 1, no. 20 (Saturday, March 12, 1814): 289–293, "Lewis' Expedition." Brief notice of publication of the *History,* followed by an unsigned account of Lewis's death, with a poem on the same subject.

The Port Folio (Philadelphia) 3, no. 4 (April 1814). Back cover carries notice of the *History of the Expedition* "Just Published by Bradford and Inskeep . . . In Two Volumes." The journal contains three excerpts from the 1814 text, as follows: pp. 353–5 "Anecdote of the Sokulk Indians" (corresponding to vol. 2, pp. 20–22); pp. 355–57 "Description of Natural Walls" (vol. 1, pp. 238–39); and pp. 357–58 "Ravenous Appetite of the Shoshonese" (vol. 1, pp. 374–76). This early selection is presumably by *The Port Folio*'s editor, Paul Allen, who had taken the Philadelphia edition through the press.

The Port Folio, 1814, back cover, with advertisement for Philadelphia 1814.

The Stranger (Albany) 1, no. 22 (Saturday, April 9, 1814): 321–328. "Review. Art. V. History of the Expedition under the command of Captains Lewis and Clark, to the sources of the Missouri, &c. Philadelphia, Bradford & Inskeep. 1814. 2 vols. octavo. pp. 992." Review of Philadelphia 1814. First part of review only.

The Western Gleaner, or Repository for Arts, Sciences and Literature (Pittsburgh) 1, no. 5 (April 1814): 293–301, "Life of Captain Lewis." (Letter of Thomas Jefferson, August 18, 1813, to Paul Allen.) Photocopy at Lewis & Clark College. Jefferson's life of Lewis is also reprinted in *The Port Folio* 4, no. 2 (August 1814): 137-147 with an editorial comment by Paul Allen.

The Western Gleaner, or Repository for Arts, Sciences and Literature (Pittsburgh) 1, no. 6 (May 1814): 350-75, "The History of the Expedition . . . ." Photocopy in Lewis & Clark College Collection.

The Analectic Magazine (Philadelphia) 5 (1815): 127–149, 210–234. Review: "*History of the Expedition* under the command of Captains Lewis and Clark, to the sources of the Missouri, thence across the Rocky Mountains and down the River Columbia to the Pacific Ocean. Performed during the years 1804-5-6. By order of the government of the United States. Prepared for the press by Paul Allen, Esquire. 2 vols. 8vo. Philadelphia. 1814." Signed by "B."

Lewis & Clark College Collection: Chuinard: Re-backed early leather, tree calf, map with many tape repairs; repairs also to p. 112, where the folding map is tipped in. Stamp of James Foshay on front boards. Shaw: Original boards, untrimmed, with map. Re-backed/replaced spines. Tweney: Rebound in full leather, with raised bands; map backed in linen. Wendlick: Rebound in half calf with marbled boards; map in excellent condition. Ownership inscription of Isaac Chauncey.

5a.2 Longman, London 1814
TRAVELS | TO THE | SOURCE OF THE MISSOURI RIVER | AND ACROSS THE | *AMERICAN CONTINENT* | TO THE | PACIFIC OCEAN. | PERFORMED | BY ORDER OF THE GOVERNMENT OF THE UNITED STATES, | IN THE YEARS | 1804, 1805, AND 1806. | [rule] | BY CAPTAINS LEWIS AND CLARKE. | [rule] | Published from the Official Report, | AND | ILLUSTRATED BY A MAP OF THE ROUTE, AND OTHER MAPS. | [rule] | London: | PRINTED FOR LONGMAN, HURST, REES, ORME, AND BROWN, | *PATERNOSTER-ROW.* | [rule] | 1814.

Collation: One volume, 4to., 31 cm. [i] half title; ii printer's notice; [iii] title page, with blank verso; [v]–xiv preface by Thomas Rees; [xv]–xxiv contents pages; [1]–663, text; [664] publisher's advertisement. Page 323 is misprinted as 223. Large folded map tipped in before title page: "A Map of Lewis and Clark's Track Across the Western Portion of North America, from the Mississippi to the Pacific Ocean."

Plates: Facing 49 (referenced to pp. 47 and 364 respectively) "Ancient Fortification on the Missouri," and "Great Falls of Columbia River"; facing 191 (and referenced to that page) "Great Falls of the Missouri"; facing 379 (referenced to pp. 379 and 398 respectively) "Lower Falls of the Columbia," and "Mouth of Columbia River." The map and plates all bear a publication date of April 28, 1814, and are re-engraved from those in the American edition. All except "Great Falls on the Missouri" are presented in horizontal format, with elaborate flourishes in the titling, and with legends reading generally in the same plane. Their engraver was Samuel John Neele (1758–1824). The folding map, re-engraved by Neele after the Samuel Lewis map of Biddle-Allen 1814, "omits the 'Southern Pass' on Henry's route, and has 'Lake Riddle' for Lake Biddle. Otherwise it is the same, except for a few minor variations" (Wheat, 2:59, n. 13). The map is printed on a paper superior to that of the Philadelphia editions. It was reprinted September 1, 1979, from the original copperplate by the Friends of the Library, American Philosophical Society, Philadelphia, in a limited edition of 160 copies, of which 150 were for sale.

References: Coues, cxxv; Graff, 2480; Paltsits, lxxvii; Wagner-Camp-Becker, 13:2.

Description: The text of this elegant British edition follows Philadelphia 1814 closely. Its editor, Thomas Rees, describes it [xiv] as "printed nearly verbatim" from sheets supplied by the American publishers, the only liberty taken being "the correction of a few inadvertent grammatical or typographical errors." Rees's preface includes President Jefferson's message of February 19, 1806, and an extract from Lewis's Fort Mandan letter to the President of "April 17th [i.e. 7th] 1805." It also makes reference to the Jefferson pamphlet of 1806 (though not to its 1807 London printing), to the surreptitious 1809 London edition (see 4a.2), and to the 1808 London edition of Gass's *Journal*. Omitted in this edition are Allen's original preface, Jefferson's seventeen-page "Life of Lewis," and the eighty-eight page ethnographic and scientific appendix drawn up by Lewis. The advertisement pages in the Wendlick copy are complete to March 1814.

Notices: *Monthly Magazine* 37, no. 257, Supplementary Number (July 30, 1814): 581–611. Review: "Travels to the Source of the Missouri River, and across the American Continent, to the Pacific Ocean. Performed by Order of the Government of the United States, in the Years 1804, 1805, and 1806. By Capts. Lewis and Clarke. Published from the Official Report. And Illustrated by a Map of the Route, and other Maps. 4to. Price 2l. 12s. 6d." Excerpts from the 1814 one-volume quarto, with editorial commentary: "it contains real portraits of human nature, teaching us duly to estimate the value of every degree of civilization, and enabling us to feel all those points in which, in spite of education, we are still but savages."

The Edinburgh Review, or Critical Journal (Edinburgh, reprinted in New York for Eastburn, Kirk & Co.) 24 (1815): 412-438. "Art IX. Travels to the Source of the

Missouri River, and across the American Continent to the Pacific Ocean; performed By Order of the Government of the United States, in the Years 1804, 1805, 1806. By Captains LEWIS and CLARKE. Published from the Official Report. Longman & Co. London, 1814." Coues (cxxiii) gives the author as Gordon.

The Quarterly Review (London) 12 (October 1814, January 1815): 317–368. "Art II. Travels to the Source of the Missouri River, and across the American Continent to the Pacific Ocean. Performed by order of the Government of the United States in the Years 1804, 1805, and 1806. By Captains Lewis and Clarke. Published from the Official Report, and illustrated by a Map of the Route, and other Maps. London; Longman and Co. 4to. pp. 662." Coues (cxxiii) gives the author as Robert Southey (British Poet Laureate in 1815).

Coues (cxxiii) lists additional notices of this London 1814 edition in *Southern Quarterly Review* 8: 191, and *Methodist Quarterly Review* 2: 556. Not at Lewis & Clark College, and not viewed.

Lewis & Clark College Collection: Chuinard: Rebound in the late nineteenth century in half leather with marbled boards. Previously owned by Chicago Historical Society. Lacks half title. Tweney: Rebound in a fine English binding (Bath, England), untrimmed, but shaved or sanded. Wendlick: Untrimmed, early boards, boxed. Signature of J. Perry on title page. Four pages of advertisements are tipped in to front endpaper, and sixteen pages of advertisements ("Corrected to March, 1814") are tipped in to back endpaper. Wendlick: Map restrike from original plate. Framed and displayed.

5a.3 Longman, London 1815

TRAVELS | TO THE SOURCE OF | THE MISSOURI RIVER | AND ACROSS THE | *AMERICAN CONTINENT* | TO | THE PACIFIC OCEAN. | PERFORMED BY ORDER OF | THE GOVERNMENT OF THE UNITED STATES, | IN THE YEARS | 1804, 1805, AND 1806. | [rule] | BY CAPTAINS LEWIS AND CLARKE. | [rule] | PUBLISHED FROM THE OFFICIAL REPORT, | AND ILLUSTRATED BY A MAP OF THE ROUTE, | AND OTHER MAPS. | [rule] | *A NEW EDITION, IN THREE VOLUMES.* | VOL. I. [II.] [III.] | [rule] | *LONDON:* | PRINTED FOR LONGMAN, HURST, REES, ORME, AND BROWN, | PATERNOSTER-ROW. | 1815.

Collation: Three volumes, 8vo., 21.5 cm. Vol. 1: [i] title page, with printer's notice on verso; [iii]–xix Thomas Rees preface; [xx blank]; [xxi]–xxvi contents pages; [xxvii] index of maps with blank verso; [1]–411 text. Vol 2: blank leaf; [iii] title page with printer's notice on verso; v–xii contents pages; [1]–434 text. Vol. 3: blank leaf; [iii] title page with printer's notice on verso; v–xii contents pages; [1]–394 text.

Plates: Vol. 1: Facing title page, the large folding map by Neele; facing 86 "Ancient Fortification on the Missouri"; facing 356 "Great Falls of the Missouri." Vol. 2: Facing 277 "Great Falls of Columbia River"; facing 302 "Lower Falls of the Columbia"; facing 338 "Mouth of Columbia River." Vol. 3: Map and plates identical throughout to those in the one-volume London edition, 5a.2, and retaining page references to that earlier edition.

References: Coues, cxxvi–cxxvii; Graff, 2481; Paltsits, lxxviii; Wagner-Camp-Becker, 13:3.

Description: A resetting of the one-volume quarto of 1814, following that edition closely.

French Translation: A translation of part of vol. 2 of the 1815 or 1817 English editions (or possibly the Dutch edition, 5a.4) appeared in the serial publication *Nouvelles Annales des Voyages*, published in Paris by Gide fils from 1819 to 1870. The translation appeared in vol. 8 (1821), pp. 119–165, of the journal, then titled *Nouvelles Annales des Voyages, de la Géographie et de l'Histoire, ou Recueil des Relations Originales Inédites*. Under the title "Indiens du Fleuve Colombia, Extrait du Voyage de Lewis et Clarke," it covers descriptions of the Shoshone, Flathead, and Columbia River Indians, beginning from chapter 16 of 5a.3 (or 5a.5), pp. 161ff. A footnote makes reference to the 1810 French translation of Gass's *Journal* (see 3.3) and the more recent three-volume quarto of the voyage, not yet translated into French, but without further identification. This is the first French translation of any part of the Biddle-Allen text. A full copy is part of the Lewis & Clark College Collection.

Lewis & Clark College Collection: Copies of 1815: Chuinard: Rebound in full leather with raised bands. Tweney: Rebound in half leather with marbled boards, some offsetting; map in good condition. Wendlick: Rebound in half leather with raised bands, marbled boards; large map misbound facing page [1].

5a.4 Blussé, Dordrecht 1816–18 [Color plate XVIII]

REIZE | NAAR | DE BRONNEN VAN DEN MISSOURI, | EN DOOR HET VASTE LAND VAN AMERICA | NAAR DE ZUIDZEE. | Gedaan op last van de Regering der Vereenigde Staten van America, | in de jaren 1804, 1805 en 1806. | DOOR DE KAPITEINS | LEWIS EN CLARKE. | MET EENE KAART. | [rule] | UIT HET ENGELSCH VERTAALD DOOR | N. G. VAN KAMPEN. | [rule] | EERSTE DEEL. [TWEEDE DEEL.] [DERDE en Laatste DEEL.] | [asterisk] | TE DORDRECHT, | BIJ A. BLUSSÉ & ZOON.[Third volume: BIJ BLUSSÉ EN VAN BRAAM.] | 1816. [1817.][1818.]

Collation: Three volumes, 8vo., vol. 1: [i]–xxxii, [1]–398; vol. 2: [i]–viii, [1]–390; vol. 3: [i]–xii, [1]–335.

References: Coues, cxxvii–cxxviii; Paltsits, lxxx; Wagner-Camp-Becker, 13:5.

Description: This translation by van Kampen into Dutch is presumably from the 1815 three-volume English octavo, providing a new preface but also translating that of Thomas Rees. The Jefferson message and Lewis's Fort Mandan letter from Rees's preface are included, but placed at the end of vol. 3. The appendix of the Philadelphia first edition is not reproduced. There are no plates. The map ("Kart der Reizen van Lewis en Clarke") is an elegant re-engraving of Neele's 1814–1815 foldout with much the same dimensions and many of the place and feature names translated. This engraving increases general readability throughout. However, Coues notes some errors in transcription. The engravers sign themselves "C. van Baarsel en Zoon." Willem Cornelius van Baarsel (1791–1854) worked in both Utrecht and Amsterdam, and is either the father or the son of this partnership.

The three volumes were published at yearly intervals between 1816 and 1818: the first two volumes by the firm A. Blussé & Zoon, and the third by Blussé en van Braam.

Lewis & Clark College Collection: Wendlick: Three volumes bound as two: vols. 2 and 3 bound together. Marbled boards, leather spine. Map bound at end of vol. 3. Coues, Paltsits, and Wagner-Camp-Becker all collate the map at the end of vol. 1.

5a.5 Longman, London 1817
TRAVELS | TO THE SOURCE OF | THE MISSOURI RIVER, | AND ACROSS THE | *AMERICAN CONTINENT* | TO | THE PACIFIC OCEAN. | PERFORMED BY ORDER OF | THE GOVERNMENT OF THE UNITED STATES. | IN THE YEARS | 1804, 1805, AND 1806. | [rule] | BY CAPTAINS LEWIS AND CLARKE. | [rule] | PUBLISHED FROM THE OFFICIAL REPORT, | AND ILLUSTRATED BY A MAP OF THE ROUTE, | AND OTHER MAPS. | [rule] | *A NEW EDITION, IN THREE VOLUMES.* | VOL. I. [II.] [III.]| [rule] | *LONDON:* | PRINTED FOR LONGMAN, HURST, REES, ORME, AND BROWN, | PATERNOSTER-ROW. | 1817.

Collation: Three volumes, 8vo., 22 cm. Pagination as in 5a.3, with the following exception: vol. 2: half title on page [i]. Engravings printed from the same plates as in 5a.2, presented singly as in 5a.3.

References: Coues, cxxvi–cxxvii; Paltsits, lxxviii; Wagner-Camp-Becker, 13:4.

Description: The third British edition, text reset following 5a.3. There has been some uncertainty as to whether this 1817 Longman edition was printed from standing type of 1815, or reset. Coues believed it was reissued "apparently from the same plates" as 1815, though he noted divergences "on the last two pages of vol. I." In the opinion of Paltsits "the 1817 edition is entirely reset." While the compositors of 1817 were rather faithful to their 1815 copy, minor variations in setting create different divisions of text into pages within almost every signature in vol. 1. However, the signatures of 1817 naturally tend to begin and end identically to those of 1815. Similar variations are present in the other volumes.

Evidence of resetting is common from the start of vol. 1. Page numerals in the contents section are set in a different font. On the first page of text, the signature (B) is differently positioned and a comma separating subject from verb in the first sentence is removed. On p. 2, line 7, "enterprize" becomes "enterprise." In the fourth line of p. 3, a comma is added after "watermen," to clarify a potential ambiguity. These changes of spelling and punctuation, to more lucid and perhaps more "modern" norms, are clearly purposeful rather than random. However, any question of proofing by reference to an original copy-text, or even to the London 1814 quarto, is out of the question. In all three cases noted above, London 1815 and 1814 are in agreement with Philadelphia 1814. Misprints are also visible, though not common, in 1817, for example, the first word of vol. 2, p. 61.

Further evidence of resetting is provided by the patterns of press figures in 1815 and 1817. Pressmen in eighteenth- and early nineteenth-century printing houses placed a small figure on the page to identify their work (McKerrow, 81f., Gaskell, 133f.). The text of 1815 was printed by nine pressmen, numbered 1 to 11, with 7 and 8 not employed in this edition. Printing was achieved in seventy-five stints, pressman 4 being used for twenty-one of the seventy-five (ten and eight in vols. 1 and 3 respectively, but only three in vol. 2). This information suggests that vol. 2 was printed simultaneously with either 1 or 3.

The 1817 reprint was printed in seventy-three stints by fifteen pressmen, numbered 1 to 16, with 3 not available on this occasion. Only six of the fifteen pressmen (5, 6, 7, 8, 10, and 12) printed pages in all three volumes, the other pressmen tending to work in one or both of vols. 1 and 2. This pattern may again be evidence of simultaneous printing of two of the volumes. The use of so many more presses than in 1815 may also indicate that there was a greater urgency in the production of the reprint.

Plates: There are differences in the placement of plates in copies of London 1817. In vol. 1, the folding map is placed differently in the Wendlick copy, as noted below. The first plate ("Ancient Fortification on the Missouri") faces page 86 in all three Lewis & Clark College Collection copies. The second plate ("Great Falls of the Missouri") faces 190 in Chuinard, as if attempting to follow the instruction on the plate ("p. 191") that was appropriate only for the 1814 London quarto. The Tweney copy (uncut and in original boards) places it facing 336. Wendlick has the plate facing 354 (perhaps in error for 356, as in 1815). In vol. 2, Tweney and Wendlick agree in placing "Great Falls of Columbia River" facing 277, "Lower Falls of Columbia River" facing 302, and "Mouth of Columbia River" facing 338, while the Chuinard copy has these plates opposite 191, 378, and 398, respectively. These variations may indicate different binders working from conflicting instructions.

Lewis & Clark College Collection: Chuinard: Rebound in half leather, lacks index of maps. Tall copy. Tweney: Original boards, boxed, untrimmed. Ownership inscription of George M. Shirley, 1817. Wendlick: Half leather with marbled boards, lacking vol. 2 half title; map misbound facing p.[1].

5a.6 Christie, Dublin 1817

HISTORY | OF | THE EXPEDITION | UNDER THE COMMAND OF | CAPTAINS LEWIS AND CLARKE, | TO | THE SOURCES OF THE MISSOURI, | THENCE | ACROSS THE ROCKY MOUNTAINS | AND DOWN THE | RIVER COLUMBIA TO THE PACIFIC OCEAN. | PERFORMED DURING THE YEARS 1804-5-6. | BY ORDER OF THE | GOVERNMENT OF THE UNITED STATES. | PREPARED FOR THE PRESS | BY PAUL ALLEN, ESQ. | *WITH THE LIFE OF CAPTAIN LEWIS,* | BY T. JEFFERSON, | *PRESIDENT OF THE UNITED STATES OF AMERICA.* | IN TWO VOLUMES. | VOL. I. [II.] | PHILADELPHIA: PUBLISHED BY BRADFORD AND INSKEEP; AND ABM. H. | INSKEEP, NEWYORK. | DUBLIN: | PRINTED BY J. CHRISTIE, 170, JAMES'S-STREET. | 1817.

Collation: Two volumes, 8vo., 21.5cm. Vol. 1: [i]–v title page backed with Pennsylvania copyright page; [iii]–v Allen preface; six unpaginated leaves (subscribers and plates index, four leaves of contents); [vii]–xxvii Jefferson's "Life of Lewis"; [1]–588 text. Vol. 2: [i]–xii title page and copyright, contents; [3]–544 text; [545]–643 appendix. The copy described by Coues had the unpaginated two-leaf subscribers' list following the contents in vol. 2, before the first page [3] of text. Both Lewis & Clark College copies possess the subscribers' list in vol. 1: in Chuinard after the preface, in Wendlick before the preface.

Principal Cascade of the Missouri

Plates: Vol. 1: Facing 78 "Fortification"; facing 326 "Principal Cascade of the Missouri"; facing 327 "The Falls and Portage." Vol. 2: Facing 40 "Great Falls of Columbia River"; facing 67 "The Great Shoot or Rapid"; facing 91 "Mouth of Columbia River." Map: "A Map of Lewis and Clark's Track Across the Western Portion of North America."

References: Coues, cxxviii–cxxx; Graff, 2482; Paltsits, lxxxix; Wagner-Camp-Becker, 13:6.

Description: The folding map in onion skin, facing the title page, is a reduced copy of that in Philadelphia 1814 (Coues, Paltsits). No engraver is listed for the five map plates. The artist of the "Principal Cascade of the Missouri" is the Irish-born John James Barralet (c. 1747–1815), who on July 14, 1807, gave Lewis a receipt for "the Sum of Forty Dollar for two Drawings water falls" (Jackson, *Letters,* item 295 and note 6). "Clark later stated that Barralet had made the two drawings and that they were of 'the falls of the Missouri & Columbia.' The fate of these is unknown" (Cutright, *History,* 46). While the originals may be lost, it seems certain that one of them is represented here in this engraving: the earliest known image of the Great Falls of the Missouri. It was re-engraved for the Harper Family Library edition of 1842 and subsequent reprints.

"Of all of the reissues this one is the best, being nearest the original, of which is a faithful and literal reprint . . . a little taller and slightly deeper book, with more margin, and a larger, clearer type, wider spaced between the lines so that there are only 32 lines to the page as against 36 of the princeps" (Coues). The text is indeed faithful to Philadelphia 1814, but with a tendency toward slightly heavier punctuation.

Lewis & Clark College Collection: Chuinard: Rebound in full leather, re-backed. Contains map. A very good tall copy, inscribed by J. Marsh. Wendlick: Rebound in half leather with marbled boards. Contains map.

5a.7 Mausberger, Vienna 1826

Hearne's, Mackenzie's, Lewis und | Pike's | Entdeckungsreisen | im | Innern Nord-Amerika's. | Nebst einer Beschreibung der Nordwestküste | und Neu-Spaniens. | [ornamental rule] | Von | Dr. Wilhelm Harnisch. | Mit zwey Kupfern und einer Karte. | [rule] | Wien. | Mausberger's Druck und Verlag. | 1826.

Description: A condensed narrative, clearly based on the text of one of the earlier Biddle editions, presumably prepared by series general editor Dr. Wilhelm Harnisch. The original publisher was G. Fleischer, Leipzig, publishing (1820–1829) under the series title *Die wichtigsten neuern Land- und Seereisen. Für die Jugend und anderer Leser.* The narrative of North American journeys appears in vol. 3, 1821.

Lewis & Clark College Collection: Wendlick: copy of the Viennese reprint, published by Mausberger (1826–1829) under the general title *Interessante Zimmerreise zu Wasser und zu Lande für wissbegierige Leser gebildeter Stände*, Wien, Mausberger's Druck und Verlag. 1826. The North American narratives take up the whole third volume of the five-volume series, with the Lewis and Clark Expedition occupying pp. 111–188 under the subtitle "Des Hauptmann Lewi's Reise von dem Ausfluss des Missouri zu dem Ausfluss der Columbia, nebst einer Beschreibung der Nordwestküste Amerika's." None of the plates corresponds with the expedition narrative; the folding map at rear ("Nord-Amerika"), engraved by von Ferro, shows the routes of Hearne, Mackenzie, Lewis, and Pike.

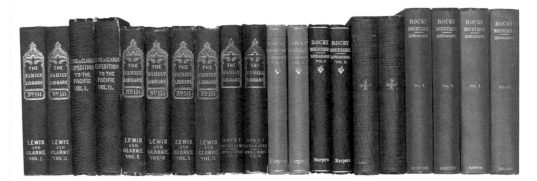

5a.8 Harper/M'Vickar, New York 1842–1917

5a.8 Harper/M'Vickar, New York [Akron] 1842–1917

HISTORY | OF | THE EXPEDITION | UNDER THE COMMAND OF | CAPTAINS LEWIS AND CLARKE, | TO | THE SOURCES OF THE MISSOURI, THENCE ACROSS THE ROCKY | MOUNTAINS, AND DOWN THE RIVER COLUMBIA TO THE | PACIFIC OCEAN: PERFORMED DURING THE | YEARS 1804, 1805, 1806, | BY ORDER OF THE | GOVERNMENT OF THE UNITED STATES. | PREPARED FOR THE PRESS | BY PAUL ALLEN, ESQ. | REVISED, AND ABRIDGED BY THE OMISSION OF UMIMPORTANT DE- | TAILS, WITH AN INTRODUCTION AND NOTES, | BY ARCHIBALD M'VICKAR. | IN TWO VOLUMES. | VOL. I. [II.] | NEW-YORK: | HARPER AND BROTHERS, 82 CLIFF-ST. | [rule] | 1842. [1845., etc.]

Note: The misprint "UMIMPORTANT" persists through all the nineteenth-century title pages of this much-reprinted edition, even when the publisher's imprint changes (around 1854, following the Cliff Street fire of December 1853) to "NEW YORK: | HARPER & BROTHERS, PUBLISHERS, | FRANKLIN SQUARE."

Collation *(through 1858)*: Two volumes, 18mo., 16 cm. Vol. 1: [i]–vi title page with copyright notice on verso; four-page publishers' preface, titled "Advertisement," and signed "H & B"; [i]–v contents pages; [vi]–li introduction by M'Vickar; [blank]; [53]–371 text. Folding map facing title page. Vol. 2: [i]–x title page backed with copyright notice, contents; [9]–338 text; [339]–395 appendix containing the natural history chapter (vol. 2, chapter 7) and some, but not all, of the original appendices (Coues, cxxxi).

Plates: Vol. 1: Facing 87 "Fortification"; facing 223 "Principal Cascade of the Missouri"; facing 234 "The Falls and Portage." Vol. 2: Facing 64 "Great Falls of Columbia River"; facing 79 "the Great Shoot or Rapid"; facing 92 "Mouth of Columbia River."

References: Coues, cxxx–cxxxi; Graff, 2483; Paltsits, lxxx–lxxxi; Wagner-Camp-Becker, 13:7.

Description: M'Vickar's edition is a selection of passages reproduced verbatim, with linking commentary by the editor. In the heavier punctuation of the quoted passages, it appears to be based on the 1817 Dublin edition rather than the 1814 Philadelphia edition. The original passages are generally surrounded with quotation marks, and omissions within them are indicated by asterisks.

Coues and Paltsits provide a listing of the twenty or so Harper and Brothers editions of this text, "most of which consisted of 250 copies" (Coues), appearing in September 1842, January 1843, May 1843, January 1844, July 1845, April 1847, May 1850, August 1851, June 1855, April 1858, November 1860, February 1868, March 1871 (vol. 2), April 1872 (vol. 1), February 1874 (vol. 2), December 1875 (vol. 1), February 1881, March 1882, July 1883, April 1886, February 1887, June 1891, and June 1901. Paltsits adds an unverified Sabin reference (item 40834) to a London 1842 M'Vickar. Most, but not all, of the editions belong to the Harper Family Library.

The engraver of the plates and folding map was W. G. Evans of New York. Map and plates derive primarily from Dublin 1817 rather than Philadelphia 1814. In the case of the map, the lineation of the title matches 1817 rather than 1814, and the map lacks the designation for the Southern Pass. Evans does have the misreading "L. Riddle" for "L. Biddle," making the same error as Neele in 1814 when following the Samuel Lewis map. Among the plates, the Evans engraving of the "Principal Cascade of the Missouri" is an inferior reproduction of John James Barralet's view, first published in the Dublin edition. It is also clear that Evans followed Dublin as one source for the remaining plates, but not exclusively. For example, in "The Falls & Portage" (1842, vol. 1, facing p. 234), Evans follows Dublin in the placement and drawing of the rapids and in supplying a river not shown in 1814 at the "Upper Pitch." However, he corrects Dublin's "1100 Yds wide" above the rapids by reference to 1814's "1400 Yds. wide." It would appear that Evans had access to plates from both editions.

Lewis & Clark College Collection: 1842, brown cloth (Wendlick). Owner inscription "James Blake 1842." Vol. 1, p. xiii, shows a binding signature (vol. 1.–B). Folding map in vol. 1. This is the September 1842 first edition.

1842–3, black cloth (Tweney). Title page dates vol. 1: 1842, vol. 2: 1843. Folding map. Binding signature on 1, xiii. This edition, a reprint outside the Harper Family Library series, with plainer spine and blind-stamped front and back cover, is printed from the same type as the Harper Family Library series. This must be the January 1843 second edition.

1845, brown cloth (Wendlick). Folding map. Binding signature on 1, xiii. This is the July 1845 fifth edition.

Undated, brown cloth (Tweney). No date on title page (the reprint of the original copyright page on verso carries an unchanged date of 1842). Title page still locates offices at Cliff Street. Folding map. The binding signature on 1, xiii, has been deleted, cutting off the tail of "p" in "Enterprise." This undated edition must follow 1845 and precede 1854, the date of the move to Harper's new offices at Franklin Square, built after their Cliff Street building burned in December 1853 (Horsford, 194). This is one of the following three reprints: April 1847, May 1850, August 1851. In this copy of vol. 2, the plates facing 68 (for 64) and 92 are identical ("Mouth of Columbia River"); the plate facing 64 should have been "Great Falls of the Columbia River."

1858, brown cloth (Wendlick). Offices located at Franklin Square. Redesigned spine, with smaller title cartouche and no Family Library series number. Title at foot of spine reads "Rocky Mountains [rule] Lewis & Clarke vol. I [II]." Folding map (not present in Lewis & Clark College copy). This edition is printed from the same type as the undated edition (previous item), including the appendix, except for the copyright notice on reverse of title page, now double-leaded, as in the two following editions. No plates are included, though the original list of plates from 1842 (following the vol. 2 contents) is, of course, still present in this direct reprint. This is the April 1858 edition.

Later undated edition, purple cloth (Wendlick). This has a plainer spine, with no reference to Family Library. Title: "Rocky Mountains." Folding map. No plates. No appendix.

Later undated edition, green cloth (Tweney). Ownership inscription: "Robinson 1900." Contents identical to above item. Binding differs in using a smaller point size for publisher imprint.

1900, purple cloth, with green clover leaf on front and spine (Tweney). A. L. Fowle, New York (Criterion Library) Edition from the same plates as (or reproduction of) those of an edition between 1845 and 1854, or one of the identical editions that includes the appendix. It differs only in the title page, reset as a close approximation to the original, and in the spine attribution to Fowle's Criterion Library. Folding map. No plates are included, although the original list of plates from 1842 (following the vol. 2 contents) is still present. There is no permission notice from Harper and Brothers, who were still the publishers of the M'Vickar text (see following items). The online catalog at Online Computer Library Center (OCLC) shows A. L. Fowle's company (in business between 1857 and 1931) publishing twelve volumes in the Criterion Library, all in 1900, specializing in historical or biographical reprints. Outside the Criterion Library, there was a Makers of Literature series and the International Science Library.

1901 Red cloth (Anderson and Wendlick). Harper and Brothers. Reprint of an edition between 1845 and 1854 or one of its successors, with folding map and appendix.

1904 Orange cloth (Chuinard and Wendlick). Identical to 1901 above.

1910 *Lewis and Clarke Explorers,* attributed to "Paul Allen" (crediting the editor of 1814). Two volumes. First volume only at Lewis & Clark College. Title on title page: *Meriwether Lewis and William Clarke, Pioneers.* Werner Company 1910: D. M. MacLellan Book Company, New York & Akron. Prefatory matter closely based on M'Vickar; narrative text identical to M'Vickar, with presumed omission of appendix, and lacking map and plates. Newly illustrated, artist unknown.

1915 Harper and Brothers, two volumes in one (pp. 371, 395). Reprint of 1814, including M'Vickar materials. Not at Lewis & Clark College. Information from OCLC database.

1915 Superior Printing Company, Akron (receiving copyright from Werner in 1915). Reprint of 1910 edition. Text as above, with introduction and appendix omitted. Divided into four volumes, titled "Up the Missouri," "Captains Lewis and Clarke," "In the Rocky Mountains," and "In Camp on White Bear Island." No map, plates, or illustrations.

1917 Superior Printing Company. Copyrights Werner 1910, Superior 1916. Two volumes. Printed "For Subscribers Only." Two volumes, titled "Early American Pioneers" and "Heroes of the Northwest." New unsigned illustrations, including those from 1910.

5a.9 McClurg/Hosmer, Chicago 1902–5, 1917, 1924

HISTORY | OF | THE EXPEDITION | OF | CAPTAINS LEWIS AND CLARK | 1804-5-6 | [rule] | *REPRINTED FROM THE EDITION OF 1814* | [rule] | WITH INTRODUCTION AND INDEX | BY | JAMES K. HOSMER, LL.D., | AUTHOR OF "A SHORT HISTORY OF THE MISSISSIPPI VALLEY," | "THE STORY OF THE LOUISIANA PURCHASE," ETC.; | PRESIDENT OF THE AMERICAN | LIBRARY ASSOCIATION. | [rule] | In Two Volumes, with Portraits and Maps | VOLUME | I. [II.] | [rule] | CHICAGO | A. C. MCCLURG & CO. | 1902

Collation: Two volumes, 8vo., 22 cm. (trade), 25 cm. (large paper). Vol. 1: [i]–lvi includes a frontispiece portrait of Lewis, a new preface by Hosmer, Allen's 1814 preface, and Jefferson's "Life of Lewis"; [1]–500 text. Folding map facing p. 124. Vol. 2: [i]–[xiv] includes frontispiece portrait of Clark; [1]–583 text, including the original appendix of 1814, and a new index, the first supplied for the Biddle text.

Plates: Vol. 1: Facing 276 "Fortification"; facing 400 "The Falls and Portage." Vol. 2: Facing 104 "Great Falls of Columbia River"; facing 250 "The Great Shoot or Rapid"; facing 374 "Mouth of Columbia River." The map and plates are facsimiles of those in Philadelphia 1814.

References: Paltsits, lxxxiii–lxxxiv.

Description: The text follows Philadelphia 1814 closely, with infrequent punctuation variants. There were five trade editions and one limited large-paper edition by A. C. McClurg & Co. The first trade edition was published on October 15, 1902, and the second trade edition (noted as such on title page) on January 15, 1903. The single large-paper edition, limited to seventy-five copies, appeared in 1904. (Hosmer's edition of Patrick Gass's *Journal* was also issued by McClurg in 1904 in a trade edition as well as a limited edition of seventy-five. Formats and bindings were identical to the *Expedition* volumes described here.) The next trade edition, noted as the third on its title page, appeared in 1905; the fourth (noted as such) in 1917; and a final trade edition (called the fourth in error on the title page, but correctly described as the fifth on the copyright page) appeared in 1924. All of the trade editions are top-edge gilt, and all but the last trade edition are in two colors of cloth: a light brown with a darker brown spine. The 1924 edition is uniformly bound in dark brown cloth. The large-paper edition is bound in gray boards with an off-white spine.

Lewis & Clark College Collection:
1902 trade: Two copies (Tweney and Wendlick).
1903 trade: One copy (Wendlick).
1904 large paper: Three copies (Chuinard, Tweney, Wendlick).
1905 trade: One copy (Wendlick).
1917 trade: One copy (Wendlick).
1924 trade: One copy (Wendlick).

The Corps of Discovery is also mentioned in Hosmer's *The History of the Louisiana Purchase*, a 1902 volume from D. Appleton and Company, New York.

5a.10 New Amsterdam Book Company, New York 1902
HISTORY | OF | THE EXPEDITION | UNDER THE COMMAND OF | CAPTAINS LEWIS | AND CLARK | TO | THE SOURCES OF THE MISSOURI, ACROSS THE ROCKY | MOUNTAINS, DOWN THE COLUMBIA RIVER | TO THE PACIFIC IN 1804-6 | *A REPRINT OF THE EDITION OF 1814 TO* | *WHICH ALL THE MEMBERS OF THE* | *EXPEDITION CONTRIBUTED* | WITH MAPS | IN THREE VOLUMES | VOL. I. [II.] [III.] | NEW AMSTERDAM BOOK COMPANY | PUBLISHERS: NEW YORK, 1902.

Collation: Three volumes, 16mo., 18 cm. Vol. 1: [i]–xxxiii, including the Allen preface and Jefferson's "Life of Captain Lewis"; 35–416 text. Vol. 2: [i]–ix, 11–410 text. Vol. 3: [i]–xi, 13–382 text; four unnumbered pages of advertisements. Folding map, reproducing the Samuel Lewis/Samuel Harrison original of 1814, in a pocket inside the back cover. Vol. 1 has a frontispiece of Lewis, vol. 2 of Clark.

Plates: Vol. 1: Facing 108 "Fortification"; facing 347 "The Falls and Portage." Vol. 2: Facing 210 "Great Falls of Columbia River"; facing 234 "The Great Shoot or Rapid"; facing 257 "Mouth of Columbia River."

Reference: Paltsits, lxxxiii–lxxxiv.

Description: The text is faithful to the original, including all of its accompanying documents, appendices, plates and map. The spelling "Clarke" is normalized to "Clark" throughout, and other minor spelling changes are made. Nevertheless, this was an important attempt to provide a general readership with a close approximation of the first edition in pocket format. Three editions appeared in

1902, two trade editions (one with a more elaborate binding, as described below) and a large-paper limited edition of 210, printed from the same type, and with its pocketed map printed on a sheet with larger margins. See 5a.14 for listing of copies held by the Lewis & Clark College Collection.

5a.11 Barnes, New York 1903

HISTORY *of* THE EXPEDI- | TION *under the* COMMAND *of* | CAPTAINS LEWIS *&* CLARK | TO THE | SOURCES OF *the* MISSOURI, ACROSS | *the* ROCKY MOUNTAINS, DOWN | *the* COLUMBIA RIVER TO | *the* PACIFIC IN 1804-6 | A REPRINT OF THE EDITION OF 1814 | TO WHICH ALL THE MEMBERS OF | THE EXPEDITION CONTRIBUTED | *WITH MAPS* | IN THREE VOLUMES | VOL. I. [II.] [III.]. | NEW YORK | A. S. BARNES AND COMPANY | 1903

Description: The above edition, identical in text and illustrations, but with a new title page, and with the map tipped in at the end of vol. 3 rather than pocketed, appeared in 1903, from A. S. Barnes and Company. The edition was part of their Classics in American History series, and was listed first in their advertisement. See 5a.14 for listing of copies held by the Lewis & Clark College Collection.

5a.12 Barnes/McMaster, New York 1904

HISTORY *of* THE EXPEDI- | TION *under the* COMMAND *of* | CAPTAINS LEWIS *&* CLARK | TO THE | SOURCES OF *the* MISSOURI, THENCE ACROSS | *the* ROCKY MOUNTAINS AND DOWN *the* | RIVER COLUMBIA TO *the* PACIFIC OCEAN | Performed During the Years 1804-5-6, by Order of the | Government of the United States | A COMPLETE REPRINT OF THE BIDDLE | EDITION OF 1814, TO WHICH ALL THE | MEMBERS OF THE EXPEDITION CONTRIBUTED | *WITH AN ACCOUNT OF THE LOUISIANA* | *PURCHASE* | *By* | PROF. JOHN BACH MCMASTER | AND | NOTES UPON THE ROUTE | *WITH ILLUSTRATIONS AND MAPS* | Vol. I [II] [III] | NEW YORK | A. S. BARNES AND COMPANY | 1904

Description: This 1904 edition, again in three volumes from Barnes, but now in their Trailmakers series, used the same text and plates. Two new additions were the introduction on the Louisiana Purchase by John Bach McMaster, and, according to Paltsits (lxxxiv), the introductory notes in each volume to the expedition route by Ripley Hitchcock. The folding map is tipped in facing the title page (Wendlick). Another set (Chuinard) of the same edition lacks the Trailmaker designation on spine, half-title advertisement, and map, but is otherwise identical. See 5a.14 for listing of copies held by the Lewis & Clark College Collection.

5a.13 Nutt, London 1905

A London edition in the following year, in identical format and contents, differs only in the title page imprint as follows:

PUBLISHED BY | DAVID NUTT | AT THE SIGN OF THE PHOENIX | LONG ACRE, LONDON | 1905 | *All rights reserved.*

The map is again tipped in at the end of vol. 3 (Tweney; lacking in Wendlick). See 5a.14 for listing of copies held by the Lewis & Clark College Collection.

5b.1 The Coues-Anderson
Manuscript Transcript of
the Journals

Left: Codex E
Falls and Portage of the
Missouri River

Right: Codex N
Lewis's Route from
Traveler's Rest to the
Missouri River

5a.14 Allerton, New York 1922

This Barnes/McMaster text appears one final time in a 1922 reprint (map at end of vol. 3) in the American Explorers Series from Allerton Book Company, New York.

Lewis & Clark College Collection: 1902 New Amsterdam, large-paper limited edition, three sets: Chuinard (no. 127 of 210; map facsimile in onion skin), Tweney (no. 152 of 210), and Wendlick (no. 107 of 210).

1902 New Amsterdam, trade edition, four sets: gray cloth with black stamping and red titling, "Commonwealth Library" on back cover (Chuinard, Tweney, Wendlick), maroon cloth with gilt stamping, back cover plain, "Daintily bound," in the words of the publisher's advertisement (Wendlick). Map in pocket, vol. 3.

1903 Barnes, one set: green cloth with red stamping, gilt titling. Map tipped in, end of vol. 3 (Wendlick).

1904 Barnes, two sets: maroon cloth, gilt titling (Chuinard and Wendlick), differences noted above.

1905 Nutt, two sets: reddish-brown cloth, gilt titling (Tweney and Wendlick).

1922 Allerton, one set: brown cloth with gilt titling, dust jacket in moss green with extensive advertisements (Wendlick).

5b Elliott Coues
5b.1 The Coues-Anderson Manuscript Transcript of the Journals [Color plate XIX]

Description: The thirty codices are arranged into sixteen boxes, a total of 2,798 pages. Page size is 22.5 x 14.5 cm. The manuscript is a close hand-written transcript of the Lewis and Clark journals. The transcript ("an exact copy, word for word, letter for letter, and point for point") was begun in December 1892 by "expert copyist" Mary Anderson at the request of Elliott Coues (Cutright, *History*, 89), and was completed in 1893. It was acquired by George Tweney in the spring of 1970 from Douglas Parsonage, a New York book dealer, who had recently succeeded Lathrop Harper, the brother of the late Francis Harper (Tweney, *Elliott Coues*).

The transcript is written throughout in pen on Coues notepaper, mostly blank, but some sheets bearing letterhead of Coues's Smithsonian address. Watermarks: HOLYOKE PAPER CO and *HOLYOKE PAPER COMPANY*. It contains interlined editorial notes in pencil by Coues. The quoted notations below are the summaries of each codex by copyist Mary Anderson, with additional comments by Elliott Coues.

Abbreviations accompanying figures: A34, etc.: original codex letter with page number; C-A23, etc.: Coues-Anderson manuscript, with page number; M2, 278, 280, etc: Moulton *Journals*, with volume and page number(s), and with figure names from Moulton. Title pages are not included in the page counts.

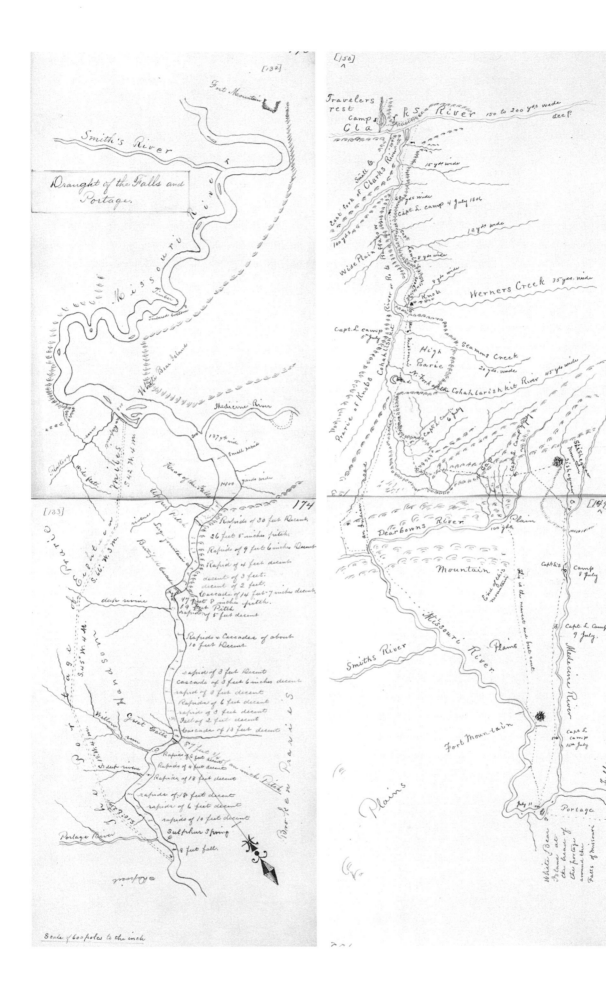

Codex A: May 13–August 14, 1804 (Clark).
"Lewis and Clark. Codex A. Journal, complete, May 13–Aug. 14, 1804, By William Clark. 92 leaves = 184 pages of the original MS., making folios 1–120 of this copy, By Mary B. Anderson, 1893. N.B. Figures in circles, thus, 116 [circled], indicate pagination of the original. All *penciling* is my memoranda of places, distances, etc., foreign to the inked text. Elliott Coues. 1893."

Figure: Manitou on a rock, June 5, 1804 (A34; C-A23; M2, 278, 280).

Codex Aa: Fragment of journal, May 20 and May 15, 1804 (Lewis).
"Lewis and Clark. Codex A.a. A fragment, May 20 and May 15, 1804. By Meriwether Lewis. copied By Mary B. Anderson, folios 1–6, Dec. 1892. Compared with the original MS. Elliott Coues."

Codex B August 15–October 3, 1804 (Clark).
"Lewis and Clark. Codex B. Journal, complete, Aug 15–Oct. 3, 1804. By William Clark. 90 leaves = 180 pages of the orig. MS., making folios 1–87 of this copy. By Mary B. Anderson, 1893."

Codex Ba Fragment of journal, September 16–17, 1804 (Lewis).
"Lewis and Clark. Codex Ba. A fragment, ("the Antelope") Sept. 16 and 17, 1804. By Meriwether Lewis. Copied By Mary B. Anderson, folios 1–8, Dec. 1892. Compared with original MS. Elliott Coues."

Codex C "The Brown Book," October 1, 1804–April 7, 1805 (Mainly by Clark); February 3–13 (Lewis); Invoices, etc. (by another hand).

"Lewis and Clark. Codex C. "The Brown Book," being the Mandan Journal, Oct. 1, 1804–Apr. 7, 1805. Mainly By William Clark– Feb. 3–13 By Meriwether Lewis– Invoices, etc. by another hand. Orig. leaves 137 = 274 pages, copied in folios 1–201 By Mary B. Anderson 1893."

Figures: War hatchet, January 28, 1805 (C158; C-A98; M3, 280); Battle ax, February 5, 1805 (C165; C-A104; M3, 287); Mississippi River and Tributaries in present Minnesota, undated, winter 1804–5 (C255; C-A182: M3, 366).

Codex D April 7–May 23, 1805 (Lewis).
"Lewis and Clark. Codex D. Journal, complete, Apr. 7–May 23, 1805. By Meriwether Lewis. Copied in folios 1–157, By Mary B. Anderson, 1983."
P. 155 completes the May 23, 1805, entry. Pages 156 and 157 represent the final page (140) of the original, headed "Remarks for June 1805." The upper part of Anderson's p. 156 is torn away, and is supplied in photocopy from microfilm of the original manuscript. (See also M4, 347–8, for a variant text of this material.)

Codex E May 24–July 16, 1805 (Lewis).
"Lewis and Clark. Codex E. Journal, complete, May 24–July 16, 1805. Missouri R. from North Mountain Cr. to the 'Gates of the Rocky Mts.' By Meriwether Lewis. Copied in folios 1–206 By Mary B. Anderson, 1983."

Figure: Falls and Portage of the Missouri River, ca. July 4, 1805 (E132/133; C-A173/174; M4, 360).

Codex F July 17–August 22, 1805 (Lewis).
"Lewis and Clark. Codex F. Journal complete, July 17–Aug. 22, 1805. From the 'Gates of the Rocky Mts.' To the Shoshone Indians. By Meriwether Lewis. Copied in folios 1–207 By Mary B. Anderson, 1983. [See with Codex F–Codices Fa, Fb, Fc, Fd, Fe.]"

Figures: Shoshone Smoking-pipe (F99; C-A132; M5, 82); Shoshone Fish Weir, August 21, 1805 (F147; C-A198; M5, 136).

Codex Fa Fragment of journal, August 1–4, 1805 (Lewis).
"Lewis and Clark. Codex Fa. Fragment of Journal, Aug. 1–4, 1805. Exploration of a Fork of Jefferson R. By Meriwether Lewis. Orig. folios 4, written to 6 1/2 pages, copied in folios 1–7, By Mary B. Anderson, Dec. 1892. Compared with original, Elliot Coues. [Follows Codex F.]"

Codex Fb Fragment of journal, August 23–26, 1805 (Lewis).
"Lewis and Clark. Codex Fb. Fragment of Journal, Aug. 23–26, 1805, The Shoshone Indians, By Meriwether Lewis. orig. folios 13, written to 25 1/4 pages Copied in folios 1–27. By Mary B. Anderson, Dec. 1892. Compared with original– Elliott Coues. [Follows Codex Fa–both go with Codex F.]"

Codex Fc Fragment of journal, September 9–10, 1805 (Lewis).
"Lewis and Clark. Codex Fc. Fragment of Journal, Sept. 9 and 10, 1805. 'Traveller's Rest.' By Meriwether Lewis. Copied in folios 1–4, By Mary B. Anderson, Dec. 1892. Compared with original, Elliott Coues. [Follows Codex Fb.]"

Codex Fd Fragment of journal, September 18–22, 1805 (Lewis).
"Lewis and Clark. Codex Fd. Fragment of Journal, Sept. 18–22, 1805. Bitter-root Mts. By Meriwether Lewis. Orig. folios 4 = 8 pages, copied in folios 1–9, By Mary B. Anderson, Dec. 1892. Compared with original, Elliott Coues. [Follows Codex Fc.]"

Codex Fe Two fragments: weather diary April–June 1805 and weather diary July–September 1805.

"Two Fragments 1. Weather Diary, Lewis, Apr–June, 1805. 2. Weather Diary, Lewis, July–September 1805. See Explanations on 2 following folios. Copied by Mary B. Anderson, Dec. 1892." [12 pages.]

"Text of 'remarks' copied, without tabulated figures by M. B. A., Dec. 1892."

"NB. This Meteorological Register consists of two parts, here united as *Codex Fe*, the dates being continuous. Apr. May, June 1805. Part first, five leaves of the original, here nine leaves, is part of Lewis Codex D. This belongs at end of Codex D, from which it was torn out; and remarks for June 1805 are on p. 140 of Codex D. Part Second, for July, Aug., Sept., 1805, being three leaves of the original, here six leaves, is similarly a part of a Lewis(?) Codex. *Note*. In making this copy the *tabular* figures of the original (thermometer etc.) are omitted: but all the text, of 'remarks' apposite these tables, and further 'remarks' on separate pages, is given. Elliott Coues. (Dec. 1892)".

Codex G July 2–October 10, 1805 (Clark).
"Lewis and Clark. Codex G. Journal, complete, July 2d–Oct. 10, 1805. Great Falls of Missouri R. To the Columbia R. By William Clark, Copied By Mary B. Anderson, 1893." [152 pages.]

Codex H October 11–November 19, 1805 (Clark).
"Lewis and Clark. Codex H. Journal, complete, Oct. 11–Nov. 19, 1805. Down the Columbia. By William Clark. Copied By Mary B. Anderson, 1893." [146 pages.] Transcript complete as originally numbered. It lacks three pages of maps, at the start of the original manuscript. These are described in Anderson's transcript of Biddle's fly-leaf note, but the maps were either not completed, or were removed before the pages were numbered by Coues/Anderson. Facsimiles of the equivalent maps in the original journals have been laid in the box.

Figure: Confluence of Snake and Columbia Rivers, Washington (H33; C-A30; M5, 297).

Codex I Miscellaneous (Clark):
"Lewis and Clark. Codex I. Miscellaneous, as follows: 1. Itinerary, Ft. Mandan to the Pacific. 2. Weather Diary, April 1805–Jan 1806. 3. Journal, Nov. 19, 1805–Jan. 21, 1806. 4. Estimate of the Western Indians. By William Clark. Copied By Mary B Anderson, 1893." [166 pages.]

Figures: Tongue Point, Oregon, Winter 1805–6 (I11;C-A12; M6, 460); Conic Hat, December 29, 1805 (I80; C-A86; M6, 143); Arrow, January 15, 1806 (I119; C-A127; M6, 209); Bone Fishhook and Line, January 16, 1806 (I122; C-A129; M6, 213); Digging Instrument, January 23, 1806 (I135;C-A143; M6, 232); Conic Hat, January 29, 1806 (I144; C-A152; M6, 247); Double-edged Knife, January 29, 1806 (I144; C-A153; M6, 247). The chart of the Mouth of the Columbia River (I152, M6, 52) is omitted in the Anderson copy, with no break in page numbering.

Codex Ia Fragment of journal, November 29–December 1, 1805 (Lewis)
"Lewis and Clark. Codex Ia. Fragment, Journal Nov. 29–Dec.1, 1805. The Netul River. By Meriwether Lewis. 2 copies follow–see explanation inside Copied by E. C. and M. B. A. Dec. 1892." "Following is 5 leaves torn out of one of the *small* oblong Note-books, written 8 pages full of Lewis' manuscript, back of one leaf blank but for a slight sketch of Point Adams, front of another leaf written across lengthwise in another hand 'Capt. Lewis rough notes, when he left Capt. Clark near the mouth of Columbia for a few days to examine the S.W. side.' Copied by me v. l. p.[verbatim litteratim punctuatim] Dec. 12 '92–E. C." The Coues copy is four pages, Anderson's copy is six pages plus the sketch of Point Adams. Total of both copies: eleven pages plus three title pages.

Figure: Point Adams, Oregon, ca. December 1, 1805 (Ia7; C-A8, Anderson; M6, 102).

Codex J January 1–March 20, 1806 (Lewis)
"Lewis and Clark. Codex J. The Clatsop Journal, Jan. 1–Mar. 20, 1806. By Meriwether Lewis. Copied by Mary B. Anderson, 1893." [193 pages.]

Figures: Two Swords, a Bludgeon and a Paddle, January 1, 1806 (J1; C-A1; M6, 152); Arrow, January 15, 1806 (J25; C-A29; M6, 207); Bone Fishhook and Line, January 16, 1806 (J28; C-A32; M6, 212); Digging Instrument, January 24, 1806 (J40; C-A48; M6, 234); Conic Hat and Double-edged Knife, January 30, 1806 (J48; C-A59; M6, 250); Paddle, Small Canoe, February 1, 1806 (J52; C-A64; M6, 264); Canoe with High Bow and Most Common Canoe, February 1, 1806 (J52; C-A65; M6, 264); Canoe with Carved Images, February 1, 1806 (J53; C-A66; M6, 266); Fir Leaf (Douglas fir, *Pseudotsuga taxifolia*), February 9, 1806 (J65; C-A82; M6, 291); Maple Leaf (vine maple, *Acer circinatum*), February 10, 1806 (J66; C-A84; M6, 294); Fern Leaf (Christmas fern, *Polystichum munitum*), February 13, 1806 (J71; C-A90; M6, 304); Head of a vulture (California condor, *Gymnogyps californianus*), February 17, 1806 (J80; C-A100; M6, 323); Pine Cone (Sitka spruce, *Picea sitchensis*), February 18, 1806 (J83; C-A104; M6, 326); Eulachon (*Thaleichthys pacificus*), February 24, 1806 (J93; C-A118; M6, 343); Head of Cock of the Plains (sage grouse, *Centrocercus urophasianus*), March 2, 1806 (J107; C-A135; M6, 369); Head of a White Gull (northern fulmar, *Fulmaris glacialis*), March 7, 1806 (J115; C-A146; M6, 389); Head of a Brant (greater white-fronted goose, *Anser albifrons*), March 15, 1806 (J131; C-A167; M6, 417); White Salmon Trout (coho salmon, *Oncorhynchus kisutch*), March 16, 1806 (J133; C-A169; M6, 422).

Codex K March 21–May 23, 1806 (Lewis)
"Lewis and Clark. Journal K. Journal, Fort Clatsop to Camp Chopunnish, Mar. 21–May 23, 1806. By Meriwether Lewis. Copied by Mary B. Anderson, 1893." [194 pages.]

Figures: Iron Scimitar, March 29, 1806 (K14, C-A18, M7, 29); Confluence of Willamette and Columbia Rivers, April 3, 1806 (K28/29; C-A36; M7, 63); Two Views of a Canoe, April 6, 1806 (K33; C-A42; M7, 80); Plan of Chinookan House, April 6, 1806 (K39; C-A49; M7, 85); Bone Fishhook, April 26, 1806 (K83; C-A105, M7, 170); Fish Net, May 18, 1806 (K139; C-A176; M7, 270);

Codex L May 24–August 8, 1806 (Lewis)
"Lewis and Clark. Codex L. Journal, complete, May 24–Aug. 8, 1806. with Weather Diaries, &c. Exploration of Maria's River, etc. By Meriwether Lewis. Copied by Mary B. Anderson, 1893. Codices La and Lb belong to this Codex, at pages 81 and 144 respectively. Pages 45–150 (3 folios), which were torn out, I have reinserted, making orig. folios 150. Elliott Coues." [169 pages.]

Codex La Fragment of journal, July 3–15, 1806
"Lewis and Clark. Codex La. Fragment, Journal, July 3–15, 1806. ('Pass Codex,' being discovery of L. and C. Pass. Belongs in Codex L., at orig. page 81.) By Meriwether Lewis. Copied by Mary B. Anderson, Dec. 1892." [18 pages.] The small sketch of Monture (Seaman's) Creek, Powell County, Montana (La4, M8, 91) is not copied by Anderson.

Codex Lb Fragment of journal, August 9–12, 1806 (Lewis)
"Lewis and Clark. Codex Lb. Fragment, Journal, Aug.9–12, 1806. "Cruzatte's Shot." By Meriwether Lewis. (his last) Copied by M. B. Anderson. Dec 1892." ". . . A Fragment, belonging with Codex L, at p.144 Shooting of Lewis by Cruzatte. . . . E. C." [7 pages.]

5b.1 The Coues-Anderson Manuscript Transcript of the Journals

Above: Codex J
Most Common Canoe

Below: Codex J
Head of a vulture

Codex M June 7–August 14, 1806 (Clark)
"Lewis and Clark. Codex M. Journal, complete June 7–Aug. 14, 1806. The Yellowstone River. By William Clark. Copied by Mary B. Anderson, 1983." [188 pages.]

Figure: Snake and Missouri rivers and their Connections, May 29–31, 1806 (M1/2; C-A2; M7, 316/317).

Codex N August 15–September 25, 1806 (Clark)
"Lewis and Clark. Codex N. Journal, complete, Aug. 15–Sept. 225, 1806. With various other matters. By William Clark. Copied by Mary B. Anderson. 1893." [128 pages.]

Figures: Bon Homme Island on the Missouri River, Bon Homme County, South Dakota and Knox County, Nebraska, September 1, 1806 (N81, C-A84; M8, 339); Bon Homme Island on the Missouri River, Bon Homme County, South Dakota and Knox County, Nebraska, September 1, 1806 (N82, C-A85; M8, 340); Lewis's Route from Traveler's Rest to the Missouri River, ca. July 3–11, 1806 (N149/150; C-A122/123; M8, 105).

Codices 0 and P are in the same box.

Codex O Astronomical Observations, May 18, 1804–March 30, 1805
"Lewis and Clark. Codex O. Astronomical Observations, May 18, 1804–Mar. 30, 1805. Geographical Notes, No dates. Copied by Mary B. Anderson, 1893." [109 pages.]

Codex P Natural History Notes, etc.; April 9, 1805–February 17, 1806
"Lewis and Clark. Codex P. Natural History Notes, &c., &c. April 9, 1805–February 17, 1806. Not in handwriting of L. or C. Collate with Codices D to N. Copied by Mary B. Anderson, 1893." [112 pages.]

Figure: Digging Instrument, January 23, 1806 (P92; C-A73; M6, 232, (note 4). (This figure is copied from I135/C-A143 above.)

Codices Q, R, S, and T are in the same box.

Codex Q Misc. Natural History, 1804–1806
"Lewis and Clark. Codex Q. Miscellaneous Natural History, 1804–1806. By Lewis, Clark, and another hand. Copied by Mary B. Anderson, 1893." [70 pages.]
Figure: Iron Scimitar, March 29, 1806 (Q88; C-A34; M7, 29 and 31, note 13). (This figure is copied from K14/C-A18 above.)

Codex R Misc. Natural History, May 1804–March 1806
"Lewis and Clark. Codex R. Miscellaneous Natural History, May 1804–Mar. 1806. By Lewis, Clark, and another hand. Copied by Mary B. Anderson. 1893." [62 pages.]

Figure: Large "convolvalist" leaf (hedge bindweed, *Convolvulus sepium L.*), July 17, 1804 (R37; C-A14; M3, 459, 467).

Codex S Two Letters by Meriwether Lewis
"Lewis and Clark. Codex S Two Letters, By Meriwether Lewis. Copied by Elliott Coues, Dec. 10, 1892.
a) Sept. 23 1806, Rough Draft of letter announcing return of the Expedition to President Jefferson.

b) Fragment of a letter, Sept. 1806, on discovery of the Yellowstone, etc."
[19 pages.]

Codex T Unidentified fragment not in Clark's hand, one loose sheet. "Lewis and Clark. Codex T. unidentified fragment. Copied by Elliott Coues [Dec. 12, 1892], copied again by Mary B. Anderson, Dec. 1892." Total of both copies, three pages, with three title pages. (See M8, 414f., note 1.)

5b.2 Elliott Coues Edition 1893

HISTORY OF THE EXPEDITION | UNDER THE COMMAND OF | LEWIS AND CLARK, | *To the Sources of the Missouri River, thence across the Rocky Mountains and* | *down the Columbia River to the Pacific Ocean, performed during* | *the Years 1804-5-6,* | *by Order of the* | GOVERNMENT OF THE UNITED STATES. | A NEW EDITION, | FAITHFULLY REPRINTED FROM THE ONLY AUTHORIZED EDITION OF 1814, WITH COPIOUS | CRITICAL COMMENTARY, PREPARED UPON EXAMINATION OF UNPUBLISHED | OFFICIAL ARCHIVES AND MANY OTHER SOURCES OF INFORMATION, | INCLUDING A DILIGENT STUDY OF THE | ORIGINAL MANUSCRIPT JOURNALS | AND | FIELD NOTEBOOKS OF THE EXPLORERS, | TOGETHER WITH | A New Biographical and Bibliographical Introduction, New Maps | and other Illustrations, and a Complete Index, | BY | ELLIOTT COUES, | *Late Captain and Assistant Surgeon, United States Army,* | *Late Secretary and Naturalist,* | *United States Geological Survey,* | *Member of the National Academy of Sciences, etc.* | IN FOUR VOLUMES. | VOL. I. [II. III. IV.] | NEW YORK. | FRANCIS P. HARPER. | 1893.

Collation: Four volumes, 8vo., 24.5 cm. (trade), 26.5 (large paper). Vol. 1: Two unnumbered leaves (half title, portrait of Lewis); [i]–xiv title, copyright notice, dedication, preface, and contents, followed by Allen's 1814 preface; facsimile of Lewis letter facing xv; xv–lxii Jefferson's "Life of Lewis," with Coues's supplement; facsimile of Clark letter facing lxiii; lxiii–xcvii memoir of Clark by Coues; xcix–cvi memoir of Patrick Gass by Coues; cvii–cxxxii bibliographical introduction by Coues; [1]–352 text. Vol. 2: Two unnumbered leaves (half title, portrait of Clark); [i]–vi title and contents; 353–820 text. Vol. 3: [i]–vi title and contents; 821–1213 text; 1215–1298 appendices by Lewis and Clark. Vol. 4: [i]–v title and contents; five unpaginated plates from 1814; genealogical tables of William Clark (two unnumbered foldouts); 1299–1364 index; three maps in back pocket: facsimile of map from Lewis at Fort Mandan to Jefferson; 1814 Samuel Lewis map from Clark; a modern map (in color) by Coues.

References: Graff, 2484; Paltsits, lxxxi–lxxxii; Wagner-Camp-Becker, 13:7.

Description: The edition consisted of one thousand numbered copies, of which copies 1 to 200 were printed on handmade paper, and copies 201 to 1,000 on fine book paper. Title pages of large-paper edition in two colors. The edition reprinted by Dover 1965, 1970, 1979, 1980. A hardbound reprint by Dover/Peter Smith appeared in the 1970s. Four volumes were bound as three, containing all of the material of the 1893 publication, but with the maps and genealogical tables differently organized in foldouts.

To Alfred J. Hill,
who followed the Lewis and Clark
Expedition on paper in 1893,
with his friend and fellow-traveller,
Elliott Coues.

St. Paul,
Sept. 11, 1893.

Lewis and Clark's Expedition.

VOLUME I.

Lewis & Clark College Collection: Large-Paper Edition: Chuinard: no. 188;
rebound with new leather spine, all maps present, but some repaired with tape.
Photograph of Elliott Coues pasted to front free endpaper of vol. 1. Tweney:
Editor's presentation copy, out of series. Inscribed by Coues in every volume to
Alfred J. Hill, who "helped me more than any other individual" (Preface, viii).
The dedication reads: "To Alfred J. Hill, who followed the Lewis and Clark expe-
dition on paper in 1893, with his friend and fellow-traveller, Elliott Coues. St.
Paul, Sept. 11, 1893." A later owner was Frank L. Hadley. All maps are present.
Wendlick: no. 152; in original binding. All maps present.

Trade Edition: Chuinard: no. 828; set shows minimal wear and is missing the Coues color map. A previous owner was William D. Fenton, Oregon corporate lawyer (1853–1925), "a leading spirit in the movement for holding the Lewis and Clark Exposition in Portland in 1905" (Lockley, 2:81). Wendlick: no. 927; set is in fine condition with all maps, and in original box. Purchased at the Roger Larson sale, February 24, 1995.

5b.3 Other Publications by Coues on Lewis and Clark

"An Account of the Various Publications Relating to the Travels of Lewis and Clarke, with a Commentary on the Zoological Results of Their Expedition." *Bulletin of the United States Geological and Geographical Survey of the Territories,* No. 6– Second series. Washington [Government Printing Office]: Department of the Interior February 8, 1876: [417]–444.

"Description of the Original Manuscript Journals and Field Notebooks of Lewis and Clark, on which was based Biddle's History of the Expedition of 1804–6, and which are now in the possession of the American Philosophical Society in Philadelphia 1893." A paper read before the American Philosophical Society, January 20, 1892, reprinted March 4, 1893, in *Proceedings of the American Philosophical Society* 32, no. 140: [17]–33.

A Letter by Elliott Coues Concerning the plotting of Lewis & Clark's courses along the Missouri River and of Coues' hope that the Journals would soon be published in full Addressed to Wendell Phillips Garrison Literary Editor of 'The Nation' April 11, 1895. Seattle: Farmhouse Press, 1993. Unpublished one-page letter from the collection of L. F. Javete, presented as a keepsake to the members of the Book Club of Washington, December 1993. An edition of two hundred copies.

In Memoriam Sergeant Charles Floyd. Report of the Floyd Memorial Association Prepared on Behalf of the Committee on Publication by Elliott Coues. Sioux City: Press of Perkins Bros. Company, 1897. 58 pages. Tweney: inscribed to Col. R. J. Durrett by Elliott Coues.

"Notes on Mr. Thomas Meehan's paper on the plants of Lewis and Clark's Expedition across the Continent, 1804-1806." *Proceedings of the Academy of Natural Sciences of Philadelphia, 1898,* Part 2 (April–September): 291–315.

5c James Davie Butler

5c.1 James Davie Butler, *The Journal of Charles Floyd* 1894

THE NEW FOUND JOURNAL | OF CHARLES FLOYD, | A SERGEANT UNDER CAPTAINS LEWIS AND CLARK. | BY | JAMES DAVIE BUTLER. | [rule] | FROM PROCEEDINGS OF THE AMERICAN ANTIQUARIAN SOCIETY, AT THE SEMI- | ANNUAL MEETING, HELD IN BOSTON, APRIL 25, 1894. | [rule] | Worcester, Mass., U. S. A. | PRESS OF CHARLES HAMILTON, | 311 MAIN STREET. | 1894.

Collation: [i] title, verso blank; [iii]–15 introduction; 16–30 appendix.

5d.1 Thwaites, *Original Journals*, 1904–5, 4(2): frontispiece

Description: Photocopy of the original. The appendix contains three items: a transcript of the "Proposals for printing by subscription Robert Frazer's Journal," (6.3, item for 1806); the text of a letter accompanying Floyd's *Journal* from Clark to Major Croghan from Fort Mandan, April 2, 1805 (Jackson, *Letters*, item 148); and the text of Floyd's *Journal*. All three original manuscripts are now at the Wisconsin Historical Society. Floyd's *Journal* appears also in the editions of Thwaites (5d) and Moulton (5h).

5c.2 Other Publications by Butler on Lewis and Clark

"John Colter." *Magazine of American History with Notes and Queries* 12 (July 1884): 83–86.

Thwaites, Reuben Gold. "List of Writings of James Davie Butler, LL.D." *Transactions of Wisconsin Academy of Sciences, Arts and Letters* 15, no. 2 (1907): 906–911.

5d Reuben Gold Thwaites

5d.1 Thwaites, ***Original Journals***, 1904–5 [Color plates XX & XXI]

ORIGINAL JOURNALS | OF THE | LEWIS AND CLARK | EXPEDITION | 1804-1806 | PRINTED FROM THE ORIGINAL MANUSCRIPTS | in the Library of the American Philosophical Society and | by Direction of its committee on Historical Documents | TOGETHER WITH | MANUSCRIPT MATERIAL OF LEWIS AND CLARK | from other sources, including Note-Books, Letters, Maps, etc., | and the Journals of Charles Floyd and Joseph Whitehouse | NOW FOR THE FIRST TIME PUBLISHED IN FULL | AND EXACTLY AS WRITTEN | *Edited, with Introduction, Notes, and Index, by* | REUBEN GOLD THWAITES, LL.D. | Editor of "The Jesuit Relations and Allied Documents," etc. | VOLUME ONE [TWO-EIGHT] | NEW YORK | DODD, MEAD & COMPANY | 1904 [1905]

The above is a transcript of the title page (one-color) of the eight-volume trade edition, undivided into parts. Vols. 1 and 2 are dated 1904 (July and November); vols. 3 to Atlas are 1905 (January, February, March, July, September, October). The two special fifteen-part editions of the same years have the third and fourth lines of the title and the publisher's name in red (two hundred copies) or orange (fifty copies), and in the division into volumes and parts. Since the half title of the trade edition announces it as being "In seven volumes and an atlas" with no parallel announcement on the special half titles, the specials presumably appeared before the trade edition.

Description: One thousand copies were printed in 1904–5, in three editions:
a) Large paper: Two hundred numbered copies in fourteen parts and an atlas, on Van Gelder handmade paper with Karl Bodmer prints. Binding in green buckram with gilt titling and ornaments. 32 cm.
b) Edition de luxe: Fifty numbered copies in fourteen parts and an atlas, on Imperial Japan paper with many of the Bodmer plates hand-tinted in color. Bound in tan buckram with gilt titling and ornaments, and inset cover portraits of Lewis and Clark. 32 cm.

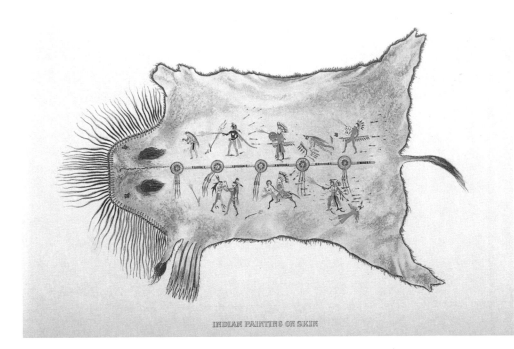

INDIAN PAINTING ON SKIN

5d.1 Thwaites, *Original Journals*, 1904–5, 4(1):28

c) Seven hundred and fifty copies, the trade edition, in seven volumes and an atlas, in red buckram with gilt titling and ornaments related to those on the specials. 25 cm. The individual volumes of the trade edition are printed from the same type as the large-paper edition, with each two-part volume of the special edition bound as one volume.

Contents of the eight volumes are as follows:
1: Introduction, Paltsits Bibliography, beginning of Lewis and Clark Journals
2: Lewis and Clark Journals continued
3: Lewis and Clark Journals continued
4: Lewis and Clark Journals continued
5: Lewis and Clark Journals continued
6: Lewis and Clark Scientific Data
7: Journals of Sergeant Floyd and Private Joseph Whitehouse, other documents, index
8: Atlas

This edition is notable for its thorough Introduction (1, xvii–lx), covering the history of the expedition and earlier exploration, and a detailed account of the original journals and their various editions. This is followed (1, lxi–xciii) by the comprehensive Paltsits Bibliography, which was, at the time, the definitive survey of the literature. This edition is also the first to present many ancillary materials for the first time. Perhaps most striking are the fifty-three facsimiles of original maps, mostly by Clark, covering almost every step of the route. In its maps and numerous illustrations, the Thwaites edition is an outstanding source of visual materials relating to the expedition. The trade edition reproduces all of the text figures of the large-paper edition, and some facsimiles of documents and map sketches in the text, but omits many of the full-page illustrations.

5d.1 Thwaites, *Original Journals*, 1904–5, 5(2): 320.

FACSIMILE OF AN INDIAN PAINTING

Plates, listed by Vol. (Part), Page: In the two large-paper editions, a selection of the plates, many of them Bodmer's "portraits of Indians, scenes of Indian life, and . . . views of Western scenery . . . reproduced from Maximilian's Atlas" (1, xv) are supplied in duplicate, with the top copy hand-colored. In five cases in Wendlick (1(1), 64; 2(1), 58; 2(2), 346; 4(1), 28; and 6(1), 110) the duplicate copy is missing, in one case with minor damage to the previous bound page. The plates were apparently hand-colored after binding. A list of these double plates, with their facing page numbers, follows.

1(1), 10 Indian Utensils and Arms; 1(1), 64 Wahk-Tä-Ge-Li, a Sioux Warrior; 1(2), frontispiece Abdih-Hiddisch, a Minatarre Chief; 1(2), 136 Sketch Plan of Fortification; 1(2), 150 Pachtüwa-Chtä, an Arrikkara Warrior; 1(2), 166 Màndeh-Pàhchu, a young Mandan Indian; 1(2), 244 Noàpeh, an Assiniboin Indian; 1(2), 336 Scalp Dance of the Minatarre Indians; 2(1), 98 Mehskeme-Sukahs, Blackfoot Chief; 2(1), 170 The Great Falls and Portage, from Clark's note-book; 2(1), 176 The Great Falls and Portage, from Lewis's note-book; 2(2), frontispiece Woman of the Snake Tribe; 2(2), 210 The Handsome Falls of the Missouri River, sketch-map by Clark; 2(2), 218 The Great Fall of the Missouri River, sketch-map by Clark; 2(2), 228 The Upper Falls of the Missouri River, sketch-map by Clark; 2(2), 346 Indian Utensils and Arms; 3(1), 4 Indian Utensils and Arms; 3(1), 118 Columbia River and its waters, showing Indian Fishing Establishments, sketch-map by Clark; 3(1), 130 Junction of Columbia and Lewis's Rivers, sketch-map by Clark; 3(2), frontispiece Indian Utensils and Arms; 3(2), 158 Long and Short Narrows of the Columbia River, sketch-map by Clark; 3(2), 172 Great Rapids of the Columbia River, sketch-map by Clark; 3(2), 234 Mouth of the Columbia River, sketch-map by Clark; 4(1), 28 Indian painting on skin; 4(2), frontispiece Mato-tope adorned with the insignia of his warlike deeds; 5(1) No color plates; 5(2), frontispiece

Tatsicki-Stomick, Piekann Chief; 5(2), 186 Mexkemahuastan, Chief of the Gros-ventres of the Prairies; 5(2), 188 A Blackfoot Indian on horseback; 5(2), 202 Chief of the Blood Indians; 5(2), 224 Assiniboin Indians; 5(2), 274 Crow Indians; 5(2), 286 Sih-Chidä and Mahchsi-Karehde, Mandan Indians; 5(2), 320 Facsimile of an Indian painting; 5(2), 338 Pehriska-Ruhpa, a Minitaree or big-bellied Indian; 5(2), 354 Pehriska-Ruhpa, Minitaree Warrior in the costume of the Dog Dance; 5(2), 368 Mató-Tope, a Mandan Chief; 6(1), 110 Dacota Woman and Assiniboin Girl; 6(2), frontispiece Psihdjä-Sàhpa, a Yanktonan Indian; 6(2), 140 Koutani Indian; 6(2), 270 Indian Utensils and Arms; 7(1), 54 Indian Utensils and Arms; 7(2), frontispiece Missouri Indian.

A further edition in seven volumes and a map case, a facsimile of the 1904–5 edition, appeared in 1959 in an edition of 750 (seven hundred numbered copies for sale) by Antiquarian Press, New York. The binding is red buckram. This edition was reprinted in 1969 and [1990] by Arno Press, with an introduction by Bernard DeVoto. The 1969 reprint is in green or red buckram covers, with gold-stamped ornaments on the spine, and a facsimile journal leaf in a front cover panel. The [1990] reprint is in plain green cloth. In 2001, Digital Scanning, Inc., published an eight-volume reproduction from a copy of the large-paper limited edition of 1904–5, in cloth and paper. The map volume (vol. 8) presents the maps in reduced form, not as foldouts.

Lewis & Clark College Collection: Large Paper: Three sets. Chuinard no. 3 of 200, Tweney unnumbered/200, Wendlick unnumbered/200.

De luxe: Three sets. Chuinard no. 32 of 50, Tweney no. 24 of 50, Wendlick no. 12 of 50.

Trade: Two sets. Chuinard, Tweney.

1959: Three sets. Chuinard, no. 160 of 700, Tweney no. 79 of 700 (in original onion skin wraps), Wendlick unnumbered.

1969 Arno: Five sets. Green: Chuinard, Tweney, Wendlick, Anderson. Red: Wendlick.

1990 Arno: One set.

2001: One set.

Lewis & Clark College also possesses a photocopy of the prospectus for the original 1904–5 publication.

5d.2 Other Publications by Thwaites on Lewis and Clark
"Lewis and Clark: Discoverers of Empire." *Christendom* (1902–3): 520–527. Not at Lewis & Clark College.

"The Story of Lewis and Clark's Journals." *Annual Report of the American Historical Association for the Year 1903. House of Representatives 58th Congress, 2nd Session, Document 745.* Washington: Government Printing Office, 1904. Vol. 1 (of two): 105–129.

A Brief History of Rocky Mountain Exploration, with Especial Reference to the Expedition of Lewis and Clark. New York: D. Appleton and Company, 1904. In the Expansion of the Republic series.

"Newly Discovered Personal Records of Lewis and Clark. With Illustrations from the Documents and from Family Relics." *Scribner's Magazine* 35, no. 6 (June 1904): 685–700. Also in facsimile reprint from Shorey Book Store, Seattle, Washington, 1971.

"Overland a Century Ago: the Lewis and Clark Expedition as a Feature in Westward Expansion and the Significance of the Present Centennial Exposition in Portland, Oregon." *Sunset Magazine* 15 (1905): 213–224. Not at Lewis & Clark College.

"William Clark: Soldier, Explorer, Statesman." *Missouri Historical Society Collections*, 2, no. 7 (October 1906): 1–24.

5e Milo M. Quaife, *Journals of Lewis and Ordway* 1916

Milo M. Quaife, *The Journals of Captain Meriwether Lewis and Sergeant John Ordway Kept on the Expedition of Western Exploration, 1803-1806.* Edited with Introduction and Notes. Publications of the State Historical Society of Wisconsin Collections 22, 1916.

Collation: [1]–7 title, image of Sacajawea statue, contents and list of illustrations; 9–10 preface; 13–28 historical introduction; 31–402 text; 405–444 index.

Description: These two journals, printed for the first time, are transcribed from original manuscripts among the papers of the Biddle family at the American Philosophical Society. The Lewis journal ([29]–76) is that of the trip from Pittsburgh to the camp on the River Dubois, August 30–December 12, 1803. Sergeant Ordway's journal ([77]–402) extends from May 14, 1804, to September 23, 1806. Like Whitehouse's journal, it shares material with that of Patrick Gass (Cutright, Appendix A). A second printing, from the same publisher in 1965, omits the half-tone illustrations and presents two redrawn maps.

The first edition was reproduced in facsimile by the National Historical Society, Harrisburg, Pennsylvania, 1994.

Lewis & Clark College Collection (1916 edition): Chuinard: As issued, with his signature on front free end paper. Tweney: As issued, with signature of Herman L. Ekem, October 3, 1916, on front free end paper. Wendlick: As issued. There are copies of 1965 from all three collections also at Lewis & Clark College.

5f Works of Donald Jackson Relating to Lewis and Clark
5f.1 *Letters of the Lewis and Clark Expedition*

Letters of the Lewis and Clark Expedition with Related Documents, 1783-1854. Urbana: University of Illinois Press, 1962. (Second printing with minor additions, University of Illinois Press, 1963. Second edition, with additional documents and notes, two volumes in slipcase, University of Illinois Press, 1978.)

Description: A monumental edition of all known letters relating to the Corps of Discovery, gathered from more than thirty different repositories. Along with the pioneering surveys of Coues, Paltsits, and Thwaites, Jackson's work is an indispensible source for students of the expedition.

5f.2 Other Publications by Jackson on Lewis and Clark
Books

Thomas Jefferson & the Stony Mountains: Exploring the West from Monticello. Urbana, Chicago, London: University of Illinois Press, 1981.

Among the Sleeping Giants: Occasional Pieces on Lewis and Clark. With a foreword by Savoie Lottinville. Urbana and Chicago: University of Illinois Press, 1987.

Articles

"Some Books Carried by Lewis and Clark." *The Bulletin of the Missouri Historical Society* 16, no. 1 (October 1959): 3–13.

"A New Lewis and Clark Map." *The Bulletin of the Missouri Historical Society* 17, no. 2, part 1 (January 1961): 117–32.

"Some Advice for the Next Editor of Lewis and Clark." *The Bulletin of the Missouri Historical Society* 24, no. 1 (October 1967): 52–62.

"On Reading Lewis and Clark." *Montana: The Magazine of Western History* 17, no. 3 (July 1968): 2–7.

"Historian Finds Lewis and Clark Article Dated and Inaccurate." *Montana: The Magazine of Western History* 22, no. 1 (January 1972): 82.

"A Footnote to the Lewis and Clark Expedition." *Manuscripts* 24, no. 1 (Winter 1972): 3–22.

"Thomas Jefferson and the Pacific Northwest." *We Proceeded On* (Winter 1974–1975). Reprinted in *We Proceeded On* (May 1998).

"Meriwether Lewis comes home." *We Proceeded On* (December 1976).

"Call Him a Good Old Dog, But Don't Call Him Scannon." *We Proceeded On* (July–August 1985). Reprinted in *We Proceeded On* Supplementary Publication 2A (March 1986); Supplementary Publication 10 (September 1990); Supplementary Publication 12 (July 1997).

5g Ernest Staples Osgood
5g.1 Ernest Staples Osgood, The Clark *Field Notes*
The Field Notes of Captain William Clark 1803-1805. Edited with an Introduction and Notes by Ernest Staples Osgood. New Haven and London: Yale University Press, 1964.

Collation: [i]–[xii] title, preface, acknowledgements, contents, short titles. xiii–[xxxviii] introduction and note on the text; [1]–326 text; 327–335 index.

Description: Yale Western Americana series, 5. Transcript and facsimiles of documents in the Western Americana Collection at Yale University.

Lewis & Clark College Collection: Beinecke: Presented to Lewis and Clark College by Frederick William Beinecke, June 12, 1966. Housed in a green leather Moroccan clamshell box. Inscribed by Ernest Staples Osgood. Chuinard: Inscribed to Chuinard by author. Tweney: As issued. Wendlick copy: As issued.

5g.2 Other Publications by Osgood on Lewis and Clark

"Clark on the Yellowstone 1806." *Montana*: *The Magazine of Western History* 17, no. 3 (July 1968): 8–29.

"A Prairie Dog for Mr. Jefferson." *Montana: The Magazine of Western History* 19, no. 2 (April 1969): 54–56.

"Our Dog Scannon: Partner in Discovery." *Montana*: *The Magazine of Western History* 26, no. 3 (July 1976): 8–17. Also printed as "Our Dog Scannon—Partner in Discovery." *We Proceeded On* Supplementary Publication 12, 1977, reprinted 1990, 1997.

5h Gary E. Moulton

5h.1 Gary E. Moulton, Journals 1983–2001

Moulton, Gary E., ed. *The Journals of the Lewis and Clark Expedition*. Thirteen volumes. Lincoln: University of Nebraska Press, 1983–2001. Vol. 1, Atlas of the Lewis & Clark Expedition; vol. 2, August 30, 1803–August 24, 1804; vol. 3, August 25, 1803–April 6, 1805; vol. 4, April 7–July 27, 1805; vol. 5, July 28–November 1, 1805; vol. 6, November 2, 1805–March 22, 1806; vol. 7, March 23–June 9, 1806; vol. 8, June 10–September 26, 1806; vol. 9, The Journals of John Ordway, May 14, 1804–September 23, 1806, and Charles Floyd, May 14–August 18, 1804; vol. 10, The Journal of Patrick Gass, May 14, 1804–September 23, 1806; vol. 11, The Journals of Joseph Whitehouse, May 14, 1804–April 2, 1806; vol. 12, Herbarium of the Lewis & Clark Expedition; vol. 13, Comprehensive Index.

Description: Gary Moulton's thirteen volumes gather all known journals and related manuscript materials from the Corps of Discovery, in scholarly editions, with detailed footnotes, and including all of the manuscript maps and all known herbarium sheets. This twenty-two-year-long project is the current standard reference text for the expedition.

5h.2 Other Publications by Moulton on Lewis and Clark
Books

Moulton, Gary E. *American Encounters: Lewis and Clark, the People, and the Land*. Lincoln, Nebraska: Center for Great Plains Studies, University of Nebraska, 1991.

Reveal, James L., Gary E. Moulton, and Alfred E. Schuyler. *The Lewis and Clark Collections of Vascular Plants: Names, Types, and Comments*. Philadelphia: Academy of Natural Sciences of Philadelphia, 1999. Offprint from *Proceedings of the Academy of Natural Sciences of Philadelphia* 149 (January 29, 1999): 1–64.

Moulton, Gary E., James E. Potter, and Debra Brownson. *Lewis and Clark on the Middle Missouri*. Lincoln: Nebraska State Historical Society, 2001. Essay first appeared in *Nebraska History*. Not in Lewis & Clark College Collection.

Articles
"The Journals of the Lewis and Clark Expedition: Beginning Again." *We Proceeded On* (November 1980).

Wood, W. Raymond and Gary E. Moulton. "Prince Maximilian and New Maps of the Missouri and Yellowstone Rivers by William Clark." *The Western Historical Quarterly* 13, no. 4 (October 1981): 373–386.

"The Specialized Journals of Lewis and Clark." *Proceedings of the American Philosophical Society* 127, no. 3 (1983): 194–201.

"Another Look at William Clark's Map of 1805." *We Proceeded On* (March 1983).

"Mapping the North American Plains." *Great Plains Quarterly* 4, no. 1 (January 1984): 3–4.

"A Note on the White Pirogue." *We Proceeded On* (May 1986).

"New Documents of Meriwether Lewis." *We Proceeded On* (November 1987).

"Knife River Indian Villages." *We Proceeded On* (August 1988).

Moulton, Gary E. and James J. Holmberg. "What We Are About: Recently Discovered Letters of William Clark Shed New Light on the Lewis and Clark Expedition." *The Filson Club Historical Quarterly* 65, no. 3 (July 1991): 387–403.

"Journey's End: The Editor of the Lewis and Clark Journals Looks Back on His 20-year Adventure With the Corps of Discovery." *We Proceeded On* (November 2000).

Chapter Six

General Histories, Centennial Publications, and Children's Literature, 1803–1905

Essay 207

Bibliography 222

6a General Histories and Centennial Publications

6b Juvenile Literature

6c Newspaper and Journal Articles

General Histories, Centennial Publications, and Children's Literature, 1803–1905

Decades passed before historians and other writers integrated the story of the Corps of Discovery into historical, travel, and juvenile literature.

"These expeditions are so laborious and hazardous that men of science, used to the temperature and inactivity of their closet, cannot be induced to undertake them."

Thomas Jefferson to Constantine Francois de Volney, February 11, 1806

Although public interest in the adventures and explorations of the Corps of Discovery was intense between 1803 and 1820, relatively few historians addressed its labors in the nineteenth century. The popularity of the Biddle-Allen narrative, reprinted in numerous editions (especially as abridged in the Harper Family Library in 1842), and the several printings of the Gass *Journal* between 1807 and 1815, appeared to meet market demand. However, Benjamin Smith Barton's failure to write the third volume identifying the expedition's scientific contributions created a great gap in one of the most important aspects of Lewis and Clark's labors. Barton's death, his widow's confusion about the disposition of his papers, apparent loss of Lewis's Indian vocabularies collected during the expedition, and dispersal of the team's ethnographic, zoological, and botanical specimens meant that few people, if any, even knew about or expected to assess the expedition's scientific contributions.[1] Lack of information contributed to the dearth of historical assessment.

However, Frederick Pursh (1774–1820), a German-born naturalist, crafted a notable contribution to the botany of the expedition with publication (in two volumes octavo) of *Flora Americae Septentrionalis* (1814). In his preface, Pursh explained how he became involved in 1807 with botanical materials collected by the Corps of Discovery. He wrote:

> . . . I had the pleasure to form an acquaintance with Meriwether Lewis, Esq., then Governor of Upper Louisiana, who had lately returned from an expedition across the Continent of America to the Pacific Ocean, by the way of the Missouri and the great Columbia rivers, executed under the direction of the Government of the United States. A small but highly interesting collection of dried plants was put into my hands by this gentleman, in order to describe and figure those I thought new, for the purpose of inserting them in the account of his Travels, which he was then engaged in preparing for the press. This valuable work, by the unfortunate and untimely end of its author, has been interrupted in its publication . . . .

Pursh explained that part of the Lewis herbarium was destroyed in the flooding of a cache near the Great Falls of the Missouri. "The loss of this first collection is the more to be regretted," he wrote, "when I consider that the small collection communicated to me, consisting of about one hundred and fifty specimens, contained not above a dozen plants well known to me to be natives of North America, the rest being either entirely new or but little known, and among them at least six distinct and new genera."[2]

Pursh traveled in the Western Hemisphere between 1799 and 1811. During his dozen years of field work, he met many of the leading figures interested in North American botany. These included Lewis; John and William Bartram, Benjamin Smith Barton, M.D., and Bernard McMahon of Philadelphia; Henry Mühlenberg, M.D., of Lancaster; David Hosack, M.D., of New York; Professor William D. Peck of Cambridge; and John Le Conte of Georgia. Pursh's plan was

1   The disposition of the collections, especially the scientific specimens, is ably discussed in "The Fate of the Lewis and Clark Booty," Cutright, *Lewis and Clark*, 349–392.

2   Pursh, *Flora Americae Septentrionalis*, x–xi.

3 Pursh, *Flora Americae Septentrionalis*, xi–xv.

4 Moulton, *The Journals*, 12:4. Cutright gave the number as 124, *Lewis and Clark*, 363.

5 Pursh also prepared four papers on North American plants, which were read to the Linnean Society in London. On January 12, 1812, his "Four New Genera of Plants" reported on *Lewisia rediviva*, *Clarkia pulchella*, *Calochordus* [sic] *elegans*, and *Tigarea Aubl. guj. tridentata*, four species Lewis collected in the Columbia watershed. McKelvey, *Botanical Exploration*, 77–78.

6 Cutright, *Lewis and Clark*, 364–366; Meehan, "The Plants," 13–14; Coues, "Notes on Mr. Thomas Meehan's Paper," 292.

7 Taylor, *Cyclopaedia of Modern Travel*, 129–194.

to coauthor with Hosack a periodical with colored plates taken from living plants, similar to *Curtis's Botanical Magazine*. Illness intervened and Pursh, hoping to find recovery, sailed to the West Indies. Upon his return, conditions had changed. Publication of botanical data seemed unlikely with the coming of the War of 1812–14. He thus decided to take his notes and specimens—including numerous herbarium sheets from Meriwether Lewis—and settle in England. There, he could consult collections and libraries to prepare his major publication.[3]

Pursh's *Flora* described 130 plants collected by Lewis and Clark, duly identified as "*in Herb. Lewis.*" Thirteen of twenty-seven plates in his book were drawn from the expedition's herbarium. Further, Pursh created the genera *Lewisia* and *Clarkia* and specially named several species: Lewis's wild flax (*Linum lewisii*), Lewis's monkey flower (*Mimulus lewisii*), Lewis's syringa (*Philadelphus lewisii*), and ragged robin (*Clarkia pulchella*).[4] Pursh established considerable credential for Lewis as a pioneering botanist in the American West.[5]

Sadly, the Lewis and Clark herbarium remained largely forgotten for decades. In 1842, Edward Tuckerman, an American botanist, purchased in England a number of Lewis's specimens. The opportunity was the sale of the collections of A. B. Lambert, a collaborator with Pursh. Tuckerman returned the sheets to the United States and, in 1856, gave most of them to the Academy of Natural Sciences in Philadelphia. The remainder of the expedition's herbarium, which had been left in the hands of Barton in 1810, remained forgotten until 1896. Thomas Meehan, a botanist at the Academy of Natural Sciences, mounted a diligent search at the American Philosophical Society and found the long-missing specimens. These sheets were also transferred to the Academy of Natural Sciences, where they remain today.[6]

In 1856, Bayard Taylor (1825–1878) included "Lewis and Clarke's Journey to the Pacific Ocean" in his nearly one-thousand-page *Cyclopaedia of Modern Travel: A Record of Adventure, Exploration and Discovery, for the Past Fifty Years*. Taylor argued that the nineteenth century was "emphatically an age of exploration and discovery," a time to use the "light of science" to illuminate explorer accounts. "The pencil, the compass, the barometer, and the sextant accompany him," he wrote; "Geology, botany, and ethnology are his aids." The volume included travel narratives from all over the world and three sections touching on the American West: the travels of Lewis and Clark, John Frémont, and Ida Pfeiffer. For the most part, Taylor paraphrased or described the journey of the Corps of Discovery. He attempted no assessment of the significance of the expedition on the nation, on science, or on the tribes encountered. The account constituted nearly ten percent of Taylor's book.[7]

Taylor was descended from a line of wealthy Quakers and was born in Kennett Square, Pennsylvania. As a young man, he wrote poetry. From 1844 to 1846, he traveled in Europe and wrote articles for the *New York Tribune* about his experiences, later collected and published as *View Afoot, or Europe Seen with Knapsack and Staff* (1846). In 1849–50, Taylor explored California to observe the gold rush for the *Tribune*. His collected essays became *Eldorado, Or Adventures in the Path of Empire* (1850). In 1852, Taylor traveled in Asia Minor and Egypt and in 1853, he joined Matthew Perry's naval expedition to Japan. He recorded events for Perry and also filed dispatches with the *Tribune*. Taylor's life was one of almost constant globetrotting, writing, and lecturing. He wrote several travel books, worked as secretary of the American legation in St. Petersburg, translated *Faust* into English (published in 1879 in the United States, England, and Germany), penned volumes of poetry, and edited in eight volumes the *Illustrated Library of Travels* (1871–74). His interest in the Lewis and Clark Expedition, therefore, was in line with his lifelong commitment to travel literature and distant places.[8]

Thomas Bulfinch (1796–1867) devoted half of *Oregon and Eldorado; or, Romance of the Rivers* (1866) to the Lewis and Clark Expedition. However, his pairing of exploration narratives was incongruous. The Corps of Discovery's adventures joined accounts of Walter Raleigh, Madam Godin, Lieutenant Herndon, and Henry Walter Bates in exploring the Amazon. The theme of travel on rivers was a flimsy excuse to marry these subjects.[9]

Bulfinch was attracted to the adventures of Lewis and Clark because his father, Charles Bulfinch, was a principal investor in the maritime trading firm that, in 1787, dispatched Robert Gray and John Kendrick on the *Washington* and the *Columbia* to the Northwest Coast. Gray, on a second voyage for the company in 1792, entered the Columbia River and named it for the vessel he then commanded. Bulfinch argued that Gray's "discovery" of the river was "the point most relied upon by our negotiators in a subsequent era for establishing the claim of the United States to the part of the continent through which that river flows." The Lewis and Clark Expedition explored the Oregon Country, a region to which Bulfinch felt a strong, personal connection. "We shall tell the story of their adventures nearly in the language of their own journal," he wrote. Bulfinch presented almost 230 pages gleaned from the Biddle-Allen narrative to recount the expedition's history. Comparison of the Bulfinch essays to that written by Biddle and Allen, however, confirms that Bulfinch freely abridged their work. In spite of lodging the narrative in quotation marks, he rewrote entire passages and crafted a largely new narrative.[10]

Educated at the Boston Latin School, Phillips Exeter Academy, and Harvard University, where he graduated in 1814, Bulfinch settled in 1818 in Washington, D.C. His father worked as architect of the capitol. In 1835, Bulfinch returned to Boston, failed in business, and settled down as a bank clerk. This position sustained his primary interest in writing. Bulfinch was the author of numerous books on fables, chivalry, and history; *Oregon and Eldorado* was his only travel book. The volume was published shortly before Bulfinch's death by J. E. Tilton and Company, a small Boston publishing house operating between 1859 and 1874.[11] Founded by John E. and Stephen W. Tilton at 161 Washington Street, it published children's books, works on drawing and gardening, sermons, and several volumes of Bulfinch's works.[12]

Decades passed before the Lewis and Clark Expedition became part of historical writing about the development of the United States. A number of historians glossed over the story, treating it largely as a sidebar or a Jeffersonian project. The first in-depth treatment of the expedition in terms of exploration of the West was penned by a Californian. In 1857, Hubert Howe Bancroft (1832–1918), a merchant, publisher, and historian in San Francisco, began assembling the largest nineteenth-century library of Western Americana. He collected books, maps, newspapers, government documents, and oral histories from Panama to the Arctic, and from the Rockies to the Pacific. Bancroft built a matchless collection; then, having hired dozens of assistants to develop a subject index to his materials, he commenced writing a detailed assessment of the Pacific Slope. Five pioneering volumes addressed what few historians had even previously considered: *The Native Races*. Additional titles covered the

8 "Bayard Taylor," *Appletons' Cyclopedia of American Biography*, 6:40–42.

9 Bulfinch, *Oregon and Eldorado*.

10 Ibid., 1–19.

11 Kunitz and Haycraft, *American Authors*, 116.

12 Wilkie, "J. E. Tilton and Company," *Dictionary of Literary Biography*, 49:466.

history of Central America, Mexico, the North Mexican States, Texas, California, and other states and territories north to Alaska and east to Colorado and Wyoming. Although the thirty-nine volumes bore Bancroft's name on the spine, thirteen members of his staff were contributing authors. Bancroft wrote approximately ten of the volumes.[13]

The *History of the Northwest Coast*, vols. 27 and 28 of "Bancroft's Works" (also printed as vols. 22 and 23 of the "History of the Pacific States of North America") addressed maritime and land-based exploration. The second part of the Northwest Coast history, of which Bancroft wrote the first 315 pages, devoted three chapters—eighty-six pages—to the Lewis and Clark Expedition. Bancroft saw the expedition as characterized by "humanity, courage, perseverance, and justice honorable alike to officer and soldier." Yet his assessment was not positive: "But for thrilling experiences, for deeds of great daring, for heart-rending suffering, for romantic adventure we must look elsewhere." Bancroft pointed to the absence of scientists in the Corps of Discovery and generally lamented the lack of coverage on the flora, fauna, and the land. However, he concluded that such investigations would surely have added another year to the expedition and that, as it stood, Jefferson's hopes were fulfilled. The footnotes appended to the three essays were filled with bibliographic commentary and suggested related reading. Sacagawea and York gained passing mention, the former in relation to the expedition members meeting her band of Shoshone and the latter in a footnote erroneously reporting his death in Virginia in 1878.[14]

Adolphus W. Greely (1844–1935) embraced danger, survived, and wrote to generations of Americans about heroic deeds of those in public service. Born in Newburyport, Massachusetts, Greely was the son of a shoemaker. His life of adventure commenced when he enlisted in the 19th Massachusetts Regiment to serve in the Union Army. Following the Civil War, he was stationed at Fort Laramie, Wyoming, spent the years 1876 to 1879 laying two thousand miles of telegraph line in Texas, Dakota, and Montana, and in 1881 commenced three years of grueling duty in the Lady Franklin Bay Expedition to establish circumpolar meteorological stations. Greely also helped map the northwest coast of Greenland and Ellesmere Island. Only seven of his party survived the expedition. Greely returned to the United States in 1887 to become a chief signal officer and in 1891, head of the U.S. Weather Bureau. In 1888, he became a founder of the American Geographical Society.[15]

Greely was also an ambitious writer. He wrote numerous technical volumes on weather and books for general readers. His early titles included *Three Years of Arctic Service* (1885), *Proceedings of the Lady Franklin Expedition* (1888), and *Men of Achievement: Explorers and Travellers* (1894). This latter volume included fourteen chapters, of which one was "Captain Meriwether Lewis and Lieut. William Clark, First Transcontinental Explorers of the United States." Greely penned brief biographies of the two leaders and wrote an overview of their travels. Perceptively, he assessed the changes flowing up the Missouri in 1806. "As Lewis descended the Missouri," he wrote, "he saw that the tide of travel and adventure was already following in his track, and two daring Illinoisians, Dickson and Hancock, were at the mouth of the Yellowstone on a hunting trip." Greely saw the expedition as a "second to none ever undertaking in the United States" and a pivotal factor, when joined with Gray's "discovery" of the Columbia River, in helping transform the country into a continental nation.[16]

13 Caughey, *Hubert Howe Bancroft*, 253–277.

14 Bancroft, *History of the Northwest Coast*, 2:29, 84–85.

15 "Adolphus Washington Greely," *The National Cyclopedia of American Biography*, 42:18–19.

16 Greely, *Men of Achievement*, 159–160.

Olin Dunbar Wheeler (1852–1925), a native of Ohio, actively researched sites along the route of the expedition at the turn of the twentieth century and wrote several publications related to the history of the Corps of Discovery. Educated at Baldwin University, Allegheny College, and Cornell University, Wheeler came west to work from 1874 to 1879 as a cartographer for John Wesley Powell in the surveys of the Colorado River. From 1879 to 1881, he was involved in administration of the Tenth Census of the United States in Nevada. He then entered business, first as an office manager and, from 1892 to 1909, as director of advertising for the Northern Pacific Railway in St. Paul. Wheeler grasped the importance of "heritage tourism" to increasing passenger revenues for the railroad. As such, his publications were both historical and promotional.[17]

During Wheeler's tenure as its director of advertising, the Northern Pacific published annually a volume called *Wonderland*. This handsomely illustrated, paper-bound book of approximately 130 pages was "descriptive of the region tributary to the Northern Pacific Railway." "When it was determined to make the leading chapter of the *Wonderland* for 1900 an abridged narrative of the journey of those explorers," wrote Wheeler, "it became necessary to more particularly visit many places that were important and critical points in their exploration." By railroad, steamboat, wagon, pack train, and on foot, Wheeler and his photographers traveled the Lewis and Clark route.[18] Wheeler's expedition of 1899 was probably the first to retrace the Lewis and Clark route from the mouth of the Missouri to the Pacific.[19] He employed historic images, maps, and photographs to illustrate the route and its condition in 1900. The maps identified the trails the explorers traveled and showed their proximity to modern towns and railroads.[20]

Wheeler was zealous in tracing the footsteps of the Corps of Discovery. He climbed Pompey's Pillar on the Yellowstone River, visited Lolo Hot Springs, camped at Glade Creek at the headwaters of the Lochsa, and interviewed native informants and knowledgeable persons about sites along the trail. Illustrative of Wheeler's approach is his account of research in coastal Oregon.

> In 1899 I visited the site of old Fort Clatsop. There were with me, Wm. Chance, Judge J. Q. A. Bowlby, Geo. W. Lounsberry, Geo. Noland, and Silas B. Smith, all of Astoria and vicinity, and Geo. H. Himes and Geo. M. Weister, of Portland. Several of these were old residents, and thoroughly familiar with the early history of the region. There is, evidently, no question as to the point we visited being the identical spot where the fort stood, although there is now nothing to indicate it except Lewis and Clark's own description as to its location.

Silas Smith, an attorney in Astoria, was the grandson of Chief Cobaway of the Clatsop tribe, a man identified in the expedition journals as Comowool. Smith was educated in local schools and at Dartmouth College. As one of Wheeler's informants, Smith drew on oral accounts of the Clatsops both to identify the fort's location as well as to recount Cobaway's dealings with the explorers. Wheeler's research also took him to the shores of the Pacific. Smith recalled: "Mother often told of Lewis and Clark making salt near Tillamook Head, at the place now known as Seaside." Wheeler, Smith, and the others found and photographed the remains of the salt works.[21]

In *Wonderland 1901*, an issue featuring Yellowstone and the Custer Battlefield, Wheeler wrote "One of Lewis and Clark's Men." Ella Fields, a daughter of William Bratton of the Corps of Discovery, had read Wheeler's account of the expedition

"I took a run the other day up Lewis & Clark's river as it is called to the place of the W[inter] encampment. . . . The site of their log hut is still visible, the foundation logs rotting where they lay."

George Gibbs to Laura Wolcott Gibbs, April 13, 1853

17 "Olin Dunbar Wheeler," *Who Was Who in America*, 4:1001.

18 Wheeler, *The Trail*, 1:v–vi.

19 From September to November 1893, Elliott Coues traveled parts of the expedition route along the Missouri to Fort Mandan and up the Yellowstone River. He also visited the Great Falls, Lewis & Clark Pass, Gibbon's Pass, and the Bitterroot Valley. Cutright and Brodhead, *Elliott Coues*, 364–365.

20 Wheeler, *Wonderland 1900*.

21 Ibid., 58–63.

published in 1900. She forwarded to him biographical details about her father and some fascinating documents, including two signed by Meriwether Lewis. Wheeler reproduced these materials in his article.[22]

With the advent of centennial observations of the Corps of Discovery, Wheeler wrote (in two volumes) *The Trail of Lewis and Clark.* An ambitious expansion of his overview essay penned for *Wonderland 1900*, the project grew with extensive quotations gleaned from the journals of expedition members. Wheeler's assessment of the contributions of Lewis and Clark held no surprises: "The Lewis and Clark expedition was the precursor of the railway which, in the last half-century, has revolutionized and transformed the West and the Northwest, and the present active expansion of our Oriental commerce, rendered possible by the railway, emphasizes the importance of the achievements of the explorers."[23] Also in 1904—on the eve of the opening of the Lewis and Clark Centennial Exposition in Portland, Oregon—Wheeler wrote "The Lewis and Clark Renaissance," an article in *Wonderland 1904*. The essay was primarily bibliographical and lifted up for readers a number of new volumes as well as old titles about the expedition.[24]

Irrepressible in his promotion of tourism based on history and scenic wonders, Wheeler returned to the Corps of Discovery a final time to write *The Lewis & Clark Exposition* (1905). The work, which was an illustrated pamphlet of sixty-four pages with maps, gave only limited attention to the expedition and focused, instead, on the amenities of Portland, tourist sites in the exposition's vicinity, the economy of the Pacific Northwest, and features of the fair.

By 1905, Wheeler was fully committed to the elevation of Sacagawea to heroine status. He wrote: "Sacágawea, the Birdwoman, stands out in a peculiarly strong and striking way and invests the exploration with a tinge of flavor that would be sadly lacking were it not for her sturdy, wholesome, virtuous personality. Her white sisters of the Northwest propose to honor her virtues and sacrifices by a statue at the Exposition."[25]

Ignoring the expedition of Alexander Mackenzie or Spanish exploration of northern Mexico and the Southwest, Noah Brooks (1830–1903) boldly titled his book *First Across the Continent: The Story of the Exploring Expedition of Lewis and Clark in 1803–4–5* (1901). Brooks was born in Maine, where his family was engaged in shipbuilding. At the age of seventeen he moved to Boston to study art but instead became enamored of writing. He lived briefly in Illinois, where he failed both at the cabinet business and at farming. During the Republican campaign of 1856, Brooks met Abraham Lincoln and forged a warm friendship. In 1859, Brooks moved to Marysville, California, where he became a newspaper publisher and contributor of articles to the *Overland Monthly*. Between 1862 and 1865, Brooks was an intimate of the White House and filed 258 news stories on Lincoln during the Civil War, most of them in the *Sacramento Union,* for which he was a correspondent. Brooks returned to California after the Civil War to work as a journalist and editor, but in 1871 went to work in New York City, writing for several major newspapers. Brooks wrote two volumes of juvenile fiction, *The Boy Emigrants* (1876) and *The Boy Settlers* (1891), and many other titles.[26]

Brooks asserted that the Lewis and Clark Expedition was the "foundation of the history of the great Northwest and the Missouri Valley." To recount their adventures, he wrote a brief narrative and quoted extensively from the Biddle-Allen edition of the journals. This Corps of Discovery sent out by the president set the stage for "the hardy American emigrant, trader, adventurer, and home-seeker," he claimed.

22 Wheeler, "One of Lewis and Clark's Men," 87–94.

23 Wheeler, *The Trail*, 2:384.

24 Wheeler, "The Lewis and Clark Renaissance," 101–108.

25 Wheeler, *Lewis and Clark Centennial Exposition*, 17.

26 McKerns, "Noah Brooks," *American National Biography*, 3:620–621.

In Brooks's estimation, the expedition helped establish American sovereignty, farms, cities, industry, and activity in what had been a wilderness. "Let the names of those two men long be held in grateful honor by the American people," he concluded.[27]

Eva Emery Dye (1855–1947) developed a fascination with the adventures of the Lewis and Clark Expedition similar to that of the Wheeler, but she approached it from a different perspective. While his research was field-based and focused on encouraging tourism, Dye's was driven by documentary work and concerned with crafting a literary epic. An 1882 graduate of Oberlin College, Dye and her attorney husband settled in 1890 in Oregon City, Oregon, at the falls of the Willamette River. Inspired since her college days to be a writer, Dye first turned to the Hudson's Bay Company in the Pacific Northwest and wrote a book on its principal figure, *McLoughlin and Old Oregon* (1900). Seeking to become the "Homer of the West," she found the Lewis and Clark Expedition a potential epic. She perceived William Clark to be a major American hero. Between 1899 and 1902, she pursued her subjects, writing hundreds of letters and crisscrossing the country to track down descendants of Clark and members of the Lewis family in her quest for original materials and insights.[28]

Dye wrote *The Conquest: The True Story of Lewis and Clark*, published in 1902 by A. C. McClurg & Company of Chicago. It was her third book, following *McLoughlin* and a volume for younger readers entitled *Stories of Oregon* (1900). The "Note of Acknowledgment" confirmed Dye's research zeal, especially her work with C. Harper Anderson, a nephew of Meriwether Lewis; Mrs. Meriwether Lewis Clark and Mrs. Jefferson K. Clark, widowed daughters-in-law of William Clark; and more than twenty of Clark's nieces and nephews. Further, she mentioned Reuben G. Thwaites, who facilitated access to the manuscripts, and descendants of expedition members Patrick Gass, Nathaniel Pryor, Charles Floyd, John Ordway, William Bratton, George Shannon, and George Drouillard, who provided other information. On its surface, Dye's book appeared to be history and, by many, was received as such. In reality, *The Conquest* was historical-romance fiction, with dialog created by Dye to meet specific objectives. In her "Foreword," Dye noted: "Other lands record the drama of kings; ours is the drama of a people. A Homeric song, the epic of a nation, clusters around the names of Lewis and Clark and the border heroes of their time: their story is the Iliad of the West."[29] Dye thought this novel might catapult her to the first rank of American literature. Her ambitions were high but her attainment fell short.

Dye's effort to create an epic revolved primarily around the life of William Clark. Book 1, "When Red Men Ruled," covered Clark's birth, upbringing, and friendship with Meriwether Lewis. In Book 2, "Into the West," Dye discussed the expedition—168 pages, carefully documented but romantically written, about the Corps of Discovery. Book 3, "The Red Head Chief," mostly concerned Clark's later years in the fur trade and as superintendent of Indian Affairs in St. Louis. Dye stressed the heroic, especially the valor of Clark and the contributions of Sacajawea. In fact, no writer did more than Dye to craft the persona of Sacajawea, the "bird woman," in the popular mind of the twentieth century. The popularity of Dye's novel, a work reprinted nine times between 1902 and 1918 and again in 1922, 1924, and 1936, established both the common spelling of the woman's name as well as her role as a guide. In the pivotal meeting with the Shoshones at the headwaters of the Beaverhead River, Dye described the young woman: "Tripping lightly

"No wonder the land was excited at the report of Lewis and Clark. All at once the unknown mysterious West stood revealed as the home of natural resources. Their travels became the Robinson Crusoe of many a boy who lived to see for himself the marvels of that trans-Mississippi."

Eva Emery Dye,
The Conquest (1902)

27 Brooks, *First Across the Continent*, 360–361.

28 Bartlett-Brown, "Eva Emery Dye"; Powers, *History of Oregon Literature*, 404–411.

29 Dye, *The Conquest*, v–vi, x.

into the willow lodge, Sacajawea was beginning to interpret, when lifting her eyes to the chief, she recognized her own brother, Cameahwait. She ran to his side, threw her blanket over his head, and wept upon his bosom." Dye concluded: "Sacajawea, too, was a Princess, come home now to her Mountain Kingdom."[30] In Dye's novel, Sacagawea was the "Bird Woman," the guide, and "the modest Shoshone princess" who brought an element of domesticity to the labors of the Corps of Discovery.[31]

Dye became president of the Sacajawea Statue Association that, in 1904–05, raised money to commission Alice Cooper of St. Louis to sculpt an imagined likeness of the Shoshone woman and her infant child. Susan B. Anthony, Anna Shaw, M.D., Eva Emery Dye, and three male speakers dedicated the statue in July 1905. A centerpiece of the Lewis and Clark Centennial Exposition, the statue subsequently found an obscure home in Washington Park in the hills west of downtown Portland, Oregon. To a number of regional suffrage advocates, Sacajawea was the epitome of a woman leading men into greater accomplishments. Sarah Evans captured the moment: "The picture will never fade from the memory of those who saw Miss Anthony and Dr. Shaw standing on the platform with the sun lighting up their silver hair like an aureole and their faces radiant with hope, as "The Star Spangled Banner" sung by an Indian boy raised a tumult of applause while the flag floated away revealing the idealized mother and babe."[32]

In 1904, Sidona Viola Johnson (b. 1875) compiled *A Short History of Oregon* for A. C. McClurg & Company of Chicago. Johnson's essays were gleaned from other histories. She drew the assessment of the Lewis and Clark Expedition from Chapter 9, "Overland Journeys to the Pacific," *History of the Willamette Valley* (1884).[33] The "Lewis and Clark Expedition" was one of twenty-six chapters in Johnson's book and was supported by a folding plate, "Map of the United States Showing the Lewis and Clarke Route and the 'Oregon Country.'"[34] The book contained two foldout facsimiles of Jefferson letters: the first penned December 4, 1783, about exploring the West, and the second, a letter of credit to Lewis written on July 4, 1803.[35] James R. Robertson, a reviewer, observed: "a compilation is of less value than a book written directly from the sources, and that it is a difficult matter to preserve a thoroughly logical arrangement of material and subordination of detail."[36] Robertson found the book clearly wanting. Johnson's other publications included articles in 1906 in the *Pacific Monthly*; none was related to the Lewis and Clark Expedition.[37]

Another book addressing Lewis and Clark—as well as Radisson, La Vérendrye, Hearne, and Mackenzie—appeared in 1904. Agnes C. Laut (1871–1936) wrote *Pathfinders of the West*. Laut was born and educated in Canada. Because of ill health, she spent many of her summers in the Selkirks and Canadian Rockies. The setting inspired her interest in the fur trade and western exploration. She worked for several Canadian and American newspapers and magazines and wrote sixteen books.[38] *Pathfinders of the West* was her fourth book and dealt almost entirely with explorers of the Canadian plains and Rockies. Laut devoted the eleventh and final chapter to Lewis and Clark, a superficial summary of the expedition's travels. The American expedition was an appendage to her primary account of the voyageurs. Laut, however, concluded that her cast of characters consisted of all "hero-types, who flung themselves against the impossible—and conquered it."[39]

In 1905, in the full rush of excitement about the Lewis and Clark Centennial Exposition in Portland, Frank Bond (1856–1940) wrote the *Brief Account of the Lewis and Clark Expedition from St. Louis, Missouri, to the Mouth of the Columbia River,*

30 Dye, *The Conquest*, 227–228.

31 Dye and her husband were also pivotal players in Oregon's Chautauqua programs. Epstein, "Gladstone Chautauqua," 391–403.

32 Edwards, *Sowing Good Seeds*, 238–239.

33 Lang, *History of the Willamette Valley*, 133–144.

34 Johnson, *A Short History of Oregon*, 302.

35 Ibid.

36 Robertson, "Reviews," 330.

37 Johnson, "Relief Work," *Pacific Monthly* 15, 746–748, "Houseboating," *Pacific Monthly* 16, 215–228.

38 "Agnes Laut," *Who Was Who in America*, 2:709.

39 Laut, *Pathfinders of the West*, 333.

Oregon and Return, 1804–1806. Born in Iowa and holding degrees from the State University of Iowa in 1880 and 1884, Bond settled in Cheyenne, Wyoming. He served on the city council and, in 1890, was elected to the House of Representatives of the first legislature in the new state. In 1907, Bond was named chief clerk of the General Land Office and lived the rest of his life in Washington, D.C.[40] Bond's *Brief Account*–a pamphlet of seven pages with map–was written for the government exhibit at the exposition. The pamphlet had remarkable durability. It was reprinted in 1926, 1952, 1954, 1969, and 1973.

Another centennial publication paired Lewis and Clark with John C. Frémont. G. Mercer Adam (1839–1912) and Charles Wentworth Upham (1802–1875) wrote *Makers of American History: The Lewis & Clark Exploring Expedition, 1804–'06; John Charles Fremont* (1905). Adam wrote on Lewis and Clark and edited Upham's biography of Frémont published in 1859.[41] Adam was a Canadian author, born in Scotland and educated at Edinburgh, where he entered the publishing business. He immigrated to Toronto in 1859 to run a bookstore for Blackwoods, where he eventually became owner of the firm. Following a period of employment in New York, Adam returned to Toronto in 1878 and the following year founded the *Canada Educational Monthly*. In 1880, he also began editing the *Canada Monthly*. Adam wrote several books on Canadian history and *The Life of David Crockett* (1903).[42] His essays on the Lewis and Clark Expedition were primarily long extracts from the journals, gleaned from the edition of the Biddle-Allen narrative published in 1902 by the New Amsterdam Book Company. Adam deemed the expedition "interesting and highly useful."[43] However, his book added no new insights.

Ripley Hitchcock (1857–1918), art historian, journalist, friend of author Stephen Crane, and historical writer, penned two works addressing the Lewis and Clark Expedition. The first was *The Louisiana Purchase and the Exploration, Early History and Building of the West* (1903). In this volume, Hitchcock devoted part 2, chapters 9–19, to the labors of Lewis and Clark. "The journey which they made," he wrote, "is one of the world's greatest explorations, and its story has become a classic among the travel tales of history."[44] This section of the book was printed as a separate volume, *The Lewis and Clark Expedition* (1905), to respond to readers during the centennial. The volume's frontispiece was a photograph of the model of the Sacajawea statue erected at the exposition in Portland.[45]

William Rheem Lighton (1866–1923) was yet another writer who responded to market potentials with *Lewis and Clark: Meriwether Lewis and William Clark* (1901). Born in Lycoming County, Pennsylvania, Lighton grew up in Nebraska and began writing when he was thirteen. A sometime lawyer, newspaperman, and court reporter, he ultimately found his calling as a free-lance writer. Lighton became best known as an advocate of a "back-to-the-land" philosophy. Lighton, his wife Laura, and their four children settled in 1908 at Fayetteville, Arkansas, where they established Happy Hollow Farm. An article on this project in the *Saturday Evening Post* (January 22, 1910) and his book, *Happy Hollow Farm* (1914), brought Lighton considerable attention. Lighton also wrote the screen play for "Water, Water Everywhere," one of Will Rogers's first movies.[46]

At the turn of the twentieth century, Houghton, Mifflin & Company of Boston and New York launched The Riverside Biographical Series. Andrew Jackson, Benjamin Franklin, Thomas Jefferson, and William Penn were among the initial profiles. Lighton's *Lewis and Clark* became vol. 8 in the series. Each book ran

40 "Frank Bond," *Who Was Who in America, Special Library Edition*, 1:114.

41 "Charles Wentworth Upham," *Appletons' Cyclopaedia*, 6:212.

42 "Graeme Mercer Adam," *Appletons' Cyclopaedia*, 1:11.

43 Adam and Upham, *Makers of American History*, 187–188.

44 Harlow, "James Ripley Wellman Hitchcock," *Dictionary of American Biography*, 9:76–77; Hitchcock, *The Louisiana Purchase*, 195.

45 Hitchcock, *The Lewis and Clark Expedition.*

46 "Lighton Family Papers."

about 140 to 160 pages and was printed in both trade and school editions. Lighton used the journals of Lewis, Clark, and Gass to craft this work. "In this brief narrative," he concluded, "we have just touched the hilltops of the adventures of the expedition." Lighton wrote descriptively and uncritically about Lewis and Clark. He expressed no realization about the longer-term impacts of the expedition on Native Americans. The Corps of Discovery "explored the wilderness that stretched from the mouth of the Missouri River to where the Columbia enters the Pacific," he wrote, and "dedicated to civilization a new empire."[47] Lighton's book was reprinted in Portland in 1905 in conjunction with the Lewis and Clark Centennial Exposition and again in 1929. The manuscript is in the Lighton family papers in the University of Arkansas library.[48]

Amy Jane Maguire helped create an initial twentieth-century persona of Sacagawea, a perspective confirmed by her title *The Indian Girl Who Led Them (Sacajawea),* published in 1905. Maguire was a stenographer working for *The Oregonian* (Porland) at the time of the Lewis and Clark Centennial Exposition.[49] The fair and her commitment to women's rights shaped her writing. Maguire opened her book by invoking Eva Emery Dye's idea of a statue of the Indian woman to stand beside that of William Clark at the crest of the Continental Divide. She conceived of Sacagawea as having "a life romantically set and eventful" but beset with drudgery. Prior to meeting the Corps of Discovery, the woman's life became the invented childhood tale of "Bird-child" and "Prairie-flower," her closest companion. The racism of Maguire's account lay not only in her treatment of native peoples but also in her descriptions of York, a man "having drolleries that were a never failing source of entertainment." She reduced him to a minstrel figure, simple and funny. Lewis's Newfoundland dog even gained a new name, "Rover."[50] The author concluded that "as long as the story of the Northwest lives it will tell of the true service of an Indian girl, and of the love of land and kindred, the loyalty, heroism and ambition that were a part of her wild nature."[51]

A number of writers found stories in the adventures of Lewis and Clark as material for juvenile readers. Isaac Taylor (1759–1829) was a major contributor to English children's literature in the early nineteenth century. He was both an author and illustrator and fostered a family of writers creating the genre. Taylor was born in London, educated at Brentford Grammar School, and brought up in his father's studio as an engraver. His forte was in landscape and portraiture. His father secured the commission to execute many of the plates in Abraham Rees's *Cyclopedia of Arts and Sciences,* and this excited his interest in travels and exotic subjects. Taylor became a minister in the 1790s, but his first love was writing and engraving book illustrations. He and his wife had eleven children, six of whom survived childhood. The Taylors read at meals to instruct their children. They even engraved charts upon which the children filled in completed tasks. These activities led to Taylor's commitment to write and illustrate volumes that would educate younger readers. He wrote *Self-Cultivation Recommended* (1817), *Advice to Teens* (1818), and *Characters Essential to Success in Life* (1820). He also launched a series of books, *Scenes in Europe* (1818), *Scenes in Asia* (1819), *Scenes in Africa* (1820), and *Scenes in America* (1821).[52]

The full title of each of the latter series was *Scenes . . . For the Amusement and Instruction of Little Tarry-at-Home Travellers.* The American volume included eighty-four engravings, three per page. Each is fanciful, though some appear inspired by plates in the 1810 edition of *A Journal of the Voyages and Travels of a Corps of Discovery,*

47 Lighton, *Lewis and Clark*, 1, 146.

48 "Lighton Family Papers."

49 *Portland City Directory 1905*, 716.

50 Maguire, *The Indian Girl*, 3, 20, 22.

51 Ibid., 3, 20, 87.

52 Seccombe, "Isaac Taylor," *Dictionary of National Biography*, 19:415–416; Harris, *Contributions*, 2, 7.

the Patrick Gass journal.[53] *Scenes in America* covered the travels of Columbus, Cortez, Balboa, Pizarro, Lewis and Clark, and Samuel Hearne and ranged from Patagonia to Onalaska. Taylor was fascinated with Sacagawea's reunion with the Shoshone and a childhood friend. He wrote the first poem to invoke her name:

> Sacajawea, sister, friend,
> > Art thou come again to life!
> Will thy bitter sorrows end,
> > Wanderings, sufferings, toil, and strife.
> Oft beneath the pine's high bough
> > Frisk'd we, when the sun was bright;
> Chas'd the jumping squirrel now;
> > Caught the fire fly's flickering light.
> Joys of childhood, doubly dear
> > Now the cares of life intrude:
> Sweet remembrance, vivid, clear,
> > Comfort in my solitude.[54]

Taylor's book had a long life. J. Harris and Son, London, reprinted it in 1822, 1824, and 1830. It was translated into Dutch and printed in Amsterdam in 1829 and 1852. The volume was printed by Silas Andrus in Hartford, Connecticut, in 1825, 1828, 1830, 1848, and 1851, and by W. Alling in 1841 in Rochester. Part of the charm of *Scenes in America* was undoubtedly Taylor's handsome engravings.

William Bingley (1774–1823) wrote *Travels in North America from Modern Writers With Remarks and Observations* (1821), part of a series of world travels "related in a series of daily instructions, from a parent to his children." The North American volume contained a number of quite ordinary traveler tales: Isaac Weld's voyage up the Hudson, Basil Hall's journey from Niagara to Philadelphia, Henry Fearon's trip from Philadelphia to Pittsburgh, and Morris Birbeck's expedition from Pittsburgh to the Illinois Territory. More noteworthy were narratives about the travels of Andre Michaux, John Bartram, and Zebulon M. Pike. A section of the volume, "Western Territory of America," included three accounts of Lewis and Clark's travels (pp. 184–228) and one of Pike's trip to Santa Fe. For example, in the "Sixteenth's Day's Instruction," Bingley wrote, "On the 29th of June, Captain Clarke left the canoes, and went on to the falls, accompanied by a black servant, named York, an Indian and his wife, with her young child." He told of the narrow escape of Clark and the Charbonneau family from a flash flood, a dramatic moment of misadventure.[55]

Orphaned at a young age, Bingley nevertheless gained a good education. He earned a bachelor's degree in 1799 and a master's degree in 1803 at St. Peter's College, Cambridge. While a student, he traveled extensively and wrote *A Tour Round North Wales* (1800). Although a cleric, Bingley passed most of his days as a writer. His project to write a history of Hampshire finally collapsed when the manuscript exceeded six thousand pages and Bingley had to advise his subscribers of his inability to finish the project. In 1816, he moved from Hampshire to London where he wrote furiously. Between 1819 and 1822, Bingley published six volumes of modern travels, including the narrative about Lewis and Clark and others in North America.[56]

Solomon Bell's *Tales of Travels West of the Mississippi* (1830, reprinted 1836) was the first children's book printed in the United States to address the Lewis and Clark Expedition. The volume was published by Gray and Bowen, Washington Street, Boston, and was illustrated with engravings and a somewhat fanciful map

53 Taylor, *Scenes in America*.

54 Ibid., 72–73.

55 Bingley, *Travels in North America*, 207–208.

56 Courteney, "William Bingley," 2:517.

showing Fort Mandan, Fort Clatsop, and tribal distribution.[57] Bell wrote advice "To My Little Readers." He counseled them to refer to the map, believe the truth of the accounts, and be both instructed and amused. Chapters 2 to 28 recounted the expedition. York and "Mrs. Chaboneau" both appeared in the narrative. Bell then spliced to the history of the Corps of Discovery two other western adventures: a brief account of Stephen H. Long's explorations of the Arkansas River and the captivity narrative of John Jewitt, a prisoner of the Nu-chal-nuth Indians at Nootka Sound. Bell rendered no interpretation of these events. He only described, but did so with good attention to the details of the primary accounts upon which he based his book.[58]

Solomon Bell was the pseudonym for William Joseph Snelling (1804–1848). Snelling was born in Boston, the only son of Colonel Josiah Snelling and Elizabeth (Bell) Snelling. His mother died when he was an infant. His father left him in the care of relatives and headed west, where he built Fort Snelling in Minnesota. William Snelling attended Dr. Stearns's Academy in Medford, Massachusetts, and entered West Point in 1818. After two years of study at the military academy, Snelling, then age sixteen, set out for the West to find his father. Between 1820 and 1827, he led an adventuresome life in the fur trade. He served as guide and interpreter for Stephen H. Long, married a girl of French and Indian descent (who died the following winter), and was involved in conflicts with the Indians in 1826 and 1827.[59] In 1828, Snelling settled in Boston and spent the remainder of his short life as a writer. In addition to *Tales of Travels*, he also wrote *Tales of the North West; or Sketches of Indian Life and Character* (1830), a volume based on his adventures in the fur trade. The following year, Snelling published *Truth; a New Year's Gift for Scribblers*. The volume was a satire in couplets, following the manner of Pope and Byron. Snelling sought to drive bad poets from Boston with this witty work. In 1831, he also wrote *The Polar Regions of the Western Continent Explored*, a narrative about the voyages of Franklin, Kotzebue, and Parry to the far north.[60]

Snelling's subsequent life was troubled. He repeatedly attacked literary and political enemies, but these efforts only seemed to multiply his misfortunes. In 1835, under the pseudonym of William Apes, he wrote *Indian Nullification of the Unconstitutional Laws of Massachusetts*. The book was a defense of the Mashpee Tribe. During this period, Snelling's life careened out of control. His alcohol dependency led to a four-month jail term and declining health. However, he emerged feisty and published *The Rat-Trap; or Cogitations of a Convict in the House of Correction* (1837). A second marriage in 1838 brought stability. Snelling lived for a time in Chelsea, where he edited the *Balance*. In 1848, he became editor of the *Boston Herald*. However, he died a few months later at age forty-four.[61]

Henrietta Christian Wright (1854–1899) was a prolific writer of children's books who resided in East Brunswick, New Jersey. The daughter of Seth G. and Rachel (Slover) Wright, Henrietta was the youngest and sole survivor of six children. She worked as a school teacher and began writing in the 1880s. Her early books were fairy stories. She also wrote articles for *Scribner's Magazine*, *The North American Review*, and *The Atlantic Monthly*. Wright's *Children's Stories in English Literature*, *Children's Stories in American Literature*, and *Children's Stories of the Great Scientists* were her efforts to glean materials and introduce younger readers to major authors. *Children's Stories of American Progress* (1886, 1895, 1906, 1911, and 1914) briefly recounted the Lewis and Clark Expedition's travels.[62]

57 Bell, *Tales of Travels*.

58 Ibid.

59 Long did not name Snelling in his 1819–20 party but enumerated "J. R. Bell, Capt. Lieut. Artillery, Journalist." Since Snelling did not graduate from West Point nor receive a commission, it may be that biographers have confused him with Captain Bell, or that Snelling accompanied Long on his trip to the sources of the St. Peter's (Minnesota) River after his return from the Rockies. Thwaites, *Early Western Travels*, 14:25; 15:191; 17:97.

60 Woodall, "William Joseph Snelling," 29, no. 3:281–283.

61 Ibid., 285.

62 "East Brunswick History"; "Henrietta Christian Wright," cdl.library.cornell.edu/ moa/browse.author/w.176; "Henrietta Christian Wright," freepages.genealogy. rootsweb.com/~popfraley/ FowlerHillyer/pafg34.htm.

In 1898, the Educational Publishing Company of Boston published *Pioneers of the West: Lewis and Clark*. A slender volume of thirty-one pages, the book was vol. 5, no. 99, in the Young Folk's Library of Choice Literature. Interestingly, the anonymous writer expended twenty-nine pages to get the expedition to the Clearwater River and told of the remainder of the trip and return in nine short paragraphs.[63]

Nellie F. Kingsley is the biographically elusive author of two books for younger readers. The first, *Four American Explorers* (1902), contained biographies of Lewis, Clark, Frémont, and Kane. The volume was part of The Four Great Americans Series edited by James Baldwin. The roster of subjects included inventors, educators, pioneers, writers, poets, patriots, naval heroes, and other dead, white males. The section on Lewis and Clark covered 132 pages, most of which was a summary of the journey. The publisher, Werner School Book Company/American Book Company, reprinted this section as a separate work, *The Story of Captain Meriwether Lewis and Captain William Clark* (1902). Kingsley had earlier co-authored with Katherine Beebe *The First Nature Reader* (1896), another publication of Werner School Book Company.[64]

Paul E. Werner joined Belford, Clarke and Company and R. S. Peale and Company in 1892 to create the Werner School Book Company at 160–174 Adams Street in Chicago. By 1895, the company was printing and reprinting standard and popular literary works and a number of textbooks. The Werner Company moved in 1897 to Akron, and slipped into receivership in 1898, the year it published Frederic Remington's *Frontier Sketches*. In 1902, the American Book Company, a leading textbook publisher, bought out Werner.[65]

Pioneer Boys of the Great Northwest, or, With Lewis and Clark Across the Rockies (1904) was an inauspicious venture into juvenile fiction that was based on the expedition. The title page identified the author as Captain Ralph Bonehill, the pseudonym of Edward Stratemeyer (1862–1930). Stratemeyer wrote: "The expedition, taken as a whole, was one of the most romantic possible to imagine. Consequently the author has found it necessary to introduce but little that is not true, in building up this story, which he fondly trusts will likewise add to their fund of historical knowledge."[66] In spite of this claim, however, Stratemeyer promptly introduces Fred Feltham and Oscar Sampson, two sixteen-year-olds who become "chums," and join the expedition. Wonder of wonders, high in the Rockies, the boys eventually find and free young Jefferson Feltham, a captive of the Indians who was carried west from Kentucky. "As it was out of the question to think of returning east alone," wrote Stratemeyer, "the Felthams and Sampson resolved to remain with the Lewis and Clark expedition. The course was down the Columbia, part of the way in canoes, and they reached the mouth of that great stream in the middle of November. During that time the three boys kept together all the time, and had great sport, hunting, fishing, and camping out."[67] The expedition had suddenly been transformed into an adventuresome trek for teenage boys!

Edward Stratemeyer transformed himself, too—into a master craftsman in writing and publishing juvenile fiction. Born in Elizabeth, New Jersey, to German immigrant parents, he began writing and printing stories as a teenager. He settled in 1890 in Newark, where he owned and operated a stationery store and a newspaper. He churned out dime novels, westerns, and mysteries. In 1899, he founded the Rover Boys, a highly popular series of formula books for boys. Writing under his own name and as Captain Ralph Bonehill and Arthur M. Winfield, he

63 *Pioneers of the West.*

64 Kingsley, *Four American Explorers*, 1–132; *The Story of Captain Meriwether Lewis.*

65 Bennett, "The Werner Company," 49(2):480.

66 Bonehill, *Pioneer Boys*, v.

67 Ibid., 304–305.

68 Johnson, "Edward Stratemeyer," *American National Biography*, 20:922–923.

69 "Death Takes Flower Lover," *San Francisco Chronicle*, June 25, 1930.

established the Stratemeyer Literary Syndicate to promote additional book series and sales. This firm eventually published eighty-five series of books, including the Bobbsey Twins, Tom Swift, Nancy Drew, and the Hardy Boys. Stratemeyer wrote an estimated two hundred books and stories and laid out the plot and characters for more than seven hundred others. At his death in 1930, the firm had published an estimated twenty million volumes.[68]

In July 1905, Katherine Chandler (1876–1930) penned the "Preface" to *The Bird-Woman of the Lewis and Clark Expedition* (1905), a volume for first- and second-graders published by Silver, Burdett and Company. A graduate of Stanford University, Chandler also wrote in 1905 *In the Reign of Coyote: Folklore from the Pacific Coast,* published by Ginn & Company.[69] Chandler presented Sacajawea as the expedition's guide. "She showed the white men the way into the West," Chandler wrote. "There were no roads in the West then. That was one hundred years ago. This Indian woman took the white men across streams. She took them over hills. She took them through bushes." Allegedly because she traveled like a bird guiding the party, the Corps of Discovery named her "Bird-Woman." Chandler wanted American school children to know that without Sacajawea, the expedition would not have completed its mission.

The first century of general histories, centennial publications, and juvenile literature addressing the Lewis and Clark Expedition was uncritical, amateurish, and overtly commercial. The exceptions were Pursh's *Flora Americae Septentrionalis*, Bancroft's history, and—in spite of his overt promotion of tourism—the works of Olin Dunbar Wheeler. Wheeler, at least, did field-based research and brought to readers a wealth of visual information to enhance understanding of the expedition's route and labors. The authors of juvenile literature stressed that the members of the Corps of Discovery were heroes and harbingers of "civilization." So, too, did the centennial volume authors, such as Adam, Hitchcock, Lighton, and Maguire. Even when they talked about deeds and valor, they seldom buttressed their claims with specific examples.

The question arises—what was missing in these works? The answer is complex. It is answered only in some of the interpretive studies crafted in the past thirty years by essayists plumbing the history of the expedition, the personalities of its members, and their dealings with nature and Native Americans. None of the writers up to 1904 plumbed the complex character of Meriwether Lewis. None looked into his periods of abject silence, his proclivities to rush ahead of the main party to "be first" at the Great Falls, Continental Divide, Cape Disappointment, or to reach the site of Fort Clatsop. None probed his inability to write the narrative boldly announced in his prospectus for a three-volume work about the expedition. None addressed the expedition's scientific activities—not even the observations of flora and fauna or the ethnographic data appearing in the Biddle-Allen narrative based on the journals of Lewis and Clark. Few seemed aware of the efforts of Elliott Coues (in his 1893 edition of the Biddle-Allen narrative) to assess the scientific contributions of the party. And singularly, none of the writers grasped that this expedition both opened contact with dozens of tribes, bands, and villages, yet was also the portent of the undoing of Indian dominion over the interior of the American continent and time-tested ways of life.

The general histories, centennial publications, and children's literature were, for the most part, sub-literary works. They were narrow in vision, sometimes racially biased, and often overtly commercial. As such, they are representative of an era when patriotism and romanticism shaped the presentation of the past and writers made but limited efforts to examine human events for wider meaning. These publications stressed the roles of heroes and heroines, but usually failed to analyze the construction that put such people on pedestals and covered over their faults or blemishes. The underlying assumption in many of these works was that the American West was a largely unoccupied wilderness, or, at best, the home of savages doomed to extinction at the hands of noble progenitors of progress and civilization. In many people's minds, the Lewis and Clark Expedition was redeeming the West by giving it a future.

These publications, in a very real sense, are worth comparing to the flood of articles, books, videos, taped "car tours" and related products of the Lewis and Clark bicentennial. They are fair warning of what not to do. The question remains: will the present generation do better?

"Some men don't belong in the wilderness: Charbonneau. Some don't belong in civilization: John Colter. And a few, having spent time in both, find they no longer have a home in either world."

Clay Jenkinson, *The Character of Meriwether Lewis* (2000)

General Histories, Centennial Publications, and Children's Literature, 1803–1905: Bibliography

This section records all known nineteenth-century Lewis and Clark Expedition materials not already described in this volume, as well as newspaper items in the Lewis & Clark College Collection. Bibliographical citations, and brief annotations when necessary, have been provided for each item. Detailed collations can be found in the National Union Catalog. Items marked with asterisks are not present in the Lewis & Clark College Collection.

6a General Histories and Centennial Publications

1814

Pursh, Frederick. *Flora Americae Septentrionalis; or, a Systematic Arrangement and Description of the Plants of North America. Containing, Besides What Have Been Described by Preceding Authors, Many New and Rare Species, Collected During Twelve Years Travels and Residence in that Country.* Two vols. London: White, Cochrane, and Co. [Color plate XXIII] Includes twenty-four hand-colored engravings by W. Hooker, titled (capitalization as in Pursh) *"Monarda Kalmiana"; "Milium amphicarpon"; "Claytonia lanceolata"; "Berberis Aquifolium"; "Berberis nervosa"; "Conostylis Americana"; "Solanum heterandrum"; "Lilium pudicum"; "Helonias tenax"; "Rhexia cilosa and Rhexia lutea"; "Clarkia pulchella"; "Gaultheria Shallon"; "Gaultheria serpyllifolia"; "Mylocarium ligustrinum"; "Tigarea tridentata"; "Rubus spectabilis"; "Caltha flabellifolia"; "Gerardia fruticosa"; "Gerardia quercifolia"; "Mimulus Lewisii"; "Lupinus villosus"; "Psoralea esculenta"; "Lupinaster macrocephalus";* and *"Prenanthes Serpentaria."* Pursh based many of his botanical descriptions and sketches on the specimens collected by Lewis and Clark.

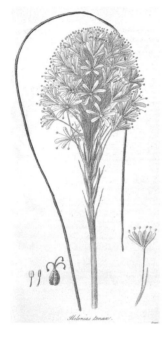

6a 1814 *Flora Americae Septentrionalis,* "Helonias tenax"

1856

Taylor, Bayard. *Cyclopaedia of Modern Travel: A Record of Adventure, Exploration and Discovery, for the Past Fifty Years, Comprising Narratives of the Most Distinguished Travelers Since the Beginning of This Century.* Cincinnati: Moore, Wilstach, Keys & Co. Illustrated with maps and engravings. Lewis and Clark Expedition-related material on pp. 129–194. Reprinted in New York by Moore, Wilstach, Keys & Co., 1860, 1861, 1864, and 1869.

1866

Bulfinch, Thomas. *Oregon and Eldorado; or, Romance of the Rivers.* Boston: J. E. Tilton and Co.

1884

Bancroft, Hubert Howe. *History of the Pacific States of North America.* San Francisco: A. L. Bancroft & Co. Vols. 22–23: Northwest Coast. Vol. 1, pp. 1543–1800. Vol. 2, pp. 1800–1846. Pages 1–86 of vol. 2 are devoted to the Lewis and Clark Expedition. There were a number of variant issues of this work with identical text, but with alternative titles, including *The Works of Hubert Howe Bancroft,* where the corresponding volumes are 27 and 28.

1894

Greely, Adolphus W. *Men of Achievement: Explorers and Travellers.* New York: Charles Scribner's Sons. Reprinted by Scribner's in 1897, 1902, and 1904; reprinted in Freeport, New York, by Books for Libraries Press, 1973.

1900

Hosmer, James K. *Sacajawea Statue Association: Oregon, Washington, Idaho, Montana, Dakota, Nebraska, Utah, Colorado.* Portland, Oregon: The Association, Mann & Beach.

Wheeler, Olin D. *Wonderland 1900: Descriptive of the Region Tributary to the Northern Pacific Railway and Including More Particularly the Story of Lewis & Clark's Great Exploration of the Northwest in 1804–1806.* St. Paul, Minnesota: Northern Pacific Railway. Pages 1–76 are subtitled "On the Trail of Lewis and Clark."

1901

Brooks, Noah. *First Across the Continent: The Story of the Exploring Expedition of Lewis and Clark in 1804-5-6.* New York: C. Scribner's Sons. Reprinted by Scribner's in 1910, 1912, 1917, 1922, 1924, 1926, 1927, and 1935.

Lighton, William R. *Lewis and Clark: Meriwether Lewis and William Clark.* Riverside Biographical Series, no. 8. Boston and New York: Houghton, Mifflin and Co., 1901. Reprinted in an exposition edition in Portland, Oregon, by J. K. Gill, 1905. Reprinted by Houghton, Mifflin, 1929.

Wheeler, Olin D. *Wonderland 1901: Descriptive of That Portion of the Northwest Tributary to the Northern Pacific Railway, and Particularly Relating the History of the Unique Trademark of the Northern Pacific and Describing Yellowstone Park and Custer Battlefield.* St. Paul, Minnesota: Northern Pacific Railway. Pages 87–94 are subtitled "One of Lewis and Clark's Men" (William Bratton).

1902

Dye, Eva Emery. *The Conquest: The True Story of Lewis and Clark.* Chicago: A. C. McClurg. Reprints: A. C. McClurg, 1911 (fifth ed.), 1912, 1914 (seventh ed.), 1918 (eighth ed.); Grosset & Dunlap, 1914; Doubleday, Page & Co., 1922, 1924; Binfords & Mort, 1936; Wilson-Erickson, Inc., 1936.

1904

Johnson, Sidona V. *A Short History of Oregon: Early Discoveries–The Lewis and Clark Exploration–Settlement–Government–Indian Wars–Progress.* Chicago: A. C. McClurg & Co.

Laut, Agnes C. *Pathfinders of the West: Being the Thrilling Story of the Adventures of the Men Who Discovered the Great Northwest: Radisson, La Vérendrye, Lewis and Clark.* New York: Grosset & Dunlap. Also printed by Grosset & Dunlap in 1906; reprinted by Macmillan in 1914, 1918, 1922, 1927, 1930, 1932, and 1937; reprinted by Books for Libraries, 1969.

Wheeler, Olin D. *The Trail of Lewis and Clark: A Story of the Great Exploration Across the Continent, 1804–06; with a Description of the Old Trail, Based upon Actual Travel Over it, and of the Changes Found a Century Later.* Two vols. New York: G. P.

Putnam's Sons. First edition bound in gold-stamped red cloth and also in blue cloth. Reprinted in New York by Putnam, 1926, and bound in black-stamped royal blue cloth; reprinted in New York by AMS Press, 1976.

Wheeler, Olin D. *Wonderland 1904: Descriptive of the Northwest.* St. Paul, Minnesota: Northern Pacific Railway. Pages 101–108 are subtitled "The Lewis and Clark Renaissance."

1905

Adam, G. Mercer, and Charles Wentworth Upham. *Makers of American History: The Lewis & Clark Exploring Expedition, 1804–'06; John Charles Fremont.* New York: The University Society.

Bond, Frank. *Brief Account of the Lewis and Clark Expedition from St. Louis, Missouri, to the Mouth of the Columbia River, Oregon and Return, 1804–1806.* Washington D.C.: Govt. Printing Office. Exhibit of the Department of the Interior, General Land Office, by Frank Bond, chief clerk, General Land Office for the Lewis and Clark Centennial Exposition. Reprinted 1926, 1952, 1954, 1969, 1973.

Hitchcock, Ripley. *The Lewis and Clark Expedition.* Boston: Ginn & Co. With illustrations and maps. The text was first printed in Hitchcock's *The Louisiana Purchase and the Exploration, Early History and Building of the West.* Boston: Ginn & Co., copyright 1903, published 1903, reprinted 1904.

Maguire, Amy Jane. *The Indian Girl Who Led Them (Sacajawea).* Portland, Oregon: J. K. Gill.

Wheeler, Olin D. *The Lewis & Clark Exposition: Portland, Oregon, June 1 to October 15, 1905.* St. Paul, Minnesota: Northern Pacific Railway. Lewis & Clark College Collection copy listed as fifth edition.

6b Juvenile Literature

1821

Bingley, Rev. William. *Travels in North America from Modern Writers. With Remarks and Observations; Exhibiting a Connected View of the Geography and Present State of that Quarter of the Globe.* London: Harvey and Darton. "Designed for the use of young persons." Lewis and Clark material, pp. 184–228. Reprinted in London by Harvey and Darton, 1823.

Taylor, Isaac. *Scenes in America, For the Amusement and Instruction of Little Tarry-at-Home Travellers.* London: Harris and Son. [Color plate XXII] Includes twelve Lewis-and-Clark-related plates, captions capitalized as follows: "46. Captains Lewis and Clarke at the Pacific Ocean"; "47. Child preserved from Fire"; "48. Clarke's escape from a Flood"; "49. Meeting of two Indian Women"; "50. Consulting the Medicine Stone"; "51. The Pipe of Peace"; "52. Indian Sagacity"; "53. Hunting the Buffalo on the Ice"; "Catching Deer in a Pound"; "The Rattle-snake"; "The Humming Bird"; "The Fire Fly." Some of these appear to be derived from the plates in the 1810 Gass *Journal.* First edition in Lewis & Clark College Collection. Reprinted in London by J. Harris and Son, 1822, 1824, 1830; reprinted in Hartford, Connecticut, by Silas Andrus, 1825, 1828, 1830, 1848, 1851; reprinted in Rochester

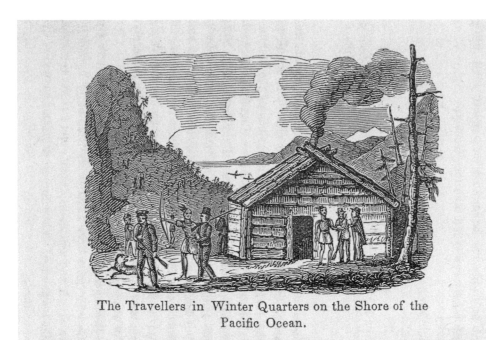

The Travellers in Winter Quarters on the Shore of the
Pacific Ocean.

6b **1830** *Tales of Travels
West of the Mississippi:*
the earliest known printed
image of Fort Clatsop,
Oregon.

by W. Alling, 1841; reprinted in facsimile from the first edition in Yorkshire by
S.R. Publishers, and in New York by Johnson Reprint Corporation; reprinted in
Dutch under the title *Merkwaardigheden uit alle bekende landen van Amerika, voor hen
die, tot eene leezame uitspanning, in het hoekje van den haard, door vreemde naar de 5de
Engelsche uitgave.* Amsterdam: Beijerinck, 1829, and in Zaandam by H.F. van der
Scheer, 1852.

1830
Bell, Solomon. *Tales of Travels West of the Mississippi.* Boston: Gray and Bowen.
Solomon Bell was the pseudonym of William Joseph Snelling. Includes a map
and numerous engravings, many signed "GLB." Those relating to the expedition
are as follows: Frontispiece "COUNCIL WITH THE INDIANS"; facing 5
"PRAIRIE ON FIRE" and "BUFFALO, OR BISON"; facing 6 "INDIANS
HUNTING BUFFALOES" and "GRISLY BEAR"; facing 8 "AMERICAN ELK";
facing 11 "Captains Lewis and Clark setting out with their men on their expedition
to the Pacific Ocean"; 14 [Rattlesnake]; 15 [Pelican, Parakeet]; facing 17 "The
Common Deer of America, called Virginia or Fallow Deer."; 17 [Wild Turkey,
Beaver, Swan]; 18 [Wolf]; facing 20 "COUNCIL, OR TALK WITH THE INDI-
ANS" (same plate as frontispiece); 25 [Plains Indian Tepees]; facing 27 "Sergeant
Pryor going to the Dahcotah Camp"; 28 [Two Vignettes of Pipes]; facing 31
"AN INDIAN ON HORSEBACK, ATTACKING AN ENEMY"; facing 33
"ANTELOPES" and "A PRAIRIE DOG VILLAGE"; facing 39 "ROCKY MOUN-
TAIN GOAT" and "THE BOY IN THE PRAIRIE"; facing 45 "MULE OR
BLACK-TAILED DEER"; facing 47 "PANTHER"; facing 49 "BUFFALOES
FALLING OVER A PRECIPICE"; facing 65 "ARGALI SHEEP"; facing 75
"VILLAGE OF THE ECHELOOTS"; facing 81 "The Travellers in Winter Quarters
on the Shore of the Pacific Ocean"; facing 87 "MACNEIL AND THE BEAR";
facing 89 "MEETING WITH THE BLACKFOOT INDIANS." The volume
consists of "Lewis and Clark's Travels" (pp. 1-105), "Long's Expedition," and
"Jewitt's Narrative." Reprinted in Boston by Russell, Shattuck, 1836.

1886

Wright, Henrietta Christian. *Children's Stories of American Progress.* Illustrated by J. Steeple Davis. New York: Charles Scribner's Sons. Reprinted in New York by Scribner's in 1895, 1906, 1911, and 1914.

1898

Educational Publishing Co. *Pioneers of the West: Lewis and Clark.* Young Folk's Library of Choice Literature, vol. 5, no. 99. Boston: Educational Publishing Co.

1902

Kingsley, Nellie F. *Four American Explorers: Captain Meriwether Lewis, Captain William Clark, General John C. Frémont, Dr. Elisha K. Kane, A Book for Young Americans.* The Four Great Americans Series, no. 8. New York: Werner School Book Co., American Book Co.

——. *The Story of Captain Meriwether Lewis and Captain William Clark for Young Readers.* Baldwin's biographical booklets. New York: Werner School Book Co.; American Book Co.

1905

Bonehill, Ralph. *Pioneer Boys of the Great Northwest, or, With Lewis and Clark Across the Rockies.* New York: Stitt Publishing Co. Copyright 1904, first edition 1905, reprinted by the Chatterton-Peck Co. in 1908.

Chandler, Katherine. *The Bird-Woman of the Lewis and Clark Expedition: A Supplementary Reader for First and Second Grades.* New York, Boston, Chicago: Silver, Burdett and Co.

6c Newspaper and Journal Articles

1803

November 26: *Columbian Centinel & Massachusetts Federalist,* Boston, p. 2, col. 1. A report from Louisville, Kentucky, announcing the expedition's departure from Louisville.

1804

June 16: *Boston Weekly Magazine,* p. 135, col. 2. "Domestick" item notes that Captain Lewis is in Pittsburgh on May 5, accompanied by Indian chiefs. The chiefs are confirmed by the next item, but Lewis was actually in St. Louis on this date (see Jackson, *Letters,* items 116, 117).

July 4: *The Connecticut Courant,* Hartford, p. 2, col. 5. This article notes that twelve chiefs of the Osage Nation have arrived in Kentucky on their way to Washington to see Jefferson. Lewis and Clark are mentioned as having sent the chiefs. A brief description of the expedition is also included.

1805

January 16: *Columbian Centinel & Massachusetts Federalist,* Boston, p. 2, col. 1. A brief announcement that the expedition members had traveled 850 miles on the Missouri with no problems, and were expected to winter with the Mandan Indians.

January 17: *The Independent Chronicle,* Boston, p. 2, col. 2. "By the Mails" notes that on August 19, Captain Lewis was up the Missouri, wintering with the Mandan Indians. Dateline January 7.

July 17: *Louisiana Gazette* (New Orleans). A detailed report on the progress of the expedition, based on dispatches sent from Fort Mandan. Contains the reference to Mackenzie noted in 1a.12. Reprinted in Nasatir, 2:760–64.

1806

November 4: *The Balance and Columbian Repository*, Hudson (New York), p. 351, col. 2. This article is part of a letter written to Thomas Jefferson, describing Lewis and Clark's winter at Fort Clatsop and the Columbia River.

November 5: *Columbian Centinel & Massachussets Federalist*, Boston. An announcement of Lewis and Clark's arrival in St. Louis, with a brief description of the expedition.

November 5: *The Witness*, Litchfield (Connecticut), p. 2, col. 3. "Domestic News" announces that the Lewis and Clark Expedition returned from its journey and arrived in St. Louis. The article briefly describes the expedition and mentions Lewis's plans to return to Washington.

November 8: *New Hampshire Sentinel*, Keene, p. 3, col. 1. Under "Domestic" is an extract of a letter from St. Louis dated September 23, 1806, announcing the arrival of Lewis and Clark at St. Louis.

November 12: *The National Aegis*, Worcester (Massachusetts), p. 3, col. 1. One paragraph, announcing the arrival of Lewis and Clark in St. Louis. It gives a brief description of the expedition, and notes that the explorers' journals will be published.

December 2: "Proposals For Publishing by Subscription Robert Frazer's Journal, From St. Louis, in Louisiana, to the Pacific Ocean . . ." printed as an extra in the *National Intelligencer*, Washington D.C., December 2, 1806, and the *Providence Gazette*, December 9, 1806 (Wagner-Camp-Becker, 5a). The manuscript proposal, possibly in Frazer's hand, is at the Wisconsin Historical Society (Paltsits, lxxxv). The printed extras are not in the Lewis & Clark College Collection. However, the collection contains a photocopy of the manuscript.

December 10: *The Witness*, Litchfield (Connecticut), p. 3, col. 3. This article notes the accomplishments of the Lewis and Clark Expedition and describes it as a success.

December 12: *The Repertory* (Boston), p. 1, para. 2. The same article as the previous item in *The Witness*, December 10, 1806.

December 13: *Freeman's Friend*, Saco (Maine), p. 2, col. 1. An announcement that Lewis and Clark have arrived in St. Louis. Includes a brief description of the expedition.

1807

July 7: *General Advertiser*, Philadelphia, p. 4, col. 1. Prospectus for three-volume octavo publication of "Lewis and Clark's Tour to the Pacific Ocean." Publisher: C. & A. Conrad. Signed M. Lewis, June 15.

August 15: *Columbian Centinel & Massachusetts Federalist*, Boston. Proposals for three-volume octavo publication of "Lewis & Clarke's Tour, to the Pacific Ocean," dated July 25.

"Notice of intention of Captain Meriwether Lewis to publish in three volumes, octavo, 'Lewis and Clarke's Tour to the Pacifick Ocean, through the interior of North America, during the years 1804, 1805, 1806. Performed by order of the government of the United States.'" *The Monthly Anthology, And Boston Review* 4 (1807): 285. Unreported early notice of Lewis's intent to publish a three-volume official account of the Lewis and Clark Expedition.

[Adams, John Quincy]. "On the Discoveries of Capt. Lewis," *The Monthly Anthology, And Boston Review, Containing Sketches and Reports of Philosophy, Religion, History, Arts and Manners* 4 (1807): 143–4. Poem of tribute to Meriwether Lewis, anonymous work of John Quincy Adams, written in parody of Joel Barlow's "On the Discoveries of Captain Lewis."

Barlow, Joel. "On the Discoveries of Captain Lewis," *The American Register, or, General Repository of History, Politics, & Science for 1806–7*, vol. 1(1807). Poem partly reprinted by Albert Furtwangler in Ronda, *Voyages of Discovery*, 229ff.

1812
Wilson, Alexander. "Particulars of the Death of Capt. Lewis," *The Port Folio* (Philadelphia) 7, no. 1 (January 1812): 34-47.

1846
"Indian Houses on Columbia River," *American Penny Magazine and Family Newspaper* (July 25, 1846): 387. A short piece on Lewis and Clark from the Biddle/Allen edition.

1876
Wright, Marcus J. "Sketch of Gov. Merriwether Lewis," *Ware's Valley Monthly* (June 1876). *

1893
Jefferson, Thomas. "Meriwether Lewis," *Old South Leaflets* 2, no. 44. Letter of Thomas Jefferson, August 18, 1813, to Paul Allen, and an extract from the journals of August 12, 1805. Undated, but Paltsits (lxxxix) lists the publication date as 1893, and also lists another version of the publication as a part of the *Old South Leaflets*, eleventh series, no. 6, 1893. Reprinted in New York by Burt Franklin, 1970.

1898
Meehan, Thomas. "The Plants of Lewis and Clark's Expedition Across the Continent, 1804–1806," *Proceedings of the Academy of Natural Sciences of Philadelphia* (January-March 1898): 12–49.

1902
Gillette, P. W. "The Lewis and Clark Expedition in Three Parts," *The Pacific Monthly* 7, no. 1 (July 1902): 3–9; no. 2 (August 1902): 51–58; no. 3 (September 1902): 110–17.

1904
"New Material Concerning the Lewis and Clark Expedition: Unpublished Letters and Portraits of William Clark, from the Family Records," *The Century Illustrated Monthly Magazine* 68, new series 46 (April 1904–November 1904): 872–76. *

Powers, H. C. "Equipment of the Lewis and Clark Exploring Expedition," *Proceedings of the Academy of Science and Letters of Sioux City, Iowa* 1 (1903–1904): 75–84.

Chapter Seven
A Twentieth-Century Publications Checklist

7a Books Relating to the Corps of Discovery, 1906–2001

7b Pamphlets, Magazines, and Scholarly Journals from the Lewis & Clark
   College Collection

7c Theses and Dissertations

A Twentieth-Century Publications Checklist

7a Books Relating to the Corps of Discovery, 1906–2001

This section attempts to provide a complete listing of books relating directly to the Corps of Discovery from 1906 to 2001. Items in this section are arranged by year, and alphabetically by author within each year. Each volume is identified by author, title, place of publication, and date. Items marked with asterisks are not currently included in the Lewis & Clark College Collection. Bibliographical information for books not held at Lewis & Clark College is derived from records in the WorldCat database. Brief descriptive annotations have been provided for books when the titles are not self-explanatory.

1908

McBeth, Kate C. *The Nez Perces Since Lewis and Clark*. New York, Chicago, Toronto, London, and Edinburgh: Fleming H. Revell Co. A history of the Nez Perce, beginning with their interactions with Lewis and Clark, written by a missionary who spent twenty-seven years with the tribe.

1910

Allen, Paul. *Meriwether Lewis and William Clarke: Pioneers of the Great American Northwest: Daring and Successful Explorers–Discoverers of the Head-Waters of the Columbia River*. Great Sovereigns, Heroes and Pioneers series. New York and Akron, Ohio: Werner Co., D.M. MacLellan Book Co. See section 5a.8.

Meyers, Mrs. Peter M. *The Coming of the White Men*. Milwaukie Land Co.

1911

Grinnell, George Bird. *Trails of the Pathfinders*. New York: Charles Scribner's Sons. "The chapters in this book appeared first as part of a series of thirty-six articles under the same title that were contributed to *Forest and Stream*," February 27, 1904–October 21, 1905. Reprinted by Scribner's in 1913.

1912

Herndon, Carrie P. *The Lewis and Clark Expedition*. Instructor Literature series, no. 209. Dansville, New York: F.A. Owen Co.; Chicago, Illinois: Hall & McCreary.

1914

Koch, Frederick H. *The Book of a Pageant of the North-West*. Grand Forks, North Dakota: University of North Dakota. Script for a theatrical performance, with a section about the Lewis and Clark Expedition.

1915

Allen, Paul. *In Camp on White Bear Island: Conflict with Indians: Singular Adventures of the Captains Lewis and Clarke and Command of the U.S. Soldiers in the Vast Unexplored West*. Akron, Ohio: The Superior Printing Co. See section 5a.8. Text from edition (Section 5a.1, etc.) originally edited by Biddle and Allen.

———. *In the Rocky Mountains: Great Difficulties and Dangers Encountered by Captains Lewis and Clark: Discoveries of the Headwaters of the Columbia River Graphically Told*. Akron, Ohio: The Superior Printing Co. See also section 5a.8.

——. *Stirring Adventures "Up the Missouri" with Lewis and Clarke: Pioneers of the Great Northwest.* Akron, Ohio: The Superior Printing Co. See also section 5a.8.

——. *Captains Lewis and Clarke of the United States Army: Daring and Successful Explorers of the American Northwestern Territory Truthfully told in easy Narrative.* Akron, Ohio: The Superior Printing Co. See also section 5a.8.

Biddle, Nicholas, and Paul Allen, eds. *History of the Expedition Under the Command of Captains Lewis and Clarke, to the Sources of the Missouri: Thence Across the Rocky Mountains and Down the River Columbia to the Pacific Ocean: Performed During the Years 1804, 1805, 1806, by Order of the Government of the United States.* New York: Harper. A 1915 edition of the 1842 publication, two vols. in one, with an introduction and notes by Archibald M'Vickar. See section 5a.8 (this edition not in the Lewis & Clark College Collection).

Scott, Laura Tolman. *Sacajawea (The Bird Woman): The Unsung Heroine of Montana 1805–1806.* Armstead, Montana: Montana Federation of Women's Clubs.

1916

Hough, Emerson. *The Magnificent Adventure: This Being the Story of the World's Greatest Exploration, and the Romance of a Very Gallant Gentleman: A Novel.* Illustrated by Arthur I. Keller. New York and London: D. Appleton and Co. Fictional account of the Lewis and Clark Expedition. Also printed in New York by Grosset & Dunlap, 1916.

Quaife, Milo M., ed. *The Journals of Captain Meriwether Lewis and Sergeant John Ordway Kept on the Expedition of Western Exploration, 1803–1806.* Vol. 22 of the State Historical Society of Wisconsin Collections. Madison: State Historical Society of Wisconsin. Reprinted by the State Historical Society of Wisconsin, 1965; reprinted in Harrisburg, Pennsylvania, by the National Historical Society, 1994. This work was the first publication of Ordway's journal and Lewis's Ohio River journal. See section 5e.

1917

Allen, Paul. *Lewis and Clarke: Early America Pioneers,* vol. 1., and *Lewis and Clarke: Heroes of the Northwest,* vol. 2. Sovereigns and Pioneers of History series, "Edition Chateaubriand." [Akron, Ohio]: The Superior Printing Co., "Printed for Subscribers Only." See also section 5a.8.

Hosmer, James K., ed. *History of the Expedition of Captains Lewis and Clark, 1804–5–6, Reprinted From the Edition of 1814.* Two vols. Fourth edition. Chicago: A. C. McClurg. Reprinted in a fifth edition by A. C. McClurg, 1924. See section 5a.9.

Sabin, Edwin L. *Opening the West With Lewis and Clark.* Philadelphia and London: J. B. Lippincott Co. Reprinted as *Vilda västerns portar öppnas: med Lewis och Clark uppför Missouri, över Klippiga bergen till Stilla havet och åter 1804–06.* Okända äventyr series. Stockholm: H. Geber, 1938. Swedish translation of *Opening the West with Lewis and Clark* (translation not in the Lewis & Clark College Collection).

1918

Schultz, James Willard. *Bird Woman (Sacajawea) the Guide of Lewis and Clark: Her Own Story Now First Given to the World by James Willard Schultz.* Boston and New York: Houghton Mifflin Co. Reprinted in Kooskia, Idaho, by Mountain Meadow Press, 1999. Narrative account of the story of Sacajawea.

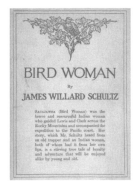

Wolfrom, Anna. *Sacajawea, the Indian Princess: The Indian Girl Who Piloted the Lewis and Clark Expedition Across the Rocky Mountains. A Play in Three Acts.* Kansas City, Missouri: Burton Publishing Co. *

1920

Skinner, Constance L. *Adventurers of Oregon: A Chronicle of the Fur Trade.* New Haven: Yale University Press; Toronto: Glasgow, Brook & Co.; London: Humphrey Milford, Oxford University Press. Includes a section on Lewis and Clark with maps and plates.

Voorhees, Luke. *Personal Recollections of Pioneer Life on the Mountains and Plains of the Great West.* Cheyenne, Wyoming. Includes "Appendix. The Voorhees family inherits the famous Lewis & Clark manuscripts" by Reuben Gold Thwaites. Closely based on Thwaites's article, "Newly discovered records of Lewis and Clark," printed in *Scribner's Magazine* 35 (June 1904): 685–700. Reissued as *Some Pioneer Recollections of George Lathrop and Luke Voorhees*, Philadelphia: George W. Jacobs, 1927.

Wagner, Henry R. and Charles L. Camp. *The Plains & the Rockies: A Critical Bibliography of Exploration, Adventure and Travel in the American West, 1800–1865.* San Francisco: John Howell-Books. Reprinted and expanded 1921, 1937, 1953, 1969, 1972, and 1982 (fourth edition, Robert H. Becker, editor). Includes extensive bibliographic information on early Lewis and Clark publications.

1922

Biddle, Nicholas, and Paul Allen, eds. *History of the Expedition Under the Command of Captains Lewis & Clarke to the Sources of the Missouri, thence across the Rocky Mountains and down the River Columbia to the Pacific Ocean, Performed During the Years 1804–5–6 by Order of the Government of the United States: A Complete Reprint of the Biddle Edition of 1814 to which all the Members of the Expedition Contributed, with an account of the Louisiana Purchase by Rev. John Bach McMaster and Notes upon the Route.* Three vols. with illustrations and maps. New York: Allerton Book Co. See section 5a.14.

1923

Carlton, Mabel Mason. *Lewis and Clark: Pathfinders of the Great Northwest.* Boston: John Hancock Mutual Life Insurance Co. Reprinted in 1925 and 1950 by John Hancock. Described in 1925 edition as "Issue No. 106." Short narrative of Lewis and Clark.

1924

Marks, Constant R. and Albert M. Holman. *Pioneering in the Northwest.* Sioux City, Iowa: Deitch & Lamar Co. Includes a chapter titled "Life of Sargeant Chas. Floyd."

Oppenlander, J. H. *The Columbia River Guide and Panorama, from Portland to The Dalles: Myths, Legends, History, Geology, Lewis & Clark Notations.* Penland Guide series. Portland, Oregon: J. H. & H. F. Oppenlander. *

Wade, Mary H. *The Trail Blazers: The Story of the Lewis and Clark Expedition.* Boston: Little, Brown, and Co. Reprinted by Little, Brown in 1933. A children's story based on the Lewis and Clark Expedition.

1925
Flandrau, Grace. *A Glance at the Lewis and Clark Expedition.* St. Paul: Great Northern Railway. Reproduced in facsimile by the Shorey Book Store, Seattle, 1971, 1973. Short overview of the expedition, intended for railroad passengers.

Sims, Elmer Harper. *Sacajawea and the Lewis and Clark Expedition, an Epic.* Coeur d'Alène, Idaho: Press Publishing Co. *

1926
Vinton, Stallo. *John Colter Discoverer of Yellowstone Park: An Account of His Exploration in 1807 and of His Further Adventures as Hunter, Trapper, Indian Fighter, Pathfinder and Member of the Lewis and Clark Expedition.* Edition of five hundred copies. New York: Edward Eberstadt. Also printed in a limited edition of thirty copies on large paper, Edward Eberstadt, 1926; reprinted in a limited facsimile edition, Mansfield Centre, Connecticut, by Martino Publishing, 1999.

Wheeler, Olin D. *The Trail of Lewis and Clark, 1804–1904: A Story of the Great Exploration Across the Continent in 1804–06; with a Description of the Old Trail, Based Upon Actual Travel Over It, and of the Changes Found a Century Later.* Two vols. with two hundred illustrations. Second edition. New York and London: G. P. Putnam's Sons. A reprint of the first, 1904 edition. See section 6a.

1927
Flandrau, Grace. *The Lewis and Clark Expedition.* St. Paul: Great Northern Railway. Reproduced in facsimile by the Shorey Book Store, Seattle, 1971. Short overview of the expedition for the use of railroad passengers; expanded from Flandrau's 1925 work *A Glance at the Lewis and Clark Expedition.*

1929

Defenbach, Byron. *Red Heroines of the Northwest.* Caldwell, Idaho: The Caxton Printers. A compilation of stories about three Indian women, including Sacagawea. Reprinted by the Caxton Printers, 1935.

McSpadden, J. Walker. *Pioneer Heroes.* New York: Thomas Y. Crowell. Includes a chapter on Lewis and Clark.

Vincent, William David. *Contributions to the History of the Pacific Northwest: The Lewis and Clark Expedition.* Spokane Study Club Series A. Pullman: State College of Washington.

1931
Ghent, W. J. *The Early Far West: A Narrative Outline, 1540–1850.* New York and Toronto: Longmans, Green & Co., 1931. Includes a section on Lewis and Clark.

Smyth, Clifford. *Lewis and Clark: Pioneers in America's Westward Expansion Movement.* Builders of America series. New York and London: Funk & Wagnalls Co.

Voorhis School for Boys. *The Magnificent Adventure: A Drama of the Lewis and Clark*

Expedition. San Dimas, California: Viking Print Shop, Voorhis School for Boys. Compiled by the Voorhis School for Boys, Class of 1931. *

1932
Crawford, Polly Pearl. *Lewis and Clark's Expedition as a Source for Poe's "Journal of Julius Rodman."* Texas Studies in English, 12. Austin, Texas: University Press. *

1933
Hebard, Grace Raymond. *Sacajawea: A Guide and Interpreter of the Lewis and Clark Expedition, With an Account of the Travels of Toussaint Charbonneau, and of Jean Baptiste, the Expedition Papoose*. Glendale, California: The Arthur H. Clark Co. Reprinted by Arthur H. Clark, 1957 and 1967; reprinted in a limited facsimile edition in Mansfield Centre, Connecticut, by the Overland Trails Press, 1999. This work is historical, but has been found to contain errors and misinformation.

Mansfield, J. Carroll. *Pioneers of the Wild West*. High Lights of History series. Cleveland and New York: The World Syndicate Publishing Co.

1934
Wilson, Charles Morrow. *Meriwether Lewis of Lewis and Clark*. With illustrations and maps. New York: Thomas Y. Crowell Co. Reprinted in the same year. Biography of Meriwether Lewis.

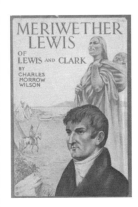

1935
Hall, Charles Gilbert. *The Great Adventure*. Illustrated by Paul Laune. Our Changing World Series. New York: Thomas Nelson and Sons. Children's book.

Hueston, Ethel. *Star of the West: The Romance of the Lewis and Clark Expedition*. Indianapolis and New York: Bobbs-Merrill Co. Also printed in the same year in New York by A. L. Burt. Narrative account of the Lewis and Clark Expedition.

1936
Churchill, Claire Warner. *South of the Sunset: An Interpretation of Sacajawea the Indian Girl That Accompanied Lewis and Clark*. Illustrated by Agnes C. Lehman. New York: The Junior Literary Guild and Rufus Rockwell Wilson. There are two versions of this book, one printed by Rufus Rockwell Wilson, and the other by The Junior Literary Guild and Rufus Rockwell Wilson. Children's book based on the story of Sacagawea.

Hewes, Agnes Danforth. *The Codfish Musket*. Illustrated by Armstrong Sperry. New York: Junior Literary Guild and Doubleday, Doran. Reprinted in New York by Doubleday, 1941 and 1947. Children's book.

1937
Davis, Julia. *No Other White Men*. New York: E. P. Dutton & Co. Also printed in Chicago by Cadmus Books, E.M. Hale and Co., 1937, and in London by J. Murray, 1937; reprinted in New York by Dutton in 1938, 1941, 1946, 1950, 1951, 1954, and 1965; reprinted in New York by Comet Books, 1949, illustrated by Richard Powers; reprinted in New York by Scholastic Books, 1965.

Gregg, Kate L. *Westward with Dragoons: The Journal of William Clark on His Expedition to Establish Fort Osage, August 25 to September 22, 1808.* Fulton, Missouri: The Ovid Bell Press. School edition.

Moorehead, Blanche Woods. *New World Builders: Thrilling Days With Lewis and Clark.* Illustrated by Armstrong Sperry. New York: The Junior Literary Guild and the John C. Winston Co.

Seymour, Flora Warren Smith. *Meriwether Lewis, Trail Blazer.* Illustrated by Norman Price. New York, London: D. Appleton-Century Co.

1938
Anderson, Sarah Travers Lewis (Scott). *Lewises, Meriwethers and Their Kin: Lewises and Meriwethers With Their Tracings Through the Families Whose Records are Herein Contained: Compiled From Family Papers and From Reliable Sources.* Richmond, Virginia: The Dietz Press. Reprinted in 1984, Baltimore: Genealogical Publishing Co.

Gass, Patrick. *Excerpt from Journal of the voyages & travels of a corps of discovery, under the command of Capt. Lewis and Capt. Clarke of the army of the United States, from the mouth of the river Missouri through the interior parts of North America to the Pacific Ocean, during the years 1804, 1805, and 1806.* [San Francisco]: Grabhorn Press for C. Hoffman. Cover reads: *Christmas greetings from Carl Hoffman, 1938.* From the edition printed for Mathew Carey, Philadelphia, 1812. See section 3.7. *

Gould, Dorothy Fay. *Beyond the Shining Mountains.* Portland, Oregon: Binfords & Mort. This book contains minimal information relating to Lewis and Clark, but it includes an otherwise unrecorded image captioned "Lewis & Clark at the mouth of the Columbia River" and titled "Oregon Territory." Gould noted in her 1937 University of Washington master's degree thesis, titled *Analysis of Ten Important Private Collections of Northwest Material, Studied from 1930 to 1937, with a Discussion of their Critical Value,* that the image was found in the private collection of Mrs. William Pitt Trimble of Seattle. It was "Pasted in front of one volume of Lewis and Clark, published in Philadelphia by Nicholas Biddle, in 1814." (*Analysis,* 29). Gould's notes describe the image as colored.

Johnson, Grace. *Colter's Hell: A Story of the Yellowstone.* Los Angeles: Maple Publishers. A novel based on the history of Yellowstone Park, including John Colter's experiences in the region.

1939
Howard, Bonnie C. and Ruth Higgins. *On the Trail With Lewis and Clark.* Illustrated by Paul Laune. New York, Boston, Chicago, and San Francisco: Silver Burdett Co.

Isely, Bliss. *Blazing the Way West.* New York, London, Charles Scribner's.

1940
Criswell, Elijah Harry. *Lewis and Clark: Linguistic Pioneers.* Vol. 15, no. 2 of the University Studies, A Quarterly of Research. Columbia: The University of Missouri. This publication was also printed with the title page: "Submitted in Partial Fulfillment of the Requirements for the Degree of Doctor of Philosophy in the

Graduate School of the University of Missouri. As published in *The University of Missouri Studies* Vol. 15, no. 2 of the University Studies. Columbia: The University of Missouri." Reprinted under the title *Lewis & Clark–Pioneering Linguists*. Bozeman, Montana: Headwaters Chapter of the Lewis & Clark Trail Heritage Foundation, 1991; reprinted in a limited facsimile edition of 175 copies, Mansfield Centre, Connecticut, Martino Publishing, 2000. This publication is a detailed analysis of the vocabulary used by Lewis and Clark and its derivation; it also includes a useful lexicon.

Schaare, C. Richard. *The Expedition of Lewis & Clark in Picture and Story.* New York: Cupples & Leon Co. Children's book.

1941
Curl, Grace Voris. *Young Shannon, Scout with Lewis and Clark.* Illustrated by Paul Lantz. First edition. New York: Harper & Brothers. Second edition published in the same year. Children's book.

1942
Peattie, Donald Culross. *Forward the Nation.* New York: G. P. Putnam's Sons. Also reprinted as an Armed Services edition in New York by Editions for the Armed Services, 1942; published in German as *Das mädchen Sacadjevia; expeditionsbericht von der ersten durchquerung Nordamerikas.* Translated by Elsa von Heinrich. Wolfsberg: Ploetz, 1948 (first edition only in Lewis & Clark College Collection).

1943
Emmons, Della Gould. *Sacajawea of the Shoshones.* Portland, Oregon: Binfords & Mort. A fictional account of Sacagawea and the Lewis and Clark Expedition, in different issues with identical pages. Lewis & Clark College Collection copies are bound as follows: in dark orange with red stamping and an orange dustjacket; in a light blue cover; and bound in yellow with orange stamping and a dust jacket featuring images from the motion picture *Far Horizons*. Also published in a Spanish edition under the title *Sacajawea*, translated by Fernando de Diego de la Rosa. La Nave, series B, no. 106. Madrid: La Nave, 1949 (English edition only in Lewis & Clark College Collection).

1945
Fletcher, Robert Henry. *American Adventure: Story of the Lewis and Clark Expedition.* Illustrated by Irvin Shope. New York: American Pioneer Trails Association.

Seymour, Flora Warren. *Bird Girl: Sacagawea.* Illustrated by Edward C. Caswell. Indianapolis and New York: Bobbs-Merrill Co. Reprinted under title *Sacagawea, American Pathfinder.* Illustrated by Robert Doremus. Childhood of Famous Americans series. New York: Aladdin Books, 1991; reproduced in Braille by the Kansas Instructional Resource Center for the Blind & Visually Impaired, two vols., 1991. Children's book (first edition only in Lewis & Clark College Collection).

1946
Bebenroth, Charlotta M. *Meriwether Lewis: Boy Explorer.* Illustrated by Al Fiorentino. Childhood of Famous Americans series. Indianapolis and New York: Bobbs-Merrill Co. Reprinted by Bobbs-Merrill, 1953, 1962; reprinted in New York by Aladdin Paperback, 1997. Children's book (Lewis & Clark College Collection does not include 1997 reprint).

Hawthorne, Hildegarde. *Westward the Course: A Story of the Lewis and Clark Expedition.* New York, London, Toronto: Longmans, Green and Co. Reprinted in 1951 by Longmans, Green and Co. (Lewis & Clark College Collection includes first edition only).

Mirsky, Jeannette. *The Westward Crossings: Balboa, Mackenzie, Lewis and Clark.* New York: Alfred A Knopf. Reprinted in London by A. Wingate, 1951; reprinted by the University of Chicago Press, 1970 (Lewis & Clark College Collection includes first edition only).

Nevin, Evelyn C. *The Lost Children of the Shoshones.* Illustrated by Manning De V. Lee. Philadelphia: The Westminster Press.

1947

Bakeless, John. *Lewis & Clark: Partners in Discovery.* New York: William Morrow & Co. Reprinted by William & Morrow, 1948; reprinted by William Morrow, 1966; reprinted in facsimile at Magnolia, Massachusetts, by Peter Smith, 1970, 1976; reprinted for the Dover Books on Travel series in New York by Dover Publications and in London by Constable, 1996. A biographical account of both Lewis and Clark, focusing on the story of the expedition (Lewis & Clark College Collection includes first edition only).

1948

Kennerly, William Clark. *Persimmon Hill: A Narrative of Old St. Louis and the Far West.* As told to Elizabeth Russell. Norman: University of Oklahoma Press. Includes biographical information about William Clark.

McCreight, Major Israel. *Sac-a-ja-wea, America's Greatest Heroine: From the Lewis and Clark Diaries.* Sykesville, Pennsylvania: Napp Printing Co.

Reid, Russell, ed. *Lewis and Clark in North Dakota: The Original Manuscript Journals and the Text of the Biddle Edition During the Time the Expedition Remained in North Dakota.* Bismarck, North Dakota. Reprinted from *North Dakota History* 14–15, State Historical Society of North Dakota, 1947–1948. Reprinted by the State Historical Society of North Dakota, 1988.

Van Every, Dale. *The Shining Mountains.* New York: Julian Messner.

1949

Smith, Robert Wallace. *The Song of Sakakawea (Bird-Woman): The Indian Guide and Interpretress of the Lewis and Clark Expedition.* Dallas, Texas: The Kaleidograph Press. A poetic interpretation of the story of Lewis and Clark.

1950

Bakeless, John. *The Eyes of Discovery: The Pageant of North America as Seen by the First Explorers.* Philadelphia, New York: J. B. Lippincott Co. A historical account of North America as it would have appeared to explorers, including Lewis and Clark.

Forrest, Earle R. *Patrick Gass: Lewis and Clark's Last Man with the War Records of Descendants of Patrick Gass in World War I and World War II.* Independence, Pennsylvania: Mrs. A. M. Painter. Reprinted in 1984.

Maudlin, Clark M. *Louisiana Purchase: Lewis and Clark Expedition from the Diary of Sergeant Patrick Gass.* Anaconda: Founders Club of Montana. *

Pollard, Lancaster. *Lewis and Clark at Fort Clatsop.* Seaside, Oregon: Clatsop County Historical Society. Reprinted and revised in 1962 by the Clatsop County Historical Society (Lewis & Clark College Collection includes 1962 revision).

Salisbury, Albert and Jane Salisbury. *Two Captains West: An Historical Tour of the Lewis and Clark Trail.* Illustrated by Carter Lucas. Limited edition of 350 copies in slipcase. Seattle: Superior Publishing Co. Also printed the same year in Seattle by Superior Publishing Co. in variant bindings with variant jackets; printed the same year in New York by Bramhall House. Reprinted under the title *Lewis & Clark: The Journey West* in New York by Promontory Press, 1990, 1993 (Lewis & Clark College Collection includes all editions except Promontory Press, 1993).

1951

Daugherty, James. *Of Courage Undaunted: Across the Continent with Lewis and Clark.* New York: The Viking Press. Reprinted in Sandwich, Massachusetts, by Beautiful Feet Books, 1967; reprinted by Viking Press, 1967; reprinted in large print in New York by Marshall Cavendish, and in Lakeville, Connecticut, by Grey Castle Press, 1991. Children's book (Lewis & Clark College Collection includes first edition only).

Davis, Lottie Wright. *Records of Lewis, Meriwether and Kindred Families: Genealogical Records of Minor, Davis, Wells, Gilmer, and Clark Families.* Columbia, Missouri: Nelson Heath Meriwether.

Neuberger, Richard L. *The Lewis & Clark Expedition.* New York: Random House, Landmark Books. Also published the same year in Chicago by Spencer Press, Landmark Books. A children's book based on the Lewis and Clark Expedition; published in Spanish under the title *La Expedicion de Lewis y Clark.* Illustrations by Winold Reiss. Translated into Spanish by Lorenzo Garza. México: Collecion Infantil, LILA, Editorial Intercontinental, S. A., 1958.

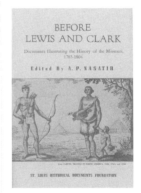

1952

Harris, Burton. *John Colter: His Years in the Rockies.* New York and London: Charles Scribner's Sons.

Nasatir, Abraham P., ed. *Before Lewis and Clark: Documents Illustrating the History of the Missouri, 1785–1804.* Two vols. St. Louis: St. Louis Historical Documents Foundation. Reprinted in cloth by University of Oklahoma Press, 1990, and in paper by Books on Demand, Ann Arbor, Michigan, 2002.

1953

Burroughs, Raymond Darwin. *Exploration Unlimited: The Story of the Lewis and Clark Expedition.* The Cass Lectureship series. Detroit: Wayne University Press.

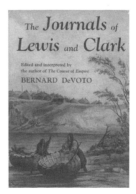

DeVoto, Bernard, ed. *The Journals of Lewis and Clark.* Maps by Erwin Raisz. Boston: The Riverside Press for Houghton Mifflin Co. Reprinted by Houghton Mifflin as a Sentry edition, 1953, 1963; reprinted in London by Eyre and Spottiswood, 1954; reprinted by Houghton, Mifflin as a part of the American Heritage Library, 1981; reprinted in a limited edition as a part of the 100 Greatest Masterpieces of American Literature series in Franklin Center, Pennsylvania by the Franklin Library, 1982; reprinted by Houghton Mifflin, 1997 (Lewis & Clark College Collection includes first edition, the 1953 Sentry edition, and the London 1954 edition). This single-volume edition of selections from the Lewis and Clark journals provides a compilation of the important journal entries.

Stevens, James, Robert Macfarlane, and Kenn E. Johnson. *Lewis and Clark: Our National Epic of Exploration, 1804–1806*. Tacoma, Washington: Washington State Historical Society. Item is undated, but was published between 1953 and 1956, as part of the Northwest Lewis and Clark sesquicentennial by the Northern Pacific Railway Co.

1954
Farnsworth, Frances Joyce. *Winged Moccasins: The Story of Sacajawea*. Illustrated by Lorence F. Bjorklund. New York: Julian Messner. Multiple printings by Julian Messner, 1955–68; reprinted as a library edition in Englewood Cliffs, New Jersey by Responsive Environments, 1954 (Lewis & Clark College Collection includes the first and second editions). Children's book.

1955
Bialk, Elisa. *Giant of the Rockies: A Story About John Colter*. Cleveland and New York: The World Publishing Co.

McClelland, John M. *Lewis and Clark in the Fort Columbia Area*. Ilwaco, Washington: Tribune Publishing Co.

McKelvey, Susan Delano. *Botanical Exploration of the Trans-Mississippi West, 1790–1850*. Jamaica Plain, Massachusetts: The Arnold Arboretum of Harvard University. Includes an assessment of Lewis and Clark's botanical contributions. Reprinted by Oregon State University Press, 1991.

Meriwether, Nelson Heath. *Supplement: Lewis, Meriwether and Kindred Families*. Columbia, Missouri: Nelson Heath Meriwether.

Nelson, Vera Joyce. *Moccasin Prints West: A Legend of the Nez Perces at the Time of Lewis and Clark*. [n.p.]: Vera Joyce Nelson.

Osborne, Kelsie Ramey. *Peaceful Conquest: Story of the Lewis and Clark Expedition*. Illustrations by Colista Dowling. Portland, Oregon: Lewis and Clark Sesquicentennial Committee for Oregon and Old Oregon Trail, Inc. Issued in boards and in wraps.

Pollard, Lancaster. *Lewis and Clark at Seaside*. Seaside, Oregon: Seaside Chamber of Commerce for the Lewis and Clark Festival. No publication date is provided, but 1955 is inferred, as this was the Lewis and Clark sesquicentennial celebration year.

1956
Holbrook, Stewart H. *The Columbia*. Vol. 50 of the Rivers of America series. Illustrated by Ernest Richardson. Special Lewis and Clark limited edition of 2,300 copies. New York and Toronto: Rinehart and Co.

1957

Wheat, Carl I. *Mapping the Transmississippi West, 1540–1861.* Five vols. San Francisco: Institute of Historical Cartography, 1957–1963. Reprinted in Storrs-Mansfied, Connecticut: Maurizio Martino Publisher; Parsippany, New Jersey: About Books, 1995. Includes information on many maps carried and drawn by Lewis and Clark.

1958

Ewers, John C. *The Blackfeet: Raiders on the Northwestern Plains.* Norman, Oklahoma: University of Oklahoma Press. Includes a section on Lewis and Clark.

Fisher, Vardis. *Tale of Valor: A Novel of the Lewis and Clark Expedition.* Garden City, New York: Doubleday & Co. Reprinted as a Giant Cardinal edition in New York by Pocket books, 1960; reprinted in Mattituck, New York, by the American Reprint Co., 1976 (Lewis & Clark College Collection includes first edition only).

Gass, Patrick. *A Journal of the Voyages and Travels of a Corps of Discovery, Under the Command of Capt. Lewis and Capt. Clarke of the Army of the United States, From the Mouth of the River Missouri Through the Interior Parts of North America to the Pacific Ocean, During the Years 1804, 1805 and 1806.* Limited edition of two thousand copies. Minneapolis, Minnesota: Ross & Haines, Inc. Reprint of the 1810 Gass, with a biography and photographs by Earle R. Forrest. See section 3.4.

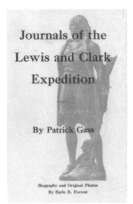

1959

Govan, Thomas Payne. *Nicholas Biddle: Nationalist and Public Banker, 1786–1844.* Chicago: University of Chicago Press. A biography of Nicholas Biddle, first editor of the Lewis and Clark journals.

Haines, Madge and Leslie Morrill. *Lewis and Clark, Explorers to the West.* Illustrated by William Hutchinson. Makers of America series. New York: Abingdon Press.

Lewis, Meriwether. *David Thompson and the Lewis and Clark Expedition: An Unpublished Account of the Lewis and Clark Expedition Written by Captain Meriwether Lewis and Copied by David Thompson of the North West Company.* Introduction by Peter Grossman. Vancouver, British Columbia: Library's Press.

Meriwether, Nelson Heath. *Addenda to the Supplement: Lewis, Meriwether and Kindred Families.* Columbia, Missouri: Nelson Heath Meriwether.

Mumey, Nolie. *Sacajawea, the Great American Indian Heroine Who Accompanied Lewis and Clark Up the Missouri River in 1804–1805; Buried in Wyoming.* Denver Brand Book 14. Denver, Colorado: Westerners.

Munves, James. *We Were There with Lewis and Clark.* Illustrated by Robert Glaubke. New York: Grosset & Dunlap. A children's book based on the Lewis and Clark Expedition.

Stoutenburg, Adrien and Laura Nelson Baker. *Scannon, Dog with Lewis and Clark.* New York: Charles Scribner's Sons.

Thwaites, Reuben Gold, ed. *Original Journals of the Lewis and Clark Expedition, 1804–1806.* Eight vols. New York: Antiquarian Press. Edition limited to 750 copies, of which 700 numbered copies were for sale. See section 5d.

1960

Bordwell, Constance. *March of the Volunteers: Soldiering with Lewis and Clark.* Portland, Oregon: Beaver Books, Reed College. Narrative interwoven with selections from the Thwaites edition (section 5d) of the journals.

Hult, Ruby El. *Guns of the Lewis and Clark Expedition.* Tacoma, Washington: Washington State Historical Society.

Seibert, Jerry. *Sacajawea: Guide to Lewis and Clark.* Illustrated by Lorence Bjorklund. Piper Books series. Boston: Houghton Mifflin, 1960. Reprinted under the title *Northwest Adventure* in Chicago by Science Research Associates, 1963 (Lewis & Clark College Collection does not include reprint). Children's book.

Stearns, Harold G. *On the Trail with Lewis & Clark in Montana: April 26, 1805–September 13, 1805; June 29, 1806–August 7, 1806.* Harlowton, Montana: Times-Clarion Publishers. Date not shown; 1960 provided by Online Computer Library Center (OCLC) WorldCat database.

1961

Burroughs, Raymond Darwin, ed. *The Natural History of the Lewis and Clark Expedition.* Michigan State University Press. Reprinted by Michigan State University Press, 1995, with a new introduction by Robert Carriker. This work contains passages from the journals with commentary by the editor, and is the only significant publication to deal exclusively with the zoological studies of Lewis and Clark.

Kennedy, Michael Stephen. *The Assiniboines: From the Accounts of the Old Ones Told to First Boy (James Larpenteur Long).* Illustrations by William Standing. Norman, Oklahoma: University of Oklahoma Press. Includes stories about the Lewis and Clark Expedition.

Lewis, Meriwether. *The Lewis and Clark Expedition.* Reprint of the 1814 Biddle-Allen edition, unabridged in three vols., with an introduction by Archibald Hanna. Philadelphia and New York: J. B. Lippincott Co. Issued as hardcover in box, and in wraps.

1962

Bakeless, John. *The Adventures of Lewis and Clark.* North Star Books 29. Boston: Houghton Mifflin Co.

Biddle, Nicholas, and Paul Allen, eds. *The Journals of the Expedition Under the Command of Capts. Lewis and Clark to the Sources of the Missouri, Thence Across the Rocky Mountains and Down the River Columbia to the Pacific Ocean, Performed During the Years 1804-5-6 by Order of the Government of the United States.* Reprint of the 1814 edition edited by Nicholas Biddle, with an introduction by John Bakeless, and illustrated in color and black and white with watercolors and drawings by Karl Bodmer and other contemporary artists. New York: The Limited Editions Club. Two vols. in slipcase.

——. *The Journals of the Expedition Under the Command of Capts. Lewis and Clark to the Sources of the Missouri, Thence Across the Rocky Mountains and Down the River Columbia to the Pacific Ocean, Performed During the Years 1804-5-6 by Order of the Government of the United States.* New York: The Heritage Press. Two vols. in slipcase. Content same as previous entry.

——. *The Journals of the Expedition Under the Command of Capts. Lewis and Clark to the Sources of the Missouri, Thence Across the Rocky Mountains and Down the River Columbia to the Pacific Ocean, Performed During the Years 1804–5–6 by Order of the Government of the United States.* Edited by Nicholas Biddle, with an introduction by John Bakeless. Illustrated. Two vols. Norwalk, Connecticut: The Easton Press. Collector's Edition bound in leather (green and brown). Reprinted by the Easton Press, 1989 (Lewis & Clark College Collection does not include 1989 reprint).

Daniels, Jonathan. *The Devil's Backbone: The Story of the Natchez Trace.* American Trails series. New York: McGraw-Hill. Includes information relating to Meriwether Lewis's death along the Natchez Trace.

Fisher, Vardis. *Suicide or Murder? The Strange Death of Governor Meriwether Lewis.* Denver: Alan Swallow. Also published same year in paper, Chicago: Sage Press, Swallow.

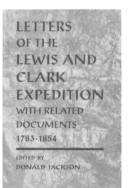

Jackson, Donald, ed. *Letters of the Lewis and Clark Expedition with Related Documents, 1783–1854.* Urbana: University of Illinois Press. Reissued in a second printing with minor additions, University of Illinois Press, 1963; second edition, with additional documents and notes, two vols. in slipcase, University of Illinois Press, 1978. An invaluable reference set that includes most known documents relating to Lewis and Clark, with footnotes.

Koch, Elers. *Lewis and Clark Across the Bitterroot Range.* Missoula, Montana: USDA Forest Service, Northern Region. *

National Park Service. *A Proposed Lewis and Clark National Wilderness Waterway Montana.* Omaha, Nebraska: Department of the Interior, National Park Service, Midwest Region Office. Lewis & Clark College Collection copies are dated February 1962, noting revisions made October 1962, and an addendum dated May 1967. The report is a supplement to appendix 7 of the Corps of Engineers-Department of the Interior Joint Report on the Missouri River between Fort Peck Reservoir and Fort Benton, Montana.

1963
Bakeless, John. *West to the Pacific: The Story of Lewis and Clark.* A Ladder edition. New York: Pyramid Books. Originally titled *The Adventures of Lewis and Clark* by John Bakeless, 1962; adapted by Lou Munson. *

Britt, Albert. *Toward the Western Ocean: The Story of the Men who Bridged the Continent, 1803–1869.* Barre, Massachusettes: Barre Publishing Co.

Dick, Everett. *Tales of the Frontier: From Lewis and Clark to the Last Roundup.* Lincoln, Nebraska: University of Nebraska Press. Reprinted by University of Nebraska Press, 1970.

Eifert, Virginia S. *George Shannon, Young Explorer with Lewis and Clark.* Illustrated by Manning De V. Lee. New York: Dodd, Mead.

Henry, Will. *The Gates of the Mountains.* New York: Random House. Reprinted by Random House, 1980; reprinted in New York by Bantam Books, 1991; reprinted in New York by Leisure Books, 1999 (Lewis & Clark College Collection includes first edition only).

Polking, Kirk. *Let's Go with Lewis and Clark.* Let's Go series. Illustrated by Albert Micale. New York: Putnam. *

Wilkie, Katharine E. *Will Clark: Boy in Buckskins.* Illustrated by William Moyers. Indianapolis, New York: Bobbs-Merrill Co. Reprinted as *Will Clark, Boy Adventurer* in New York by Aladdin Paperbacks, 1997 (Lewis & Clark College Collection includes first edition only). Children's book.

1964

Bakeless, John, ed. *The Journals of Lewis and Clark.* New York: A Mentor Book, The New American Library. Single-volume abridgement of the Lewis and Clark journals.

Bowman, Gerald. *With Lewis and Clark Through the Rockies.* Illustrated by Lunt Roberts. Adventures in Geography series. London: Frederick Muller. Reprinted by Frederick Muller, 1965.

Garver, Frank Harmon. *Lewis and Clark in Beaverhead County.* Dillon, Montana: Western Montana College of Education. Reprint from *Dillon Examiner* (Dec. 10, 1913).

Link, Louis W. *Lewis and Clark Expedition, 1804–1806: From St. Louis, Missouri, to Pacific Ocean and Return, with Particular Reference to the Upper Missouri and Yellowstone Rivers.* Cardwell, Montana.

Meriwether, Nelson Heath. *The Meriwethers and their Connections.* Columbia, Missouri: The Artcraft Press. Reprinted in Baltimore for the Meriwether Society by Gateway Press, 1991.

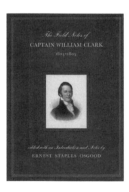

Osgood, Ernest Staples, ed. *The Field Notes of Captain William Clark.* New Haven and London: Yale University Press. The first published edition of Clark's field notes; includes facsimiles of the manuscripts. Lewis & Clark College Collection also has the prospectus for this volume. See section 5g.1.

Skarsten, M. O. *George Drouillard: Hunter and Interpreter for Lewis and Clark and Fur Trader, 1807–1810.* Western Frontiersmen series, no. 11. Glendale, California: The Arthur H. Clark Co. The only biography of Drouillard. Lewis & Clark College has publisher's galley proofs, as well as correspondence between Skarsten and Arthur H. Clark.

Space, Ralph S. *Lewis and Clark through Idaho, 1805–1806.* Lewiston, Idaho: Tribune Publishing Co. Includes excerpts from the journals, with commentary by Space. Publication date is approximate.

West, Helen B. *Meriwether Lewis in Blackfeet Country.* Browning, Montana: Museum of the Plains Indian. Reprinted by the Lewis & Clark Foundation in 1984.

1965

Blassingame, Wyat. *Sacagawea: Indian Guide.* Illustrated by Edward Shenton. Champaign, Illinois: Garrard Publishing Co. Children's book.

Chuinard, Eldon G. *The Medical Aspects of the Lewis & Clark Expedition.* Corvallis, Oregon: Friends of the Library, Oregon State University.

Coues, Elliott, ed. *History of the Expedition Under the Command of Lewis and Clark.* Three vols. New York: Dover Publications. Reprint of the original edition printed by Francis P. Harper in 1893 in four volumes (see section 5b). Bound as three vols. in this edition, containing all the material of the 1893 publication, but arranged differently. This Dover version was reprinted in 1965, 1970, 1979, and 1980. A hardbound edition was reprinted by Dover/Peter Smith and appeared (undated) in the 1970s.

Department of the Interior. *The Lewis and Clark Trail: A Proposal for Development.* Washington, D.C.: Government Printing Office.

Dillon, Richard. *Meriwether Lewis: A Biography.* New York: Coward-McCann, Inc. Reprinted as a paperback in New York by Capricorn Books, 1968; reprinted 1988 in Santa Cruz by Western Tanager Press with a new foreword by Stephen Ambrose.

Tomkins, Calvin. *The Lewis and Clark Trail.* Introduction by Stewart L. Udall. New York: Harper & Row.

1966
Cramer, Zadok. *The Navigator.* Eighth edition. Great Americana series. Readex Microprint. A facsimile of the 1814 edition published in Pittsburgh. Includes an appendix with information about Lewis and Clark summarized from Gass's journal. See section 3.1.

Lewis and Clark Trail Commission. *The Lewis and Clark Trail: An Interim Report to the President and to the Congress.* Washington, D.C.: Government Printing Office.

Lewis, Meriwether. *The Expedition of Lewis and Clark.* Great Americana series. Two vols. Readex Microprint. A facsimile of *History of the Expedition Under the Command of Captains Lewis and Clark,* 1814 Philadelphia, edited by Nicholas Biddle and Paul Allen. Reprinted by Readex, 1974.

Montgomery, Elizabeth Rider. *World Explorers: Lewis and Clark.* Illustrated by Edward Shenton. Champaign, Illinois: Garrard Publishing Co. Children's book.

1967
Andrist, Ralph K. *To the Pacific With Lewis and Clark.* New York: American Heritage Publishing. Also printed as a part of the American Heritage Junior Library in Mahwah, New Jersey, by Troll Associates, 1967.

Frazier, Neta Lohnes. *Sacajawea: The Girl Nobody Knows.* New York: David McKay Co. Children's book.

Holm, Don. *Christmas at Fort Clatsop.* A Buffalo Book: Beaverton, Oregon: Don Holm.

Loomis, Noel M. and Abraham P. Nasatir. *Pedro Vial and the Roads to Santa Fe.* Norman, Oklahoma: University of Oklahoma Press. Includes a chapter on Lewis and Clark addressing the Spanish reaction to the expedition.

Voight, Virginia Frances. *Sacajawea.* Illustrated by Erica Merkling. New York: Putnam. *

1968

Brown, Stuart E. *The Guns of Harpers Ferry.* Berryville, Virginia: Virginia Book Co. Includes a discussion of the guns carried by Lewis and Clark.

Cutright, Paul Russell. *Meriwether Lewis: Naturalist.* Portland, Oregon: Oregon Historical Society. Combines two articles from the *Oregon Historical Quarterly* into a single volume: 69, no. 1 (March 1968): 5–28; 69, no. 2 (June 1968): 148–70.

De Kay, Ormonde. *The Adventures of Lewis and Clark.* Illustrated by John Powers Severin. New York: Step-Up Books, Random House. Children's book.

1969

Coues, Elliott, ed. *Lewis & Clark Expedition, 1804–1806: A Brief Synopsis Taken From the Original Diaries of Members of the Lewis and Clark Expedition, as Written in the Interesting Volumes of Elliott Coues, Captain and Assistant Surgeon, United States Army.* Omaha, Nebraska: U.S. Army Corps of Engineers. The text of this volume was printed ca. 1941 in the *Crossroads* newsletter as a series titled "First Missouri River Inspection Trip: Lewis & Clark Expedition Explores the 'Big Muddy.'" It is a digest version of the *History of the Expedition* edited by Coues in 1893 (see section 5b). The publication has been extensively rearranged and cut. Reprinted in 1976, with no date of publication listed; 1976 is inferred by the term "Bicentennial Edition." Reprinted as a "Fiftieth Anniversary Edition" in 1984, at Omaha by the Army Corps of Engineers; the volume may have been originally printed in 1934.

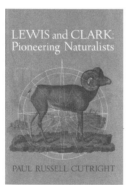

Cutright, Paul Russell. *Lewis and Clark: Pioneering Naturalists.* Urbana, Chicago, London: University of Illinois Press. Reprinted as a Bison Book by University of Nebraska Press, 1989. This was the first comprehensive assessment of Lewis and Clark's work as naturalists.

Eide, Ingvard Henry. *American Odyssey: The Journey of Lewis and Clark.* Chicago, New York, San Francisco: Rand McNally & Co. Reprinted in paperback by Rand McNally, 1979. Large-format book with many photographs of the trail.

Howard, Harold P. *Mystery of Sacajawea: Indian Girl With Lewis and Clark.* Stickney, South Dakota: Harold P. Howard. Reprinted in 1973.

Lewis and Clark Trail Commission. *The Lewis and Clark Trail: Final Report to the President and to the Congress.* Washington, D.C.: U.S. Government Printing Office.

Thwaites, Reuben Gold, ed. *Original Journals of the Lewis and Clark Expedition, 1804–1806.* Eight volumes, with an introduction by Bernard DeVoto. New York: Arno Press. Bound in both red and green buckram. Reprinted by Arno, 1990. See section 5d.

1970

Brown, Dee Alexander. *The Lewis and Clark Expedition: An Illustrated Keepsake Album.* Gettysburg, Pennsylvania: National Historical Society. Reprinted in Harrisburg, Pennsylvania, by Historical Times, 1982.

Cappon, Lester J. and Alfred C. Berol. *History of the Expedition Under the Command of Captains Lewis and Clark, Philadelphia, published by Bradford and Inskeep, 1814: A Census of Extant Copies in Original Boards.* New York: Columbia University Libraries.

Chidsey, Donald Barr. *Lewis and Clark: The Great Adventure.* New York: Crown Publishers.

Clarke, Charles G. *The Men of the Lewis and Clark Expedition: A Biographical Roster of the Fifty-one Members and a Composite Diary of their Activities from All Known Sources.* Western Frontiersmen series, 14. Glendale, California: The Arthur H. Clark Co. Reprinted by Arthur H. Clark, 2001. Includes biographical information on most members of the expedition.

Rees, John E. *Madame Charbonneau: The Indian Woman who Accompanied the Lewis and Clark Expedition, 1804–6: How She Received Her Indian Name and What Became of Her.* Salmon, Idaho: Lemhi County Historical Society.

Snyder, Gerald. *In the Footsteps of Lewis and Clark.* Washington, D.C.: National Geographic Society.

Space, Ralph S. *The Lolo Trail: A History of Events Connected with the Lolo Trail.* Lewiston, Idaho: Printcraft Printing. Reprinted in multiple later printings by Printcraft Printing. Reissued with new title: *The Lolo Trail: A History and a Guide to the Trail of Lewis and Clark.* Second edition, Missoula, Montana: Historic Montana Publishers, 2001.

1971

Bernard, Charles Richard, William Brune, and James Langdon. *In the Footsteps of Lewis and Clark: A Directed Inquiry.* Memphis: Rhodes College; Department of English. "Under the direction of Prof. Jack Farris, Southwestern English Department." *

Flug, Arthur and Seymour Litman. *Stories of the Westward Movement.* The Social Studies Readers. River Forest, Illinois: Laidlaw Brothers. Includes a section on Lewis and Clark.

Foote, Stella. *Pompeys Pillar of the Lewis and Clark Trail.* Billings, Montana: Reporter Printing & Supply Co.

Hays, Wilma Pitchford. *The Meriwether Lewis Mystery.* Philadelphia: The Westminster Press.

Howard, Harold P. *Sacajawea.* Norman, Oklahoma: University of Oklahoma Press. Reprinted multiple times by University of Oklahoma Press, including 1973, 1979. The story of Lewis & Clark, with a focus on Sacajawea.

Ray, Verne F. *Lewis and Clark and the Nez Perce Indians.* The Great Western series, no. 10. Washington, D.C.: Potomac Corral, The Westerners. Issued in boards and in wraps.

Thwaites, Reuben Gold. *Newly Discovered Personal Records of Lewis & Clark.* Seattle: Shorey Book Store. Facsimile reprint of article in *Scribner's Magazine*, June 1904. Reprinted by Shorey, 1974.

1972

Jones, Roy F. *Wappato Indians of the Lower Columbia River Valley.* Privately printed by Roy F. Jones. Includes two chapters on Lewis and Clark.

1973

Barnes, Esther. *Lovely Sacajawea.* Illustrated by Donna Hayes. Boise, Idaho: Joslyn & Rentscler Lithoprinters. Bound in boards and in wraps. Children's book.

Biddle, Nicholas, and Paul Allen, eds. *History of the Expedition Under the Command of Captains Lewis & Clarke to the Sources of the Missouri, Thence Across the Rocky Mountains and Down the River Columbia to the Pacific Ocean, Performed During the Years 1804–5–6 by Order of the Government of the United States: A Complete Reprint of the Biddle Edition of 1814 to Which All the Members of the Expedition Contributed with an Account of the Louisiana Purchase by Rev. John Bach McMaster and Notes Upon the Route.* The American Explorers series. With illustrations and maps in three vols. New York: AMS Press.

Gilbert, Bil. *The Old West: The Trailblazers.* New York: Time-Life Books. Includes a section on Lewis and Clark.

Lange, Robert E. *Bibliographical Index to the Literature of the Lewis and Clark Expedition.* Portland, Oregon: Robert Lange. Prepared for distribution to members of the Oregon Chapter, Lewis & Clark Heritage Foundation.

Stiles, Glee Druyor. *The Drouillard to Druyor Family History with Related Facts.* Genealogical study of the Drouillard family.

1974

Bureau of Outdoor Recreation. *The Lewis and Clark Trail: A Potential Addition to the National Trails System: Summary of Findings and Alternatives.* Denver, Colorado: Bureau of Outdoor Recreation, Mid-Continent Region. Lewis & Clark College also holds the preliminary draft of this report.

Grant, Matthew. *Lewis and Clark: Western Trailblazers.* Gallery of Great Americans series. Illustrated by John Keely and Don Pulver. Mankato, Minnesota: Creative Education.

Holloway, David. *Lewis & Clark and the Crossing of North America.* New York: Saturday Review Press. Reprinted in Japan by Excalibur, 1974; reprinted in London by Purnell Book Services, 1974 (Saturday Review edition only in Lewis & Clark College Collection).

Lacy, Dan Mabry. *The Lewis and Clark Expedition, 1804–06: The Journey that Opened the American Northwest.* A Focus Book. New York: Watts. *

Thomson, Ruth. *Lewis and Clark.* Illustrated by Joan Dolbier. London: Macdonald and Co. *

1975

Allen, John Logan. *Passage Through the Garden: Lewis and Clark and the Image of the American Northwest.* Urbana, Chicago, London: University of Illinois Press. Reprinted by University Microfilms, 1986; reprinted in New York by Dover, 1991, under title *Lewis and Clark and the Image of the American Northwest.*

Appleman, Roy Edgar, comp. *Lewis and Clark: Historic Places Associated With Their Transcontinental Exploration (1804–06)*. The National Survey of Historic Sites and Buildings, vol. 13. Robert G. Ferris, ed. Washington: U.S. National Park Service. Reprinted by the Lewis & Clark Trail Heritage Foundation and the Jefferson National Expansion Historical Association, 1993, 2000.

Berthold, Mary Paddock. *Including Two Captains: A Later Look Westward*. Detroit: Harlo.

Blevins, Winfred. *Charbonneau: Man of Two Dreams*. Los Angeles: Nash Publishing. Fictional work based on the life of Jean Baptiste Charbonneau.

Bureau of Outdoor Recreation. *The Lewis and Clark Trail: A Proposed National Historic Trail*. Washington, D.C.: U.S. Department of the Interior.

1976
Bureau of Outdoor Recreation. *Final Environmental Impact Statement: The Lewis and Clark Trail, A Potential Addition to the National Trails System*. U.S. Department of the Interior.

Cutright, Paul Russell. *A History of the Lewis and Clark Journals*. Norman, Oklahoma: University of Oklahoma Press. Reprinted in a limited facsimile edition of 150 copies, Mansfield Centre, Connecticut, Martino Publishing, 2000. Documents the history of the Lewis and Clark manuscripts and their publication.

Muhly, Frank, comp. *Historical Signboards on the Lewis and Clark Trail*. [Philadelphia]: Frank Muhly.

Ruby, Robert H. and John A. Brown. *The Chinook Indians: Traders of the Lower Columbia River*. Norman, Oklahoma: University of Oklahoma Press. Includes a section on Lewis and Clark.

Seattle Art Museum. *Lewis and Clark's America: A Voyage of Discovery* and *A Contemporary Photo Essay*. Two vols. in slipcase. Seattle: Seattle Art Museum. Includes artwork and photographs of the Lewis and Clark trail.

Wainwright, Nicholas B. *Andalusia: Countryseat of the Craig Family and Nicholas Biddle and His Descendants*. Philadelphia, Historical Society of Pennsylvania.

Wheeler, Olin. *The Trail of Lewis and Clark, 1804–1904: A Story of the Great Exploration Across the Continent in 1804–06; with a Description of the Old Trail, Based Upon Actual Travel Over It, and of the Changes Found a Century Later*. Two vols. New York: AMS Press. A facsimile of the 1904 edition. See section 6a, 1904.

1977
Meyer, Roy W. *The Village Indians of the Upper Missouri: The Mandans, Hidatsas, and Arikaras*. Lincoln and London: University of Nebraska Press.

Muench, David and Dan Murphy. *Lewis and Clark: Voyage of Discovery*. Las Vegas: KC Publications. Reprinted by KC Publications in 1984.

Skold, Betty Westrom. *Sacagawea*. Minneapolis: Dillon Press.

Steffen, Jerome O. *William Clark: Jeffersonian Man on the Frontier*. Norman, Oklahoma: University of Oklahoma Press. Second printing by University of Oklahoma Press, 1977.

1978

Burt, Olive Woolley. *Sacajawea.* Visual Biography series. New York: Watts. *

Muench, David and Archie Satterfield. *Lewis & Clark Country.* Wilsonville, Oregon: Beautiful America Publishing Co.

Satterfield, Archie. *The Lewis & Clark Trail.* Illustrated by Marilyn Weber. Harrisburg, Pennsylvania: Stackpole Books. A guide to the Lewis and Clark Trail with an account of the expedition. Reprinted by Stackbole Books, 1981; reprinted in Lincoln, Nebraska, by iUniverse.com, Inc., 2000.

Stein, R. Conrad. *The Story of the Lewis and Clark Expedition.* Illustrated by Lou Aronson. Cornerstones of Freedom series. Chicago: Childrens Press. Reprinted by the Children's Press, 1997 (reprint not in Lewis & Clark College Collection). Children's book.

1979

Chuinard, Eldon G. *Only One Man Died: The Medical Aspects of the Lewis and Clark Expedition.* Western Frontiersmen series, 19. Glendale, California: The Arthur H. Clark Co. Reprinted by the Arthur H. Clark Co, 1980; reprinted in Fairfield, Washington, by Ye Galleon Press, 1987, 1997. The first full-length publication to deal exclusively with medical issues of the expedition. Lewis & Clark College has publisher's galley proofs and correspondence between Chuinard and Arthur H. Clark.

Clark, Ella E. and Margot Edmonds. *Sacagawea of the Lewis and Clark Expedition.* Berkeley, Los Angeles, London: University of California Press. Reprinted in paperback by the University of California Press, 1983.

Jassem, Kate. *Sacajawea, Wilderness Guide.* Illustrated by Jan Palmer. Mahwah, New Jersey: Troll Associates. Also reproduced in Braille in Richmond, Virginia, by Instructional Materials and Resource Center, Virginia Department for the Visually Handicapped, 1979; reprinted 2000, 2001.

Lee, Robert Edson. *The Dialogues of Lewis and Clark: A Narrative Poem.* Boulder, Colorado: Associated University Press. A poem based on the Lewis and Clark journals.

Madsen, Brigham D. *The Lemhi: Sacajawea's People.* Caldwell, Idaho: The Caxton Printers.

Waldo, Anna Lee. *Sacajawea.* New York: Avon. First edition, large-paper version in wraps; also issued in a smaller paperback version. Fictional work, loosely based on the life of Sacagawea. Reprinted in Dutch as *Sacajawea: Geluk en Tragiek in Het Leven Van Een Indiaanse,* Den Haag/Antwerpen: NBC, 1980, and again as *Sacajawea,* Amsterdam/Brussel: Elsevier, 1980.

1980

Gattia, Alarico, et al. *Lewis et Clark: l'Amérique d'est en ouest.* Series: La découverte du monde en bandes dessinées; no. 19. Paris: Bandes dessinées Larousse. *

Hawke, David Freeman. *Those Tremendous Mountains: The Story of the Lewis and Clark Expedition*. New York, London: W.W. Norton & Co. Reprinted as a Norton paperback in New York, 1985, 1998 (reprints not in Lewis & Clark College Collection).

Horne, Esther Burnett. *Oral Tradition of Sacajawea*. Wahpeton, North Dakota: Horne. *

Huffman, Marian. *Sacajawea*. Illustrated by Brian Bateman. Havre, Montana: Griggs Printing and Publishing.

Johnson, Ann Donegan. *The Value of Adventure: The Story of Sacagawea*. First edition. La Jolla, California: Value Communications. *

Viles, Don. *North America's Faked History of the Lewis & Clark Expedition*. Garibaldi, Oregon: North America Historiography. Reprinted in 1981. Originally published in serial form in the *Nehalem Bay (Oregon) Fishrapper*.

1981
Cutright, Paul Russell and Michael J. Brodhead. *Elliott Coues: Naturalist and Frontier Historian*. Urbana, Chicago, London: University of Illinois Press. Biography of Elliott Coues, one of the early editors of the Lewis and Clark journals. See section 5b.

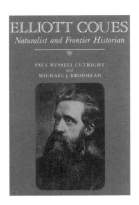

Hogrogian, Robert. *Sacajawea*. Illustrated by John Coutney. People to Remember series. [Hawthorne, New Jersey]: January Productions. *

Jackson, Donald. *Thomas Jefferson & the Stony Mountains: Exploring the West from Monticello*. Urbana, Chicago, London: University of Illinois Press. A study of Thomas Jefferson's vision of a transcontinental exploration, including a large section on Lewis and Clark.

Missouri Historical Society. Division of Library and Archives. *The Lewis and Clark Expedition: A Guide to the Holdings in the Division of Library and Archives of the Missouri Historical Society*. St. Louis, Missouri: The Society. *

Raymond, James. *Lewis & Clark: Northwest Glory*. Wayne, Pennsylvania: Miles Standish Press, Dell Publishing.

Rogers, Ann. *Lewis and Clark in Missouri*. St. Louis: Meredco. Reprinted in an expanded edition by Meredco, 1993.

1983
Copeland, Peter F. *The Lewis and Clark Expedition Coloring Book*. New York: Dover Publications, Inc.

Foley, William E. and C. David Rice. *The First Chouteaus: River Barons of Early St. Louis*. Urbana and Chicago: University of Illinois Press. Includes a section on Lewis and Clark's interactions with the Chouteaus.

Halsey, Cheryll and Robert R. Beale. *Lewis and Clark and the Shahaptian Speaking Americans*. Limited edition of one thousand copies. Fairfield, Washington: Ye Galleon Press.

Moulton, Gary E., ed. *The Journals of the Lewis and Clark Expedition.* 13 vols. Lincoln: University of Nebraska Press, 1983–2001. Vol. 1, Atlas of the Lewis & Clark Expedition; vol. 2, August 30, 1803–August 24, 1804; vol. 3, August 25, 1803–April 6, 1805; vol. 4, April 7–July 27, 1805; vol. 5, July 28–November 1, 1805; vol. 6, November 2, 1805–March 22, 1806; vol. 7, March 23–June 9, 1806; vol. 8, June 10–September 26, 1806; vol. 9, the Journals of John Ordway, May 14, 1804–September 23, 1806, and Charles Floyd, May 14–August 18, 1804; vol. 10, the Journal of Patrick Gass, May 14, 1804–September 23, 1806; vol. 11, the Journals of Joseph Whitehouse, May 14, 1804–April 2, 1806; vol. 12, Herbarium of the Lewis & Clark Expedition; vol. 13, Comprehensive Index. This edition of the Lewis & Clark journals incorporates documents that had previously been published separately. The set is heavily annotated. Atlas reprinted by University of Nebraska Press, 1999.

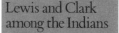
Moulton, Gary E., ed.
The Journals of the Lewis and Clark Expedition.

1984
Ronda, James P. *Lewis and Clark among the Indians.* Lincoln, Nebraska: University of Nebraska Press. Reprinted by the University of Nebraska Press, 1985, 1988.

Thom, James Alexander. *From Sea to Shining Sea.* New York: Villard Books, 1984. Also published in New York by Ballantine Books, 1984.

Willingham, William F. and Leonoor Swets Ingraham, eds. *Enlightenment Science in the Pacific Northwest: The Lewis and Clark Expedition.* Lewis & Clark College: Portland, Oregon. A one-day symposium held on February 18, 1984, at Lewis and Clark College. Includes topical essays on Lewis and Clark and a bibliography of Lewis and Clark publications compiled by Eldon Chuinard.

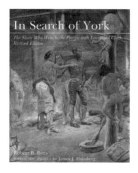

1985
Betts, Robert B. *In Search of York: The Slave Who Went to the Pacific with Lewis and Clark.* Boulder: Colorado Associated University Press. Reprinted with new information by University Press of Colorado and the Lewis and Clark Trail Heritage Foundation, 2001. The only full-length academic work to deal with the life of York.

Bohner, Charles. *Bold Journey: West with Lewis and Clark*. Boston: Houghton Mifflin Co. Reprinted in German under the title *Drei Schiffe westwärts*. Edition: 1. Aufl. Würzburg: Arena, 1989; reprinted in the Houghton Mifflin social studies trade book set and in large print, 1991; reprinted in Braille in San Rafael, California, by Transcribing Mariners, 1991 (first edition only in Lewis & Clark College Collection).

McGrath, Patrick. *The Lewis and Clark Expedition*. Turning Points in American History. Morristown, New Jersey: Silver Burdett Co. Children's book.

Sabin, Francene. *Lewis and Clark*. Illustrated by John Lawn. Mahwah, New Jersey: Troll Associates. Reproduced in Braille in Visalia, California, Sequoia Transcribers, Specialists in Braille, and in Richmond, Virginia, Instructional Materials and Resource Center, Virginia Department for the Visually Handicapped, 1985 (Braille copies not in Lewis & Clark College Collection).

1986
Bergantino, Robert N. *Atlas of the Lewis and Clark Expedition from the Yellowstone River to the Summit of Lolo Pass, 1805–1806.* Butte, Montana: R. N. Bergantino.*

Dattilio, Daniel J. *Fort Clatsop, The Story Behind the Scenery*. Edited by Russell D. Butcher. Las Vegas: KC Publications. Reprinted 1993 (reprint not in Lewis & Clark College Collection).

O'Dell, Scott. *Streams to the River, River to the Sea: A Novel of Sacagawea*. Boston: Houghton Mifflin Co. Reprinted in Dutch under the title *Wild Water*. Series: Totem: avontuur. uit het Engels vertaald door Louis Thijssen; omslagillustratie Annemarie van Haeringen. Tielt: Lannoo, 1988. Reprinted in New York by Ballantine Books, 1988; reprinted in four vols., Braille, Milwaukee, Wisconsin, Volunteer Services for the Visually Hadicapped, 1988; reprinted in Portuguese under the title *Ribeiros para o rio, rio para o mar*, Caminho Jovens series, 12; translated by António Pescada, Lisboa: Caminho, 1989; reprinted in large print in Boston by G.K. Hall, 1989; reprinted in German under the title *Vogelmädchen*, edition: Ungekürzte Ausg. München: Deutscher Taschenbuch Verlag, 1992. Lewis & Clark College Collection includes first edition.

Olmsted, Gerald W. *Fielding's Lewis and Clark Trail*. New York: Fielding Travel Books.

Reid, Russell. *Sakakawea: The Bird Woman*. Bismarck, North Dakota: State Historical Society of North Dakota.

Saindon, Bob. *The Boy from Locust Hill: A Childhood Biography of Meriwether Lewis*. Helena, Montana: Bob Saindon.

1987
Blumberg, Rhoda. *The Incredible Journey of Lewis and Clark*. New York: Lothrop, Lee & Shepard Books. Reproduced in Braille, Kansas City, Missouri, Beth Shalom Sisterhood Braille Committee, 1987; reprinted in New York by Scholastic, 1993; reprinted in New York by Beech Tree, 1995 (reprints not in Lewis & Clark College Collection).

Duncan, Dayton. *Out West: An American Journey.* New York: Viking. Reprinted in New York by Penguin Books, 1988; reprinted by University of Nebraska Press, 2000.

Gleiter, Jan, and Kathleen Thompson. *Sacagawea.* Illustrated by Yoshi Miyake. Raintree Stories series. Milwaukee: Raintree Children's Books. Reprinted in Chinese under the title *Sakajiawei: Mei xi tan xian nü xiang dao.* Taibei Shi: Lu qiao wen hua shi ye you xian gong si, 1991; reprinted in Austin, Texas, by Raintree Steck-Vaughn, 1991, 1995. *

Jackson, Donald. *Among the Sleeping Giants: Occasional Pieces on Lewis and Clark.* Foreword by Savoie Lottinville. Urbana and Chicago: University of Illinois Press.

1988
Anderson, Irving W. *A Charbonneau Family Portrait: Biographical Sketches of Sacagawea, Jean Baptiste, and Toussaint Charbonneau.* Fort Clatsop Historical Association: National Memorial, National Park Service, U.S. Department of the Interior. Revised edition printed in 1992.

Bramstedt, Christine Turpin. *Ballad of Seaman: Dog of the Lewis and Clark Expedition.* Alton, Illinois: Stimark Publications. *

Brown, Marion Marsh. *Sacagawea: Indian Interpreter to Lewis and Clark.* Chicago: Childrens Press.

Hagood, J. Hurley and Roberta Roland Hagood. *George Shannon (peg-leg): A Story of Courage Personified.* Hannibal, Missouri: The Author. *

Lavender, David. *The Way to the Western Sea: Lewis and Clark Across the Continent.* New York: Harper & Row. Reprinted as an Anchor paperback in the same year and in 1990; reprinted by University of Nebraska Press, 2001.

Petersen, David and Mark Coburn. *Meriwether Lewis and William Clark: Soldiers, Explorers, and Partners in History.* People of Distinction Biographies series. Chicago: Childrens Press. Errata slip included. *

Zadra, Dan. *Lewis and Clark: Western Trailblazers.* Illustrated by John Keely and Don Pulver. We the People series. Mankato, Minnesota: Creative Education. *

1989
Baker, Troy. *Plants of Fort Clatsop, From the Journals of Lewis & Clark.* Astoria, Oregon: Fort Clatsop Historical Association.

Bergon, Frank, ed. *The Journals of Lewis and Clark.* Penguin Nature Library. New York: Viking. A condensed version of Lewis and Clark's journals, focusing on entries relating to natural history. Reprinted in New York by Penguin Books, 1995; reprinted under the title *Pathfinders of the American West: The Journals of Lewis & Clark* in London by the Folio Society, 2000 (reprint by the Folio Society not in Lewis & Clark College Collection).

Bryant, Martha F. *Sacajawea: A Native American Heroine.* Edited by Hap Gilliland, illustrated by Heather Sargent. Billings, Montana: Council for Indian Education. *

Charbonneau, Louis. *Trail: The Story of the Lewis & Clark Expedition.* New York: Doubleday. Reprinted in a condensed version by the Reader's Digest Association, 1989.

Fisher, Ronald K. *West to the Pacific: The Story of the Lewis and Clark Expedition.* Edited by Merle Wells. Coeur d'Alène, Idaho: Alpha Omega.

Hoyle, Robert J. *Lewis and Clark Routes Between the Bitterroot Valley and the Columbia River.* Lewiston, Idaho: Robert J. Hoyle.

McCorkle, Jack. *Sacajawea: The Great Divide.* Cleveland, Ohio: Modern Curriculum Press. *

Rowland, Della. *The Story of Sacajawea, Guide to Lewis and Clark.* Illustrated by Richard Leonard. A Dell Yearling Biography. New York: Dell Publishing Co. Reproduced in Braille, Springfield, Illinois, by Illinois Instructional Materials Center, 1989; reprinted as part of the Famous Lives series in Milwaukee, Wisconsin, by Gareth Stevens, 1995; reprinted by Houghton Mifflin in Boston, 1997; reprinted in a large-print edition by the American Printing House for the Blind, 1997.

1990
Johnson, Mabel. *The Work-a-Day Detail of the Lewis and Clark Expedition.* Boring, Oregon: Quality Paperbacks.

Kiesling, Sanna Porte. *The Lewis and Clark Expedition.* Illustrated by Dan White. Highlights from American History. Helena, Montana: Twodot and Falcon Press. *

Swayne, Zoa L. *Do Them No Harm! An Interpretation of the Lewis and Clark Expedition Among the Nez Perce Indians.* Edited by Carol Ann Goodrich Bates. Orofino, Idaho: Legacy House.

Upton, Harriet. *Trailblazers.* Illustrated by Luciano Lazzarino and edited by Arlene C. Rourke. Vero Beach, Florida: Rourke Publications. Describes the exploration of the American West during the early 1800s, and includes information relating to Lewis and Clark, John Colter, Joe Walker, and Thomas Nuttall. *

1991
Cavan, Seamus. *Lewis and Clark and the Route to the Pacific.* World Explorers series. New York: Chelsea House Publishers.

Fitz-Gerald, Christine Maloney. *Meriwether Lewis and William Clark.* The World's Great Explorers series. Chicago: Childrens Press. *

Moulton, Gary E. *American Encounters: Lewis and Clark, the People, and the Land.* Lincoln, Nebraska: Center for Great Plains Studies, University of Nebraska.

1992
Ingoglia, Gina. *Sacajawea and the Journey to the Pacific: A Historical Novel.* Illustrated by Charles Shaw. Disney's American Frontier series, no. 7. New York: Disney Press.

Otfinoski, Steven. *Lewis and Clark: Leading America West.* New York: Fawcett Columbine. *

Porter, Donald Clayton. *Hawk's Journey.* Bantam edition. White Indian series, book 23. New York: Bantam Books.

Stetoff, Rebecca. *Lewis and Clark.* Junior World Biographies. Philadelphia: Chelsea House Publishers.

1993

Biddle, Nicholas and Paul Allen, eds. *The Journals of the Expedition Under the Command of Capts. Lewis and Clark to the Sources of the Missouri, Thence Across the Rocky Mountains and Down the River Columbia to the Pacific Ocean, Performed During the Years 1804–5–6 by Order of the Government of the United States.* Edited by Nicholas Biddle, with an introduction by June Namias and foreword by John Bakeless. Two vols. Norwalk, Connecticut: The Easton Press. Collectors' edition. Republished with slipcases the same year by the Heritage Press, Norwalk, Connecticut.

Burns, Ron. *The Mysterious Death of Meriwether Lewis: A Novel.* New York: St. Martins Press.

Christian, Mary Blount. *Who'd Believe John Colter?* Illustrated by Laszlo Kubinyi. First edition. New York: Macmillan Publishing Company; Toronto: Maxwell Macmillan Canada; New York: Maxwell Macmillan International.

Coues, Elliott. *A Letter by Elliott Coues: Concerning the Plotting of Lewis & Clark's Courses Along the Missouri River and of Coues' Hope that the Journals Would Soon Be Published in Full: Addressed to Wendell Phillips Garrison, Literary Editor of "The Nation," April 11, 1895.* Limited edition of two hundred copies. Seattle: Farmhouse Press.

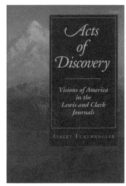

Furtwangler, Albert. *Acts of Discovery: Visions of America in the Lewis and Clark Journals.* Urbana and Chicago: University of Illinois Press. Reprinted by University of Illinois Press, 1999. Essays about Lewis and Clark.

Howard, Ella Mae. *Lewis and Clark Exploration of Central Montana: Marias River to the Gates of the Mountains.* Illustrations by Tom English and Robert Moritz, maps by Robert Bergantino, cover by Robert Orduna. Great Falls, Montana: Lewis and Clark Interpretive Association. Multiple later printings (Lewis & Clark College has fourth printing, 1998).

McBeth, Kate. *The Nez Perces Since Lewis and Clark.* Introduction by Peter Iverson and Elizabeth James. Moscow, Idaho: University of Idaho Press.

Noonan, Jon. *Lewis and Clark.* Illustrated by Yoshi Miyake. New York: Crestwood House; Toronto: Maxwell Macmillan Canada; New York: Maxwell Macmillan International.

Robinson, Sheila C. *Along the Lewis & Clark Trail in North Dakota.* Coleharbor, North Dakota: S. Robinson. Includes reprints of excerpts taken from several works. *

Roop, Peter and Connie Roop. *Off the Map: The Journals of Lewis and Clark.* Illustrated by Tim Tanner. New York: Walker and Co. A compilation of excerpts from the journals of Lewis and Clark. *

1994

Carlson, Nolan. *Lewis & Clark and Davey Hutchins.* Illustrated by Becky Bryant. Hillsboro, Kansas: Hearth Publishers. A novel about the Lewis and Clark Expedition.

Carter, W. Hodding. *Westward Whoa: In the Wake of Lewis and Clark*. New York: Simon & Schuster.

Chandler, David Leon. *The Jefferson Conspiracies: A President's Role in the Assassination of Meriwether Lewis*. New York: William Morrow and Co.

Fanselow, Julie. *The Traveler's Guide to the Lewis & Clark Trail*. Helena, Montana: Falcon Press. Revised edition printed by Falcon Press, 1998.

Hatch, Lynda. *Lewis and Clark*. Illustrated by Ted Warren. Pathways of America series, Carthage, Illinois: Good Apple. A social studies activity book for grades 4–8. *

Knox, Bob. *Dave and Jane's Adventures with Lewis and Clark*. New York: Rizzoli International Publications. Children's book, with selected excerpts from the journals of Lewis and Clark.

Kroll, Steven. *Lewis and Clark: Explorers of the American West*. Illustrated by Richard Williams. New York: Holiday House.

Raphael, Elaine, and Don Bolognese. *Sacajawea: The Journey West*. Drawing America series, "Cartwheel Books." New York: Scholastic.

Steber, Rick. *Lewis and Clark*. Illustrated by Don Gray. Traveling Companion series, vol. 4. Prineville, Oregon: Bonanza.

Twist, Clint. *Lewis and Clark: Exploring North America*. Beyond the Horizons series. Austin: Raintree Steck-Vaughn. Reprinted in London by Evans, 1994; reprinted in Braille, San Rafael, California, Transcribing Mariners, 1994 (Lewis & Clark College has first edition).

1995
Benson, Guy Meriwether, William R. Irwin, and Heather Moore. *Exploring the West from Monticello: A Perspective in Maps from Columbus to Lewis and Clark*. Charlottesville: University of Virginia Library. The Catalog of an Exhibition of Maps and Navigational Instruments, University of Virginia, July 10 to September 26, 1995.

Botkin, Daniel B. *Our Natural History: The Lessons of Lewis and Clark*. New York: G. P. Putnam's Sons. Reprinted as a Perigree edition, New York, by Berkley Publishing Group, 1996.

Hamilton, Irene Nakai. *Sacajawea: Translator and Guide*. Illustrated by Troy Anderson. Beginning Biographies series. Morristown, New Jersey: Modern Curriculum Press. Reprinted in Spanish under title *Sacajawea: Traductora y Guía*. Morristown, New Jersey: Modern Curriculum Press, 1995. *

Howard, Harold P., et al. *Pocahontas, Sacajawea, Sarah Winnemucca of the Northern Paiutes*. New York: MJF Books.

Kessler, Dorothy Simmons. *Lewis & Clark: The Fincastle Connection*. Fincastle, Virginia: Historic Fincastle Inc. *

Strong, Emory and Ruth Strong. *Seeking Western Waters: The Lewis and Clark Trail from the Rockies to the Pacific.* Edited by Herbert K. Beals. Portland: Oregon Historical Society Press. A compilation of journal entries during Lewis and Clark's time in the Columbia River Basin, together with photographs and text. Lewis & Clark College Collection also has typescript review copy.

Young, Judith A. *The Story of George Shannon, the Youngest Member of the Lewis and Clark Expedition.* Bothell, Washington: Education Resource Network. *

1996

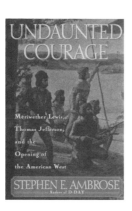

Ambrose, Stephen E. *Undaunted Courage: Meriwether Lewis, Thomas Jefferson, and the Opening of the American West.* New York: Simon & Schuster. Also reprinted in a new edition that includes two new chapters on Lewis's interaction with Native Americans. Simon & Schuster, Touchstone, 1997.

Hall, Eleanor J. *The Lewis and Clark Expedition.* World History series. San Diego: Lucent Books. *

Hedstrom, Deborah. *From East to West with Lewis & Clark.* Illustrated by Sergio Martinez. My American Journey series. Sisters, Oregon: Questar. *

Lewis & Clark. Kids Discover series, vol. 6, no. 9. [New York]: Kids Discover. *

Kessler, Donna J. *The Making of Sacagawea: A Euro-American Legend.* Tuscaloosa: University of Alabama Press.

Nell, Donald F. and John E. Taylor. *Lewis and Clark in the Three Rivers Valleys, Montana, 1805–1806: From the Original Journals of the Lewis and Clark Expedition.* Tucson, Arizona: The Patrice Press and Bozeman, Montana: Headwaters Chapter, Lewis and Clark Trail Heritage Foundation. A compilation of the Lewis and Clark journal entries from the Three Rivers Valleys, Montana, together with annotations, maps, and photographs.

Wood, Gertrude. *Lewis and Clark in Cass County.* [Nebraska]: G. Wood. *

1997

Bowen, Andy Russell. *The Back of Beyond: A Story About Lewis and Clark.* Illustrated by Ralph L. Ramstad. A Carolrhoda Creative Minds book. Minneapolis: Carolrhoda Books. Reprinted by Carolrhoda Books, 1998.

Colter-Frick, L. R. *Courageous Colter and Companions.* Washington, Missouri: L. R. Colter-Frick.

Duncan, Dayton and Ken Burns. *Lewis & Clark: The Journey of the Corps of Discovery: An Illustrated History.* New York: Alfred A. Knopf. Companion volume to the PBS television series *Lewis & Clark: the Journey of the Corps of Discovery.* Reprinted in London by Pimlico, 1998; reprinted in paperback in New York by Knopf, 1999 (reprints not in Lewis & Clark College Collection).

Fenlason, Ed and Mel Gemmill. *The Hills By the Headwaters: From the Moccasin Tracks of Lewis & Clark & Colter to the Wagon Tracks of the Homesteaders & Ranchers to the Steel Tracks of the Jawborne Railroad; 1800s History Around the Horseshoe Hills of Gallatin County, Montana.* Belgrade, Montana: E and M Books.

Lourie, Peter. *In the Path of Lewis and Clark: Traveling the Missouri*. Parsippany, New Jersey: Silver Burdett Press. Description of the author's trip up the Missouri River with a comparison to the Lewis and Clark Expedition.

MacGregor, Carol Lynn, ed. *The Journals of Patrick Gass: Member of the Lewis and Clark Expedition*. Missoula, Montana: Mountain Press Publishing Co. See Chap. 3.

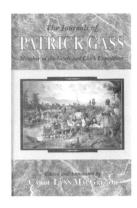

Sachatello-Sawyer, Bonnie. *Lewis and Clark*. New York: Scholastic Professional Books. Children's curriculum guide.

Sanford, William R., and Carl R. Green. *Sacagawea: Native American Hero*. Legendary Heroes of the Wild West series. Springfield, New Jersey: Enslow Publishers.

Scheuerman, Richard D. and Arthur Ellis, eds. *The Expeditions of Lewis & Clark and Zebulon Pike: North American Journeys of Discovery*. Illustrated by James LeGette. Madison, Wisconsin: Demco. A selection of primary source materials and study guides. *

Shaughnessy, Diane and Jack Carpenter. *Sacajawea, Shoshone Trailblazer*. Famous Native Americans series. New York: PowerKids Press.

St. George, Judith. *Sacagawea*. New York: Putnam. *

Thomasma, Kenneth. *The Truth About Sacajawea*. Illustrated by Agnes Vincent Talbot. Jackson, Wyoming: Grandview Publishing Co.

Van Steenwyk, Elizabeth. *My Name is York*. Illustrated by Bill Farnsworth. Flagstaff, Arizona: Rising Moon/Books for Young Readers from Northland Publishing. Children's book.

White, Alana J. *Sacagawea: Westward with Lewis and Clark*. Native American Biographies series. Springfield, New Jersey: Enslow Publishers.

1998
Ambrose, Stephen E. *An Epic American Exploration: The Friendship of Lewis and Clark*. [Minneapolis]: Associates of the James Ford Bell Library.

——. *Lewis & Clark: Voyage of Discovery*. Photographs by Sam Abell. Washington, D.C.: National Geographic Society.

Barth, Gunther Paul, ed. *The Lewis and Clark Expedition: Selections From the Journals, Arranged by Topic*. The Bedford Series in History and Culture. Boston: Bedford Books.

Dear, Elizabeth A. and Charles M. Russell. *The Grand Expedition of Lewis & Clark as Seen by C. M. Russell*. Great Falls, Montana: C. M. Russell Museum. Second edition printed by C. M. Russell Museum, 2000. *

Discovery Writers and Jeanne O'Neill, et al. *Lewis & Clark in the Bitterroot*. Stevensville, Montana: Stoneydale Press.

Fifer, Barbara, Vicky Soderberg, and Joseph Mussulman. *Along the Trail with Lewis and Clark*. Great Falls, Montana: Montana Magazine. Reprinted 2000. New edition 2001, Farcountry Press.

Fradin, Dennis B. *Sacagawea: The Journey to the West*. Illustrated by Nora Koerber. Remarkable Children series. Parsippany, New Jersey: Silver Press.

Gustafson, R. W. *The Dog Who Helped Explore America*. Conrad, Montana: R. W. Gustafson. Children's story of the Lewis and Clark Expedition.

Hull, Bette Meine. *Lewis and Clark in Beaverhead County, Montana*. Dillon, Montana: Tourism and Recreation Department of Western Montana College of the University of Montana. *

Lewis and Clark Trail Heritage Foundation, Inc. *An American Legacy: The Lewis and Clark Expedition: Curriculum and Resource Guide for Middle and Junior High Schools (grades 5–9)*. Great Falls, Montana: Lewis and Clark Trail Heritage Foundation, Inc. *

Morley, Jacqueline. *Across America: The Story of Lewis & Clark*. Illustrated by David Antram. London and New York: Franklin Watts.

Peterson, Donald A. *Early Pictures of the Falls: A Lewis and Clark Portrait In Time*. Great Falls, Montana: Portage Route Chapter, Lewis and Clark Trail Heritage Foundation. Includes photos courtesy of Cascade County Historical Society, Montana Historical Society, and Don Nell. Journal entries reprinted from Moulton's *Journals of Lewis and Clark*.

Rogers, Ken. *Sakakawea and the Fur Traders*. Bismarck, North Dakota: Bismarck Tribune. *

Ronda, James P., ed. *Voyages of Discovery: Essays on the Lewis and Clark Expedition*. Helena, Montana: Montana Historical Society Press.

Schmidt, Thomas. *The Lewis & Clark Trail*. Washington, D.C.: National Geographic Society. National Geographic guidebook.

Streissguth, Thomas. *Lewis and Clark: Explorers of the Northwest*. Historical American Biographies series. Springfield, New Jersey: Enslow Publishers.

Thorp, Daniel B. *Lewis & Clark: An American Journey*. New York: MetroBooks.

Warner, Doten. *Following the Lewis and Clark Trail: A Vacation Guide for Campers*. Lutz, Florida: Perseverance Publishers.

Welden, Amelie and Jerry McCann. *Girls Who Rocked the World: Heroines from Sacajawea to Sheryl Swoopes*. Milwaukee, Wisconsin: Gareth Stevens. *

1999
Botkin, Daniel B. *Passage of Discovery. The American Rivers Guide to the Missouri River of Lewis and Clark*. New York: Perigree Books.

Discovery Writers and Jean Clary et al. *Lewis & Clark on the Upper Missouri*. Stevensville, Montana: Stoneydale Press.

Edwards, Judith. *Lewis and Clark's Journey of Discovery in American History*. Springfield, New Jersey: Enslow Publishers.

Gale, Kira. *Lewis & Clark at Council Bluff: A Guide to Lewis & Clark in the Omaha-Council Bluffs Area*. Omaha, Nebraska: Omaha History Center & Coffee Lounge. *

Haney, Rich. *Sacajawea: Her True Story*. R. Haney. Issued in hardcover and softcover.

Hastings, Patricia B. *Quilting the Journeys of Lewis & Clark: A Pattern Book for Making "Lewis & Clark in the Bitterroot."* Stevensville, Montana: Stoneydale Press. First in a series.

Highsmith Press. *The Journey of Lewis and Clark: A Teacher's Resource Booklet*. Fort Atkinson, Wisconsin: Highsmith. Teacher's resource booklet contains lesson plans and reproducible student-activity assignments. *

Hosmer, James K., ed. *Gass's Journal of the Lewis and Clark Expedition: Reprinted from the Edition of 1811, with Facsimiles of the Original Title page and the Five Original Illustrations, a Reproduction of a Rare Portrait of Gass, and a Map of the Lewis and Clark Route*. Five-hundred-copy limited edition facsimile of the 1904 printing (3.12). Mansfield Centre, Connecticut: Lone Wolf Press.

Houk, Rose. *The Lewis & Clark Expedition*. Westward Expansion series, no. 1. St. Louis, Missouri: Jefferson National Parks Association. *

Karwoski, Gail Langer. *Seaman: The Dog Who Explored the West With Lewis & Clark*. Illustrated by James Watling. Atlanta: Peachtree Publishers.

Moeller, Bill and Jan Moeller. *Lewis & Clark: A Photographic Journey*. Missoula, Montana: Mountain Press.

Reveal, James L., Gary E. Moulton, and Alfred E. Schuyler. *The Lewis and Clark Collections of Vascular Plants: Names, Types, and Comments*. Philadelphia: Academy of Natural Sciences of Philadelphia. First printed in the *Proceedings of the Academy of Natural Sciences of Philadelphia* 149 (January 29, 1999): 1–64.

Roop, Peter and Connie Roop. *Girl of the Shining Mountains: Sacagawea's Story*. New York: Hyperion Books for Children.

Schmidt, Thomas and Jeremy Schmidt. *The Saga of Lewis & Clark: Into the Uncharted West*. A Tehabi Book. New York: DK Publishers.

Smith, Roland. *The Captain's Dog: My Journey with the Lewis and Clark Tribe*. San Diego, New York, London: Gulliver Books, Harcourt Brace & Co. Children's book. Reprinted as a paperback edition by Harcourt Brace, 2000 (reprint not in Lewis & Clark College Collection).

Stevens, Sydney. *D is for Discovery: The A-B-C's of the Lewis & Clark Expedition's Winter on the Pacific Coast, 1805–1806*. Illustrated by Pat Fagerland. Oysterville, Washington: The Author. *

Sullivan, George. *Lewis and Clark*. New York: Scholastic Reference. Reprinted 2000.

Torrance, Harold. *Lewis and Clark: Across a Vast Land*. Carlisle, Massachusetts: Discovery Enterprises. A historical play. *

Walcheck, Kenneth C. *The Lewis & Clark Expedition: Montana's First Bird Inventory through the Eyes of Lewis and Clark*. Great Falls, Montana: Lewis and Clark Interpretative Association, Inc. *

Adler, David A. *A Picture Book of Sacagawea.* Illustrated by Dan Brown. New York: Scholastic; New York: Holiday House.

Bergen, Lara Rice. *The Travels of Lewis & Clark.* Illustrated by Patrick O'Brien. Explorers & Exploration series. Austin, Texas: Steadwell Books. *

Bruchac, Joseph. *Sacajawea: The Story of Bird Woman and the Lewis and Clark Expedition.* San Diego: Silver Whistle.

Carter, Edward C., ed. *Three Journals of the Lewis & Clark Expedition, 1804–1806.* Philadelphia: American Philosophical Society. A facsimile of original expedition journals from the collections of the American Philosophical Society.

Cleary, Rita. *River Walk: A Frontier Story.* Five Star Standard Print Western series. Unity, Maine: Five Star; Bath: Chivers. Reprinted in New York by Leisure Books, 2001.

The Double Eagle Guide to Camping Along the Lewis and Clark Trail. Two vols. A Double Eagle guide. Billings, Montana: Discovery Publishing. A trail guide featuring descriptions of camping areas along the trail. *

Evenson, Teri, Lauren Lesmeister, and Jeffrey W. Evenson. *The Lewis & Clark Cookbook: With Contemporary Recipes.* Bismarck, North Dakota: Whisper'n Waters. Includes quotations from the Lewis and Clark journals and artwork by Bodmer, Clymer, Russell, and Peale. Reprinted by Whisper'n Waters, 2001. *

Fernandez, Vivian. *The Golden Dollar: Legend of Sacagawea.* Illustrated by Mark McIntyre and Allen Davis. Lake Mary, Florida: B Plus Marketing. Reprinted 2002. *

Fifer, Barbara. *Going Along with Lewis & Clark.* Helena, Montana: Montana Magazine.

Foucrier, Annick and Philippe Jacquin. *Meriwether Lewis & William Clark: La Traversée d'un Continent, 1803–1806.* Biographies Américaines series. Paris: M. Houdiard. *

Gunderson, Mary. *Cooking on the Lewis and Clark Expedition: Exploring History through Simple Recipes.* Mankato, Minnesota: Blue Earth Books.

Gustafson, R. W. *York: The Slave Who Helped Explore America.* Conrad, Montana: R. W. Gustafson.

Haan, Wanda. *Exploring with Lewis and Clark.* Skokie, Illinois: Rand McNally. *

Hastings, Patricia B. *Quilting the Journeys of Lewis & Clark: A Pattern Book for Making "Lewis & Clark on the Upper Missouri."* Stevensville, Montana: Stoneydale Press. Second in a series.

Hauser, David. *The Only True America: Following the Trail of Lewis and Clark.* San Jose, California: Writer's Showcase.

Herbert, Janis. *Lewis and Clark for Kids: Their Journey of Discovery with 21 Activities.* Chicago: Chicago Review Press.

Hunsaker, Joyce Badgley. *Sacagawea: Beyond the Shining Mountains with Lewis and Clark*. Boise, Idaho: Tamarack Books.

Jacob, J. G. *The Life and Times of Patrick Gass: Now Sole Survivor of the Overland Expedition to the Pacific, Under Lewis and Clark, in 1804–5–6; also, a Soldier in the War with Great Britain, from 1812 to 1815, and a Participant in the Battle of Lundy's Lane. Together with Gass' Journal of the Expedition Condensed; and Sketches of Some Events Occurring During the Last Century in the Upper Ohio Country, Biographies, Reminiscences, etc.* Mansfield Centre, Connecticut: Lone Wolf Press. Facsimile reprint of the 1859 edition. See section 3.11.

Jenkinson, Clay S. *The Character of Meriwether Lewis: Completely Metamorphosed in the American West*. Reno, Nevada: Marmarth Press.

Jones, Landon Y., ed. *The Essential Lewis and Clark*. New York: Harper Collins, Ecco Press. A brief abridgement of the Lewis and Clark journals.

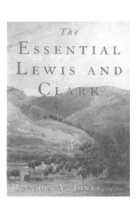

Kozar, Richard. *Lewis and Clark*. Explorers of the Louisiana Purchase series. Philadelphia: Chelsea House Publishers.

Lasky, Kathryn. *The Journal of Augustus Pelletier: The Lewis and Clark Expedition*. My Name is America series. New York: Scholastic. Children's book.

Leininger, Tracy M. *The Land Beyond the Setting Sun: The Story of Sacagewea*. Illustrated by Kelly Pulley and Lisa Reed. The Beautiful Girlhood Collection. San Antonio, Texas: His Seasons. Children's book.

Long, Benjamin. *Backtracking by Foot, Canoe, and Subaru Along the Lewis and Clark Trail*. Seattle: Sasquatch Books. *

Montgomery, M. R. *Jefferson and The Gun-Men: How the West Was Almost Lost*. New York: Crown and Three Rivers Press.

Patzman, Barbara J. *Would You Have Gone With Lewis and Clark? The Story of the Corps of Discovery for Young People*. Bismarck, North Dakota: United Printing and Mailing. *

Plamondon, Martin. *Lewis and Clark Trail Maps, A Cartographic Reconstruction*. Pullman, Washington: Washington State University Press. Maps of Lewis and Clark overlaid with modern maps. Vol. 2 published in 2001.

Poole, Kristin. *After Lewis and Clark: Explorer Artists and the American West*. Ketchum, Idaho: Sun Valley Center for the Arts. Exhibition at Ketchum, Idaho, July 14–September 29, 2000, and Boise Art Museum (Boise, Idaho), October 2, 2000–February 11, 2001. *

Rodger, Tod. *Bicycle Guide to the Lewis & Clark Trail*. Harvard, Massachusetts: Deerfoot Publications. *

Rogers, Ken. *Lewis & Clark: Art of the Upper Missouri*. Bismarck, North Dakota: The Tribune. *

Ronda, James P. *Jefferson's West: A Journey with Lewis and Clark.* [Charlottesville, Virginia]: Thomas Jefferson Foundation.

Sierra Club. *Wild America: Protecting the Lands of Lewis & Clark.* San Francisco, California: Sierra Club. *

Thom, James Alexander. *Sign-talker: The Adventure of George Drouillard on the Lewis and Clark Expedition: A Novel.* New York: Ballantine Books. A narrative account of the Lewis and Clark expedition from the perspective of George Drouillard, based on original documents.

Thomas, George. *Lewis and Clark Trail—The Photo Journal: Up the Missouri, Down the Columbia and Back.* Missoula, Montana: Pictorial Histories Publishers.

Watson, Kathy and Stuart Watson. *The Lewis & Clark Expedition: A Traveler's Companion for Oregon and Washington.* [Oregon]: Kathy and Stuart Watson. *

2001

Benge, Janet and Geoff Benge. *Meriwether Lewis: Off the Edge of the Map.* Heroes of History series. Lynnwood, Washington: Emerald Books.

Bowen, Peter. *Cruzatte and Maria: A Gabriel Du Pré Mystery.* New York: St. Martin's Minotaur.

Devillier, Christy. *Lewis and Clark.* Edina, Buddy Books, First Biographies series. Minnesota: Abdo Publishers.

Eyerly, Pete, Keith Haupt, and Joe Haug. *From the Eye of the Eagle: A Contemporary Aerial Perspective of Lewis & Clark's Historic Path Across America.* Community Communications. *

Faber, Harold. *Lewis and Clark.* New York: Benchmark Books/Marshall Cavendish. Copyright states 2002 as date of publication, Library of Congress lists 2001.

Fazio, James R. *Across the Snowy Ranges: The Lewis and Clark Expedition in Idaho and Western Montana.* Photographs by Mike Venso, cartography by Steve F. Russell. Bicentennial Commemorative Edition. Moscow, Idaho: Woodland Press.

Graetz, Rick, Susie Beaulaurier Graetz, and Larry Mayer. *Lewis & Clark's Montana Trail.* Montana series, no. 8. Helena, Montana: Northern Rockies Publishing. *

Hargrove, Julia and Gary Mohrman. *Fort Clatsop: The Journey of Lewis and Clark.* Historic Monuments series. Carthage, Illinois: Teaching & Learning Co.

Hastings, Patricia B. *Quilting the Journeys of Lewis & Clark: A Pattern Book for Making "Lewis & Clark to the Pacific."* Third in a series. Stevensville, Montana: Stoneydale Press.

Lourie, Peter. *On the Trail of Sacagawea.* Honesdale, Pennsylvania: Boyds Mills Press.

Marcovitz, Hal. *Sacagewea: Guide for the Lewis and Clark Expedition.* Philadelphia: Chelsea House Publishers.

McMurtry, Larry. *Sacagawea's Nickname: Essays on the American West.* New York: New York Review Books. Includes three essays relating to the Lewis and Clark Expedition.

Milton, Joyce and Shelly Hehenberger. *Sacajawea: Her True Story*. All Aboard Reading series. New York: Grosset & Dunlap.

Moulton, Gary E., James E. Potter, and Debra Brownson. *Lewis and Clark on the Middle Missouri*. Lincoln, Nebraska: Nebraska State Historical Society. Essay first appeared in *Nebraska History*. *

North Dakota Parks & Recreation Department. *North Dakota Plant Species Documented on the Lewis & Clark Expedition*. Bismarck, North Dakota: North Dakota Parks & Recreation Department. *

Paton, Bruce C. *Lewis & Clark: Doctors in the Wilderness*. Golden, Colorado: Fulcrum Publishers.

Plamondon, Martin. *Lewis and Clark Trail Maps, A Cartographic Reconstruction. Volume II, Beyond Fort Mandan (North Dakota/Montana) to Continental Divide and Snake River (Idaho/Washington)-Outbound 1805; Return 1806*. Pullman, Washington: Washington State University Press. Vol. 1 published in 2000.

Quiry, Patricia Ryon. *The Lewis and Clark Expedition*. Minneapolis: Compass Point Books.

Ronda, James P. *Finding the West: Explorations with Lewis and Clark*. Albuquerque: University of New Mexico Press.

Rosen, Daniel and Ronald Himler. *Lewis and Clark: Into the Wilderness*. New York: McGraw-Hill School Division. *

Santella, Andrew. *Lewis and Clark*. New York: Franklin Watts.

Scheuerman, Richard D. *The Expeditions of Lewis & Clark and Zebulon Pike: North American Journeys of Discovery Travelogue*. Second edition. Madison, Wisconsin: Demco. Selected primary source materials and sixty interpretive study guides. *

Schuler, Harold H. *Lewis & Clark in the Pierre and Fort Pierre Area*. Pierre, South Dakota: Pierre Convention & Tourism Bureau. *

Tenney, Jeffrey W. *Corps of Discovery: A Novel Based on the Lewis and Clark Expedition of 1803–1806*. New York: Writer's Showcase, 2001.

Tinling, Marion. *Sacagawea's Son: The Life of Jean Baptiste Charbonneau*. Missoula, Montana: Mountain Press.

Thwaites, Reuben Gold, ed. *Original Journals of the Lewis & Clark Expedition as Published in 1904*. Facsimile of the fifteen-volume 1904 limited edition, condensed into eight volumes. Scituate, Massachusetts: Digital Scanning, Inc. Issued in both hardcover and paperback. See section 5d.1 for description of the original edition.

Watercourse. *Lewis & Clark Educator's Resource Guide: A Review of Lewis and Clark Materials*. Bozeman, Montana: The Watercourse and Project WET. *

Undated Publications
Carson, Kevin and Dennis Ditmanson. *Lewis & Clark Coloring Book*. Fort Clatsop, Oregon: Fort Clatsop Historical Association.

Denslow, Ray V. *Meriwether Lewis: Missouri's First Royal Arch Mason*. Missouri: Grand Chapter Royal Arch Masons.

Northern Colorado Teachers of the National Citizenship Education Program. *The Lewis and Clark Expedition*. Federal Words Agency, Works Projects Administration of Colorado.

Northern Pacific Railway. *The Storied Northwest: Explored and Made Known by Lewis & Clark, Opened and Developed by Northern Pacific Railway*. St. Paul: Northern Pacific Railway Co. Olin Wheeler is quoted in this publication. No date of publication is listed. Online Computer Library Center lists various speculative dates of publication, including 1916, 1920, 1921, 1922, and 1924.

7b Pamphlets, Magazines, and Scholarly Journals from the Lewis & Clark College Collection

The quantity of Lewis and Clark articles published in magazines, newspapers, organizational newsletters, and scholarly journals is enormous, and cataloging has never been attempted. This listing of articles and ephemera is not a comprehensive catalog, but rather a presentation of the items at Lewis & Clark College. All items listed below can be found in Lewis & Clark College's Special Collections.

1906
Thwaites, Reuben Gold. "William Clark: Soldier, Explorer, Statesman." *Missouri Historical Society Collections* 2, no. 7 (October 1906): 1–24. Includes black and white plates of Thwaites and Clark.

1907
Hebard, Grace Raymond. "Pilot of First White Men to Cross the American Continent: Identification of the Indian Girl Who Led the Lewis and Clark Expedition Over the Rocky Mountains." *Journal of American History* 1 (July–September, 1907): 465–84.

1909
Garver, Frank Harmon. "The Story of Sergeant Charles Floyd." *Proceedings of the Mississippi Valley Historical Association for the Year 1908–1909* (Iowa City, Iowa) 2.

Teggart, Frederick J. "Notes Supplementary to Any Edition of Lewis and Clark." *Annual Report of the American Historical Association for the Year 1908* (Washington, D.C.). Excerpt from the report.

1916
Abel, Annie Heloise. "A New Lewis and Clark Map." *The Geographical Review* (New York) 1, no. 5 (May 1916).

1919
Wood, Ruth Kedzie. "The Lewis and Clark Expedition." *The Mentor* serial 178, 7, no. 6 (May 1, 1919). Reprinted 2000.

1920

Gray, Charles Gilmer. "Lewis and Clark at the Mouth of Wood River." *Journal of the Illinois State Historical Society* 13, no. 2 (July 1920): 180–91.

1925

Beard, Joseph Howard. "The Medical Observations and Practice of Lewis and Clark." *The Scientific Monthly* 20, no. 5 (May 1925): 506–26.

Flandrau, Grace. "The Verendrye Expeditions in Quest of the Pacific." Great Northern Railway. Reprinted from *Oregon Historical Quarterly* 26, no. 2 (June 1925).

1926

Holman, Frederick V. "Lewis and Clark Expedition at Fort Clatsop." *Oregon Historical Quarterly* 27, no. 3 (September 1926): 266–78.

1927

Crawford, Helen. "Sakakawea." *North Dakota Historical Quarterly* 1, no. 3 (April 1927).

Reid, Russell. "Birds and Mammals Observed by Lewis and Clark in North Dakota." *North Dakota Historical Quarterly* 1, no. 4 (1927). Reprinted in *North Dakota History* 66, no. 2 (Spring 1999).

1928

Freeman, Lewis R. "Trailing History Down the Big Muddy: In the Homeward Wake of Lewis and Clark." *The National Geographic Magazine* 54, no. 1 (July 1928): 73–120.

Stanley, Leo Leonidas. "Medicine and Surgery of the Lewis and Clark Expedition." *Medical Journal and Record* (March 7, 21, April 4, May 16, June 6, 20, and July 4, 1928). Also reprinted as a sixty-four-page pamphlet, 1928.

True, Rodney H. "Some Neglected Botanical Results of the Lewis and Clark Expedition." *Proceedings of the American Philosophical Society* 67, no. 1 (1928): 1–20.

1931

Meany, Edmond S. "Doctor Saugrain Helped Lewis and Clark." *The Washington Historical Quarterly* 22, no. 4 (October 1931): 295–311.

1934

Hazlitt, Ruth. *Historical Reprints: The Journal of Francois Antoine Larocque. Sources of Northwest History* 20. Missoula: State University of Montana. Reprinted from *The Frontier* 14, nos. 3 and 4, and 15, no. 1.

1938

Brown, John G. "Annal Open Question on Name of Landmark: Term 'Pompeys Pillar' May be Investigation of Historians Who Embellished Writings of Clark Referring to Pompy's Tower." *The Billings Gazette* (November 13, 1938).

1940

Koch, Elers. "Lewis and Clark Route Retraced Across the Bitter-roots." *Oregon Historical Quarterly* 41 (June 1940): 160–174.

1944

Clarke, Charles G. "The Roster of the Expedition of Lewis and Clark." *Oregon Historical Quarterly* 45, no. 4 (December 1944): 289–305.

Kingson, C. S. "Sacajawea as Guide: The Evaluation of a Legend." *Pacific Northwest Quarterly* 35, no. 1 (January 1944): 3–18.

1945

Adelman, Seymour. "Equipping the Lewis and Clark Expedition." *The American Philosophical Society Library Bulletin* (1945): 39–44.

1947

Larsell, O. "Medical Aspects of the Lewis and Clark Expedition." *Surgery, Gynecology and Obstetrics* 85 (November 1947): 663–669.

1948

Caywood, Louis R. "The Exploratory Excavation of Fort Clatsop." *Oregon Historical Quarterly* 49, no. 3 (September 1948): 205–210.

Finley, Helen Deveneau et al. "The Missouri Reader: The Lewis and Clark Expedition." *Missouri Historical Review,* parts 1, 2, and 3.

Forrest, Earle E. "Patrick Gass: Carpenter of the Lewis and Clark Expedition." *The Missouri Historical Society Bulletin* 4, no. 4 (July 1948): 217–222.

1952

DeVoto, Bernard. "The Turning Point for Lewis & Clark." *Harper's Magazine* 205, no. 1228 (September 1952): 36–43.

1954

Bakeless, John E. "Lewis and Clark's Background for Exploration." *Journal of the Washington Academy of Sciences* 44, no. 2 (November 1954): 334–38.

Ewers, John C. "The Indian Trade of the Upper Missouri Before Lewis and Clark: An Interpretation." *The Missouri Historical Society Bulletin* 10, no. 4, part 1 (July 1954): 429–446.

Friis, Herman R. "Cartographic and Geographic Activities of the Lewis and Clark Expedition." *Journal of the Washington Academy of Sciences* 44, no. 2 (November 1954): 338–351.

Jensen, Dana O., ed. "Folio of Lewis and Clark Material." *The Missouri Historical Society Bulletin* 10, no. 4, part 1 (July 1954): 504–511.

——. "St. Louis Celebrates: The World Fair of 1904." *The Missouri Historical Society Bulletin* 11, no. 1, part 1 (October 1954): 54–72.

Lewis, Grace. "Financial Records: 'Expedition to the Pacific Ocean.'" *The Missouri Historical Society Bulletin* 10, no. 4, part 1 (July 1954): 465–489.

Loos, John Louis. "William Clark's Part in the Preparation of the Lewis and Clark Expedition." *The Missouri Historical Society Bulletin* 10, no. 4, part 1 (July 1954): 490–503.

McDermott, John Francis. "William Clark: Pioneer Museum Man." *Journal of the Washington Academy of Sciences* 44, no. 2 (November 1954): 370–373.

Neuberger, Richard L. "The Lochsa, Realm of History and Grandeur." *Montana Magazine of History* 4, no. 3 (Summer 1954): 1–9.

Ray, Verne F. and Nancy Oestreich Lurie. "The Contributions of Lewis and Clark to Ethnography." *Journal of the Washington Academy of Sciences* 44, no. 2 (November 1954): 358–370.

Rudd, Velva E. "Botanical Contributions of the Lewis and Clark Expedition." *Journal of the Washington Academy of Sciences* 44, no. 2 (November 1954): 351–356.

Setzer, Henry W. "Zoological Contributions of the Lewis and Clark Expedition." *Journal of the Washington Academy of Sciences* 44, no. 2 (November 1954): 356–357.

1955
Christopherson, Edmund. "Expedition, West." *Montana: The Magazine of Western History* 5, no. 3 (July 1955): 38–46.

DeVoto, Bernard. "An Inference Regarding the Expedition of Lewis and Clark." *Proceedings of the American Philosophical Society* 99, no. 4 (August 30, 1955): 185–194.

Duboc, Jessie L. "Yellowstone Adventure." *Montana: The Magazine of Western History* 5, no. 3 (July 1955): 28–33.

Jefferson, Thomas. "Letter from President Jefferson to Capt. Lewis." *Montana: The Magazine of Western History* 5, no. 3 (July 1955): 19.

Larsell, Olaf. "Medical Aspects of the Lewis and Clark Expedition." *Oregon Historical Quarterly* 56, no. 3 (September 1955): 211–225.

Neuberger, Richard L. "I Will Believe." *Montana: The Magazine of Western History* 5, no. 3 (July 1955): 1–2.

Overland, Helen Howard. "Fabled Friendship: The Story of the Two Great Leaders." *Montana: The Magazine of Western History* 5, no. 3 (July 1955): 3–18.

Shope, Irvin S. "The Lewis and Clark Trail, 1804–06." *Montana: The Magazine of Western History* 5, no. 3 (July 1955): 34–35.

Smith, James S. and Kathryn Smith. "Sedulous Sergeant, Patrick Gass." *Montana: The Magazine of Western History* 5, no. 3 (July 1955): 20–27.

Toole, K. Ross, ed. "What Are the Facts? Did William Clark Leave Indian Descendants?" *Montana: The Magazine of Western History* 5, no. 3 (July 1955): 36–37.

1956
Phelps, Dawson A. "The Tragic Death of Meriwether Lewis." *The William and Mary Quarterly*, third series, 13, no. 3 (1956).

1957
Hall, Courtney R. "Jefferson on the Medical Theory and Practice of His Day." *Bulletin of the History of Medicine* 31, no. 3 (May–June 1957): 235–245.

Smith, M. J. *John Colter*. Park County Chapter, Wyoming Historical Society.

1958

Burke, Redmond A. and Robert Q. Kelly. "The Lewis-Clark Expedition Papers: The Genesis of a Case." *The American Book Collector* 8, no. 7 (March 1958): 3–10.

Karolevitz, R. F. "Sacajawea: Heroine of the Lewis & Clark Expedition." *True West* (August 1958): 4–6, 28–30.

Lewis, Grace. "The First Home of Governor Lewis in Louisiana Territory." *The Missouri Historical Society Bulletin* 14, no. 4, part 1 (July 1958): 357–368.

Rees, John. "The Shoshoni Contribution to Lewis and Clark." *Idaho Yesterdays* 2, no. 2 (Summer 1958): 2–13.

1959

Bahmer, Robert H. and Paul M. Angle. "The Case of the Clark Papers." *Minnesota History* 36, no. 6 (June 1959): 216–229.

Jackson, Donald D. "Some Books Carried by Lewis and Clark." *The Missouri Historical Society Bulletin* 16, no. 1 (October 1959): 3–13.

Neuberger, Richard L. "The Legacy of Lewis and Clark." *Think* (June 1959).

Will, Drake W. "The Medical and Surgical Practice of the Lewis and Clark Expedition." *Journal of the History of Medicine and Allied Sciences* 14, no. 3 (1959).

1960

Jones, Roy F., ed. *Clark County History*, 1. Vancouver, Washington: Pioneer Printing.

1961

Bell, Burnby M. "The Lewis and Clark Expedition." *Astoria Sesquicentennial: 1811–1961*. Astoria, Oregon: 4.

Drury, Clifford M. "Letters to the Editor: Sacajawea's Death—1812 or 1884?" *Oregon Historical Quarterly* 62, no. 3 (September 1961): 288–291.

Jackson, Donald. "A New Lewis and Clark Map." *The Missouri Historical Society Bulletin* 17, no. 2, part 1 (January 1961): 117–132.

1962

Curtis, K. D. "York, the Slave Explorer." *Negro Digest* (May 1962): 1–16.

1963

Cutright, Paul Russell. "I Gave him Barks and Saltpeter." *American Heritage* 15, no. 1 (December 1963): 58–61.

McDermott, John Francis, ed. "The Western Journals of Dr. George Hunter, 1796–1805." *Transactions of the American Philosophical Society* 53, part 4 (1963).

Reid, Russell. "Sakakawea: The Bird Woman." *North Dakota History* 30, nos. 2 and 3.

1964

Barbour, William R. "The Guns of Lewis and Clark." *Gun Digest*, eighteenth edition (1964).

"Books for the Western Library." *Journal of the West* 3, no. 3 (July 1964): 401, 426.

Cutright, Paul Russell. "Lewis and Clark and Du Pratz." *The Missouri Historical Society Bulletin* 21, no. 1 (October 1964): 31–35.

Garver, Frank Harmon. "Lewis and Clark in Beaverhead County." Dillon, Montana: Western Montana College of Education, Beaverhead Printers. Reprint of the *The Dillon Examiner* (December 10, 1913).

Loos, John L. "They Opened the Door to the West." *The Humble Way* 3 (1964): 364.

Peebles, John J. "Rugged Waters: Trails and Campsites of Lewis and Clark in the Salmon River Country." *Idaho Yesterdays* 8, no. 2 (Summer 1964): 2–17.

Petersen, William J. "The Lewis and Clark Expedition." *The Palimpsest* 45, no. 3 (March 1964).

Poole, Edwin A. "Charbono's Squar." *The Pacific Northwesterner* 8, no. 1 (Winter 1964).

1965
Clarke, Charles G. "The Roster of the Lewis and Clark Expedition." *Daughters of the American Revolution Magazine* 99, no. 9 (November 1965): 878–882.

Cutright, Paul Russell. "Lewis and Clark and Cottonwood." *The Missouri Historical Society Bulletin* 12, no. 1 (October 1965): 35–44.

Everhart, William C. "So Long, St. Louis, We're Heading West." *National Geographic* 128, no. 5 (November 1965): 643–669. Includes a special section on Sacagawea.

Yates, Ted. "Since Lewis and Clark." *The American West* 2, no. 4 (Fall 1965): 22–30.

1966
Beidleman, Richard G. "Lewis and Clark: Plant Collectors for a President." *Horticulture* 44, no. 4 (April 1966): 28–29, 36–37.

Cutright, Paul Russell. "Jefferson's Instructions to Lewis and Clark." *The Missouri Historical Society Bulletin* 12, no. 3 (April 1966): 302–320.

———. "Meriwether Lewis Prepares for a Trip West." *The Missouri Historical Society Bulletin* 23, no. 1 (October 1966): 3–20.

DeLorean, John Z. "The Lewis and Clark Route." *Pontiac Safari* 7, no. 4 (July–August 1966): 14–15.

Fjosee, Wayne. "Comments on Lewis' Exploration of the Marias River." *Archaeology in Montana* 7, no. 3 (July–September 1966).

Mattes, Merrill J. "On the Trail of Lewis and Clark with Thomas Hart Benton." *Montana: The Magazine of Western History* 17, no. 3 (July 1966): 6–22.

Murfitt, Rex. "Lewisias." *Horticulture* 44, no. 7 (July 1966): 30.

Peebles, John J. "Lewis and Clark in Idaho." Idaho Historical Series, 16. Idaho Historical Society.

Tompkins, Calvin. "Annals of Law: The Lewis and Clark Case." *The New Yorker* 42, no. 36 (October 29, 1966): 105–148.

West, Helen B. "Lewis and Clark Expedition: Our National Epic." *Montana: The Magazine of Western History* 17, no. 3 (July 1966): 2–5.

1967

Brodhead, Michael J. "Elliott Coues: The Naturalist as Historian of the American West." *The Trail Guide* 12, no. 1.

Cutright, Paul Russell. "Lewis and Clark Begin a Journey." *The Missouri Historical Society Bulletin* 24, no. 1 (October 1967): 20–35.

——. "The Odyssey of the Magpie and the Prairie Dog." *The Missouri Historical Society Bulletin* 23, no. 3 (April 1967): 215–228.

——. "Well-Traveled Plants of Lewis & Clark." *Frontiers: A Magazine of Natural History* 31, no. 3 (February 1967): 80–83.

Jackson, Donald. "Some Advice for the Next Editor of Lewis and Clark." *The Missouri Historical Society Bulletin* 24, no. 1 (October 1967): 52–62.

Lee, Fred L. "Sha Ha Ka: Lewis and Clark's Mandan Friend." *The Trail Guide: Kansas City Posse, The Westerners* 12, no. 3 (September 1967).

Stevenson, Elizabeth. "Meriwether and I." *The Virginia Quarterly Review* 43, no. 4 (Autumn 1967): 580–591.

1968

Appleman, Roy E. "The Lost Site of Camp Wood." *Journal of the West* 7, no. 2 (April 1968): 270–274.

Cutright, Paul Russell. "Lewis and Clark Indian Peace Medals." *The Missouri Historical Society Bulletin* 24, no. 2 (January 1968): 160–167.

——. "Lewis on the Marias 1806." *Montana: The Magazine of Western History* 18, no. 3 (July 1968): 30–43.

——. "Meriwether Lewis: Botanist." *Oregon Historical Quarterly* 69, no. 2 (June 1968): 148–170.

——. "Meriwether Lewis: Zoologist." *Oregon Historical Quarterly* 69, no. 1 (March 1968): 5–28.

Hill, Richard H. "The Lewis and Clark Expedition–Where Did It Start?" *The Filson Club History Quarterly* 42, no. 2 (April 1968): 182–184.

Jackson, Donald. "On Reading Lewis and Clark." *Montana: The Magazine of Western History* 18, no. 3 (July 1968): 2–7.

Keating, Bern. "Today Along the Natchez Trace, Pathway Through History." *National Geographic* 134, no. 5 (November 1968): 641–667.

McNeill, Joseph P. and Christine A. McNeill. "Medicine's Role in the Corps of Discovery and the Northwest." *Texas Reports on Biology and Medicine* 26, no. 1 (Spring 1968).

Medical Research Foundation of Oregon. "Questions Formulated by Dr. Benjamin Rush for the First Medical Research in Oregon." *Annual Report, 1968.* Medical Research Foundation of Oregon: Portland, Oregon.

Osgood, Ernest S. "Clark on the Yellowstone 1806." *Montana: The Magazine of Western History* 18, no. 3 (July 1968): 8–29.

1969
Cutright, Paul R. "Lewis and Clark: Portraits and Portraitists." *Montana: The Magazine of Western History* 19, no. 2 (April 1969): 37–53.

Osgood, Ernest S. "A Prairie Dog for Mr. Jefferson." *Montana: The Magazine of Western History* 19, no. 2 (April 1969): 54–56.

1970
Anderson, Irving W. "J. B. Charbonneau, Son of Sacajawea." *Oregon Historical Quarterly* 71, no. 3 (September 1970): 246–264.

Adreon, William Clark. "William Clark of the Village of St. Louis, Missouri Territory." Paper presented before the St. Louis Westerners. Lewis and Clark Heritage Foundation.

Brown, Mark H. "Reflections on a Threatened Treasure." *Montana: The Magazine of Western History* 20, no. 3 (July 1970).

Goosman, Mildred. "Karl Bodmer: Earliest Painter in Montana." *Montana: The Magazine of Western History* 20, no. 3 (July 1970).

Lepley, John G. "The Prince and the Artist on the Upper Missouri." *Montana: The Magazine of Western History* 20, no. 3 (July 1970).

Snoddy, Donald D. "Medical Aspects of the Lewis and Clark Expedition." *Nebraska History* 51, no. 2 (Summer 1970): 115–152.

1971
Allen, John L. "Lewis and Clark on the Upper Missouri: Decision at the Marias." *Montana: The Magazine of Western History* 21, no. 3 (July 1971).

Will, Drake W. "Lewis and Clark: Westering Physicians." *Montana: The Magazine of Western History* 21, no. 4 (October 1971): 2–17.

Zochert, Donald. "This Nation Never Saw a Black Man Before." *American Heritage* 22, no. 2 (February 1971): 8–10. Article about York.

1972
Adreon, William. "Dedication of Gravesite of Jean Baptiste Charbonneau: Danner, Oregon, August 6, 1971." Photocopy of dedication speech.

Anderson, Irving. "He Rests at the End of the Trail." *Our Public Lands* 22, no. 2 (October 1972): 18–19.

Chuinard, E. G. "Letters to the Editor." *Montana: The Magazine of Western History* 22, no. 2 (April 1972). Letter to the editor concerning "Westering Physicians."

Churchill, Sarah. "Locust Hill Virtually Unknown: Meriwether Lewis Home at Ivy Seldom Visited." *The Jefferson Journal* (December 7, 1972).

Clarke, Charles G. "Thirty-Eight Horses and a Branding Iron." *The Branding Iron: The Los Angeles Westerners Corral* 106 (June 1972).

Cutright, Paul Russell. "The Journal of Private Joseph Whitehouse: A Soldier with Lewis and Clark." *The Missouri Historical Society Bulletin* 27, no. 3 (April 1972): 143–161.

Hail, Jane Wood. "Drugs Helped Assure Success for Lewis and Clark." *Walgreen World* 39, no. 6 (June 1972): 6–7.

Jackson, Donald. "A Footnote to the Lewis and Clark Expedition." *Manuscripts* 24, no. 1 (Winter 1972): 3–22.

———. "Historian Finds Lewis and Clark Article Dated and Inaccurate." *Montana: The Magazine of Western History* 22, no. 1 (January 1972): 82.

1973
Anderson, Irving. "Probing the Riddle of the Bird Woman." *Montana: The Magazine of Western History* 23, no. 4 (October 1973): 2–17.

Brodhead, Michael J. "A Soldier-Scientist in the American Southwest: Being a Narrative of the Travels of Elliott Coues, Assistant Surgeon, U.S.A." *Historical Monograph* (The Arizona Historical Society) 1.

Chatters, Roy Milton. "The Enigmatic Lewis and Clark Air Gun." *The Record* 34: 50–53.

Chuinard, E. G. "How Capt. Clark Paddled up the Willamette River to the Future Site of Portland." *The Portland Magazine* 56, no. 36 (September 7, 1973): 30.

Erickson, Vernon. "Lewis and Clark on the Upper Missouri." *North Dakota History: Journal of the Northern Plains* 40, no. 2 (Spring 1973): 34–37.

McDermott, John Frances. "Gallipolis as Travelers Saw It, 1792–1811." *The Ohio State Archaeological & Historical Quarterly* 48, no. 4 (October 1939).

1974
Cutright, Paul Russell, Clifford M. Drury, and Tom McCall. "Letters to the Editor: The Life and Death of Bird Woman." *Montana: The Magazine of Western History* 24, no. 2 (January 1974): 80. Excerpt included in October 1973 *Montana: The Magazine of Western History*.

Dodge, James, ed. "Retracing Lewis and Clark through CZ Country." *Crown Zellerbach Resource* 3, no. 2: 5–10.

Halliburton, R. "John Colter's Bare Escape." *American History Illustrated* 9, no. 7 (November 1974): 12–17.

Rehder, Dudley D. "Voyage of Discovery." *Water Spectrum* 6, no. 3: 10–18.

Snyder, Gerald S. "The Girl of History Who Became a Woman of Fable." *Westways* 66, no. 3 (March 1974): 36–39, 71–74.

Stacey, Joseph, ed. "Lewis and Clark." *Arizona Highways* 50, no. 11 (November 1974): 38–42.

1975
Appleman, Roy E. "Joseph and Reubin Field, Kentucky Frontiersmen of the Lewis and Clark Expedition and Their Father, Abraham." *The Filson Club History Quarterly* 49, no. 1.

Chuinard, E. G. "Thomas Jefferson and the Corps of Discovery." *The American West* 12, no. 6 (November 1975): 4–13.

Steffen, Jerome O. "William Clark: A Reappraisal." *Montana: The Magazine of Western History* 25, no. 2 (April 1975): 52–61.

1976
Anderson, Irving W. "Fort Manuel: Its Historical Significance." *South Dakota History* 6, no. 2 (Spring 1976): 131–151.

——. "Toussaint Charbonneau, a Most Durable Man." *South Dakota History* 6, no. 2 (Spring 1976): 152–185.

Chuinard, Eldon G. "The Actual Role of the Bird Woman." *Montana: The Magazine of Western History* 26, no. 3 (July 1976): 18–29.

——. "Lewis and Clark and the Bicentennial." *Journal of the American Medical Association* 236, no. 5 (August 2, 1976).

Dickson, Frank H. "Hard on the Heels of Lewis and Clark." *Montana: The Magazine of Western History* 26, no. 1 (January 1976): 14–25.

Gillette, David D. "Thomas Jefferson's Pursuit of Prehistoric Fauna." *Frontiers* 40, no. 3 (Spring 1976): 16–21.

Osgood, Ernest S. "Our Dog Scannon: Partner in Discovery." *Montana: The Magazine of Western History* 26, no. 3 (July 1976): 8–17.

Saindon, Bob. "The River Which Scolds at All Others." *Montana: The Magazine of Western History* 26, no. 3 (July 1976): 2–7.

Walcheck, Ken. "Montana Wildlife 170 Years Ago." *Montana Outdoors* 7, no. 4 (July/August 1976): 15–30.

Werner, Wilbur. "Letters to the Editor." *Montana: The Magazine of Western History* 26, no. 4 (October 1976). Responses to articles on Sacajawea and Lewis and Clark.

1977
Chuinard, Eldon G. "Letters to the Editor." *Montana: The Magazine of Western History* 27, no. 2 (April 1977): 71. Response to criticism in previous issue (27, no. 1).

Fisher, Sherry R. "In the Footsteps of Lewis and Clark." *Vista* 13, no. 3 (November 1977): 33–36.

Stewart, Henry M. "The American Air Gun School of 1800, With Corollary Verification of the Lewis-and-Clark Air Rifle Maker." *Monthly Bugle* (February 1977).

Walcheck, Ken. "For the Missouri Breaks: A Wild Future." *Montana Outdoors* 8, no. 5 (July/August 1977): 15–22.

Yaple, James. "Letters to the Editor." *Montana: The Magazine of Western History* 27, no. 1 (January 1977): 75. Criticism of Chuinard's article (26, no. 3).

1978

Abrams, Rochonne. "The Colonial Childhood of Meriwether Lewis." *The Missouri Historical Society Bulletin* 34, no. 4 (July 1978): 218–227.

Anderson, Irving W. "Sacajawea, Sacagawea, Sakakawea?" *South Dakota History: South Dakota State Historical Society and Board of Cultural Preservation Quarterly* 8, no. 4 (Fall 1978): 303–311.

McDermott, John Francis. "William Clark's Struggle with Place Names in Upper Louisiana." *The Missouri Historical Society Bulletin* 34, no. 3 (April 1978): 140–150.

Schroer, Blanche. "Sacajawea." *In Wyoming* 10, no. 5 (December 1978): 22–42.

1979

Abrams, Rochonne. "Meriwether Lewis: Two Years with Jefferson, the Mentor." *The Missouri Historical Society Bulletin* 36, no. 1 (October 1979): 3–18.

Ellis, Dick. "The Land Where Rivers Join." *Montana Outdoors* 10, no. 3 (May/June 1979): 8–12.

Hammarsten, James F. "Physicians and the Lewis and Clark Expedition." Speech given in Boise, Idaho.

Strong, Emory. "Lewis and Clark in Skamania County, 1805–1806." *Skamania County Heritage* 7, no. 4 (March 1979) and 8, no. 1 (June 1979).

Voelker, Robert G. "Lewis and Clark's Fabulous Journey." *NRTA* [National Retired Teachers' Association] *Journal* 30, no. 149 (May/June 1979): 25–29.

1980

Allen, John L. "Montana Reviews." *Montana: The Magazine of Western History* 30, no. 2 (April 1980): 74–75. Review of *Only One Man Died* by E. G. Chuinard.

Anderson, Irving W. "A Charbonneau Family History." *The American West* 17, no. 2 (March/April 1980): 4–13, 58–64.

Goddard, Donald. "Sculptor Harry Jackson's Sacagawea." *The American West* 17, no. 2 (March/April 1980): 14–15, 56.

Jackson, Donald. "Jefferson, Meriwether Lewis, and the Reduction of the U.S. Army." *Proceedings of the American Philosophical Society* 24, no. 2 (April 1980).

Nichols, William. "Lewis and Clark Probe the Heart of Darkness." *The American Scholar* 49, no. 1 (Winter 1979–80): 94–104.

Schroer, Blanche. "Boat-Pusher or Bird Woman? Sacagawea or Sacajawea?" *Annals of Wyoming* 52, no. 1 (Spring 1980): 46–54.

1981

Bishop, Beverly D. "The Writingest Explorers: Manuscripts of the Lewis and Clark Expedition." *Gateway Heritage* 2, no. 2 (Fall 1981): 22–29.

Bolas, Deborah W. "Books from an Expedition: A Publications History of the Lewis and Clark Journals." *Gateway Heritage* 2, no. 2 (Fall 1981): 30–35.

Crawford, Anthony R. "Exploring the Wilderness: The Lewis and Clark Expedition." *Gateway Heritage* 2, no. 2 (Fall 1981): 8–21.

Fields, Wayne D. "The Meaning of Lewis and Clark." *Gateway Heritage* 2, no. 2 (Fall 1981): 2–7.

Holt, Glen E. "After the Journey was Over: The St. Louis Years of Lewis and Clark." *Gateway Heritage* 2, no. 2 (Fall 1981): 42–48.

Kushner, Howard I. "The Suicide of Meriwether Lewis: A Psychoanalytic Inquiry." *The William and Mary Quarterly* third series, 38, no. 3 (July 1981): 464–481.

Snow, Jan. "Lewis and Clark in the Museum Collections of the Missouri Historical Society." *Gateway Heritage* 2, no. 2 (Fall 1981): 36–41.

Wood, W. Raymond. "The John Evans 1796–97 Map of the Missouri River." *Great Plains Quarterly* 1, no. 1 (Winter 1981): 39–53.

Wood, W. Raymond and Gary E. Moulton. "Prince Maximilian and New Maps of the Missouri and Yellowstone Rivers by William Clark." *The Western Historical Quarterly* 12, no. 4 (October 1981): 373–386.

1982

Ahsahta Press. *A Calendar of Indigenous Wonders.* Boise: Ahsahta Press. Extracts from the *Journals of Lewis and Clark* edited by Thwaites, and the field notes of William Clark.

Chatters, Roy M. "The Discovery of the Lewis and Clark Expedition Medal." *Bunchgrass Historian* 10, no. 2 (June 1982): 3–9.

Hirasuna, Delphine, ed. "Lewis and Clark." *The Potlatch Story* 22, no. 2 (November 1982): 4–7.

Jefferson, Thomas. Form carried by Lewis and Clark, to be filled out and presented to friendly Indian chiefs as they might meet on their way to the Pacific. New Haven, Connecticut: Beinecke Rare Book Library. One hundred fifty facsimile reproductions made by Beinecke Rare Book Library for the 14th annual meeting of the Lewis and Clark Trail Heritage Foundation, August 8–10, 1982, Philadelphia.

Saindon, Bob. *Authentic Cutout Models of the Three Historic Forts of the Lewis and Clark Expedition.* Helena, Montana: Bob Saindon.

Walcheck, Ken. "With Pen & Plant in Hand." *Montana Outdoors* 13, no. 4 (July/August 1982): 30–37.

1983

Foley, William E. "The Lewis and Clark Expedition's Silent Partners: The Chouteau Brothers of St. Louis." *Missouri Historical Review* 77, no. 2 (January 1983): 131–146.

Holmgren, Virginia C. "Bird Watching with Lewis and Clark." *Bird Watcher's Digest* 6, no. 1 (September 1983): 20–25.

Lewis and Clark Trail Heritage Foundation. *Clark's Lookout, Proposed State Monument: Application for Coal Tax Park Funds*. Beaverhead County, Montana: Beaverhead County Commissioners.

Moulton, Gary E. "The Specialized Journals of Lewis and Clark." *Proceedings of the American Philosophical Society* 127, no. 3: 194–201.

Van Geothem, Larry. "Following the Course of Lewis and Clark." *Odyssey* 16, no. 4 (Summer 1983): 24–29.

1984

Allen, John L. "Patterns of Promise: Mapping the Plains and Prairies, 1800–1860." *Great Plains Quarterly* 4, no. 1 (January 1984): 5–28.

Bedini, Silvio A. "The Scientific Instruments of the Lewis and Clark Expedition." *Great Plains Quarterly* 4, no. 1 (January 1984): 54–69. Includes reviews of Moulton's *Atlas of the Lewis and Clark Expedition*, p. 70.

Halsey, Ashley Jr. "The Air Gun of Lewis and Clark." *American Rifleman* 132, no. 8 (August 1984): 36–37, 80–82.

Moulton, Gary E. "Mapping the North American Plains." *Great Plains Quarterly* 4, no. 1 (January 1984): 3–4.

Ronda, James P. "A Chart in His Way: Indian Cartography and the Lewis and Clark Expedition." *Great Plains Quarterly* 4, no. 1 (January 1984): 43–53.

Wood, W. Raymond. "Mapping the Missouri River through the Great Plains, 1673–1895." *Great Plains Quarterly* 4, no. 1 (January 1984): 29–42.

1985

Ehrlich, George. "The 1807 Plan for an Illustrated Edition of Lewis and Clark." *The Pennsylvania Magazine of History and Biography* 109, no. 1 (January 1985): 43–57.

Henrikson, Stephen E. "This Place of Encampment: Fort Clatsop." *American History Illustrated* 20, no. 5 (September 1985): 22–33.

Olson, Kirk. "A Lewis & Clark Rifle?" *American Rifleman* (May 1985).

Thompson, Larry S. "Montana's Explorers: The Pioneer Naturalists." *Montana Geographic Series* 9. Helena: Montana Magazine.

1986

Fent, Cindy. "Some Medical Aspects of the Lewis and Clark Expedition." *North Dakota History* 53, no. 1 (Winter 1986): 24–28.

Larson, Marion J. "Trail's End: The Lewis and Clark Expedition Comes Alive at Fort Stevens State Park." *Oregon Coast* 5, no. 4 (June 1986): 16–17.

Majors, Harry M. "Lewis and Clark Enter the Rocky Mountains: North Fork Salmon River." *Northwest Discovery: The Journal of Northwest History and Natural History* 7, nos. 30 and 31 (April and May 1986).

1987

Heckrotte, Warren. "Aaron Arrowsmith's Map of North America and the Lewis and Clark Expedition." *The Map Collector* 39 (Summer 1987): 16–22.

Majors, Harry M. "Lewis and Clark Among the Sayleesh Indians: Ross Hole." *Northwest Discovery: The Journal of Northwest History and Natural History* 7, nos. 32 and 33 (January and February 1987): 126–246.

——. "Lewis and Clark in the Bitterroot Valley." *Northwest Discovery: The Journal of Northwest History and Natural History* 7, nos. 34 and 35 (March and April 1987): 246–386.

Willard, John, ed. "With William Clark on the Rochejohne." *Hoofprints from the Yellowstone Corral of the Westerner* 17, no. 1 (Spring-Summer 1987): 3–32.

1988

Brown, Dee. "What Really Happened to Meriwether Lewis?" *Columbia* 1, no. 4 (January 1988): 43–45.

Johnson, Mabel. "The Preparation." Vol. 1, *The Work-a-Day Detail of the Lewis and Clark Expedition.* Quality Paperbacks: Boring, Oregon.

Moulton, Gary E. "Lewis and Clark: Our National Epic of Exploration Worthy of Monumental Editing Task." *Nebraska Alumnus* 84, no. 2 (March/April 1988): 8–11.

Rogers, Ann. "William Clark: A Commemoration." *Gateway Heritage* 9, no. 1 (Summer 1988): 12–15.

1989

Gilbert, Bil. "The Incredible Odyssey of the President's Beasts." *Audubon* 91, no. 1: 100–114.

Kobler, John. "The Patriot Doctor." *Constitution* (Spring 1989): 63–67.

Large, Arlen J. "Following the Lewis & Clark Trail." *Friendly Exchange* 9, no. 1 (Spring 1989): 10–16.

Leonard, Bruce Jr. "Passage to the Pacific." *Trailer Life* 49, no. 3 (March 1989): 99–102, 149–150.

Ronda, James P. "Dreams and Discoveries: Exploring the American West, 1760–1815." *The William and Mary Quarterly* third series, 46, no. 1 (January 1989): 145–162.

1990

Beless, James W. "Meriwether Lewis—Explorer and Mason." *The Scottish Rite Journal, Southern Jurisdiction* 98, no. 3 (March 1990): 20–28.

1991

Moulton, Gary E. and James J. Holmberg. "What We Are About: Recently Discovered Letters of William Clark Shed New Light on the Lewis and Clark Expedition." *The Filson Club Historical Quarterly* 65, no. 3 (July 1991): 387.

1992

Simon-Smolinski, Carole. *Lewis and Clark Among the Nez Perce: An Elderhostel*

Class. Prepared for the 24th annual meeting of the Lewis and Clark Trail Heritage Foundation.

Tweney, George H. *Elliot Coues on Lewis and Clark—A Discovery*. Prepared for the 24th annual meeting of the Lewis and Clark Trail Heritage Foundation.

1993
Saindon, Bob. "Lewis and Clark on the Upper Missouri." *Nakodabi: The Assiniboine People* 1, no. 3 (Winter 1993): 10–15.

Woodwell, William H. "Who Shot Meriwether Lewis?" *The George Washington University Magazine* 3, no. 3 (Spring 1993): 18–22.

1995
Hoyle, Robert J. "Lewis and Clark's Course and Distance Records: Did Clark Use Them in Mapping the Route to the Pacific Ocean?" Accompanied by a letter to George Tweney from Paul Russell Cutright, dated October 21, 1974, and a photocopy of a letter from Cutright dated December 2, 1974.

1997
Moulton, Candy et al. "Lewis and Clark: Explorers for a Nation." *Persimmon Hill* 25, no. 4 (Winter 1997): 16–36.

2000
Beckham, Stephen Dow. "Models for Leadership for Modern Times: Jefferson, Lewis and Clark." *Open Spaces: Views from the Northwest* 3, no. 1.

Preston, Richard S. "The Accuracy of the Astronomical Observations of Lewis and Clark." *Proceedings of the American Philosophical Society* 144, no. 2 (June 2000): 168–191.

U.S. Public Law 106–507. *An Act to Provide for the Posthumous Promotion of William Clark of the Commonwealth of Virginia and the Commonwealth of Kentucky, Co-Leader of the Lewis and Clark Expedition, to the Grade of Captain in the Regular Army.*

We Proceeded On

We Proceeded On is the quarterly publication of the Lewis and Clark Trail Heritage Foundation. The magazine was first published in 1975, and is still in print as of 2002. Each issue contains multiple articles dealing with Lewis and Clark Expedition-related topics, many by recognized Lewis and Clark scholars. The Lewis and Clark Trail Heritage Foundation has also issued supplements to the magazine, which contain longer essays; a complete list of the supplements is given below.

Supplementary Publication 1, October 1976. *Proceedings of the Eighth Annual Meeting, August 15–18, 1976, Great Falls, Montana*. Includes "President's Message" by Wilbur P. Werner; "Status of Missouri River Breaks Wild and Scenic River Legislation" by Edwin Zaidlicz; "Sacagawea and Sacagawea Spring" by E.G. Chuinard, M.D.; "The Expedition's Journals—Captain Lewis's Discovery and Description of the Great Falls of the Missouri River" by Robert E. Lange; and "The White Pirogue of the Lewis and Clark Expedition" by Robert Saindon.

Supplementary Publication 2, July 1977. Osgood, Ernest Staples. *Our Dog Scannon—Partner in Discovery*. Reprinted from *Montana, The Magazine of Western History*, Summer 1967.

Supplementary Publication 2A, March 1986. Jackson, Donald. *Call Him a Good Old Dog, but Don't Call Him Scannon*.

Supplementary Publication 3, July 1978. Biddle, Henry J. *Beacon Rock on the Columbia: Legends and Traditions of a Famous Landmark*. A reprint of Biddle's 1925 monograph concerning the acquisition and preservation of the 800-foot-high landmark on the Columbia River. Lewis and Clark described the geologic formation in 1805–1806. Annotations by Robert E. Lange.

Supplementary Publication 4, December 1980. *Three Papers Presented at the Foundation's 12th Annual Meeting, Omaha, Nebraska, and Sioux City, Iowa, August 20–22, 1980*. Includes "Sergeant Floyd and the Floyd Memorial at Sioux City, Iowa" by Edward Ruisch; "Some Thoughts on the Death of Sergeant Charles Floyd" by E.G. Chuinard; and "Expansion of the Fur Trade Following Lewis and Clark" by Charles E. Hanson Jr.

Supplementary Publication 5, August 1981. Lange, Robert E., comp. *Thirteenth Annual Meeting Visit to the Missoula County Courthouse, The Edgar Samuel Paxson Murals*. The visit to the Missoula, Montana, courthouse was an event during the Heritage Foundation's annual meeting. This publication provides biographical information about Montana artist Edgar Paxson, and descriptions of two of the eight Paxson murals in the courthouse that depict incidents related to the expedition in the Missoula area.

Supplementary Publication 6, July 1982. Cutright, Paul Russell. *Contributions of Philadelphia to Lewis and Clark History*. A study of the activities related to the expedition in Philadelphia, both before and after the expedition. Includes information on Nicholas Biddle's contributions to the publication of a narrative based on the captains' journals.

Supplementary Publication 7, May 1984. *Lewis's Woodpecker and Clark's Nutcracker*. Two 8" x 10" color images (with captions) of birds reproduced from color paintings by Marie Nonmast Bohlen.

Supplementary Publication 8, November 1984. Fritz, Harry W. *Meriwether Lewis and William Clark and the Discovery of Montana*. Transcript of a paper presented at the 16th annual banquet of the Heritage Foundation, Great Falls, Montana, August 8, 1984.

Supplementary Publication 9, August 1990. Ronda, James P. *Westering Captains: Essays on the Lewis and Clark Expedition*. Robert E. Lange, ed. Collection of eight essays relating to the Lewis and Clark Expedition.

Supplementary Publication 10, September 1990. Osgood, Ernest S. and Donald Jackson. *The Lewis and Clark Expedition's Newfoundland Dog*. Two monographs: "Our Dog Scannon—Partner in Discovery" by Ernest S. Osgood and "Call Him Good Dog, But Don't Call Him Scannon" by Donald Jackson.

Supplementary Publication 11, May 1992. Yater, George H. and Carolyn S. Denton. *Nine Young Men From Kentucky*. A collection of biographical sketches of the nine expedition members from Kentucky and of Clark's manservant York.

Supplementary Publication 12, February 1997. *An Overview of Facts and Fiction About the Famous Newfoundland Dog*. Reprints Supplementary Publication 2 and 2A.

Supplementary Publication 13. Benson, Guy Meriwether. *Exploring the West from Monticello*. Limited edition by the University of Virginia Library as catalog of an exhibition at its Alderman Library. Supplementary publication number does not appear on the item.

Supplementary Publication 14, February 2000. Fazio, James R., ed. *The Mystery of Lost Trail Pass: A Quest for Lewis and Clark's Campsite of September 3, 1805*. Includes essays by Robert N. Bergantino, J. Wilmer Rigby, Hadley B. Roberts, Steve F. Russell, and James R. Wolf.

7c Theses and Dissertations

Information for the theses and dissertations listed in this section was compiled from Dissertation Abstracts and WorldCat databases. Items marked with asterisks are not in the Lewis & Clark Collection.

1920
Rees, John E. "Letter, Salmon, Idaho, to Charles H. Burke, Washington, D.C." Dissertation concerning the identity, name, and history of Sacagawea.*

1927
Clark, Frank Henry. "Lewis and Clark Expedition." Master's thesis, Boston College.*

1931
McGrath, Francis Joseph. "Lewis and Clark Expedition." Master's thesis, Boston College.*

1936
Criswell, Elijah Harry. "Lewis and Clark—Linguistic Pioneers." Two vols. Ph.D. diss., Columbia: University of Missouri (reprinted as issue of University of Missouri Studies; see section 7a, 1940).

1939
Baird, Helen D. "The Use and Accuracy of Accounts of the Lewis and Clark Expedition in Children's Literature Published from 1806 through December 1938." Two vols. Master's Essay, Columbia University.

1953
Bragg, William Frederick. "Sacajawea's Role in Western History." Master's thesis, University of Wyoming.

Loos, John L. "A Biography of William Clark, 1770–1813." Two vols. Ph.D. diss., Washington University. Reproduced in facsimile by University Microfilms, 1978.

1957
Firtch, William Horace. "Adventure to the West: A Story of the Lewis and Clark Expedition." Master's thesis, San Diego State College.*

1962

Godfrey, Larry. "A Survey of 20th Century Novels Based on the Lewis and Clark Expedition." Master's thesis, St. Louis, Missouri: Washington University.

1967

Abrams, Rochonne Weintraub. "The Lewis and Clark Journals: Their Contribution to American Literature." Master's thesis, Washington University, Department of English. *

1970

McDonald, Mary Jane. "The Lewis and Clark Expedition: The Return Trip." Ph.D. diss., Saint Louis University. Microfilm of typescript. Ann Arbor, Michigan: University Microfilms. Reproduced by University Microfilms, 1978, 1980.

1971

Keller, Linda Quinne. "Jefferson's Western Diplomacy: The Lewis and Clark Expedition." Master's thesis, Charlottesville, Virginia: University of Virginia.

Wilkinson, Katherine Ann. "Lewis and Clark Retraced: Crossing the Continental Divide." Master's thesis, University of Minnesota. *

1973

Alleman, Paula Fenza. "The Life-History of Jean Baptiste Charbonneau: An Anthropological Analysis." Master's thesis, Dekalb, Illinois: Northern Illinois University.

1974

Cohick, Nancy. "Thomas Jefferson's Object and Philosophy for the Lewis and Clark Expedition." Departmental honors thesis, La Verne, California: University of La Verne.

1980

Anderson, Douglas Alan. "The Explanation of the West: Exploration, Expectation and Uncertainty from Lewis and Clark to Frederick Law Olmsted." Ph.D. diss., University of Virginia. *

1981

Ritter, Michael L. "The Early Career of Jean Baptiste Charbonneau, 1805 to 1842." Master's thesis, Sonoma State University.

1986

Simpson, Mary Charlotte. "Benjamin Capps and the "Sacajawea" Plagiarism Case." Master's thesis, University of North Texas, 1986. *

1989

Hamilton, M. B. "Some Studies, 1986–1989: Lyrics, Long Poems, and the Lewis and Clark Journals." Master's thesis, University of Montana. *

1990

MacGregor, Carol Lynn. "The Patrick Gass Journal of the Lewis and Clark Expedition." Master's thesis, Boise State University. Includes the text of Patrick Gass's journal. Missoula, Montana: Mountain Press, 1997.

1991

Pepe, Albert R. "The Lewis and Clark Expedition: The Preparation Period and Early Passage: A Thesis Submitted to the School of Graduate Studies." Master's thesis, Southern Connecticut State University.

1993

Kessler, Donna J. "Sacagawea: A Uniquely American Legend." Ph.D. diss., Emory University. Reproduction by UMI Dissertation Services, 1994. Published as *The Making of Sacagawea: A Euro-American Legend*. Tuscaloosa: University of Alabama Press, 1996.

1996

Blair, Elizabeth Marie. "Divided Light." (Original Writing; Poetry, Meriwether Lewis, William Clark). Ph.D. diss., University of Illinois at Chicago. *

1997

Garrison, Kirk Alan. "Lewis and Clark at Fort Clatsop: A Winter of Environmental Discomfort and Cultural Misunderstandings." Master's thesis, Portland State University. *

Hallaron, Scott L. "The Lewis and Clark Odyssey and the Decimation of the American Bison." Master's research paper, Department of History, Southern Illinois University at Carbondale. *

Wisneski, Richard Lawrence. "Travelers In a Wilderness: Conflicting Identities In America, 1760–1812." Ph.D. diss., Michigan State University. Discussion of travel narratives by Jonathan Carver, Hector Crevecoeur, William Bartram, Meriwether Lewis, and William Clark.

1998

Patten, William Jeffrey. "Sacagawea: The History of a Myth." Master's thesis, Portland State University. *

Warner, Joan K. "The Rhetoric of Imperialism in the Lewis and Clark Journals: Camp Dubois to the Mandan Villages." Master's thesis, English Department, South Dakota State University.

Waters, Patricia. "Mr. Jefferson's Literary Pursuit of the West: The Journals of Lewis and Clark." Ph.D. diss., Knoxville: University of Tennessee. Reproduced by University Microfilms, 1999.

1999

Kimaid, Michael A. "If we want it, I warant it will soon be ours": How the Success of the American Corps of Discovery Signaled the Demise of Spanish Empire on the North American Continent. Master's thesis, Bowling Green State University. *

Thompson, Carolyn K. "A Literature-Based ESL Curriculum: The Great Lewis and Clark Expedition." Master's thesis, Eastern Washington University. Curriculum included, based on the book The Incredible Journey of Lewis and Clark by Rhoda Blumberg. *

2000

Bockelmann, Scott. "Exploring the Lewis and Clark Expedition in an Eighth Grade Social Studies Class Using Multiple Intelligences." Master's research paper, University of Northern Iowa. *

Sumption, Linda Jan. "A wayless way": Patterns of Adventure in Nineteenth-Century American Travel Narratives. Ph.D. diss., City University of New York.

2001

Buckley, Jay Harry. "William Clark: Superintendent of Indian Affairs at St. Louis, 1813–1838 (Missouri)." Ph.D. diss., University of Nebraska–Lincoln.

Davis, Kristen. "The Lewis and Clark Expedition in Textbooks and Children's Literature: the Native American Perspective." Master's thesis, Whitworth College.

Gevock, Nick J. and Drew Winterer. "Fishing with Silas: An Angler's Guide to the Lewis and Clark Trail." Master's thesis, University of Montana. *

Sources Cited

Adam, G[raeme] Mercer and Charles Wentworth Upham. 1905. *Makers of American History: The Lewis & Clark Exploring Expedition, 1804–'06; John Charles Fremont.* New York: The University Society, Inc.

"Adolphus Washington Greely." 1958. In *The National Cyclopedia of American Biography,* 42:18–19. New York: James T. White & Co.

"Agnes C. Laut." 1943. In *Who Was Who in America, Special Library Edition,* 2:709. Chicago: A. N. Marquis Co.

Allen, John Logan. 1975. *Passage Through the Garden: Lewis and Clark and the Image of the American Northwest.* Urbana, Chicago, London: University of Illinois Press.

Allgemeine Deutsche Biographie. 1907. Vols. 10 and 53. Leipzig: Verlag von Duncker & Humblot.

American State Papers. Documents, Legislative and Executive, of the Congress of the United States, from the First Session to the Second Session of the Fifteenth Congress, Inclusive: Commencing March 3, 1789, and Ending March 3, 1819. 1832. Vol. 12. Washington, D.C.: Gales and Seaton.

Ames, Gregory. 1986. "Dodd, Mead and Company." In *American Literary Publishing Houses, 1638–1899, Part 1, A-M, Dictionary of Literary Biography,* Peter Dzwonkoski, ed., 49:126–130. Detroit: Gale Research Co.

Anderson, Mary B., transcriber. 1892–93. "The Coues-Anderson Manuscript Transcript of the Journals." Lewis & Clark College Special Collections, Portland, Ore.

Armbrust, Crys. 1991. "David Nutt." In *British Literary Publishing Houses, 1820–1880. Dictionary of Literary Biography,* Patricia J. Anderson and Jonathan Rose, eds., 106:228–229. Detroit: Gale Research Co.

Arrowsmith, Aaron. 1802. "A Map Exhibiting all the New Discoveries in the Interior Parts of Northa America." London: Aaron Arrowsmith.

"Articles of War–1778." www.cvco.org/sigs/reg64/articles. Viewed May 9, 2002.

Baltimore Directory for the Year 1812 . . . . 1812. Baltimore: B. W. Sower & Co.

Baltimore Directory and Register for 1814–15 . . . . 1815. Baltimore: J. C. O'Reilley.

Baggerman, Arianne. 2000. *Een lot uit de loterij Familiebelangen en uitgeverspolitiek in de Dordtse firma A. Blussé en Zoon, 1745–1823.* Den Haag: Sdu Uitgevers.

Bancroft, Hubert Howe. 1884. *History of the Northwest Coast, Vol. 2, 1800–1846.* San Francisco: A. L. Bancroft & Co., Publishers.

Bartlett–Browne, Sheri. 2002. "Eva Emery Dye." Ph.D. diss., St. Paul: University of Minnesota.

Barton, Benjamin Smith. 1797. *New Views of the Origin of the Tribes and Nations of America.* Philadelphia: John Bioren for the Author.

———. 1803. *Elements of Botany: Or Outlines of the Natural History of Vegetables.* Philadelphia: The Author.

———. 1812. "New Views of the Origin of the Tribes and Nations of America." *The Port Folio,* New Series 7, no. 6 (June): 507–526.

Bautz, Friedrich William. 1990. "Wilhelm Harnisch." In *Biographisch-Bibliographiches Kirchenlexikon,* 2:570. www.bautz.de/bbkl/h/harnisc. . . . Viewed March 1, 2002.

"Bayard Taylor." 1899. In *Appletons' Cyclopedia of American Biography.* James Grant Wilson and John Fiske, eds. 1:40–42. New York: D. Appleton and Co.

Bedini, Silvio A. 1999. "Andrew Ellicott." In *American National Biography,* John A. Garraty and Mark C. Carnes, eds., 7:415–416. New York and London: Oxford University Press.

Bell, Solomon. 1830. *Tales of Travels West of the Mississippi*. Boston: Gray and Bowen. Reprint Boston: Russell, Shattuck, 1836.

Benjamin Franklin Ells." N.d. Ancestry WorldTree, wysiwyg://129/http://pedigree.ance... view.d11ti=O&ind11456&file=39875. Viewed August 17, 2001.

Bennett, Ruth H. 1986. "The Werner Company." In *American Literary Publishing Houses, 1638–1899, Part 2: N-Z, Dictionary of Literary Biography*, Peter Dzwonkoski, ed., 49:480–481. Detroit: Gale Research Co.

Benson, Guy Meriwether, William R. Irwin, and Heather Moore. 1995. *Exploring the West from Monticello: A Perspective in Maps from Columbus to Lewis and Clark*. Charlottesville, Va.: University of Virginia Library.

Bergantino, Robert N. 2001. "Revisiting Fort Mandan's Longitude: Lewis doubted his data, but the fault was in his calculations." *We Proceeded On* 27, no. 4 (November): 19–26.

Bertuch, Friedrich J. 1815. *Neue Bibliothek der wichtigsten Reisebeschreibungen zur Erweiterung der Erd- und Völkerkunde*. Weimar: Im Verlage des H.S. privil. Landes-Industrie-Comptoirs.

Biddle, Nicholas and Paul Allen. 1814. *History of the Expedition Under the Command of Captains Lewis and Clark, to the Sources of the Missouri, Thence Across the Rocky Mountains and Down the River Columbia to the Pacific Ocean. Performed During the Years 1804-5-6. By Order of the Government of the United States*. 2 vols. Philadelphia: Bradford and Inskeep; New York: Abraham Inskeep.

Bierman, E. Benjamin. 1904. "Lebanon County in Our State Legislature." *Publications of the Lebanon County Historical Society* 2, no. 13: 353–396.

Bingley, William. 1821. *Travels in North America, from Modern Writers. With Remarks and Observations; Exhibiting a Connected View of the Geography and Present State of that Quarter of the Globe*. London: Harvey and Darton.

Biographies of Successful Philadelphia Merchants. 1864. Philadelphia: James K. Simon.

Bonehill, Captain Ralph (Edward Stratemeyer). 1905. *Pioneer Boys of the Great North-west, or, With Lewis and Clark Across the Rockies*. New York: Stitt Publishing Co.

Bradford, Samuel Fisher. 1800–14. "Bradford Family Papers." Philadelphia: The Historical Society of Pennsylvania.

Bradsher, Earl Lockridge. 1966. *Mathew Carey: Editor, Author and Publisher, A Study in American Literary Development*. New York: AMS Press, Inc.

Briggs, Asa. 1995. "T. Longman." In *The British Literary Book Trade, 1700–1820*. James K. Bracken and Joel Silver, eds., 176–183. Detroit: Gale Research Co.

Brigham, Clarence Saunders. 1962. *History and Bibliography of American Newspapers, 1690–1820*. 2 vols. Worcester: American Antiquarian Society.

Brodhead, Michael J. 1999. "Elliott Coues." In *American National Biography*, John A. Garraty and Mark C. Carnes, eds., 5:577–578. New York and London: Oxford University Press.

Brooks, Noah. 1901. *First Across the Continnt: The Story of the Exploring Expedition of Lewis and Clark in 1804-5-6*. New York: C. Scribner's Sons. Reprint New York: C. Scribner's Sons, 1910, 1912, 1917, 1922, 1924, 1926, 1927, 1935.

Brown, Philip Arthur Henry. 1982. *London Publishers and Printers, 1800–1870*. London: British Library.

Buck, Solon Justus. 1932. "James Kendall Hosmer." In *Dictionary of American Biography*, Dumas Malone, ed., 9:244–245. New York: Charles Scribner's Sons.

Bulfinch, Thomas. 1866. *Oregon and Eldorado; or, Romance of the Rivers*. Boston: J. E. Tilton and Co.

Butler, James Davie. 1884. "John Colter." *Magazine of American History* 12 (July): 83–86.

——. 1895. "The New Found Journal of Charles Floyd, a Sergeant Under Captains Lewis and Clark." *American Antiquarian Society Proceedings*, New Series 9: 225–252.

Cappon, Lester J. 1962. "Who is the Author of *History of the Expedition under the Command of Captains Lewis and Clark* (1814)?" *William and Mary Quarterly* 19 (April): 257–268.

Cappon, Lester and Alfred C. Berol. 1970. *History of the Expedition Under the Command of Captains Lewis and Clark, Philadelphia, Published by Bradford and Inskeep, 1814: A Census of Extant Copies in Original Boards.* New York: Columbia University Libraries.

Carey, Mathew. 1810. *Catalogue of Books.* Philadelphia: Mathew Carey.

——. 1813. *Narrative of the Proceedings of Edward Gray, Samuel F. Bradford, and Robert Taylor, Previous and Subsequent to the Bankruptcy of C. & A. Conrad & Company.* Philadelphia: M. Carey.

Caughey, John Walton. 1946. *Hubert Howe Bancroft: Historian of the West.* Berkeley and Los Angeles: University of California Press.

Cazden, Robert E. 1984. *A Social History of the German Book Trade in America to the Civil War.* Columbia, S.C.: Camden House, Inc.

"Celebrated Historian of Oregon City Discoverer of Lewis and Clark Diary." 1923. *The Oregonian*, Portland, November 11.

"Charles Wentworth Upham." 1898–1900. In *Appletons' Cyclopedia of American Biography*. James Grant Wilson and John Fiske, eds., 6:212. New York: D. Appleton and Co.

Chase, Philander D. 1999. "Friederich Wilhelm von Steuben." In *American National Biography*, John A. Garraty and Mark C. Carnes, eds., 20:689–691. New York and London: Oxford University Press.

Chuinard, Eldon G. 1979. *Only One Man Died: The Medical Aspects of the Lewis and Clark Expedition.* Glendale: Arthur H. Clark Co.

Clark, William and Meriwether Lewis. "Manuscript Journals." Library of the American Philosophical Society, Philadelphia. Microfilm.

Clarkin, William. 1984. *Mathew Carey: A Bibliography of His Publications, 1785–1824.* New York and London: Garland Publishing Inc.

Clerke, Agnes Mary. 1921–22a. "Nevil Maskelyne." In *Dictionary of National Biography*, Leslie Stephen and Sidney Lee, eds., 12:1299–1301. London: Oxford University Press.

——. 1921–22b. "Richard Kirwan." In *Dictionary of National Biography*, Leslie Stephen and Sidney Lee, eds., 11:228–230. London: Oxford University Press.

Cole, Richard Cargill. 1986. *Irish Booksellers and English Writers, 1740–1800.* London: Mansell Publishing, Ltd.; Atlantic Highlands, N.J.: Humanities Press International, Inc.

A Collection of Modern and Contemporary Voyages and Travels: Containing, I. Translations from Foreign Languages, of Voyages and Travels Never Before Translated. II. Original Voyages and Travels Never Before Published. III. Analyses of New Voyages and Travels Published in England. 1807. London: Richard Phillips.

"Columbia College." 1855. In *Cyclopedia of American Literature.* www.columbia.edu/cu/columbiana/cchist.html. Viewed March 5, 2002.

Coote, Charles Henry. 1921–22. "Aaron Arrowsmith." In *The Dictionary of National Biography*, Leslie Stephen and Sidney Lee, eds., 1:595–596. London: Oxford University Press.

Coues, Elliott. 1876. "An Account of the Various Publications Relating to the Travels of Lewis and Clarke, with a Commentary on the Zoological Results of Their Expedition." *Bulletin of the United States Geological and Geographical Survey of the Territories*, 2d series, no. 6: 417–444.

——. 1892–93. Letters to Henry Phillips Jr. Philadelphia: American Philosophical Society.

———. 1893. "Description of the Original Manuscript Journals and Field Notebooks of Lewis and Clark, on Which Was Based Biddle's History of the Expedition of 1804-06, and Which Are Now in the Possession of the American Philosophical Society in Philadelphia." *Proceedings, American Philosophical Society* 3: 17–33.

———. 1898. "Notes on Mr. Thomas Meehan's Paper on the Plants of Lewis and Clark's Expedition Across the Continent." *Proceedings of the Academy of Natural Sciences of Philadelphia*, part 2 (April–September): 292.

Coues, Elliott, ed. 1893. *History of the Expedition Under the Command of Lewis and Clark, To the Sources of the Missouri River, thence across the Rocky Mountains and Down the Columbia River to the Pacific Ocean, performed during the Years 1804-5-6, by Order of the Government of the United States.* 4 vols. New York: Francis P. Harper.

Courteney, Wiliam Prideaux. 1921–22. "William Bingley." In *Dictionary of National Biography*, Leslie Stephen and Sidney Lee, eds., 2:517. London: Oxford University Press.

Cramer's Pittsburgh Magazine & Almanack, for the Year of Our Lord 1810. Pittsburgh: Cramer, Spear & Eichbaum.

Cramer, Zadok. 1814. *The Navigator: Containing Directions for Navigating the Monongahela, Allegheny, Ohio and Mississippi Rivers . . . Containing an Account of Louisiana, and of the Missouri and Columbia Rivers, as Discovered by the Voyage Under Capts. Lewis and Clark.* Pittsburgh: Cramer, Spear and Eichbaum.

Crane, Elaine Forman and Sarah Blank Dine, eds. 1991. *The Diary of Elizabeth Drinker, Vol. 3, 1803-1807.* Boston: Northeastern University Press.

Croll, P. C. 1909. "Lebanon County Imprints." *Pennsylvania Bibliographies, No. 2.* N.p.: Pennsylvania Federation of Historical Societies.

Curwen, Henry. 1873. *A History of Booksellers, the Old and the New.* London: Chaatto and Windus.

Cutright, Paul Russell. 1964. "Lewis and Clark and Du Pratz." *Missouri Historical Society Bulletin* 21 (October): 31–35.

———. 1969. *Lewis and Clark: Pioneering Naturalists.* Urbana and Chicago: University of Illinois Press. Reprint Lincoln and London: University of Nebraska Press, 1989.

———. 1976. *A History of the Lewis and Clark Journals.* Norman, Okla.: University of Oklahoma Press.

Cutright, Paul Russell and Michael J. Brodhead. 1981. *Elliott Coues: Naturalist and Frontier Historian.* Urbana and Chicago: University of Illinois Press.

Dahlinger, Charles. 1916. *Pittsburgh: A Sketch of Its Early Social Life.* New York and London: G. P. Putnam's Sons.

Davis, Kathleen R. 1986. "A. C. McClurg and Company." In *American Literary Publishing Houses, 1638-1899, Part 1: A-M, Dictionary of Literary Biography*, Peter Dzwonkoski, ed., 49:297–298. Detroit: Gale Research Co.

"Death Takes Flower Lover" [Katherine Chandler obituary]. 1930. *San Francisco Chronicle*, June 25.

Discoveries Made in Exploring the Missouri, Red River and Washita, by Captains Lewis and Clark, Doctor Sibley, and William Dunbar, Esq. With a Statistical Account of the Countries Adjacent . . . . 1806. Natchez, Miss.: Andrew Marschalk.

Documents Accompanying a Bill Making Compensation to Messieurs Lewis and Clarke, and Their Companions, Presented the 23d January, 1807. 1807. Washington City: A. & G. Way.

Documents Relating to the Purchase and Exploration of Louisiana. 1904. Boston and New York: Houghton, Mifflin & Co.

Douglas, Bessie P. 1928. *The Families of Joshua Williams of Chester County, PA. and John McKeehan of Cumberland County, PA. with Some Allied Familes.* Minneapolis: Augsberg Press.

Dye, Eva Emery. 1902. *The Conquest: The True Story of Lewis and Clark*. Chicago: A. C. McClurg & Co.

"East Brunswick History." N.d. www.westfieldnj.com/whs/history/eastbrunswick.Viewed February 11, 2002.

Edwards, G. Thomas. 1990. *Sowing Good Seeds: The Northwest Suffrage Campaigns of Susan B. Anthony*. Portland, Ore.: Oregon Historical Society.

Ellicott, Andrew. 1803. *Journal of Andrew Ellicott, Late Commissioner on Behalf of the United States During Part of the Year 1796, the Years 1797, 1798, 1799, and Part of the Year of 1800: For Determining the Boundary Between the United States and the Possessions of His Catholic Majesty In America . . . .* Philadelphia: Thomas Dobson.

Epstein, Donald B. 1979. "Gladstone Chautauqua: Education and Entertainment, 1893–1928." *Oregon Historical Quarterly* 80, no. 4: 391–403.

Espinasse, Francis. 1921–22. "Ephraim Chambers." In *Dictionary of National Biography*, Leslie Stephen and Sidney Lee, eds., 4:16–17. London: Oxford University Press.

Exman, Eugene. 1965. *The Brothers Harper: A Unique Publishing Partnership and Its Impact Upon the Cultural Life of America from 1817 to 1853*. New York: Harper & Row, Publishers.

Feather, John. 1988. *A History of British Publishing*. London and New York: Routledge.

Field, Thomas W. 1991. *An Essay Towards an Indian Bibliography. Being a Catalogue of Books, Relating to the History, Antiquities, Languages, Customs, Religion, Wars, Literature, and Origin of the American Indians . . . .* William S. Reese, Intro. Reprint of 1873 edition. New Haven: William Reese Co.

Fischer, E. 2000. "Philipp Reclam, Jun." In *Lexikon des Gesamten Buchwesens, LGB2*, 6:203–204. Stuttgart: Verlag Anton Hiersemann.

Fisher, William, comp. 1812a. *An Interesting Account of the Voyages and Travels of Captains Lewis and Clark, in the Years 1804, 1805, and 1806 . . . .* Baltimore: Anthony Miltenberger.

———. 1812b. *New Travels Among the Indians of North America; Being a Compilation, Taken Partly from the Communications Already Published, of Captains Lewis and Clark, to the President of the United States . . . .* Philadelphia: James Sharan.

———. 1813. *An Interesting Account of the Voyages and Travels of Captains Lewis and Clarke, in the Years 1804-5, & 6 . . . .* Baltimore: P. Mauro.

"Frank Bond." 1943. In *Who Was Who in America, Special Library Edition*, 1:114. Chicago: A. N. Marquis Co.

Frank, P. R. 1988. "Anton Doll." In *Lexikon des Gesamten Buchwesens*, 2:336. Stuttgart: Verlag Anton Hiersemann.

"Friedrich Justin Bertuch: Schriftsteller, Übersetzer, Verleger und Fabrikant." N.d. In *Geschichte Mitteldeutschland Dresa-Projektgruppe*, www.mdr.de/geschichte/pers nen/124507.html Viewed April 6, 2002.

Gale, Robert L. 1999. "Reuben Gold Thwaites." In *American National Biography*, John A. Garraty and Mark C. Carnes, eds., 21:637–638. New York and London: Oxford University Press.

Gaskell, Philip. 1972. *A New Introduction to Bibliography*. New York & Oxford: Oxford University Press.

Gass, Patrick. 1807. *A Journal of the Voyages and Travels of a Corps of Discovery, Under the Command of Capt. Lewis and Capt. Clarke of the Army of the United States . . . .* Pittsburgh: Zadok Cramer. Reprint London: J. Budd, 1808; Philadelphia: Mathew Carey, 1810, 1811, 1812.

———. 1810. *Voyage des Capitaines Lewis et Clarke, Depuis l'embouchre du Missouri, jusqu'a l'entrée de la Colombia Dans l'océan Pacifique; Fait Dans les Années 1804, 1805 et 1806, Par Ordre du Gouvernement des États-Unis . . . .* Paris: Arthus-Bertrand.

———. 1814. *Tagebuch einer Entdeckungs-Reise durch Nord-America, von der Mündung des Missuri an bis zum Einfluss der Columbia in den stillen Ocean, gemacht in den Jahren 1804, 1805 und 1806, auf Befehl der Regierung der Vereinigten Staaten, von den beiden Capitäns Lewis und Clarke.* Weimar: Verlag des H. S. privil. Landes-Industrie-Comptoirs.

———. 1847. *Lewis and Clarke's Journal to the Rocky Mountains in the Years 1804, -5, -6; as Related by Patrick Gass, One of the Officers in the Expedition.* Dayton, Ohio: Ells, Claflin & Co.

———. 1904. *Gass's Journal of the Lewis and Clark Expedition, by Sergeant Patrick Gass, One of the Persons Employed in the Expedition.* James Kendall Hosmer, introduction. Chicago: A. C. McClurg & Co.

[George Way.] N.d. Ancestry.com, individual database search result. Search.ancest...prox=1&ti=0&gss=angs&Gs=Way+George. Viewed August 17, 2001.

Glazier, Michael, pub. *The Congressional Journals of the United States: The Journal of the House of Representatives and the Senate.* Facsimile reprints, arranged by presidential administration, multiple vols. Wilmington, Del.: Michael Glazier, Inc.

"Graeme Mercer Adam." 1899. In *Appletons' Cyclopedia of American Biography,* James Grant Wilson and John Fiske, eds., 1:11. New York: D. Appleton and Co.

Graff, Everett D. See Storm, Colton.

Green, James N. 1999. "Matthew Carey." In *American National Biography,* John A. Garraty and Mark C. Carnes, eds., 4:381-383. New York and London: Oxford University Press.

Harlow, Alvin F. 1933. "James Ripley Wellman Hitchcock." In *Dictionary of American Biography,* Dumas Malone, ed., 9:76-77. New York: Charles Scribner's Sons.

Harnisch, Wilhelm, ed. 1826. *Interessante Zimmerreise zu Wasser und zu Lande für wisbegierige Leser gebildeter Stände.* Wien: Mausberger's Druck und Verlag.

Harris, G. Edward. 1965. *Contributions Toward a Bibliography of the Taylors of Ongar and Stanford Rivers.* Hamden, Conn.: Archon Books, the Shoe String Press.

Hazlitt, Ruth, ed. 1934. "The Journal of Francois Antoine Larocque from the Assiniboine River to the Yellowstone-1805." *Sources of Northwest History No. 20.* Missoula: State University of Montana.

Heckrotte, Warren. 1987. "Aaron Arrowsmith's Map of North America and the Lewis and Clark Expedition." *The Map Collector* 39 (Summer): 16-20.

Heinemann, Albrecht von. 1955. *Ein Kaufmann der Goethezeit: Friedrich Justin Bertuchs Leben und Werk.* Weimar.www.mdr.de/geschichte/archiv/personen/bertuch.html. Viewed April 6, 2002.

"Henrietta Christian Wright." N.d. cdl.library.cornell.edu/moa/browse.author/w.176. Viewed February 11, 2002.

———. N.d. freepages.genealogy.rootsweb.com/~popfraley/FowlerHillyer/pafg34.htm. Viewed June 3, 2002.

History of the Expedition of Captains Lewis and Clark 1804-5-6 Reprinted from the Edition of 1814. 1902. Intro. by James K. Hosmer. 2 vols. Chicago: A. C. McClurg. Reprint 1904.

History of the Expedition Under the Command of Captains Lewis and Clarke, to the Sources of the Missouri, Thence Across the Rocky Mountains, and Down the River Columbia to the Pacific Ocean. Performed During the Years 1804-5-6. By Order of the Government of the United States. 1814. Paul Allen, ed. 2 vols. Philadelphia: Bradford and Inskeep; New York: Abraham Bradford.

History of the Expedition Under the Command of Captains Lewis and Clarke, to the Sources of the Missouri, Thence Across the Rocky Mountains, and Down the River Columbia to the Pacific Ocean. Performed During the Years 1804-5-6. By Order of the Government of the United States. 1842. Intro. and notes by Archibald M'Vickar. New York: Harper & Brothers, Publishers.

History of the Expedition Under the Command of Captains Lewis and Clark to the Sources of the Missouri, Across the Rocky Mountains, Down the Columbia River to the Pacific in 1804–6. A Reprint of the Edition of 1814 to Which all the Members of theExpedition Contributed with Maps in Three Volumes. 1902. New York: New Amsterdam Book Co., Publishers. Reprint, New York: A. S. Barnes and Co., 1903.

History of the Expedition Under the Command of Captains Lewis & Clark to the Sources of the Missouri, Across the Rocky Mountains, Down the Columbia River to the Pacific in 1804–6. A Reprint of the Edition of 1814 to Which All the Members of the Expedition Contributed With Maps in Three Volumes. 1904. An Account of the Louisiana Purchase by John Bach McMaster; intros. by Ripley Hitchcock. New York: A. S. Barnes and Co. Reprint, London: David Nutt, 1905; New York: Allerton Book Co., 1922.

Review of *History of the Expedition Under the Command of Captains Lewis and Clark . . . .* 1814. In *The Stranger* 1, no. 22 (April 9): 321–328.

Review of *History of the Expedition Under the Command of Captains Lewis and Clarke . . . .* 1814. In *The Western Gleaner, Or, Repository for Arts, Sciences and Literature* 1, no. 6 (May): 350–375.

Review of *History of the Expedition Under the Command of Captains Lewis and Clark . . . .* 1815. In *The Analectic Magazine, Containing Selections from Foreign Reviews and Magazines, Together With Original Miscellaneous Compositions* 5: 127–149, 210–234.

Hitchcock, Ripley. 1903. *The Louisiana Purchase and the Exploration Early History and Building of the West.* Boston: Ginn & Co.

——. 1905. *The Lewis and Clark Expedition.* Boston: Ginn & Co.

The Hive: Or, a Collection of Thoughts on Civil, Moral, Sentimental & Religious Subjects: Selected from a Number of the Best Authors in the English Language . . . . 1804. Frederick-town, [Maryland]: John P. Thomson.

Hodge, Frederick Webb. 1899. "Diary, July 7–August 22" MS 430, papers of Frederick Webb Hodge. Los Angeles: Southwest Museum.

Horsford, Howard C. 1986. "Harper and Brothers." In *American Literary Publishing Housse, 1638–1899, Part 1: A-M, Dictionary of Literary Biography,* Peter Dzwonkoski, ed., 49:192–198. Detroit: Gale Research Co.

Howe, Ellic, ed. 1947. *The London Compositor: Documents Relating to Wages, Working Conditions and Customs of the London Printing Trade, 1785–1900.* London: Bibliographical Society, London.

Howes, Wright. 1962. *U.S.Iana (1650–1950).* New York: R.R. Bowker Co. for the Newberry Library. Reprint, revised and edited, Pine Mountain, Ga.: WHR Books, 1994.

"Hubbard Lester." N.d. www.familysearch.org/Eng/Search/IGI/Individualrecord.asp? recid=2804 6090&Idsnn=12. Viewed August 1, 2001.

"Indiens du Fleuve Colombia, Extrait du Voyage de Lewis et Clarke." 1821. In *Nouvelles Annales des Voyages de la Géographie et l'Histoire, ou Recueil des Relations Originales Inédites* 8: 119–165.

Issitt, John. 1998. "Introducing Sir Richard Phillips." *Paradigm* 26 (October).

Jackson, Donald. 1959. "Some Books Carried by Lewis and Clark." *Missouri Historical Society Bulletin* 16, no. 1 (October): 3–13.

——. 1981. *Thomas Jefferson & the Stony Mountains: Exploring the West from Monticello.* Carbondale: University of Illinois Press. Reprint Norman, Okla: University of Oklahoma Press, 1993.

——. 1998. "The Race to Publish Lewis and Clark." In *Voyages of Discovery: Essays on the Lewis and Clark Expedition,* James Ronda, ed., 209–228. Helena, Mont.: Montana Historical Society.

Jackson, Donald, ed. 1978. *Letters of the Lewis and Clark Expedition with Related Documents 1783–1854.* 2d ed. 2 vols. Urbana: University of Illinois Press.

Jacob, J. G. 1859. *The Life and Times of Patrick Gass, Now Sole Survivor of the Overland Expedition to the Pacific, Under Lewis and Clark, in 1804–5–6 . . . .* Wellsburg, Va.: Jacob & Smith.

"James Davie Butler." 1891. In *The National Cyclopedia of American Biography*, 9:190–191. New York: James T. White & Co.

Jefferson, Thomas. 1814. "Life of Captain Lewis." *The Western Gleaner, Or, Repository for Arts, Sciences and Literature* 1, no. 5 (April): 293–301.

Johnson, Deidre A. 1999. "Edward Stratemeyer." In *American National Biography*, John A. Garraty and Mark C. Carnes, eds., 20:922–23. New York and London: Oxford University Press.

Johnson, Sidona V. 1904. *A Short History of Oregon Early Discoveries–the Lewis and Clark Exploration–Settlement–Government–Indian Wars–Progress.* Chicago: A. C. McClurg & Co.

——. 1906a. "Relief Work at Portland." *Pacific Monthly* 15: 746–748.

——. 1906b. "Houseboating in the Pacific Northwest." *Pacific Monthly* 16: 215–228.

The Journal of the Executive Proceedings of the Senate of the United States of America: From the Commencement of the First, to the Termination of the Nineteenth Congress. 1828. Vol. 1. Washington, D.C.: Duff Green, Wilmington, Del. Michael Glazier, Inc.

The Journal of the House of Representatives, Thomas Jefferson Administration 1801–1809. Volume 2, Seventh Congress, Second Session, December, 1802–March, 1803. Wilmington, Del.: Michael Glazier, Inc.

The Journal of the House of Representatives, Thomas Jefferson Administration 1801–1809. Volume 3, Eighth Congress, First Session, October, 1803–March, 1804. Wilmington, Del.: Michael Glazier, Inc.

The Journal of the House of Representatives, Thomas Jefferson Administration 1801–1809. Volume 6, Ninth Congress, Second Session, December, 1806–March, 1807. Wilmington, Del.: Michael Glazier, Inc.

The Journal of Lewis and Clarke, to the Mouth of the Columbia River Beyond the Rocky Mountains, in the years 1804–5, & 6 . . . . 1840. Dayton, Ohio: B.F. Ells.

The Journal of the Senate of the United States of America Including the Journal of the Executive Proceedings of the Senate. Thomas Jefferson Administration 1801–1809. Volume 2, Seventh Congress, Second Session, December, 1802–March 1803. Wilmington. Del.: Michael Glazier, Inc.

The Journal of the Senate Including the Journal of the Executive Proceedings of the Senate. Thomas Jefferson Administration 1801–1809. Volume 3, Eighth Congress, First Session, October, 1803–March, 1804. Wilmington, Del.: Michael Glazier, Inc.

The Journal of the Senate Including the Journal of the Executive Proceedings of the Senate, Thomas Jefferson Administration 1801–1809. Volume 5, Ninth Congress, First Session, December, 1805–April, 1806. Wilmington, Del.: Michael Glazier, Inc.

The Journal of the Senate Including the Journal of the Executive Proceedings of the Senate, Thomas Jefferson Administration 1801–1809. Volume 6, Ninth Congress, Second Session, December, 1806–March 1807. Wilmington, Del.: Michael Glazier, Inc.

Review of *Journal of the Voyages and Travels of a Corps of Discovery . . . .* 1809. In *The Quarterly Review* (London) 1 (February and May):293–304. Reprint London: 1827, 293–304.

Kagle, Steven E. 1999. "Paul Allen." In *American National Biography*, John A. Garraty and Mark C. Carnes, eds., 1:337–338. New York and London: Oxford University Press.

Kaiser, Gerhard R. N.d. "Friedrich Justin Bertuch als Verleger." www.weimar-klassik.de/projekte/index.html. Viewed April 6, 2002.

Kelly, P[atrick]. 1796. A Practical Introduction to Spherics and Nautical Astronomy . . . . London: J. Johnson and G. G. and J. Robinson.

Kingsley, Nellie F. 1902a. *Four American Explorers: Captain Meriwether Lewis, Captain William Clark, General John C. Frémont, Dr. Elisha K. Kane, A Book for Young Americans.* New York: Werner School Book Co.

———. 1902b. *The Story of Captain Meriwether Lewis and Captain William Clark for Young Readers.* New York: Werner School Book Co.: American Book Co.

Kirwan, Richard. 1784. *Elements of Mineralogy.* London: P. Elmsly.

Kunitz, Stanley J. and Howard Haycraft, eds. 1938. *American Authors, 1600–1900: A Biographical Dictionary of American Literature.* New York: H. W. Wilson Co.

Lang, Herbert O., ed. 1885. *History of the Willamette Valley, Being a Description of the Valley and Its Resources, With an Account of Its Discovery and Settlement by White Men, and Its Subsequent History; Together with Personal Reminiscences of Its Early Pioneers.* Portland, Ore.: Geo. H. Himes, Book and Job Printer.

Lange, Robert E. 1972. *Bibliographical Index to the Literature of the Lewis and Clark Expedition.* Portland, Ore.: Oregon Lewis and Clark Trail Heritage Foundation.

Laut, Agnes C. 1904. *Pathfinders of the West: Being the Thrilling Story of the Adventures of the Men Who Discovered the Great Northwest: Radisson, La Vérendrye, Lewis and Clark.* New York: Grosset & Dunlap.

The Laws of the United States of America. 1803. Vol. 6. Washington, D.C.: [n.p.]

The Laws of the United States of America. 1807. Vol. 8. Washington, D.C.: [n.p.]

Lee, Sidney, ed. 1896. "Thomas Rees." In *Dictionary of National Biography*, 47:401–402. London: Elder & Co.

Lester, Hubbard. 1809. *The Travels of Capts. Lewis & Clarke, by Order of the Government of the United States, Performed in the Years 1804, 1805, & 1806 . . . .* Philadelphia: Hubbard Lester.

"Lighton Family Papers: Correspondence, Photographs, Manuscripts, and Other Papers. 1828–1987." MS Collection MC 779, University of Arkansas, Fayetteville. /www.uark.edu:80/libinfo/speccoll/lightonaid.html. Viewed February 15, 2002.

Lighton, William R. 1905. *Lewis and Clark: Meriwether Lewis and William Clark.* Boston and New York: Houghton Mifflin and co., 1901. Reprint Portland, Ore.: J.K. Gill.

Lockley, Fred. 1928. *History of the Columbia River Valley from the Dalles to the Sea.* 3 vols. Chicago: S. J. Clarke Publishing Co.

Louisiana Gazette and New-Orleans Advertiser. June 9, 1814–February 21, 1815.

Luckhardt, Virginia E. 1949. *Notable Printers of Early Pittsburgh.* Master's thesis. Pittsburgh: Carnegie Library School.

MacGregor, Carol Lynn, ed. 1997. *The Journals of Patrick Gass: Member of the Lewis and Clark Expedition.* Missoula, Mont.: Mountain Press Publishing Co.

Mackenzie, Alexander. 1801. *Voyages From Montreal, on the River St. Lawrence, Through the Continent of North America, to the Frozen and Pacific Ocean; In the Years 1789 and 1793. . . .* London: T. Cadell, Jun. and W. Davies, Cobbett and Morgan. Reprint Edinburgh: W. Creech, 1802; New York: G. F. Hopkins, 1802.

Maguire, Amy Jane. 1905. *The Indian Girl Who Led Them (Sacajawea).* Portland, Ore.: J. K. Gill.

Mayer, Anton. 1883–87. *Wiens Buckdrucker-geschichte, 1482–1882, Herasugegeben von den Buckruckeren Wiens.* Wien: Verlag des Comites zur Feier der Vierhundertj. Einfuhrung der Buckdruckierkunst in Wien, Wilhelm Frick, Druck von F. Jasper.

McCulloch, William. 1921. "William McCulloch's Additions to Thomas's History of Printing." *American Antiquarian Society Proceedings* 31, New Series no. 1: 89–247.

McKelvey, Susan Delano. 1955. *Botanical Exploration of the Trans-Mississippi West, 1790–1850*. Jamaica Plain: Arnold Arboretum of Harvard University. Reprint Corvallis, Ore.: Oregon State University Press, 1991.

McKerns, Joseph P. 1999. "Noah Brooks." In *American National Biography*, John A. Garraty and Mark C. Carnes, eds., 3:620–21. New York and London: Oxford University Press.

McKerrow, Ronald B. 1927. *An Introduction to Bibliography for Literary Students*. Oxford: Clarendon Press. Reprint 1967.

McMurtrie, Douglas C. 1936. *A History of Printing in the United States: The Story of the Introduction of the Press and of Its History and Influence During the Pioneer Period in Each State of the Union. Vol. 2, Middle & South Atlantic States*. New York: R. R. Bowker Co.

McVickar, Edward and William Constable Breed. 1906. *Memoranda Relating to the McVickar Family in America*. New York: The Authors.

Meehan, Thomas. 1898. "The Plants of Lewis and Clark's Expedition Across the Continent, 1804–1806." *Proceedings of the Academy of Natural Sciences of Philadelphia* (January–March): 13–14.

Message from the President of the United States, Communicating Discoveries Made in Exploring the Missouri, Red River and Washita, by Captains Lewis and Clark, Doctor Sibley, and Mr. Dunbar; with a Statistical Account of the Countries Adjacent. 1806. Washington, D.C.: A. & G. Way, Printers. Reprint New York: Hopkins and Seymour, 1806.

Miller, Daniel. [1910]. "The German Newspapers of Lebanon County." In *Publications of the Lebanon County Historical Society* 5, no. 4: 131–150.

Miller, John. 1779. *An Illustration of the Sexual System, of Linnæus*. [John Miller]: London.

Miner, William Harvey. 1902. *The Literary Collector* 3: 204–209.

Missouri River Commission. 1892–95. *Map of the Missouri River From its mouth to Three Forks, Montana, in Eighty-four Sheets*. N.p.: Missouri River Commission.

M'Keehan, David. 1800. *An Address Delivered at Greensburgh, Westmoreland County, in the State of Pennsylvania, on Saturday, February 22, 1800, the Anniversary of the Birth of the Late Illustrious Hero, Statesman and Citizen, George Washington*. Washington, Pa: Colerick.

The Monthly Anthology, And Boston Review. 1806.

Moulton, Gary, ed. 1983–2001. *The Journals of the Lewis & Clark Expedition*. 13 vols. Lincoln, Nebr.: University of Nebraska Press.

Nasatir, Abraham P., ed. 1952. *Before Lewis and Clark: Documents Illustrating the History of the Missouri, 1785–1804*. 2 vols. St. Louis: St. Louis Historical Documents Foundation.

National Intelligencer and Washington (D.C.) Advertiser, 1806–29.

"New Publications for 1814." *The Edinburgh Annual Register*, xxvi–xxvii.

The Weekly Inspector, New York, December 6, 1806.

Norona, Delf and Charles Shelter, eds. 1958. *West Virginia Imprints, 1790–1863: A Checklist of Books, Newspapers, Periodicals and Broadsides*. Moundsville, W.Va.: West Virginia Library Association.

O'Donoghue, Freeman Marius and George Simonds Boulger. 1921–22. "John Miller." In *Dictionary of National Biography*, Leslie Stephen and Sidney Lee, eds., 13:413–415. London: Oxford University Press.

"Olin Dunbar Wheeler." 1961–68. *Who Was Who in America*. 4:1001. Chicago: Marquis Who's Who.

Palmer, John McAuley. 1930. *Washington, Lincoln, Wilson: Three War Statesmen*. Garden City: Doubleday, Doran & Co., Inc.

Paltsits, Victor Hugo. 1904 (1905). "Bibliographical Data." In *Original Journals of the Lewis and Clark Expedition, 1804-1806*, Reuben Gold Thwaites, ed., 1:lxi-xciii. New York: Dodd, Mead & Co. Reprint, New York: Arno Press, 1953, 1969.

Perry, Marilyn Elizabeth. 1999. "James Mackay." In *American National Biography,* John A. Garraty and Mark C. Carnes, eds., 14:245-246. New York and London: Oxford University Press.

Peterson, Merrill D., ed. 1984. *Thomas Jefferson: Writings*. New York: The Library of America/Penguin Books.

Poulson's American Daily Advertiser, Philadelphia, 1811-25.

The True American Commercial Advertiser, Philadelphia, April 30, 1807.

Phillips, George. 1822. *Travels in North America*. Dublin: Christopher Bentham. Reprint Dublin: Brett Smith, 1824; London: C. J. G. & F. Rivington, Booksellers to the Society for Promoting Christian Knowledge, 1831; London: R. Clay for the Society for Promoting Christian Knowledge, 1846.

Pioneers of the West:Lewis and Clark. 1898. Boston: Educational Publishing Co.

Plomer, Henry Robert. 1900. *A Short History of English Printing, 1476-1898*. London: Kegan Paul, Trench, Trubner & Co., Ltd.

Plomer, Henry Robert, G. H. Bushnell, and E. R. McC. Dix. 1932. *A Dictionary of the Printers and Booksellers Who Were at Work in England, Scotland, and Ireland from 1726 to 1775*. Oxford: Bibliographical Society at the Oxford University Press.

"Political Cabinet." 1806-7. Appendices to *The Monthly Anthology, And Boston Review* 3 and 4.

Portland City Directory 1905. Portland, Ore.: R. L. Polk & Co., Publishers.

Powers, Alfred. 1935. *History of Oregon Literature*. Portland, Ore: Metropolitan Press, Publishers.

Preston, Richard S. 2000. "The Accuracy of the Astronomical Observations of Lewis and Clark." *Proceedings of the American Philosophical Society* 144, no. 2 (June): 168-191.

Purple, Samuel S. 1873. *Bradford Family: Genealogical Memorials of William Bradford, The Printer*. New York: Privately Printed.

Pursh, Frederick. 1814. *Flora Americae Septentrionalis; or, a Systematic Arrangement and Description of the Plants of North America. Containing, Besides What Have Been Described by Preceding Authors, Many New and Rare Species, Collected During Twelve Years Travels and Residence in that Country*. 2 vols. London: White, Cochrane, and Co.

Quaife, Milo Milton, ed. 1915. "Extracts from Capt. McKay's Journal-and Others." *Proceedings of The State Historical Society of Wisconsin* no. 171: 185-210.

———. 1916. *The Journals of Captain Meriwether Lewis and Sergeant John Ordway Kept on the Expedition of Western Exploration, 1803-1806*. Madison: The State Historical Society of Wisconsin.

Rees, Thomas. 1896. *Reminiscences of Literary London from 1779 to 1853, With Interesting Anecdotes of Publishers, Authors and Book Auctioneers of that Period, &c., &c*. London: Suckling & Galloway.

Reese, William. 2001. *206 New Acquisitions in Western Americana*. New Haven: Wm. Reese Co.

Die Reisen der Capitaine Lewis und Clarke; unternommen auf Befehl der Regierung der Vereinigten Staaten in den Jahren 1804, 1805 und 1806. . . . 1811. Jacob Stöver: Libanon [Lebanon], Penn.

Reize naar de Bronnen van den Missouri, en door het vaste Land van America naar de Zuidzee. Gedaan op last van de Regering der Vereenigde Staten van America, in de jaren 1804, 1805 en 1806, Door de Kapiteins Lewis en Clarke. Met Eene Kaart. 1816-1818. Dordrecht: A. Blussé en Zoon, vols. 1-2; Blusse & Van Braam, vol. 3.

Report of the Committee of Commerce and Manufactures, Who Were Instructed, By a Resolution of This House, of the 18ᵗʰ.Ult. "To Enquire into the Expediency of Authorising the President of the United States, to Employ Persons to Explore Such Parts of the Province of Louisiana, as He May Deem Proper. 1804. [Washington, D.C.: n.p.]

Resultate der Reise der Capitäne Lewis und Clarke den Missuri entlang bis zur Sud-See. Allgemeines historisches Archiv herausgegeben . . . . 1811. Leipzig: Carl Heinrich Reclam.

Rivington, Septimus. 1919. *The Publishing Family of Rivington.* London: Rivingtons.

Robertson, James R. 1905. "Reviews." *The Quarterly of the Oregon Historical Society* 6: 330–331.

Ronda, James P., ed. 1998. *Voyages of Discovery: Essays on the Lewis and Clark Expedition.* Helena, Mont.: Montana Historical Society Press.

Rowland, Mrs. Dunbar [Eron Rowland]. 1930. *Life, Letters and Papers of William Dunbar of Elgin, Morayshire, Scotland, and Natchez, Mississippi, Pioneer Scientist of the Southern United States.* Jackson: Press of the Mississippi Historical Society.

"Royal Navy Articles of War–1757." N.d. www.hmsrichmond.org/rnarticles.htm. Viewed May 9, 2002.

Rudner, Lawrence A. and Hans A. Heynau. 2001. "Revisiting Fort Mandan's Latitude: Lewis got it *almost* right." *We Proceeded On* 27, no. 4 (November): 27–30.

Sabin, Joseph. 1868. *A Dictionary of Books Relating to America, From its Discovery to the Present Time.* Reprint (2 vols): Mansfield Centre, Conn.: Martino Fine Books, 1998.

Sayre, Gordon. N.d. "A Biographical Outline. Antoine-Simon Le Page du Pratz, The History of Louisiana." www.darkwing.uoregon.edu/~gsayre/LPDP.html. Viewed April 21, 2002.

Scharf, J. Thomas. 1882. *History of Western Maryland: Being a History of Frederick, Montgomery, Carroll, Washington, Alleghany, and Garret Counties. . . .* 2 vols. Philadelphia: Louis H. Everts.

Schneller, Beverly. 1992. "*The Monthly Magazine,*" *Encyclopedia of Romanticism: Culture in Britain, 1780s–1830s,* Laura Dabundo, ed., 382. New York and London: Garland Publishing.

Schütz, J. B., ed. *Neue historische und geographische Gemählde, oder Charakteristiken merkwürdiger Personen und Darstellungen wichtiger Begebenheiten unserer Zeit; nebst Schilderungen der durch die neuesten Schicksale ausgezeichneten, neu entdeckten oder näher untersuchten Länder und Völker.* 1811. Wien: Anton Doll.

Seccombe, Thomas. 1921–22. "Isaac Taylor." In *Dictionary of National Biography.* Leslie Stephen and Sidney Lee, eds., 19:415–416. London: Oxford University Press.

Shade, William G. 1999. "Nicholas Biddle." In *American National Biography,* John A. Garraty and Mark C. Carnes, eds., 2:734–736. New York: Oxford University Press.

Sharan, James. 1808. *The Adventures of James Sharan: Compiled from the Journal Written During His Voyages and Travels in the Four Quarters of the Globe.* Baltimore: James Sharan.

Shaw, Ralph R. and Richard H. Shoemaker. 1958–1963. *American Bibliography: A Preliminary Checklist for 1801–1819.* New York: The Scarecrow Press.

Shenk, Hiram H. 1930. *A History of the Lebanon Valley in Pennsylvania.* 2 vols. Harrisburg, Pa: The National Historical Association, Inc.

Shuffleton, Frank. 1986. "M. Carey and Company." In *American Literary Publishing Houses, 1638-1899, Part 1, A-M,* 49:72–80. *Dictionary of Literary Biography,* Peter Dzwonkoski, ed. Detroit: Gale Research Co.

Siebert, Frank T. 1999. *The Frank T. Siebert Library of the North American Indian and the American Frontier, Part II.* Sale catalog of October 28, 1999. New York: Sotheby's.

Silbey, Joel H. 1999. "Duff Green." In *American National Biography,* John A. Garraty and Mark C. Carnes, eds., 9:484–485. New York: Oxford University Press.

Silver, Rollo G. 1953. *The Baltimore Book Trade, 1800–1825.* New York: The New York Public Library.

Slatkin, Carole Anne. 1999. "Alexander Wilson." *American National Biography*, John A. Garraty and Mark C. Carnes, eds., 23:554–556. New York: Oxford University Press.

Smith, Margaret Bayard. 1796–1840. "The Papers of Margaret Bayard Smith." Microfilm no. 18,941-8P. Washington, D.C.: Library of Congress.

Sobel, Dava. 1995. *Longitude: The True Story of a Lone Genius Who Solved the Greatest Scientific Problem of His Time.* New York: Walker Publishing Co., Inc.

Society of Gentlemen. 1765. *A New and Complete Dictionary of Arts and Sciences . . . .* 8 vols. in 4. London: W. Owen.

Sowerby, E. Millicent. 1955. *Catalogue of the Library of Thomas Jefferson.* 5 vols. Washington, D.C.: The Library of Congress.

Starr, Eileen. 2001. "Celestial Navigation Basics: How the captains found latitude and (sometimes) longitude." *We Proceeded On* 27, no. 4 (November): 12–18.

Stewart, Watson. N.d. *Personal Memoirs of Watson Stewart.* Sect. 2: "Making His Way." Kansas Collection Articles, www.KanColl.org. Viewed April 2002.

Storm, Colton, comp. 1968. *A Catalogue of the Everett D. Graff Collection of Western Americana.* Chicago: Newberry Library, University of Chicago Press.

Streeter, Thomas Winthrop. 1967–70. *The Celebrated Collection of Americana Formed by the Late Thomas Winthrop Streeter, Morristown, New Jersey: Sold by Order of the Trustees.* 7 vols. New York: Parke-Bernet Galleries, Inc.

Sullivan, Robert B. "Benjamin Rush." 1999. In *American National Biography* John A. Garraty and Mark C. Carnes, eds., 19:72–75. New York and London: Oxford University Press.

Taylor, Bayard. 1856. *Cyclopedia of Modern Travel: A Record of Adventure, Exploration and Discovery, for the Past Fifty Years, Comprising Narratives of the Most Distinguished Travelers Since the Beginning of This Century.* Cincinnati: Moore, Wilstach, Keys & Co.

Taylor, Isaac. 1821. *Scenes in America, For the Amusement and Instruction of Little Tarry-at-Home Travellers.* London: Harris and Son.

Thomas, Davis and Karin Ronnefeldt, eds. 1976. *People of the First Man: Life Among the Plains Indians in Their Final Days of Glory, The Firsthand Account of Prince Maximillian's Expedition; Up the Missouri River, 1833–34.* New York: E. P. Dutton & Co., Inc.

Thomas, Phillip Drennon. 1999. "Benjamin Smith Barton." In *American National Biography*, John A. Garraty, and Mark C. Carnes, eds., 2:287–288. New York: Oxford University Press.

Tiefer, Charles. 1989. *Congressional Practice and Procedure.* New York: Greenwood Press.

Todd, William Burton. 1972. *A Directory of Printers and Others in Allied Trades: London and Vicinity 1800–1840.* London: Printing Historical Society.

Travels in the Interior Parts of America; Communicating Discoveries Made in Exploring the Missouri, Red River and Washita, by Captains Lewis and Clark, Doctor Sibley, and Mr. Dunbar; with a Statistical Account of the Countries Adjacent. 1807. London: Richard Phillips.

The Travels of Capts. Lewis & Clarke, from St. Louis, by Way of the Missouri and Columbia Rivers, to the Pacific Ocean; Performed in the Years 1804, 1805 & 1806 . . . . 1809. London: Longman, Hurst, Rees, and Orme.

Travels to the Source of the Missouri River and Across the American Continent to the Pacific Ocean. Performed by Order of the Government of the United States, in the Years 1804, 1805, and 1806, by Captains Lewis and Clarke . . . . 1814. London: Longman, Hurst, Rees, Orme, and Brown.

Review of *Travels to the Source of the Missouri River, and Across the American Continent to the Pacific Ocean; Performed by Order of the Government of the United States, in the Years 1804, 1805, 1806 . . . .*1815. *The Edinburgh Review, Or Critical Journal* 24 (November 1814–February 1815): 412–438.

Thwaites, Reuben Gold, ed. 1904–05. *Original Journals of the Lewis and Clark Expedition 1804–1806 from the Original Manuscripts . . . .* 8 vols. New York: Dodd, Mead & Co.

———. 1905. *Early Western Travels, 1748–1846, a Series of Annotated Reprints of Some of the Best and Rarest Contemporary Volumes of Travel, Descriptive of the Aborigines and Social and Economic Conditions in the Middle and Far West, During the Period of Early American Settlement.* 32 vols. Cleveland: Arthur H. Clark Co.

Tweney, George H. 1993. "Elliott Coues on Lewis and Clark: A Discovery." *We Proceeded On* 19, no. 1 (February): 11–16.

Vancouver, George. 1798. "A Chart shewing part of the Coast of N.W. America." In *A Voyage of discovery to the North Pacific ocean, and Round the World.* London: N.p.

Van der Aa, 1876a. A. J. "Abraham Blussé" and "Abraham Blussé de Jonge." In *Biographisch Woordenboek der Nederlanden, Bevattende Levensbeschrijvingen van Zoodanige Personen, die Zich Op Eenigeriei Wijze in ons Vanderland Hebben Vermaard Gemaakt,* 2:666–671. Haarlem: J. J. Van Brederode.

———. 1876b. "Pieter van Braam." In *Biographisch Woordenboek der Nederlanden, Bevattende Levensbeschrijvingen van Zoodanige Personen, die Zich Op Eenigeriei Wijze in ons Vanderland Hebben Vermaard Gemaakt,* 3:1139–1141. Haarlem: J. J. Van Brederode.

———. 1879. "Nicholas Godfried Van Kampen." In *Biographisch Woordenboek der Nederlanden, Bevattende Levensbeschrijvingen van Zoodanige Personen, die Zich Op Eenigeriei Wijze in ons Vanderland Hebben Vermaard Gemaakt,* K:15–25. Haarlem: J. J. Van Brederode.

Wagner, Henry R. and Charles L. Camp. 1982. *The Plains & the Rockies: A Critical Bibliography of Exploration, Adventure and Travel in the American West, 1800–1865.* 4th ed. Robert H. Becker, ed. San Francisco: John Howell-Books.

Wallace, Henry Edward. 1904. *Sketch of John Inskeep, Mayor, and President of the Insurance Company of North America, Philadelphia.* Philadelphia: Reprint from *The Pennsylvania Magazine of History and Biography.*

Weinreb, Ben and Christopher Hibbert, eds. 1983. *The London Encyclopedia.* London: Macmillan.

Welsh, Mary Ann. 1957. "Andrew Marschalk: Mississippi's First Printer." Master's thesis. Oxford, Miss.: University of Mississippi.

Wendlick, Roger. 2002. "In Search of the White Earth." *Oregon Chapter Newsletter*, Lewis and Clark Trail Heritage Foundation (February): 4–10

Wesseling, Klaus Gunther. 1992. "Friedrich August Koethe." In *Biographisch-Bibliographisches Kirchenlexikon,* 4:298–299.

The Western Miscellany. 1848. (Dayton, Ohio) 1 (July).

Wheat, Carl I. 1957–63. *Mapping the Transmississippi West 1540–1861.* 6 vols. San Francisco: The Institute of Historical Cartography. Reprint 1958–60.

Wheeler, Joseph Towne. 1938. *The Maryland Press, 1777–1790.* Baltimore: The Maryland Historical Society.

Wheeler, Olin Dunbar. 1900. *Wonderland 1900: Descriptive of the Region Tributary to the Northern Pacific Railway and Including More Particularly the Story of Lewis & Clark's Great Exploration of the Northwest in 1804–1806,* 1–76. St. Paul, Minn.: Northern Pacific Railway.

——. 1901. "One of Lewis and Clark's Men." *Wonderland 1901: Descriptive of That Portion of the Northwest Tributary to the Northern Pacific Railway, and Particularly Relating the History of the Unique Trademark of the Northern Pacific and Describing Yellowstone Park and Custer Battlefield*, 87–94. St. Paul, Minn.: Northern Pacific Railway.

——. 1904a. *The Trail of Lewis and Clark, 1804–1904: A Story of the Great Exploration Across the Continent in 1804–06; With a Description of the Old Trail, Based Upon Actual Travel Over It, and of the Changes Found a Century Later*. 2 vols. New York and London: G. P. Putnam's Sons.

——. 1904b. "The Lewis and Clark Renaissance." *Wonderland 1904: Descriptive of the Northwest*, 101–108. St. Paul, Minn.: Northern Pacific Railway.

——. 1905. *Lewis and Clark Centennial Exposition, Portland, Oregon, June 1 to October 15, 1905*. St. Paul, Minn.: Northern Pacific Railway.

"Wilhelm H. Harnisch." 1907. *Allgemeine Deutsche Biographie*, 10: 614–617. Leipzig: Verlag von Duncker & Humblot.

Wilkie, Everett C. Jr. 1986. "J. E. Tilton and Company." In *American Literary Publishing Houses, 1638–1899, Part 1: A-M*, 49, no. 2:466–67. *Dictionary of Literary Biography*, Peter Dzwonkoski, ed. Detroit: Gale Research Co.

Wilkinson, Carol Ann. 1986. "A. S. Barnes and Company." In *American Literary Publishing Houses, 1638–1899, Part 1: A-M*, 49:40–42. *Dictionary of Literary Biography*, Peter Dzwonkoski, ed. Detroit: Gale Research Co.

"William Fisher." N.d. www.familysearch.org. Viewed August 13, 2001.

Williams, Gwyn A. 1979. *Madog: The Making of a Myth*. New York and London: Oxford University Press.

Winsor, Justin, ed. 1888. *Narrative and Critical History of America*, 7:556–558. Cambridge: The Riverside Press for Houghton, Mifflin and Co., Boston and New York.

Wood, W. Raymond and Thomas D. Thiessen. 1985. *Early Fur Trade on the Northern Plains: Canadian Traders Among the Mandan and Hidatsa Indians, 1738–1818: the Narratives of John Macdonell, David Thompson, Francois-Antoine Larocque, and Charles McKenzie*. W. Raymond Wood and Thomas D. Thiessen, eds. Norman, Okla.: University of Oklahoma Press.

Woodall, Allen E. 1933. "William Joseph Snelling: A Review of His Life and Writings." *University of Pittsburgh Bulletin* 29, no. 3: 281–286.

Wright, Charles Henry. 1903. *Genealogy of the Claflin Family, Being a Record of Robert Mackclothlan, of Wenham, Mass[.] and of His Descendants, 1661–1898*. New York: William Green.

Index

In the following index, page numbers in roman type lead to items discussed in the text, and those in italic type indicate illustrations. Plates are indexed with roman capitals.

Items in section 7b, the twentieth-century articles, are indexed by author's name only. Those wishing to research this checklist by title or key word are invited to access its electronic form at the Web site of Lewis & Clark College's Watzek Library at library.lclark.edu. Follow the link to "Rare Books."

A

Abel, Annie Heloise, 266
Abrams, Rochonne, 276, 283
Academy of Natural Sciences, 8, 53, 208, 228
"An Account of the Various Publications," 162, 195
Across America, 260
Across the Snowy Ranges, 264
Act Authorizing Jefferson to Take Possession, 76-77
"An Act for Extending the External Commerce," 68, 76
"An Act Making Compensation," 86
Acts of Discovery, 256, *256*
Adam, G. Mercer, 215, 224
Adams, John, 15
Adams, John Quincy, 68, 95, 228
Adelman, Seymour, 268
Addenda to the Supplement, 241
Adler, David A., 262
Adreon, William Clark, 273
"Adventure to the West," 282
Adventurers of Oregon, 233
The Adventures of James Sharan, 127
The Adventures of Lewis and Clark (1962), 242-243
The Adventures of Lewis and Clark (1968), 246
After Lewis and Clark, 263
Algonquin, 53, 123, 138
Alleman, Paula Fenza, 283
Allen, John Logan, 36-37, 55, 62, 248, 273, 276, 278
Allen, Paul, 150-151, 153, 171-173, 180, 183, 231-233, 242, 248, 256
Allerton Book Company, 168, 186
Allgemeine Erdkunde, 111
Allgemeines Archiv für Ethnographie, 124
Allgemeines Historisches Archiv, 124, 135-136
Alling, W., 217, 224-225
Along the Lewis & Clark Trail in North Dakota, 256
Along the Trail with Lewis and Clark, 259
Alston, Willis, 72-73
Ambrose, Stephen E., 258, 259

"America" (Mackenzie), 53. *See also* "A Map of America"
"America Between Latitudes 40 and 70 North." *See* "A Map of America"
American Adventure, 237
American Book Company, 219, 226
American Encounters, 202, 255
An American Legacy, 260
American Odyssey, 246
American Penny Magazine, 228
American Philosophical Society, 21, 26, 28, 68, 92, 162-164, 168, 208
The American Register, 228
American State Papers, 73, 79, 85
"Amerique Septentrionale" (d'Anville), 40
Among the Sleeping Giants, 201, 254
The Analectic Magazine, 154, 173
Andalusia, 249
Anderson, Douglas Alan, 283
Anderson, Irving W., 20-21, 254, 273, 274, 275, 276
Anderson, Mary B., 21, 163-165, 186-193
Anderson, Sarah Travers Lewis (Scott), 236
Andrews, E. T., 52
Andrist, Ralph K., 245
Andrus, Silas, 217, 224
Angle, Paul M., 270
The Annual Review, 112
apocrypha. *See* surreptitious
Appleman, Roy E., 249, 272, 275
Appleton, D. and Company, 167
Arikara (Ricara), 153
Arrowsmith, Aaron, 39-40, 56-57, 134-135, 151, plate IV
Arthus–Bertrand, 22, 96, 106-108, *107*
Articles of War, 29-30, 48-49
Assiniboin, 36
The Assiniboines, 242
astronomy, 31-33, 35-36, 38, 54-55, 60, 63, 192
Astronomy Notebook, 63, 192
Atlas of the Lewis & Clark Expedition (Moulton), 37, 39-40, 202
Atlas of the Lewis and Clark Expedition from the Yellowstone River (Bergantino), 253
Aurora, 91

B

Baarsel en Zoon, C., 159
The Back of Beyond, 258
Backtracking by Foot, 263
Bahmer, Robert H., 270
Baird, Helen D., 282
Bakeless, John, 238, 242-244, 268
Baker, Laura Nelson, 241
Baker, Troy, 254
The Balance and Columbian Repository, 227
Baltimore, nineteenth-century publications, 127-129, 138-141
Baltimore American, 84
Bancroft, Hubert Howe, 15, 18, 168, 209-210, 222
Bancroft Library, 18

Barbour, William R., 270
Barlow, Joel, 228
Barnard, J. G., 71, 81-82, 154
Barnes, A. S. and Company, 167-168, 185-186
Barnes, Alfred Smith, 167
Barnes, Esther, 248
Barralet, John James, 156, 179, 181
Bärtgis, Matthias, 125, 137
Barth, Gunther Paul, 259
Barton, Benjamin Smith, 26, 28, 33-34, 37, 41, 43, 46-47, 52-54, 68, 147-148, 153
Beale, Robert R., 251
Beard, Joseph Howard, 267
Bebenroth, Charlotta M., 237
Becket, T., 45-46
Beckham, Stephen Dow, 16, 18, 280
Bedini, Silvio A., 278
Before Lewis and Clark, 239, *239*
Beidleman, Richard G., 271
Beinecke, Frederick William, 16
Beinecke Library, 16
Beless, James W., 279
Bell, Burnby M., 270
Bell, Solomon, 217-218, 225
Benge, Janet and Geoff, 264
"Benjamin Capps and the 'Sacajawea' Plagiarism Case," 283
Bensley, T., 52
Benson, Guy Meriwether, 37, 55, 257, 282
Bentham, Christopher, 142
Bergantino, Robert N., 253, 282
Bergen, Lara Rice, 262
Bergon, Frank, 254
Bernard, Charles Richard, 247
Berol, Alfred C., 172, 247
Berthold, Mary Paddock, 249
Bertuch, Friedrich Justin, 100-101, 114, 124
Betts, Robert B., 252
Beyond the Shining Mountains, 236
Bialk, Elisa, 240
Bibliographical Index to the Literature of the Lewis and Clark Expedition, 248
Bicycle Guide to the Lewis & Clark Trail, 263
Biddle, Henry J., 281
Biddle, Nicholas, 70-71, 92, 98, 147-151, 163, 171-172, 232-233, 242, 248, 256
Biddle-Allen, 20, 147-168, 171-186, 209, plate XVII. *See also History of the Expedition*
A Bill Making Compensation, 84-86, *85*
Bingley, William, 217, 224
"A Biography of William Clark, 1770–1813," 282
Bird Girl: Sacagawea, 237, *237*
Bird Woman (Sacajawea) the Guide of Lewis and Clark (Houghton Mifflin, 1918), 233, *233*
The Bird-Woman of the Lewis and Clark Expedition (1905), 220, 226
Bishop, Beverly D., 277
Blackfeet, 91
The Blackfeet, 241
Blair, Elizabeth Marie, 284
Blassingame, Wyat, 244

Blazing the Way West, 236
Blevins, Winfred, 249
Blumberg, Rhoda, 253
Blussé, Abraham, 157
Blussé, A. en Zoon, 157, 159, 176-177
Blussé en van Braam, 157, 159, 176-177
Blussé, Pieter, Jr., 157
Blussé, Pieter, Sr., 157
Blussé, Pieter van Braam, 157
Bockelmann, Scott, 285
Bodmer, Karl, 97, 169, 196-199, *196-199,*
    plates XX and XXI
Bohlen, Marie Nonmast, 281
Bohner, Charles, 253
Bolas, Deborah W., 277
Bold Journey, 253
Boley Law Library, 16, 75
Bolognese, Don, 257
Bolton, Herbert Eugene, 18-19
Bon Homme Island (two Lewis/Clark
    manuscript maps), 192
Bond, Frank, 214, 224
Bonehill, Ralph, 226. *See also* Stratemeyer
The Book of a Pageant of the North-West, 231
Booth, Brian and Gwyneth, 20
Bordwell, Constance, 242
Boston, nineteenth-century publications,
    52, 72, 217, 219, 225
Boston Weekly Magazine, 226
Botanical Exploration, 208, 240
botany, 33-34, 47-48, 52-53, 147, 192, 202,
    207-208
Botkin, Daniel B., 257, 260
Bowen, Andy Russell, 258
Bowen, Peter, 264
Bowman, Gerald, 244
The Boy from Locust Hill, 253
Brackenridge, Henry M., 93-94
Brackenridge, Hugh Henry, 92-93
Bradbury, John, 148
Bradford and Inskeep, 34, 149, 160, 162,
    171-173, 178-179
Bradford, Samuel Fisher, 125, 149, 152
Bradford, Thomas, 152
Bradford, William, 125, 152
Bragg, William Frederick, 282
Bramstedt, Christine Turpin, 254
Bratton, William, 211-212
Brettell & Co., 95
Brettell, John, 95
Brettell, Thomas & Company, 95
*Brief Account of the Lewis and Clark
    Expedition,* 214-215, 224
*A Brief History of Rocky Mountain
    Exploration,* 200
Britt, Albert, 243
Brodhead, Michael J., 164, 251, 272, 274
Brooks, Noah, 212-213, 223
Broughton, William, 40, 59
Brown, Dee, 246, 279
Brown, John A., 249
Brown, John G., 267

Brown, Marion Marsh, 254
Brown, Mark H., 273
Brown, Stuart E., 246
Browne, D., 58
Brownson, Debra, 265
Bruchac, Joseph, 262
Brune, William, 247
Bryant, Martha F., 254
Buckley, Jay Harry, 285
Budd & Bartram, 35, 54
Budd & Calkin, 95
Budd, John, 95, 106
Buffon, Georges L., 157
Bulfinch, Thomas, 209, 222
Bureau of Outdoor Recreation, 248, 249
Burke, Redmond A., 270
Burns, Ken, 258
Burns, Ron, 256
Burr, Aaron, 68
Burroughs, Raymond Darwin, 239, 242
Burt, Olive Woolley, 250
Butler, James Davie, 166, 195-196

C

Cadell and Davies, 47, 53
Camp, Charles L., 233
Camp Dubois, 30, 37, 121
In Camp on White Bear Island, 231
Cappon, Lester J., 150, 172, 247
The Captain's Dog, 261
Captains Lewis and Clarke, 232
Carey, Mathew, 97-98, 104, 108-112, 117,
    148-149, 152, plates IX and X
Carlson, Nolan, 256
Carlton, Mabel Mason, 233
Carpenter, Jack, 259
Carr, Robert, 26, 152
Carson, Kevin, 265
"Carte de la Louisiane" (de l'Isle), 40, 58
"Carte du Rio Colombia" (de Mofras), 22
"Carte Pour Servir au Voyage" (Tardieu),
    96-97, *107,* 108, 114
Carter, Edward C., 262
Carter, W. Hodding, 257
cartographers and engravers: Arrowsmith,
    Aaron, 39-41, *56,* 56-57, 134-135, 151;
    Barralet, John James, 156, 179, 181;
    Carey, Mathew, 97-8, 112, plates IX and
    X; Clark, William, 7, 39, 98, 151, 154,
    169, 171, 174-176, 179, 181, 184-185,
    187; 188, 191-193, 197; Cook, James,
    40, 58, *59;* d'Anville, Jean Baptiste
    Bourguignon, 40; de l'Isle, Guillaume,
    40, 58; de Mofras, Duflot 22; du Pratz,
    Antoine-Simon, 37, 45, *45,* 55-6; Ellicott,
    Andrew, 40, 54, *55, 61;* Evans, John,
    36-38, 61, 63; Evans, W. G., 181; Frazer,
    Robert, 90; Grosvenor, 115, 141; Harrison,
    Samuel, 151, 172, 184; Hooker, W., 222;
    Jefferys, Thomas, 43-44; King, Nicholas,
    39-41, 57, 70, 78; Lewis, Meriwether, 39,
    40, *187,* 188, 191; Lewis, Samuel, 98, 135,

151, 172, 174, 181, 184, 193; Mackay,
    James, 36-38, 37-38, 60, 63; Mackenzie,
    40, 53, 60; Miller, John, 29, 41, 47, *48;*
    Mitchell, John, 40, 57; Moore, E. F., 116;
    Neele, Samuel John, 108, 123, 133-135,
    154, 159, 174-178, 181; Senex, John, 26,
    58, *58;* Smither, James, 98; Soulard,
    Antoine, 38-39, 62; Tardieu, J. B., 96-97,
    106-8, *107,* 114; Thompson, David, 40,
    57; van Baarsel, Willem Cornelius, 176,
    plate XVIII; Vancouver, George, 39-41,
    56-57, 59, plate V; von Ferro, 160, 180;
    Whimper, 143
cartography, 36-42. *See also* maps, eighteenth
    and nineteenth century
Carver, Jonathan, 102, 121-122, 124
Casa-Calvo, Marqués of, 53
Catlin, George, 15
Caughey, John Walton, 17-19
Caughey, LaRee, 17-19
Cavan, Seamus, 255
Caywood, Louis R., 268
Centinel of Liberty (Georgetown), 68
Chambers, Ephraim, 26, 44, 155
Chandler, David Leon, 257
Chandler, Katherine, 220, 226
The Character of Meriwether Lewis, 91, 221, 263
A Charbonneau Family Portrait, 21, 254
Charbonneau, Louis, 254
Charbonneau: Man of Two Dreams, 249
Charbonneau, Toussaint, 73, 97
Charleston, South Carolina, 48
"Chart of the NW Coast of America"
    (Cook), 40, 58, *59*
"A Chart shewing part of the Coast"
    (Vancouver), 40-41, 59, plate V
Chatters, Roy M., 274, 277
Cheetham, James, 53
Chidsey, Donald Barr, 247
children's literature to 1905, 215-220, 224-226
Children's Stories of American Progress, 226
The Chinook Indians, 249
Chippewa, 35-36, 53, 122
Christian, Mary Blount, 256
Christie, J., 156-157, 178-179
Christmas at Fort Clatsop, 245
Christopherson, Edmund, 269
Chuinard, Eldon G. (Frenchy) M.D., 17, 20,
    244, 250, 273, 274, 275, 280, 281
Chuinard, Robert, 17
Churchill, Claire Warner, 235, 273
Clark, Ella E., 250
Clark, Frank Henry, 282
Clark, S., 51
Clark, William: as cartographer, 7, 39, 98, 151,
    154, 169, 171, 174-176, 179, 181, 184-
    185, *187;* 188, 191-193, 197; as fictional
    subject, 213-214; journals and field notes,
    25, 27, 30-31, 41, 46, 49, 169, 170, 186-
    193, 201-202; letters, 25, 44. 71, 73, 74,
    83, 96, 121, 125-126, 134; publication
    of 1814 edition, 147-152; reports, 36, 54,

69-71, 74, 121, 122, 160

Clarke, Charles G. 247, 268, 271, 274

Clarkia pulchella, plate XXIII

Clary, Jean, 260

Clatsop, 211

Clay, Richard, 131

Cleary, Rita, 262

Coale, E. J., 172

Cobbett and Morgan, 53

Coburn, Mark, 254

The Codfish Musket, 235

Cohick, Nancy, 283

A Collection of Modern and Contemporary Voyages, 71, 82

Collins, John, 30

Colter, John, 166, 196

Colter-Frick, L. R., 258

Colter's Hell, 236, *236*

The Columbia, 240

Columbia River, 34, 60, 99, 123

The Columbia River Guide, 233

Columbian Centinel & Massachusetts Federalist, 76, 82, 226-227

The Coming of the White Men, 231, *231*

Commissioners of Longitude, 52

Committee of Commerce, 69

Confidential Request for Funds, 68, 75-76

Confluence of the Willamette and Columbia Rivers (Lewis/Clark manuscript map), 191

Congressional Globe, 116

The Connecticut Courant, 76, 226

The Conquest, 169, 213-214, 223, *223*

Conrad, C. & A., 148-149, 172, 227

Conrad, John, 26, 91, 147, 149

Contributions to the History of the Pacific Northwest, 234

Cook, James, 40, 57-58, *59*, 96, 122, 152

Cooking on the Lewis and Clark Expedition, 262

Cooper, Alice, 214

Copeland, Peter F., 251

Corps of Discovery, 7, 37, 40-41, 42, 67, 71-74, 90, 102, 104-105, 121

Corps of Discovery: A Novel, 265

Coues, Elliott, 21, 121, 126, 149-151, 156, 161-166, 168, 177, 179, 181, 186-195, 211, 245-246, 256

Coues-Anderson Manuscript, 21, 163-166, 186-193, *187*, *191*, plate XIX

Courageous Colter and Companions, 258

Cramer, Spear & Eichbaum, 93, 94, 105, 153

Cramer, Zadok, 89-94, 104-105, 245

Cramer's Almanac, 93-94

Crawford, Anthony R., 277

Crawford, Helen, 267

Crawford, Polly Pearl, 235

Cree, 36, 122-123

Creech, W., 47, 53

Criswell, Elijah Harry, 236, 282

Croswell, William, 52

Crow, 41

Cruzatte and Maria, 264

Cruzatte, Pierre, 91

Cuming, Fortescue, 93

Curl, Grace Voris, 237

Curtis, K. D., 270

Custis, Peter, 69

Cutright, Paul Russell, 121-123, 131, 164, 168, 246, 249, 251, 270, 271, 272, 273, 274, 281

Cyclopaedia of Modern Travel, 208, 222

Cyclopædia, or an Universal Dictionary, 26, 45, 155, 216

D

D is for Discovery, 261

Daniels, Jonathan, 243

d'Anville, Jean Baptiste Bourguignon, 40

Dattilio, Daniel J., 253

Daugherty, James, 239

Dave and Jane's Adventures, 257

David Thompson and the Lewis and Clark Expedition, 241

Davis, J. Steeple, 226

Davis, Julia, 235

Davis, Kristen, 285

Davis, Lottie Wright, 239

Dayton, Ohio, nineteenth-century publications, 101-102, 114-115, 131-132, 141

Dear, Elizabeth A., 259

Dearborn, Henry, 26, 69, 72-73

de Carondelet, Baron, 37

Defenbach, Byron, 234

de Hondt, P. A., 45

De Kay, Ormonde, 246

de l'Isle, Guillaume, 40, 57-58

DeLorean, John Z., 271

de Mofras, Duflot, 22

Denslow, Ray V., 266

Denton, Carolyn S., 282

Department of the Interior, 245

"Description of the Original Manuscript Journals," 164, 195

The Devil's Backbone, 243

Devillier, Christy, 264

DeVoto, Bernard, 239, 268, 269

The Dialogues of Lewis and Clark, 250

Dick, Everett, 243

Dickson, Frank H., 275

Dictionary of Arts and Sciences, 26, 27, 41, 43-45, *44*, plate II

A Dictionary of Books Relating to America, 168

Dillon, Richard, 245

Dippold, Hans Karl, 124, 135-136

Directions for Preserving the Health of Soldiers, 28, 46-47

Discoveries Made in Exploring the Missouri, 70, 81

Discovery Writers, 259, 260

Ditmanson, Dennis, 265

"Divided Light," 284

Do Them No Harm, 255

Dobson, Thomas, 26, 35, 54, 149

Documents Accompanying a Bill, 72-73, 84-85, *85*

Documents Relating to the Purchase, 78

Dodd, Frank H., 169

Dodd, Mead & Company, 168-170, 196-199

Dodd, Moses W., 169

Dodge, James, 274

The Dog Who Helped Explore America, 260

Doll, Alois, 99

Doll, Anton, 98-100, 111

Dordrecht, Netherlands, nineteenth-century publications, 157-159, 176-177

The Double Eagle Guide, 262

Draper, Lyman, 166, 168

Drouillard, George, 244

The Drouillard to Druyor Family History, 248

Drury, Clifford M., 270

Duane, William & Son, 69, 72-73, 77-78, 83, 86

Dublin, nineteenth-century publications, 97, 129, 142, 156, 178-179

Duboc, Jessie L., 269

Duflot de Mofras' Travels, 22

du Lac, Perrin, 71, 100

Dunbar, William, 57, 69-71, 74, 78, *80*, 81, 83, 105, 121

Duncan, Dayton, 254, 258

Dunlap, John, 46-47

du Pratz, Antoine-Simon Le Page, 27-28, 37, 41, 43, 45-46, 53, 55-56, 124

Dye, Eva Emery, 169, 213-214, 216, 223

E

"The Early Career of Jean Baptiste Charbonneau," 283

The Early Far West, 234

Early Pictures of the Falls, 260

Early Western Travels, 168

Eaton, John, 102

The Eclectic Review, 112

The Edinburgh Review, 135, 155, 159, 174-175

Edmonds, Margot, 250

Educational Publishing Company, 219, 226

Edwards, Judith, 260

Eells, Benjamin, 131

Ehrlich, George, 278

Eichbaum, William, 93-94

Eide, Ingvard Henry, 246

Eifert, Virginia S., 243

Eldorado, 208

Elements of Botany, 33-34, 41, 47, 52-53, plate I

Elements of Mineralogy, 30, 41, 49-50

Ellicott, Andrew, 26, 34-35, 39-40, 43, 51, 54-55, 60-61

Elliott Coues, 251, *251*

Ellis, Arthur, 259

Ellis, Dick, 276

Ells, Benjamin Franklin, 101, 131, 141

Ells, Claflin, & Co., 101-102, 114-115

Elmsly, P., 49

Emmons, Della Gould, 237

Encyclopaedia (French), 26

Encyclopaedia; or, A Dictionary of Arts, 26

engravers. *See* cartographers and engravers

Enlightenment, 7-8, 41, 42

Enlightenment Science in the Pacific Northwest, 252

An Epic American Exploration, 259

Erickson, Douglas, 19
Erickson, Vernon, 274
An Essay Towards an Indian Bibliography, 168
The Essential Lewis and Clark, 263, *263*
Evans, John, 36-38, 61, 63
Evans/Mackay, *Journal Extracts*, 36
Evans, Sarah, 214
Evans, W. G., 181
Evening Fire-Side, 71, 78
Evenson, Jeffrey W., 262
Evenson, Teri, 262
Everhart, William C., 271
Ewers, John C., 241, 268
Excerpt from Journal of the Voyages, 236
La Expedicion de Lewis y Clark, 239
*The Expedition of Lewis & Clark in Picture
    and Story*, 237
The Expedition of Lewis and Clark
    (Readex Microprint, 1966, 1974), 245
*The Expeditions of Lewis & Clark and
    Zebulon Pike*, 259, 265
"The Explanation of the West," 283
Exploration du Territoire de l'Orégon, 22
Exploration Unlimited, 239
"Exploring the Lewis and Clark
    Expedition," 285
Exploring the West from Monticello, 37, 55, 257
Exploring with Lewis and Clark, 262
Eyerly, Pete, 264
The Eyes of Discovery, 238

F
Faber, Harold, 264
Falls and Portage of the Missouri
    (Lewis/Clark manuscript map), 188, *187*
Fanselow, Julie, 257
Farnsworth, Frances Joyce, 240
Fazio, James R., 264
Fenlason, Ed, 258
Fent, Cindy, 278
Fernandez, Vivian, 262
Fidler, Peter, 39, 56-57
Field, Thomas, 168
The Field Notes of Captain William Clark,
    16, 201-202, 244
Fielding's Lewis and Clark Trail, 253
Fields, Wayne D., 277
Fifer, Barbara, 259, 262
Final Environmental Impact Statement, 249
Finding the West, 265
Finley, Helen Deveneau, 268
First Across the Continent, 212-213, 223
The First Chouteaus, 251
Firtch, William, 282
Fisher, Ronald K., 255
Fisher, Sherry R., 275
Fisher, Vardis, 241, 243
Fisher, William, 101, 125-126, 128, 131,
    138-140
"Fishing with Silas," 285
Fitz-Gerald, Christine Maloney, 255
Fjosee, Wayne, 271

Flandrau, Grace, 234, 267
Flathead, 159
Fleischer, Gerhard, 159, 180
Fletcher, Robert Henry, 237
Flora Americae Septentrionalis, 207-208, 222,
    222, plate XXIII
Floyd, Charles, 73, 89-90, 166, 195-196, 202
Flug, Arthur, 247
Foley, William E., 251, 277
*Following the Lewis and Clark Trail:
    A Vacation Guide*, 260
Foote, Stella, 247
Forrest, Earle R., 104, 115, 238, 268
Fort Clatsop, 17, 27, 31, 35, 41, 97, 133, 163,
    211, *225*, 227
Fort Clatsop, The Story Behind the Scenery, 253
Fort Mandan, 36, 41, 54, 69-71, 73-74, 78, 83,
    90, 96, 121-122, 124, 125, 133, 226-227
"Fort Mandan Miscellany," 36
Forward the Nation, 237
Foucrier, Annick, 262
Four American Explorers, 219, 226
Fowle, A. L., 182
Fradin, Dennis B., 260
Frazer, Robert, 89, 227
Frazier, Neta Lohnes, 245
Free Library, 89
Freeman, Lewis R., 267
Freeman, Thomas, 69
Freeman's Friend, 84, 227
Freneau, Philip, 92
Friedrichstadt (Fredericktown), Maryland,
    nineteenth-century publications, 125, 137
Friis, Herman R., 268
Fritz, Harry W., 281
From East to West with Lewis & Clark, 258
From Sea to Shining Sea, 252
From the Eye of the Eagle, 264
Furtwangler, Albert, 228, 256

G
Gale, Kira, 260
Gales and Seaton, 79, 85
Gallatin, Albert, 25-26, 39-40
Garnett, John, 52
Garrison, Kirk, 284
Garver, Frank Harmon, 244, 266, 271
Gass, Patrick, 20, 89-117, 122, 163, 202,
    236, 241
Gass's Journal (Hosmer), 102, 117, 167, 261
The Gates of the Mountains, 243
Gattia, Alarico, 250
Gemmill, Mel, 258
General Advertiser, 227
"A General History of the Fur Trade," 91
"A General Map of Uper Louisiana"
    (Soulard), 38-39
George Drouillard, 244
George Shannon, 243
George Shannon (peg-leg), 254
Gevock, Nich J., 285
Ghent, W. J., 234

Giant of the Rockies, 240
Gibbs, George, 211
Gide Fils, 159, 176
Gideon, Jacob, 68
Gilbert, Bil, 248, 279
Gillette, David D., 275
Gillette, P. W., 228
Girl of the Shining Mountains, 261
Girls Who Rocked the World, 260
A Glance at the Lewis and Clark Expedition, 234
Gleiter, Jan, 254
Gmelin, Johann, 48
Goddard, Donald, 276
Godfrey, Larry, 283
Going Along with Lewis & Clark, 262
The Golden Dollar, 262
Goodrich, Silas, 35
Goosman, Mildred, 273
Gould, Dorothy Fay, 236
Govan, Thomas Payne, 241
Graetz, Rick, 264
Graetz, Susie, 264
Grant, Matthew, 248
Gray and Bowen, 217, 225
Gray, Charles Gilmer, 267
Gray, Edward, 149
Gray, Robert, 59, 209
The Great Adventure, 235
Great Falls of the Missouri, 41, *179*, *187*, 207
Great Plains Quarterly, 278
Greely, Adolphus W., 210, 223
Green, Carl R., 259
Green, Duff, 67-68, 75
Greenwich meridian, 31, 33, 39
Greenwich Observatory, 31
Gregg, Kate L., 236
Grinnell, George Bird, 231
Groff, Joseph, 68
Grosvenor, 115, 141
Grosvenor, C. H., 115
Gunderson, Mary, 262
The Guns of Harpers Ferry, 246
Guns of the Lewis and Clark Expedition, 242
Gustafson, R. W., 260, 262

H
Haan, Wanda, 262
Hagood, J. Hurley, 254
Hagood, Roberta Roland, 254
Hail, Jane Wood, 274
Haines, Francis D. Sr., 19
Haines, Madge, 241
Hall, Charles Gilbert, 235
Hall, Courtney R., 269
Hall, Eleanor J., 258
Hallaron, Scott L., 284
Halliburton, R., 274
Halsey, Ashley Jr., 278
Halsey, Cheryll, 251
Hamilton, Charles, 195-196
Hamilton, Irene Nakai, 257
Hamilton, M. B., 283

Hammarsten, James F., 276
Haney, Rich, 261
Hanna, Archibald, 242
Hanson, Charles E., 281
Hardy, P. D., 143
Hargrove, Julia, 264
Harnisch, Dr. Wilhelm, 159-160, 180
Harper and Brothers, 160-162, 167, 180-183
Harper Family Library, 22, 160-161, 179
Harper, Francis P., 149, 161-162, 164-166,
    186, 193-195
Harper, James, 161
Harper, John, 161
Harper, Lathrop, 165, 186
Harris and Son, 217, 224
Harris, Burton, 239
Harrison, John, 31-32
Harrison, Samuel, 151, 172, 184
Harrison, William Henry, 37, 60, 96, 134
Harvey and Darton, 224
Hastings, Patricia B., 261, 262, 264
Hatch, Lynda, 257
Haug, Joe, 264
Haupt, Keith, 264
Hauser, David, 262
Hawke, David Freeman, 251
Hawk's Journey, 255
Hawthorne, Hildegarde, 238
Hay, John, 38, 63
Hayes, Anna, 16
Hayes, Edmond, 16
Hays, Wilma Pitchford, 247
Hazlitt, Ruth, 267
Hearne, Samuel, 39, 152, 160
Hearne's, Mackenzie's, Lewis und Pike's
    Entdeckungsreisen, 159-160, 180
Hebard, Grace Raymond, 235, 266
Heckrotte, Warren, 57, 279
Hedstrom, Deborah, 258
Hehenberger, Shelly, 265
Henrikson, Stephen E., 278
Henry, Will, 243
herbarium, 8, 202, 207-208
Herbert, Janis, 262
Heriot, George, 98
Herndon, Carrie P., 231
Hewes, Agnes Danforth, 235
Higgins, Ruth, 236
Highsmith Press, 261
Hill, Richard H., 272
The Hills By the Headwaters, 258
Himler, Ronald, 265
Hirasuna, Delphine, 277
Histoire de la Louisiane, 28, 124
Histoire Naturelle, 157
An Historical Account of the Most
    Celebrated Voyages, 152
Historical Signboards, 249
"Historical Sketches," 69-70
The History of Louisiana (du Pratz), 28, 37,
    41, 43, 45-46, *45, 55
History of the Expedition (Philadelphia, 1814),

16, 74, 93-94, 121, 125, 148-154, 171-173,
    172, 245, plate XVII
History of the Expedition (Dublin, 1817),
    156-157, 161, 178-179, *179*, 181
History of the Expedition (Harper/M'Vickar
    series, 1842-1917), 22, 160-161, *180*, 180-183
History of the Expedition (Coues, 1893-1965),
    126, 167, 193-195, *194*, 245
History of the Expedition (Hosmer, 1902-1924),
    167, 183-184
History of the Expedition (New Amsterdam,
    1902), 184-185
History of the Expedition (Barnes, 1903-1904),
    167, 185
History of the Expedition (McMaster series,
    1904-1922), 167, 185-186
History of the Expedition (Harpers,1915), 183, 232
History of the Expedition (A. C. McClurg,
    1917), 184, 232
History of the Expedition (A. C. McClurg,
    1924), 184, 232
History of the Expedition (Allerton Book Co,
    1922), 186, 233
History of the Expedition (AMS, 1973), 248
History of the Expedition: a Census of Copies 247
A History of the Lewis and Clark Journals, 121,
    131, 168, 249
The History of the Louisiana Purchase, 167
History of the Northwest Coast, 168, 210, 222
History of the Pacific States, 18, 222
Hitchcock, Ripley, 167, 185, 215, 224
Hoff, J., 172
Hogrogian, Robert, 251
Holbrook, Stewart H., 240
Holloway, David, 248
Holm, Don, 245
Holman, Albert M., 233
Holman, Frederick V., 267
Holmberg, James J., 279
Holmgren, Virginia C., 278
Holt, Glen E., 277
Hooker, W., 222
Hopkins, G. F., 70, 79-80
Hopkins and Seymour, 70, 79-80
Horne, Esther Burnett, 251
Hosmer, James Kendall, 102, 104, 117, 167,
    183-184, 223, 232, 261
Hough, Emerson, 232
Houk, Rose, 261
Howard, Ella Mae, 256
Howard, Bonnie C., 236
Howard, Harold P., 246, 247, 257
Howell, Warren R., 17
Hoyle, Robert J., 255, 280
Hubbard, Rev. J., 132
Hubbard, William, 123
Hudson's Bay Company, 39, 57
Hueston, Ethel, 235
Huffman, Marian, 251
Hull, Bette Meine, 260
Hult, Ruby El, 242
Hunsaker, Joyce Badgley, 263

Hunter, George, 69, 71, 74, 121
Hurst, Thomas, 155

I

"If We Want It," 284
An Illustration of the Sexual System, 29, 41,
    47-48, *48*, plate III
An Illustration of the Termini Botanici, 29, 41, 47
In Memoriam Sergeant Charles Floyd, 195
In Search of York, 252, *252*
In the Footsteps of Lewis and Clark, 247
In the Footsteps of Lewis and Clark:
    A Directed Inquiry, 247
In the Path of Lewis and Clark, 259
In the Rocky Mountains, 231
Including Two Captains, 249
The Incredible Journey of Lewis and Clark, 253
The Independent Chronicle, 226, *226*
The Indian Girl Who Led Them, 216, 224
"Indiens du Fleuve Colombia," 159, 176
Information Respecting the History, 15
Ingoglia, Gina, 255
Ingraham, Leonoor Swets, 17, 252
Inskeep, Abigail, 152
Inskeep, Abraham H., 152, 171, 178
Inskeep, John Jr., 151-153
Interessante Zimmerreise, 159-160, 180,
An Interesting Account (1812), 128, 139-140,
    plate XVI
An Interesting Account (1813), 128-129,
    131-132, 140-141
Introduction to Spherics. See Practical
    Introduction to Spherics
Isely, Bliss, 236
Israel, John, 93
Irwin, William R., 257

J

Jackson, Andrew, 67-68, 71
Jackson, Donald, 25, 92, 170, 200-201, 243,
    251, 254, 270, 272, 274, 276, 281
Jacob, J. G., 102, 104, 116-117, 263
Jacob & Smith, 102, 116
Jacquin, Philippe, 262
Jassem, Kate, 250
Jefferson and the Gun-Men, 263
The Jefferson Conspiracies, 257
Jefferson library and papers, 25, 26, 28, 40
Jefferson, Thomas, 7, 15, 17, 20, 22, 25-27,
    35-37, 46, 52-54, 62, 67-84, 96-98, 100,
    121, 125, 127, 147, 151, 157, 207, 214,
    228, 269, 277
Jefferson's Instructions to Lewis and Clark,
    22, 25, 31-33, 38, 43, 52, 73-74
Jefferson's Report to Congress, 69-72, 77-82
Jefferson's West, 264
"Jefferson's Western Diplomacy," 283
Jefferys, Thomas, 43-44, *44*
Jenkinson, Clay S., 91, 221, 263
Jensen, Dana O., 268
The Jesuit Relations, 168
Jeunehomme, Vᵉ, 96

John Colter (Burton Harris), 239
John Colter Discoverer of Yellowstone Park, 234
John Howell Books, 17
Johnson, Ann Donegan, 251
Johnson, Grace, 236
Johnson, J., 50-51
Johnson, Kenn E., 240
Johnson, Mabel, 255, 279
Johnson, Sidona V., 214, 223
Jones, John, 143
Jones, Landon Y., 263
Jones, Roy F., 248, 270
The Journal of Andrew Ellicott, 32, 35, 54-55, 55, 60, *61*
The Journal of Augustus Pelletier, 263
The Journal of Lewis and Clarke (1840), 131-132, 141-142
The Journal of the Executive Proceedings of the Senate, 67-68, 75-76
The Journal of the House of Representatives, 67, 69, 75-77, 83, 86
The Journal of the Senate, 67, 69, 75, 77-79, 83, 86
A Journal of the Voyages and Travels (1807), 89-96, 104-105, *105,* 110, 122, 134, 153
A Journal of the Voyages and Travels (1808), 106
A Journal of the Voyages and Travels (1810, first state), 108-110
A Journal of the Voyages and Travels (1810, second state), *109,* 110-111, 216-217, 224, plates IX and X
Journal of the Voyages and Travels (1811), 111, 117
Journal of the Voyages and Travels (1812), 112, plate XII
A Journal of the Voyages and Travels (Ross & Haines, 1958), 241, *241*
The Journals of Lewis and Clark (Houghton Mifflin, 1953), 239, *239*
The Journals of Lewis and Clark (Mentor Books, 1964), 244
The Journals of Lewis and Clark (Viking, 1989), 254
The Journals of Lewis and Ordway, 200, 232
The Journals of Patrick Gass, 259, *259*
The Journals of the Expedition (The Heritage Press, 1961), 242
The Journals of the Expedition (The Limited Editions Club, 1961), 242
The Journals of the Expedition (Easton Press, 1962, 1989, 1993), 243, 256
The Journals of the Lewis and Clark Expedition (Moulton), 37, 104, 148, 170, 202, 252, *252*
The Journey of Lewis and Clark: A Teacher's Resource Booklet, 261
juvenile literature. *See* children's literature

K

"Kaart der Reizen" (van Baarsel), 176, XVIII
Kamm, Caroline (Gray), 15
Karolevitz, R. F., 270
Karwoski, Gail Langer, 261
Keating, Bern, 272
Keller, Linda, 283

Kelly, Patrick, 31-32, 50-51, *51*
Kelly, Robert Q., 270
Kennedy, Michael Stephen, 242
Kennerly, William Clark, 238
Kerr, Robert, 48
Kessler, Donna J., 258, 284
Kessler, Dorothy Simmons, 257
Kidd, James, 22
Kiesling, Sanna Porte, 255
Kimaid, Michael A., 284
King, Nicholas, 39-41, 54-55, 57-60, 70, 78
Kingsley, Nellie F., 219, 226
Kingson, C. S., 268
Kinistanoes. *See* Knisteneaux
Kirwan, Richard, 30, 31, 41, 49-50
Knisteneaux, 36, 53, 122-123
Knox, Bob, 257
Kobler, John, 279
Koch, Elers, 243, 267
Koch, Frederick H., 231
Koethe, Friedrich August, 124, 135-136
Kozar, Richard, 263
Kroll, Steven, 257
Kushner, Howard I., 277

L

Lacy, Dan Mabry, 248
Lake Biddle, 174, 181
Lake Riddle, 174, 181
Lallemant, A. J. N., 96, 106, 108
The Land Beyond the Setting Sun, 263
Landes–Industrie–Comptoirs, 100-101, 112-114
Langdon, James, 247
Lange, Robert E., 20, 248, 280, 281
Large, Arlen J., 279
Larocque, Francois-Antoine, 41
Larsell, Olaf, 268, 269
Larson, Marion J., 278
Lasky, Kathryn, 263
Laut, Agnes C., 214, 223
Lavender, David, 254
The Laws of the United States, 73, 76
Lea & Blanchard, 98
Lebanon, Pennsylvania, eighteenth and nineteenth-century publications, 123-124, 136
Ledyard, John, 96, 152
Lee, Fred L., 272
Lee, Robert Edson, 250
Leininger, Tracy M., 263
Leipzig, nineteenth-century publications, 124, 135-136, 159, 180
The Lemhi: Sacajawea's People, 250
Leonard, Bruce Jr., 279
le Page. *See* du Pratz
Lepley, John G., 273
Lesmeister, Lauren, 262
Lester, Hubbard, 122, 124, 126-127, 133-134, 136, 138, 155, plate XIII
Let's Go with Lewis and Clark, 244
A Letter by Elliott Coues, 195, 256

Letters of the Lewis and Clark Expedition, 200-201, 243, *243*
"Letter, Salmon, Idaho," 282
Lewis and Clark (Abdo Publishers, 2001), 264
Lewis and Clark (Bonanza, 1994), 257
Lewis and Clark (Cavendish, 2001), 264
Lewis and Clark (Chelsea House Publishers, 1992), 255
Lewis and Clark (Chelsea House Publishers, 2000), 263
Lewis and Clark (Crestwood House, 1993), 256
Lewis and Clark (Franklin Watts, 2001), 265
Lewis and Clark (Good Apple, 1994), 257
Lewis & Clark (Kids Discover, 1996), 258
Lewis and Clark (Lighton, 1905), 215, 223
Lewis and Clark (Macdonald, 1974), 248
Lewis and Clark (Scholastic, 1999), 261
Lewis and Clark (Scholastic Professional Books, 1997), 259
Lewis and Clark (Troll Associates, 1985), 253
Lewis & Clark: A Photographic Journey, 261
Lewis & Clark: Across a Vast Land, 261
Lewis and Clark Across the Bitterroot Range, 243
Lewis and Clark Among the Indians, 252, *252*
Lewis & Clark: An American Journey, 260
Lewis & Clark and Davey Hutchins, 256
Lewis & Clark and the Crossing of North America, 248
Lewis and Clark and the Image of the American Northwest. See Passage through the Garden
Lewis and Clark and the Nez Perce Indians, 247
Lewis and Clark and the Route to the Pacific, 255
Lewis and Clark and the Shahaptian Speaking Americans, 251
Lewis & Clark: Art of the Upper Missouri, 263
Lewis & Clark at Council Bluff: A Guide to Lewis & Clark in the Omaha-Council Bluffs Area, 260
Lewis and Clark at Fort Clatsop, 239
"Lewis and Clark at Fort Clatsop: A Winter of Environmental Discomfort," 284
Lewis and Clark at Seaside, 240
The Lewis and Clark Centennial Exposition, 20, 166, 212, 214, 216
The Lewis and Clark Collections of Vascular Plants, 202, 261
Lewis & Clark College, 15-22
Lewis & Clark Coloring Book (Fort Clatsop Historical Association), 265
The Lewis & Clark Cookbook: With Contemporary Recipes, 262
Lewis & Clark Country, 250
Lewis & Clark: Doctors in the Wilderness, 265
Lewis and Clark: Early America Pioneers, 232
Lewis & Clark Educator's Resource Guide: A Review of Lewis and Clark Materials, 265
The Lewis and Clark Expedition (Hitchcock 1905), 167, 224
Lewis and Clark Expedition (Cardwell, 1964), 244
"Lewis and Clark Expedition" (Clark, 1927), 282
The Lewis and Clark Expedition (Compass Point

Books, 2001), 265

The Lewis and Clark Expedition (Dansville, 1912), 231

The Lewis and Clark Expedition (Great Northern Railway, 1927), 234

The Lewis and Clark Expedition (Hitchcock, 1905), 167, 215, 224

The Lewis and Clark Expedition (J. B. Lippincott Company, 1961), 242

The Lewis & Clark Expedition (Jefferson National Parks Association, 1999), 261

The Lewis and Clark Expedition (Lucent Books, 1996), 258

"Lewis and Clark Expedition" (McGrath, 1931), 282

The Lewis & Clark Expedition (Random House, 1951), 239

The Lewis and Clark Expedition (Silver Burdett, 1985), 253

The Lewis and Clark Expedition (Twodot, 1990), 255

Lewis and Clark Expedition (Works Projects Administration of Colorado), 266

The Lewis and Clark Expedition: A Guide to the Holdings, 251

The Lewis & Clark Expedition: A Traveler's Companion for Oregon and Washington, 264

The Lewis and Clark Expedition: An Illustrated Keepsake Album, 246

The Lewis and Clark Expedition Coloring Book, 251

The Lewis and Clark Expedition, 1804–1806: A Brief Synopsis, 246

The Lewis and Clark Expedition, 1804–06: The Journey that Opened, 248

"The Lewis and Clark Expedition in Textbooks," 285

The Lewis & Clark Expedition: Montana's First Bird Inventory, 261

The Lewis and Clark Expedition: Our National Epic of Exploration, 240

The Lewis and Clark Expedition: Selections From the Journals (Bedford Books, 1998), 259

"The Lewis and Clark Expedition: The Preparation," 284

"The Lewis and Clark Expedition: The Return Trip," 283

The Lewis and Clark Expedition's Newfoundland Dog, 281

Lewis and Clark Exploration of Central Montana, 256

Lewis and Clark: Explorers of the American West, 257

Lewis and Clark: Explorers of the Northwest (Enslow Publishers, 1998), 260

Lewis and Clark, Explorers to the West, 241

Lewis and Clark: Exploring North America, 257

The Lewis & Clark Exposition (Wheeler, 1905), 212, 224

Lewis and Clark for Kids: Their Journey of Discovery with 21 Activities, 262

Lewis and Clark: Historic Places, 249

Lewis and Clark in Beaverhead County, 244

Lewis and Clark in Beaverhead County, Montana, 260

Lewis and Clark in Cass County, 258

Lewis and Clark in Missouri, 251

Lewis and Clark in North Dakota, 238

Lewis & Clark in the Bitterroot, 259

Lewis & Clark in the Fort Columbia Area, 240

Lewis & Clark in the Pierre and Fort Pierre Area, 265

Lewis and Clark in the Three Rivers Valleys, Montana, 258

Lewis and Clark: Into the Wilderness, 265

Lewis and Clark journals, 21

"The Lewis and Clark Journals: Their Contribution to American Literature," 283

Lewis and Clark: Leading America West, 255

Lewis and Clark: Linguistic Pioneers, 236, 282, 282

Lewis & Clark: Northwest Glory, 251

"The Lewis and Clark Odyssey and the Decimation of the American Bison," 284

Lewis and Clark on the Middle Missouri, 203, 265

Lewis & Clark on the Upper Missouri, 260

Lewis & Clark: Our National Epic of Exploration, 1804–1806, 240

Lewis & Clark: Partners in Discovery, 238, *238*

Lewis and Clark: Pathfinders of the Great Northwest, 233

Lewis and Clark: Pioneering Naturalists, 246, *246*

Lewis and Clark: Pioneers in America's Westward Expansion Movement, 234

"Lewis and Clark Retraced," 283

Lewis and Clark Routes Between the Bitterroot Valley and the Columbia River, 255

Lewis & Clark: The Fincastle Connection, 257

Lewis & Clark: The Great Adventure, 247

Lewis & Clark: The Journey of the Corps of Discovery: An Illustrated History, 258

Lewis and Clark through Idaho, 244

The Lewis & Clark Trail (1978), 250

The Lewis and Clark Trail (Harper & Row, 1965), 245

The Lewis & Clark Trail (National Geographic Society, 1998), 260

The Lewis and Clark Trail: An Interim Report, 245

The Lewis and Clark Trail: A Potential Addition, 248

The Lewis and Clark Trail: A Proposal for Development, 245

The Lewis and Clark Trail: A Proposed National Historic Trail, 249

Lewis and Clark Trail Commission, 245-246

The Lewis and Clark Trail: Final Report, 246

Lewis and Clark Trail Heritage Foundation, 17, 19-20, 260, 278

Lewis and Clark Trail Maps, A Cartographic Reconstruction, 263

Lewis and Clark Trail Maps, A Cartographic Reconstruction. Volume II, 265

Lewis and Clark Trail–The Photo Journal, 264

Lewis and Clark: Voyage of Discovery (KC Publication, 1977), 249

Lewis & Clark: Voyage of Discovery (National Geographic Society, 1998), 259

Lewis and Clark: Western Trailblazers (Creative Education, 1974), 248

Lewis and Clark: Western Trailblazers (Creative Education, 1988), 254

Lewis and Clarke's Journal to the Rocky Mountains, 101, 114-115, 141

Lewis and Clark's America: A Voyage of Discovery and *A Contemporary Photo Essay,* 249

Lewis and Clark's Expedition as a Source for Poe's "Journal of Julius Rodman," 235

Lewis and Clark's Journey of Discovery in American History (Enslow Publishers, 1999), 260

Lewis and Clark's Montana Trail, 264

Lewis et Clark: l'Amérique d'est en ouest, 250

Lewis, Grace, 268, 270

Lewis, Meriwether: as cartographer, 39, 40; as naturalist, 7-8, 17, 27, 47-48, 53, 157, 192, 202, 207-208; astronomy notebook, 63, 192; death of: 147-148, 151; instructions to, 7, 22, 25, 31, 33, 38, 40, 54; journals, 41-42, 56, 89-91, 163, 186-193, 200, 202, 241-242, 245; letters, 46, 82, 121, 124; library assembly, 25-26, 28-29, 32-63; prospectus of 1807, 72, 91, 147, 227-228; reports, 36, 46, 54, 69-71, 73-74, 121, 122, 151-152, 160

Lewis, Samuel, 98, 135, 151, 172, 174, 181, 184, 193

Lewises, Meriwethers and Their Kin, 236

Lewis's Route from Traveler's Rest to the Missouri, (Lewis/Clark manuscript map), 192, *187*

Library Company, 28, 43, 92, 102

Library of Congress, 28, 40, 75, 90, 102

The Life and Times of Patrick Gass, 102, 104, 116-117, 262

"Life of Captain Lewis," 74, 94, 151, 153, 156, 171, 173, 174

"Life-History of Jean Baptiste Charbonneau," 283

Lighton, William R., 215-216, 223

Link, Louis W., 244

Linnæus, Carolus, 29, 34, 47-48, 97

Linnean Society, 26, 208

The Literary Collector, 168

"A Literature-Based ESL Curriculum: The Great Lewis and Clark Expedition," 284

Litman, Seymour, 247

The Lolo Trail: A History and A Guide, 247

The Lolo Trail: A History of Events, 247

London, eighteenth and nineteenth-century publications, 26, 27, 29-31, 43-60, 71, 81-82, 95-96, 121, 123, 131-135, 143, 154-156, 173-178, 217, 224

Long, Benjamin, 263

longitude, calculations of, 31-33, 39-40, 50-52, 54-55

Longman, Hurst, Rees, and Orme, 123, 134-135, 154, 155
Longman, Hurst, Rees, Orme, and Brown, 155-156, 173-178
Longman, Thomas, 155
Loomis, Noel M., 245
Loos, John L., 268, 271, 282
The Lost Children of the Shoshones, 238, *238*
"Louisiana" (Arrowsmith/Lewis), 134-135
"Louisiana" (du Pratz), 45, *45*, 55
"Louisiana" (1812 Carey), 97, plate XII
Louisiana Gazette, 53, 227
Louisiana Purchase, 68-69, 121, 168, 185
The Louisiana Purchase (Hitchcock, 1903/04), 167, 215
The Louisiana Purchase and the Exploration, 224
Louisiana Purchase: Lewis and Clark Expedition, 239
Louisiana Gazette, 92
Louisiana Territory, 37-38, 68, 70, 74, 76-77, 93, 99, 100, 121, 123
Lourie, Peter, 259, 264
Lovely Sacajawea, 248
Lurie, Nancy, 269

M

Macfarlane, Robert, 240
MacGregor, Carol Lynn, 92, 97, 102, 104, 259, 283
Mackay, James, 36-38, 60, 63
Mackay-Evans, *Journal Extracts*, 63
Mackay-Evans exploration, 61
Mackenzie, Alexander, 35-36, 39-41, 47, 53-54, 57, 59-60, 70, 91, 94, 122-123, 126, 134, 138, 160
Mackinlay, J., 49
Macon, Nathaniel, 68
Madame Charbonneau, 247
Madog, 38
Madsen, Brigham D., 250
The Magnificent Adventure (1916), 232
The Magnificent Adventure (1931), 234
Maguire, Amy Jane, 216, 224
Majors, Harry M., 278, 279
Makers of American History, 215, 224
The Making of Sacagawea, 258
Mandan, 36-38, 72-74, 226
Mansfield, J. Carroll, 235
Manuscript Map of Western North America (King), 39-41. *See also* Map of the Western Part
"A Map Exhibiting all the New Discoveries" (Arrowsmith), 39-41, *56*, 56-57, plate IV
"A Map of America between Latitudes 40 and 70 North" (Mackenzie), 40, 53, 60
"A Map of Lewis and Clark's Track" (Clark), 7, 171, 174-176, 179, 181, 184-185, 193
"A Map of Louisiana and of the River Mississipi" (Senex), 58, *58*
"A Map of Louisiana, with the course of The Missisipi" (du Pratz), 37, 45, 55-56
"A Map of the British and French Dominions"

(Mitchell), 40
"Map of the Country" (anonymous), 122, 133-134
"Map of the Country" (Neele), 123, 133-135, plate XIV
"A Map of the Discoveries Made by Capts. Cook & Clarke" (Carey 1809), 98
"A Map of the discoveries of Capt. Lewis & Clark" (Frazer ms.), 90
Maps of the Mississippi and Ohio Rivers (Ellicott), 40, 54, *55, 61*
Map of the Missouri (Evans), 61
Map of the Missouri (Mackay), 60
Map of the Missouri to the mouth of the Osage (Soulard), 62
Map of the Missouri River, 165
"Map of the Washita River" (King/Dunbar), 70, 78
Map of the Western Part of North America (King), 39-41, 57
Map of Upper Louisiana (Soulard), 62
"Map of Virginia" (Samuel Lewis), 98
"A map showing the Great Bend of the Missouri" (Thompson), 40
mapmakers, *see* cartographers and engravers
Mapping the Transmississippi West, 36, 241
maps, eighteenth and nineteenth century:
"America Between Latitudes 40 and 70 North" (Mackenzie), 40, 53, 60, *see also* "A Map of America;" Bon Homme Island (two Lewis/Clark manuscript maps), 192; "Carte de la Louisiane" (de l'Isle), 40, 58; "Carte du Rio Colombia" (de Mofras), 22; "Carte Pour Servir au Voyage" (Tardieu), 96-97, *107*, 108, 114; "Chart of the NW Coast of America" (Cook), 40, 58, *59*; "A Chart shewing part of the Coast" (Vancouver), 40-41, 59, plate V; Confluence of the Willamette and Columbia Rivers (Lewis/Clark manuscript map), 191; Falls and Portage of the Missouri (Lewis/ Clark manuscript map), *187*, 188; "Kaart der Reizen" (van Baarsel), 176, plate XVIII; Lewis's Route from Traveler's Rest to the Missouri (Lewis/Clark manuscript map), *187*, 192; "Louisiana" (Arrowsmith/Lewis), 134-135; "Louisiana" (du Pratz), 45, *45*, 55; "Louisiana" (Carey 1812), 97, 112, plate XII; Manuscript Map of Western North America (King), 39-41. *See also* Map of the Western Part; "A Map Exhibiting all the New Discoveries" (Arrowsmith), 39-41, *56*, 56-57, plate IV; "A Map of America between Latitudes 40 and 70 North" (Mackenzie), 40, 53, 60; "A Map of Lewis and Clark's Track" (Clark), 7, 171, 174-176, 179, 181, 184-185, 193; "A Map of Louisiana and of the River Missis-sipi" (Senex), 58, *58*; "A Map of Louisiana, with the course of The Missisipi" (du Pratz), 37, 45, 55-56;

"A Map of the British and French Dominions" (Mitchell), 40; "Map of the Country" (anonymous), 122, 133-134; "Map of the Country" (Neele), 123, 133-135, plate XIV; "A Map of the Discoveries Made by Capts. Cook & Clarke" (Carey 1809), 98; "A Map of the discoveries of Capt. Lewis & Clark" (Frazer ms.), 90; Maps of the Mississippi and Ohio Rivers (Ellicott), 40, 54, *55, 61*; Map of the Missouri (Evans), 61; Map of the Missouri (Mackay), 60; Map of the Missouri to the mouth of the Osage (Soulard), 62; *Map of the Missouri River*, Missouri River Commission 1893-4), 165; "Map of the Washita River" (King/Dunbar), 70, 78; Map of the Western Part of North America (King), 39-41, 57; Map of Upper Louisiana (Soulard), 62; "Map of Virginia" (Samuel Lewis), 98; "A map showing the Great Bend of the Missouri" (Thompson), 40; Mississippi River and Tributaries, (Lewis /Clark manuscript map), 188; New Discoveries (Arrowsmith), *see* "A Map Exhibiting all the New Discoveries;" "Nord-Amerika mit Bezeichnung der Entdeckungsreisen" (von Ferro), 160, 180; Snake and Missouri Rivers (Lewis/Clark manuscript map), 192; "A Topogra[phical] Sketch" (Soulard), 38-39, 62
March of the Volunteers, 242
Marcovitz, Hal, 264
Marks, Constant R., 233
Marschalk, Andrew, 70, 81-82
Mattes, Merrill J., 271
Maudlin, Clark M., 239
Maskelyne, Nevil, 31-33, 51-52
Mauro, Philip, 128-129, 140
Mausberger, Anton, 160, 180
Mavor, William Fordyce, 152
Maximilian, Prince. *See* von Wied-Neuwied
Maxwell, James, 125, 138, 171
Mayer, Larry, 264
McBeth, Kate C., 231, 256
McCann, Jerry, 260
McClelland, John M., 240
McClurg, A. C. & Co., 102, 117, 183-184, 214, 223
McCorkle, Jack, 255
McCreight, Major Israel, 238
McDermott, John Frances, 269, 270, 274, 276
McDonald, Mary Jane, 283
McGrath, Francis Joseph, 282
McGrath, Patrick, 253
McKelvey, Susan Delano, 208, 240
McMaster, John Bach, 167-168, 185
McMurtry, Larry, 264
McNeil, Christine A., 272
McNeill, Joseph P., 272
McSpadden, J. Walker, 234
Mead, Edward S., 169

Meany, Edmond S., 267
The Medical Aspects of the Lewis & Clark Expedition, 244
Medical Inquiries and Observations, 28, 47
Medical Repository, 71, 78, 112
Medical Research Foundation, 273
Meehan, Thomas, 228
"Memoire sur la Louisiane," 27
Men of Achievement, 210, 223
The Men of the Lewis and Clark Expedition, 247
The Mentor, 266
Meriwether Lewis (Dillon), 245
Meriwether Lewis and William Clark, 255
Meriwether Lewis and William Clark: Soldiers, Explorers, and Partners in History, 254
Meriwether Lewis and William Clarke (Werner, 1910), 183, 231
Meriwether Lewis: Boy Explorer, 237
Meriwether Lewis & William Clark: La Traversée d'un Continent, 262
Meriwether Lewis in Blackfeet Country, 244
Meriwether Lewis: Missouri's First Royal Arch Mason, 266
The Meriwether Lewis Mystery, 247
Meriwether Lewis: Naturalist, 246
Meriwether Lewis of Lewis and Clark, 235, *235*
Meriwether Lewis: Off the Edge of the Map, 264
Meriwether Lewis, Trail Blazer, 236
Meriwether, Nelson Heath, 240-241, 244
The Meriwethers and their Connections, 244
Merkwaardigheden, 225
Message from the President of the United States (A. & G. Way, 1806), 36, 62-63, 69-70, 74, 77-78, 89, 100, 121, plate VI
Message from the President of the United States (Hopkins and Seymour, 1806), 70, 79-80, *80*
Methodist Quarterly Review, 175
Meyer, Roy W., 249
Meyers, Mrs. Peter M., 231
Miller, John, 29, 41, 47-48, plate III
Miltenberger, Anthony, 128-129, 139
Milton, Joyce, 265
Miner, William Harvey, 168
Mirsky, Jeannette, 238
Mississippi River and Tributaries (Lewis/Clark manuscript map), 188
Missouri Historical Society, 36, 251
Missouri Historical Society Bulletin, 268
Missouri River, 36-42, 56, 60-63, 67, 71-72, 99, 121-122, 158, 165, *187*, 226
Mitchell, John, 40, 57
M'Keehan, David, 89-92, 100, 102, 104-106, 110-111, 117
M'Millan, B., 50
Moccasin Prints West, 240
Moeller, Bill and Jan, 261
Mohrman, Gary, 264
Montgomery, Elizabeth Rider, 245
Montgomery, M. R., 263
The Monthly Anthology and Boston Review, 71-72, 82-83, 105, 112, 228
Monthly Magazine, 174

Mooney, Michael, 8, 19
Moore, E. F., 116
Moorehead, Blanche Woods, 236
Morier, Jacob, 100, 114, 159
Morley, Jacqueline, 260
Morrill, Leslie, 241
Moulton, Candy, 280
Moulton, Gary E., 37, 39-40, 104, 148, 170, 202-203, 252, 255, 261, 265, 278, 279
"Mr. Jefferson's Literary Pursuit," 284
Muench, David, 249, 250
Muhly, Frank, 249
Müller, Johann Sebastian. *See* Miller, John
Mumey, Nolie, 241
Munroe & Francis, 72
Munves, James, 241
Murfitt, Rex, 271
Murphy, Dan, 249
Murray, John, 106
Mussulman, Joseph, 259
M'Vickar, Archibald, 160-161, 180-183
My Name is York, 259
The Mysterious Death of Meriwether Lewis, 256
Mystery of Sacajawea, 246

N

Narrative and Critical History of America, 168
A Narrative of the Indian Wars, 123
Narrative of the United States Exploring Expedition, 15
Nasatir, Abraham P., 239, 245
Natchez, nineteenth-century publications, 70-71, 81-82, 100, 121
Natchez (tribe), 28
Natchez Trace, 147
The National Aegis, 227
National Intelligencer, 68, 72-73, 84-86, 90-91, 227
National Intelligencer Extraordinary, 20, 72, 84, plate VII
National Park Service, 243
The Natural History of the Lewis and Clark Expedition, 242
Nautical Almanac, 31-33, 52
Nautical Ephemeris, 51-52
The Navigator, 93, 105, 245
Neele, Samuel John, 108, 133-135, 154, 159, 174-178, 181
Nell, Donald F., 258
Nelson, Vera Joyce, 240
Neuberger, Richard L., 239, 269, 270
Neue Bibliothek der wichtigsten Reisebeschreibungen, 100, 114, 124
Neue historische und geographische Gemählde, 98-99, 111, plate XI
Nevin, Evelyn C., 238
New Amsterdam Book Company, 166-167, 184-185, 186, 215
A New and Complete Dictionary. See Dictionary of Arts and Sciences
The New Cyclopaedia, 26
New Discoveries (Arrowsmith). *See* "A Map

Exhibiting all the New Discoveries"
The New Found Journal of Charles Floyd, 166, 195-196
A New General Atlas, 58
New Hampshire Sentinel, 82, 84, 227
New Orleans, nineteenth-century publications, 92
New Travels Among the Indians (Philadelphia, 1812), 125, 138-139
New Views of the Origin of the Tribes, 33, 53-54
New World Builders, 236
New York, nineteenth-century publications, 70, 79-80, 121, 160-161, 180-183
Newly Discovered Personal Records, 247
Newman, John, 73
Nez Perce, 123
The Nez Perces Since Lewis and Clark, 231, 256
Nicholas Biddle, 241
Nichols, William, 276
No Other White Men, 235
Noble, R., 53
Noonan, Jon, 256
"Nord-Amerika mit Bezeichnung der Entdeckungsreisen" (von Ferro), 160, 180
North American Indians, 15
North America's Faked History, 251
North Dakota Parks & Recreation Department, 265
North Dakota Plant Species Documented on the Lewis & Clark Expedition, 265
North West Company, 37, 41
Northern Colorado Teachers of the National Citizenship Education Program, 266
Northern Pacific Railway, 266
Northwest Discovery, 279
Northwest Passage, 7
"Notes on Mr. Thomas Meehan's Paper," 195
Notes on the State of Virginia, 98, 127, 151
Nouvelles Annales des Voyages, 159, 176
Nutt, David, 168, 185-186

O

O'Dell, Scott, 253
Of Courage Undaunted, 239
Off the Map: The Journals of Lewis and Clark, 256
Old South Leaflets, 228
The Old West: The Trailblazers, 248
Olmsted, Gerald W., 253
Olson, Kirk, 278
Omnium Gatherum, 71, 83
On the Trail of Sacagawea, 264
On the Trail with Lewis and Clark, 236
On the Trail with Lewis & Clark in Montana, 242
O'Neill, Jeanne, 259
Only One Man Died, 17, 250
The Only True America: Following the Trail of Lewis and Clark, 262
Opening the West With Lewis and Clark, 232
Oppenlander, J. H., 233
Oral Tradition of Sacajawea, 251
Ordway, John, 30, 89-90, 92, 200, 202
Oregon and Eldorado, 209, 222

Oregon Historical Quarterly, 272
*Original Journals of the Lewis and Clark
    Expedition* (Thwaites, 1904), 17, 168-170,
    196-199, *196-198,* plates XX and XXI
*Original Journals of the Lewis and Clark
    Expedition* (Thwaites, Antiquarian Press),
    199, 241
*Original Journals of the Lewis and Clark
    Expedition* (Thwaites, Arno), 199, 246
*Original Journals of the Lewis & Clark
    Expedition as Published in 1904* (Thwaites,
    DSI), 199, 265
Orme, Cosmo, 155
Osage, 72, 153, 226
"Osage River map," 39
Osborne, Kelsie Ramey, 240
Osgood, Ernest Staples, 16, 170, 201-202, 244,
    273, 275, 281
Otfinoski, Steven, 255
Our Natural History, 257
Out West: An American Journey, 254
Overland, Helen Howard, 269
Owen, William, 26-27, 41, 43
Owen's Dictionary. See Dictionary of Arts and Sciences

P
Palladium, 71, 134
Paltsits, Victor Hugo, 97, 168, 177, 181, 197
Pamplin, Dr. Robert B. Jr., 19
The Panhandle Farmer, 102
The Panoplist, 82
Paris, nineteenth-century publications,
    96-97, 106-108
Parsonage, Douglas, 165, 186
Part of the Coast of NW America
(Vancouver).
See "A Chart shewing"
Passage of Discovery, 260
Passage Through the Garden, 36-37, 248, *248*
Pathfinders of the West, 214, 223
Paton, Bruce C., 265
"The Patrick Gass Journal," 283
Patrick Gass: Lewis and Clark's Last Man,
    104, 238
Patten, William, 284
Patterson, Robert, 26, 32, 36, 43, 51, 63
Patzman, Barbara J., 263
Peaceful Conquest, 240
Peattie, Donald Culross, 237
Pedro Vial and the Roads to Santa Fe, 245
Peebles, John J., 271
Pepe, Albert R., 284
Persimmon Hill, 238
Personal Recollections of Pioneer Life, 233
Petersen, David, 254
Petersen, William J., 271
Peterson, Donald A., 260
Phelps, Dawson A., 269
Philadelphia, 21
Philadelphia, eighteenth and nineteenth-century
    publications, 35, 52-54, 70, 91, 97-98,
    101, 108-112, 122-124, 133-134, 138-139,

148-153, 171-173
Phillips, George, 121, 129-132, 142-143, 155
Phillips, Henry, 163-165
Phillips, Richard, 71, 81-82
A Picture Book of Sacagawea, 262
Pike, Zebulon M., 100, 154, 160, 162, 165, 217
Pioneer Boys of the Great Northwest, 219, 226
Pioneer Heroes, 234
Pioneering in the Northwest (Deitch & Lamar
    Co., 1924), 233
Pioneers of the West, 219, 226
Pioneers of the Wild West, 235
Pittsburgh Gazette, 71, 89, 91-92, 104
Pittsburgh Magazine Almanack, 93
Pittsburgh, nineteenth-century publications,
    89-94, 104-105
The Plains & the Rockies, 16, 233
Plamondon, Martin, 263, 265
Plants of Fort Clatsop, 254
Pocahontas, Sacajawea, Sarah Winnemucca, 257
"Political Cabinet," 82-83
Polking, Kirk, 244
Pollard, Lancaster, 239-240
Pompeys Pillar, 247
Poole, Edwin A., 271
Poole, Kristin, 263
The Port Folio, 34, 91, 148, 150, *173,* 173, 228
Porter, Donald Clayton, 255
Potter, James E., 265
Powell, Lawrence Clark, 15
Powers, H. C., 228
A Practical Introduction to Spherics, 31, 35, 50-51, *51*
Preston, Richard, 280
printers and publishers, nineteenth-century:
    Alling, W., 217, 224-225; American Book
    Company, 219, 226; Andrews, E. T., 52;
    Andrus, Silas, 217, 224; Arthus-Bertrand,
    22, 96, 106-108, *107;* Barnard, J. G., 71,
    81-82, 154; Bärtgis, Matthias, 125, 137;
    Barton, Benjamin Smith, 33-34, 47, 52-53,
    68, 147-148, 153, plate I; Becket and de
    Hondt, 45; Becket, T., 45-46; Bensley,
    T., 52; Bentham, Christopher, 142;
    Blussé, Abraham, A. en Zoon, en van
    Braam, 157, 159, 176-77; Bradford &
    Inskeep, 34, 149, 160, 162, 171-173,
    178-179; Bradford, Samuel Fisher and
    William 125, 149, 152; Bretell, Thomas
    & Company, 95; Browne, D, 58.; Budd
    & Bartram, 35, 54; Budd, John, 95,
    106; Cadell and Davies, 47, 53; Carey,
    Mathew, 97-98, 104, 108-112, 117, 148-
    149, 152, plates IX and X; Carr, Robert,
    26, 152; Chambers, Ephraim, 26, 44, 155;
    Christie, J., 156-157, 178-179; Clark, S.,
    51; Clay, Richard, 131; Coale, E. J., 172;
    Cobbett and Morgan, 53; Commissioners
    of Longitude, 52; Conrad, C. & A., 148-
    149, 172, 227; Cramer, Zadok, 89-94, 104-
    105, 245; Cramer, Spear & Eichbaum,
    93, 94, 105, 153; Creech, W., 47, 53; de
    Hondt, P. A., 45; Dobson, Thomas, 26,

35, 54, 149; Doll, Anton, 98-100, 111;
    Duane, William & Son, 69, 72-73, 77-78,
    83, 86; Dunlap, John, 46-47; Educational
    Publishing Company, 219, 226; Fleischer,
    Gerhard, 159, 180; Ells, Benjamin
    Franklin, 141; Ells, Claflin & Company,
    101, 114-115; Elmsly, P, 49.; Fisher,
    William, 101, 125-126, 128, 131, 138-
    140; Gales and Seaton, 79, 85; Gray and
    Bowen, 217, 225; Green, Duff, 67-68, 75;
    Hamilton, Charles, 195-196; Harper and
    Brothers, 160-162, 167, 180-183; Harris
    and Son, 217, 224; Harvey and Darton,
    224; Hoff, J., 172; Hopkins, G. F., 70,
    79-80; Hopkins & Seymour, 70, 79-80;
    Inskeep, Abraham, 152, 171, 178; Jacob,
    J. G., 102, 104, 116-117, 263;
    Jeunehomme, V^e, 96; Johnson, J., 50-51;
    Landes-Industrie-Comptoirs, 100-101,
    112-114; Lester, Hubbard, 122, 124, 126-
    127, 133-134, 136, 138, 155; Longman,
    Hurst, Rees and Orme, 123, 34-135, 154-
    155; Longman, Hurst, Rees, Orme and
    Brown, 155-156, 173-178; Mackinlay, J.,
    49; Marschalk, Andrew, 70, 81-82; Mauro,
    Philip, 128-129, 140; Mausberger, Anton,
    160, 180; Maxwell, James, 125, 138, 171;
    Miller, John, 29, 41, 47; Miltenberger,
    Anthony, 128-129, 139; M'Keehan,
    David, 89-92, 100, 102, 104-106, 110-111,
    117; Munroe & Francis, 72; Murray, John,
    106; Noble, R., 53; Owen, William, 26,
    41, 43; Phillips, George, 121, 129-132,
    142-143, 155; Phillips, Richard, 71, 81-82;
    Reclam, Anton Philipp, 124; Reclam,
    Carl Heinrich, 124, 135-136; Rees,
    Abraham, 26, 44, 155, 216; Richardson,
    W., 51; Rivington, C. J. G. & F., 131, 143,
    155; Rivington, F. and C., 50; Robinson,
    G. G. and J., 50; Schnee, Jacob, 123;
    Sharan, James, 101, 125-128, 138-139;
    Smith, Samuel Harrison, 67-69, 72-73,
    75-76; Society for Promot-ing Christian
    Knowledge (S. P. C. K.), 131, 143; Stöver,
    Jacob and John Casper, 123-125, 136-137;
    Stower, C., 123; Tilton, J. E. and Company,
    209, 222; Way, A. & G., 67-68, 70, 72, 75,
    77, 83-84, 86; Way and Gideon, 68; Way
    and Groff, 68; Werner Company, 183,
    219, 226; White, Cochran, and Company,
    222; Wilson, John, 11, 11; Young, W. P., 48
*Proceedings of the State Historical Society
    of Wisconsin,* 168
Proposals For Publishing by Subscription
    Robert Frazer's Journal, 227
*A Proposed Lewis and Clark National
    Wilderness,* 243
Providence Gazette, 84, 227
Pryor, Nathaniel, 89-90
publishers. *See* printers and publishers
Pursh, Frederick, 89, 147, 207-208, 222,
    plate XXIII

Q

Quaife, Milo M., 90, 200, 232
The Quarterly Review, 95-96, 106, 112, 135, 155, 159, 175
Quilting the Journeys of Lewis & Clark, 261, 262, 264
Quiry, Patricia, 265
Quivera Society, 18

R

Raphael, Elaine, 257
Ray, Verne F., 247, 269
Raymond, James, 251
Reclam, Anton Philipp, 124
Reclam, Carl Heinrich, 124, 135-136
Records of Lewis, Meriwether and Kindred Families, 239
Red Heroines of the Northwest, 234, *234*
Rees, Abraham, 26, 44, 155, 216
Rees, John, 247, 270, 282
Rees, Josiah, 154
Rees, Owen, 154-155
Rees, Thomas, 154-155, 159, 174, 176
Reese, William, 20, 100
Regulations for the Order and Discipline of the Troops, 29-30, 48-49
Rehder, Dudley D., 274
Reid, Russell, 238, 253, 267, 270
Reise durch Persien, 100
Reise in die Beyden Louisianen, 100
Die Reisen der Capitaine Lewis und Clarke (1811), 123-124, 136-137, *137,* plate XV
Die Reisen der Capitaine Lewis und Clarke (1812), 125, 137-138
Reize naar de Bronnen van den Missouri, 20, 157-159, 176-177
The Repertory (Boston), 71, 78, 81-82, 84, 227
Report of the Committee of Commerce, 77
Request for Compensation, 115-116
Resultate der Reise, 124, 136
Reveal, James L., 261
"The Rhetoric of Imperialism," 284
Rice, C. David, 251
Richardson, W., 51
Rigby, J. Wilmer, 282
Ritter, Michael, 283
River Walk: A Frontier Story, 262
Rivington, C. J. G. & F., 131, 143, 155
Rivington, F. and C., 50
Roberts, Hadley B., 282
Robertson, James R., 214
Robinson, G. G. and J., 50
Robinson, Sheila C., 256
Rodger, Tod, 263
Rogers, Ann, 251, 279
Rogers, Ken, 260, 263
"A Roll of the Men," 73, 84-85, *85*
Ronda, James, 228, 252, 260, 264, 265, 278, 279, 281
Roop, Connie, 256, 261
Roop, Peter, 256, 261

Rosen, Daniel, 265
Rowland, Della, 255
Royal Society (London), 26, 32
Ruby, Robert H., 249
Rudd, Velva E., 269
Ruisch, Edward, 281
"Rules of Health," 28
Rush, Benjamin, 26, 28, 43, 46
Russell, Charles M., 259
Russell, Steve F., 282

S

Sabin, Edwin L., 232
Sabin, Francene, 253
Sabin, Joseph, 168
The Saga of Lewis & Clark, 261
Sacagawea, 21, 73-74, 167, 212-214, 216-217
Sacagawea (Dillon, 1977), 249
Sacagawea (Putnam, 1997), 259
Sacagawea (Raintree, 1987), 254
"Sacagawea: A Uniquely American Legend," 284
Sacagawea: Beyond the Shining Mountains, 263
Sacagewea: Guide for the Lewis and Clark Expedition, 264
Sacagawea: Indian Guide, 244
Sacagawea: Indian Interpreter to Lewis and Clark, 254
Sacagawea: Native American Hero, 259
Sacagawea of the Lewis and Clark Expedition, 250
"Sacagawea: The History of a Myth," 284
Sacagawea: The Journey to the West (Silver Press, 1998), 260
Sacagawea: Westward with Lewis and Clark, 259
Sacagawea's Nickname, 264
Sacagawea's Son: The Life of Jean Baptiste Charbonneau, 265
Sacajawea (Arthur H. Clark, 1933), 235
Sacajawea (Putnam, 1967), 245
Sacajawea (Howard, 1971), 247
Sacajawea (Watts, 1978), 250
Sacajawea (Avon, 1979), 250, *250*
Sacajawea (Griggs, 1980), 251
Sacajawea (January Productions, 1981), 251
Sacajawea (Griggs, 1980), 251
Sacajawea: A Native American Heroine, 254
Sac-a-ja-wea, America's Greatest Heroine, 238
Sacajawea and the Journey to the Pacific, 255
Sacajawea and the Lewis and Clark Expedition, 234
Sacajawea: Guide to Lewis and Clark, 242
Sacajawea: Her True Story, 261
Sacajawea: Her True Story (Grosset, 2001), 265
"Sacajawea: Heroine of the Lewis & Clark Expedition" (1958), *270*
Sacajawea of the Shoshones, 237
Sacajawea, Shoshone Trailblazer, 259
Sacajawea Statue Association, 167, 214, 223
Sacajawea (The Bird Woman) (Montana Federation of Women's Clubs, 1915), 232
Sacajawea: The Girl Nobody Knows, 245

Sacajawea, the Great American Indian Heroine, 241
Sacajawea: The Great Divide, 255
Sacajawea, the Indian Princess, 233
Sacajawea: The Journey West, 257
Sacajawea: The Story of Bird Woman, 262
Sacajawea: Traductora y Guía, 257
Sacajawea: Translator and Guide, 257
Sacajawea, Wilderness Guide, 250
"Sacajawea's Role," 282
Sachatello-Sawyer, Bonnie, 259
Sagittaria sagittifolia, 34, plate I
Saindon, Robert, 253, 275, 277, 280
Sakajiawei: Mei xi tan xian nü xiang dao, 254
Sakakawea and the Fur Traders, 260
Sakakawea: The Bird Woman, 253
"Sakakawea: The Bird Woman" (1963)
Salisbury, Albert and Jane, 239
Sanford, William R., 259
Santella, Andrew, 265
Satterfield, Archie, 250
Scannon, Dog with Lewis and Clark, 241
Scenes in America, 217, 224-225, plate XXII
Schaare, C. Richard, 237
Scharf, J. Thomas, 125
Scheuerman, Richard D., 259, 265
Schmidt, Jeremy, 261
Schmidt, Thomas, 260, 261
Schnee, Jacob, 123
Schoolcraft, Henry Rowe, 15
Schroer, Blanche, 276
Schuler, Harold H., 265
Schultz, James Willard, 233
Schütz, J. B., 98-99, 111
Schuyler, Alfred E., 261
Scott, Laura Tolman, 232
Scull, John, 93
Seaman: The Dog Who Explored the West, 261
Seattle Art Museum, 249
Seeking Western Waters, 258
Seibert, Jerry, 242
Senex, John, 26, 58
Setzer, Henry W., 269
Seymour, Flora Warren, 236, 237
Shannon, George, 148, 150
Sharan, James, 101, 125-128, 138-139
Shaughnessy, Diane, 259
Shaw, Dorothy, 16
Shaw, Laurence L., 16
The Shining Mountains, 238
Shope, Irvin S., 269
A Short History of Oregon, 214, 223
Shoshone, 73, 99, 159
Sibley, John, 69, 74, 83, 121
Sierra Club, 264
Sign-talker, 264
Simon-Smolinski, Carole, 279
Simpson, Mary, 283
Sims, Elmer Harper, 234
Sioux, 122
Skarsten, M. O., 244
Sketches, Historical and Descriptive, 98

Sketches of a Tour, 93
Skinner, Constance L., 233
Skold, Betty Westrom, 249
Smith and Maxwell, 91
Smith, Brett, 142
Smith, J. A., 102
Smith, James S., 269
Smith, Kathryn, 269
Smith, M. J., 269
Smith, Margaret Bayard, 68
Smith, Robert Wallace, 238
Smith, Roland, 261
Smith, Samuel Harrison, 67-69, 72-73, 75-76
Smith, Silas B., 211
Smither, James, 98
Smyth, Clifford, 234
Snake and Missouri Rivers (Lewis/Clark
    manuscript map), 192
Snelling, William Joseph, 218, 225
Snoddy, Donald D., 273
Snow, Jan, 277
Snyder, Gerald, 247, 274
Society for Promoting Christian
    Knowledge, 131, 143
Society of Gentlemen, 43
Soderberg, Vicky, 259
"Some Books Carried," 25
"Some Studies, 1986-1989," 283
The Song of Sakakawea, 238
Soulard, Antoine, 38-39, 62
South Dakota History, 275
South of the Sunset, 235
Southern Quarterly Review, 175
Southey, Robert, 156, 175
Space, Ralph S., 244, 247
SPCK. See Society for Promoting
Spear, John, 93
St. George, Judith, 259
St. Louis, 38
Stacey, Joseph, 275
Stanley, Leo Leonidas, 267
Star of the West, 235
"A Statistical View of the Indian Nations,"
    36, 54, 69, 74, 82, 122, 124
Stearns, Harold G., 242
Steber, Rick, 257
Steffen, Jerome O., 249, 275
Stein, R. Conrad, 250
Stetoff, Rebecca, 255
Stevens, James, 240
Stevens, Sydney, 261
Stevenson, Elizabeth, 272
Stewart, Henry M., 275
Stiles, Glee Druyor, 248
Stirring Adventures "Up the Missouri," 232
Stoddard, Amos, 98
The Storied Northwest, 266
Stories of the Westward Movement, 247
The Story of Captain Meriwether Lewis
    and Captain William Clark, 226
The Story of George Shannon, 258
The Story of Sacajawea, Guide to Lewis

and Clark, 255
The Story of the Lewis and Clark Expedition,
    250
The Story of the Louisiana Purchase, 102
Stoutenburg, Adrien, 241
Stöver, Jacob, 123-125, 136-137, plate XV
Stöver, John Casper, 123
Stower, C., 123
The Stranger, 153, 173
Stratemeyer, Edward, 219-220, 226
Streams to the River, River to the Sea, 253
Streissguth, Thomas, 260
Strong, Emory, 258, 276
Strong, Ruth, 258
Suicide or Murder? 243
Sullivan, George, 261
Sumption, Linda Jan, 285
Superior Printing Company, 183
Supplement: Lewis, Meriwether and Kindred
    Families, 240
surreptitious publications, 101, 121-143;
sources of, 133
"A Survey of 20th Century Novels," 283
Swayne, Zoa L., 255
Systema Naturae, 47-48

T
Tabeau, Pierre Antoine, 100
Tables, for Readily, 52
Tables Requisite (Garnett), 52
Tables Requisite (Maskelyne), 32-33, 51-52
Tagebuch einer Entdeckungs-Reise durch
    Nord-America, 100, 112-114, 113
Tale of Valor, 241
Tales of the Frontier, 243
Tales of Travels West of the Mississippi,
    217-218, 225, 225
Tardieu, J. B., 96-7, 106-108, 107, 114
Taylor, Bayard, 208-209, 222
Taylor, Isaac, 216-217, 224-225, plate XXII
Taylor, John E., 258
Taylor, Robert, 149
Teggart, Frederick J., 63, 266
Telegraphe and Daily Advertiser, 134
Tenney, Jeffrey W., 265
32nd Congress, 1st Session, House Report
    No. 56, 115
33rd Congress, 1st Session, House Report
    No. 215, 116
Thom, James Alexander, 252, 264
Thomas, George, 264
Thomas, I., 52
Thomas Jefferson & the Stony Mountains,
    25, 201, 251
"Thomas Jefferson's Object and
    Philosophy," 283
Thomasma, Kenneth, 259
Thompson, Carolyn K., 284
Thompson, David, 40, 57
Thompson, Kathleen, 254
Thompson, Larry S., 278
Thomson, Ruth, 248

Thorp, Daniel B., 260
Those Tremendous Mountains, 251
Three Forks of the Missouri, 97, 133
Three Journals of the Lewis & Clark
    Expedition, 262, 262
Throckmorton, Arthur, 15
Thwaites, Reuben Gold, 17, 90, 166, 168-170,
    196-200, 213, 241, 246, 247, 265, 266
Tillamook Head, 30
Tilton, J. E. and Company, 209, 222
Tilton, John E., 209
Tilton, Stephen W., 209
Tinling, Marion, 265
To the Pacific With Lewis and Clark, 245
Tomkins, Calvin, 245, 271
Toole, K. Ross, 269
"A Topogra[phical] Sketch," 38-39, 62
Torrance, Harold, 261
Toward the Western Ocean, 243
The Trail Blazers, 234
The Trail of Lewis and Clark, 212, 223-224,
    234, 249
Trail: The Story of the Lewis & Clark
    Expedition, 254
Trailblazers, 255
Trails of the Pathfinders, 231
The Traveler's Guide, 257
"Travelers in the Wilderness," 284
traveling library, 7, 23-63
Travels in North America (Dublin, 1822),
    121, 129-130, 142
Travels in North America (Dublin, 1824),
    129-130, 142
Travels in North America (London, 1831),
    131, 143, 155
Travels in North America (London, 1846),
    131, 143
Travels in North America, from Modern Writers,
    217, 224-225
Travels in the Interior Parts of America, 71, 81-82
The Travels of Capts. Lewis & Clarke
    (Philadelphia, 1809), 122-123, 124, 127,
    133-134, plate XIII
The Travels of Capts. Lewis & Clarke (London,
    1809), 123, 134-135, 155, plate XIV
The Travels of Lewis & Clark, 262
Travels Through the Canadas, 98
Travels Through the Interior Parts, 121-122, 124
Travels Through the Two Louisianas, 71
Travels to the Source of the Missouri River
    (London, 1814), 135, 154-156, 173-175,
Travels to the Source of the Missouri River
    (London, 1815), 175-176
Travels to the Source of the Missouri River
    (London, 1817), 177-178
True, Rodney H., 267
True West, 270
Truteau, Jean Baptiste, 36, 62-63, 100
Truteau Journal Extracts, 36, 62-63
The Truth about Sacajawea, 259
Tuckerman, Edward, 208
Turton, William, 48

Tweney, George, 21, 165-6, 186, 280
Twist, Clint, 257
Two Captains West, 239

U

Undaunted Courage, 258, *258*
University of Pennsylvania, 33
Untitled map of the Missouri River, 37
Upham, Charles Wentworth, 215, 224
Upton, Harriet, 255
U.S. Congress, 67-69, 72-86
"Use and Accuracy of Accounts," 282

V

The Value of Adventure: The Story of Sacagawea, 251
van Baarsel, Willem Cornelius, 176, plate XVIII
van Braam, Pieter, 157
van Braam Blussé, Pieter. *See* Blussé
van Every, Dale, 238
Van Geothem, Larry, 278
van Kampen, Nicholas Godfried, 157-159, 176
Van Steenwyk, Elizabeth, 259
Vancouver, George, 39-41, 56-57, 59, plate V
Vater, Johann Severin, 124, 136
Vienna, nineteenth-century publications, 98-100, 111, 159-160, 180
Views of Louisiana, 93-94
Vilda västerns portar öppnas, 232
Viles, Don, 251
The Village Indians of the Upper Missouri, 249
Vincent, William David, 234
Vinton, Stallo, 234
vocabularies, Indian languages, 36, 53-54, 91, 122-123, 138, 153
Voelker, Robert G., 276
Voight, Virginia Frances, 245
von Ferro, 180
von Linné, Karl. *See* Linnæus
von Steuben, Frederich W. A., 29-30
von Wied-Neuwied, Prince Maximilian, 97
Voorhees, Luke, 233
Voorhis, Eleanor Glasgow, 169
Voorhis, Julia Clark, 169
Voorhis School for Boys, 234
Voyage des Capitaines Lewis et Clarke, 96, 106-108, *107*, 114, plate VIII
A Voyage of Discovery (Vancouver), 59
A Voyage to the Pacific Ocean, 58
The Voyages and Travels of Captains Lewis and Clarke (Philadelphia, 1812), 139
Voyages of Discovery, 260
Voyages from Montreal, 35-36, 39, 41, 47, 53-54, 60, 70, 91, 94, 122, 134, 138

W

Wade, Mary H., 234
Wagner-Camp-Becker bibliography, 16
Wagner, Henry Raup, 233
Wainwright, Nicholas B., 249
Walcheck, Kenneth C., 261, 275, 276, 277

Waldo, Anna Lee, 250
Wappato Indians, 248
Ware's Valley Monthly, 228
Warfington, Richard, 73
Warner, Doten, 260
Warner, Joan K., 284
The Washington 89, 21
Washington, D.C., nineteenth-century publications, 68-70, 72, 75-79, 83-86
Watercourse, 265
Waters, Patricia, 284
Watson, Kathy and Stuart, 264
Watzek Library, 15-22, 75
Way, A. & G., 67-68, 70, 72, 75, 77, 83-84, 86
Way and Gideon, 68
Way and Groff, 68
Way, Andrew Jr., 67, 73
Way, George, 67, 73
The Way to the Western Sea, 254
"A Wayless Way," 285
We Proceeded On, 20, 280-282, *280*
We Proceeded On, Supplementary Publications, 280-282
We Were There with Lewis and Clark, 241
The Weekly Inspector (New York), 72, 84
Weimar, nineteenth-century publications, 100-101, 112-114
Welden, Amelie, 260
The Wellsburg Herald, 102
Wellsburg, West Virginia, 101, 116-117
Wendlick, Roger, 19-21, 50
Werner Company, 183, 219, 226
Werner, Paul E., 219
Werner, Wilbur, 275, 280
West, Helen B., 244, 272
West to the Pacific: The Story of Lewis and Clark, 243
West to the Pacific: The Story of the Lewis and Clark Expedition, 255
Western World (Frankfort, Kentucky), 71
The Western Gleaner, 94, 153, 173
The Western Miscellany, 101
The Westward Crossings, 238
Westward the Course, 238
Westward Whoa, 257
Westward with Dragoons, 236
Weyland, Philipp Christoph, 100, 112-114
Wheat, Carl I., 36, 55, 241
Wheeler, Olin D., 211, 223-224, 234, 249
Whimper, 143
White, Alana J., 259
White, Cochrane, and Co., 222
Whitehouse, Joseph, 40, 89-90, 202
"Who is the Author of *History of the Expedition*?" 150
Who'd Believe John Colter? 256
Die Wichtigsten Neuern Land- und Seereisen, 159-160, 180
Wilbur, Marguerite Eyer, 22
Wild America: Protecting the Lands of Lewis & Clark, 264
Wilkes, Charles, 15

Wilkie, Katharine E., 244
Wilkinson, Katherine, 283
Will Clark: Boy in Buckskins, 244
Will, Drake W., 270, 273
William and Mary Quarterly, 279
William Clark: Jeffersonian Man on the Frontier, 249
"William Clark: Superintendent of Indian Affairs," 285
Willingham, William F., 252
Wilson, Alexander, 151, 228
Wilson, Charles Morrow, 235
Wilson, John, 131, 141
Winged Moccasins, 240
Winsor, Justin, 168
Winterer, Drew, 285
Wisneski, Richard, 284
Wistar, Caspar, 26, 35, 43, 62
With Lewis and Clark Through the Rockies, 244
The Witness, 84, 227
Wolfrom, Anna, 233
Wolf, James R., 282
Wonderland 1900-1904, 211-212, 223-224, *224*
Wood, Gertrude, 258
Wood, Ruth Kedzie, 266
Wood, W. Raymond, 277, 278
Woodard, Keith, 19
Woodbridge, Hensley C., 21
Woodwell, William H., 280
Worcester, Massachusetts, 195
The Work-a-Day Detail, 255
World Explorers, 245
Would You Have Gone With Lewis and Clark? 263
Wright, Henrietta Christian, 218-219, 226
Wright, Marcus J., 228
Wythe, George, 25

Y

Yale University, 16, 39
Yaple, James, 276
Yater, George H., 282
Yates, Ted, 271
York, 73-74
York: The Slave Who Helped Explore, 262
Young, Judith A., 258
Young Shannon, 237
Young, W. P., 48

Z

Zadra, Dan, 254
Zaidlicz, Edwin, 280
Zochert, Donald, 273